D0880611

Murders, Mysteries and History
of
Lorain County, Ohio,
1824–1956

Don Hilton

authorHOUSE®

AuthorHouse™
1663 Liberty Drive
Bloomington, IN 47403
www.authorhouse.com
Phone: 1 (800) 839-8640

© 2018 Don Hilton. All rights reserved.

No part of this book may be reproduced, stored in a retrieval system, or
transmitted by any means without the written permission of the author.

Published by AuthorHouse 04/19/2018

ISBN: 978-1-5462-3590-3 (sc)
ISBN: 978-1-5462-3589-7 (e)

Print information available on the last page.

Any people depicted in stock imagery provided by Getty Images are models,
and such images are being used for illustrative purposes only.
Certain stock imagery © Getty Images.

This book is printed on acid-free paper.

Because of the dynamic nature of the Internet, any web addresses or links contained in
this book may have changed since publication and may no longer be valid. The views
expressed in this work are solely those of the author and do not necessarily reflect the views
of the publisher, and the publisher hereby disclaims any responsibility for them.

- FOR BROTHER JON -

Who, in all certainty, surely wanted to commit murder.

I am getting the feeling that booze, divorce papers,
and weapons are a lethal mixture.
But I can't understand "I loved her so I killed her."

- Kevin Weidenbaum -

THANKS TO

Do people even read the thanks? I hope so!

Mr. Andy Young, editor emeritus, and *The Chronicle-Telegram,* Elyria, Ohio. Permission to use their articles made this book 'way easier to write and much more enjoyable to read.

The Lorain County Office of the Clerk of Courts, Records Division (especially Bobbi and Cherri) for their expertise, patience, good humor, and being sure that at least one of their microfilm readers was always working. The Lorain County Recorder's Office whose wonderful deed books allowed me to figure out who was where and when.

The Lorain County Historical Society, Elyria, Ohio, for helping me learn how to track people through time. The Spirit of '76 Museum in Wellington, Ohio. They have tons of cool stuff!

The Lorain Public Library, the Elyria Public Library, the Oberlin Public Library, and the Grafton-Midview Public Library as places to meet, read, and research. *Everything is **not** on the Internet!*

Mr. Daniel Brady, compendium of Lorain County trivia. If he didn't know something, he always knew who did.

Ms. Che Gonzalez, a long-time friend. She steered me true when it came to questions of race and ethnicity.

Ms. Margaret Christian, first met in the course of research. Our honest conversations on how the world works helped keep me on the straight and narrow.

Retired Elyria Police Detective Al Leiby and Oberlin Police Patrolman Bashshar Wiley for information needed to both begin and finish a particular set of stories.

Mr. David Woodruff, proud Carolinian, for providing enough on fingerprinting to keep me from sounding like a complete doof. I wish he was around to read this book.

Mr. Kevin Weidenbaum: Wielder of The Red Pen. Blame "grammerical" missteps on me not paying close enough attention to his notes. Blame factual mistakes, along with the typos you are certain to find, on me not paying close enough attention to the world.

Artist Kat Sikora for the wonderful cover illustration set upon part of a seriously altered Art Leiby photo. You'll recognize the story—for sure!

Finally... Every paper source I used was created by people in the government, courts, or newspapers who were just doing their jobs. You're all long gone, but I grew to recognize your handwriting and editorial styles. So, for all of the interconnected pieces of information, I thank the record-keepers of the past, present, and future. You might think yourself unimportant, but the world needs each and every one of you!

CONTENTS

PREFACE XIII

A NOTE ON NAMES XV

STRUCTURE XVII

BEFORE LORAIN COUNTY XIX

1824 – 1829: COUNTY POPULATION = 3,695 1

1830 – 1839: COUNTY POPULATION = 5,696 4

1840 – 1849: COUNTY POPULATION = 18,467 7

1850 – 1859: COUNTY POPULATION = 26,086 10

1860 – 1869: COUNTY POPULATION = 29,744 13

1870 – 1879: COUNTY POPULATION = 30,308 21

1880 – 1889: COUNTY POPULATION = 35,526 28

1890 – 1899: COUNTY POPULATION = 40,294 55

1900 – 1909: COUNTY POPULATION = 54,857 89

1910 – 1919: COUNTY POPULATION = 75,037 162

1920 – 1929: COUNTY POPULATION = 90,612 203

1930 – 1939: COUNTY POPULATION = 109,206 273

1940 – 1949: COUNTY POPULATION = 112,390 340

1950 – 1956: COUNTY POPULATION = 148,162 398

AND THERE YOU HAVE IT 426

BY THE NUMBERS: EVEN IF YOU DON'T LIKE MATH 427

ETHNICITY AND RACE ARE SLIPPERY 431

THE GENTLER SEX 433

Modus Operandi.. 434

Court Reporting 435

A Tale of Two Counties 437

Sources and Sundries 439

List by Location.. 443

Master Lists:... 444

PREFACE

The perpetrators of murder often seem like you and me. Regular folk pushed a little too far by the circumstances of life. People who drank too much or fell in with a bad crowd: otherwise innocent, except for listening to the wrong whispering voice and resorting to violence when they might have simply walked away.

That is not always the case. Murder can often be foreseen with fair ease. This is particularly true for people, mostly women, involved in abusive relationships. They are, in turn, controlled, threatened, shoved, struck, beaten, and murdered. Murdered, especially, when they try to escape their abuser. That pattern is repeated with depressing regularity throughout this book.

A man who can hit is a man who can kill. If you're the victim in a violent relationship, please get out as safely as you can. If you're committing the violence, please understand that your behavior is not normal. Find counseling before you end up spending the better part of your life behind bars as the killer of another human being, or find yourself dead because of it.

It's far better, and much easier to avoid trouble than try to stop it once it starts. If you have children, be sure they know to stay away from people who treat them badly. Be sure they can identify the early, tell-tale signs of control and abuse. Be sure they think highly enough of themselves to escape. Be sure they can defend themselves against those who persist. Please. Be sure.

A Note on Names

Nobody knows exactly how to spell Lorain County names. Court recorders, newspaper reporters, census takers, everyone has a different version of who is who. Is it Ericsen or Erickson? Dobesak or Dovisek? Kovacz or Kovach? Making matters worse, immigrants tend to "Americanize" themselves, especially when their home countries are at war with the United States. Georg Decher transforms into George Decker, Giuseppe Garbaccioto becomes Joe Garby, and Ibrahim Khoury is now Abe Corry.

Newspapers of the past are terrible with names. An article might start off with one spelling, shift to another half-way through, and end up with something different. You might expect official legal records to be better, but they're not. Sure, spellings *might* be correct, but such old documents are hand-written. The difference between a Palgot, Poigat, or a Peiget is often impossible to tell.

What this adds up to is a mess so tangled that you can't even find death certificates. Is the person killed John Washnac? Or was it Wasnok? Or, maybe, Wasnik, Wasniak, Washak, or Washek? The guy accused of killing him is Joe... Sknoicki, Skoneski, Soneski, Skroneski? You get the idea.

Despite the misspellings, Lorain County readers *will* see names they recognize. Everyone should "judge slowly." If you are part of a family included in these stories, please remember that there is a good chance that what's presented will not gibe with the stories you've perhaps heard. The information herein is from newspapers and court records—but that doesn't mean that the book is always right.

Don't be ashamed if you're surprised to find a relative in these pages. It's common for people to choose not to remember such things. The circumstances surrounding the death of a murder victim are often forgotten. As for perpetrators: all families have skeletons in their closets (mine sure does). I've always found my worst-behaving kinfolk the most intriguing.

As someone I greatly admire once told me, "I'd rather be a bad example than no example at all!"

STRUCTURE

This book is organized by the decades listed just below (those **bolded** are the most deadly). Local history does not happen in a vacuum so passing years have a few sentences describing what was going at the time. These include items such as inventions, books, songs, wars, elections, and the births of some well-known (or not) Ohioans. Common criminal charges for the year are listed as "Popular in the docket."

Years	Murders
1824-1829	0
1830-1839	0
1840-1849	1
1850-1859	0
1860-1869	2
1870-1879	5
1880-1889	4
1890-1899	17
1900-1909	**46**
1910-1919	35
1920-1929	**65**
1930-1939	33
1940-1949	23
1950-1956	20

There is no reason for you to read this book in any particular order. Not everyone likes a slow start, so feel free to skip around.

A few crimes get a "just the facts" treatment. Most have enough information for a couple of paragraphs or a page or two. Some murders end up with several pages. It depends on the circumstances and how tell-able I found the story.

Scattered throughout the book are newspaper articles that caught my eye. Many have to do with the crimes described or are broadly related to the topic at hand. Others have nothing to do with anything else but were just too interesting or entertaining to omit. To me, at least.

I sometimes comment or add notes in or at the end of a story or article. **These appear in a different font so you know it's me.**

In the last chapters there's a compilation of Lorain County murder data for the period covered by this book. You might find it entertaining or enlightening. There are also instructions on how to find a murder *you* may be interested in researching, and at the very end, various indices of the killings described.

Scattered throughout are a few short essays on specific topics tied to the crimes described. Some are fact-based, others I've used to express my opinions with which not everyone will agree. If you're one of those people, please feel free to write your own doggone book!

Before Lorain County...

A Short and Painless History

Generally speaking, land in the United States that's east of Ohio is divided by the traditional survey technique of "metes and bounds." This imprecise system is based on descriptions of often-shifting criteria: "Proceed forty rods north from the large pile of rocks that forms the southeast corner of the property to the stream and thence several hundred rods counter to the flow until reaching a split pine marking the northeast corner." Such vague boundaries clog the courts with cases created by the confusion over the ownership of land. They also interfere with commerce by complicating the construction of the infrastructure that's required for growth.

Leaders of the nascent U.S. hoped a more "scientific" method of survey would help bring order to the settlement of any lands added from the great Northwest Territories. But, like many scientific endeavors, it required an arbitrary starting point.

Near East Liverpool, Columbiana County, Ohio, close by the three-way intersection of the states of Ohio, Pennsylvania, and the northern tip of West Virginia, there is a small monument that honors *The Point of Beginning*: This is the spot where, in 1785, the young U.S. Government began using its "Public Land Survey System" to subdivided any newly acquired lands. From that starting point, master latitudes and longitudes were struck and, from there, much of the rest of the country was measured.

Survey parties were often the first pioneers of new lands. Working their way through the wilderness, they divided what they found into numbered sections, townships, and ranges. Nearly all of Ohio, including its northern tier, was surveyed under the Public Land System. While the boundaries of many of our neat, regular townships were in place *before* White settlers arrived, the history of each township is unique. Each deserves a book of its own. You should start working on yours, if it hasn't already been written!

These townships, some already settled and named, were taken from larger, pre-existing counties, and in 1824, jig-sawed together to form Lorain County which then evolved as it gained and lost townships over time. The outside borders of the county were set in 1846. Internal political boundaries continue to evolve.

RaCe and rAcE

I capitalize all words my sources used to describe a person's race or nationality *except in cases of direct quotes*. You'll see Colored and colored, Black and black, White and white, and so on. Some quoted newspaper articles are strongly racist. Apologies to the offended, but I never trust anyone who sanitizes the past.

1789: The world is supposed to end, according to Cardinal Pierre d'Ailly. It doesn't. North Carolina. George Washington (Virginia Nonpartisan) wins the first U.S. Presidential Election. (100% of the vote—sort of. Elections weren't quite the same back then). Hold on… Go back and check out that date. Up until 1789, the government of the United States of America operated under the *Articles of Confederation*. There was no such thing as a "chief executive office." From 1774 to 1788, fourteen men served a total of sixteen terms as *President of the Continental Congress*. John Hancock is likely the only name you'd recognize. He served twice in that role, though he never showed up for his second term.

1790: Rhode Island.

1791: The first ten Amendments were made to the *U.S. Constitution: First:* Freedom of religion, speech, press, assembly, and petition. *Second:* Militias and the right to keep and bear arms. *Third:* Prevention of quartering soldiers in times of peace or war without regard to law or owner's permission. *Fourth:* Protection from unreasonable searches and seizures. *Fifth:* Right to legal due process, trial, prevention of retrial on same charge, compensation for seized property, and freedom from self-incrimination. *Sixth:* A speedy trial by impartial jury, facing accusers, with legal counsel. *Seventh:* Jury trials at a federal level and prohibition of a court overturning a jury's finding of fact. *Eighth:* Prevention of cruel and unusual punishment. *Ninth:* "Unenumerated rights" of citizens not specified by other laws. *Tenth:* Restricting federal governmental power to only those specified in the Constitution and granting remaining power to the states. Vermont.

1792: George Washington (Virginia Nonpartisan) wins the Presidential Election with 100% of the vote—again—sort of. Kentucky.

1795: The world is supposed to end, according to Nathaniel Halhed. It doesn't. Amendment to the *U.S. Constitution: Eleventh:* Prohibits jurisdiction of federal courts over cases in which a state is sued by an individual from another state or another country. The *Treaty of Greenville* opens Ohio lands.

1796: John Adams (Massachusetts Federalist) wins the Election with 53.4% of the popular vote. Tennessee.

1800: Settlement in what becomes northern Ohio brings Irish and Scots Protestants. Thomas Jefferson (Virginia Democratic-Republican) wins the Election with 61.4% of the popular vote. $1,000 is worth $18,870 modern (2017), based on the U.S. Inflation Rate, according to the Bureau of Labor Statistics.

1802, April 30: U.S. President Thomas Jefferson signs into law a bill to *begin* establishment of a new state in the Ohio territory. That November, a State Constitutional Convention meets in Chillicothe, Ohio, and adopts the state's *1802 Constitution.* A "General Assembly" is given most of the power with very few checks and balances from a weak Governor and judiciary. But fear not! Ohioans may rewrite the *State Constitution* every twenty years.

1803: February 19: Thomas Jefferson signs into law a bill providing that Ohio has become one of the United States. There is no resolution declaring the state, just recognition of existence. March 1: Ohio becomes the 17th state when its General Assembly meets in the capital, Chillicothe.

1804: Amendment to the *U.S. Constitution: Twelfth:* Provides a separate vote for a Vice Presidential candidate. Ohio passes laws restricting the movement of Blacks. Thomas Jefferson (Virginia Democratic-Republican) wins the Election with 72.8% of the popular vote.

1805: The world is supposed to end, according to Presbyterian Minister Christopher Love. It doesn't. The *Fort Industry Treaty* does away with Native American claims to farmlands. End of the First Barbary War. The "Shores of Tripoli!" $1,000 is worth $19,936 modern.

1808: First mail passes through what will become Lorain County via the "Lake Route." James Madison (Virginia Democratic-Republican) wins the Election with 64.7% of the popular vote.

1810: For various and sundry political reasons, Zanesville becomes the Ohio State Capital. Inmates begin constructing a newer Ohio Penitentiary in Columbus. $1,000 is worth $19,057 modern.

1812: War sort of stirs up northern Ohio. For various and sundry political reasons, Chillicothe re-becomes the Ohio State Capital. James Madison (Virginia Democratic-Republican) wins the Election with 50.4% of the popular vote. Louisiana.

1814: The world is supposed to end, according to Joanna Southcott. It doesn't. First Post Office at the mouth of Black River. John Reid is the Master. Five Native American tribes in Ohio make peace with the U.S. and declare war on Britain. The Village of Cleaveland, located at the mouth of the Cuyahoga River, is incorporated.

1815: The newest Ohio Penitentiary along the Scioto River in Columbus begins taking prisoners. The Second Barbary War. $1,000 is worth $15,245 modern.

1816: The State Assembly meets in Ohio's brand-new capital of Columbus and has remained since. James Monroe (Virginia Democratic-Republican) wins the Election with 68.2% of the popular vote. Indiana.

1817: The Erie Canal spurs westward immigration. Native Americans are gone from what will become Lorain County. The First Seminole War in what will be Florida. Mississippi.

1818: Post Office in the village of Elyria with Heman (not "Herman") Ely as the Master. Illinois.

1819: First July 4th celebration in the "county." Shipbuilding begins at the mouth of the Black River. Alabama.

1820: Population of what will become Lorain County is an estimated 1,694. William Tecumseh Sherman is born in Lancaster, Fairfield County, Ohio. James Monroe (Virginia Democratic-Republican) wins the Election with 80.6% of the popular vote. Maine. $1,000 is worth $19,936 modern.

1821: Missouri.

1822: Future U.S. President Ulysses Grant is born in Point Pleasant, Clermont County, Ohio. Future President Rutherford Hayes is born in Delaware, Delaware County, Ohio. The "Columbus Penitentiary of Ohio" is renamed the "Ohio Penitentiary in Columbus." December 26: Lorain County is formed from chunks of Medina, Huron, & Cuyahoga Counties, but not yet organized. Courts are held in Medina for the next 13 months.

1823: Alexander Twilight, a "person of color" receives a bachelor's degree from Middlebury College in Middlebury, Vermont. The Arikara Indian War (Missouri River). The State of Ohio, after considering Black River and Sheffield, chooses Elyria as the seat of the soon-to-be County of Lorain, or, as it might have been named, Colerain. To help sway the decision, Heman Ely offers land and $2,000 for a court house and jail. On Valentine's Day, the construction of the court house begins at the northeast corner of Middle and Broadway. This one-floor, wood-framed building serves the public until 1828. A two-story jail is built on the Public Square corner of 3rd and Middle. Looking like an over-sized house, one half holds the jailer and his family. The other half, for law-breakers, is lined with hewn logs and contains a total of ten, high-ceilinged, 8' x 12' cells. This serves as the county lock-up for nearly 70 (!) years.

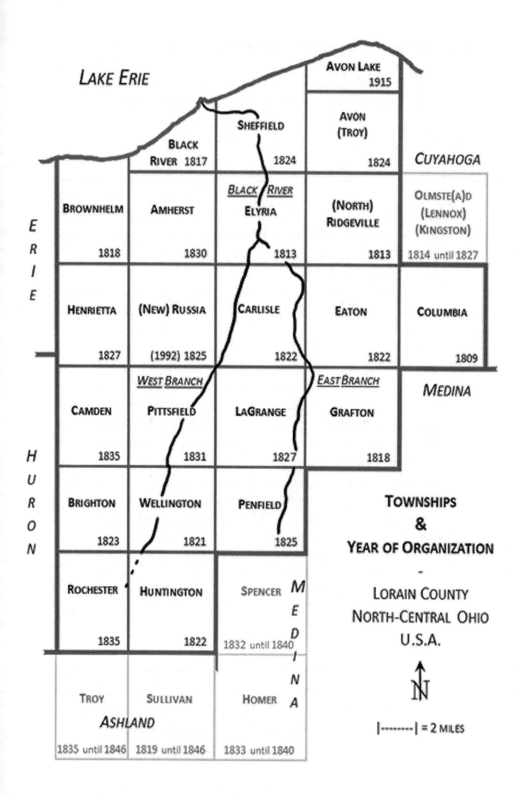

LAKE ERIE

AVON LAKE 1915

AVON (TROY) 1824

SHEFFIELD 1824

BLACK RIVER 1817

CUYAHOGA

BROWNHELM 1818

AMHERST 1830

BLACK RIVER ELYRIA 1813

(NORTH) RIDGEVILLE 1813

OLMSTE(A)D (LENNOX) (KINGSTON) 1814 until 1827

E R I E

HENRIETTA 1827

(NEW) RUSSIA (1992) 1825

CARLISLE 1822

EATON 1822

COLUMBIA 1809

WEST BRANCH

EAST BRANCH

MEDINA

CAMDEN 1835

PITTSFIELD 1831

LAGRANGE 1827

GRAFTON 1818

H U R O N

BRIGHTON 1823

WELLINGTON 1821

PENFIELD 1825

ROCHESTER 1835

HUNTINGTON 1822

SPENCER 1832 until 1840

M E D I N A

TROY 1835 until 1846

SULLIVAN 1819 until 1846

HOMER 1833 until 1840

ASHLAND

TOWNSHIPS & YEAR OF ORGANIZATION - LORAIN COUNTY NORTH-CENTRAL OHIO U.S.A.

N

|--------| = 2 MILES

1824 – 1829: County Population = 3,695

1824: Lorain County Courts open for business. The "old" Republican Party splits into the National Republicans and Democratic-Republicans. The Bureau of Indian Affairs is created within the U.S. War Department. John Quincy Adams (Massachusetts Democratic-Republican) wins the Election with 30.9% of the popular vote. Well… not really. Andrew Jackson wins the popular vote (41.4%), but his 99 electoral votes are not enough to take the race. Adams is selected by the U.S. House of Representatives thanks, in large part, to an endorsement of another candidate, Speaker of the House Henry Clay. When Adams goes on to name Clay as his U.S. Secretary of State, Andy Jackson is *greatly* displeased and charges corruption.

Please keep in mind that newspaper article are always quoted verbatim. Mistakes in structure, spelling, or punctuation remain.

1824, February 25: *Sandusky Clarion:*

Melancholy Affair—A daughter of one Mr. Onstine, of Black River township, Lorain county, was engaged to be married to a Mr. Crawford, which being contrary to the wishes of her brother, he declared if she married him he would kill her. She was, however, shortly afterwards married. Young Mr. Onstine had previously quarreled with another of his brothers-in-law, and on the 11th, inst. He threatened to go down and flog him. His sister that married Mr. Crawford was on a visit to her sister, when he came, and they both prevailed on his brother-in-law not to fight, and took a club away from Onstine. He then took up a stone, and aiming a backhanded blow at his brother-in-law, hit his young sister, Mrs. C. in the breast. She lingered until about 3 o'clock the next morning, when she expired. We have not heard of his being apprehended.

Hold on… This appears in the next *Clarion:*

Sir—The writer of the article headed "Melancholy Affair," must have been grossly misinformed, or very ignorant as respects the transaction detailed. It is true Mr. Onstine and his brother-in-law quarreled, but no one that is acquainted with the circumstances pretends that Mrs. Crawford received any injury in the affray, unless proceeded from exertion or affright.

I give you this early notice that you may, by publishing this or a part of it, counteract the unfavorable impression that has gone abroad to Mr. Onstine's injury. Respectfully, yours, E. REDINGTON.

There's a good chance that the writer of this letter was a relative of Judge H.G. Redington who will sit on the Lorain County Common Pleas Court from 1914 to 1929.

SORORICIDE: Killing one's sister.

1825: Quincy Adams Gillmore is born in Black River, Lorain County. Educated at West Point, he will become the first to effectively use rifled cannon, destroying Confederate Fort Pulaski. He will also lead racially integrated Civil War troops and is part-inspiration for the 1989 movie *Glory*. $1,000 is worth $23,561 modern.

1826:. *The American Temperance Society* forms in Boston, Massachusetts. The first U.S. railway company in Quincy, Massachusetts. The HMS Beagle sets sail with a curious Charles Darwin along for the ride.

1827: Olmsted Township is detached from Lorain County and attached to Cuyahoga County to the east. Stagecoach service comes to Elyria. The Winnebago Indian War.

1828: Lorain County gets its second courthouse. Built on the southern portion of Elyria's Public Square, the red-brick building, fronted by a pediment and four large pillars, is 45 x 66 feet in size and topped with a cupola holding a bell rung by the sheriff to announce the start of court sessions (and by parishioners of St. Andrew's Church holding services there). The first floor holds county offices. The second, the court room. The structure is eventually painted or parged a light color. The Cherokees publish the first American-Indian newspaper. Adult White males may now vote in most U.S. states. They used to have to own land or pay taxes. Andrew Jackson (Tennessee Democrat) wins the Election with 55.9% of the popular vote.

1829: The State of Georgia declares it illegal for Cherokees to hold political assemblies. The first "real" county newspaper, the *Lorain Gazette*, is published on Friday, July 24th. News of the day: Patriotic bluster. Complaints about the

Post Office. Advertisements with questionable truths. And this: "Conceit and ignorance are a most unhappy combination, for none are so invincible as the half-wit, who knows just enough to excite their pride, but not so much to cure their ignorance." Not much changes, it seems.

1830 – 1839: County Population = 5,696

1830: Lorain County's first high school, in Elyria, with Reverend Monteith as Superintendent. William IV succeeds brother George as the King of England. French King Charles X is knocked from his seat by revolution. *The Indian Removal Act* pushes those sort of folks west of the Mississippi. Panama is part of the newly independent country of Columbia. $1,000 is worth $25,408 modern.

1831: Virginia, Southampton County: Slave Nate Turner leads a short-lived revolt for freedom. Turner is skinned. Slavery in the United States grows ever more repressive. You can't trust a slave who knows how to read and write. Can you? Future President James Garfield is born in Orange Township, Cuyahoga County, Ohio. Cleaveland becomes Cleveland when one of its newspapers finds its masthead has room for only nine letters, or when some surveyor can't spell the name right on a map.

GENOCIDE: Systematic death of a group based on ethnic, racial, religious, or national characteristics.

DOMINICIDE: Killing one's master.

1832: Codeine is isolated. U.S. Vice President John Calhoun resigns due to differences with his boss, Andrew Jackson. The Black Hawk Indian War.

1833: Escaping the moral decay of Lorain County's northern population, Presbyterian ministers John Shipherd and Philo Stewart wander south to the wilderness of Russia Township where (as the story goes) not being killed by a bear convinces them they're in the right place to found the *Oberlin Collegiate Institute*. To gain funding from eastern liberals, Oberlin College (as it is renamed in 1850) becomes the first truly coeducational and racially integrated institute of higher learning in the U.S. Future President Benjamin Harrison is born in North Bend, Hamilton County, Ohio. Andrew Jackson (Tennessee Democrat) wins the Election with 54.7% of the popular vote.

1834: Cyrus McCormick patents the mechanical reaper. Henry Blair is the first African American to obtain a U.S. patent—for a corn planter. The new Ohio Penitentiary in Columbus begins taking prisoners (including women)

4

from the old pen a mile away on Scioto Street. The new O.P.'s high, stone, fortress-like walls expand over its lifetime and hold prisoners in its downtown location on Spring Street until August of 1984. Starting in 1972, the prison in the state's capital will be replaced by the Southern Ohio Correctional Facility in Lucasville, Ohio, but won't be demolished until the 1990s.

1835: "The Toledo War" between Ohio and Territory of Michigan over the upper-left corner of Ohio and control of the mouth of the Maumee River. Lots of posturing, but no battles of any consequence. Sounds much like football to me. The argument is settled in 1836: Ohio gets the Maumee. Michigan, much a da YUPE. The start of the Second Seminole Indian War. Attempted assassination of President Andrew Jackson. In the Docket: Applications for Tavern Licenses. Annual cost is $5.00 and there looks to be few, if any, refusals. Being caught without a license brings fine of $10.00 and the possibility of a short time in jail. $1,000 is worth $26,446 modern.

1836: The world is supposed to end, according to John Wesley, one of the founders of the Methodist Church. It doesn't. The village of Black River, Lorain County, becomes Charleston. Texas declares independence—from Mexico. Remember the Alamo? In the Docket: Many, many, many requests for citizenship. Martin Van Buren (New York Democrat) wins the Election with 50.8% of the popular vote. Arkansas.

1837: At the age of 18, Victoria becomes Queen of England after her grandfather, three uncles, and father all drop dead over the course of 17 years. The U.S. state of Georgia passes legislation that makes it illegal to sell firearms that can be concealed. The law is later declared unconstitutional. The Patriot War in the Great Lakes. There was shooting offshore, on Lake Erie. The Procter & Gamble Company is formed in Cincinnati, Ohio to manufacture soap and candles from the tallow produced by the city's meat packing industry. The Steamboat Association is formed in Charleston, Lorain County. A lantern, placed at the end of a dock, is the beginning of the Lorain Lighthouse. In the Docket: Retailing Without a License. Michigan.

1838: Kicking, head-butting, eye gouging, and biting are eliminated from boxing. The paddle-steamer *Great Western* crosses the Atlantic in a record 15 days. The *Great Removal* forces five tribes of Native Americans to new territories west of the Mississippi. Victoria Woodhull is born in Homer, Licking County, Ohio. Don't know who she is? Shame on you!

1839: In Afghanistan: the British invade and install Shuja Shah as their puppet. In Algeria: Abd-el-Kader declares a holy war against the French. In China: the British invade after authorities in Canton destroy opium stocks. In Columbus: the Ohio Statehouse opens for business. In New Rumley, Harrison County, Ohio: George Custer is born. In the Docket: Shooting with Intent to Kill (but no killings that I can find).

1840 – 1849: County Population = 18,467

1840: Homer and Spencer Townships are detached from southern Lorain County and attached to western Medina County. Victoria marries first cousin Albert. Her image is also married to the first postage stamp! Catherine Brewer is the first woman in the U.S. to earn a bachelor's degree when she graduates Wesleyan College in Macon, Georgia. William Henry Harrison (Ohio Whig) wins the Election with 52.9% of the popular vote and serves as President for exactly one month before dying of pneumonia. Vice-President John Tyler takes over and has better luck. Of *eleven* U.S. presidents between 1841 and 1921, *seven* of them are Ohioans: Ulysses Grant, Rutherford Hayes, James Garfield, Benjamin Harrison, William McKinley, William Taft, and Warren Harding. *Three* die in office: Garfield, 20th, shot in 1881; McKinley, 25th, shot in 1901; Harding, 29th, dies suddenly in 1923 of, most folks think, congestive heart failure. In the Docket: Keeping a tavern without a License. $1,000 is worth $26,997 modern.

Remember, now, a "?" in a listing means I was unable to find that information:

1840, late spring or early summer: Trial: 1840, June 26: Location: ? Victim: ? Suspect: Lavinia (Lovinia) Gilmore. Charge: Murder, maybe. Plea: Not guilty. Jurors: Joseph Smith, Edmond R. Leavitt, Reuben Wallace, Noah Eldred. Lewis D. Boyton, Norman Fels, Ransom Gibbs, Lott Chapman, Amos St. Clark, and William W. Dryer.

Judge J.W. Willey. Prosecuted by Eliphalis H. Leonard. No mention of a defense attorney. Outcome: Not Guilty.

I searched the *Elyria Lorain Standard*, Norwalk's *Huron Reflector*, and the *Sandusky Clarion* newspapers. All of them carry news of murders from across the U.S. and its Territories. None of them mention this crime. I suspect I'm reading the docket incorrectly but it's include, just in case.

Judge J.W. Willey (appointed):

Often seen as "Wiley," John Wheelock Willey was born (1797) in New Hampshire, educated at Dartmouth, Massachusetts, and studied law in New York. A "quick-witted Democratic," he served in the Ohio House of Representatives (1827–1830), then in the Ohio Senate (1830–1832). As the first mayor of Cleveland, Ohio (starting in 1836), Willey helped write both the municipal charter and many of that city's original laws. In 1840, he was appointed as presiding judge of the 14th Judicial District by Ohio Governor

Wilson Shannon (also a Democrat). Judge Willey did not serve for long. He died on July 9, 1841.

1841: The Amistad slaves are free. Poe's *Murders in the Rue Morgue* is, arguably, the first detective story.

1842: Care to vote? The Ohio Supreme Court says it's cool, as long as you are a man, of the age of majority, and contain a "preponderance of White blood" as decided by local authorities. In the Oberlin area, where nearly all of Lorain County's non-White citizens live, "preponderance" mostly means "any at all." Remember, females with any kind of blood need not bother. Crawford Long uses ether as a general anesthetic. The British abandon the first Anglo-Afghan war as "unwinnable." We're slow learners, huh? The border between the U.S. and Canada is negotiated. China's island of Hong Kong is granted to the British as a result of the earlier "Opium Wars."

1843: The world is supposed to end, according to preacher Harriet Livermore. It doesn't. Brunel's *SS Great Britain* is the first ocean-going ship with an iron hull. She's also the first with a propeller and the largest ship of her time. Charles Dickens publishes *A Christmas Carol*. It snows in Lorain County on June 1. *We* complain about the weather? William McKinley is born in Niles, Trumbull County, Ohio.

1844: According to Baptist preacher William Miller, the world is supposed to end by March 21. Then, April 18. Then, October 22. It doesn't. Public outcry stops the Ohio Penitentiary from punishing poor behavior with whippings and starvation. They are replaced by being hung by the wrists, near-drownings by water tortures, cagings in small steel boxes, and once the technology becomes available, electrically-driven abuse with a device referred to as "the hummingbird." These adjustments to attitude are meted out in the basement of the prison chapel: "Heaven above, but a hell beneath." None of that stuff is on the public tours, mind you. Samuel Morse sends "What hath God wrought." The *next day's* edition of the *Baltimore (Maryland) Patriot* newspaper carries stories transmitted by the new technology. Dr. Horace Wells uses nitrous oxide as an anesthetic. James K. Polk (Tennessee Democrat) wins the Election with 50% of the popular vote.

1845: We ponder weak and weary. Gum-bands (rubber-bands to most a y'ins) are patented in England by Stephen Perry. A Naval School opens in Annapolis, Maryland. Rules for a game that becomes baseball are developed by Alexander Cartwright. The idea of "Manifest Destiny" gains ground. Looks like we're headed for the left coast! The Lorain County Agricultural Society is formed. Florida. Texas. $1,000 is worth $30,854 modern.

1846: The U.S. declares war on Mexico. Reaching that point is complicated, but the conflict serves as a training ground for military leaders that will take the part of both sides in the U.S. War of Secession. The sultry Sax. The Smithsonian Institute. Lorain County's shape is set as the southern townships of Sullivan and Troy are reassigned to Ashland County. Iowa.

1847: Harriet Livermore, the preacher who predicted the end of the world four years ago? Well, she's sure she's right this time. She's not. First bank in Lorain County: "Lorain Bank of Elyria." The first birth with labor pangs eased by chloroform—rumors are Jane Carstairs christens her baby "Anaesthesia." Baptismal records show "Wilhelmina." The British limit the working day to 10 hours. For women and children, that is. The Cayuse Indian War (Oregon) begins. Inventor Thomas Alva Edison is born in Milan, Erie and Huron counties, Ohio.

1848: *Oh! Susanna* by Stephen Collins Foster. The Mexican-American War ends, and the U.S. reaches from sea to shining sea. The French revolt— again. There are uprisings in Sicily, Rome, Vienna, and Prague, to name a few. Zachary Taylor (Louisiana Whig) wins the Election with 47.3% of the popular vote. Wisconsin.

1849: Elizabeth Blackwell is the first woman to earn a degree in medicine from a U.S. school (Geneva Medical College, New York). The British are on the move in India. Anti-British sentiment is so high in the U.S. that, when Englishman William Macready appears as Macbeth in New York, a mob attacks the theater. Many are injured and twenty-two are killed. There's a tragedy for you.

1850 – 1859: COUNTY POPULATION = 26,086

1850: "Berea Sandstone" becomes a building material. After being held four times, the "County Fair" moves from Elyria to Oberlin. On December 16, the village of Wellington welcomes the first of many trains. The Taiping Rebellion (China) begins. Zach Taylor dies in office. It's Millard Fillmore's turn. California. $1,000 is worth $30,136 modern.

1851: The "County Fair" moves from Oberlin to Wellington. The ophthalmoscope is invented. Verdi's *Rigoletto*. The start of the Apache Indian Wars. On June 17, Ohio adopts its *1851 Constitution*. It rebalances power by granting more authority to the state's executive and judicial branches. Many previously-appointed offices, including those for judge and district attorney, are now filled by election.

1852: The "County Fair" moves from Wellington to Elyria, for good, it seems. Ohio makes it illegal for children under 18 and women to work more than 10 hours a day and for children younger than 12 to work in mines. First railroad to Elyria is completed. Franklin Pierce (New Hampshire Democrat) wins the Election with 50.8% of the popular vote.

1853: Russia occupies two Ottoman territories on the west coast of the Black Sea. The vaccination of infants against smallpox is now mandatory in Britain. Parents are fined or imprisoned if they fail to comply.

1854: The U.S. Republican Party (re)forms on an anti-slavery platform. The U.S. buys much of what becomes southern Arizona from Mexico because it's way cheaper than war. The Bombardment of Greytown (Caribbean). John Snow uses geography to prove a London cholera epidemic is caused by tainted water from a public well.

1855: The "old" Ohio Penitentiary, down on Scioto Street in Columbus, is pulled apart after serving several years as an armory. In Lorain County, John M. Langston becomes the first Black man in the U.S. to be nominated and elected by popular vote when he wins the position of Township Clerk in Brownhelm Township. $1,000 is worth $26,997 modern.

1856: Abolitionist John Brown and his mob murder five men in Kansas. His pappy, Owen, was on Oberlin's board of trustees from 1835-1844. Moses Fleetwood "Fleet" Walker is born in Mt. Pleasant, Jefferson County, Ohio. He will attend Oberlin College in the early 1880s and become the first Black ("Mulatto," actually, his mother was White) major league ball player as a catcher for the American Association team, the Toledo Blue Stockings in 1884. The Puget Sound Indian War. The Rogue River Indian War. The Filibuster War (Nicaragua). In China, it's the start of the Second Opium War. Granville Woods is born in Columbus, Ohio. He'll go on to improve the telephone and telegraph, among other things. James Buchanan (Pennsylvania Democrat) wins the Election with 45.3% of the popular vote.

That Boy's a Hexadecaroon

Anybody with any sense who stomps around in the history of the U.S. finds abhorrent wonder in the length slave holders reached to justify their ownership of humans who happened to be covered with dark skin. Some of the most disturbing are "good Christians" claiming their Godly values undamaged because "Black Africans have no souls."

Theological arguments aside, the biggest problem with that approach was that Black Africans didn't stay that way.

Throughout their lives, slaves in the U.S. were beasts of burden with no more rights than a farm animal. There is no argument: Black slave women and girls (and men and boys) were subject to routine sexual abuse and rape. No big surprise. That's what always happens when one group has absolute power over another.

Simply put… "You always know who the mother is." Slave women bore slave babies. Nearly every, single "mixed-blood" slave child was treated the same as any other farm animal, often worse for being a reminder.

"Mulatto" started as a term to describe a person who was half Black and half something else, typically White, but maybe Native American, for instance. The word eventually came to mean a person of mixed race. There were lots of such people during slave times. The 1860 U.S. census classified well over a half-million people as "Mulatto," and that was probably an underestimate since the census couldn't be trusted with such things.

Beyond a biracial Mulatto, things got complicated. A "Quadroon" was one-quarter Black. Octoroon, one-eighth. Quintroon, one-sixteenth: dark skin, light skin, redbone, yellow, high yellow, passing. It didn't take too many generations for the enslaved to look much the same as the enslaver.

11

This posed an interesting challenge. How much Black blood did it take to make a person Black? Stated another way, how much White blood did it take to give a Black slave a soul?

1857: Louis Pasteur identifies germs as the cause of illness. Native troops in India are issued Enfield Rifle cartridges from England which are, against the specific orders of local British commanders, pre-greased with beef tallow and pig lard. This, along with other religious insults, kicks off the First War of Indian Independence. The Utah Indian War. J. Lee Richmond is born in Sheffield, Lorain County. Playing for a variety of baseball teams in the Major Leagues, he will become the first person to pitch a no-hitter. Clarence Darrow is born in Kinsman, Trumbull County, Ohio. Future U.S. President William Taft is born in Cincinnati, Ohio.

1858: Wellington is invaded by Oberlin which nobody seems able to forget. The Third Seminole Indian War. The Yakima Indian War (Washington Territory). The Navajo Indian Wars begin. Mexican Civil War. The First War of Indian Independence comes to an end on the sub-continent. British rule grows more brutal. Europe happily meddles in China's affairs thanks to winning the Second Opium War. Minnesota.

1859: Ohio makes it illegal to carry concealed weapons with a law that holds tight 'til 1974. The First and Second Cortina Wars in Texas and Mexico. Romania is formed from Wallachia and Moldavia. Abolitionist John Brown is captured while trying to seize arms from the Federal Arsenal at Harper's Ferry, (West) Virginia. Oberlinian Lewis Sheridan Leary (24) is one of the seventeen killed in the raid. Leary's fellow townsmen, Shields Green (23) and John A. Copeland (25) are hung two weeks after Brown is. All three Oberlinians are Black. Oregon.

1860 – 1869: County Population = 29,744

1860: The census shows more than 500 Blacks living in Lorain County. All but 50 live in, or within, two miles of Oberlin. Florence Nightingale opens her school of nursing. Annie Oakley is born in Darke County, Ohio. The Paiute Indian War (Nevada). The Reform War (Mexico). Abraham Lincoln (Illinois Republican) wins the Election carrying 39.7% of the popular vote and *no* electoral votes from southern states. On December 20, we become the *dis*-United States when South Carolina secedes from the Union. $1,000 is worth $28,171 modern.

1860, July 11, Wednesday: Location: Columbia Township. Victim: John Squires Jr. (14, cousin). Suspect: Wallace Walrath (19, cousin). Victim is the son of farmer John Squires, Sr. Suspect is an occasional farmhand. The boys are known to be quarrelsome.

The night of the crime they argue before heading to bed. Cousin Wallace arises in the early morning hours, takes a rifle that is in the room and strikes the sleeping John, "burying the barrel in the right side of his head, and breaking the skull four inches in length and nearly two inches wide."

Wallace returns to bed, gets up the next morning, and starts his chores. When asked where his cousin is he replies that he has killed him. Squire Senior rushes upstairs to find his son "apparently lifeless" with coagulated blood oozing from his head. Physicians are called. The case is deemed hopeless.

Sheriff Burr holds a preliminary hearing at the Squire farm. Wallace Walrath says he has no memory of making the strike and must've done it in his sleep. He is taken into custody and placed in the Elyria Jail.

Hold on... Despite the assurance of the doctors of his certain death, John Jr. recovers. No crime is found. Those involved refuse to divulge the nature of the argument. The episode is written off as youthful exuberance.

Outcome: Case dismissed.

PARRICIDE: the killing of a close relative.

Call The Cops

Through this book you'll see "constables" and "marshals" as part of local law enforcement. As time goes on, they become local police reporting to their own municipal judges and courts. Sheriffs and deputies, in contrast, work for the county court system.

1861: The U.S. pulls apart. After South Carolina's 1860 exit, Mississippi, Florida, Alabama, Georgia, and Louisiana leave the Union. Then Texas, followed by Virginia, Arkansas, North Carolina, and finally, Tennessee. Slave states remaining are Missouri, Kentucky, Maryland, and Delaware. Kansas becomes a state. The "Confederate States of America" with Jefferson Davis, of Mississippi, as their Provisional President, and Richmond, Virginia, as their capital. Ohio makes it illegal for Whites and Blacks to marry each other. Prince Albert dies and Queen Victoria begins mourning. Lagos, Nigeria, is annexed as a British Colony when England is unable (unwilling?) to end the lucrative slave trade. Alexander II decrees that all Russian serfs are free as long as, y'know, they don't get no fancy ideas. A bankrupt Mexico stops paying international debts. In the Docket: Selling Liquor without a License and Assault and Battery, including "Biting Ear With Intent to Disfigure."

1861, April 12: Fort Sumter: Kill/wound/capture/missing = 0
1861, July 21: First Manassas: 4,690 (it takes a while to get cranking)

1862: The world is supposed to end according to preachers John Cummings and Joseph Morris. The predictions are made separately. Both are incorrect. Mary Jane Patterson receives a degree from Oberlin College becoming the first African-American female college graduate in the U.S. Want 160 acres of western farm land? The *Homestead Act* gives it to any family willing to farm it for five years, previous tenants notwithstanding. The French, Spanish, and British invade a bankrupt Mexico to collect the loan interest owed them. Isn't it funny how money helps form alliances?

1862, February 12: Fort Donelson: 17,398 killed/wounded.
1862, April 6: Shiloh: 23,741.

1862, April 14, Monday: Location: Grafton Township near Grafton Station. Victim: Orson Burton. Suspect: William Fryar.

Burton works alongside the railroad. Fryar stops to talk. Both drink whiskey. They argue. Fryar breaks Burton's skull with several blows with "a bludgeon." Fryar flees. Burton's body is found by an unnamed person.

Stereotypically, William Fryar returns to the scene of the crime as Coroner Gates and coroner's jury are investigating. Fryar confesses and is taken before "Esq. Faxon" (perhaps Elyria's John H. Faxon?). *The Elyria Independent Democrat* says the charge is murder in the first degree. The Docket lists murder in the second degree. Prosecutor: Washington W. Boyton. Judge: S. Burke. Plea: Not guilty. *Changed to:* Guilty of manslaughter. Outcome: Ohio Penitentiary, 18 months, plus court costs of $40.28.

Awa Wi' Ye!

County authorities deliver you to the high, stone walls of the Ohio Penitentiary. You are taken by prison staff and searched for weapons. Your vital statistics are collected along with, depending on the era, descriptions of identifying marks, Bertillion measures, fingerprints, and photographs. The hair on your head and face are cut as closely as possible and, depending on the effect of the trimming, a second set of photos might be made.

You are stripped naked, sprayed with water, ensured a good scrubbing, deloused, and provided a set of "regulation zebra stripes." From there it's off to the prison hospital for a medical exam: Are you lame? Do you have pneumonia? Tuberculosis? Cancer? Bad heart action? Skin infections? Lunacy? Any of cupid's diseases?

Then, it's up to the Chaplain for a check on your moral situation: What is your religious affiliation? You do have one, don't you? Are you married? Divorced? Widowed? Have children? Do you smoke? An acceptable habit, for a man. Drink? Too bad. Sorry. Not in here.

After gaining your serial number, you're back with a Deputy Warden and thence to your cell. Your location depends on a combination of your sentence and the just-completed evaluation; hard labor, regular work, idle, sick, or insane. Housing also depends on your sex. The few women prisoners (about 20 out of 2,000) are placed in their own dormitory and, for safety's sake, kept separate from the general male population. No matter where you end up you hope for reasonable company, or at the very least, to be with people who are not too violent.

Life is hard because it's meant to be. Official punishments for violation of the rules range from the mild—loss of minor privileges—all the way up to physical torture. Misdeeds against other prisoners produce unofficial retributions that include rebukes and shunnings, to beatings, rapes, and death.

But all is not lost… You're in a very big place, and there's plenty of work to be done. Do you have a trade? You may be enlisted to help maintain the prison in which you are kept. Are you well educated? Then, perhaps you can work within the penitentiary's sizable bureaucracy. There are a few trusted individuals lucky enough to run errands outside the penitentiary walls. You could be one of them.

No matter your standing there's time off your sentence if you can manage to keep your nose clean. At first, each year of good behavior cuts a couple months, but the longer you stay out of trouble, the more time you earn: A decade of being good gets you three years and eight months closer to your release. Plus, there's always hope for parole, or maybe the Governor will commute your sentence to time served.

It *does* happens, you know.

Judge Stevenson Burke:
S. Burke was born in St. Lawrence County, New York on November 26, 1826. His family moved to Ridgeville, Lorain County, when he was about eight years old. Smart and ambitious, he worked his way through Ohio Wesleyan University, was admitted to the Ohio bar in 1848, and gained a reputation as a sharp trial lawyer. Burke was elected to the Court of Common Pleas in Lorain County in 1862 and served until 1869, when he resigned to resume his practice of law. Many of his cases as a litigator involved the corporate laws surrounding the growing railway industry. Burke died on April 24, 1904.

1862, May 31: Seven Pines: 13,736 killed/wounded.
1862, June 27: Gaines' Mill: 15,500.
1862, July 1: Malvern Hill: 8,500.
1862, August 28: Second Manassas: 22,180.
1862, September 17: Antietam: 23,100.
1862, October 8: Perryville: 7,407.
1862, December 13: Fredericksburg: 17,929.
1862, December 31: Stones River: 23,515.

1863: The world is supposed to end according to preacher John Wroe. It doesn't. *Four score and seven years ago…* Mobs of women in the Confederate States' Capital of Richmond, Virginia, destroy shops in protest over the high price of food. West Virginia. The first Ohio monument to Civil War dead is placed in Bristolville, Bristol Township, Trumbull County, in honor of thirteen "Defenders of the Union." The small stone monument, topped with a draped urn, is still there, a few steps north of the intersection of Ohio Routes 88 and 45. Complaints about the Lorain County Courthouse, particularly its "poor ventilation," grow more common.

1863, January 9: Ark. Post: 6,547 killed/wounded.

1863, April 30: Chancellorsville: 30,500 (estimate)

1863, May 18 - July 4: Vicksburg: 19,233.

1863, May 21 - July 9: Port Hudson: 12,208.

1863, July 1: Gettysburg: 51,000.

1863, September 19: Chickamauga: 34,624.

1863, November 23: Chattanooga: 12,485.

1864: Lorain County's first Public Library (Elyria). Karl Marx emerges as a political leader in London, England. The French make Austrian Archduke Maximilian the Emperor of Mexico. The *Geneva Convention* sets standards for the treatment of war wounded. Abraham Lincoln (Illinois National Union) wins the Election with 55.0% of the popular vote among those states that participate. A long-range attempt on Lincoln's life leaves his hat with a bullet hole. Nevada.

1864, May 5: The Wilderness: 29,800 killed/wounded.

1864, May 8: Spotsylvania Courthouse: 30,000.

1864, May 13: Resaca: 5,547.

1864, May 31: Cold Harbor: 15,500.

1864, July 22: Atlanta: 12,140.

1864, July 30: The Crater: 5,300.

1864, August 18: Globe Tavern: 5,879.

1864, October 19: Cedar Creek: 8,575.

1864, November-December: Sherman's March to the Sea.

1864, November 30: Franklin: 8,587.

1864, December 15: Nashville: 6,602

1865: Amendment to the *U.S. Constitution: Thirteenth:* Prohibition of slavery and other forms of "involuntary servitude." Abraham Lincoln visits Richmond, Virginia. Lee surrenders at Appomattox, Virginia. Lincoln is assassinated. Andrew Johnson becomes President. Southern states begin passing "Black Codes" to limit the freedoms of ex-slaves, including forbidding them from owning firearms. The first branch of the first version of the Ku Klux (Klan) is founded by Confederate War veterans in Pulaski, Tennessee—on Christmas Day (**Happy Birthday, Jesus!**). British women begin organized agitation for the right to vote. Future President Warren

Harding is born in Corsica (Blooming Grove), Morrow County, Ohio. $1,000 is worth $14,398 modern.

1865, March, 13, Monday: Location: Black River Township, Rochester Depot, James Long's Hotel. Victim: George Mitchell. Suspect: James Long.

A "dancing party" is being held at Long's Hotel, which the suspect keeps with his mother (the father is away in the armed service).

One John Taylor and victim Mitchell are musicians at the party, which breaks up peacefully around midnight. John Taylor and James Long's mother argue about the amount of money owed to the musicians. The son takes up the argument and denounces the musicians "with horrid oaths and used the most insulting epithets, ordering them to leave which they did."

Outside, the victim, George Mitchell loudly tells John Taylor he won't take that kind of talk from anybody. James Long hears the remark, re-opens the door, and repeats himself. Mitchell turns and starts towards Long who produces a "single-barrel" pistol and fires.

Shot in the eye and through the head, George Mitchell dies almost instantaneously. Victim Mitchell is a veteran soldier who served three years in the Civil War with his two brothers, Adelbert and Sidney. Honorably discharged about three months prior, the victim is known to be quiet, peaceable, and temperate. Friends state that he sent all his war pay back to his widowed mother.

James Long is arrested and held in lieu of $1,500 bail. Prosecutor: John C. Hale. Judge: S. Burke. Charge: Murder in the first degree. Plea: Not guilty. Found: Guilty of murder in the second degree. Outcome: Ohio Penitentiary, 10 years, plus cost of $244.54.

1865, April 6: Sailor's Creek: 9,980 killed/wounded.
1865, April 9: Lee's Surrender at Appomattox.
1865, May 10: Union Army captures Confederate States' President Jefferson Davis in Irwinville, Georgia, as he's making a run for Mexico.

1865, June 2: The U.S. Civil War comes to a formal close with the surrender of General Edmund Kirby Smith, commander of Confederate forces west of the Mississippi. The grim statistics:

    620,000 Killed.
    467,000 Wounded.
    400,000 Captured/Missing.

The Great State of Ohio sent 60% of her men, aged 18 to 45 to the war: The highest percentage of any northern state, for a total of almost 320,000 (including 5,000 free Blacks). Of the total, 6,835 were killed in action and another 28,640 were wounded. What would we sacrifice so much for today?

1866: What do you do with too much milk? Wellington, Ohio, starts making lots and lots of cheese. Lucy Hobbs is the first (schooled) female doctor of dental surgery when she graduates from the Ohio College of Dental Surgery in Cincinnati, Ohio. A *Civil Rights Act* is passes in Congress to guarantee the legal protection of African-Americans. The Navajo Indian Wars end. The Kingdom of Italy is formed.

1867: Wilbur Wright is born in Dayton, Ohio. Joseph Lister develops antiseptic surgical methods—ever hear of "Listerine?" Padded gloves are introduced to boxing. *Slave Songs of the United States* is the first collection of "Negro Spirituals" published for White folks. Lorain County's first street lights (Elyria) are fired with kerosene. Wellington's first jail is built by volunteers and presented to the village. The U.S. buys Alaska from Russia for $7.2 million. Many folks think it's a bad deal. A Republican Congress passes the *Reconstruction Acts*. They divide the south into military districts and enforce the right to vote for all male citizens, no matter their color. Women need not bother. Remember Maximilian, the Emperor of Mexico? Well, he's shot and killed. Karl Marx publishes "Das Kapital." Canada comes to life as its own country. Parcheesi. Future ball-player Denton True (Cy(clone)) Young is born in Gilmore, Tuscarawas County, Ohio. Charles Turner is born in Cincinnati, Ohio, and grows up to discover that insects can hear and learn. Nebraska. Colorado.

1868: Amendment to the *U.S. Constitution: Fourteenth:* Guarantees equal rights to all born or naturalized U.S. citizens (including ex-slaves). It ensures due-process at a state level and guarantees equal protection under the law. Mid-term elections bring "Radical Reconstruction Republicans" into power. The dismissal of Civil War-time Secretary of War Edwin Stanton brings President Andrew Johnson pretty darned close to being booted from his office by the Senate. Cuba rebels against Spain. A Civil War monument of an eagle capping an obelisk is placed in Huntington Township on the southeast corner of Ohio Routes 58 and 162. Custer massacres more than a hundred Native Americans beside the Washita River. Harvey Firestone is born in

Columbiana, Columbiana County, Ohio. U.S. Grant (Illinois Republican) wins the Election with 52.7% of the popular vote.

1869: Cincinnati, Ohio, fields the first baseball team in which every player is a paid professional. They win all their games that season. Former Confederate President Jeff Davis won't be prosecuted for treason. John Menard is the first African American to speechify in Congress. U.S. patent for the first plastic: celluloid. Tom Edison gets one for his voting machine. And so does William Semple, another Ohio boy, for chewing gum. Failed Oberlin geology student, Major John Powell (Ret.) and his left arm head down the Colorado River. He left his right arm at Shiloh. The first train chugs from the right coast to the left. The Suez Canal opens for business. There are now nine, instead of seven, judges on the U.S. Supreme Court. John Heisman is born in Cleveland, Ohio.

1870 – 1879: County Population = 30,308

1870: Amendment to the *U.S. Constitution: Fifteenth:* Prohibits the use of race, color, or prior standing of servitude in determining who might vote in elections. Women need not bother. Ada Kepley is the first woman to graduate from an accredited law school (Union College of Law in Chicago, Illinois). Through this decade, the first declared Muslim immigrants begin to arrive in the U.S., first from Syria-Lebanon, later from Europe and India. France declares war on Prussia because Otto von Bismarck fiddles with the text of the Ems Dispatch. Revolution in France. Again. One of the first board games: *Snakes and Ladders.* $1,000 is worth $17,998 modern.

1870, October 13, Thursday: Location: ?. Victim: Jones. Suspect: Jones. Act: Murder. Charge: ? Outcome: ?
   I'm not even sure if this was a Lorain County murder. The newspapers are difficult to decipher. There was nothing in the docket.

1870, November 24: Location: Ridgeville Township. Victim: John P. Mieden. Body buried in Avon's Catholic Cemetery is exhumed on January 13, 1871. Coroner Faxon holds an inquest. Organs of chest "mostly in a normal condition." Brain is "too much softened to bear examination." Stomach contents show the man died of acute arsenic poisoning.

   Mary, 45, wife of 14 years, testifies that Meiden died after a trip to Cleveland to sell apples. She says that her husband stated, upon return, that he did not feel well and that he began vomiting and purging about an hour after going to bed. He worked on the farm for part of the next day and died the day after that while suffering a great deal of pain.

   Authorities discover the dead man was needlessly jealous of his wife's relationship with her childhood friend Nicholas Schleifeinbaum, to the point of banning him from the Mieden home. Schleifeinbaum is closely questioned and, while admitting to having fought with Meiden, he denies having anything to do with the death of the husband of his good friend, Mary.

   Outcome: Unsolved.

1871: Oberlin builds a Civil War monument on the southeast corner of Professor and West College. Lorain County sandstone quarries find a huge market in Chicago, Illinois, after a cow there kicks over a lantern. The National Rifle Association is founded by veterans of the Civil War with the motto "Firearms Safety, Education, Marksmanship, Training, Shooting for Recreation." U.S. Expedition to Korea. Afghan philosopher Jamal al-Din urges violence against western influence. Rome becomes the capital of Italy. President Grant suppresses the Ku Klux Klan with a new *Civil Rights Act*. Orville Wright is born in Dayton, Ohio. Washington gets its "D.C."

1872: The Lakeshore & Tuscarawas railroad reaches what will soon be the Village of Lorain. Native American territories are cut by the Missouri, Kansas, and Texas Railroad. The Modoc Indian War in California and Oregon. Pearl (Zane) Grey is born in Zanesville, Ohio. Ohio-born Victoria Woodhull runs for president but Ulysses Grant (Illinois Republican) wins the Election with 55.6% of the popular vote.

1873: The Village of Lorain is incorporated. Voters reject changes to the Ohio State Constitution. Among the more radical proposals denied: Allowing women to run for seats on local school boards and restrictions on municipal debt. The U.S. Congress authorizes federal postage stamps. The Comstock Law makes it illegal to send obscene, lewd, or lascivious material through the U.S. Mail. Strauss and Davis patent copper-rivet-reinforced blue jeans. Susan B. Anthony is fined $100 for voting in the previous year's presidential election (perhaps for the aforementioned Ohioan, Victoria Woodhull). Cable cars in San Francisco. Buda and Pest join.

1873, November 13, Thursday: Location: ? Victim: ? Suspect: John Williams. Act: ? Charge: ? Plea: ? Outcome: Nollied by Prosecutor Charles W. Johnson.

What is "Nollied?"

Various issues cause the dismissal of criminal cases: Lack of evidence, a change in testimony, death of a witness, inability to bring a suspect to trial, or charging the wrong person. Only the prosecution can declare a "nolle prosequi." The judge almost always agrees and orders a docket entry of "nolle prose" which is Latin for "forget about it." Court Recorders shorten the formal phrase to "nollied."

1874: Charleston City Incorporated. First load of coal to Lorain County steel mills. Germany makes the smallpox vaccine compulsory. U.S. troops land in Hawai'i "to protect the King." The Red River Indian War in Texas.

The *National Woman's Christian Temperance Union* (NWCTU) gets it start in Cleveland, Ohio.

1875: In Wellington, Ohio, A. Willard paints a picture every U.S. citizen has seen. Congress outlaws segregation on public transport, in hotels, and in restaurants. That does not mean it isn't done. State's rights, after all. Electric dental drill gains a patent. The first Catholic Cardinal in the U.S.—John McCloskey. The first 9-inning shutout Chicago (1) St. Louis (0). Alexander Bell transmits sound via wire. Las Cuevas War in Texas and Mexico. $1,000 is worth $12,597 modern.

1875, October 28: *Elyria Constitution:*

A Fatal Quarrel:

Two colored men of Oberlin, Cash Scott and Drury Cooper, living on adjacent lots, have for some time been bitter enemies. Scott, in order to shut out his domicile from the view of his neighbor, built a high board fence between the lots. But Cooper did not take kindly to the obstruction, so on Saturday, he proceeded to saw down the fence.

Scott with the assistance of a boy named Vaughn, tried to stop him, when a fight ensued. Cooper hit Vaughn with a stone, when Vaughn turned on him and struck him four hard blows in the breast with a billy[club], and then ran away, and Cooper set to work again sawing at the fence, but shortly afterwards dropped down dead.

A postmortem examination was held and the jury returned a verdict that death resulted from a rupture of a blood vessel near the heart caused by excitement and exercise. Scott and Vaughn were not arrested. Wonder whether the exercise of that billy did not have something to do with that rupture.

OR...

1875, November 30: *The Elyria Democrat:*

Oberlin. A Sudden Death:

The people of this place were startled on Saturday, October 23d, by the report that Mr. Drury Cooper was dead.

As near correct as the facts, are which can now be

gathered, it seems that a high and tight board fence had been erected within a few days previous, on the lot line between Mr. Cooper and Mr. Vaughan. Mr. Cooper's house being within a few feet of the line, the house on the north was almost cut off by the fence.

Under advice that the height of a fence was four feet only, and being unable to reduce the fence to that height by protest or persuasion, he proceeded to saw off the boards so that the fence should have only the prescribed height by statute.

This excited the ire of the Vaughan interest, and the two young lads of the family, Cassius Scott and Lewis Vaughan, came out for the protection of the fence as it had been built. Some hard words passed between the parties, and perhaps a scuffle, as one report is.

However that may be, Mr. Cooper warned the Vaughan lad to let his saw alone, he being on the side opposite from where Mr. Cooper stood, hitting it with a stick. The report further is, that he came around on the sidewalk, to a point near to, and on the same side with Mr. Cooper, and while Mr. Cooper was engaged in sawing the fence, two little children of Mr. Cooper, standing near their father, (one five and the other seven years of age) said they saw a large ball come and strike their father upon the breast, and he, instantly fell and died.

A coroner's inquest was held and the decision was, that he died from a disturbance of the heart.

The hurried manner in which the inquest was held, and the time of day, it being after night-fall, together with some other facts that have come to the surface since, seem to throw a shade of suspicion that the whole of the truth in the matter has not yet been brought to the light.

An examination of the lads was held before Esq. Harris, but nothing definite was brought in proof against them, and they were discharged.

Drury and Racheal Cooper's home in Oberlin was on South Water (now South Park) one block from Groveland. Ex-slave and Civil War vet John Vaughn (Vaughan) and his wife, Lethe Ann were on Groveland. Louis (Lewis) Vaughn was their son while Cassius (Cash) Scott was Mrs. Vaughn's son by a previous marriage—they were the two lads antagonizing Drury Cooper.

Cassius Scott was eventually charged with murder and indicted by the January, 1876, Lorain County Grand Jury. A criminal trial prosecuted by George P. Metcalf in front of Judge Boyton found him innocent.

The cause of the argument that prompted the building of the high, wooden fence mentioned in the newspapers seems unknown.

Judge Washington Wallace Boyton:

W.W. Boyton (Republican) was born to a farm family in Lorain County's Russia Township. A precocious child, he was teaching school at the age of sixteen. Boyton studied law at the Elyria office of his uncle, Elbridge Boyton and joined the Ohio Bar in 1856.

He was voted in as the Lorain County Prosecuting Attorney (1859-1863) and served a term in the Ohio State House of Representative where he tried (and failed) to give men the right to vote, regardless of color of blood. Boyton was appointed to the judgeship of Lorain County by Ohio Governor Rutherford B. Hayes (Republican) and then elected to the same position in 1871. He resigned in 1876 when he was elected to the Ohio Supreme Court where he served for half a decade before resigning due to poor health and the crummy pay. Among Boyton's many local accomplishments are helping to found and serving as president of the Elyria Memorial Hospital. Boyton died on June 27, 1916. He can now be found in the Elyria Cemetery.

1876: The ballet *Swan Lake*. Turkish irregular troops massacre more than 15,000 Bulgarians. France and Britain control the finances of Egypt's government. Victoria is "Empress of India." Susan B. Anthony's *Woman's Declaration of Rights* is just in time for the country's Centennial Celebration. She eventually gets a dollar for this, and other efforts. "Mr. Watson, come here!" Custer collects what's due. Buffalo Hunters' Indian War (Texas and Oklahoma, against the Comanche and Apache). The Great Sioux Indian War in Montana, Dakota, and Wyoming. Rutherford Hayes (Ohio Republican) is president with 47.9% of the popular vote (*see 1877*). New York Democrat Samuel Tilden wins 50.9% of the votes but still loses the election.

1877: The Republican party ends support of southern, post-Civil War reconstruction to secure southern electoral votes needed to win the contested presidential election for Rutherford Hayes. Welcome Jim Crow to the table! A near-nationwide strike of railway workers against wage cuts. Helen Magill is the first woman in the U.S. to earn a Ph.D., in her case, in Greek, from Boston University, Boston, Massachusetts. Nez Perce Indian War (various western states). San Elizario Salt War is an uprising of militia in Texas. A bill is introduced in the Ohio Legislature to "give juries discretion to sentence persons convicted of murder in the first degree to the Penitentiary for life." This takes the form of being "guilty of with a recommendation of mercy." Prior to this, all those convicted of first degree murder suffered a mandatory sentence of death.

1878: The British invade Afghanistan—again. More than 13,000 people of the lower Mississippi River die of Yellow Fever. The first U.S. telephone exchange in New Haven, *Connect*icut. George Coy is the first full-time operator. Ivory Soap by William Proctor. The first fire pole is installed in a New York City firehouse. Cheyenne Indian War (various mid-west states). Bannock Indian War (various western states).

1879: Work begins on Lorain County's new Courthouse. Lorain High School graduates its first class. The White River Indian War (Ute, in Colorado). Sheepeater Indian War (Shoshone in Idaho). Victorio's Indian War (Apache in Mexico). The Senate passes *The Chinese Bill* restricting ship captains to no more than fifteen Chinese passengers bound for this country on any U.S. boat. The *Elyria **Republican** (Feb 20, 1879)* says:

> The Senate has passed the Chinese Bill by a small majority.
> It imposes heavy penalties upon ship-owners or masters who
> bring more than fifteen Chinamen to our shores on any single
> voyage. Will any person say what right we have to proscribe the
> Chinese, more than the Germans, the Irish, or the inhabitants
> of any other nation with whom we are on terms of amity? We
> regard it as an act of exclusion unworthy of the great nation
> we proudly boast of.

1879, May 29: Trial: 1879, October ?: Location: ? Victim: Joseph Cook. Suspect: Thomas Faulkner (Falkner). Suspect Faulkner has been a drunkard his entire adult life with no friends or relatives this side of the Atlantic. Victim Cook is known to habitually beat and abuse Faulkner who finally explodes into "the rage of a maniac" and strikes Cook several blows on the head with an old axe.

Thomas Faulkner is so drunk at the time of arrest that he doesn't know what he did, let alone why. General consensus is that the killer should be treated gently because of the combination of his drunkenness and maltreatment at the hands of his victim. Prosecutor: George P. Metcalf. Judge: John C. Hale. Charge: Murder in the first degree. Plea: Not guilty. Found: Guilty as charged, with mercy. Outcome: Life in the Ohio Penitentiary.

Judge John Cushman Hale:

Born in Orford, New Hampshire, March 3, 1831, J.C. (Republican) was raised on his family's farm until the age of 19. Educated in public schools, he graduated in the 1857 class of Dartmouth College, then moved to Cleveland, Ohio.

School teacher Hale read law in the office of Judge Samuel B. Prentiss and was admitted to bar in July, 1861. Three months later he was practicing in Elyria. In two years he was elected to the first of two consecutive 3-year terms as Lorain County's Prosecuting Attorney, serving from 1863-1869.

Near the end of his second term as prosecutor, Hale was elected Judge of the Common Pleas Court twice, from 1867 to September, 1883, when he resigned to continue the practice of law, in Cleveland, in partnership with former Lorain County Judge W. W. Boynton. John C. Hale also served 12 years as a judge in the Eighth District Circuit Court, starting in 1893, after which he retired.

J.C. Hale died June 9, 1922.

1880 – 1889: County Population = 35,526

1880: People in Avon start planting vineyards. Tom's incandescent light bulb. Memphis, Tennessee, is the first city in the U.S. to separate its storm and sanitary sewers. Wabash, Indiana, is the first entirely lit with electricity. Charles Jones is the first to hit 2 home runs in 1 inning. John Lee Richmond is the first to pitch a no-hitter in major league baseball—against Cleveland. Sousa takes over the U.S. Marine Band. *The Great White Way!* James Garfield (Ohio Republican) wins the Election with 48.3% of the popular vote. $1,000 is worth $22,734 modern.

1881: Watson meets Holmes for the first time. Kansas goes dry. *The Greatest Show on Earth.* American Red Cross. B.T. Washington's Tuskegee Institute. The OK Corral. The American Federation of Labor. The British withdraw from Afghanistan—again. James Garfield is shot and dies two months later, more from crummy medical care than anything else. Chester Arthur is President. After decades of complaints, the "new" Lorain County Courthouse opens for business, sheet-steel dome, figure of justice, and all. Its face of sandstone from Amherst's quarries lasts a long, long time. After decades of complaints it will be replaced, in 2004, by the relatively huge, 7-floor, Lorain County Justice Center across Court Street. The "old" stone courthouse still stands in (reduced) use when this book is published.

1881, May 20: *Oberlin Weekly News*

> A SAD AFFAIR
>
> Shooting of Constable Frank Stone
>
> --His Dangerous Condition
>
> A large proportion of the readers of the News who reside in this vicinity, have doubtless heard something before this of the exciting events which took place in our usually quiet village last week about the hour that the paper went to press.
>
> The assault upon Constable Frank Stone by Robert "Butler" Durham who was a prisoner in his charge; the interference of Butler's brother Tom and his father, Samuel Durham; the subsequent attempt to arrest Tom; the shooting of the constable by Samuel Durham; the constable's critical condition, and the imprisonment of the old man and Butler— are matters which have been the exciting topic of conversation

for the past week. The flying reports have been so conflicting and in some instances so much exaggerated that a connected narrative may still be of interest.

THE PRELIMINARY SKIRMISH

On Wednesday evening of last week [May 11] Frank Cobb and Butler Durham were together about the barns north of the Union School House and had an altercation, in which Durham gave Cobb a pounding.

RESISTING AN OFFICER

On the following day young Cobb made an affidavit before Justice Myers, charging Durham with assault and battery. A warrant was issued and placed in the hands of Constable Frank Stone. Knowing his customer, Mr. Stone invited Mr. A.K. Bacon to accompany him to make the arrest, which he did with a horse and buggy.

They found their man on South Water Street [Park] and as he agreed to come along quietly, Mr. Bacon drove home. When Mr. Stone and Durham were opposite Penfield carriage shop on Mill Street [Vine], the prisoner refused to go any further. His father and his brother Tom, who were laying a floor in the carriage blacksmith shop came to his assistance and things began to look ugly. Stone called for assistance and the employees of the shop, with G.W. Whitney and others, responded and the scene became lively. Within a brief space of time, Butler threw Stone twice striking him in the face after he was down each time until the blood flowed freely. Tom drew a hatchet upon I.H. Brown, who attempted to interfere. Accounts differ as to the weapon flourished by the old man. Butler finally escaped, and Stone sent a pistol ball after him without effect.

FOUR MORE WARRANTS

Constable Stone then returned to the office of Justice Myers and procured warrants for the arrest of Tom Durham and his father [Samuel] on a charge of resisting an officer, and two more warrants for Butler—one charging him with resisting an officer and the other with assault and battery for striking him.

A RACE

Soon after seven o'clock [PM], Stone saw Tom Durham sitting upon a goods box in front of the Worcester block, called upon two or three men to assist, crossed the street, and when near him, said "I have a warrant for you." Tom started south upon a run saying "Catch me first." Stone followed, firing his revolver after the fugitive and calling upon the bystanders to assist. The race was a sharp one, Stone firing five shots before Tom reached home at No. 26 Mechanic Street [Locust], but it appears that only one shot took effect, making a slight wound in the skin on his back.

The route taken was south on South Main Street across the open lots in the rear of Lane's old blacksmith shop and the Methodist church to Groveland, thence east to South Pleasant and south to Mechanic Street, the pursued and the pursuers taking across another corner to the Durham place, a little east of South Pleasant.

Tom ran to the house, told his father that he had been shot, and excitedly began to gather up stones to throw at his pursuers.

THE CONSTABLE SHOT

Mr. Stone, being full of energy and somewhat impulsive, determined to capture his man, led the pursuit and was followed by quite a company of men. As the officer left the sidewalk to cross the street in the direction of the house, the old man [Samuel] Durham stepped toward the front door, placed one knee on the floor, rested his rifle against the door, and, saying "You shot my boy and I will shoot you," took aim at Stone's breast and fired, the ball passing in at the breast and out under the left arm. Mr. Stone did not fall or at first realize the extent of his injury, but soon found the blood flowing and began to feel faint. He told those around him that he was shot, and asked them to take hold of him. He was carried to the house of Mr. Darling close by, and soon after to his own home No. 58 South Professor Street.

Doctors Johnson Allen and Wm. C. Bunce, and a little later, Dr. Wm. Bunce were present, and gave him all the attention in their power.

THE CITIZENS ARM

The report of the shooting spread rapidly, several men were sworn in as special constables and, armed with revolvers, proceeded to the house to make sure of the arrest of the Durhams. Mr. O.F. Carter taking the lead, requested the crowd to keep back while he went in and talked with the old man, the latter showing no disposition to make any further resistance. While these events were in progress, a telegram was sent to Sheriff Corning at Elyria, but fortunately that official drove into town soon after the shooting took place, and proceeded directly to the house, where he arrived just as Mr. Carter was holding the consultation with Durham. He immediately placed the old man under arrest and took him to the depot, where he was placed in the baggage room until the arrival of the train, which was over an hour late, when he was taken to Elyria and placed in jail.

TOM DURHAM

was allowed to remain at home that night, promising to appear before the Justice the next morning, which he did, and after a brief examination was ordered to enter into a recognizance in the sum of $100 for his appearance – J.W. Worcester becoming his bondsman; but the prisoner finally changed his plea "guilty", and the case was continued till Monday, Tom promising to assist in the capture of Butler who had left on Thursday night. On Monday Tom appeared again, and was fined $10 for resisting an officer and $10.75 costs.

THE ARREST OF BUTLER

On Friday about 10 o'clock a dispatch was received from Norwalk stating that Butler had been there at 6 o'clock that morning. A telegram was immediately sent to the marshal of that city to arrest and hold him. About noon the marshal telegraphed that he had got his man. Constable Cameron took the 5 p.m. train and went up to Norwalk and brought Butler back on the evening train, taking him directly through to Elyria, where he was lodged in jail.

On Saturday Samuel Durham and his son Butler were both brought before J.H. Faxon, J.P., at Elyria. The old man Durham was held for his appearance at court on a charge of shooting with intent to kill, and Butler on two charges of assault and battery and one for resisting an officer. Not being able to secure bail they were both returned to jail. Court will convene next week and their cases will come before the grand jury.

THE DURHAMS.

Samuel Durham is a colored man with some admixture of White blood, sixty six years of age. He is a large, bony man, a carpenter by trade, and has not been especially troublesome as a citizen, except in defense of his boys, in which, he seemed willing to go to any length, right or wrong.

Tom has been considered the most peaceable one of the family, and seldom got into trouble, but takes his brothers part. He is a strong built young man, and also works at carpentering sometimes.

Butler [about 15, at this time] has been a source of annoyance to citizens and officers for years past. A regular bull-dog in disposition, with muscles like iron, he was ready to pound any man that came across his path, and was a troublesome customer for an officer to arrest. At one time he evaded all efforts of the Marshal to bring him in and Detective Goodrich, of Cleveland, was called upon, who succeeded in getting the fellow in the lockup, but narrowly escaped a blow over the head with a bar of iron. On another occasion he broke out of the lock-up, doing considerable damage, and was gone for some months. Altogether, he is a hard case.

The charge of cowardice, to which other officials have been subjected, for being afraid to arrest the Durhams, had, no doubt, some effect upon the mind of Constable Stone when he determined to take his prisoners, at all hazards.

THE CONSTABLE

Frank Stone is a good citizen, has been the agent of the United States Express Company at this place for several years, and has had considerable experience as an officer. His misfortune in this case has excited universal sympathy, and the perpetrator of the dastardly act is universally condemned.

Mr. Stone has been lying in a critical condition since he was wounded, and appears to be gradually failing. He has lost a great deal of blood, and nothing but his strong constitution can save him. Upon the first examination, Doctors Johnson and Allen were of the opinion that his lungs were not seriously injured, but the Doctors Bunce claimed that the ball passed through the left lung, and having attended him since, are still of the same opinion.

Samuel Durham is first charged with, and indicted for, shooting Stone with intent to kill. This is changed to murder in the first degree when the Constable dies on June 4. Samuel Durham pleads not guilty. The criminal trial starts November 28 in front of Judge Hale. Prosecution is George P. Metcalf, A.B. Webber, and E.G. Johnson. Defense is I.E. Webster, of Oberlin, and J.H. Dickson. Outcome: Found guilty of murder in the second degree. The mandatory sentence is life in the Ohio Penitentiary in Columbus. A new trial is requested and refused.

Samuel Durham proves to be such a good prisoner that *the warden* of the Ohio Penitentiary pushes for his release from jail. Ohio Governor James E. Campbell grants the pardon in December of 1891. Durham, in his late 70s, dies in October of 1897.

1881, August 5: *Oberlin Weekly News:*

John Walker, a Mulatto, who has been making his home at the house of Lewis Clark, No. 100 East College street, this village, and has been working for J.W. Mesroe of Russia township disappeared from Mr. Mesroe's on Thursday morning, July 28th. Search was made for him in this and surrounding towns, his brother, who came from Nashville, Tenn., in response to a telegram, assisting, and a reward was offered for his recovery. On Thursday morning of this week Newton Stone, a young man of this place, while out hunting squirrels on the farm of Alfred Harris, in the neighborhood where he had been at work, found the missing man suspended from the limb of a tree, with a strip of basswood bark around his neck, his feet about four feet from the ground. The friends were notified, and the remains were brought in and interred in the cemetery Thursday Evening.

The "J.W. Mesroe of Russia township" was Jonathan Mesrole, owner of 109 acres in present-day New Russia Township, on Pyle-South Amherst Road,

half-way between the zig-zag north of Route 511 and Russia Road. The location of the "farm of Alfred Harris" proved elusive. There was an Alfred Harris who owned property on the south side of Morgan Street, in Oberlin. Maybe he was leasing property?

I found no other any references to this very lynch-like hanging, but those considering this scant coverage proof of a cover-up should keep in mind that, on July 2, 1881, Charles Guiteau shot U.S. President Garfield and that the wounded Garfield lingered for months before dying. The local weekly papers were filled with little else. It would be an interesting project to see what might have been written in private sources about John Walker. Why don't one of you do that?

The man who found the hanging Walker, Newton Stone, was a first-generation Oberlinian and about 20 years old at the time. He appears in the papers a few times after his harrowing experience, sometimes as "Black," sometimes "mulatto," but mostly for drinking and having too good a time.

The dead man's board-keeper, Lewis Garrard Clarke, was an "escaped Kentucky octoroon slave" who, along with his wife, Emily, were early "colored" settlers in Oberlin. Clark claimed his published life's story to be part-inspiration for Harriet Beecher Stowe's book *Uncle Tom's Cabin*.

1882: Vaccine for rabies. A mad-dog-bitten boy receives its first application three years later. *The Chinese Exclusion Act* is a 10-year moratorium on the importation of laborers from that country. Ohio's *Pond Bill* goes into effect. It requires substantial private bonds for the establishment of taverns and ties the breaking of liquor laws to the loss of those bonds. It also levies high annual taxes on tavern owners. This and "Sunday Laws" (no booze on that day) are the state's first serious attempt at controlling the sale and use of alcohol. The drinking crowd takes a dim view of these new restrictions. This is the first year reliable sources of "extra-judicial killings" are available. There are 113 lynchings in the U.S.: 49 Blacks, 64 others, per the Tuskegee Institute, 1979.

1882, June 23: *The Daily Advocate (Newark, Ohio):*

> Remarkable Phenomenon: A Tidal Wave Sweeps the Shore of Lake Erie at Cleveland. Considerable Damage Done—Two Men Washed off the Shore.
>
> CLEVELAND, June 23.—A remarkable tidal-wave swept the lake front here at six o:clock this morning. From the best information known it was about two miles wide and 11 feet higher than the surface of the lake. It came in the wake of a dense and angry looking black gray cloud, which moved sullenly from the north west over the city...

This the one of the best, early accounts I found of what's called an "Edge Wave," or "Seiche" (sayish). Caused by a confluence of weather and strong winds, this natural sloshing of water about the relatively shallow Lake Erie basin can be magnified by local shoreline geography into impressive and sometime fatal results.

1882, April 7, Friday, early evening:

Florence Hance Fishburn loves her husband Tom. Her brothers and Tom's parents owned property across from each other in Eaton Township, just north of the curves on Island Road—it is as if fate brought them together. She is nine years younger than Tom, but the difference in age has never been an issue. Folks say they are "well-paired."

A teen-aged Florence was petrified with fear when her 24-year-old Tom signed up for duty in the War of Rebellion. Off he went in January of 1862 to join Company B of the Union Ohio Volunteers. She was relieved when he, along the rest of his troop, was assigned to stand guard over the thousands of Confederate soldiers held in the Johnson's Island Union Prison in Sandusky Bay. Tom complained some about his duty, especially during the long, cold winters, but she was comforted to know he was safe from the fighting and fewer than a hundred miles from home.

Tom is discharged three years later "on expiration of term of service." Florence is proud of him even though, like so many others, he went in as a private and came out the same. The two are married shortly after his return and she begins bearing children. First, there's son, Almond, in 1866, and then Joseph three years later. Florence adores her children, as she should. It troubles her that Tom lacks her depth of feeling.

You see, sometime after son Joseph's birth, Tom expresses jealousy over Florence's affection for their children, saying she loves them more than him. She can't understand his anger. It's a mother's duty to love her children with all her heart, isn't it?

Florence is panicked in June of 1871 when her husband ups and leaves without warning. She spends weeks not knowing if he's dead or alive until a friend happens to encounter Tom working as a farmhand in Michigan. He returns home shortly thereafter but, strangely enough, refuses to offer any explanation for his disappearance.

As time passes Tom begins to regard his wife "with an expression that is terrible to behold." By 1875, his family and hers have grown concerned enough with Tom's behavior to convince him to undergo treatment at the lunatic asylum in Newburgh, Ohio, a few miles south of the city of Cleveland.

It's her old, loving husband who returns home some months later, and the two start afresh. Over the next four years Tom builds his growing family one of the nicest homes on Island Road. She bears another son, Charles in 1879 and a daughter, with whom she shares her name, three years later.

It's then that Tom starts sliding back into old behaviors, suffering many moody attacks. There is no violence, but he is bound and determined to make Florence miserable. Like the three days he hides himself in his haymow, actively avoiding those searching for him. Just like his episode in Michigan, Tom returns to his work as if nothing ever happened.

He begins to haunt Florence, always lurking nearby, frightening her with silent stares and threatening behavior. It grows so bad that their eldest son, Almond, sits up at night, loaded shotgun in hand, guarding his mother against attack.

Tom seems to calm himself. A fairly pleasant, early spring Friday passes with nothing untoward between wife and husband. Supper has been served and eaten. Almond, the oldest, leaves to visit a friend. Joe, the 13-year-old, entertains his toddler brother, Charlie, and baby sister in the sitting room.

Florence is cleaning dishes at the sink. The kids hear their dad enter the house through the kitchen door. There's the clatter of chopped wood tossed into its box followed by a loud thump. Joe hurries to the kitchen to see his mother on the floor, his father striking her head with a stout stick. Once discovered, the man runs into the gathering night.

The boy rushes to the front yard, screaming with all his might. Almond hears the call and hurries home. The two reenter the kitchen to find a blood-covered Charlie trying to lift their wounded mother from the floor.

One of the two older boys runs across the road to their Uncle Ed Hance, who notifies Sheriff Corners and calls for Coroner Jefferies. The coroner brings Marshal Sudro to the scene of the crime. They find that Tom has struck Florence four times, once to the left temple and thrice to the back of the head. Each blow fractured her skull.

The 35-year-old woman never regains consciousness and is dead within a few hours.

The immediate property and buildings are searched but darkness prevents any discovery. A thorough investigation begins as soon as there is morning light. Tracks are soon uncovered.

The murder weapon is found about 150 feet west of the house. It's a green basswood club about 3 inches square, 29 inches long, and covered with spots of blood and hair.

The trackers arrive at a rail fence about a quarter-mile out and are surprised to find some amount of blood where Tom clambered across. They note that their quarry had traveled at great speed to the fence. After that point, he began to slow.

There is a second crossed fence, smeared with a great deal of blood. Then, a third that Tom was unable to climb. He's found lying face-down with his hands beneath him. The party cautiously approaches.

Tom is rolled to his back. His pursuers are shocked by the sight. His right hand holds his pocketknife, the blade worn and terribly dull. His left hand and wrist are hacked nearly to pieces. He had also tried to cut his throat, sawing with his old knife until he severed his windpipe, instead.

The funeral for Mr. and Mrs. Fishburn is held by Rev. Mr. Scott on Sunday, April 9, at 10:30am at the Disciple Church. The service is attended by a vast crowd. The bodies are buried, side-by-side, in the cemetery on Butternut Ridge.

Say the papers: "What sudden impulse led him to this terrible deed is known only to the Infinite's mind."

The Fishburn family persists in Lorain county. One of them, Walter, plays a part in establishing and maintaining the Grafton Prison Farm.

1883: A Civil War monument of an eagle with outspread wings is set by the Woman's Relief Corps in Elyria's Ridgelawn Cemetery. The U.S. Supreme Court says the *Civil Rights Act of 1875* is unconstitutional. Edison strings the first overhead wires to light Roselle, New Jersey. Alabama is the first state in the U.S. to enact an anti-trust law. Buffalo Bill puts on his first Wild West Show. The first baseball "Ladies' Day" (the New York City Gothams beat the Cleveland Spiders, 5-2). The first run of the Orient Express, sans murder. There are 130 lynchings in the U.S.: 53 Blacks, 77 others.

1883, July 18, Saturday, just past midnight: Location: Wellington. Victim: George Brenner (43), Marshal of Wellington and night-watchman at time of death. Suspects: Augustus F. Tirey and John Young. Charge: Murder in the first degree. 1883, December 13, Thursday: Tirey is on trial for murder in Judge E.P. Green's court. E.G. Johnson is Tirey's counsel. It's Prosecutor David J. Nye and assistant, J.H. Dickson, for the State.

The witnesses:

Luther Winchell: Lives in Wellington Township, a couple miles east of the village. He saw the accused and two other men the mid-morning the day before the killing. The men were together, going west. They passed within feet of where he stood.

Addison E. Sheldon: Lives in Wellington Township, about a mile east of the village. The accused and one other man came to his home about noon, the day before the murder, wanting something to eat. After leaving, the two went west, came back and went east, and then south.

Henry Biggs: Agent for W&LE Railroad (Wheeling and Lake Erie). He left work the day before the murder at about 9:00pm. He returned about 6:00am the morning of the killing to find his office broken into and the money drawer and its contents gone.

Mrs. Caroline Brenner: Wife of murdered man. Last saw her husband alive a few minutes before midnight, just before he was killed, when he came into her room and told her he was starting his rounds as night-watchman. She heard a pistol report shortly thereafter. She got out of bed, looked out the window, and saw her husband running west, in pursuit of a small man. Her husband fired twice. The other man fired twice. She could see the muzzle flash of shots directed at her husband. Then, she heard someone cry "I am shot!" Mrs. Brenner ran from her home and met her husband at the railroad crossing. He said to her, "I am shot, get the doctor." She helped him upstairs, to bed. He was dead in about five minutes.

Dr. T.M. McLaren: Wellington physician. He performed the post-mortem on the victim, Mr. Brenner. The pistol ball passed into the neck under the right ear, cutting off the anterior part of the windpipe, severing the carotid artery on the left side, and passing in the direction of the shoulder where it lodged beneath the left shoulder blade.

Frank Chapman: A clerk for the CCC&I Railroad (Cleveland, Columbus, Cincinnati, and Indianapolis). His second-floor sleeping room faces, and is about 200 feet south of the depot. He heard two pistol shots about half-past midnight the morning of July 18. The last shot was fired south of the depot. A small man ran towards his house, came within 25 feet, then turned and ran north. Chapman went immediately to the telegraph office, and then to Brenner's. The marshal was already dead. Searching the area, he found one of the victim's bedroom slippers about 20 feet from the corner. Also discovered, near the Brenner home, the man's dropped lantern and revolver with two chambers fired. Chapman saw footprints both north and south of the railroad platform, measured them and then covered them to keep them undisturbed.

O.P. Chapman: Wellington cheese dealer. He heard of Brenner's death and went to the depot where he saw tracks in mud, heading south. He noticed that the right heel track was deeper than the left and that the footprints reversed direction and headed north. Chapman followed them all the way to Oberlin, getting there shortly after daylight. There, he saw Tirey in jail, took his boots, and fitted them to the tracks. Sure enough, the heel of right boot was about a half-inch longer than that of the left.

Geo. Couch: Wellington undertaker. Between midnight and 1:00am he heard of Brenner's shooting, went to his home, found him dead, and examined the body. He saw tracks as previously described and examined their appearance. The day of the killing, he compared the boots taken from the accused in prison with the prints in the mud and found them to fit exactly. He examined the revolver taken from Tirey and found it fully loaded, though three chambers were freshly stained with gunpowder.

John Brister: Local farmer living two miles north of the center of Pittsfield on Oberlin Road. The day Brenner was shot happened to be the last day of haying season. Brister spotted the accused, Tirey, walking "middling fast" towards Oberlin and because it was almost daylight, the farmer says, he could see distinctly. States the man on trial "did not look as clean as he does now" but that he was the man on the road that morning.

S.T. Tufts: A Clevelander who is an engineer on a local freight for LS&MS Railroad (Lake Shore and Michigan Southern). His train was headed west on July 18. At his 9:17 morning stop in Oberlin, he was told of Brenner's death and given a description of the suspect. Tufts saw and recognized Tirey, sitting between two freight cars. Tirey "came up on deck" at the engineer's request and said he was heading towards Fremont (the seat of Sandusky County, Ohio, about 60 miles to the west). Tirey rode 3.5 miles to Kipton when Tufts arrested him with help from D.D. Seely, his brakeman. The accused was carrying a loaded revolver which was marked "A.F.T." When the Brenner killing was mentioned, Tirey said "I did not shoot him." Tufts also noted the accused boots: They had the ankles cut out of them.

D.D. Seely: A brakeman on Tufts' train. He saw Tirey on a boxcar about a mile west of Oberlin. Tirey got off at Kipton, and that's where Seely and Tufts arrested him. They took the accused's revolver from his pocket. The train left with another brakeman. Officers from Oberlin came to collect Tirey. Both brakeman Seely and Engineer Tufts received portions of the reward that was offered.

H.P. Whitney: Citizen and Deputy Sheriff of Oberlin. He went to Kipton by buggy and took charge of the accused, transporting him to Oberlin and then Wellington. In court, he identifies the revolver as the one Seely gave him. Three chambers had the appearance of having been recently discharged. A straight razor was also found on Tirey.

John Young: *He had been charged with murder alongside Tirey.* In return for his testimony on the killing, the State is allowing him to plead guilty to burglary. Young is 28 years old and fresh from the Western Penitentiary (near Pittsburgh, Pennsylvania) after serving five-and-a-half years for burglary.

Young says he met Tirey in Mansfield, Ohio. The two came up the NYP&O Railroad (New York, Pennsylvania, and Ohio) to Wadsworth and from there to Wellington, arriving July 17. They were a mile east of the village that afternoon, and southeast of the depot by evening. The two were traveling with a man named "Jim," the third person some witnesses describe seeing. Near Wellington, he and Tirey gave Jim a pocketbook with $10 in it and told him to go into the village and buy everyone something to eat. Jim left and never returned.

Later that evening, Tirey and Young went to the W&LE depot. Young said he wanted to break in; Tirey did not. Young tried to cut the glass, but could not, and so he kicked in the pane of glass, entered the depot, and stole what he could, amounting to about 35 cents. The accused murderer, Tirey stood back about forty feet and took no part in the robbery. The two then went up the track a few rods (about 50 feet), sat, and talked over a plan to rob a clothing store. It seems that Tirey wanted a suit of clothes and especially new boots since the ones he was wearing fit so poorly that he had to cut the sides open to keep them from hurting his ankles.

Young left to find a store they could burgle and found a likely candidate on the right-hand side of the street. He then returned to Tirey. The two stayed along the track until near midnight. At that time, both went into town with Tirey carrying a 6-foot long pinch bar they found along the CCC&I tracks.

Marshal Brenner suddenly appeared from a livery along the street and confronted them saying "What are you doing this time of night?"

Young and Tirey did not answer. Brenner put his lantern up in Young's face. Young saw Brenner's revolver and panicked, gave Brenner a shove and ran away. Tirey ran off, too, but in a different direction. For some reason, Brenner chased Tirey.

Young had hurried only 35 feet before he heard a shot. He turned to see Brenner running near the railroad's hitching-posts. Then there were two more shots in rapid succession. Yes, both Young and Tirey were armed, but only Tirey was chased and only Tirey shot at Brenner.

The next time Young saw Tirey it about 10:00 the next morning on July 18 when they met in the lockup.

Henry Chapman: He works as a Turnkey in the Elyria Jail and is called to testify, over defense objections.

Chapman, in taking care of prisoners, enters the jail area three or four times a day. Tirey arrived at the Elyria Jail from Wellington on July 18 and was confined on the east side, upstairs, and was given the range of the corridor in daytime. Chapman went to the corridor at about 6:00pm. The jailer passed through the first door, locked it behind him, put the key in his hip pocket, and entered the room.

While Chapman was removing the lower lock of Tirey's door, the prisoner struck him over the head with a "heavy piece of scantling" that turned out to be one of the legs from the corridor sink. The blow cut a long gash in Chapman's head and knocked him to his knees. Tirey struck again as Chapman gained his feet, but the jailer warded off the blow and used his fists to knock the prisoner to the floor.

Tirey was then dragged into his cell. Since the attack, the accused is kept in his cell at all times, except when washing up in the morning.

The accused murderer, Augustus F. Tirey, in his own defense: He had turned 18 last May. He was born and raised in Indiana and has two sisters; one married, the other a nun. Also a 22-year-old brother, of whom he has lost track. He has been in Terre Haute, Indiana, with his married sister for most of the time over the past three years.

Tirey describes how he's been traveling over the last several months. First to Elmira, in south-central New York, where he worked for about nine months, then to Meadville, in northwest Pennsylvania, then to Silver Creek, Ohio (near Wadsworth, in Medina County). It was in Silver Creek that he met John Young and the other man, "Jim."

The three of them traveled to Medina, where they stayed the night. The next morning they made their way to Wellington "on the mud road" (present day Ohio Route 18) as the first part of a trip back to his sister's in Terre Haute. The three stopped east of Wellington, then went on to the W&LE crossing, where they also stopped for a spell. They arrived at the village about 2:00pm. He walked into town, then back to meet the others.

He and Young gave Jim a purse with $10 in it, to buy supplies. Jim left, but never came back. He and Young stayed at the W&LE depot until suppertime, then went to the crossing and sat down. A bell struck 9:00pm while they were sitting there.

Tirey maintains that he left Wellington about 10:00pm for Oberlin. Followed a wagon road. Got to Oberlin between midnight and 1:00am. He says he had nothing to do with the robbery or shooting.

He did not go up the road at 4:00am as John Brister had testified. Instead, he arose in Oberlin at 8:00 the next morning and hopped the freight going west. He was arrested by railroad men at the next station, hauled back to Oberlin and, from there, Wellington.

He did not fire at Brenner. In fact, he never even saw him. Young was lying about him wanting to rob a clothing store, and he never told Young he wanted new boots or a suit of clothes.

On cross examination Tirey is unable to give any details of any of his travels. He did not know the year or month he left Indiana, when he got to New York, and couldn't even say if it was winter or summer. Tirey couldn't describe the work he did, nor say how much he was paid.

Say the papers: "The witness denied all knowledge of any towns he passed through, and overwhelmed his counsel with mortification at the boldness with which he uttered his self-evident lies." The general consensus is that the only truth he utters is that he attacked his jailer to get keys and escape.

J.H. Dickson closes for the State, speaking two hours of Marshal Brenner's exemplary life and his love of family, and the premeditative characteristics of Tirey's dastardly crime.

Defense attorney C.W. Johnston starts their close maintaining, among other things, that evidence could not convince a jury beyond a reasonable doubt that Tirey killed Brenner.

Defense attorney E.G. Johnson then stands. He is expected to continue the close. Instead he declares to the court that his client is willing to change his plea from not guilty of murder in the first degree to guilty of murder in the second and asks if that can be accepted.

Prosecution lawyers consult with the family of the slain man and decide it would be best to accept the proposition.

Judge E.P. Green instructs the jury to retire and return a verdict of murder in the second degree. Both Tirey and Young are sent back to jail.

Friday afternoon, December 14, sentence is passed on Augustus Tirey and John Young. Except for their chains, the two young men look like they haven't a care in the world as they talk and smile as they await sentencing.

Young's counsel, George. P. Metcalf says a few words on behalf of his client. Young stands for a sentence of nine years hard labor. Tirey gets life in prison. Both are silent.

The next day they are transported to Columbus "where they will soon be forgotten, save by the friends of those whom they so brutally murdered."

Local papers use the crime as fodder for articles for and against the U.S. Constitution's Second Amendment, the right to bear arms.

1886, July 29: Tirey, in the Ohio Penitentiary in Columbus, has attempted suicide twice in the past week. He somehow obtained matches with which he set his bedding on fire. He lay down on the burning bed and covered himself with a quilt. The fire is discovered, and he is pulled from the bed and cell before he is seriously injured. Tirey then tries again with an unsuccessful attempt to hang himself using a pillow cover from his bed. The article notes that he has been confined for some time in the "insane department."

1895, March 21: A 30-year-old Tirey is reported as dying in the Ohio Penitentiary.

Judge Edwin P. Green:

Farm boy Edwin Green was born in Stockbridge, Vermont, on March 10, 1829. He attended public schools, was a teacher in rural schools of both New Hampshire and New York, and completed his reading of law in the office of Humphry, Upson, and Edgerton, in Akron, Ohio.

Green was admitted to the Ohio Bar in 1853. That next year he was elected Clerk of Courts for Summit County, Ohio. Green was first elected as a judge in the Lorain County Courts in October of 1883 (filling a vacancy left by Newell D. Tibbals.). Then, he was elected for another full term of five years.

He resigned from the bench in January, 1891, because of poor health, and took up his practice in Akron, only to leave it because of illness. Green was not known as a fiery speaker, but was a solid lawyer and good judge known for his sense of humor, kind nature, and warm-heartedness. E.P. died in Akron, December 24, 1894, at the age of 65, "after a struggle with disease lasting many years."

During his time on the Lorain County bench the local press always called him "E.P." In his death notice, the Elyria papers listed him as "J.P." Green. How soon we forget.

1883, September 21, Friday, 10:30pm:

It's late morning and Elyrian L.B. Smith sighs as he writes a check for $100 to Catherine Ryan and her son James. Another loan. Smith can't figure how the two ever manage to pay him back, but he knows it's by the hard work of the woman. All Jimmy does is drink and gamble.

About noon, that same day, Elyria Savings Bank teller Arthur Hecock scrutinizes the check given him by his two Irish-accented customers. Hecock knows neither, but he does recognize the signature of L.B. Smith. The teller counts out $100 even and places it on the counter. It's the young Mr. Jimmy Ryan who picks it up, folds it in half, and sticks it in his pocket.

About 8:30 that evening, Orrin Dole, detective for the Lake Shore and Michigan Southern Railroad (LS&MS) is out and about. Dole's not walking a beat. No sir. Those days are behind him. But he is paying attention.

Like all Friday nights, Broad Street is bustling, even with the threat of rain. As Dole strolls along, he spots a couple of troublemakers: The young punk Clevelander, Bobby Bruce, and that Jimmy Ryan fellow from Carlisle Township. Detective Dole shakes his head. Bruce's crooked, lying ways and Ryan's drunken, quarrelsome attitude are bad enough apart. When combined... Dole smiles grimly. Were he were a betting man, he'd put odds on one or the other, or most likely both, being in jail by tomorrow morning.

Nineteen-year-old John Henings and his pal Fred Moe are enjoying a beer at Frederick's Saloon where they watch an already half-lit Bob Bruce play his harmonica and bones. The two young men would like to stay, but can't be out late. Both have morning duty as hostlers for respectable families on Fifth Street. Henings works for Mr. Clauss, and Moe for Mr. Forbes.

Fred Town, telegraph line repairman, and fellow Elyrian, James Melin, arrive in town by train from Oberlin about 10:00pm. They figure it'd do no harm to stop for a beer. Thirty minutes later the two start for their homes, walking south on West Avenue.

At the alley between Second and Third streets, they approach an obviously inebriated Jimmy Ryan, who's talking to an equally tipsy Robert Bruce. They don't catch the whole conversation, but hear Ryan call Bruce a "son of a bitch." Then, "You've been fooling me long enough, and now go on, or I'll give it to you."

Town and Melin figure it's an argument between drunken friends and take no steps to intervene. Besides, it's starting to rain. There's no use getting wet over it, is there?

Close to midnight, a sharp rap on the Clauss' barn door wakes hostler

John Henings. John hears Bobby Bruce calling, and that fellow's always trouble. Henings rolls over, pulls his blankets up over his shoulder, and ignores the calls for help. A smart lad, there.

Henings' friend, Fred Moe, over at Alex Forbes', doesn't ignore the knocks and opens the barn door to an agitated Bobby Bruce who rushes in carrying a large and bloody-looking jack-knife in his hand. In the year since they met, Moe has come to understand that Bruce is a chronic liar, so he doesn't put much stock in the wild yarn the rain-soaked man acts out about stabbing a man over on West Avenue.

Bruce calms as he tells his story, winding up with "Fred, if I am arrested tomorrow morning, I want you to swear that I came here at 9 o'clock."

Moe agrees to let the obviously exhausted Bruce sleep in his bed. Bruce wants to keep the darkly-stained knife with him, but Moe refuses that request. Bruce promptly falls asleep and is still dreaming when Fred Moe is summoned by his boss, Mr. Forbes, around 5:00am the next morning to pick up an order at a downtown butcher's shop.

The well-known Elyria businessman, Dan W. Hyland, leaves his home at Middle Avenue and Eighth on the morning of September 22 at 5:20, sharp. He drives his rig, clippity-clop, down Middle then up Fifth to West Avenue to pick up his friend, Assistant Postmaster M.A. Elder. As he makes the right turn onto West, Hyland notices some large, dark stains on the sidewalk, but doesn't give them much thought.

Mr. Hyland pulls to a stop across from the front of the Elder home. Mr. Elder exits his gated yard, saying his good mornings as he gingerly crosses the muddy street and climbs aboard. Hyland snaps the reigns and away they go, towards downtown. A couple hundred feet along West Avenue, between Fourth and Third, they spy a man, face-down on the sidewalk. A drunkard, no doubt, filled with liquor and passed out. Not the first rascal of his kind the two gentlemen have seen on an early Saturday morning.

It takes a moment for Hyland's wartime experience to kick in. With all he's been through, he knows a dead man when he sees one! He and Elder check the body, being careful not to disturb it or its surroundings. Then it clicks—the large stains a couple blocks back must've been blood. This unfortunate man must've ruptured a vessel with drink and then bled out.

Elyria Police and Lorain County Coroner R.E. Braman are summoned. In front of a growing crowd, the dead man is rolled to his back. It's the 40-year-old, Jimmy Ryan. His face and clothing are covered with blood. There is a single stab wound, about an inch wide, on the left side of the neck and under the ear. Whatever caused the injury passed through the lower portion of the carotid artery. The cause of death is as it appears: Loss of blood.

There are no weapons or money on the body; the only items in Jimmy's pockets are his handkerchief and a large, unsmoked cigar.

Authorities easily back-track the trail of blood as it zig-zags down the sidewalk nearly 500 feet along West Avenue to the front of the J.J. Burrows' residence on the north corner of West and Fifth. There, investigators find evidence of the crime and the striking of the deadly blow, though there is no indication of any great struggle.

Apparently, after being stabbed, the bleeding Ryan headed back in the direction of Elyria, looking for help. The blood trail indicated rapid movement, until, "weak and faint, he fell where he was found stiff and stark."

Just as the investigation gets started, along comes Fred Moe who, after making his run to the butcher, happens to return by way of West Avenue. Fred slows, understandably curious about the early morning ruckus, and sees Jimmy Ryan dead on the ground. Fred shudders when he hears how and when the corpse was found. It would've been *him* who discovered the body if he hadn't've taken Middle Avenue on his early morning errand.

Then a terrible thought strikes the young man. He urges his horse home to its barn and wakes the still-sleeping Bobby Bruce. Fred asks if the story he heard the night before, the one about the stabbing, was true.

Bobby Bruce tells him it was. Yes. Absolutely. God's own truth.

Fred Moe describes to Bruce what he saw over on West Avenue. Bobby pales, turns, and in silence, walks from the barn.

Mind racing, Fred Moe takes care of his morning chores, then walks the few blocks to the scene of the murder. He's surprised to find Bobby Bruce in the crowd that's milling about. Bruce says nothing about the crime but, as he turns to head for town, he says to Fred Moe, "For God's sake, don't tell anybody about this."

News of the crime spreads through Elyria like lightning. Hordes of people gather on West Avenue, making the walk between where Jimmy Ryan was found and the corner at Fifth where the stabbing took place. Many pick up small stones or brightly-colored autumn leaves as souvenirs.

Ryan's body is taken to the Morse Brothers Undertakers on Cheapside (the east side of the Square along Middle Avenue). The dead man is put on display, still dressed in bloody clothes with the fatal wound clearly visible. Hundreds view the corpse in the next few hours.

Says the *Elyria Republican,* Jimmy Ryan's killing is "a forcible illustration of the fact that among the human race are creatures no better than the wild savage beasts of earth, and upon whose murderous nature the influence of high civilization is completely lost."

While Jimmy Ryan is being placed in his casket, 21-year-old John Kretzel, low man on the totem pole at DeGraw's Saloon, rolls his eyes and shakes his head. Drinkers are understandably few at 7:00am, and it's just his luck to be stuck playing audience to the over-animated and lying-like-usual Bobby Bruce.

Bruce downs a couple stiff ones as he describes how he had "done one man up" and would do the same to another man if he squealed on him, and with the same knife to boot. Bobby then takes his leave to eat breakfast down the street at Hardy's Restaurant. It's shortly after that meal, a few minutes before 8:00am, when none other than the observant Railroad Detective Orrin Dole finds Bruce on Court Street, sitting by the Beebe Hotel.

Dole starts with the fact that Jimmy Ryan is dead. There's no response from Bobby. The detective questions him about his perhaps being with Jimmy Ryan the night before. Bruce emphatically denies having seen the victim and, in point of fact, claims that he doesn't even know a person with that name. Dole, having seen them together, knows that's a lie. He pulls the small and slight man to his feet and hauls him the short distance to the Court House where he is presented to Prosecutor D.J. Nye.

Elyria Police are summoned. An examination of Bruce's clothing reveals what appears to be blood on his left coat-sleeve and handkerchief. Bruce says he's had trouble in recent days with recurring nosebleeds. He laughs at the notion that his large pocket-knife is blood-stained. Cops should know the difference between blood and tobacco juice!

All the same, it takes only a few hours of hard questioning for Bobby Bruce to confess to killing Jimmy Ryan, but Bruce claims the killing was done in self-defense. Trouble is, there's not a mark on him. When asked why he happened to have an open knife when Ryan jumped him, Bruce replies that he "was using it to clean his nails."

Then Bruce changes his story. While he was robbing the drunken Ryan of his bank roll, the man suddenly attacked him. Bruce says he made a slash with his knife, took the money, and ran, first to Clauss' barn, where John Henings didn't let him in, and then the Forbes' place, where he spent the night with Fred Moe.

Bobby Bruce is brought to his preliminary hearing in front of 'Squire

Doolittle that afternoon. Bruce pleads not guilty to the charge of murder in the first degree.

Local newspapers have nothing less than a field day with the crime. All of them push for harsher punishments, better control of the liquor trade, temperance, and sometimes, even complete prohibition.

Says *The Elyria Weekly Republican (Sept 27, 1883):*

> How can it be expected that human life will be safe when such depraved wretches exist upon the earth, and with so many chances of escape from the gallows when they should justify, and for the safety of mankind, be compelled to suffer the extreme penalty of the law?

In the same paper, the *Women's Christian Temperance Union* declares:

> One finished product of the saloon business lay cold and silent in ghastly death at the morgue on Saturday morning. An able-bodied man, who, had he not been "full," could have defended himself against his assailant, but was overpowered and murdered for money, by a poor, miserable outlaw, and left on the pavement on one of our principle streets. His father was a drunkard before him: so Jim Ryan died, and was buried like a beast. Who is to be the next victim?

Bobby Bruce's preliminary hearing on September 29 is filled to overflowing. While being unshackled, the prisoner glances around the room, seemingly without concern. Anybody he knows is given a bow "with a smile of recognition that one would not expect from a person called to answer the terrible charge of murder in the first degree." Bruce pleads not guilty and is remanded to jail.

The criminal trial begins Friday, November 30, 1883, in Judge E.P. Green's court. E.G. Johnson is defense counsel. The State is represented by Prosecutor D.J. Nye assisted by former judge John C. Hale. Seating the jury takes a day and a half because many people have scruples against executing Bruce should he be proven guilty of the charges against him.

Testimony begins on Monday, December 3. The first two days of the trial are spent exposing the jury to the facts of the matter. The State carefully builds its case against Bobby Bruce, bringing in one eyewitness after another, establishing a timeline, motive, means, and opportunity.

Coroner R.E. Braman and Dr. W.F McLean describe the examination of the crime scene and the corpse of Jimmy Ryan. John Henings and Fred Moe tell their stories of Bruce's late-night visit.

The defense works to establish the fact that Bobby Bruce, despite his reputation, is a hard-working and sober man of good conduct. Bruce's boss and co-workers at Beebe's, proprietor C.C. Briggs, Mrs. Sadie Briggs, and clerk Charles Waterman, all very well known to the community, describe the defendant as a person who can hold a job and do what's expected of him. Many of those same witnesses testify to the quarrelsome personality of the victim, Jimmy Ryan, especially when he was drinking, and everyone agrees that was pretty much most of the time.

On December 5, Robert Bruce takes the stand in his own defense. His story: He is 20 years old with a birthday coming up on December 22. He was born in Canada and was four months old when he came to the United States. His family moved first to Cleveland, where they stayed until he was 7 and thence to Youngstown, where he lived for another 7 years.

At about age 14, Bobby came alone to Elyria to work as a bootblack. He had no place to stay, so he lived where he could, like the barn in back of Beebe's. Around that same time, his mother moved back to Cleveland where he'd visit, sometimes staying as long as a year, working at blacking boots and peddling newspapers.

Of late, he had returned to Elyria where he had worked several jobs, sometimes two or more at a time, usually as a bell-boy or clerk at the Beebe for Mr. Briggs and the Black River for Mrs. Farrell. Later at Wolcott's in Amherst, then back to Elyria and the Metropolitan. He also worked a stint with Mr. Mussey on Fifth Street taking care of his horses. That was how he met John Henings and Fred Moe.

Bobby Bruce says he was working at the Metropolitan when he first met the murdered man, Jimmy Ryan, who wanted a bottle of whiskey on credit. When Bruce refused to give him the liquor, Ryan threatened to "take it out" of him and stormed from the building. Bruce's boss told him the drunken, angry man was "Ryan, the fighting fellow and a hard case."

Bruce tells how, the night of the killing, he'd been at Frederick's Saloon, dancing and playing for change. He left there, meeting a fairly drunk Jimmy Ryan on the street. Jimmy half-recognize him as a friend and suggested having a drink. After that, Ryan departed the saloon, heading out West Avenue.

Bruce's words (*The Elyria Weekly Republican, December 13, 1883*):

I was walking slowly but still overtook Ryan at Second

Street. We exchanged hellos. Ryan asked where I was going. I told him my home on Fifth. He said "you are a son-of a b---- and a liar."

We quarreled long, up the street, and I took out my knife to cut some tobacco. He said "you are the fellow who worked at the Metropolitan and refused to trust me." I told him he had better go home and then he grabbed me—got me by the throat and choked me against the fence. I tried to get away and said to him, "for God's sake don't choke me to death."

I cried murder once or twice and then struck him with the knife. He let go and I ran because I thought he was following me. I went to Hening's and then Moe's who I told not to tell anybody because I was afraid, not because I was threatening him.

I did not know the man was dead until Moe told me the next morning. I had no friends and told Moe not to speak of it. I said what I did because I was scared and didn't know what to do.

I didn't think I had hurt Ryan so badly. I just hit him where I could.

The morning of the fourth and last day of testimony is spent with more character building for the defense and rebuttals by the State. The courtroom remains packed through trial and closing arguments.

Following a weekend recess, Judge Green charges the jury. They take the case at 4:00, Monday afternoon.

After a night's deliberation, the good people of Lorain County return their verdict, declaring Robert Bruce guilty of murder in the second degree.

In response, "a visible smile of gratification lit the countenance of the prisoner, who will spend the remainder of his life in the penitentiary, unless previously released by executive clemency."

1884, August 21: *Elyria Republican:*

Of the eighty-three male prisoners who are sentenced to life in the penitentiary, three are from Lorain County: Robert Bruce, Samuel Durham, and Augustus Tirey. This is three times her share, as there are eighty-three counties in the state. But then, they never hang murderers in this county!

1886, June 10: Bruce is used in the *Elyria Republican* as a bad example of what happens when action is not taken against "sneaking ruffians." In this case, two young men who waylaid and robbed a man on Washington Avenue as he returned from escorting a young lady home.

1887, October 27: Amid local efforts to gain a parole or pardon for Bobby Bruce comes this letter to the editor of *The Elyria Democrat* from local attorney, William. G. Sharp:

> I am informed that a report is in circulation to the effect that I have used my influence to secure the pardon of one, Robert Bruce who, a few years ago it will be remembered, was sent to the penitentiary for life for the murder of James Ryan. I am somewhat surprised that such a story should gain any credence, for it is wholly untrue and indeed I have used all honorable means to oppose any executive clemency being extended to Bruce. The misapprehension probably arises from the fact that a petition asking for his pardon was some time ago circulated among our people, which obtained some signatures. A letter is on file in Gov. Foraker's office in which I state reasons why the executive pardon should be with-held in this case.

1889, July 18: "Robert Bruce, the ex-convict, who killed Ryan six years ago, has been pardoned, and has taken his residence in Canada. He had better go among the Camanches [*sic*]." Actually, Bruce found work with the Edison Electric Light Company in Montreal.

1895, April 15: Back in Cleveland, Bruce is arrested for assault with attempt to rob an "intoxicated old man" on Rockwell Street in that city. An officer reports Bruce struck the old man and removed something from his pockets.

1898, December 30: Bruce, back in prison for reasons unknown to us, is part of a Christmas play put on for Ohio Penitentiary authorities. He is "well-liked by prison officials."

I could not find the ultimate end of Bobby Bruce, but both he and Jimmy Ryan should be remembered as being the perpetrator and victim of the first murder I found within the city of Elyria.

Also... The northern blocks of Elyria's Middle Avenue were nicknamed "Cheapside" for the street that hosts the financial district of London, England.

And... There was never any mention of Ryan's wad of money being found.

1884: The village of Grafton places a Civil War monument of a soldier at parade rest in the Butternut Ridge Cemetery (Butternut Ridge and Durkee

Road). Britain reduces the amount of money a person must have in order to qualify to vote. Now, not-so-rich people can exercise the right—as long as they're men. Germany's mucking about in Africa. So is Spain, as they begin to colonize the western Sahara. Burton "Barney" Shotton is born in Brownhelm Township. Known for his running speed during his time in baseball, he will go on to help win two National League pennants during his time with the Brooklyn Dodgers in the late 1940s. Grover Cleveland (New York Democrat—the first of his party since the Civil War) wins the Election with 48.9% of the popular vote. 211 lynchings in the U.S.: 51 Blacks, 160 others.

1885: In Ohio, it's decided that all state executions will take place at the Ohio Penitentiary in Columbus. In Iowa, Dr. W.W. Grant carves the first appendectomy scar into Mary Gartside (22). In D.C., the dedication of the Washington Monument, 37 years after its start. AT&T. United States' Salvation Army. The Boston Pops Orchestra. Ft. Wayne, Indiana gets the first gasoline pump. Huckleberry Finn begins conning his friends. 184 lynchings: 74 Blacks, 110 others. $1,000 is worth $24,450 modern.

1886: BB Guns. Chicagoans demonstrate against police brutality where city cops are more than willing to prove the point by killing many protesters. Work begins on the Ohio State Reformatory, a few miles north of Mansfield, Richland County. A practical refining process for the expensive metal, aluminum, is invented by Oberlinian Charles Hall in his backyard lab, but it would be bad form to forget Professor Frank Jewett and Frenchman Paul L.T. Héroult, wouldn't it? James T. Brand is born in Oberlin. His tenure on the Oregon State Supreme Court will be interrupted in 1947 so he can help judge a portion of the Nuremberg Trials for Nazi War Crimes. Cleveland Stone Co. Incorporated. 138 lynchings: 74 Blacks, 64 others.

1887: Kipton places a Civil War monument of a Soldier at parade rest in the park at 6th and State. Metal fatigue (and strong west winds) will eventually encourage the proud warrior to stand not quite upright. Ohio repeals her law that makes it illegal for Whites and Blacks to marry each other. The next state to do so will be California—*in 1948!* First contact lenses by Adolf Fick in Germany. Victoria's "Golden Jubilee." In Paris, construction begins on Eiffel's Tower. France brings Cambodia and Vietnam together as "French

Indochina." Native Americans are stripped of their tribal lands by *The Dawes Act*. 120 lynchings: 70 Blacks. 50 others.

1887, February 24: Location: Oberlin, Train Depot. Victim: Unknown, White male infant. Buried in Oberlin cemetery.

According to the *Elyria Daily Telephone* (March 2, 1887):

> Dr. W.F. Bunce, of Oberlin, performed the postmortem examination upon the body of the infant which was so foully murdered at Oberlin a few days past. The infant was cruelly smothered, probably in its bed, and suspicion points to parties who, it is thought, have been connected with affairs of this kind before, as it is not the first occurrence of the kind in Oberlin. The sleuth-hounds of justice now have a chance to do some fine work.

Outcome: Unsolved.

INFANTICIDE: Killing a child less than one year old.

1888: Three years after a tax levy was approved, the City of Elyria erects a Civil War monument of a Union standard bearer in Ely Park. Richmond, Virginia, has the first successful electric street car system in the U.S. Americans get a whole 'nother reason to cuss when the game of golf is demonstrated by Scotsman John Reid in Yonkers, New York. Eastman Kodak. Hailstones kill 250 in Delhi, India. *Casey at the Bat*. Vincent now has only one ear. Benjamin Harrison (Indiana Republican) wins the Election with 47.8% of the popular vote. 137 lynchings: 69 Blacks, 68 others.

1889: First commercial fishing companies in Lorain County. The Lorain County Historical Society is organized. Oklahoma Land Run on property previously granted to Native Americans. In Paris, Eiffel's Tower is open to the public. Most folks don't like it very much. North Dakota. South Dakota. Montana. Washington (the state). 170 lynchings: 94 Blacks, 76 others.

1889, April 3: *The (Wellington) Enterprise:*

> A sad case of infanticide was developed in this place [Oberlin] last week. India Johnson, a girl about eighteen years of age, who came to Oberlin from Harmar, Ohio, near

Marietta, five months ago, has been employed as a domestic at No. 7 College Plan, which is a highly respectable board house for young ladies. She was unwell last week and on Friday afternoon [March 29], while caring for her room, the lady of the house found a dead infant in the slop jar, which had been set away and covered with some clothing. A stocking had been drawn tightly around its neck. The girl admitted that it had been born Wednesday night. Prosecuting Attorney Webber was notified, and came from Elyria Saturday. An inquest and post-mortem examination was ordered. Drs. Allen, Wilson, Noble, and W.C. Bunce, made the examination at Ransom's the undertaking firm, and the inquest was held by Justice Dale, acting as corner [*sic*]. It was decided that the child's death was caused by strangulation. No arrest has yet been made as the girl is not able to be moved. LATER—The girl disappeared between 9 and 11 o'clock Wednesday evening, and her present location is unknown.

Outcome: Charge nollied by Prosecutor Amos R. Webber with no explanation provided.

1890 – 1899: County Population = 40,294

1890: The Pine Ridge Indian Campaign, Wounded Knee, South Dakota. The first one. Vaccines for tetanus and diphtheria. The ballet *Sleeping Beauty*. Eddie Rickenbacker lands among the living in Columbus, Ohio. Bill Morrison, Des Moines, Iowa, builds the first American electric automobile. It's a 6-passenger wagon that'll reach 14 miles per hour. In the Docket: There are so many cases of "Selling & Furnishing Intoxicating Liquor to a Minor" and "Selling & Furnishing Liquor to a Person in the Habit of getting Intoxicated" that the Clerk of Courts begins using a stamp to enter the charges instead of writing them in by hand. Wyoming. 96 lynchings: 85 Blacks, 11 others. $1,000 is worth $25,917 modern.

1890, February 4, Tuesday: Location: South Water Street (South Park), Oberlin. Victim: Henry Blakeley (Blakenay). Suspect: Henry Waring. Act: Gunshot. Both victim and suspects are "young colored men." They are friends and "of respectable character." The newspapers are unable to provide a detailed account of the shooting, but it *seems* as if there is some sort of an argument between Waring and Blakeley over the affection of a daughter of Mrs. R.J. Cooper, "A very respectable colored lady living at No. 35 South Water." The two men visited her together to discuss a series of letters the young lady had received that, it turns out, Blakely had written. The men leave the Cooper house. Two shots are heard and Blakely is found on the corner of Groveland and Water (Park) with a bullet wound to the back. Dr. W.C. Bunce (South Main) probes for, but cannot find the ball. Blakely dies two days later, but not before telling police that he was shot by Waring. Authorities are unable to untangle the story because of multiple, conflicting witnesses.

Charge: Murder. Plea: Not guilty. Indicted April 30, 1890, for murder in the second degree. Judge: E.P. Green. Prosecutor: A.R. Webber. Defense: C.A. Metcalf, E.G. Johnson, and J.C. Hale. Testimony makes it no clearer who held the gun that fired the fatal shot. Outcome: Waring is found guilty of manslaughter. Sentence: Ohio Penitentiary, 1 year and costs.

July 23, 1890: *The Elyria Daily Chronicle:*

> A petition for the pardon of Henry Waring, who was recently sent to the penitentiary for one year for being implicated in the shooting of Henry Blakenay, has been circulated and signed by many of the most prominent citizens of Oberlin. His previous good character as shown during the trial and the

doubts surrounding the case rendered the circulation of the petition an easy matter. This is an illustration of the value of a good reputation, which every young man would do well to consider.

And this:

Sickly sentimentalism prompts this effort to get Waring out of the penitentiary—Why not get the old man Durham out?
See: 1881, May 20.

1890, July 20, Sunday evening: Location: Oberlin, Grafton Street, a short distance east of the southern termination of South Water (South Park). Victim: Clinton D. Hutchinson (28) farmer and teamster from Pennsylvania. Suspect: Bonsor Jacobs, an expert at shoeing horses, with a shop on South Main Street.

The two men are involved in an ongoing quarrel over the location of a shared property line and the fence along it. In the final iteration, Hutchinson has stacked lumber against the fence, an act to which Jacobs strenuously objects. Hutchinson is invited to the Jacob's barn so they can settle the argument once and for all. Hutchinson's wife pleads with him not to go. He ignores her and is shot in the mouth. The ball breaks two teeth and lodges in the neck somewhere behind the right tonsil.

The wounded Hutchinson races in his own horse and buggy into town to visit Dr. W.C. Bunce. He nearly overturns the rig at the corner of South Water and Vine. Thrown out and to the ground, blood gushing from his mouth, Hutchinson gains his feet and then runs the remaining quarter-mile to the doctor's office. W.C. Bunce and his father, W., manage to slow the bleeding but cannot find the projectile.

Hutchinson cannot speak, but writes the following while seated on the operating table:

He put some things away from the line fence and then came to the fence and began to tell me not to put anything there and called me names and said he was going to fix me before I got through with him. He was or had been drinking. He said I should come out behind the barn and he would talk to me. He went around and pulled up and shot me. *(The Oberlin Weekly News, July 24, 1890)*

Jacobs surrenders immediately when authorities arrive at his farm. He is released on $1,000 bail, or $1,500, depending on the source. When Hutchinson dies two days later, Jacob's is re-arrested and charged with murder. Jacobs is described as a "hardworking, honest man." The papers are convinced that he was acting in self-defense.

Hutchinson is made out to be the exact opposite. During the trial, witnesses lambaste the victim (and his wife) as liars and "poor neighbors."

Charge: Murder in the second degree. Plea: Not guilty. Prosecutor: A.R. Webber. Judge: E.P. Green. Outcome: Guilty of manslaughter. Sentence: Two years in the Ohio Penitentiary in Columbus. Out on parole as of November 18, 1891.

1890, December 9: *The Norwalk Daily Reflector:*

> Double Tragedy at Wellington:
>
> Our neighboring village of Wellington is stirred from center to circumference over the murder of one of her prominent citizens and the prompt suicide of the murderer. The murdered man is S.L. Sage, who for many years has kept a grocery store, and was a highly respected citizen. The murderer, David Hoke, was also an old and well known citizen. He was formerly a carriage maker and earned good wages, and it is reported that he had saved and accumulated considerable property. For the past ten weeks he has been employed by Sage to deliver groceries.
>
> About two weeks ago Sage mistrusted that he was stealing groceries, and finally accused him of it. Hoke at first denied, but at last confessed his guilt and promised to settle the matter Monday. Hoke went to the store, and the two men became involved in an altercation about the settlement and Hoke pulled a revolver and shot Sage through the head. He then ran in to a back room of the store and shot himself through the mouth. He died in about ten minutes; and Sage died about six o'clock the same evening.
>
> Sage was the father-in-law of H.M. Battles, formerly proprietor of the Norwalk bus line, and both the murdered man and the murderer stood high in the community.

As stated in the article above, neither of these men were young. The body of victim Samuel Louis Sage (63) was returned to his hometown of Huntington's Evergreen Cemetery to be placed next to his wife, Elizabeth

Wolcott Sage. Probate records show her dying of "Rheumatism" just five months prior to the shooting death of her husband.

David Hoke (65) was buried in Wellington's Greenwood cemetery. His wife, Anne E. Manley Hoke joined him in 1902.

1891: U.S. Congress legislates the Court of Appeals into existence. SPAM! American Express Traveler's Checks. A self-starter for the automobile is patented. So is the motion picture camera. Basketball starts at the Springfield, Massachusetts YMCA thanks to Canadian James Naismith. Lorain County gets its first Electric Power & Light Co. Railroad watches everywhere in the U.S. are required to be much more accurate when out-of-synch timepieces are the root cause of the death of several men in a collision between the Number 14 Fast Mail Train and the Toledo Express near Kipton, Camden Township. The Garza Revolution in Texas and Mexico. 184 lynchings: 113 Blacks, 71 others.

1892: Lorain City has a hospital and it's St. Joe's! "Pudge" Heffelfinger is paid $500 as the first pro football player. Despite being a flop, *The Nutcracker* will eventually give dancers a reason to costume themselves as heroic toy soldiers, mean mice, and a sampler of treats. Daisy Bell looks sweet upon a seat. The living pester the dead with Ouija Boards. The Sierra Club is formed in—where else—California. Vaccine for cholera. A link between Chickenpox and Shingles is suggested. Lowell Thomas is born in Woodington, Darke County, Ohio. Grover Cleveland (New York Democrat) wins the Election with 46.0% of the popular vote. 230 lynchings: 161 Blacks, 69 others.

1892, December 12, Monday, 10:30am:

Mrs. Bennett, who lives on Bennett Street, in Wellington, Ohio, is making a late-morning visit with her elderly neighbors, Reverend John and Lida (Eliza) Arnold, who live just down the way. She knows she can only stop by when both John and Lida are home because, to make Lida feel more secure, John locks the door when he's away—though Lida sometimes teases it's to keep the ladies from gossiping when he's gone.

The Arnolds are local folks, but relatively new neighbors, having arrived in 1880. John Arnold was an early settler of the Camden area where he lived from 1834 until 1858. Bit by the travel bug, he moved away, first to Minnesota and then Iowa. During this time, he became a preacher in the Church of the

United Brethren. Reverend Arnold no longer delivers sermons, but he will perform weddings, if you ask nicely.

The old man had volunteered for and spent three years in the service during the Civil War. After that, he'd traveled to California before finally returning to Camden Township and Wellington. Though gruff and abrupt, all the kids know him as the man who once ran the candy store.

John and Lida were married on March 4, 1891. She is his fifth wife and he, her fourth husband. Their seventy-plus years are beginning to show heavily on both of them. John's hands are so palsied that he only fills his coffee cup halfway. He suffers continual pain from what he calls "his war injury," a severe abdominal hernia. He receives an $8.00 a month pension from the government because of it.

Lida has been ailing with severe stomach pains. They've worsened with time, and she was forced to her bed at the end of this past summer. She's grown despondent over her poor health, and that worries Mrs. Bennett because Lida's family has a history of black moods. Her brother spent time in asylums, and a sister drowned herself.

Today, though somewhat wild-eyed, Lida tells Mrs. Bennett that she has been feeling a little better of late. In fact, yesterday evening, John had helped her stand and walk the six or seven steps to the bedroom door where she sat for a while before returning to bed. Her improvement, she thinks, is likely due to the new medicine, "Swamp Root," prescribed by Wellington's female physician, Dr. Warren.

The stress of caretaking shows on John. He once likened the loneliness of living with and caring for his invalid wife to being in a prison. Some of the nosier neighbors have rumored about shouted arguments between Lida and her more active husband, but Mrs. Bennett doesn't cotton to such talk. She knows what she sees: a good man patiently caring for his wife. All women should be so lucky!

After a visit of a half-hour, Mrs. Bennett says her goodbyes to the Arnolds and walks across the street to see Mrs. Heminway. A half-hour after that, Mrs. Heminway calls attention to a bare-headed Mr. Arnold who is trying to run up the walk. Mrs. Bennett hurries out to meet him and asks what was the matter.

"My wife is dying!"

As the two ladies and Arnold rush back to the house, he describes how Lida had begun struggling for breath.

The three enter the bedroom. They find Lida Arnold in her bed, lying on her back, her head inclined a little to the right with both arms extending down her body and above the bed cover that's tucked up under her chin. She is unconscious, but alive.

The women loosen the bed clothing from her chin so she can breathe. They discover a wound on the front of her throat. Blood is found on the upper portion of the wound and on the collar of her clothing.

"She has stabbed herself!" one the women exclaims.

"Why would she do that?" Reverend Arnold asks.

Mrs. Bennet sends Mrs. Heminway to find a doctor. Dr. Hathaway arrives about 15 minutes later.

Lida is still alive. Hathaway administers a "hypodermic stimulant," meanwhile sending a lady (of which, by now, there are several) for some brandy. Lida stirs a bit. As the doctor prepares a sling to remove Lida from her bed, he finds she's lying in a pool of blood that saturates the garments on the upper part of her body.

Lida is closely examined for another wound. She has none, only the small cut on her neck. Neither does she have any blood on her hands or arms. A wadded, bloody rag, the size of a man's fist, is found on the floor by the side of the bed. It is picked up and placed on a bedroom table, then tossed into the wood stove to burn.

Doctor Hathaway turns to Reverend Arnold and asks if he had found a knife in the room.

Arnold, obviously confused, replies he does not know. Then he then thrust his hands into both of his pocket and pulls a penknife from the right one saying, "Yes, here it is!" He opens the blade and, in doing so, stains his finger with what looks like blood.

The doctor tries to stop the bleeding, but cannot. Several times, Lida tries to speak to the women in the room, but her voice is inaudible. She dies shortly after noon from the loss of blood. A post mortem examination will reveal that the tiny knife wound to her throat had severed her inferior thyroid artery. The stimulant Hathaway administered probably hastened death.

Once Lida Arnold is dead, John brusquely sends Dr. Hathaway home. He asks one of the ladies, Mrs. Henry Converse, to take charge of preparing the body and says he's heading to Camden overnight to arrange for the digging of his wife's grave. He packs a few belonging and leaves his home. His next stop is a Wellington livery to procure a horse and rig for the trip.

As arrangements are made for a December 22, 1892, burial, it's discovered that Reverend Arnold had purchased the necessary undergarments and clothing some weeks before. He tells those who ask that he had bought the items because Lida had asked him to and, in all honesty, at the time, he did not think his wife had long to live.

Wellington's Mayor Couch decides the circumstances connected with Lida's death "are somewhat peculiar" and summons Coroner Braman to investigate. Arnold is surprised when he returns to his home and discovers he is under suspicion of committing murder. It is Arnold himself who insists on a full accounting of the facts.

The coroner interviews several reliable people present at Lida's death and decides to hand the matter over to the prosecutor. Within days, Reverend Arnold is arrested, hauled in front of Wellington's mayor, and charged with murder.

The March 1893 trial takes place a few days after Arnold's 77th birthday. There are seventy-five witnesses and the proceedings are a sensation for both the papers and the citizens of Lorain County. Out on $20,000 bond, the accused man appears to be in better health and spirits that he has been in months. Says the *Lorain County Reporter* (March 18, 1893):

> Mr. John Arnold, the man out on bail for wife murder, is seen at his old house occasionally, but does not meet with a very cordial reception from his former neighbors, especially those who are best acquainted with the details concerning his wife's death.

Large crowds are present throughout John Arnold's trial, with many ladies in attendance. Railroad fares between Wellington and Elyria total more than they have in months.

Arnold gets the best defense he can buy: E.G. Johnson of Elyria (whose son-in-law dies and is buried during the trial), J.H. Dickson of Elyria, and Judge Blaudin of Cleveland. The three attorneys work hard for their client.

Prosecutor A.R. Webber is assisted by W.W. Boyton, now of Cleveland, but an ex-prosecutor and ex-judge of Lorain County.

The trial is "fought vigorously on both sides," in front of Judge Nye, "with many witnesses, to say nothing of the number of spectators, filling the courtroom completely."

The defense brings in several witnesses to illustrate the good character of John Arnold while highlighting the evidence of insanity in Lida Arnold's family.

Dr. Richardson, superintendent of the Columbus Asylum (where Lida's brother had been cared for) testifies to the symptoms and causes of insanity, saying that the insane often appear much improved, as shown by their demeanor, just prior to some desperate act. Dr. Strong, also an expert in mental diseases, says that there were at least four insane members in Mrs. Arnold's immediate family. She had been confined to bed for months and in a melancholy frame of mind, and such circumstance would push her to suicide in four out of five cases.

Dr. McLean, called as an expert surgeon, testifies the wound could have been either self-inflicted, or done by somebody else but, on cross, admits that if two quarts of blood had passed over the neck leaving no trace, then some effort was made to remove it. Dr. Warren, the "lady physician" who attended Mrs. Arnold, says she visited Lida about 60 times in the latter course of her life up until about two weeks before her death. Warren says her patient never expressed any ill-will towards her husband and that he always provided for her needs. What's more, it was Mrs. Arnold herself who always wanted the front door locked when he left so she would not be disturbed.

Then Reverend Arnold takes the stand. He answers all questions put to him in a ready and candid manner.

The morning of Lida's death, he says, after Mrs. Bennett had visited, he sat near Lida's bed. She asked for his knife to "pare her fingernails." He opened it, gave it to her, and she began to work on her nails.

He left to clean out a candy pail that he had promised to Lida's sister. After doing that, he went back to his wife's room, saw, and picked the knife up from the bed and put it in his pocket.

He then noticed Lida was struggling for breath. He called her name, but could not rouse her. He ran as fast as he could for help, finding Mrs. Bennett at Mrs. Heminway's home. He arrived back at the room a few moments ahead of the ladies. The three of them untied the kerchief around his wife's neck and saw the puncture wound.

Per the *Lorain County Report* (April 1, 1893):

> One of the ladies asked me where the knife was. I said I did not know, but when I put my hand in my right pocket, I found it, brought it forth, and opened it. I saw that it was bloody. I closed it, put it in my pocket. Somebody later asked for it and I gave it to them and didn't think a thing about it until the hearing before the mayor.
>
> After she died, I changed my vest, put on an overcoat and scarf, leaned over and kissed the corpse of my wife and went

out, gave directions to prepare her body for burial. I got a horse
and buggy and went to Camden to make arrangements for her
burial in my lot there. I stayed with my nephew.

Arnold denies ever fighting with his wife. He denies ever having cross
words with her. He never called her a liar. Never had a quarrel with her.
He only locked the door at her request. Besides, the back door was always
unlocked in case his wife's brother came to visit.

The jury deliberates for days with John Arnold waiting: "It was a pitiful
sight so see the old man sitting, often alone, in his place at the trial table,
with his eyes fixed intently upon the door through which the jury departed."

Friday night, the jurors sleep on the bare floor. Matting is provided for
Saturday. Sunday night, the court brings in mattresses. On Monday morning,
they declared themselves unable to reach a verdict. It is not a point of law,
they say, but the facts that are in disagreement.

Judge Nye refuses to accept the deadlock and sends them back to continue
deliberation. Tuesday morning they are called in "and on stating to the court
there was not the slightest prospect of an agreement," they are discharged.
Each is happy to go home with $36.00 for two-weeks of duty.

It is revealed that a murder conviction was never in the cards. The jury's
first vote was eight for conviction on manslaughter and four for acquittal.
Their opinions were the same when discharged. For Conviction: C.H.
Blanchard, John Schmitkons, William Shanks, S.D. Stearns, J.B. Baumhart,
M. Matthews, A.P. Johnson, and George Litchfield. For acquittal: L. Brush,
S.W. Moon, Robert Redfern, and Charles Chandler.

The majority of the public, who considered Arnold guilty, is in an
uproar. How a jury could not convict "is a matter of wonderment to those
who followed the testimony in the case." The trial, with no judgement, has
cost upwards of $3,000 with the cost of prosecution at $2,500. All of that
comes straight out of the taxpayer's pockets. "It is questionable, all things
considered, if it is ever tried again."

The penniless and now ill Reverend John Arnold is set free. The case is
never retried and remains unresolved.

Probate Records list the cause of Lida Arnold's death as "Suicide."

Judge David J. Nye:

David Nye was born in Ellicott, Chautauqua County, New York, on
December 8, 1843. After some public and private schooling, he enrolled in

the 1866 Oberlin College preparatory class and went on to earn a Bachelor of Arts (1871) and Master of Arts (1883). His pre-law employment included farmer, teacher, and the Milan, Ohio, School Superintendent.

Nye was admitted to the Ohio Bar in August, 1872, and immediately started his practice in Elyria. From 1881 to 1884 he served as the Lorain County Prosecuting Attorney and was elected to the Common Pleas Court for two terms, starting in 1892. The second term ended in 1901. He declined the opportunity to run for a third. He sat with the strong opinion that the judgeship should be kept out of politics and vice-versa.

He returned to private practice, establishing an office with his sons. D.J. Nye died July 29, 1928. He's buried in Ridgelawn Cemetery, Elyria, Ohio.

1893: *The Anti-Saloon League* is formed in Oberlin, Ohio. It goes national two years later and becomes a driving force for laws prohibiting the use of alcohol. La Grange? Nope. It's LaGrange, but don't tell anybody! Local outbreaks of diphtheria and typhoid. The U.S. Navy and Marines take part in suppressing the Brazilian Naval Revolt and also help overthrown the Kingdom of Hawai'i. In India, Mahatma Gandhi is forced to move from a first-class train car for which he has a ticket. Bad move, fellas. France pulls Laos into its "French Indochina." Frederick Jones is born in Cincinnati, Ohio. He's best known for inventions that improve mechanical refrigeration. Lillian Gish is born in Springfield, Clark County, Ohio. After decades of complaints, Lorain County builds a new jail on the corner of Middle Avenue and Third Street. The sprawling, yet neat, two-story, red-brick building (with appropriately Victorian three-story towers) will stand until the 1980s. Top-of-the-line when it is constructed, this jail will be replaced in 1977 with a new facility on Murray Ridge Road, again after decades of complaints, and near horror-show reviews by Lorain County Grand Juries (*see 1948, June 11, for example*). 152 lynchings: 118 Blacks, 34 others.

1893, November 5, Sunday, between 9:00-10:00pm:

Mrs. Morehouse, Mrs. W.R. White, and Mrs. White's cousin, Mrs. Ellen Manning, have just left evening services at Elyria's Methodist Church. The calm of worship and unseasonably warm weather create a pleasant night, particularly for Mrs. Manning who's trying her best to recover from the emotional and social shame of a failed marriage. Not that anybody could say it was her fault.

Husband Charlie Manning had been a good man, though they did take some good-natured kidding for being sort of an odd couple. She was so tiny, and he so big and strong. Charlie made a good living as a brakeman on the railroad. It had been nice, at first. Then came the drinking. She'd confided in her cousin, Mrs. White, that Charlie was a demon when drunk. Mrs. White didn't initially agree with that assessment, but changed her tune once her tipsy cousin-in-law threatened to kill several people in their family.

Charlie had grown insanely jealous of everyone his wife knew, refusing to let her see anybody, questioning her on her whereabouts, flying into violent rages when she disobeyed. He refused to provide food or clothing and had, how did the lawyer put it? "Absented himself from their bed."

The troubles peaked a few days after Charlie's last July 4th bender. He displayed a loss of temper and irrational anger over the time his wife spent with her cousin, A.I. Osborn, Mrs. White's brother. A truly frightened Ellen took her two-year-old daughter, Edna, and fled to her parent's house to live in safety.

Filing for divorce had been one of the hardest things she had ever done. Especially seeing their names and her charges in the papers: habitual drunkenness, cruelty, and cursing. The vile names. The violence and threats of death. The legal action enraged her husband to the point that he out-and-out told her he would kill her and as many members of her family as he could. But that was behind her. She needed to start looking ahead.

The three women talk quietly as they walk with other small groups of church-goers along West Broad. As they near Gray's Shoes, at 577 Broad, a large man approaches from the shadows, grabs the tiny Mrs. Manning by her arm and yanks her away from her companions.

It's Charlie. Without saying a word, and in full view of witnesses, he produces a revolver and shoots his estranged wife in the side of her neck. He calmly turns to Mrs. White who tries to run across Broad Street. Her Sunday-go-to-meeting clothes make her nowhere near as fast as her assailant who follows, firing two shots: one to her neck, the other to her back.

Mrs. White falls to the ground.

Still armed, Charlie Manning races for cover.

Mrs. Morehouse helps Ellen Manning to the saloon of a nearby hotel where the young victim soon dies of a severed jugular. "Shot like a dog by a drunken brute" are among her last words.

Bystanders assist Mrs. White to the same hotel saloon where she fares much better. The badly bleeding wound on her neck is superficial. Like something out of a melodrama, the shot to her back was stopped by her corset stays. There she's badly bruise and nothing more.

Elyria Police turn out in force. It's Officer Larson who spots the perpetrator, not far from the scene of the crime. Upon the approach of the policeman, Charlie Manning places the barrel of the murder weapon in his mouth and fires a bullet into his own head.

The following letter is found on the suspect:

> For Publication:
>
> To all who may read about this after it is done and gone, I want to say that I married Miss Ellen I. McCabe, the first day of 1890, for love, and I want to say that I have always provided for her as well as a poor man could, most of the time earning from $60 to $90 per month. Now on the 2nd of last August she met her cousin, A.I. Osborn and he put her up to leave me, and on the Fourth of July we all met at Mrs. Thorp's and he went home with us, and my wife took him to La Grange to see a sick cousin the next day. So I made up my mind to kill her and myself, and if I had a chance I will kill Osborn, the black bastard.
>
> Hope the Lord will spare her from the fire, but as for him he needs all the hell he can get, and I shall too if I succeed in carrying out my attempt. I told her the 6th day of September that I would kill her, and I mean to do it now, as I have got a nice little daughter, and I hope the Lord will watch over her for I love her but her mother don't think any more of her than she does of me at this date. On the 7th of July I took him and my wife over to Mrs. Thorp's and then went to Elyria to get my horse shod, and Osborn told me to wait until he came down town and he would ride home with me. Instead of that he goes to where my wife was, and had her out under an apple tree all day.
>
> When I went to have my wife go home, she refused to go. It made me jealous and I called her some hard names, but we made up after that and everything was all right until that bastard came back and soaped her. Now I am too nervous to tell what I would like to, but the short of it is I always loved the woman and baby and I love her now, and to live without her I can't.

This gun belongs to Mr. Earl Hewitt, Camden, and I hope it will be returned to him.

Now I dread doing this, but I can't see any other way out of this trouble. If she would have lived with me as before I would have been a loving husband and a kind father, for no man ever loved two persons better than I love them and to live away from them both makes me crazy.

Now whoever reads this I hope will reason for I have tried to overcome this murderous attempt, and have prayed to the Lord to guide me what to do. Now the way I feel over this. If I'll kill myself and let her go. I don't want people to think I am insane, for I meant to do this ever since she would not let me talk to her on the 6th day of September. I told her I would kill both her and myself and I hope I succeed in getting all names mentioned for if Osborn and his sister [Mrs. White] had let her alone I would have been living happy with my family today instead of writing this to the public. I have gone to Elyria a good many times with the intention of locating them, and then I was going to buy a revolver and try to do the deed. I hope someone will take the little girl and put her in the orphan's home.

This is the first time I have ever carried a weapon and I will start in the morning to kiss my little girl goodbye for I do love them both. I hope this will be a warning to some others. I am too nervous to write what I would like to. My wife has told me with her arms around my neck that nothing but death should part us so I hope death will part us before she gets her divorce I would have done anything in this world to have mended this up but she wouldn't have it so the worst must come. This is for publication.

C.H. MANNING

The Murderer

I hope I succeed in ending my own life, for I don't want to be Lorain County's first man to stretch hemp. *Lorain County Reporter, November 11, 1893.*

The local papers use the murder of Ellen Manning as fodder is their ongoing battle for the prohibition of liquor.

Ellen Manning's body was returned to her parent's home in Pittsfield for the funeral and was buried in Murray Ridge Cemetery. Charlie Manning was buried in the Camden Cemetery.

Little Edna Manning is seen in the local papers once—in the summer of the next year, visiting friends with her grandmother, Mrs. V. Powers.

UXORICIDE: Killing of one's wife.

1894: The City of Lorain is incorporated—Charleston has slid away. The first sanctioned automobile race takes place in France from Paris to Rouen, over 78 miles. At an average speed of 12 mph, Count de Dion arrives first. He is disqualified because his steam car requires a passenger to stoke the firebox. The start of the first Sino-Japanese War. The first documented polio outbreak in the U.S. occurs in Rutland County, Vermont. 192 lynchings: 134 Blacks, 58 others.

Split Personality:

No matter how you look at it, Lorain County was doomed to schizophrenia. At first, both the county's interior and Lake Erie shoreline were settled at a fairly even clip, but soon enough the two regions diverged.

While attractive and fairly well drained with its ridges of sand and gravel, the problem with the extreme northern section of the county was that there was no ready source of power. Before mechanical engines were invented you needed flowing or falling water, and for that you had to move upstream. It is true that Heman Ely offered land and money for a court- and jailhouse to encourage state officials to name Elyria as the county seat, but I am willing to bet that the obvious benefit of the Black Rivers had as much, if not more to do with the decision. Narrow enough to be spanned by bridges, yet with good flows over falls of dozens of feet, the advantages were plain to see to businessmen and politicians of that era.

The City of Lorain came into its own once the trains arrived. Neatly placed between sources of raw material, shipbuilding and steel went hand-in-hand. The want of labor encouraged, and then necessitated, immigrants who arrived from all around the world. Lorain's heavy industries actively searched for and imported workers from the southern United States, Mexico, and Latin American countries. From its very beginnings the city was a mix of races and cultures.

In 1880, Elyria and Lorain combined held only 18% of the county's population. Twenty years later, it was 45%, but the growth was not even. In 1880, Elyria held twice as many people as Lorain. Twenty years later, Lorain was nearly twice the size of Elyria. It's not that the county seat was a slouch; the port city simply grew faster. The development along the county's northern edge also caused the disappearance of townships, like Black River, and was echoed in others, like Avon and Sheffield townships which pulled themselves apart because of differences in industrialization.

Elyria had its amusements, but there is no doubt that the City of Lorain was the place to go for all sorts of entertainment: clean, dubious, and illegal. It was generally accepted that Lorain was a safety valve where those looking for release might find it. Authorities there became well-versed in handling violent crimes that would've thrown the county seat into an absolute tizzy.

It is true that the majority of Lorain County murders take place in its biggest cities. It is also true that folks should never forget that it takes only a few miles to move from bright lights to star-filled skies over what is not always a peaceful earth populated by the descendants of the county's original farm settlers.

1894, July 31, Saturday, Early Evening:

It's the end of another hot, Ohio July. Joseph Schaf(f)er stops at one of Avon's many "rum-holes" for a drink. Or two. Or three.

While there, he happens to jostle the arm of one Matthew Waldecker. Words are exchanged, coats are removed, and a fight begins. Mathias Nichols, Waldecker's boss, joins the fray. It's nothing new between the three, actually more like the continuation of an old feud than anything else.

In short order the saloonkeeper turns the three farmers out into the street to finish their scrap. At first it's hard to tell who's winning, but it becomes apparent that Schaffer is beginning to receive the worst of it. Nichols manages to grab hold of Schaffer. Waldecker repeatedly kicks Schaffer in the guts, despite the beaten man's protests that he's had more than enough and is willing to yield.

Nichols lets go of Schaffer who falls to the ground. Waldecker kicks him again. One John Powdermacher has seen enough and grabs Waldecker to stop the fight. Nichols, in turn shoves Powdermacher, exclaiming "fair play, keep away!" Then Nichols turns to urge on Waldecker. "Give it to him. Kill the son of a bitch. That's it; follow him up."

Schaffer manages to gain his feet and begins staggering away. At the urging of his boss, Waldecker follows and kicks the wounded man in the stomach several more times, both before and after Schaffer once again falls to the ground.

Nichols pats Waldecker on the back when the fight's done. "You are the boy, Mattie!" The two are hauled into jail but are soon bailed on a relatively small amount of money.

Members of the crowd that gathered during the fight help Schaffer to a barn where he lay, in agony, through the night. The next morning he's carried to his widowed mother's home, in Avon, where he lingers two or three days in great distress and dies, leaving a wife and two kids.

A post mortem done by Dr. W.F. McLean, of Elyria, and Dr. Randall, of Avon, shows it was a terrible death. The whole of the dead man's abdomen is badly bruised and discolored. The large intestine is torn open by Waldecker's violent and persistent kicks. Decomposition had already set in.

Nichols and Waldecker are rearrested by Officers Boyd and Collins, then released on a bail of $500 each with a preliminary hearing scheduled for August 13. Public outcry against this second release is so severe that bail is revoked and the two are arrested a third time. At their hearing before "Squire Chapman" at the courthouse, bail is reset at $5,000. This is not met and the two are placed in jail. There are unsubstantiated reports that Nichols tries to hang himself while in custody.

The Grand Jury indicts both for murder in the second degree. They plead not guilty.

They are tried in Judge Nye's court. Prosecution is Mr. Thomas assisted by A.R. Webber. Defense is E.C. Johnson and I.A. Webster.

At trial it's revealed that Waldecker struck the first blow and then followed Schaffer into the road to finish the fight with Nichols' help. Waldecker claims he would have never have been so cruel without Nichols egging him on.

Partway thru proceedings Waldecker drops his plea of innocence and agrees to a charge of manslaughter. Nichols finishes the trial and is found guilty of manslaughter with a recommendation of mercy.

At Christmastime, Judge Nye sentences Waldecker to seven years in the Ohio Penitentiary in Columbus. He takes his sentence stoically while Nichols is considerably broken up over his sentence of just two years.

This crime is used in letters to the editor to point out the evils of drink: "The scar of the awful and damning power of liquor is burnt into our character as a people…" The *Elyria Republican* also refers to it near election-time as part of a plea for Avon Township to vote itself dry.

Two weeks after the trial ends, this appears on the front page of the *Elyria Republican:*

> Wants Heavy Damages. Webber & Stroup on Tuesday filed for Anna Mary Schaffer, a suit for $10,000 damages against Mathias Nicholas and Matthew Waldecker, for the killing of Joseph Schafer at French Creek, last summer. Mrs. Schaffer brought the suit as administratrix of the estate of Joseph Schaffer, her son, whom she believes to have been worth the sum demanded. The defendants are serving a term in the penitentiary, convicted of manslaughter.

I did not find the outcome.

1894, September ?: Location: Grafton, "Allen's Hotel." Victim: John Hoeline (stepfather). Suspect: Andrew Mertaugh (22, stepson). Suspect Mertaugh on the run from the law since November 1894. Arrested in May of 1895. Was living in Cleveland and working for a bridge construction company. Charged with murder. Brought before Magistrate Chapman on May 19, 1895. Defended in pretrial "in an able manner" by Leo Stroup. There is not enough evidence to hold the prisoner, and he is released. Outcome: Unresolved.

PARENTICIDE: Killing of one's mother or father.

1894, November 14, Wednesday:

Smoke rises over the West View property of farmer William Gletzer (35), about a mile north of Copopa, Columbia Township (the intersection of Ohio 82 and 252). Neighbors hurry to find flames engulfing Gletzer's barn, but there's no sign of the 35-year-old farmer.

The reason for this fact is apparent once what's left of the barn cools enough to be entered. Charles Handwerg, 30, Gletzer's brother-in-law, searches the structure to find and douse what he thinks are Gletzer's charred, still-smoldering remains. Only the trunk and head remain. There is a burnt rope around his neck. Holes and melted lead are found in the skull. Coroner Braman and Sheriff Ensign are summoned.

Suspicion immediately falls on the victim's ne'er-do-well stepson, 22-year-old Charlie Geska. He and Gletzer had been living on the farm and constantly arguing since the recent death of the boy's mother in a Cleveland asylum. William planned on remarrying which Charles was vehemently opposed to. The farmer gave the young man the boot.

Since then Charlie has been a vagabond, given to "sleeping in strawstacks and living a worthless sort of life." He'd been seen in the area the Monday before the fire, when he called on local blacksmith Fred Orlofsky. During that visit Charlie used some threatening language in reference to his stepfather.

Charlie Geska is arrested in Cleveland on the night of November 16 at the home of a woman who had been a housekeeper at the farm. Found on him is a letter to his grandmother, written in German. It says, in part, "I take the pen to write a few lines about the accident that happened to father and to tell how it is I am alone."

The young man appears on the verge of nervous collapse when he arrives at the Elyria jail. He claims he was in Cleveland, nowhere near the farm on the day of the blaze.

Justice B.B. Adams of Columbia Township acts as coroner at the inquest. The cause of death is determined to be "gunshot wounds at the hands of some person unknown." The investigation places the time of the shooting at 8:00pm, the night before the fire, based on the testimony of neighbor Mrs. Richard Putt who had heard shots at around that time.

The dead man's boots were found in their usual place but with blood stains upon them, so he did not walk by himself into the barn but was carried there, probably in the blood-covered carriage that sat outside the burned building. It is decided that the fire was set in hopes of covering the crime.

At the preliminary trial Charlie is defended by A.R. Webber and Lee Stoup. Charles Handwerg, the brother-in-law, testifies that he lives about a half-mile from the Gletzer farm and last saw the victim the Saturday before the murder. Handwerg went to the fire the night the barn burned, found the corpse about 1:30am, and splashed it with water to preserve what was left. Handwerg says there was what seemed to be a rope under the neck. He also states that Gletzer and Geska had their problems, but he had never heard any threats from Geska.

Dr. Stewart, of Berea, was called to the farm the morning after the fire to examine the remains. The bones of the skull were well-preserved, except for a portion above the right eye that was burned away, but the identity of the victim was not readily apparent because of the lack of flesh. Stewart had measured the skull, which contained melted lead, and compared it to Gletzer's hats and found it matched. The doctor is of the opinion the skull was that of Gletzer.

Sheriff Ensign testified that he had talked to Geska about the German-language letter that seemed to indicate prior knowledge of his stepfather's death. The young man said it was not translated properly.

Geska, the accused, says his stepfather had turned him away from the farm with no money. He had slept in a strawstack in Rockport (a now-vanished township in Cuyahoga County, along Lake Erie west of Cleveland) both Tuesday and Wednesday nights, but during both of those days, had been in Cleveland.

Columbia Township Attorney, L.Z. Tunney, testifies that he had known both men for about five years. He drops a bombshell by saying that, a week before the fire, William Gletzer had told him that Charlie had asked for one-third the property that his mother had left and that the old man had said that he told his stepson that he'd get none of the property nor any money from it—ever—no matter what happened.

Attorney Tunney is also of the opinion that the body is that of Gletzer because the trunk was that of a larger man and that one tooth in the scorched skull projects over the others, a peculiarity of Gletzer's smile.

With Grand Jury testimony complete, Charles Geska is bound over for criminal trial. Newspapers surmise that defense will try to show that the body cannot be identified as that of William Gletzer. As everyone knows, with no sure identification of the body there can be no murder.

On November 27, Charlie Geska asks Jailer Squires to send for Sheriff Ensign. Ensign arrives with his deputy to find Geska pale and haggard from several sleepless nights. Says the sheriff, "Young Geska then proceeded to make a confession which indicated that he is not the meek and innocent creature which he has claimed to be but a murderer whose deed of blood and pillage has scarcely been surpassed in the annuls of crime."

The *Elyria Republican* (December 6, 1894) reports Charlie's story:

On Thursday, November 8th, I was coming from Sandusky to Cleveland on a freight train, beating my way, when I met two tramps who hailed from Cleveland, named Charles Todd and Mike Plako. I got "in" with them and just then I was pretty mad at the old man [William Gletzer]. I wanted to get even with him. I told Todd and Plako about him, and how we could "fix" him. I wanted them to help me give father a big whipping, and told them that he had some money and I knew where we could get it after we "fixed" him. My plan was to disable him, not to kill him.

The two men agreed to my plan, but we made no arrangements that day. We met in Cleveland, however, on the following Saturday, November 10th, and on that night made arrangements to go out to West View. I met them again on the Tuesday following, November 13th, on the flats in Cleveland. We all jumped a freight and went to Berea where we got off and went cross-lots to West View, and our home.

We reached the house at 11 o'clock on Wednesday evening. I opened the kitchen door and found the old man sitting by the side of the stove reading. He wore his slippers. He looked up when I came in and asked me what business I had in there. He said "Go away." I told that I had come to stay and that I was going to stay. The other two men were outside and he did not see them.

Father went into the pantry and came out with a box, out of which a razor dropped on to the floor between the kitchen door and the pantry door. He stooped down to pick up the razor and I grabbed a shot gun, which was standing close to the kitchen door between the front room door in the kitchen, and fired as he was just reaching the razor.

His head was down and turned toward me. The full charge went into his head. I only shot once. He went down on his hands and knees, and was up again in a moment, the blood streaming out of his head in a frightful manner. He made for me, but I managed to hold him off with the gun. I did not want to be covered with the blood.

Just then the two men outside gave a yell and said that someone was coming. We all ran outside and back of the barn. Father came out of the house, though almost ready to fall from loss of blood, and cried for help as loud as he could.

We then lost sight of him for a few moments and after it had grown quiet we returned, but could find nothing of him. We hunted around and at last discovered him lying next to the front gate. He had crawled around there on his hands and knees. We found a rope, slipped it around his neck and dragged him by it to the barn. We all took a hand in this. We left the body on the floor of the barn. He was dead then.

We went into the house after disposing of the body, and

my companions went to sleep in father's bed, while I cleaned the gun and mopped the floor, removing all traces of blood. Then I went to sleep in my own bed.

On Wednesday morning before daylight we went to the barn and lifted the body up on to the hay mow, throwing the rope off. We crawled back to the house on our hands and knees, so as not to be seen. We stayed in the house all day Wednesday and that night about 8 o'clock went to the barn.

We placed a big charge of powder in the hay mow, to which we attached a fuse, lighted it and made our escape. I gave the tramps $31 in money, all there was in the house, and a watch which was my mother's.

During the scrimmage with my father, after the shooting, one of the window lights in the door was broken.

The facts corroborate at least some of the story: One of the kitchen doors shows the marks of a shot, and a pane of broken glass. Plus, one of the neighbors saw a large object, now believed to be the body, roll from the hayloft as the barn burned.

The sheriff says he has searched for Todd and Plako, the two men mentioned in the story, but he has reached the conclusion that they both are "myths," even though there is some question as to how the rather smallish Geska, by himself, could manage the large body of his dead-weighted stepfather into the hayloft.

Defense lawyers A.R. Webber and Lee Stroup are surprised by the confession, but say they can save their client from execution.

Charlie Geska is charged with murder in the first degree with his criminal trial to set to begin on Monday, March 25. Locals have considerable feeling against Geska. There are "threats of violence if Geska is given anything but a sentence of murder in the first degree."

Editorials call for more severe punishment for all crimes. The *Elyria Republican:* "There is insanity in the family. Will this old, familiar plea be made?"

The criminal trial is crowded with spectators. A large group from Columbia Township is present. Prosecutor Thomas states that he can prove that the accused shot the victim through the glass of the farmhouse's porch door and that the killing was not done in self-defense but as a premeditated act committed well out of reach of the victim.

Frank Snell, a neighbor, places Geska headed toward the scene of the crime and identifies the skull as that of William Gletzer by the nose and cheekbones. A.H. Osborn, a friend of the victim, identifies the gun used in the crime. He also contends that the remains are those of Gletzer, supporting his decision with two front teeth that project outwards.

At this point juror E.H. Manning, of Brighton, faints away, and court is adjourned until 1:00pm.

Upon reconvening, Ambers Bennett describes how he had talked to the accused only two weeks before the killing. Charlie had said a horse he had paid for was going to be taken away by his stepfather, adding that he would "get rid of the son of a bitch."

Lieutenant O'Donnell, officer at the Second Precinct on the near east side of Cleveland, Ohio, testifies that, upon arrest, the accused was carrying "a silver watch, knife, a package of smoking tobacco, pawn ticket, a pocketbook with no money in it, and a letter to his grandmother in Germany." Geska showed no surprise when apprehended at 186 Waring Street by Cleveland policemen. In fact, he admitted that he "might have done something to be arrested for."

Charlie's Elyria jailer, Frank Squires tells how the young man confessed spontaneously and that no threats were made to obtain it.

On the second day of the trial, Dr. P.W. Stewart of Berea, the first to examine the skull, tells how he had found two apertures in it from which he had taken buckshot. He states that these injuries were severe enough to cause death.

The letter found on Geska at the time of his arrest, this time translated by Reverend E.T. Bettex of St. Paul's Church in Elyria, is read into evidence. It states Charlie did not feel sorry over Gletzer's death.

Miss Pauline Ritchie is called as a point of contention between the victim and the accused. The now-dead Gletzer had asked for her hand in marriage just one month after the death of Charlie's mother. Nearly a dozen letters written by Miss Ritchie to Gletzer are read into evidence, "much to the amusement of the witness and audience." Prosecutor Thomas then reads Charlie Geska's written confession and then closes his case.

A.R. Webber, for the defense, speaks of the victim courting a woman within weeks of the death of the mother of the accused. Charlie Geska was displeased with the turn of events, and when he spoke his mind, the victim not only turned him out of the house but threatened his life, as well.

Witness Charles Handwerg testifies that the old man had found his stepson in his barn the Friday before the murder and told him he'd be shot if discovered there again

The defense calls Charlie's sanity into question. Geska's aunt cut her own throat to commit suicide while insane, and her sister, Geska's mother, died in an insane asylum. Dr. Todd, of the asylum, testified that Charlie's mother had died "of insanity that was hereditary," but no expert testimony directly addresses the sanity of the accused.

Mrs. John French and Mrs. C.W. Stoll, of Chestnut Ridge in Olmsted Township, tell of feeding the accused the week before the crime. There were two men with him at the time. One closely matched the description of one of the friends mentioned in Geska's confession.

Charles Geska, on the stand in his own defense, insists that two other men were with him. When asked why he did not call on them to help in his fight with his stepfather, he replies "I was excited." The burning of the barn was the idea of his vanished pals.

Under cross examination, the accused is unable to explain why, if the killing was in self-defense, he hid in the barn instead of calling for a doctor. When confronted with powder burns on the door, evidence of him shooting the victim through the glass, Charlie emphatically answers "no!" He denies that he wrote the letter to his grandmother that describes the "accident" that befell his stepfather before it actually happened. He denies all but one of the threats he made against the old man.

When asked if he had "finished off" Gletzer by cutting his throat, pounding his head with a club, and then using a hay knife to hack off the old man's arms and legs before burning the barn "the prisoner, squirming under the ordeal, broke down and said he had done enough already."

During close, defense lawyer Lee Stroup states that Geska had not used the hay knife to dismember the body since it was found under the body, as several witnesses at the time of the fire described. He reemphasizes that it was self-defense and not vengeance that prompted the killing. Attorney Webber details how the German-born Charlie had been taken advantage of. Deprived of a proper U.S. education and with few skills, the boy was "selfishly used for Gletzer's personal profit." The accused had worked in his dead mother's house until the victim turned him out.

The defense stresses that Geska had no motive for lying in his confession and remarks that "Lorain County had never hung a man, yet enforces the law as well as any county in the state."

Prosecutor Thomas stresses the lack of testimony as to the good character of Geska. He repeats what the victim had once told a friend: "I fear the boy and will send him back to Germany even if I have to borrow the money to pay his fare." Thomas describes the three accidental meetings Charlie recounted between him and his alleged companions as unbelievable. He states the powder marks on the door were proof that Gletzer was shot through the glass and not in self-defense, that the act was premeditated, and that Charles Geska deserves the noose.

Judge Nye charges the jury with instructions on determining the degree of murder and to the laws of evidence concerning self-defense, insanity, confessions, and conversations long after the crime had been committed, and sends the jurors to their deliberations at 4:00pm Saturday.

12:30am Sunday morning, a verdict is returned: Guilty of murder in the second degree.

When asked if he had anything to say before sentencing, attorney Webber stands and says that "he and his partner, Mr. Stroup, had told Geska that the only thing that would save him from the gallows was to tell the absolute truth to them and the jury, as a lie would hang him."

The sentence is fixed by law: Life in the Ohio Penitentiary in Columbus. Charlie holds himself in check until his counsel refers to his dead stepfather whereupon the young man bursts into tears.

A later interview with a juror reveals that, on the first ballot three were for execution, eight for second degree, and one for manslaughter. It took some argument and another vote to come to an agreement on second degree murder. The threats the young man had made, that the prosecutors made so much of, were not considered clear enough evidence for premeditation, but if the State had been successful in proving Charlie Geksa had actually fired through the door from outside the house, the verdict would have been murder in the first degree and a death sentence.

Early morning, April 10, 1895, Charlie Geska is taken to Columbus on the "Big Four Train." He retains his composure until the big gate is slammed shut behind him. When the warden asks what he'd done, the boy cries for several minutes before answering "murder."

The warden replies "that means you are in here for life."

Geska is put to work as a cigar packer, "determined to make the best of the situation." Prosecutor Thomas visits Geska at the pen in February, 1896. He's still packing cigars. Confinement is beginning to tell and Geska has grown thin and looks old before his time. He tells Thomas the outlook is dreary.

October 14, 1909: Geska is in the Penitentiary's hospital after "swallowing a medicine vial." But he does not die. In November that same year, he receives a "Thanksgiving Pardon" by the Ohio Governor. Geska, suffering from tuberculosis, faints upon hearing the news. He is taken in by a Mrs. Shellhouse who lives south of the city of Columbus, Ohio.

In October of 1909, on the James Miller farm, also in Columbia Township, two large barns and adjoining buildings burn. Human bones are found during the cleanup. Circumstances are similar to the murder of William Gletzer except there are no bullet holes in the skull and nobody in the area is missing. It's surmised that it was a tramp, sleeping in the barn, who accidentally cause the fire, was caught in the flames, and burned to death.

Who Is That Skull?

Western courts long followed the legal maxim of "no body, no murder," partially based on the 1660 case of "Campden Wonder" in which a mother and two sons were found guilty, tortured, and executed for the murder of a person who later showed up alive.

The idea of "corpus delicti" (body of crime) as referring to the actual body of a murdered person was hard for the courts to shake. Prosecutors had to have a reasonable identification of a body, or important parts thereof, before pursuing a charge of murder. This put them at a disadvantage since clever criminals knew circumstantial evidence was not enough in cases where there was no corpse.

Whether young Charles Geska, in the story above, knew this when he tried to burn his stepfather's body is a matter of question.

The identity of William Gletzer's corpse was so hard to establish because forensic science was inadequate. At the time dried blood of any kind was indistinguishable from other dark stains. Differentiating between animal and human blood wasn't possible until the early 1900s. It wasn't until the 1950s that non-destructive tests for blood and its full typing were readily available.

In 1960 it was clearly established in U.S. courts that circumstantial evidence alone could prove the guilt of murder when a body could not be found (People v. Scott, 176 Cal. App. 2d 458). The first court case in the United States that used DNA to gain a conviction took place in 1987 (Tommy Lee Andrews, of a series of sexual assaults in Orlando, Florida).

It took nearly a century for science to catch up with the needs of the State in the murder of William Gletzer.

1895: X-rays discovered by Roentgen. The U.S. Golf Association puts on the first national championships. "Banjo" Patterson and Christina Macpherson put together Australia's unofficial national anthem, *Waltzing Matilda*. The end of the first Sino-Japanese War. Sino didn't do so hot. Lenin (the Bolshevik) is arrested in St. Petersburg. The Johnson Steel Company in Lorain. 179 lynchings: 113 Blacks, 66 others. $1,000 is worth $27,571 modern.

1895, June 8, Saturday: Location: Brownhelm Township, home of Hattie Scarlet. Victim: William Champsey. Suspects: Morris Snyder and William Shepley (Shipley). Body is found in a lake at the foot of a high cliff. First thought to be a drowning victim, but a broken neck prompts further investigation. Prosecutor Thomas is assisted by W.B. Thompson of Lorain. Defense is Judge Mills, of Sandusky, and E.G. Johnson. During trial a Mrs. Scarlet causes a scene by fainting away while on the witness stand.

Charge against both: Murder in the second degree. Pleas of both: Not Guilty. Morris Snyder is found not guilty. William Shepley is found guilty of manslaughter. Outcome: Shepley sentence to Ohio Penitentiary for 2 years. Suspended until circuit court May 1897 hears appeal. Appeal for new trial refused.

1895, September ??: Location: Lorain. Victim: John Drugaen. Suspect: Michael Palgot (Pogat, Poigat). Act: Trauma. Several "Poles" are involved in a quarrel at the christening of a child. The suspect picks up a chair and strikes the victim on the head cutting a "terrible gash." The wounded man is taken care of by the police. Several men are arrested, but Drugaen identifies his attacker as Palgot who is jailed along with several of his companions (as witnesses). Drugaen dies the next day. The suspect is indicted by the November Grand Jury. Charge: Murder in the second degree. Plea: Not guilty. Outcome: Guilty of manslaughter. Sentence: 1 to 20 years in the Ohio Penitentiary

1895, October 17, Thursday: Location: Lorain. Victim: D.H. Moon (35) housewife from Urickesville, Ohio. Suspect: ?. Act: Violence. Outcome: ?

1895, November 6, Wednesday: Location: ? Victim: ? Suspect: Peter Aleck. Act: ? Charge: Murder in the second degree. Plea: Not guilty. Outcome: Guilty of manslaughter.

1896: Pittsfield dedicates a Civil War monument of an east-facing Union standard bearer near the present-day intersection of Ohio 58 and 303. The

"Skirmisher" Civil War monument is erected in Elyria's Ridgelawn Cemetery. The castle-like Ohio State Reformatory in Mansfield, Ohio, begins taking prisoners after ten years of construction (funding problems, y'see). The first inmates are put to work finishing the facility that is praised as the best of its kind. It will eventually be condemned as one of the worst. At the time of this book, the Reformatory is open to visitors. Make a visit. Vaccine for typhoid fever. The start of the 22-year Yaqui Indian Wars in Arizona and Mexico. First modern Olympic Games are held in Athens, Greece. Theodor Herzl calls for a Jewish State. Spanish Concentration Camps in Cuba. William McKinley (Ohio Republican) wins the Election with 51.0% of the popular vote. Utah. 123 lynchings: 78 Blacks, 45 others.

1896, ? ?: Location: ? Victim: ? Suspect: Elias Authoro. Act: ? Charge: Murder in the second degree. Plea: Not guilty. Outcome: Guilty as charged. Sentence: Ohio Penitentiary, 18 months.

1896, December 20: *Lorain County Coroner's Death Records:*
>   Assistant Coroner George Foster reports that *76-year-old* Maud Innis, of LaGrange, has died *in childbirth.* A great example of why you should never trust official records!

1897: Vaccine for bubonic plague. Victoria's Diamond Jubilee. The LakeShore Electric Interurban Railroad. The State of Ohio begins electrocuting murderers. First up is 17-year-old William Haas Hamilton, from Hamilton County, on April 21, 1897, for the rape and murder of his employer's wife, Mrs. William Brader. He was supposed to have been executed on April 8th, but problems with the generator forced a postponement. A few minutes later, wife murderer William Wiley is sent on to his Maker in the same fashion. A total of 315 male and female prisoners will be electrocuted until 1963, when Ohio calls a (temporary) halt to the death penalty. 158 lynchings: 123 Blacks, 35 others.

1897, January 23: *Lorain County Reporter:*
>   Statistics show that when a man commits a murder in this country there is only one chance in sixty that he will be legally hanged for the crime. This is what keeps "Judge Lynch" so long in office.

1898: National Basketball League is established in Philadelphia, Pennsylvania. Germany begins naval expansion. Charlotte Perkins' *Women and Economics.* The Hawai'ian islands are made a territory of the U.S. five years after the rulers were overthrown—by the U.S. The Philippines declare independence from Spain, with whom they are at war. On a related note, Spain cedes Puerto Rico and Cuba to the U.S. and sells us the rebellious Philippines for $20 million to conclude the Spanish-American War. Norman Vincent Peale is born in Bowersville, Greene County, Ohio. 120 lynchings: 101 Blacks, 19 others.

1898, January 27, Thursday: Location: Wellington, residence of Charles F. West. Victim: Fred Packenbush (Packbausch, Packenbausch). Suspect: Joseph Fox aka Joseph Thomas (about 21), not to be confused with Joe "Dummy" Fox, a deaf man from Oberlin who grew to be a local character of sorts.

Preliminary hearing is held the week of January 29, 1898. Criminal trial is scheduled for March 18, 1898.

Early Sunday, March 13, 1898, Fox breaks out of the County Jail in the company of Thomas Fay (attempted robbery of a North Amherst bank), Fred Wright (robbing boats in the Lorain harbor), and James Thompson (fencing stolen goods and attempting murder of a police officer).

When the prisoners are placed in their cells that night, James Thompson uses a piece of soft wood in such a way to prevent his door from locking. This gives him access to the corridor. He dismantles a window ventilator to fashion a tool he uses to break the lock on the corridor door and jimmy the cells of the other men. They are then able to reach an outside window. The four men lower themselves to the ground by using a rope made of their bed sheets. The dark and stormy night helps them escape detection.

Two hours later, Joseph Fox pounds on the front door of the jail. He says the other prisoners threatened to kill him if he had not gone along with the escape. He had hopped a freight for Toledo but "as I had no money and could get nothing to eat I decided to return here and stand trial, so took another freight and have just arrived." The other escapees are never found.

Fox's four-day trial takes place as scheduled in front of Judge Nye. Prosecution: A.R. Thomas and Clayton Chapman. Defense: Attorney Blinn and A.R. Webber. Charge: Murder. Plea: Self-defense.

Charles F. West, a Wellington farmer, employed both Fred Packenbush and Joseph Fox as laborers. He testifies that Packenbush was found unconscious in the barn and robbed of a pair of felt boots and a pair of mittens. This made Fox an immediate suspect since the two workers had previously argued over the ownership of the boots (to make matter worse, Fox had the boots and mittens in his possession when he was arrested).

According to farmer West, Fox and the victim constantly argued. The night of the murder, Packenbush was sent to the barn for an armload of firewood. When he did not return Mrs. West went looking and, shortly after 8:00pm, found the victim beaten and bleeding, sitting on the ground in the barn, groaning and unable to speak.

Mrs. West fetched her daughter. They wrapped the injured Packenbush in blankets and moved him to the house where he died about 10:30pm, never regaining consciousness.

Fox's story is that he and Packenbush got into an argument over the use of Fox's own felt boots. Packenbush had threatened to toss him from the barn to which Fox replied "I am just as big as you are." The victim rushed him and struck the first blow. When Fox hit him back, the victim grew enraged and seized "some big club, looked to me like a plow handle."

Packenbush got the better of Fox, driving him into a corner, striking him several times on the shoulders and arms, and threatening to kill him "then and there." Fox managed to obtain a weapon of his own, a "door roller" from the barn and, after exchanging several blows, knocked Packenbush to the ground.

Fox then removed his felt boots from the victim. The mittens, Fox explained, were loaned to him by Packenbush earlier in the day. He put them in his pocket and forgot he had them. He claims he didn't know Packenbush was dead until he was arrested. The man was certainly alive when he left him. Both of them were "excited and mad" during and after their fight.

After a day of deliberation the jury stands at two for murder in the first, two for murder in the second, and eight for manslaughter. Outcome: Guilty of manslaughter. Sentence: Ohio Penitentiary, 15 years at hard labor with no solitary.

Say the papers: "His pleas of self-defense and extreme youth of the prisoner probably saved him from the electrical chair. Fox is indeed lucky in getting out of this difficulty with such a light sentence."

1898, April 13: The *Superior City* is launched from the Lorain Yards of the Cleveland Ship Building Company. She is the first large steel-hulled cargo carrier to sail the Great Lakes and the biggest freshwater ship of her time (429 feet long, 50 feet wide, 25 feet high, and just over 4,785 gross tons), propeller driven, with a crew of 33.

At 10:00pm, August 20, 1920, in Whitefish Bay, Lake Superior, she is rammed on her port side, aft of amidships by the steamer *Willis L. King*. The stern of the *Superior City* blows to smithereens when her boilers contact the cold lake water. She sinks quickly, and all but four hands are lost.

One survivor is Walter Richter, of Lorain, stripped naked by the force of the blast that lifted him from his doomed ship. He is found floating to safety on a hatch cover.

1899: Camille Jenatzy is the first to officially drive faster than a mile a minute, reaching 65mph. It's an electric car. The Somalis rebel against Britain. The U.S. is involved in the Moro Rebellion (Philippines) in particular, and the Philippine-American War, in general. American Shipbuilding Co., Lorain. Lorain Harbor has a light-keeper. In the Docket: Selling Liquor to Minors. Fines are $80 and less. 106 lynchings: 85 Blacks, 21 others.

1899, April 8, Saturday: Location: Lorain, Ward 3, "On the viaduct." Victim: George Rider (Reider, Bider) (38). Suspect: Anton(e) Sagi. "Both men are Hungarians."

Sagi and his wife, Katy, are married in Cleveland in August of 1895. They have a daughter, five-year-old Helen, and run a boarding house near the Lorain Steel Mill. Bad feeling have existed between the Sagi and Rider since before Sagi applied for divorce on the grounds of adultery, claiming Rider has ruined his family. The two men meet by chance on the Lorain Viaduct. An altercation follows. Sagi pulls his revolver, shoots Rider three times, and then immediately surrenders to police. Held by Lorain Mayor Babcock for shooting with intent to kill. Bail is set at $1,000. Bail is revoked, and the charge upped to murder when medical treatment fails to save Rider's life. He is buried in the potter's field of Lorain's Elmwood Cemetery.

Sagi is placed in the county lockup because Lorain Jail officials are worried about a lynching. But, "Upon inquiry it was learned there was nothing to fear from this point, as all sympathy of the Hungarians were with the man that had done the shooting."

Sagi and his wife reconcile while he awaits trial.

His trial attorneys are E.G. Johnson and W.L. Hughes. Charge: Murder in the second degree. Plea: Not guilty. *Changed to:* Guilty of manslaughter. Sentence: Ohio Penitentiary in Columbus, 5 years.

Week of June 15, 1899, after sentencing by Judge Nye, the papers say:

> The circumstances of the case, and the fortitude with which Sagi bore his imprisonment have created for him no little sympathy and many would have been pleased had he received a lighter sentence. Sagi's wife and children visited him in the jail after he was sentenced, and he promised to return to them at the expiration of his term of imprisonment. *The Elyria Reporter, June 15, 1899.*

Mrs. Sagi, who runs the boarding house while her husband is imprisoned, continues to cater to a rough crowd.

1900, summer: Sagi is paroled. Shortly thereafter he sues for divorce from Katy, the woman for whom he killed. She gets their property. He gets custody of their daughter. Sagi and the girl move in with his elderly parents who also live in Lorain.

1900, late September: Katy countersues. Her attorney is Q.A. Gillmore. Non-support is one reason, that he's "in the penitentiary" is the other. In actuality, he's serving his sentence, but is on parole.

1902, May 22: Mr. Anton Sagi is granted a divorce on the ground of her unfaithfulness.

1902, June 26: Lorain dock hand Anton Sagi (41) files for a license to marry Mrs. Teresa Lacz(a) (18) of Lorain.

1902, June 26: Sagi is struck with a crane bucket while helping to load coal "at the Whirleys" (a high, spinning crane). His shoulder is injured and skull fractured. Recovery is "doubtful." I did not find a death notice.

1899, September 7, Thursday evening:

Thick-set, with graying black hair and mustache, Clevelander Franklin E. Wheeler has been in Lorain for about two months, doing a good business as a sales agent for the New Jersey Mutual Life Insurance Company. His unassuming and intelligent manner makes him seem about a decade older than his 43 years, but he is popular and has many friends—when sober.

Wheeler is no saint. He's divorced, is known to take a drink, or two, and is a frequent customer of Lorain native, 25-year-old Philip Meyers, of Livingston Avenue, who runs the bar adjacent to Lorain's Franklin Hotel, where Wheeler has a room.

The evening of Thursday, September 7, Wheeler and Meyers bump into each other in the hotel's dining room. Meyers takes the moment to publicly remind the older man that he owes a bar tab of $4.00. Franklin strenuously denies the bill. The young, yet veteran barkeeper persists; he knows unpaid bills are bad for business. The two men exchange a few harsh words, then go their separate ways.

Bartender Meyers takes a seat and orders dinner. Wheeler leaves the hotel and walks across the street to Chapman and Hill's general store. He tells the clerk he wants to "kill a cat" and purchases an Ivers Johnson, double-acting, .38 caliber, 5-shot revolver. Wheeler asks the salesman to load the weapon and then buys five extra cartridges, paying a dollar in total and promising to return to pay the balance.

Pocketing the revolver, Wheeler returns to the hotel and takes a seat in the dining room where he displays "unusually loud and boisterous" behavior, including singing and otherwise disturbing his fellow customers.

The waiter refuses to serve him and leaves the room to report the matter to the hotel owner, Mrs. McElroy. When she arrives to admonish Wheeler, he is gone, following Meyers, who left his seat at another table to return to his work.

Meyers enters his saloon, he takes a seat at the far end of the otherwise empty bar, and reopens the book he's been reading, *Captains Courageous*, by Rudyard Kipling. Wheeler strolls in a few moments later. Without a word, he walks about half-way across the room, takes quick aim with his brand new revolver, and fires two shots at Meyers. The first goes wide. The second flattens itself against the brick wall near the seated barkeep who, recovering his senses, leaps to his feet and dashes to the closest door, the one that leads outside.

Wheeler shoots three more times and Meyers is struck in the left arm, halfway between the elbow and shoulder; in the back through the left shoulder blade where it strikes a rib and stops near the breast bone; and through the back below the shoulder blade near the spine where it pierces the heart.

Those outside hear gunshots in rapid succession. The saloon door bursts open and out reels Philip Meyers, blood gushing from his nose and mouth.

Lorain's Dr. Kiplinger and Chester O'Neil almost collide with the dying man who collapses to the sidewalk and with a loud groan, dies. They carry him to a back room of the bar, summon doctors Mean and Van Tilberg, and alert the police.

Franklin Wheeler is no place to be found. He has wandered a few blocks to the home of Lorain's Dr. Garver. When told the doctor is not in, Wheeler says to the person answering the door, "I have just shot a man and I want to sit down here and wait for the police." When the doctor arrives, Wheeler is sitting, twirling the revolver in his hand. He appears neither excited, nor intoxicated. He is arrested and placed in the Lorain City Jail.

Lorain Police Chief Meister examines the revolver and finds all five chambers discharged. Wheeler exhibits "absolutely no emotion when questioned." When asked why he did it he says, "I intended to get even with him, but I guess I got a little too even."

A noisy crowd forms at the Franklin Hotel and begins making threats against Wheeler. Two or three hundred angry men gather at the Lorain City Jail where they are told that the shooter has been taken Wheeler by buggy to Elyria. This is a lie meant to mislead, as shortly after, Wheeler is taken down the alley behind the city jail to Bank Street and then on the electric street car to the county seat. His escort, Chief Meister and five uniformed police, are happy to arrive safe and sound. For his part, Wheeler tells those protecting him that, if the mob finds them, to let them have him so that life and property would not be put at risk on his account because, "perhaps a man might be killed whose life is worth ten such as mine."

"Unprovoked and cold-blooded murder" is what the papers call it, "For cold blooded deliberation, [this crime has] never had an equal in the criminal history of the county."

During his first few days in jail Wheeler stays in his cot with a blanket hung in from of the door to keep out the light. He refuses all visitors and finally asks the sheriff not to admit them.

When arraigned, Wheeler is the coolest man in the room as he waives a hearing and pleads not guilty to murder in the first degree. He make no arrangement for counsel, saying his friends will take care of him. It's as if he either doesn't know or doesn't care about the consequences of his actions.

Wheeler is indicted on charges of murder in the second by the Lorain County Grand Jury. It's something of a surprise, considering the circumstances of the case.

As his criminal trial grows near, Wheeler maintains his lack of fear over the consequences of his actions. "I am not afraid. I have but one life to live and when that is gone all will be over with me. I am not sure but the sooner it ends, the better."

His sentence is life in the Ohio Penitentiary in Columbus.

1901, May 23: The *Elyria Republican* reports that Wheeler has been appointed superintendent of Ohio Penitentiary schools and, though he's "still a prisoner," feels his treatment in the pen has been good. "To those who know of Wheeler's educational advantages as brought out in the evidence at his trial, his success in teaching is no surprise."

1902, January 8: Wheeler is given a watch as a Christmas present by his companions and teachers in the penitentiary school.

1905, February 1905: A petition is circulated, endorsing a pardon for Wheeler. He is a model of behavior and said to be "one of the most intelligent and trusted prisoners there."

> The people who have charge of his case claim there are a number of circumstances which make it proper for the pardon board to exercise leniency. On the other hand, Meyers was popular and not considered a person of a quarrelsome disposition. *Elyria Reporter, February 9, 1905.*

1907, February: Outgoing Ohio Governor Herrick does not pardon Wheeler but cites his exemplary behavior in prison when commuting his sentence from life to 15 years. A half-dozen years "is not sufficient punishment" for a man who took another's life, says the Governor.

1907, April: Wheeler's lawyer, L.B. Fauver, applies for a full pardon.

1907, May: Less than 8 years after committing murder, Franklin Wheeler is freed from the Columbus prison as long as he makes a monthly report there for the next two years.

Wheeler's victim, young Philip Meyers, remains dead.

1900 – 1909: County Population = 54,857

1900: Earth-shaking news—Charles Richter is born in Hamilton, Ohio. Baseball cards. Lionel Trains. Bayer starts selling Aspirin. The end of the Apache Indian Wars. Freud's *Interpretation of Dreams.* The King of Italy is assassinated. Doctors figure out that mosquitos spread Yellow Fever. William McKinley (Ohio Republican) wins the Election with 51.6% of the popular vote. 115 lynchings: 106 Blacks, 9 others. $1,000 is worth $17,571 modern.

1900, July 18, Wednesday: Location: Oberlin, Precinct 2. Victim: Kilburn Morrison (boy). Suspect: ? Act: Malnutrition. Charge: ? Plea: ? Outcome: ? Sentence: ? Buried in Oberlin's Westwood Cemetery. I found no court docket entry related to this death.

1900, August 5, Sunday:

1900, mid-July: A young woman, about 20 years old, nicely dressed and very composed, arrives at Elyria's American Hotel (West and Broad) with a baby and a nurse in tow. She informs the proprietress, Mrs. Bulleyette, that she has traveled from Cleveland under physicians orders to spend a few weeks in the country. The woman is provided with the best rooms the American has to offer.

A few days later, the same woman applies to the Elyria Township Trustees for assistance. Her name is *Miss May* Trebisky, of Cleveland, and she is caring for a soon-to-be-orphaned baby of a dying cousin named Kuchtenrither whose husband has been killed while fighting in the Philippines.

May Trebisky had promised her cousin to care for the child, but now finds she can no longer do so. She begs the trustees to place the baby in the children's home or help find a good family. The trustees take the matter under consideration and begin an investigation that leads to Mr. Starr, of Abbe Road.

Mrs. Mary Trebisky had come to work for the Starrs from a domestic service in Cleveland, Ohio. Mr. Starr and his own daughter had interviewed Mrs. Trebisky at her parent's home on Central Street, on the near east side of Cleveland. Trebisky, her mother, grandmother, and the baby had all been present.

Mr. Starr's daughter said the Trebisky family seemed to be well-off and that Mary was well-raised. Mr. Starr had agreed that Mary could bring her child to his Elyria home.

Trebisky told him that she and her husband had been married four weeks before he died and that the baby (which Starr described as then looking "sickly and half starved") had been born nine months later. She wanted a job in the country, hoping it would improve her baby's health.

Once employed, the young woman told them she was graduated from a convent. She was well-spoken and obviously well-educated. She never complained of her wages, saying she had, or would have, considerable money from her dead husband who left her property and insurance. She was a good worker and took good care of the baby, though she never showed affection for it. The baby appeared to thrive and was doing well when she suddenly asked for a short time off, saying she needed a little rest.

The Starr's found they missed Mary, and especially her baby. Said Mr. Starr, "I never saw a child that seemed to appreciate so much every little act of kindness. Whenever I came into the room where it was, it would hold out its little hands for me to take it in such a way that elicited all a person's sympathies."

This, along with other developments, leads the Township Trustees to believe Trebisky is the mother of the child. She had concocted the "orphan story" for them to rid herself of the burden of caring for the infant.

This is confirmed a few days later when it is found that Trebisky has offered money to no fewer than three other Elyrians to take care of the child "for a few days." It is decided to have the woman brought in for further investigation. She cannot be found.

On August 4, Elyria conductor, Mr. Dermie takes notice of an attractive young lady who carries her baby aboard the morning car to Ridgeville.

Once alight, she walks from one door to the next, offering sums of money to various residents to take care of the child for several days. For example, she tells Carol Peek she'll pay her $5 for a week of her time, but Mrs. Peek refuses, suspicious because the young woman carries no clothing for the child. Mrs. Sidney Butler is offered $6 a week for two weeks. Mrs. Butler also refuses.

The woman takes her baby eastward along the ridge. About an hour later she returns, empty handed, and takes the first car she can from Ridgeville back to Elyria. The streetcar conductor is, once again, Mr. Dermie. Those who see her suppose she has found someone to care for the child and think little of it until *The Elyria Reporter* describes Trebisky and her previous efforts to rid herself of her child.

Authorities are alerted. The sheriff orders a search. Police and locals question those living in every house for two miles east on the ridge. Nobody has seen anything beyond that which was already told. All abandoned buildings are closely searched, as are old wells. The Lorain County sheriff and deputy travel to Trebisky's parents in Cleveland to see if they can gather any clues. They return empty-handed.

Along with many others, Ridgeville resident Henry Blake has been hired to search for the missing baby. He and his 17-year-old son have spent a long August 6th tromping through the nearby fields, working their way through the woods, along weed-and-insect-filled ditches, and brier-grown fences. They've found nothing.

Arriving home late at night, tired and discouraged, Blake goes to bed but not immediately to sleep:

> I rolled from one side of the bed to the other, possessed of a strange uneasiness, but along after midnight, I fell into a light sleep and then I dreamed of finding the body of the babe. Something seemed to lead me down the lonely Snow [Jaycox] Road, into the cornfield and over into the wood and there I saw, in my dream, the body of the babe.
>
> I awoke with a start; the vividness of the dream impressed me as a reality. I got out of bed and dressed and awakened my son, told him I knew where the baby was and was going to find it. He went with me and I followed as nearly as possible the course taken in my dream.
>
> It was not yet light when we reached the cornfield and so we sat down by the roadside and waited for day to break. As the first streak of dawn came we started through the cornfield and as we emerged into the wood I looked ahead and there, in the breaking light, I saw the body of the babe just as I saw it in my dream. *The Elyria Reporter, August 8, 1900.*

Coroner Braman arrives, reporter in tow, on the 7:00am car to Ridgeville. Mr. Blake meets them and, with his buggy, drives them out Snow Road a half-mile north of where it is even with the center of Ridgeville. Behind "the Buck house," past a cornfield, the baby lay dead under the spreading branches of a big oak tree in Lehman's Woods.

> The spot is a lonely one. The nearest house is nearly half a mile away, and no better place could have been chosen by the desperate woman to take the life of her innocent babe.

Its pitiful cries were unheard save by the ears of its inhuman mother. It was a sight to soften the hardest heart, and the horror which everyone present felt was only equaled by the indignation expressed against one who could willfully commit such a fearful crime. *The Elyria Reporter, August 8, 1900.*

The infant is laying in the sun, eyes open, wearing disarranged clothing. One of its tiny, white kid slippers is on the ground, "Evidently having been thrown off in the poor little victim's struggle with death." When the newspaper reporter pulls up on the outer dress of the child to cover its face, its white, lace bonnet slides back to reveal a wound on the crown of its head.

The baby is placed in a basket and taken to Elyria for examination. The post mortem determines that the injury to the baby's head was not fatal. There is bruising on the neck, but neither had the child been choked. The coroner finds the infant terribly emaciated. The cause of death: starvation.

The baby is buried in the North Ridgeville Cemetery. The clothing it wore is kept as evidence, but decent burial garments, along with a casket and proper ceremony are provided by the women of Ridgeville.

It was indeed a sad sight as the little coffin was lowered into the ground, the grave surrounded by those who had gathered at misfortune's call to mourn in pity at the sad ending of the short life of the little babe who had never known a mother's tender care, whose birth was a disgrace and whose death was a crime. *The Elyria Reporter, August 15, 1900.*

The night Henry Blake dreams of finding the baby, Lorain County Deputy Salisbury is dreaming something else entirely: that he will find the mother in a crowded place that he has seen before. When told by the sheriff to bring the woman in, the deputy turns to his wife and tells her the suspect will be in custody by noon.

Sure enough, led by *his* dream, Deputy Salisbury finds and arrests Mary Trebisky in the Bessemer House, a business of ill-repute located at 810 Broadway, Lorain. She is sleeping when picked up by police. She had tried to commit suicide two nights prior by drinking carbolic acid, but the man in the room with her at the time knocked the bottle to the floor. Her mouth and throat are burnt, but she can still speak.

Upon arrest, she tells Deputy Salisbury, "I left the baby under the tree in the woods. What else could I do? But I did not harm it. I set the baby down on the grass and kissed it goodbye and went back to Elyria." She never asks if the child is alive or dead.

The woman is well-dressed and neat when hauled before Justice Lawrence. She is unconcerned and expresses no emotion until the warrant for the murder of her child is read, whereupon tears come to her eyes, and she bows her head.

When asked if she has anything to say, she looks about the room before finally replying that she does not. She is placed in the County Jail where it is observed that she seems to carry no weight from her crime.

Once in her cell, Trebisky insists that the baby was not hers and that she can prove it. Yes, she told her Elyria employer, the Starrs, that the baby was hers and was born on Christmas Day but now claims she adopted it from a foundling's home in Cleveland.

She blames the Elyria Township Trustees for the death. The trustees object. It's true they knowingly allowed her to depart, but they had no power or reason to delay or apprehend her. The trustees maintain that had Trebisky stayed in the city even one hour longer, the child would have become a ward of the county, but she chose not to.

Trebisky then changes her story, saying she had found the child in an asylum and that everyone agreed it looked like her and, for that reason, she was given permission to keep it. She readily gives the police the names of the three people who allowed her to take the baby.

She says her parents didn't know she had the child. She brought the child to the country where it would do better. She had gone to Mrs. Starr's to work so she could feed the baby but, after that, could not care for it. She tried to get others to care for the child, but could not and so abandoned it in the woods. "What else could I do?"

She is charged with murder in the second degree, which is not stern enough for many involved, but is the most severe crime that circumstances allow.

Trebisky pleads not guilty.

On August 7, the day the baby and suspect are found, a well-dressed, middle-aged man appears at the office of *The Elyria Reporter*. His name is James Trebisky, a farmer from Euclid Township, east of Cleveland.

He claims the real name of the woman suspected of abandoning the infant is "Mary Svoboda" and says he first met her about a year ago when she came to his farm to hire herself out to pick grapes. She and the farmer's son, Eddie, not yet 21, began keeping company. Trebisky senior discovered the girl "was dishonest" and forbade his son any further contact.

Last April, Mary Svoboda had Eddie Trebisky arrested, claiming he had placed her in a family way. At the time, she was in possession of a baby which she claimed was hers and Eddie's. The case against the boy never came to trial as Svoboda never appeared in court against him.

It was later found out by Trebisky senior that Svoboda had been given the baby by the Cleveland Humane Society the day before her accusation. That child died at the home of her parents in June.

Trebisky is certain Svoboda never had a child of her own. He doesn't know where she obtained the baby she abandoned in the woods, but figures she probably got it from a Cleveland orphanage to continue the deception.

That same day authorities receive a letter from Dr. J.K. Hamilton, Youngstown, Ohio. In it, he says that he is a physician of the maternity hospital on Prospect Street in Cleveland and knows Svoboda's case.

She came to his hospital as a patient, representing herself as being wealthy. She was gregarious and well-spoken. She hired a fine carriage to take herself and a nurse into Cleveland to buy expensive clothing. They refused her credit. She went to a bank to arrange a loan, which was refused.

Dr. Hamilton soon discovered that the Svoboda family were poor, laboring people. They could not afford to help their daughter pay her bills, and she was turned out. "She was either possessed of a delusion that she was wealthy, or she was an habitual liar," said the doctor. "She lied about all things. At the time I believed her to be slightly deranged."

The jailed woman's older sister comes forth to tell Probate Judge Hinman the following story: In April, 1900, May/Mary Trebisky/Svoboda delivered her own child in a Cleveland maternity home for unwed mothers. That baby died in June and was buried by its grandparents. Soon after the baby's death, Mary Svoboda left home.

Upon a return visit, Mary was carrying a baby. When asked, she told her family that it belonged to a woman for whom she was working.

The family heard no more about it until they saw the accounts of the case in the paper. Svoboda's sister states that the baby that died in the woods was from an asylum. When asked by Judge Hinman if she thought Mary was sane, the sister gives him the address of a physician who had previously declared her to be of unsound mind. The sister thinks the death of the first child preyed upon Mary's mind and that's why she, by some means, managed to obtain the second child that was abandoned near Ridgeville.

The Lorain County Humane Society declares that story is exactly backwards. That the baby (a boy) who died at the Svoboda home was from the Cleveland branch of the Society, given to the suspect who claimed to be married and had the recommendations of two Woodland Avenue physicians. But the baby left in the woods was the suspect's own child.

When Judge Hinman and the suspect's sister make a visit to the jail, Trebisky/Svoboda goes violently insane, scratching her face and tearing out her hair until she is forcibly restrained. After a bit, she calms down and asks about her father and mother. She tells her visitors that she had no choice in doing what she did. After a few minutes she flies back into hysterics, shouting, "When I get out of here, I will kill the man who caused me all my first trouble and then kill myself!"

It's obvious to Judge Hinman that the jailed woman, while intelligent and shrewd, is not normal. She holds herself totally unaccountable for her actions. *The Elyria Reporter* questions if it is correct to keep her in prison if she's insane, even if she's in "the woman's ward."

Prosecutor Lee Stroup says that until the court finds her insane, she's in the place she should be and until the courts makes a determination, she'll be treated as any other person under the same charge. He states that A.R. Webber has been assigned as her defense and assures the press she is in good hands.

Then, the Elyria Township Trustees get sucked into the mess.

August 15, *The Elyria Reporter:* Trustees are not to blame for the death of the baby. They have laws and rules they must follow. They offered to take the woman and child in, to give aid, and were seeking her out to do so when she took her baby and disappeared. They had nothing to do with the crime and in no way should be blamed for it.

August 16, *Elyria Republican:* Trustees are to blame. They could have offered aid when it was first requested and then started their investigation instead of letting the woman leave to complete her onerous task. None of this would've happened had they helped when first approached.

August 16, *The Elyria Democrat:* The trustees should have erred on the side of charity rather than to refuse help under the law.

August 22, *The Elyria Reporter:* The [Elyria] *Republican* and *Democrat* [newspapers] both knew well enough of the circumstances of the case before the crime was committed. Why didn't they act to save the child when no law restrained them?

August 23, *The Elyria Republican:* There is no law to compel individuals to take action in cases of need. That is the Township's job, but the laws that provide such action are to be followed no matter the case.

The *final* version of Mary Svoboda's story, according to police and court authorities, is this.

On April 23, 1900, Svoboda, representing herself as "Mrs. Blaha," makes an application to General Agent Rickseeker of the Cleveland Humane Society for an infant child. She uses two forged physician recommendations to help the process along. This is the child she uses as leverage against Eddie Trebisky. It was this baby who died in June at the home of Svoboda's parents and was buried by them.

On June 23, 1900, she applies for another child, this time using the name Mrs. Mary Trebisky. This application holds forged signatures of two people known by the Humane Society, but the baby is provided by the hospital ward of the Cleveland orphanage "Infant's Rest." When told the infant is sickly, Svoboda replies "it is just what she wants." This child is the one she takes to the Starr's home in Elyria and the baby that is eventually left in the woods to die.

Why two babies? The first one was to blackmail Eddie Trebisky, whom she loved, into marrying her. That baby died while waiting for the case to come to court, so she obtained the second to continue the ruse. Once she'd been discovered, the second baby became a burden. She tried all she knew to get rid of the infant, but couldn't find a taker. Not knowing what else to do, she abandoned the child in the woods north of Ridgeville.

It's unknown whether Svoboda ever actually had a child of her own.

In late August, when confronted with all that the authorities have learned, the suspect does not confirm or deny any of it but asks, "How did you find it all out?" As ever, she is unconcerned with her crime or any possible consequences.

A month later, Probate Judge Hinman holds a sanity hearing for Mary Svoboda. Her [unnamed] family physician allows that he has never considered her of good mental balance. Elyria physician Charles H. Cushing, who had examined her in the County Jail after her arrest, said she claimed she didn't recall anything of abandoning the baby until it came to her one night during a terrible storm. He did not consider her to be of sound mind. A large number of other witnesses are called. Not a single one will testify that the woman is sane.

Decides Judge Hinman:

> There can be no question as to Mary Svoboda's mental condition. That she was wholly unaccountable for actions both previous to and after the commission of the terrible deed,

I have not the slightest doubt. The evidence is conclusive. It would be impossible to convict the prisoner of the crime charged, and her trial would cause the county useless expense. *The Elyria Reporter, Sep. 26, 1900.*

He sends her to Cleveland's Newburgh Asylum, so she can be close to her family. Total cost of proceedings is $34.47.

But we're not done, yet...

1901, April 17: Less than a year after her confinement at Newburgh, Mary's back in the area. She is working as a dressmaker in Lorain and is newly married to J.E. Hilt to whom she told stories of inheriting money from wealthy relatives who just died. He gives her $600 in diamonds to entice her to marry. Then he goes to Cleveland to arrange for the sale of his wife's property only to find out Mary has lied to him. The address is part of the Huntington Estate. He now wants his freedom back, not to mention the diamonds.

1901, April 23: *Elyria Republican:*

> Chapter Steen-Hundred in the Wondrous Adventures of Mary Svoboda.
>
> Mary Hilt, nee Svoboda, who became notorious in Elyria in connection with the abandonment of her adopted child in Ridgeville last summer, has added another adventure to her already long list.
>
> She appears as prosecuting witness against Officer Zinsmeister, of Lorain, in a breach of discipline case which charges him with frequenting disorderly houses.
>
> If she maintains her reputation for a variegated and fancy liar, it should not be hard to break her testimony.
>
> Her new husband, by the way, who at last accounts was about to sue for divorce, appears to be reconciled again.

And then... Mary up and vanishes from the papers.

PAEDOCIDE: Killing a child or children.

"It Would Hold Out Its Little Hands"

In four different newspapers I found a total of twenty-one separate articles referring to this story. Twenty of them consistently use the third-person, gender-neutral pronoun "it" to refer to the infants who died under Mary Svoboda's care.

Consider the above quote from Mary's employer, Mr. Starr: "Whenever I came into the room where it was, it would hold out its little hands for me to take it in such a way that elicited all a person's sympathies." What person or newspaper in today's world would refer to a child as an "it?"

The ease with which Svoboda obtained "her" babies may be astonishing, but remember the time frame. In 1900 America, any city of any size contained an over-abundance of illegitimate and/or abandoned children along with multiple "orphanages" set up to handle them.

Some such institutions operated for the public good. Others were money-making ventures, actively advertising for infants: "For Adoption at Birth. Full Surrender. No Questions Asked." And: "It's cheaper and easier to buy a baby for $100.00 than to have one of your own." A heartbreakingly large number of such businesses were grotesque "baby-farms" that shocked the general public, even in that time period.

Few things have changed as much as our general views surrounding the value of children and the importance of legitimacy. Babies, once considered little more than chattel and blank slates of flesh and bone, are now cherished by society as a whole. Unwed mothers and their children, once scorned, hidden, and denied basic rights, now hardly register a second thought.

I'd bet that many fatherless children now living in the U.S. don't even know what the word "illegitimate" means. This may indicate woefully shallow vocabularies, but it's better than the way things used to be.

Probate Judge Edgar Hiram Hinman:

Edgar Hinman was born in Portage County, Ohio, on December 16, 1846. As a child, his family moved to Oberlin, Ohio, where he attended public schools. He graduated from the Ann Arbor (Michigan) Law School (1864), then served with the 150th Ohio Volunteers in the U.S. Civil War.

Admitted to the Ohio Bar in 1869, he practiced law, first in Oberlin, then Amherst, where he served as mayor for nearly a decade. Following his election in 1881 to Probate Court, he moved to Elyria. He assumed his duties in February of 1882, then won each election to serve continuously for 30 years. "Most likeable," he gradually became "undoubtedly the best known man in Lorain County."

Judge Hinman retired in 1907, "due to suffering from wounds received in the Civil War," in his side and hip "which have never healed and never will." E.H. died in the late morning of June 5, 1912 at the age of 65, after an illness of several months. Common Pleas Court Judge Lee Stroup closed the Lorain County Courts for two days in honor of Hinman's service. He is buried in Elyria's Ridgelawn Cemetery.

1900, August 1: *Elyria Republican:*

> First to Buy an Automobile.
>
> Oberlin Physician to Employ It in His Travels.
>
> The first man in this county to purchase an automobile lives in Oberlin. He is Dr. W.H. Pyle.
>
> The carriage is operated by steam with gasoline for fuel. It will carry three persons with comfort. The doctor will use the vehicle in the course of his professional work. It represents an investment of about $800.
>
> A year ago those steam wagons—locomobiles, as the type is called—were put on the market at $600, but big orders from abroad sent the price to $650 and later to $700. Nowadays people wishing to purchase them must wait many months before their orders are executed. Indeed to such an extent are the automobile factories in this country behind their orders that it is no uncommon thing for impatient customers to pay a premium to others more patient for the privelege [*sic*] of being served earlier.

Dr. Pyle (W.H. or H.W.) went on to lead a fairly interesting life. I encourage interested Oberlinians to do a little research on the topic.

1901: The City of Lorain erects, in its Public Square, a Civil War monument comprised of a fountain capped with a statue of a soldier at parade rest. Blood is classified as A, AB, and O by Karl Landsteiner. The American Baseball League, formed a year earlier from the Western League, goes national. Ping Pong. Queen Victoria dies; Long live Edward VII. *Bill Bailey, Won't You Please Come Home?* After three years of U.S. military rule, Cuba becomes independent—certain restrictions apply. Arthur Griffin, Sinn Fein, and an independent Ireland. Another blast furnace for the Lorain Steel Plant. National Tube is a subsidiary of U.S. Steel. Regular rail passenger service begins between Oberlin and Norwalk. Clark Gable is born in Cadiz, Harrison

County, Ohio. McKinley is assassinated. Teddy Roosevelt is President. 130 lynchings: 105 Blacks, 25 others.

1901, April:

Thirty-something Bill Gurnhill moves from Penfield Township to LaGrange, buying a slightly dilapidated farm near the intersection of what will become Whitney and Indian Hollow roads. The man's a hard worker, but he exhibits some undesirable traits. Just ask his ex-wife, Hannah, who files for divorce in August of 1900 just after the arrival of an obviously half-Gurnhill baby to their neighbor, spinster Emma Edward.

In April of 1901, Gurnhill digs to rebuild the sagging foundation of one of his out-buildings. He encounters a large, wooden keg buried more than two feet down. Excited, he pulls it to the surface, and cracks open the lid to find, not treasure, but a mass of lime-rotted bones and decayed flesh. The gruesome contents are packed in a way that suggests dismemberment.

Samples are taken to Elyria doctor P.D. Reefy who pronounces them human, but too far gone to determine the sex. Says he:

> There is no telling how long the barrel has been buried, but there is no doubt from appearances that it has been under the ground for many years. The place where it was found is dry and the process of decomposition is very slow. Possibly twenty-five years may have elapsed since the crime, if crime there was, in connection with the burial. *The Elyria Reporter, June 12, 1901.*

Gurnhill had purchased the farm from Mr. and Mrs. William Gibson. Mrs. Gibson was married to the previous owner, Frank Hastings, who died on the property. In the years prior, there were several other owners who are either dead or cannot be located by authorities.

William Wilcox, living close to the south, remembers an old lady in the neighborhood who told stories of a unnamed peddler who went missing at night on nearby roads. His wandering horse was found the next day. It took months to find his robbed and hidden wagon. A brother of the peddler searched the vicinity and came away satisfied there had been a murder.

Others think the body may be that of Lisle Cadmus, an old man of Brunswick Township, Medina County, who left to visit a neighbor and was never heard from again. "He disappeared completely," folks said, "as though the earth had opened and swallowed him."

As for Dr. Reefy, he recalls a boarder the Hastings once had, a young man named Brown, who was studying medicine. Reefy thinks the barreled remains represent a grave robbing, re-interred after dissection. "There was some good reason why the body of a human being was cut up, packed into a small barrel with a quantity of lime, and buried deep in the earth," says the good doctor. "But what that reason was may never be known."

William Gurnhill (36) and Emma Edwards (31) marry in December of 1901. Both suffer relatively early deaths. Their children are, at first, scattered across the U.S. but most are ultimately gathered back to Lorain County where descendants remain.

1901, July 3: *The Elyria Reporter:*

> Ghosts on the Rampage in Carlisle Township:
>
> It is asserted that for many years Indian Hollow in Carlisle township has been the scene of many a ghostly revelry, and there are people living today who every time they pass that lonely spot recall the tales old gossips used to tell of how a beautiful Indian maiden, whose lover was killed in battle on the eve of their marriage, jumped from the high bank of the river near where the school house now stands and dashed out her young life on the cruel rocks beneath. And it is said that ever since that time the spirit of the Indian maiden and that of her warrior-lover have hovered around the spot they loved so well in life. This was the story that once was told. But now an Elyria man who is not an occultist and who says there are no such things as ghosts, claims to have seen the Indian spirits holding a camp-fire in front of the old deserted stone house on the west side of the road.

1901, July 3: *The Elyria Reporter:*

> Arose and Sang:
>
> Supposed Dead Man Suddenly Came to Life.
>
> An amusing incident is reported from the village of Wellington. A stranger was found lying by the roadside in the outskirts of the village apparently dead, and later a team which he was supposed to have driven was found wandering in the streets. A physician was hastily summoned, who pronounced the man dead, giving the cause of death as heart disease. The body was taken to an undertaking establishment and was being prepared for burial when suddenly the supposed dead man rose

up and began to sing. The undertaker, who is also mayor of the town, ordered the village marshal to arrest the warbler and lock him up in jail. Later the man was given a hearing before the mayor-undertaker, and was fined $5 and costs for disturbing the peace of the village by singing.

I think there may be some confusion, here: A.G. Couch was the undertaker. His son, G.L. Couch was the mayor. Father and son also owned a furniture factory in Wellington.

1901, October 30, Wednesday:

Big Joe Kovacs' (Kovacz) wife and 12-year-old daughter are due to arrive from Hungary in the next week and that won't be soon enough.

After all his extra hours in the Lorain mill and saving every last dime for their passage, Joe'll be happy beyond words to move out of the cramped room above Kucas' Saloon in South Lorain that he shares with two other guys. It's not the room that so bad. It's his roommates. The three of them have been together for far too long.

Well, if Joe tells the truth, John Masco isn't such a bad guy. He's quiet and keeps to himself. But John Nagi (Nagy), is really getting to him: short, smart-mouthed, always stomping around. He's able enough to work around the Bessemer at the mill, but plays his damned peg leg for all it's worth. And Nagi's always telling lies and spreading rumors which drives Joe crazy. You get to know a guy when you spend so much time together, and Joe has come to the conclusion that he doesn't like the "little, one-legged cripple."

On the other hand, nobody will be happier than John Nagi when Joe leaves. The big man bullies him something fierce. Calls him names. Makes fun of his wooden leg. Pushes him around. Tells him to shut up.

Like Nagi, the trio's third man, John Masco, is also happy that Joe'll be moving out. Things have been more tense than usual, but John figures it'll blow over like it always does. All everyone needs to do is hold their tempers, keep quiet, and stay out of each other's way for a few more days.

The night of the 30th, Nagi's wooden leg pounding across the room and down the hall rouses John Masco. He lights a lamp and yells when he finds Joe Kovacs bloody in bed, stabbed several times to his body and face.

Saloon-owner Mrs. Kucas enters the room to find the cause of the disturbance, shouts in surprise, and rushes out to call the police.

Masco and another renter, Andrew Berczik, try to comfort the badly bleeding man. Andrew asks what he did to cause Nagi to stab him. Big Joe mumbles a few words and loses consciousness. He dies a few minutes later.

Nagi is arrested and makes the following statement:

> I arose Sunday morning and after breakfast I began to patch my clothes. I saw Kovacs and we were friendly. Kovacs went away. In the afternoon I was sitting out in the yard mending my shoes. Kovacs came up to me and wanted to know why I had been talking about him. He said, I said he had lice and began kicking me. I called for help. He kicked me several times and said he would kill me. I went up to my room after he left and got my clothes ready to move.

> After supper I went to bed but was still afraid and went down stairs and asked Mr. Kucas what I should do. He said, "is there no knives here?" I said there was and took one from the table and went to bed.

> John Masco was in another bed in the room. After a half hour later Kovacs came in. He was muttering to himself. There was no light in the room but we could see some. He saw me lying in bed and said, "now I'll fix you." I said to him he had better lie down and leave me alone. Kovacs picked up some of my clothes and threw them in my face. I jumped out of bed and grabbed him. He then struck me in the breast.

> We stood so his back was to the bed. I being lame put all my weight against him and threw him back on the bed. I fell on top and then struck him with the knife. I do not know how many times I struck him. Mrs. Kucas came in. She screamed, as Masco had lit the lamp and she could see what had happened. I went down stairs with her. Then I went out into the yard. There I threw the knife away. I told Mrs. Kucas to call the police so they could take care of me. *The Elyria Republican, October 24, 1901.*

Mrs. Kucas tells police that her first indication of trouble were the sounds of the struggle. She says Nagi went past her, exiting the building and tossing the knife away. She followed, grabbed him by the ear, and led him back into the building.

Her story is completely at odds with Nagi's. She says, of the two, Kovacs was first to bed around 6:00pm and that Nagi followed two hours later.

Shortly after, she heard some commotion in the room, the principal sound being the stomping from Nagi's wooden peg leg.

John Masco has nothing to tell police about the stabbing. A very heavy sleeper, he missed the entire thing.

Nagi is bound over to the Grand Jury without bail. During those proceedings, the *5-year-old* son of Mr. and Mrs. Kucas testifies that he saw Nagi take the knife from the kitchen before going upstairs and that he did it quietly when there were no grownups nearby.

The papers suspect the charge will be murder in the second degree. The Grand Jury returns an indictment for murder in the first.

Nagi's criminal trial takes place the second week of December in front of Judge Nye. It's slow going since most of the testimony is in Hungarian and through interpreters.

The Coroner's Report states that the most severe of the half-dozen stab wounds were inflicted to the victim's left side so he was sleeping on his right. In that case, the suspect leaned over the bed and struck downward.

The prosecution, Lee Stroup and W.B. Thompson of Lorain, work to prove that Nagi went up to the room intending to kill Kovacs in revenge for being kicked. They contend that the victim was asleep when killed. Why would Nagi strike blows to the victim's back if they were done in self-defense? How could there have been a fight as Nagi claimed if their other roommate, John Masco, didn't awake to the scuffle? The prosecution goes on to say that Kovacs was a "big, strong man" while Nagi is a "small man and a cripple." If Nagi were telling the truth, Kovacs would've fought back and escaped with only injuries. Plus, Nagi was dressed; Kovacs was not. That was a clear indication as to who was the aggressor.

After heated arguments between the lawyers, witness Andrew Berczik is allowed to give Kovacs' last words: "I have done nothing. He rushed upon me and stabbed me in my bed."

Defense attorneys A.R. Webber of Elyria and C.F. Adams of Lorain earn their pay by injecting as much doubt as possible into who started the trouble. At close, defense lawyer Webber's speech to the jury is a plea for sympathy and mercy. He works Nagi's small size and wooden leg for all they're worth and plays up the kicking attack made earlier in the day by the much larger and stronger victim.

After a day's worth of deliberation, the jury finds Nagi guilty of murder in the second degree. Rumors are that on the first vote the jury was about evenly split between first degree, second degree, and manslaughter.

It isn't certain that Nagi understands what is going on at his sentencing. He has nothing to say. But "the most pathetic feature of the case is the spectacle of Kovacs' wife and twelve-year-old daughter. They were upon the ocean when the tragedy occurred and arrived in Lorain about a week later."

Upon sending him to Columbus for life, "Judge Nye advised him to behave himself in the penitentiary and said that if he evidenced a desire to thoroughly repent of his evil deed, he would probably be pardoned out before the expiration of his sentence."

Judge Nye knew his stuff. Nagi is pardoned and paroled just before Christmas, 1913, after serving a dozen years. Former Prosecutor Lee Stroup, now a Lorain County Judge, does not oppose the action.

"The pardon board was informed that Nagi had been a model prisoner since entering the grim prison, and it is supposed that he has thoroughly reformed."

1901, December 15, Sunday: Location: ? Victim: "The Larson Boy" Suspects: Mr. and Mrs. Worden. Death due to "Bright's Disease" (generally, kidney inflammation caused by infection, autoimmune disease, or strenuous exercise) while under the care of the suspects, both of whom are Christian Scientists.

During the inquest Dr. McGarvey of Lorain declares he has treated many similar cases and never lost a patient. Mrs. Worden is quoted as saying "the child was already saved. How can a child of God die?" Outcome: No case is brought against the boy's parents because Mrs. Worden was in charge of the care. Mrs. Worden is not prosecuted because "the relevant statute is not clear enough in its terms."

1902: Teddy Bear. Newspaper ads for Bell Telephone. Radio makes its public debut. Big coal strikes begin and end. Scripps-McRae Press Association. Newspapers begin reporting "standardized news stories." A.A.A. starts in Chicago. Motion picture theaters. The Antikythera Mechanism is discovered. The U.S. buys out the French option on the Panama Canal for $40 million. The Cleveland Indians are the first to hit three consecutive home runs in the same inning: Nap Lajoie, Legs Hickman, and Bill Bradley, all off St. Louis Browns pitcher Jack Harper. It was the 6th inning of a blowout, 17-2, Cleveland. Trans-Pacific cable links Hawai'i to the U.S. 92 lynchings: 85 Blacks, 7 others.

1902, ?, ??: Location: ? Victim: ? Suspect: James Caine. Act: ?

A May 8, 1917, article in the *Elyria Evening Telegram* describes how James Caine, sent to the Penitentiary for life on a murder charge from Lorain County, had escaped in 1909 but was identified in Milwaukee, Wisconsin, after being arrested for vagrancy. It was reported that Cain had lived in that city for eight years under an assumed name but was identified by pictures in a "Rogue's Gallery" and Bertillion measurements. But... I found no local news articles or Lorain County court entries describing a murder committed by James Caine.

Biometrics, Old School

Back in the late 1800s, French police were searching for a way to identify criminals. It was Alphonse Bertillon, a French criminologist, who invented a method of accurately measuring the physical structure of a person to create a repeatable method of describing an individual.

In 1884, after French police proved the success of the "Bertillon Measures" by identifying more than 200 repeat offenders, its use quickly spread. Known criminals were measured and photographed, the start of the archives of what we now call "mugshots."

The U.S. champion of Bertillon Measures was Illinois Penitentiary Warden, R.W. McClaughry, who began the formal use of the measures to catalogue his prisoners in 1887. As the number of people categorized grew, the complexity of the measures, which first focused on the head and face, constantly increased to include other portions of the body: arms, hands, legs, and feet. It remained the most widely-used method of identifying criminals until 1903.

In that year, at Leavenworth Penitentiary in Kansas, a man named Will West was measured and photographed. It was noticed that Will West bore an uncanny resemblance to a man already in the prison whose name, oddly enough, was William West. The two men denied any family relationship, yet Will and William's Bertillion Measures were nearly identical. But their fingerprints were different. This helped spur the adoption of print identification. For a while, both prints and Bertillion Measures were recorded. Once reasonable methods of categorizing fingerprints were invented and adopted, Bertillion's system was dropped.

1902, October 2: *The Elyria Republican:*

>A Tragic Mystery:
>
>Skeleton Found, in the Woods Near Belden.
>
>No Clue As to the Identity of the Man—Morphine In His Pocket.
>
>A grewsome [sic] discovery was made last Monday by some farmer cutting timber in the woods near Belden. It was the skeleton of a man clothed in a weather stained suit of gray. The man had evidently been dead several months. His clothing, which appeared to have been of very good quality, were ruined by the exposure. There was no flesh left on the bones.
>
>In the pocket of the dead man were found a hypodermic syringe, several morphine tablets, and a bottle of whiskey. Coroner French, who was called to investigate the remains, said he had little doubt that it was a case of suicide. There are no marks of violence on the skull and no reason to doubt that morphine was the cause of death. The unknown might, however, have taken an overdose of the drug unwittingly.
>
>Nowhere about the remains was there a scrap of further evidence. A few pennies was all the money found and there were no papers. The man seemed to have been one of middle age and was about five feet eight inches in height.

The remains were eventually identified as those of former Railroad Conductor Jason E. Washburn (born 1861) of Lake Avenue, Elyria, who left home in June and had not been heard from since. He was placed in the Belden Cemetery.

There was some doubt of this identification a fortnight after burial, and that the dead man might instead might be the brother-in-law of J.W. Stone, James Baird, who also had not been heard from since June.

The Washburn family was, however, certain of their identification by sister, Mrs. Elle Washburn, based on "a peculiarity of one of the teeth" in the skull provided them by Coroner French.

I found no *obvious* connection between this Washburn and the one who, two years later, would be appointed as a Lorain County Judge.

1902, March 10, Monday: Location: Lorain, Broadway Avenue, Bank Restaurant. Victim: Will (William, Bill) McCoy (Colored). Suspect: Alex

(Peter) Tate (Colored). Shooting takes place following a game of craps during which victim and suspect "bantered each other to the point of ill feeling." As they depart via the rear door, Tate draws a revolver and fires three shots in rapid succession. Two strike McCoy in the chest, passing through his body. The suspect flees the scene.

McCoy does not immediately die and says, should he recover, he will not bear witness against the shooter since no harm was intended. But, before dying on March 12, he changes his mind, saying he was shot maliciously. As of March 27, Tate is still on the lam. Outcome: No mention of a trial.

My assumption is that Alex Tate escaped arrest.

1902, June 13, Friday: Location: Elyria Ward 1. Victim: Walter Russell (baby) from Lorain. Suspect: Frank Russell. Act: Infanticide. Outcome: ? Nothing found in court dockets.

1903: Lake Erie water to Elyria encourages growth. An "electric road" between Elyria and LaGrange is being considered. Outbreaks of smallpox across the area, especially in Vermilion. First World Series. Guantanamo Bay, even though Cuba doesn't like it much. Lenin continues his rise. The King and Queen of Serbia are assassinated. Teddy's "Big Stick" appears off shore of Panama and *poof* the U.S. is granted a ten-mile-wide corridor across the county right where a canal might be built. Crayola Crayons. Oberlin Professor E.I. Bosworth is chosen as president of the *Ohio Anti-Saloon League*. In the Docket: Operating Slot Machines. Also, winning lawsuits brought against businesses for injuries suffered at work due to negligence of employers, like George Haupt, of Lorain, who sued the B&O Railroad for $10,000 for the loss of his left hand in a planer accident. 99 lynchings: 84 Blacks, 15 others.

1903, February ?: Location: Lorain sewer. Victim: Unknown Infant. Act: Unknown. Workmen find a baby's body in Lorain sewers. "Generally believed that this is an instance of criminal practice, but it will probably be difficult to locate the guilty." Outcome: Unsolved.

1903, February ?: Location: Lorain. Victim: Baby boy. Act: Unknown. Sewer workers make the ghastly find of yet another baby's body. Case is a complete mystery. Belief is that it's murder. Outcome: Unsolved.

1903, February 14, Saturday: Location: Oberlin, the Butler home on Groveland Street. Victim: Riley D. Black (about 35, Colored) Oberlin College student/laborer from Mississippi. Suspect: James S. Butler (about 63, "negro"). Act: Gunshot.

Riley Black is a former boarder at Butler's home. There have been bad feelings between the men for about a week, some say it's due to damage to a rug in the home. Others suggest an improper relationship between Mrs. Butler and her boarder.

Black visits Saturday night to pick up some personal effects but never even enters the building. Mrs. Elizabeth Butler retrieves them and is handing the bundle to Black when James Butler appears behind her, single barrel shotgun in hand. He orders his wife back into the house and, without warning, shoots Black in the left side of his chest, just below the heart. Black falls to the porch floor and dies almost instantly. Elizabeth Butler, the only witness to the crime, runs, screaming for help.

A crowd of neighbors gather. Police arrest the small man, who is intoxicated and boasting "I always shoot to kill." An examination of the dead man show his heart and lungs shredded by the blast. The shot did not travel through him but gathered sack-like within the skin of his back.

The now-dead Black was a student at Oberlin's Theological Seminary. "Sober and industrious," he is buried from the A.D. Booth Funeral Home and Rust M.E. Church in Oberlin's Westwood Cemetery after failed attempts to contact his sister in Knoxville, Tennessee.

Suspect Butler is a disabled Civil War veteran, light-skinned enough to have enlisted before Blacks were allowed. His temper gave him trouble in the service, but he was honorably discharged and drew a large pension. "When not under the influence of liquor, he is quiet and inoffensive, but liquor transforms him into a demon." Once sober, he sits in his cell, crying. He is placed under suicide watch by Oberlin Police.

Butler is brought before Judge Fauver in Oberlin, bound over to the Grand Jury, and brought to the County Jail. He insists he was not drunk when the shooting occurred. His friends say there is more to the situation than meets the eye.

Charge: Murder in the first degree. Plea: Not guilty. Held without bond. Attorney L.B. Fauver is appointed to defend him. Hearing in "Old Library Room" with Judge Webber. Trial starts April 27, 1903. Butler is nervous during proceedings. There are few spectators in the courtroom.

Butler claims he and Black had considerable trouble with each other.

On the day of the murder they had quarreled before he used the shotgun for self-defense after being threatened with a knife. Butler claims his wife and the dead man had been intimate and that the judge should consider mercy under the "unwritten law" (that is, a cuckolded man can kill his wife's lover with impunity).

Prosecutor Lee Stroup allows James Butler to change his plea to guilty of murder in the second degree. Butler is given a mandatory life sentence by Judge Webber and ends up as number 34815 in the Ohio Penitentiary. Outcome: Butler is paroled in February, 1907, and dies five months later at the age of 65.

Judge Amos Richard Webber:

Born on January 21, 1852, in Hinckley Township, Medina County, Ohio, Webber attended public schools. A 1876 graduate of Baldwin University, Berea, Ohio, he began practicing law in Elyria, Lorain County, that same year, gradually becoming "one of the best trial lawyers of his day."

A Republican, Webber served as the Lorain County Prosecutor, (1888-1893), Common Pleas Court Judge 1901-1904 and 1922-1935, and also as a U.S. Congressman 1904-1907.

A.R. Webber died in Elyria February 25, 1948 at age 96 and was buried in Ridgelawn Cemetery, Elyria.

1903, May 1, Friday, very early morning:

Lorain Police are summoned to the rectory of St. Joseph's German Catholic Church on the southwest corner of Reid and 8th. The rectory is a small, wooden building that came along with the property when the church was built. The locks are poor and its condition is such that some of the interior doors don't close.

The parish priest, Father Charles Reichlin, is not home, having been called away to Kelleys Island to attend a funeral. Police are greeted by the priest's brother, Casimir, editor of the German-language *Lorain Post*, and the visiting Reverend Father Ferdinand Walser, a well-educated, 52-year-old German, late of Toledo. Both men smell of whiskey and appear tipsy.

Police are led to the second floor. There, with the sound of a loudly barking St. Bernard dog in the background, officers find the "very handsome and popular" Miss Agatha Reichlin, 34, laying on her side in her bed. The rectory housekeeper, she is the sister of Charles and Casimir—or was.

The left side of the woman's skull is crushed from multiple blows with a heavy, blunt object. There are four fractures, each with a wound three inches long and two inches deep. There are no signs of a struggle. An examination of the body shows no evidence of criminal assault.

At the back of the building are footprints and an old, rickety ladder reaching almost to an attic window. On the ground is a large stone used by the victim as a doorstop. It is covered with blood and matted knots of hair.

Police have a weapon, an apparent means of entry, a motive of robbery. A suspect entering the attic would have to open a door and pass through the victim's room to reach the rest of the property. The thief likely woke Agatha Reichlin who then paid with her life.

The problem with that theory is that valuables in the victim's room are undisturbed. In addition, the ladder falls short of the window by a foot-and-a-half, and there are no boot scuffs or other marks against the house as might be expected.

Father Charles Reichlin returns from Kelleys Island as quickly as possible. Reverend Father Walser makes the following statement:

> I went to bed about 11 o'clock and occupied Father Reichlin's room. During the night I was awakened by smothered cries like one in agony and pain. I listened and thought it must be the woman who slept in the next room and was probably dreaming or sick. Her brother being in the house, I decided to wait to see if he would go to her to find if she was sick. After a little I heard someone moving about and then I heard the striking of a match. I supposed that was Casimir and waited for him to come to my room. Soon the door opened and I looked that way and when the head presented itself I saw that it was not Casimir. I spoke up and said to him. "What are you doing here? Get out as fast as you can." The man turned away very quickly and I called out to Casimir that robbers were in the house. The man I saw was short, not over five feet tall. He wore a slouch [brimmed] hat, had a black coat, was slim and had a mustache. He moved lively. Casimir answered my call and it was not long until he called me and told me his sister had been murdered. I shall never forget those cries, as they went through me and left an impression. I believe that if I had not seen the man and had not discovered him he would have silenced me as well. Strangely enough before we retired last night I spoke

of locking the doors to keep out robbers. *The Elyria Chronicle, May 2, 1903.*

Casimir Reichlin adds:

I was awakened by Father Walser calling me. He cried out there were burglars in the house. I rushed to my sister's room and saw the door open leading to the attic. The fellow was making some noise and I ran into the attic and looked out of the open window. There I saw the ladder and that told me how the escape had been effected. I decided I could do nothing there and went back. I hunted around for a match and went to my sister's room to ask her if she had heard the robbers. I noticed she looked very peculiar and turned up the gas. I then saw that one eye was black and there was blood on her face. I realized she had been foully dealt with and called to Father Walser. He sent for the police and I turned things over to them. *The Elyria Chronicle, May 2, 1903.*

What they leave out: That Walser and Casimir Reichlin had arrived unexpectedly the night of the murder. Casimir had visited a nearby saloon for a gallon of whiskey, and the two drank freely after finding the body. The first police on the scene said the two men "smelled like a whiskey jug" and had the general appearance of drinking and dissipated men.

Bloodhounds arrive the next day from Ft. Wayne, Indiana. They are taken to the room of the victim (severely aggravating the now-returned Reverend Reichlin in the process). Once given the scent and taken outside, the dogs circle the area and come back to where they had started.

The ladder found at the crime scene, supposedly carried by the killer some 50 feet from the property of William Sheehan, is presented to the bloodhounds. They give no reaction. Handler Dr. T.L. Hickman tells authorities this means that the person who murdered Agatha did not use the ladder to gain entry. If the murderer's scent was present, the dogs would find and follow it. When given free reign, the animals always return to the room Father Walser used the night of the murder.

The talent of the dogs is brought into question. Dr. Hickman gives one of the investigators a head start of several minutes. The bloodhounds track him down in less time than it took for him to hide.

Once the behavior of the dogs is reported, Father Walser begins receiving telephoned death threats. Police are informed there is talk among men at the steel plant of finding and lynching the priest. He is taken into custody at 9:30am, May 2, both to protect him and because he's a suspect.

Father Walser is dazed when arrested and states "it's an outrage, you are wrong, officer, you have arrested an innocent man."

The Reichlin brothers are certain of Walser's innocence, but Prosecutor Lee Stroup points to holes in both Walser's and Casimir Reichlin's story. The men say they turned in early, but neighborhood witnesses state people were up and lights were lit in the house until just before the murder. A large and vicious St. Bernard dog living in the house raises Cain whenever anybody approaches. How could an outside man place a ladder against the side of the house, scale it, enter a window, and then get into a room without the dog knowing it? Stroup maintains that whoever committed the crime was familiar to the St. Bernard and with the floor plan of the structure. Most importantly, neither of the men actually saw what the other one did the night of the murder.

Though the Prosecutor does allow that the church's gold and silver is locked in a safe in Father Reichlin's office and might have been a possible target for a robbery and could be considered worth killing for. It was generally known that Father Charles Reichlin had traveled to Kelleys Island and that his unfortunate sister would be alone. Perhaps the last minute arrival of Casimir Reichlin and Walser was a surprise to some unknown perpetrator who was carrying out a crime without expectation of discovery.

Father Schaffeld, pastor of Elyria's St. Mary's Church states "I believe people should wait for further developments of the case and not pass their opinion until an examination has taken place, for I believe there is a little religious prejudice with it."

Agatha Reichlin is buried Monday, May 4, from a black-draped St. Joseph's. Her remains are laid out with injuries visible. Thousands of people view the remains. The church is filled to capacity. She is buried in Lorain's Calvary Cemetery (Elyria papers say it's Lake Avenue Cemetery, but that's incorrect). Her family, Charles, Zeno, Martin, and Casimir Reichlin attend.

Father Walser is released the next day due to lack of evidence. Says Sheriff Salisbury, "I feel pretty sure myself that the priest did not commit the murder." He and Prosecutor Stroup draw a correlation between the killing and several small robberies and attempted robberies in the neighborhood in the nights leading up to the murder. This includes one five blocks away at Mrs. J.M. Spencer's home on Dexter Street where a man attempted entry by way of raising a window, reaching the point of sticking his head inside the home whereupon Mrs. Spencer frightened him off.

Salisbury also mentions that a man had been spotted waiting on the steps of the church the night of the killing, raising the specter of another possible suspect.

Coroner French still thinks Father Walser is guilty because there was no robbery. He doesn't think there was any attempted entry via the ladder. In his mind, the priest is the most likely culprit. Still his inquest finds Agatha Reichlin died "at the hands of a man unknown."

Father Reichlin greets Father Walser upon his release. "I could not kill anything," Walser says. "I could not kill a chicken." He thanks officials for his courteous treatment. The next morning he states, "Although I am exonerated there will still remain in the minds of the prejudiced suspicion that I am guilty at least 'til the murderer is caught." Then escorted by other priests, Walser leaves for the Celina, Ohio, home of J.A. Roemer, a wealthy Catholic layperson who has offered material aid.

Feelings in the City of Lorain run high. Police watch the community closely. There is an obvious attempt to hush things up and keep them out of the press. Then things begin to get weird...

There is talk that Agatha's killer was an old suitor who had pressed his affections, had been spurned, and she was killed because of it. But that particular man has been in Germany for the past two months.

There are persistent rumors that Agatha and Father Charles Reichlin are not siblings, but secretly husband and wife. This idea carries on for months until a family member produces official documentation of their births.

In Sandusky, a person named Frank Kennedy, aka Frank Charles, is held on suspicion of the murder. Kennedy had stolen a pistol from a store in Bellevue, Ohio, and had blood on his shoes that he could not explain. His feet are about the size of the tracks found at the rear of the Reichlin home. When caught, he had on an entirely new set of cheap clothes, right down to his skivvies. There are many trains from Lorain and Kennedy could've easily committed the murder and been in Bellevue by morning. The suspect also matches the description of the killer given by Walser.

Lorain police dismiss the coincidences. Chief Braman says his men searched all the stations, and he doesn't believe a man could have escaped in that manner. Kennedy is not charged with the murder but is eventually sentenced by the Sandusky Courts to two years in the Fremont Penitentiary on a separate burglary conviction.

The City of Lorain is in an uproar. Citizens demand a new police chief. Authorities posit the crime was committed by some sort of Lorain "Jekyll and Hyde-like" maniac. They hint they know who it is but give no other information.

Father Patrick O'Brien of Toledo and formerly of Elyria investigates the arrest of Walser and publishes letters declaring the City of Lorain officers "bigoted" against the Catholic Church. He charges that threats of mob violence were whipped up by the police themselves:

> It would appear as though the officers of Lorain took advantage of the flimsy opportunity they had to disgrace a priest, and, through him, to disgrace the priesthood and the Catholic church.

But:

> Be it said to the credit of my old home, Elyria, Protestants and Catholics, they treated the priest-prisoner with humane respect. They sent him food from their homes and did all in their power to cheer him up during his stay among them. The people of Elyria are a credit to their town, while the officers and a bigoted section of the people of Lorain are a disgrace to Ohio. *The Elyria Chronicle, May 11, 1903.*

A $10,000 reward for the conviction of the murderer of Agatha Reichlin is put up by the Lorain Council of the Knights of Columbus. The Lorain County Commissioners add another $1,000. A wealthy KoC member from Cleveland increases it by $4,000. As the total mounts, it's suggested a commission be created to take care of the large rewards being offered for the conviction of the murderer. Considering the comments of Father O'Brien of Toledo, Mayor King of Lorain dodges the issue, saying Catholic and Protestant citizens should take care of the issue themselves.

On May 14, two weeks after the killing and with people watching from the windows of nearby homes, Agatha Reichlin's body is exhumed and examined by Drs. French, H.H. Brelsiord, and O.T. Maynard in an effort to settle disagreement among the investigators as to whether she might have been strangled. The body is described as "well preserved" and the flowers with it "looking as fresh as the day they were buried."

The doctors find there are bruises on Agatha's neck, but the cause of death were the blows to her head with the stone.

Drs. Cox and Cowley, who performed the original post-mortem, are not present for the exhumation, calling it a "dirty piece of business." They state it was something that would have been unneeded had French, Brelsiord, and Maynard attended the original autopsy as was their right.

The story is now being followed by newspapers around the world. Sheriff Salisbury is kept awake all night with calls from reporters wanting more information.

Lorain Police Detective Jake Mintz, who is working the case, says the murder was committed by a tramp. He says he knows who killed the woman but does not yet have the evidence to act. There are two parties involved and he can find them at any time. Mintz says authorities seem to have no interest in solving the case. Many Lorainites agree, saying religion and politics are involved. Lorain's Mayor King seems to support the accusations by saying the city cannot afford to keep working the case.

Detective Mintz manages to convince Coroner George French to reopen the inquest into Agatha Reichlin's death to review "new evidence:" a pair of pants, secreted away in the attic, but found via the reported dream of a woman "living far away from the crime scene:"

> In her dream she saw a scuffle, saw the girl struggling with her assailant, saw the brute choke the girl until she was black in the face and then laying her body upon the bed took a stone and struck the girl an awful blow, crushing her skull. She told of her dream the next morning and told where the murderer had hid a pair of pants in the attic. Surely enough, upon investigation, the trousers were brought to light. *The Elyria Chronicle, June 1, 1903.*

In the end, though, the story of the pants is a fake—all of it. There was no dreaming woman. In fact, there was no dream. It's just an old pair of pants owned by Casimir Reichlin that had been burnt, torn, and discarded.

The newspapers mock Detective Mintz, calling him a "Crafty Foxy Quiller." (A character in a 1900 comic opera of the same name: "the quintessence of all human intelligence.")

On July 28, Lorain City Auditor Mahoney receives a letter from the semi-famous psychic, Gustave Myer (who reportedly predicted the Hoboken Wharf Fires (June 30, 1900) and the assassination of U.S. President McKinley (September 6, 1901)):

> I find that only one person murdered Miss Agatha Reichlin and that person was a man. In his disposition he was given to

gambling, drinking, speculating, indiscriminate pleasures, fond of ease, nervous, restless and changeable, yet he is given to be quite talkative, courteous; sociable and apparently pleasing but quite eccentric and he is given to be a woman hater; and I am of the opinion that this is not the first woman he has murdered and I find furthermore that he was a married man, but that he was given to clandestine meetings and evil associations with the fair sex after marriage, which, gave rise to quarreling with his wife and separation.

I am of the opinion that her murderer being a gambler, murdered her purely for her money and I find that he was a false friend to her and am further of the opinion that she had been befriending him from time to time and had finally decided to cut him off. *The Elyria Chronicle, July 28, 1903.*

In August, Casimir Reichlin retires as the editor of the *Lorain Post* and is succeeded by Richard Fisher.

In late September, a Grand Jury opens on the Reichlin murder. It tries to reconstruct the crime at the scene. Prosecutor Stroup attempts to climb the ladder allegedly used in the crime, but it won't support his 290 pounds. A lightweight juryman, keeping his feet to the outside edges of the rungs, makes it to the top with no trouble. He swings a leg into the open window and easily enters the house (though he did not come down that way). The group visits the home from which the ladder was pilfered. They examine Agatha's room and the one Walser slept in and then return to the court to begin to hear testimony from a list of witnesses that does not include their previous suspect, Father Walser.

No indictments are produced.

In mid-October, an attempted robbery of a Lorain Hotel, the Farrell House, is made using the same M.O. of the Reichlin case: a ladder against a high, rear-facing window. Employee Augusta Urckovick holds the sash tightly closed and screams, frightening away the would-be burglars.

Years pass with no solution.

1906, September 5: An announcement is made that St. Joseph's Church will tear down the building Agatha Reichlin was murdered in and build a "fine three-story residence" for their priest who is still Father Charles Reichlin.

1907: Word is received that Father Ferdinand Walser, now a part of the

Catholic order of the Missionaries of the Precious Blood, has died in Rome City, Indiana, on February 17. Other details are not given.

Outcome: Unsolved.

1903, October 8, Thursday Morning:

Florence J. Bennett (23), a "highly educated mulatto of striking appearance" has been staying these past few days with the Bolden family on the outskirts of Oberlin.

The Boldens understand that Florence has left her husband in Covington, Kentucky (across the river from Cincinnati, Ohio) about a month back. What they don't know is that the man is actively searching for the wife who abandoned him.

One morning, John (Lee) Bennett (26) appears at their front door, having followed his wife from Covington to Cleveland, and then on to Oberlin. Bennett is bound and determined to confront the woman. There's a loud argument that involves everyone in the house. Police are called. The husband storms out.

He returns later for a reasonably calm and much longer discussion. The two reconcile, and he spends the night at the Boldens, husband and wife planning their immediate future.

Mr. Bolden leaves for work as usual on Thursday morning. At 8:00am, Mrs. Bolden leaves to run errands in Oberlin. John Bennett departs at the same time to look for work, he says. Mrs. Bolden returns an hour later to an empty house. Seeing the Bennetts' clothing in their room, she figures them to be away.

About a half-hour later she happens to go to the basement. There's a strangely sweet smell as she descends the stairs. She's horrified to find the body of Florence Bennett, cold on the floor, head crushed by a brick, and beautiful face burned nearly beyond recognition by carbolic acid "the fumes of which still impregnated the damp air of the little room."

Mrs. Bolden calls Oberlin Mayor Fauver who, once he has heard the story, concludes the husband must be the guilty party. A quick investigation leads him to believe that John Bennett has caught the 9:00am C&SW (Cleveland and Southwestern) streetcar bound for Cleveland, Ohio. A description of the suspect is telephoned to police in that city.

Cleveland officers meet the car as it arrives at 10:30am. Bennett happens to be the first person to disembark. He maintains his innocence, but his clothing smells of carbolic acid. There's blood on both his shirt-sleeves and pocket handkerchief that he blames on a morning nosebleed. He has no ready explanation for why he's carrying his wife's wedding ring or for what look like acid burns on his hands.

Bennett is arrested, returned to Oberlin, and given a preliminary hearing in front of Mayor Fauver.

He tells the following story:

> Florence and I were married at Maysville, Kentucky, four years ago (May, 1898, according to later court testimony). Soon afterward, we went to Covington, Kentucky where we lived while I worked in Cincinnati. Four weeks ago she left me. I found she had been writing to a Cleveland man who lived on Forest Street. I came to Cleveland Tuesday and went to this man's house. I was told my wife had gone to Oberlin. I went there Tuesday night. I couldn't find her that night, but learned where she was Wednesday morning. I went to Mrs. Bolden's. I was told Florence was not there.
>
> A White man, who was in the house, he seized a coat that I recognized as my wife's and ran out of the room with it. He then ordered me out of the house. I wouldn't go. I searched the rooms and found my wife. She screamed and the police were called. They didn't arrest me.
>
> After some talk with my wife I succeeded in making up with her. I stayed at the house Wednesday afternoon and night. My wife told me to come to Cleveland and find work. She said she would come to me here. She gave me one dollar and I left this morning. I did not kill her. I don't know anything about her death. *The Elyria Reporter October 9 1903.*

A druggist at Oberlin's Person's Pharmacy remembers selling a bottle of carbolic to a man he *thinks* was Bennett.

Police surmise that, once alone, the Bennetts argued. He tried to force her to drink the carbolic. She refused. He hauled her to the cellar, crushed her skull with a brick, poured the acid on her face, and fled.

Charged with murder in the first degree, John Bennett is sent to the Lorain County Jail. Lorain County Prosecutor Lee Stroup complains, "Matters have come to such a pass that people from distant points such as Kentucky come to Lorain County to commit murder knowing that a Lorain County jury has never yet hanged any one."

119

A Special Grand Jury is called on October 26 for the Bennett case to allow a criminal trial in the present session of the courts. Bennett is indicted for murder in the first degree on October 30.

Bennett pleads not guilty in front of Judge Webber. The criminal trial is to take place on December 7 with Elyria attorneys A.W. Cinneger and Q.A. Gilmore defending. The prosecutors will be Lee Stroup and L.B. Fauver (Elyria) and Frank P. O'Donnell, prosecutor of Mason County, Kentucky.

The accused grows ill in the county jail. He is attended to by physician Dr. Sheffield who declares Bennett's sickness is not serious.

It takes three days before a single juror is selected with the lawyers questioning fifty-eight people to get their twelve. Said one (who was refused), "I read all about it in a paper which did not pretend to give the facts of the case." And another (also refused), "I have formed a strong opinion concerning the defendant's guilt, but not so strong that it would require any evidence to remove it."

When complete, the jury is: George E. Bryant, U.S. Behner, D.F. Morgan, George Rendall, Harvey Winckles, Gray Harris, Wm. Milspaugh, Lewis Rowell, E.D. Dewey, Harvey C. Post, George Roth, and Avery Hardy.

The courtroom is crowded for the trial. Many of those attending are from Oberlin. Papers report that "at least half the spectators are colored."

Bennett is highly nervous, watching everything with extreme attention. Things progress slowly with the more than forty witnesses. All have much to say.

On the stand, Mrs. Lee Bolden says John Bennett arrived October 7 about 5:00am. When admitted to the house, he rushed through the upper rooms searching for his wife. He broke both furniture and a window in his violent search and in a struggle with Mrs. Bolden as she tried to hold him for the police. According to Bolden, Bennett told his wife, "If I had found you at Elmer Richardson's (the Cleveland man), I would have killed you and him, too."

When Bolden left the house the next morning, Bennett went with her, saying he was going to look for work. When she returned, short of an hour later, the murder had already been committed.

Ed Ivory, "a gambler and frequenter of houses of ill fame" from Cincinnati, Ohio, testifies. Speaking "with a candor which is remarkable," Ivory states that he met Bennett in Cincinnati not long before the murder. At that time, Bennett said that he was going to hunt up his wife and kill her and that if he found her with a man, he would shoot him, too. Ivory said Bennett had stated that, if he could get his wife into a room by herself, he would like to pour carbolic acid down her throat and let her die by degrees.

The State rests after this testimony.

Bennett takes the stand in his own defense, saying he may have told his friends he wanted to kill his wife, but he denies ever describing wanting to kill her with carbolic acid.

When asked directly if he committed murder *The Elyria Reporter* quotes him, in dialect: "No, sah, I didn't do nuffin of de kind. I done love my wife and I done want her and I done follow her 'cause I love her."

He contends that what police call "acid burns" on his hands are the result of his work with asphalt in Dayton: "De tar was hot, boiling hot."

Bennett says that the morning of the crime he had first hauled in water so Mrs. Bolden could do the wash, then he remembered his wife's clothes were Cleveland so he boarded the car to retrieve them for her. As for buying the carbolic acid, he didn't even know where Person's Drug Store was.

Bennett tells how his wife left their Kentucky home without his knowledge, leaving no word as to where she had gone. He learned through a neighbor that she had gone to visit Elmer Richardson, in Cleveland. Bennett started for the city, stopping at Springfield and Dayton, Ohio.

In Dayton he spoke with a minister about his troubles and also called on his wife's grandmother, who did not know him. The old woman told him third-hand stories of his family troubles. Stories his wife had made up about how she had been abused and maltreated by her husband.

Bennett flatly denies having anything to do with the death of his wife.

The *Elyria Chronicle* seemed to think his testimony had a favorable effect on the case, that he kept his nerve and stuck to his story under a strict cross examination. But, on Monday, December 14, after a scant two hours deliberation, the jury returns a verdict of guilty of murder in the first degree with no recommendation of mercy—it is a sentence of death.

Said one of the jurors: "It was a very unpleasant duty and we all left the room resolved never to get into such a place again."

December 12: Editorial: *The Elyria Reporter*:

> The verdict brought in by the jury in the Bennett murder case was in accordance with public opinion and gave universal satisfaction. It was feared that because this county had never convicted any one of murder in the first degree that the jury would not do so in this case or if they did bring in a verdict for first degree murder they would recommend mercy and thereby

not make it capital punishment. The crime for which Bennett was tried was one of the most premeditated and blood thirsty ever committed and the evidence showed very clearly that no other person had done the awful deed, or had any motive for doing it. The evidence produced by the prosecution was of the most incriminating nature against Bennett and showed he had threatened to take the life of the woman and his every act after reaching Oberlin was of the most convincing circumstantial evidence of his guilt.

Almost every one that expressed themselves on the crime was of the opinion that Bennett was the guilty one and that nothing less than death penalty would answer as a punishment for this most atrocious murder, and when the verdict was read entire satisfaction seemed to rest in every face in the court room.

The colored people were unanimous in their desire to have the responsibility for the crime fixed upon Bennett and that the death penalty should be given him for its commission. They firmly believed in his guilt. If the reason for this county never before having anyone convicted of first degree murder, has been because former juries have had any compunctious against being the first to bring in such a verdict, the precedent has been made, and if any former juries are called upon to sit on a murder trial they will have no fears along that line. The jury in this case are certainly to be commended for finding the verdict as they did and no one can ever say again that a person cannot be convicted of first degree murder in Lorain County. Of course it is a hard thing to do to condemn anyone to death, but as long as crime is not given the full penalty of the law when committed, it makes the criminal class more daring and more ready to commit any crime that their vicious natures prompt them to do, and when they find out that they will get just penalties for their crimes they will be more careful about committing them.

The defense immediately requests a new trial for "all the usual reasons" plus the fact that juror Gray Harris "had slept so much during the trial that it became gross misconduct." On December 30, the motion for new trial (with the accusation of sleeping withdrawn) is denied by Judge Webber.

The execution date is set for April 15, 1904. On the way to the Ohio Penitentiary in Columbus, Bennett tells Deputy Salisbury he's innocent.

1904, April 4: *The Elyria Reporter:*

> The colored citizens of Maysville, Kentucky, have addressed a petition to (Ohio) Governor Herrick for the pardon of John Bennett, sentenced to electrocution on April 15th for the murder of his wife at Oberlin last October. The petition says that Bennett always enjoyed the love and esteem of all the citizens of Maysville, his native town, and it claims that the murdered woman had provoked her husband to the terrible deed by continued unfaithfulness.

Defense applies to the State Board of Pardons in an attempt to have the death sentence commuted to life in prison. The plea is refused.

Bennett's mother begs Governor Herrick "upon bended knee" for the life of her son. It does no good.

Papers report that Bennett converted to Christianity shortly after conviction and exhorts the other killers in the death-row annex to embrace Christianity and prepare to meet their God.

On April 14, 1904, now-Sheriff Salisbury travels to Columbus to witness the execution. It starts at 12:01am, April 15. Bennett is led from the execution annex where he and other murderers have been singing hymns. He carries a Bible in his hand, stopping before "Old Sparky," Ohio's electric chair, to read the fourth verse of the twenty-third Psalm (*Yea, though I walk...*).

Bennett takes his seat. He is strapped to the chair, electrodes at head and leg. When asked for last words he replies, "Forsaking all, I take Him."

He says goodbye to his caretakers in a straightforward, almost cheerful manner. Current is applied. Once. Twice. Three times. Bennett is declared dead at 12:06am.

Ohio Penitentiary Warden Hershey permits staff and prisoners to take a collection to help pay the costs of shipping Bennett's body back to Maysville for burial.

John Bennett is the first person executed for murder in Lorain County. He is not the last...

CAPITAL PUNISHMENT: The judicial killing of a human.

Please Take Your Seat:

Starting with the founding of Ohio in 1803, criminals condemned for capital offenses were hanged in the county that found them guilty. Such executions were more-or-less public, depending on the time and place, but they were always witnessed and described by the press in fair detail, especially when the hanging didn't go well, which was discouragingly often.

To help standardize executions (and to yield more consistent results), the Ohio Penitentiary in Columbus became the state's sole site for hangings. From 1855 to 1896, the penitentiary conducted a total of twenty-eight such executions. Not all of them went without a hitch.

From *Historical Lights and Shadows of the Ohio Penitentiary, 1899 edition:*

> Bloody and ghastly was the scene of execution of Michael McDonough, the Kenton wife murderer, in the penitentiary annex on the morning of June 28, 1895…
>
> Although the drop was only seven feet, the rope nearly cut the murderer's head off and instantly the blood began to spurt. The jugular vein was severed and the crimson fluid fairly poured out from under the somber black cap. Then it fell in a shower on the stone floor beneath, making the most gruesome patter imaginable.

Even in the most successful hangings it took at least ten minutes for the executed to be declared dead. Papers routinely ran lurid stories of those who "danced" at the ends of their ropes, slowly strangling to death over the course of twenty minutes, or more.

In 1889, New York became the first state in the U.S. to use the electric chair as a form of capital punishment. Ohio was the second, in 1897, to adopt what was considered to be a more humane way of killing prisoners than the somewhat dicey proposition of stringing them up.

Ohio's stoutly built, high-backed, three legged, wooden "electrical chair" was bolted to the floor directly under the trapdoors of the gallows it replaced. Stocks and straps held the condemned tightly in place as current was applied to water-soaked legs and head.

An electrocution took only a few minutes, but like hangings, things didn't always go according to plan. From the 1907, July 19, *Elyria Chronicle:*

> Took Heavy Shock To Kill Murderer:
>
> Columbus—Not until a sheet of fire shot from the head of Henry White, negro murderer of Town Marshal Basore, of

Franklin, did the volts of the electric chair kill. Two shocks had been given the man without fatal effect. Then 1,750 volts were turned on, and white flame burst from the murderer's head.

Over its 66-year career, "Old Sparky" aka "Old Thunderbolt" took 312 men and 3 women from this world to whatever awaited them. The state's original electric chair was gifted to the Ohio Historical Society in 2002. At the time of this publication, the original chair and a replica were held by The Mansfield Reformatory Preservation Society at the Mansfield Reformatory, Richland County, Ohio.

1903, October 16: *The Elyria Reporter:*

A New Kind of Drunk.

Boy, Nine Years Old had Peculiar Habit and is Sent to the State Hospital at Toledo.

J.E. Thayer of this city has issued a public request that persons refuse his 9-year-old son gasoline. The boy has the habit of inhaling fumes until he is reduced to a stupor. He has an insatiable craving for this form of intoxication. His health is wrecked and he will be placed in the hospital in Toledo in the hope of curing his strange appetite.

1903, October 26, Monday, about 4:45pm: Location: Lorain, corner of Broadway and 6th avenues, outside Fred Barnes' saloon. Victim: Dan Richards (Richardson). Suspects: Steve Majesse, Charles Majesse, and John Vig.

Lake Sailors Frank Ferguson (48) and Dan Richards (32) serve onboard the tug *Anna R.* out of Ashtabula, Ohio. Ferguson is an engineer; Richards, a deck hand. Ferguson and Richards, along with a few of their shipmates, are in Fred Barnes' saloon. Also there is a "party of foreigners" including the suspects. One of the tug-men steps on the toe of a foreigner's shoe. The groups begin arguing.

The sailors leave the saloon. The foreigners follow and attack. In the short fight, Ferguson is stabbed under the left arm. Dan Richards has a knife thrust into in his back where it sticks and cannot be withdrawn. Police are called. Officers Pat Masterson and Dave Beatty arrest Steve Majesse, Charles Majesse, and John Vig in Paul Drescheler's bar about twenty minutes later. The suspects are held in Lorain City Jail while the stabbing victims undergo treatment.

Ferguson is taken to St. Joe's in Lorain. Richards ends up in a doctor's office where the knife is removed and his wound dressed. It looks as if both men will survive the experience. The suspects are charged with cutting to wound and released on bond to await trial.

Frank Ferguson does recover, but Dan Richards takes a turn for the worse and dies three weeks later on November 19, 1903, at 7:15pm. Within ten minutes, the Majesse brothers and John Vig are rearrested and on their way to the County Jail.

It's Charles Majesse who's indicted on second degree murder charges by the Grand Jury and bound over to a criminal trial that finds him guilty of manslaughter. He's too young for the Ohio Penitentiary in Columbus and so is sentenced to the Mansfield Reformatory for an indefinite term.

During trial a man named Benjamine Caperillo is the star prosecution witness. It's his testimony that sends Charles Majesse into the reformatory. Majesse's friends tell Caperillo that they "would get him some time."

March, 1904: The Mansfield Reformatory reports Charles Majesse is dead from pneumonia.

Hold on a second…

Reports of the young man's death are greatly exaggerated. He is released in April of 1905 on the basis of good behavior. "Majesse has been an excellent prisoner and not a mark has been placed against him for misconduct."

Several months later there is a "regular race riot" at Oak Point Park. Charles Majesse is accused of being a principal in that action.

Charged with cutting with intent to wound and kill, he is brought before Lorain Mayor King. The lack of evidence makes it impossible to send him back to Mansfield and he is released.

1903, early December: A car from the C&SW (Cleveland and Southwest Traction Company) makes the run from Norwalk to downtown Cleveland in 95 minutes.

1904: LaGrange dedicates a Civil War monument of a Union standard bearer in a traffic circle at the present-day intersection of Ohio Routes 301 & 303. He starts off facing north. Puerto Ricans cannot be refused entry into the U.S. In times of trouble, Marconi says *CQD*. The Japanese bombard Russia. They also pound around in Korea. The ice cream cone. The U.S. starts digging its version of the Panama Canal. Flyers are now Flexible! The first Buddhist Temple in the U.S.—in Los Angeles. Jules Verne publishes the novel *Master of the World*. In it, both the villain and hero travel to the wilds of Lorain County, Ohio. Orville and Wilbur fly in circles. Theodore Roosevelt (New York Republican) wins the Election with 56.4% of the popular vote. 83 lynchings: 76 Blacks, 7 others.

1904, January 26, Tuesday: Location: Elyria, on the Lake Shore's rails, a short distance east of South Main. Victim: William Henry Ennis aka Bud or Buddy Nelson ("a half-witted colored man"). Suspects: Robert Nelson (grandfather), Edna (Ota) Nelson (aunt), and Cora (Nelson) Bogart (aunt) ("all colored").

Victim is a "widely known colored character." He is unconscious when found and had been drinking heavily in Elyria the day before. Death is thought to have been caused by alcohol poisoning. The victim is found without the $20 cash he was supposed to be carrying.

Authorities think foul play is involved and bring in Coroner French who decides the cause of death is from drinking wood alcohol. Is not known if he decided to do it himself, or if it was forced upon him. The autopsy shows his stomach contains a small amount of poison "resembling coffee grounds." It is examined by Professor F. Jewett of Oberlin College with the results unreported.

The relatives tell "a story of so doubtful a character" regarding the victim's death that they are arrested. Police discover the story of him drinking in Elyria all day was a fabrication of the suspects. He never left Oberlin. Suspects had been with him shortly before his death.

The suspects are indicted for murder in the second degree in May's Grand Jury and are now boarding at "Hotel De Salisbury" (Salisbury's the County Jailer, y'know). They all plead not guilty before Judge Webber.

Q.A. Gillmore is appointed to defend the three.

February 29: Oberlin's long-time Mayor, Alfred Fauver, dies with most of the pertinent information in his head. There are no written records. Prosecution is at a loss as to how to proceed.

The accused, originally bonded at $5,000 each are now released on $1,000.

There is still no trial by June 23, 1904. The defense requests more time.

Early November, 1904: The case is nollied by request of Prosecutor Stroup due to lack of evidence. *Outcome:* Unresolved.

1904, April 9: Sheffield: Announcement of a 1,000-foot bridge over the Black River by officers of the Lake Erie and Pittsburgh Railroad.

1904, May 6: *Elyria Reporter:*

> Negroes Imported From The South.
>
> Sixty Negros, typical "South-before-the-war" specimens have been imported into Lorain from Alabama by the Pittsburgh and Lake Erie Railroad. They will be employed as laborers in the construction of the new line into Lorain. There are "mammies" and "pickaninies," wenches and young men, the workers having brought their families and all their earthly belongings with them, from the family rooster to the family banjo. They will be set to work at once.

1904, November 27, Sunday: Location: Lorain, Hill Street. Victim: Carmello Securro (Italian). Suspect: Joseph Dimente (Italian). Act: Beating. Charge: Murder in the second degree. Pleads to: Guilty of assault and battery. Outcome: Judge Neff assigns six month "in the workhouse."

Judge William Byron Neff:

Born in Preble County, southwest Ohio, April 30, 1851, Neff attended public schools in Van Wert, Ohio. He attended Ohio Wesleyan University, which he left in his senior year to study at the Cincinnati Law School where he graduated in 1876, the same year that Neff was admitted to the bar. He began his practice in Cleveland with his brother, attorney O.L. Neff.

I can find no reference to Neff being elected to a Lorain County judgeship and assume he was working here on assignment. He did serve as a Cuyahoga County Common Pleas judge until 1922 when he died at age 72 due to complications following surgery at John Hopkins Hospital, Baltimore, Maryland, on November 6.

W.B. Neff is buried in Lake View Cemetery, Cleveland, Ohio

1904, December 8, Thursday, 8:30pm: Location: Lorain, Paris Café, "a dive of the worst kind." Victim: Lulu White ("Negress" and "reputed bad woman"). Suspect: Mattie Williams (21, "Negress" from Cincinnati, Ohio). Miss White is stabbed in the heart with a pocket knife during a fight of jealous rage over one Frank Robinson, a Colored musician from Cleveland. Williams, Robinson, and witness John Chin are taken into custody and held under heavy bond.

Suspect Williams tells all on arrest, but this will not be allowed as evidence in her trial due to the circumstances of the confession. The problems are unspecified in the papers.

Williams has a tough time as the only female prisoner in the County Jail's women's wing. The solitary confinement breaks her down. She constantly shrieks "in a delirium of terror and remorse." Sheriff Salisbury asks for a special grand jury to hurry things along. Prosecutor Stroup says no can do because of the heavy case load. Says the sheriff in response, "From the woman's action I believe she will go insane."

Attorneys Q.A. Gillmore and A.W. Cinniger, both of Elyria are appointed to defense. Prosecution is Stroup and C.F. Adams, of Lorain. Williams is tried in front of Judge Washburn. The court room is crowded to the doors. There is difficulty seating a jury since possible outcomes include execution.

Stroup argues the quarrel was premeditated by the accused and that the slaying was an act of jealousy.

Doctor Cox, who attended the victim and did the autopsy, identifies the weapon. Death was caused by a stab wound to the chest, about one inch wide and one inch deep that pierced an auricle of the heart.

It proves to be a tough case for the defense. Isaac Moody, of Lorain, was a witness but not completely sober at the time of the stabbing. He had seen Ms. White, Ms. Williams, and their shared paramour, Mr. Robinson together, but did not see them drinking.

Percy Redfern was called. He did not drink because it was election night but did not see Robinson and Williams together. Redfern says the victim, Ms. White, had a gun which he, Redfern, talked her out of carrying. Other witnesses corroborate his story.

Mattie Williams takes the stand to defend herself and answers questions in a plain and straightforward manner.

February 22: The jury is charged at 6:30pm and deliberates for three hours. They return a verdict of guilty of murder in the second degree.

The defendant throws herself into the arms of her brother, faints, and has to be carried back to jail, but shows no emotion when sentenced to life in the woman's section of the Ohio Penitentiary in Columbus. A plea is made for a new trial by Attorney Gillmore. It is denied by Judge Washburn.

Before heading for prison, she is allowed out of her cell for a few minutes for a local justice-of-the-peace to marry her to a long-time lover from Sandusky, Jim O'Nelson, aka James Nelson Woods, a hotel porter. Of him, she says, "He is the only true friend I ever had and has stood by me through all my trouble; that is why I married him."

Sheriff Salisbury is now of the opinion that the stabbing was in self-defense and that it was the victim, Lulu White, who began the argument that led to her own death. Says Mattie Williams, "Someday they will see that I was not to blame in this affair and then I may be pardoned." Her new husband dedicates himself to getting his wife a new trial or pardon.

1935, August: Williams is denied parole and her term is continued until July, 1937.

In March of 1905 the owner of the Paris Café, Tom Harris, Colored, gives up his business, not because it's disreputable, but because it's not profitable.

1905, January 4: *The Elyria Reporter:*

These Three Damsels Liked To Play "Cards."

They were sitting in the jury room, three coal-black, colored women and they looked bored. They were waiting to be called in Wednesday afternoon to testify in the Mattie Williams murder case before the Grand Jury and they had worn out discussion on the matter and hung their heads.

Presently one looked up. "Sakes, alive Flossie," she said. "We layin' 'roun here and me got the cards in ma pocket." She took from her pocket a thumb-worn deck of cards and presently all three women were engaged in card playing, The sheriff looked through the door and laughed, then the deputy, then lawyers, then witnesses. They chuckled gleefully, but the women played on.

Finally Flossie saw them there and she let out a muffled scream. In a moment cards were out of sight and the three colored women hung their heads.

Judge Clarence Griffin Washburn:

A native of Huron County, Ohio, Washburn graduated University of Michigan Law School. In 1892, he served as the Solicitor of the City of Lorain. He was elected the Lorain County Clerk of Courts in 1896 and 1899. In 1904, he was appointed Common Pleas Court Judge to complete the term vacated by A.R. Webber who left the courts for the U.S. Congress. Washburn was later elected to the judgeship.

He was elected judge of the Court of Appeals of the Ninth Judicial District of Ohio in 1918, and won successive elections until retiring in 1944.

C.G. Washburn died June 14, 1956 and is buried in the Edwards Grove Cemetery, Greenwich, Huron County, Ohio.

1905: Ohio makes it illegal for boys younger than 15 and girls younger than 16 to work during the school year. The law is widely ignored. The radical union known as the Wobblies (Industrial Workers of the World) is founded in Chicago. Strikes and riots rip across Russia. Tsar Nicholas II authorizes an elected legislature even though he doesn't really want it. The cause of polio remains unknown, though researchers are convinced it's communicable. The U.S. Supreme Court upholds the constitutionality of mandatory smallpox vaccination programs (Jacobson v. Massachusetts). Local newspapers begin using "Continued on page…" instead of running undivided articles. In the Docket: Many charged with running or taking part in "Bucket Shops." These are parlors where men gather, not to buy stocks, but to bet against the shop owner on whether a stock sold on a legitimate exchange will go up or down in value. 62 lynchings: 57 Blacks, 5 others. $1,000 is worth $26,446 modern.

1905, mid-August: Location: Shawville (where the railroad crosses the Avon-Belden Road). Victim: "Unknown Hungarian." Act: Trauma.

Coroner French rules victim was robbed and thrown off one train then crushed to death by the next. Opinion based on the fact there was no money on the body. "These fellows are rarely without money and fall easy prey to tramps and thugs." Outcome: Unsolved.

1905, August 23, Wednesday, about 10:00pm: Location: Lorain, Lake Avenue, "a mile and half north of the 'Half Way House.'" Victim: Thomas McFadden (Negro plasterer). Act: Trauma. Victim is found by Henry Taft, local farmer, and Hermann Miller, his 14-year-old helper. The two are cutting brush when Taft sits down beside the road to ease his hurting feet, and young Miller spots a dead man nearby.

The body is a bloody mess with its head crushed and clothing covered with gore. One hand is raised across the face as if to ward off blows. Beside the body are found a broken fence rail and a piece of sandstone, both with blood and matted hair upon them. About 150 feet down the road, a hatchet head and shaft, separated and also bloodied, are found.

Authorities investigate. A blow from the hatchet opened a three-inch wound in the skull from which the victim's brain oozed, but death was caused by repeated blows from the fence rail and heavy stone. The dead man's pockets hold four cents, a pipe, and an empty tobacco package but Coroner French does not consider robbery the motive.

The Miller boy identifies the body as Thomas McFadden and says the man was a plasterer working for Henry Lashell, who lives near Stop 21 on the Green Line.

Mrs. Henry Lashell says the victim lived on 15th Avenue in South Lorain with his wife and kids and was sober and industrious, though he'd misbehaved in his younger years and spent time in prison.

Walter Benford, farmer, who lives a quarter-mile from the scene of the crime heard hollering about 10:00pm the night of the killing, but his wife would not allow him to investigate on his own. It took ten minutes to wake his son, George, and rouse his neighbors, Billy Deitman and Nick Sens, to go down the road together. They saw and heard nothing and figured it was nothing more than a "gang of drunken rioters" that had passed by.

Neighbor Mrs. Nelson Gleason said she heard screaming about the same time and then a voice moaning "Oh, dear! Oh, dear!" She was sure from the start that it was murder, but being alone, did not dare investigate.

Another neighbor, Mrs. Harry Braman, remembers a buggy that drove past the scene around the time the shouting began.

Police entertain a theory that the victim's widow and a boarder named Morton conspired to kill the man in order to secure his insurance and elope. The two are closely questioned along this line at the coroner's inquest but never charged.

A month passes with no new clues. Prosecutor Stoup considers offering a reward. The County Commissioners consider appointing a special detective to investigate the crime.

> The authorities feel that such a brutal murder and one which has shocked the community as this one has, should not remain a mystery, and the murderer allowed to go unpunished. For this reason a man will probably be appointed for the purpose of bringing the miscreant to justice. *The Elyria Reporter, Sep. 7, 1905.*

Police keep suggesting they have more information, but never make it public. The September 27 Grand Jury does not consider the case.

On October 19, the papers report that the victim's widow received $600 in death benefits from her husband's insurance and that police suspicion of her had caused delay in payment. But the woman provided a copy of the Coroner's Verdict: "killed by persons unknown" and that was enough of a vindication to collect. Outcome: Unsolved.

The "Half Way House" mentioned at the start of this case was a place of business and community at the intersection of Lorain and Lake Avenues—half-way between Lorain and Elyria. The structure was old back in 1905. It was demolished in 1945.

1905, October 24, Tuesday: Location: Lorain, the alley in back of the Hotel Franklin. Victim: Bert James (Lee) (Colored porter). Suspect: Joseph Torney (saloonkeeper, Colored *or* Italian depending on the edition of the paper). Trouble stated when James allegedly stole a bottle of whiskey from Torney's bar. Torney said he had sought out the victim to tell him not to come to his saloon anymore. They met in the alley where the killing happened. Torney claims he fired the shot because he was afraid.

Grand Jury indicts for murder in the first degree in late January, 1906. Plea: Not guilty. W.H. Boyd of Cleveland is defending. He says the killing was in response to an unprovoked assault and, if not acquitted, the most severe crime the accused could be found guilty of is manslaughter.

Criminal trial takes place in March 1906. There is difficulty seating jurors because of scruples against the death penalty. Forty-eight are examined before the panel is filled.

The question… Who was the aggressor? The State says it was the suspect. Defense claims self-defense. Few spectators attend the trial even though testimony is interesting and cross examinations are intense.

State witnesses, who were all close to the shooting, hotel chef Robert Anderson, Harry Bunch, stable-hand, and William Rawschert, wagoner for a furniture dealer, all incriminate the accused.

The Hotel Franklin landlord, and R.F. Powell, both of whom witnessed the shooting, said that the victim and a "negro companion" approached the accused in a threatening manner and that Torney was in actual retreat when he fired the shot. Outcome: Guilty of manslaughter. Sentence: Ohio Penitentiary, 6 years, plus cost.

1906: Wasserman's test for syphilis. Bubble Gum. The term "allergy" is first used by Vienna Pediatrician Clemens von Pirquet. German researcher Alois Alzheimer finds physical symptoms in the brain of a dead woman who suffered from dementia. The *Naturalization Act* standardizes the process for the foreign-born to become a U.S. citizen. The Pure Food and Drug Act begins to close down the patent medicine racket. Tsar Nicholas II dismisses the elected legislature that he didn't really want in the first place. Mahatma

Gandhi begins his passive campaign against British rule. Architect Philip C. Johnson is born in Cleveland, Ohio. 65 lynchings: 62 Blacks, 3 others.

1906, ? ?: Location: Lorain. Victim: Nick Rasin. Suspect: Mike Bunda. Act: Trauma. Victim is struck over head with beer glass. *Suspect is brought in front of the Grand Jury a decade later.* Charge: Murder in the second degree. Plea: Not guilty. *Changed to:* Guilty of Assault with Intent to Kill. Outcome: Ohio Penitentiary, 1 year, plus costs of $43.05.

1906, late February: Location: South Lorain, along the river. Victim: Mike Bruc. Body found, frozen, at the bottom of an embankment. Coroner French was not present at the autopsy because it had been reported to him that a man fell down the river bank and had frozen to death. He had no idea the dead man's skull was fractured until he read about it in the papers.

Blood traces found on trees in various places and on the ground where the body was found lead French to decide it was a crime. "We will leave no stone unturned." Body buried at Calvary Cemetery in Lorain.

Outcome: Unsolved.

1906, March 21, Wednesday, shortly after noon: Location: Lorain, Fifth Avenue, "Colored Boarding House." Victim: Elizabeth Elder(s) (Colored 49) housekeeper from Mississippi. Suspect: George Williams (Colored). Suspect is a hod carrier for the Bonsor Brothers and one of twenty people boarding with the victim.

Victim Elder is in the kitchen preparing lunch. Suspect Williams enters by the rear door and beckons her into a small, adjoining bedroom that also has a door that opens into the front parlor. After a few minutes, the nine or ten people in the parlor hear four shots in quick succession.

The boarders run for the front door, then return. One, George Smith, gathers a few of the others around him and enters the small room. It is apparent that Williams had seized Elder around the neck, shot her dead through the head twice with a .32 Smith and Wesson revolver: once just below the right eye and again in the left temple. Williams had then committed suicide with the same weapon. Both bodies had fallen across the bed with his left arm around her neck. The assumption is that he suggested something to which she objected, and she was shot in return.

Victim came from Columbus about sixteen years ago and was married twice, the last time nineteen years ago. Two daughters at home, Mary (14) and Malinda Elder (17), and a married son, William Triplett, who works as a porter at the John Poper and Palm Garden saloons. Elder's body is taken to Fey's morgue at 1:30pm and identified by son William.

Police discover that George Williams was married to a woman in New London, Ohio, but was passing himself off as single. When undertaker Wickens contacts the widow about the disposition of her husband's body, she replies she wanted nothing to do with him when he was alive and certainly wants nothing to do with him now that he is dead.

1907: Walter Christie drives faster than 120 mph. Street cars collide between 4th and 5th on Elyria's Middle Avenue, kicking off a chain of events that results in that city's Memorial Hospital. T.R.'s big stick shows up off shore of Honduras and marines help protect United States interests. He also sends his stick on a world tour. Australia establishes a "minimum wage" (about $75/week modern). Burgess Meredith is born in Lakewood, Lorain County, Ohio. In the Docket: "Operating stationary engine without a license" first appears. Oklahoma. 61 lynchings: 58 Blacks, 3 others.

1907, January Friday, mid-afternoon:

Sixty-something Oscar McAlpine is angry with Mary, his estranged wife. That's nothing new since it feels as if he's been angry with her almost since the day they married in 1866.

Some time ago, he left Mary and their adult children for Wisconsin. Before they parted ways, the 58-year-old Mary promised him $1,800 for his share of their property in Penfield Township. She even signed a bill of sale. But after he'd gone, she refused to send him the full amount, stiffing him for almost a third of what she agreed to pay.

He'd made the trip back to Ohio at the start of 1907 which cost him even more money, trying to get what he was rightfully owed. When he arrives, the weather is cold, unlike Oscar McAlpine who is mighty hot under the collar. He bolsters himself with a few shots of liquid courage. One last talk with Mary and things'll be settled, one way or the other.

The visit goes well for about an hour until he brings up the money she owes him. That's when the argument starts. Mary turns her back on him, ignoring him, pretending to attend to her laundry. Oscar's seething anger comes to a sudden boil. He stands, draws his .32 revolver from his back pocket, aims, and fires.

The bullet crashes through Mary's head and lodges in a pail hanging in the open pantry. She's dead before she hits the floor. Realizing what he's done, Oscar places the weapon against his side, aims at his heart, and pulls the trigger. But the shot is deflected by a rib, passes through his abdomen and comes to a stop in the muscles of his back.

His two grown sons rush into the room and take the weapon. They call Constable George Whitehead. The constable notes that there's booze on McAlpine's breath and that the shooter's own family speaks about him in the harshest of terms.

Oscar McAlpine is very much awake when he is arrested. He is calm and not the least concerned with his dead wife. Instead, he complains about the pain of his own wound and his feeling of cold. He is taken first to Wellington where his wounds are treated, then hauled to Elyria for more medical treatment and processing by the law.

Dr. Sheffield decides to leave the bullet in place. Sheriff Salisbury figures Oscar doesn't have any more than a few days. Coroner French concludes there are two reasons not to bother with an inquiry: first, it's an open and shut case. Second, the guilty man has no chance of survival. Once blood poisoning sets it, that'll be all she wrote.

Oscar McAlpine beats the odds. He recovers sufficiently to be transferred from the hospital to the Lorain County Jail. In a few months he'll be well enough for trial. Well enough, perhaps, to be sent to the electric chair.

In the meantime, Mary's body is sent home to her own parents in Wadsworth, Ohio.

In his cell, Oscar is morose and will not talk of the crime, though he is quoted as saying "I ought to have killed her thirty years ago." His mood improves with his health. He has no apparent worries over his fate, but trembles from head to foot when he pleads not guilty to murder in the first degree in a voice so quiet it can hardly be heard.

The Grand Jury indicts him as charged. McAlpine claims destitution despite the land he owns in Wisconsin. The court assigns attorney A.W. Lawrence to defend him. The lawyer asks for an assistant because of the severity of the crime.

Judge Washburn responds that he will not grant an assistant but will see to it that Prosecutor Stevens does not have one either. Fair's fair, after all.

Oscar's health is stable yet he remains so weak and feeble from his self-inflicted wounds that he asks for a wheelchair. There is speculation that he may lack the strength for the upcoming criminal trial.

The case never makes it to a jury. On February 25, 1907, Oscar McAlpine pleads guilty to murder in the second degree. Judge Washburn sentences him to life in the Ohio Penitentiary.

Oscar's twenty-something son, Vernon, is with him at sentencing. As they part, the old man takes his son's hands and says "Vern, don't you ever taste any whiskey. It will get the best of you if you do. I was one of those fools who drank it all of my life and you see what it has brought me to."

Local papers, (especially the *Elyria Chronicle*) use McAlpine's crime as an opportunity to describe the evils of drink. The next month, an anonymous letter appears in the *Chronicle* saying, in part:

> Drunk or sober he [McAlpine] was one of the most vicious men that ever lived and when the news of the murder came no one who ever knew him was in the least surprised.

It goes on to describe, not a feeble, trembling old man, but a monster who terrorized and abused his wife and family for more than three decades:

> Liquor was not the at the bottom of it all, for he was not always under the influence of liquor when committing these crimes against society. He was not in the habit of keeping liquor in his house and only occasionally went on a spree. It was simply inborn meanness and hatred of everyone who was not in his class. None of his former neighbors have a good word for him. He returned evil for good. *The Elyria Chronicle, March 5, 1907.*

McAlpine, still in his cell at the Lorain County Jail, denies the accusations, saying he drank because he was "yoked to an evil woman" who allowed one of their children, at age three, to die from summer's heat. He reveals that the revolver he used to kill his wife was never meant for her. He was carrying it, instead, to shoot a man who was a frequent visitor when he was away.

The old man shows a great deal of sorrow as Sheriff Ward and Deputy Sheriff Horn take him to Columbus in March of 1907. He is assigned to help make cigars. Eight years later, a plea for parole is refused. Six years after that Oscar McAlpine dies at the Lima State Hospital in Lima, Ohio. He is buried in the cemetery there.

1907, January 05: Sheriff Salisbury, upon retirement, is given an upholstered chair by friends in court so he can "spend his declining years in ease." He is replaced by Robert Ward.

1907, January 12, Saturday, shortly after 6:00pm: Location: Lorain, corner of Park Street and 7th Avenue. Victim: Neil (Leo) Wilson (Colored). Suspect: William (Banjo Bill) Juren. Act: A stabbing with wounds not thought to be serious. Suspect Juren vacates the city immediately after the act. Victim Wilson dies March 19.

Stares *The Elyria Reporter:* January 14: "The fight [was] over the affections of Laura Ferguson, Colored boarding house keeper." The suspect caught the victim "in the act of making love." (This is the first time I saw this phrase in the Lorain County press in relation to a murder.)

Same newspaper: March 20: "The cause was an escalating fight over the merits of a banjo. Suspect rushed victim and stabbed him several times in the left breast. The wounds did not appear all that serious until it discovered that one of the cuts punctured the left lung."

Whatever the cause, Juren followed Wilson to his room where a fight began. Juren stabbed Wilson at least a half-dozen times and then hurriedly left the house. Wilson was found shortly thereafter by another boarder. Outcome: Unresolved. Banjo Bill Juren is never found.

1907, January 17: Grand Jury is investigating the proliferation of speakeasies and illegal sales of booze in Wellington.

1907, February 19: *Elyria Chronicle:*

Thinks Authorities Should Investigate Norfa's Death. Italian Residents of Elyria Say American's Murder Would Not be Treated So Lightly.

Joe Norfa, an Italian, was sandbagged [beat over the head with a sap] and murdered, and up to the present, the county authorities have not taken any steps to apprehend the murderers.

Norfa worked on the Wabash railway construction work, and when found he was unconscious. He was taken to the hospital and the physicians said that his death was inevitable, he could not live long. He died and the coroner made a postmortem of his head, and the result of the examination was that he found that the man had been sandbagged, but that his death was due to meningitis.

The man's death was hastened by the slugging he received, and therefore the man who did it is guilty of murder. An effort should be made to capture him and the prosecuting attorney should take up and follow the case. The Italians in this district are of the opinion that the authorities are negligent in this matter. If an American had been treated as Norfa had been and a death resulted, the authorities would have immediately tried to capture his slayer.

The sandbagging was not done by an Italian. Italians do not work with sandbags. When they want to get rid of a man they use a stiletto or a revolver.

Outcome: Unsolved.

1907, March 20: There are twenty-four cases of typhoid in the Lorain Hospital. The poor quality of the county's drinking water is blamed.

1907, April 21, Sunday: Location: Lorain's American Shipbuilding yards. Victim: John T. (or A.) Koch (Kock) (worker). Suspect: William M. Brown aka Michael Kelly (security guard).

To break a protracted strike at the Lorain Shipyards, scabs are brought in from the east coast. By April 11, the strike is at a practical end, and the strike-breakers are leaving the area for other shipyards.

The shooting occurs during a tumultuous shift change coinciding with an argument between drunken armed guards. At first, it's reported victim was a fellow security guard instead of a worker.

Suspect Brown pleads not guilty at preliminary hearing, saying the shooting was accidental. He is taken to the County Jail as the Lorain City Jail is not considered secure enough for a murder suspect.

Defense is attorney Hughes. Bail is set for $3,000. Several witnesses give $100 promissory bonds to guarantee their presence at the trial including J.A. "Kentucky Joe" Wills (Willis), another guard, with whom Brown was arguing when he fired the gun. The case is postponed while witnesses are rounded up.

On April 26, while awaiting arraignment, the accused tells the victim's son, William, "I want you to feel that the death of your father was accidental and that I would do anything in the world to bring him back to you."

At the May Grand Jury it's determined that victim Koch was a strikebreaker. Brown is indicted for murder in the second degree and is "evidently very much disturbed" by this turn of events.

At the criminal trial Kentucky Joe testifies that there was no malice of the accused toward the victim. There were three or four men in the guard shanty that night. A drunken argument ensued over the question of who had the most lice in his head (yuck). In the course of the argument, the suspect pulled his revolver and fired it into the dark, accidentally striking Koch in the head and killing him.

Ray Read, another strike-breaker, tells the same story.

Brown's version is that there *was* a drunken argument, but it was not over head lice, but who could hold the most liquor. Kentucky Joe claimed that distinction, and Brown, by way of making a counterpoint, pulled his weapon and fired into the dark. For some time after, nobody even knew the victim had been shot. Brown is unshakeable in his testimony.

Jury finds the accused not guilty of murder in the second degree, but guilty of manslaughter with "many spectators surprised at success of the State in securing any conviction." Brown seems content with a three year sentence at the Ohio Penitentiary and expresses satisfaction it is for no longer. A motion for a new trial is filed and overruled.

The shipyard strike finally ends in mid-June.

1907, July 07: *The Elyria Chronicle:*

Lovers Routed by New Light: Boys and Girls Think Park Rights Have Been Invaded:

What do you know about that light in the city park. It is a downright shame for anyone to erect such a strong light in the center of a resort where young men and women meet in the evening. The man who was instrumental in making this improvement ought to have had more forethought and common sense.

While two girls were conversing on Broad Street on Thursday evening the above words were used by one of them. This is the sentiment, of many of the boys and girls who used to spoon in the city park in the evenings under the lofty shade trees of that resort.

The light which is considered a great improvement will cause the sparking school to move its headquarters. An indignation meeting of the girls was held just as soon as the new light gave its first twinkle. It was resolved that the man who was guilty of causing the electric light to be erected in the park was not a friend of the spooning organization and should be hoisted from office. The resolution was carried unanimously, and a copy of it will be sent to all their gentlemen friends.

1907, October 24, Thursday, shortly before 9:00am: Location: Lorain, 600-block Kent Street. Victim: Anna Schwarz (Schwartz) (63, wife). Suspect: John Schwarz (Schwartz) (72, husband). Mr. and Mrs. are from Switzerland. She is sitting at a desk writing a letter. Her husband, "in a fit of insanity," sticks a shotgun in her face and pulls the trigger, "scattering blood, brains and large pieces of skull in profusion about the room."

Three daughters, Catherine, Martha, and Emma, known throughout the county as the "Schwarz Singers," are visiting a neighbor at the time. This is unusual since they are not in the habit of leaving their mother and father alone together. They return home to find their mother dead. They disarm their father who is ranting and waving the weapon in the air.

Police arrive shortly after the shooting to take the man they describe as "a raving maniac" into custody. The little old man with gray hair and whiskers speaks German to his jailers and seems unaware of what he has done. Mr. Schwarz is held without bond by Lorain's Mayor King.

Dr. Van Nuys, Mr. Schwarz' regular physician says the old man is suffering from "softening of the brain and has not been in his right mind for several years. He has always been the possessor of a gun and always kept it loaded as the family knew."

The papers say "on numerous occasions he has taken the shotgun from his room and threatened various members of the family but as he never attempted violence the family felt no fear when he would bring forth the gun and threaten to kill the mother or a daughter."

It is not true what the paper said, that they had no fear, says the family. Mrs. Schwarz was terrified of the shotgun and had unsuccessfully begged her son to hide the weapon from the old man.

The coroner does not class the act as a crime due to the old man's mental state. Judge Hinman and Prosecuting Attorney Stevens are not satisfied that the old man is insane and so plan to hold a hearing on the matter after visiting him in jail.

Schwarz continues to speak only German. Authorities use another German prisoner as a translator. Schwarz claims to remember nothing of the shooting. His mind is a blank on the topic. He is observed by several doctors while in jail.

The November Grand Jury indicts him for murder in the second degree (the papers say murder in the first). The daughters force the issue of sanity by requesting an immediate inquest into their father's state of mind.

The young women testify, in part, that their father told them that his own father appeared to him in dreams three times to say his wife was unfaithful. The killer had gone so far as to suggest that the children he had helped raise were not his own.

In February of 1908, Judge Hinman declares Mr. Schwarz insane and suffering from "Pre-Senile Dementia." Outcome: Schwarz is sent to the Massillon Asylum. The case is dropped from docket on February 6, 1908.

A Note on Addresses

I have a few reasons for obscuring specific addresses for locations in which killings took place (e.g., *600-block*). First: addresses are not permanent. In fact, street names are not permanent. It'd be a shame to pin a murder on your house when it never happened there at all. Second: if a murder *did* occur in your house, maybe you don't want all your neighbors to know. Third: this is all public record. If you really want to know where a murder took place, then go look it up!

1907, November 1, Friday: Location: Lorain, 1600-block Penfield Avenue, Helen Stabler's Rooming House. Victim: Robert J. Smith. Suspect: John Goohs (Goos). The victim, Robert Smith, of Port Huron, Michigan, is an engineer on the brand-new lake steamer *J.J. Sullivan.* He is shot during a robbery in a "sporting house." Rose Martin, May Freeland, and Helen Hartsell, all soiled doves of the establishment, are witnesses.

It takes Smith several days to die. The case against John Goohs is weak from the start. The original charge against him is murder in the first degree, but Lorain's Mayor King says evidence cannot sustain that charge or even one of murder in the second, and so it's stepped down to manslaughter.

Goohs is transferred to the County Jail. Police remain satisfied with their investigation and feel they have their man. Others, who originally thought him guilty, are now unsure.

The November Grand Jury indicts on murder in the second degree. Goohs' defense, Attorney Cinniger, enters a plea of not guilty.

Prosecutor Stevens begins having severe problems when star witness John Little hangs himself while in custody in the County Jail. Then another witness, Fred Burroughs, tries to overdose on laudanum.

The criminal trial end abruptly 3:00pm, February 5, 1908, at the end of testimony about several threats made by the prosecution's last witness, "Dynamite" Burrows, towards defendant Goohs. Judge Washburn orders a stop to the proceedings and dismisses the jury due to insufficient proof that the accused had committed the crime.

The judge says the court "was quite satisfied that the state had not proved the guilt of the defendant beyond a reasonable doubt and rather than set aside any verdict the jury might return, he would do that which the law permitted, if not commanded him to do."

The prosecutor's office makes a request for a new trial on February 8, 1908. That request is withdrawn in September of that same year. Outcome: Unresolved.

Smith's ship, *J.S. Sullivan*, renamed *Clarence B. Randall* in 1963, remained in service until 1988, when she was scrapped.

1907, November 10, Sunday: Location: Eaton Township, three miles from Grafton. Victim: Benjamine Caperillo (about 35). Caperillo's body is found along the "Big Four" tracks in Eaton Township with crushed legs and neck injury, left side, three inches long, just above the collar bone and two inches near the chin, right leg badly crushed. A blood-covered stiletto is found in the right, front trouser pocket.

The coroner thinks Caperillo was murdered and placed on the tracks to cover the crime. The victim had trouble, earlier in the day, when he was involved in an argument in an Elyria saloon. It's thought a few of those men (Italians, all) followed him and committed the crime. It's also noted that Caperillo was a witness for the prosecution in the Majesse murder/manslaughter case a few years back and that threats against his life were made at that time.

The belief is that the "Black Hand or some Italian secret organization" is responsible in the killing. There are some signs that the man was drunk—a partly-filled whiskey bottle is found on his person. The victim is supposed to have been carrying $280, which is missing along with his watch. He was riding the freight to Cleveland where he was going to send the money to Italy to bring his wife and children to this country.

The lack of evidence makes it impossible to proceed. Caperillo is buried in the Grafton Cemetery. Outcome: Unsolved.

See 1903, October 26.

1907, November 13, Wednesday: Location: Green Line (C.S.&C.) car, Oberlin Road. Victim: Unknown baby. Corpse of an infant, wrapped in a neat package, is found on a Green Line car left there, it's thought, by three people who boarded south of Elyria. Police Chief Whitney and Coroner Miller investigate.

Motorman Vanderwyst recalls a stop on the Oberlin Road at which two women and a man got on and occupied the seat beneath which the package was later discovered. One woman was dressed in brown, the other in black. The one in black attracted some attention by her "apparently overwrought manner" and sat in an odd posture over top the spot the baby was later found. The trio left the car at the "Big Four" crossing, presumably to catch a train. The discovery of the package and its gruesome contents were made a few minutes later. The motorman thought it was meat, butchered and packed, at first. He alerted Wellington's Marshal upon realization it was a dead child.

Coroner Miller's judgment is that the baby was alive at birth and had been allowed to bleed to death. Cleveland and Elyria police are also involved to see if they could discover who was responsible for placing the tiny body in the Green Line car. Outcome: Unsolved.

1907, November 15, Friday, early morning: Location: Lorain, Saloon at Park and 7th Street. Victim: Lewis (Louis) Washtak (Washtue) (bar patron, 37). Suspect: Joseph J. Thomas (saloon owner). Both are Polish.

Washtak is employed at the Lorain shipyards. According to the papers, while a customer in the saloon, victim Washtak raises a ruckus and refuses to calm himself despite frequent warnings and threats of expulsion by Thomas, who owns the business. Thomas then draws a .38 revolver and threatens the victim with death if he does not leave. Washtak refuses to budge and is shot for his stubbornness. The bullet enters the front of the throat, severs the windpipe, and lodges in the back of his neck, beneath the skin.

Washtak is taken to St. Joseph's Hospital for medical attention. Doctors say he has only a few hours to live but, three days later, the shooting victim is still alive. Joseph Thomas is charged with shooting with intent to kill and is released on $5,000 bond.

Lewis Washtak dies at midnight November 18. Thomas is re-arrested on charges of murder in the second degree. Bond is upped to $10,000, which Thomas pays.

November 26, Coroner Miller states "I find that Louis Washtak met death as the result of a gunshot wound, the same having been inflicted by

John J. Thomas." The autopsy, performed by doctors Cox and McNamara, of Lorain, also finds a chunk of knife blade that had been embedded in Washtak's skull "for quite some time."

The Grand Jury indicts on murder in the second degree. The criminal trial starts the first week of February, 1908, with the jury visiting the saloon where the shooting took place.

Court room Number One is crowded to the doors with Judge Washburn presiding. Prosecutor Lee Stroup assisted by attorney Glitch. Defense is attorneys Fauver, and Adams. The best money can buy.

The trial goes slowly because of the need for interpreters. Testimony reveals that it *was* a fight, but the circumstances are far different than those reported by the papers.

It is readily evident that Washtak was being purposefully quarrelsome and making remarks calculated to cause trouble. In doing so, Washtak had boasted of his abilities as a fighter and wrestler.

Bar-owner Thomas then commented the victim might whip a child but not a man. That's when Washtak picked him up and tossed him across the bar. And that's when Thomas went to the back room of his saloon to retrieve his revolver. Upon his return, and despite being armed, Thomas was struck by the victim several times about the head with the wooden shoes used by men in the steel mills to walk on hot surfaces. Thomas then shot Washtak in self-defense.

So it becomes a trial of the victim. Defense present several witnesses, include Lorain police officers and citizens of Berea, Cuyahoga County, Ohio, all of whom testify to Lewis Washtak's leanings toward violence and bad behavior. Many of those same people laud Joseph Thomas for his peaceful disposition and respect for the law.

The case is handed to the jury at noon, February 12. While the jury is out, John Washtak, brother of the victim, along with some friends, make loud charges in the court house that the accused has used his considerable wealth to bribe the jury. The brother predicts the jury will either acquit or disagree and be hung. Enough of a ruckus is raised that Judge Washburn orders the jury placed under lock and key. The accused, who is out on bond, is slipped out the back door of the court house. Police escort him to his car by a roundabout route.

Whether or not the brother's accusation of bribery is fact, his prediction proves true. After 24 hours deliberation, jury foreman S.S. Lockwood reports that there is no hope of reaching an agreement.

Judge Washburn sends them back in for another try, but no dice. He excuses the jury. Afterward, Foreman Lockwood reports that a small majority of the jurors wanted to convict while the rest insisted on acquittal on the grounds of self-defense.

Thomas' new trial is on February 24. It proceeds much as the first with the same witnesses and the same testimony. Judge Washburn surprises everyone when he unilaterally drops the charge of murder in the second degree and limits the jury to deciding if the accused is guilty of manslaughter.

It takes 18 hours for the jury to find not guilty of manslaughter. Joseph Thomas doesn't, at first, understand the outcome. "The expression on his face never changed as the clerk read the verdict declaring him not guilty of manslaughter and it was not until his friends shook his hand that he appeared to realize he was a free man."

1907, December 14, Saturday, about 7:00pm:

Harry Sesila (Semeler, Semelar, Secila, or Cecila) is a persnickety man who likes everything just so. He thinks everything has a place, and that's where everything should be.

It so happens that everything in its place is exactly what Joe Dominski wants. That's why he hired Harry to work in his dry goods store in the 300-block of 8th Avenue, Lorain. Sure, Harry's an excitable sort of fellow and sometimes tends to blow things out of proportion, but that's a small price to pay for a man you can trust.

Sesila's boss, Dominski, is a prominent member of Lorain's Polish community and a self-made business man. Besides the store, Dominski's a contract carpenter, and when he's away, Sesila works the counter.

When business man Joe Dominski is shot and killed at his store the evening of December 14, 1907, there are but two witnesses: counter clerk Harry Sesila and store-boy Ignace Chaulsky. Sesila tells police that two men, one tall, one short, both well-dressed, came in to buy collar buttons. They paid with a small bill and then loudly argued over the change they were given, contending they'd used a 10-dollar bill for the purchase.

Dominski, who was at the back of the store, started towards the ruckus. One of the arguing men pulled a revolver and leveled it at Sesila who ducked behind the counter just as his boss arrived. The man with the weapon opened fire, shooting over Sesila's head and into a stack of boxes behind the counter. The shooter then turned the revolver on Dominski, hitting him in the leg.

Wounded, Dominski turned to run and was shot, through and through, from back to front.

The shooter and his partner emptied the cash drawer and fled with $100. In the process, little Ignace Chalusky zapukał do jego tyłka.

It *would* be a straightforward robbery and shooting, except that the high-strung Sesila is a poor eyewitness. For example, he first says the robbers shot into a stack of boxes behind the counter. But when no spent bullets are found, he admits he might be mistaken. Ignace Chaulsky has a similar, yet still conflicting story, but he is so young that nobody trusts his account.

Dominski is buried on December 20 from the "Polish Catholic Church in Lorain." Services are well attended. It takes more than two hours for people to pass by the casket. Family and friends travel in five special funeral (street) cars to the internment in Calvary Cemetery.

Lorain police initially say the murder is the work of a gang that has been robbing stores throughout the city. They then arrest but do not charge three tramps who are positively identified by Harry Sesila and Ignace Chaulsky.

The three deny the crime. They weren't even in Lorain at the time of the shooting. Investigation reveals that all can provide an alibi, which includes being locked up at the time of the murder. The three are released despite Sesila and Chaulsky insisting they are the men responsible for the crime.

In the meantime, Joe Dominski's wife has come up with her own, unnamed suspect. She is reported as watching for a specific action that will prove guilt and trigger an arrest.

The dry goods store is robbed twice more following its owner's death. Mrs. Dominski decides to sell the property to C.H. Kohn and A. Shafer, who take immediate possession. As soon as she closes the deal, she's on her way to Cleveland where she has relatives. "She is said to constantly fear for her life and the lives of her children."

Harry Sesila is arrested in late March, 1908, to face the Grand Jury as an accessory to the murder. Authorities think that he may have identified the three innocent tramps as a way to protect the real culprits. Nothing comes of the action.

In mid-April, 1908, Leon Rebovski, Mike Pitnicka, Anton Gaitha, and Stencil Dombroski, all in their 20s, are arrested with police claiming they can shed light on what happened in the Dominski killing. They are later released.

Outcome: Unsolved.

1908: Lorain Chief of Police Braman is in trouble with the courts because of seeming complicity with houses of ill fame in that city. In summer editions of the *Elyria Telegram:* "Go to breeze blown, wave washed Cedar Point." U.S. boxer Jack Johnson KOs Tommy Burns and becomes the first Black man to be the heavyweight champion. The reason you don't know who Katie Casey is because you never sing more than the chorus! Britain's Liberal Government establishes an old-age pension of five shillings a week. The Ottoman Empire is kaput. Austria uses that as an excuse to annex Bosnia-Herzegovina. China's Last Emperor is the two-year-old Puyi. The poliovirus is identified. Paul Brown, of football fame, is born in Norwalk, Huron County, Ohio. In the Docket: Abandonment of Children. William Howard Taft (Ohio Republican) wins the Election with 51.6% of the popular vote. 97 lynchings: 89 Blacks, 8 others.

1908, January 20, Monday, about 10:00pm:

Joe Doneski and Joe Sknoicki have made trouble for John Washnack before. Everyone knows there's bad blood between the three. In December of last year John swore out warrants against both Joes for threatening his life. Doneski and Sknoicki were arrested and hauled into Lorain's Mayor's Court where they plead guilty and are fined.

Monday evening, January 20, the three men bump into each other at Kelly and Tigue's Saloon, at the corner of 30th and Palm in Lorain. If they'd all been a little smarter, they would've backed away. Instead, they trade harsh words, and before you know it, John Washnack is running for his life.

He heads towards the South Lorain woods with Doneski and Sknoicki in hot pursuit. A large, loud, and somewhat drunken crowd follows. Washnack makes it more than a mile before Doneski gets close enough to "tap" him on the back of the head with a long, oak club. Washnack goes down and Doneski begins to beat him mercilessly.

Some in the crowd try to stop the one-sided battle. Sknoicki shoves them back, threatening them with the same treatment that Washnack's taking. By the time Doneski's finished, his victim's head is literally beaten to a pulp. After the last strike, those in the crowd hear Doneski say, "in Slavish," "There. I hope you die."

Joe Sknoicki is arrested almost immediately and held without bond. Joe Doneski heads for family in Pittsburgh, Pennsylvania, and cannot be found. He is arrested a week later when he sends a letter asking for money to a Lorain friend who is brave enough to turn the letter over to the authorities.

Pittsburgh police are wired and make the arrest. Like his partner in crime, Doneski is held without bond.

Investigators turn up a number of witnesses. All tell different versions of the story. Several are arrested as flight risks and held on $300 bonds. There is no doubt in the mind of Coroner S.E. Miller. He thinks both Doneski and Sknoicki are equally guilty of the crime. Miller is expected to recommend a charge of murder in the first degree.

The Grand Jury proves difficult. Witnesses give incomplete, conflicting, or changing testimonies:

> This same situation has been met with before in a number of cases. Foreigners who have been relied upon by the state as its principal witness have come into court at the trial and have shown an amazing ignorance of the accused man's connection with the crime. This has led to the belief that either money has been used or the men have been coerced by friends of the prisoner. *The Elyria Chronicle, April 9, 1908.*

After being placed on hold for the April, 1908, Republican primary election, the Grand Jury returns an indictment for murder in the first degree against Joe Doneski with Joe Sknoicki aiding and abetting. Bond for each is $3,500. Each will have his own trial.

The criminal proceedings have a rough start when Edson Hastings and Frank Whitman appear on the list of potential jurors. They're both dead.

Twin resurrections are not required when Doneski's attorneys convince him to avoid the death penalty by pleading guilty to murder in the second degree. Joe Sknoicki follows suit and pleads guilty to manslaughter.

Judge Hayden sends Sknoicki to a term "consistent with the law" at the Mansfield Reformatory.

Hayden then sentences Doneski to life in the Mansfield Reformatory. Then, realizing his mistake, the judge calls the guilty man back from his cell to resentence him to the Ohio Penitentiary in Columbus.

This sentence/resentence causes considerable consternation among lawyers on both sides of the case. Defense attorney Adams maintains that the judge's action invalidates any sentence made and submits that Doneski is now a free man. A nice try, but it doesn't work out that way.

This is the first case in which I saw local newspapers apply the word "alleged" to a murder or murderer.

Judge George Hayden:

George Hayden was born in Sharon Township, Medina County, Ohio, on April 5, 1840. He enjoyed both public and private educations, and then went on to Hiram College, Hiram, Ohio.

In 1861, Hayden enlisted in the Union Army and served under Commander (and future U.S. President) James A. Garfield. He was at the siege of Vicksburg where his brother was fatally wounded. By 1863, George Hayden was in very poor health, but recovered.

A Republican, he was elected as the Medina County Clerk of Courts for two terms, starting in 1879. Then elected to Medina County Common Pleas Court Judge in 1900. At this time the district judges were busy working through old cases and so each shared their load with the other: Judges Kohler of Summit, Hayden of Medina, and Nye of Lorain.

G. Hayden died in office on November 28, 1910, three months from finishing his term. He had been very tired and taking nitroglycerine to "improve his heart action." Hayden was buried in Spring Grove Cemetery, Medina, Ohio.

1908, January 20, Monday: Location: Lorain. Victim: John Berta (Barbo, Barta, Barto). Suspect: Steve Garvey (Garman, Garvay), Steve Cepis (Sepos), Daniel Pap (Pop), Joseph Pap (Pop), and Emery Pap (Pop). A street fight that escalates out of control. Cause of death is skull fracture. Takes several days for the victim to die. Newspaper accounts are confused because of the large number of people involved. *Italicized names* do not show up in the court docket.

January Coroner's Inquest: Witness Steve Horitz testifies that Joseph and *James* Pap struck the victim over the head while Garvey, Sepos, and Dan Pap were assaulting him. After Berta fell to the ground it was Dan Pap who struck him with a club.

April Grand Jury indicts all five on charges of murder in the second degree. Bond $3,500 each. Outcome: Steve Garvey and Joseph Pap plead guilty to manslaughter and are sent to Mansfield for 1 to 20 years.

All others are discharged by the court. Cost is "several thousand dollars."

1908, January ?: Lorain, 400-block Burton Street. Victim: The body of a newborn baby boy is found at the construction site of a new house by 9-year-old Ernest Carlisle, son of Mr. and Mrs. Charles Carlisle of Houghton Street. The lad is on his way home from school when he finds the tiny, frozen body lying in the snow several feet from the house. It is wrapped in an old, blue jacket and calico apron and covered with a newspaper. The infant's skull is fractured by a blow from a blunt object.

Coroner Miller said the baby was fully developed and at least week old when killed. Outcome: Unsolved.

Newspaper accounts say this is the "second baby murder mystery within a month." I couldn't find the other.

1908, January 31: *Elyria Telegram:*

Blames Buster and His Like.

"I believe that the circulation of these comic supplements such as the Kaztenjammer Kids and the like have a demoralizing effect upon boys and they are often led to do things by seeing these pictures which they would never think of otherwise," says Supt. Eldredge of Lorain concerning the destruction of [growing plant] vines on the school house.

1908, March 20, Friday: Location: Lorain, 10th Avenue. Victim: Joe Dovisak (Dobesak, Davisak). Suspect: Frank Dick. Victim and suspect are "fellow foreigners." Dovisak is found in a partially constructed building. Frank Dick is arrested after bragging in a barber shop near the scene of the murder that he had "done for a man."

Dick is indicted by April's Grand Jury for murder in the second degree. Plea: Not guilty. *Changed to:* Guilty of assault and battery. Outcome: County Workhouse, 60 days, plus court costs of $25.

1908, April: Stories from "United Press" start appearing in local papers. The focus of front page news shifts dramatically from regional to national. Only divorce cases of some notoriety show up on the front page.

1908, April 26, Sunday: Location: Lorain, National Tube Company. Victim: Julius Zernikow. Suspect: Thomas McLane. Act: Shooting. Police think this a "random killing." Suspect released. Outcome: Unsolved.

1908, June 27, Saturday Morning:

Lum Kee, owner of a laundry in the 900-block of Broadway, Lorain, is taken seriously ill and cannot continue his work. He appeals for help to Wong Kee, a man of some note in the Cleveland Chinese community. Wong Kee sends to Pittsburgh for Yung Pa, "a celebrated washer and ironer." Yung Pa runs the laundry on Broadway for one month, until June 27, when he is found dead, his "head beaten to jelly" with a large, iron bolt.

Police pick up one James Naylor as a witness. Naylor confesses to being part of a plot to drug and rob Yung Pa in exchange for $50, half the loot the victim was supposed to have been carrying. Naylor claims he lost his nerve and never showed up. It was his partner in the plot, a now-vanished brother-in-law Raymond Connors, who proceed alone and resorted to violence.

June 30: At Coroner Miller's inquest, Raymond Connors' wife is implicated as standing guard while the crime took place and escaping with him on an east-bound passenger train. Authorities begin their search for the Connors. It soon involves the entire region.

July 1: James Naylor is taken to the County Jail in lieu of $500 bond. Mr. and Mrs. Connors are still at large, though it is reported that police expect an arrest shortly.

July 3: A substantial fund has been collected by the "Chinese of Cleveland" to help in the search and prosecution of the suspect. The organization is headed by Wong Kee, 710 Superior Avenue, N.E., Cleveland.

July 8: Connors is claimed to have been arrested and will be brought to the city in the next week. This report turns out to be false.

July 10: Light-hearted article:

> Hero Will Save A Shirtless City: Celestial Comes Back To Lorain To Sort the Wash:

> Bushels of stained shirts and collars, which have lain in a Lorain laundry since the murder of Yung Pa are to be released by the heroism of Lum Kee, the owner of the laundry, who leaves a bed in a Cleveland hospital to sort and return the wash....The Cleveland and Pittsburgh Chinese won't go near the laundry. It is possessed with devils, the devils that choked the life out of poor Yung Pa, they insisted. Lum Kee is going to the rescue—today. *The Evening Telegram, July, 8 1908.*

October: James Naylor (now "Maylor" in the papers) is released from the County Jail after being held for 90 days awaiting the arrest of Connors and his wife (now "Conners" in the papers). Naylor says he's willing to be a witness whenever Connors is brought to justice.

December, 1908: Lorain County Sheriff Ward heads out to Allentown, Pennsylvania to pick up Connors and his wife where they have been arrested.

Their return is delayed by the fact that Pennsylvania Governor Edwin Stuart is on Christmas vacation and not available to sign the extradition papers.

December 30: The Connors arrive in Elyria. The wife wanted to be shackled to her husband, but he advised against it. Connors denies he is responsible for the death of the "chink" (**the newspaper's word**), though he was in Lorain that night and did leave on the train police said he was riding. Connors' young and rather attractive wife (the former Miss Jacobs of Elyria) is not taken into custody. Charges that she materially helped her husband in the crime have been dropped. The two have been married about eleven months.

1909, January 2: Connors is bound over to the Grand Jury under a $5,000 bond. The charge, according to the papers, is murder in the second degree. Connors smiles at wife during the proceeding as if the hearing is a joke. He is represented by Elyria attorney Q.A. Gilmore.

January 14: Many witnesses are called to Grand Jury. According to *The Evening Telegram:*

> For the first time in the history of Lorain county grand juries, it has been necessary to secure the services of Chinese interpreter, Wong Vie an intelligent Chinaman of Cleveland will translate the testimony of the Lorain Chinamen who will testify before the grand jury in the Connor murder case. Wong Vie is manager of the Gold Dragon Company Restaurant on the public square in Cleveland and speaks the English language in a very fluent manner.

The Grand Jury is out from 2:00pm, January 13 until 9:10am, the next day. At 6:30pm, after supper at the Feed Stable, they ask to review the testimony given by Alfred Donet, but defense attorney Gilmore refuses. Judge Washburn denies the jurors the testimony.

January 19: The Grand Jury indicts Raymond Connors on the charge of murder in the first degree.

March 3: At his criminal trial, following the presentation of what amounts to purely circumstantial evidence, Connors is found guilty. When the verdict is announced, the man screams in horror and faints into his wife's arms, pulling her to the ground. Both become so hysterical that they do not hear the recommendation for mercy that changes the sentence from death to life in prison.

Judge Washburn calls for Dr. French to calm Connors and his wife.

Before French arrives, the guards "force" whiskey down Connor's throat, whereupon he half-regains his senses to begin to fight the men helping him.

Once calmed, Connors is sentenced to life in the Ohio Penitentiary in Columbus plus court costs of $1,205.37.

May 13: Lorain authorities now say they're not certain that Connors is the murderer of Yung Pa.

July 14: Defense attorneys Nieding and Gilmore petition for a new trial. They charge "that the court erred in permitting certain testimony to go to the jury," that "the prosecutor made a mistake in his address to the jury," and that the "jury was guilty of improper action."

December 28: The Circuit Court reprimands Prosecutor Stevens "for language used in the Connors murder case." Despite that, the request for a new trial is refused. The life sentence stands.

1910, March 22: Dallas Washington (60), defense witness in the Connors murder trial, is found convulsing in his room. Post mortem was unremarkable. One theory among the public is that he died from alcohol poisoning; another, that he was murdered with strychnine.

1911, April, 27: It's revealed by Prosecutor Stevens that he withheld evidence during the trial that indicated that the victim, Yung Pa, had converted to Christianity and that he had been in correspondence with a number of Sunday school teachers and a variety of young women as well.

1914, January 23: Raymond Connors has become a "trusty" of the penitentiary and is allowed to come and go as he pleases. "He often being encountered on the streets of Columbus, by officers from this county."

1914, October 14: Connors seeks parole but is turned down. He is now described as "an all-around crook."

December 7: Now being called "Harry Sisson" (since that's his "real name") Connors is characterized as "a rambler, a bigamist, a thief, and a pool room shark."

It is also reported that Army Air Captain John Cochran, a local expert on all things Chinese, thinks Connors/Sisson is innocent, the real murderer was Chinese, and the killing was done in revenge against Yung Pa for a supposed role in a plot against the Chinese Emperor. Cochran offers no proof of his statements.

1915, January 11: Outgoing Ohio Governor Cox commutes Connors/Sisson's sentence from life to three to fifteen years. The man has been a model prisoner in his time at the Ohio Penitentiary in Columbus.

1909: Jigsaw puzzles. Sports columns start to appear in newspapers. The Crazy Snake Rebellion in Oklahoma. President Taft builds the first Oval office. He also sends marines to Nicaragua after two U.S. citizens are executed there. There is an assassination attempt on Taft. Britain creates its secret service in fear of German spies. In July, the Lorain County Grand Jury finds "the (criminal) dockets are indifferently kept." It's bad enough that some prisoners are released due to lack of documentation. The National Association for the Advancement of Colored People (NAACP) comes to life, partly in response to multiple lynchings in Illinois. 82 lynchings in the entire U.S.: 69 Blacks, 13 others.

1909, January 18, Monday: Location: Lorain, Joe Simarelli's (Zizarelli's, Zicarilli's) Saloon. Victim: Joseph Jas. (John) Watson (55 Colored). Suspect: John Williams. Act: Trauma. Victim Watson is an "ex-preacher and a card shark" (likely not as rare a combination as one might think). He had been the pastor of second Baptist Church of Lorain but left preaching a year ago to work as a bricklayer's helper. "In his odd hours, he gambled, being very proficient with the cards."

Ex-Reverend Watson wins all of Williams' money. There is an argument. Watson pulls a knife. Be that as it may, that argument comes to a reasonably peaceful end.

Williams leaves the saloon only to return about a half-hour later, brick in hand, which he hurls at Watson who is struck just over the right ear. He dies of a fractured skull at St. Joseph's Hospital some hours later.

April Grand Jury: Suspect is indicted for murder in the second degree. Defended by Attorney Charles Adams. Plea: Not guilty. *Changed to:* Guilty of manslaughter. Outcome: Ohio Penitentiary, 15 years, no solitary, plus costs.

1909, March 8, Monday: Location: Elyria, North Street. Victim: Earl Francis (21 Colored). Suspect: Kale Moore. Victim Francis dies of a fractured skull several hours after a brutal assault. Suspect maintains all along that he's innocent.

Story 1: Moore's wife and Earl Francis are arguing. The woman leaves the house with Francis closely following. The woman stops walking. Francis continues and is shouting his arguments at a distance when he confronts an unknown man who is standing on the street. Moore's wife calls out a warning for Francis to stay away from the man who strikes Francis to the ground with a long, umbrella-like object and then runs away.

155

Story 2: Moore's wife drags an already-unconscious Earl Francis from her home to the place where she claimed he was killed by a man who was a stranger to her.

Both stories end with Francis being carried to the Moore house by witnesses who find the suspect of the case (Kale Moore) asleep.

Moore is arrested. His wife is held as a witness and may be charged with being an accomplice.

In the April Grand Jury the defense attorney is Clayton Chapman. Coroner Miller's inquest brings no damaging testimony to light against Moore or his wife. Police are convinced the suspect and his wife are not telling the whole story. There is no indictment. Outcome: Unsolved.

1909, July 16, Friday: Location: Lorain, Joe Petro's Saloon, 2900-block Penfield Avenue. Victim: Alex Szantaj (Santay). Suspect: Joseph Petro (who lives in the 300-block of 12th Avenue).

Victim Szantaj, a well-known Lorain butcher, walks into Petro's saloon where he observe two women buying pails of beer. Szantaj makes a crude remark about the women. Petro is offended and attacks, "beating him to the floor and twisting his arms and legs." When the fight is broken up by others, it is found that Szantaj is paralyzed from the neck down.

Petro is arrested, charged with assault with intent to kill, and released on bond. Szantaj dies July 22. Coroner Miller's inquest says it's murder. Petro is rearrested and charged with murder in the second degree. He is re-released on $5,000 bond.

At the August Grand Jury, Petro arrives late. When his name is called, someone else answers "out of town" which causes a loud round of laughter. Petro is indicted for murder in the second degree. He pleads not guilty.

Victim Szantaj's widow is seriously injured when thrown from her carriage a few weeks later. Their one-year-old daughter, Helen, dies after a short illness on September 30. She is buried at the Elmwood Cemetery from the Reformed Church.

Joseph Petro's criminal trial is a debacle. The main witness for the State tells such a different version of the events which led to the death than he presented to the police and Grand Jury that it is useless to continue. Prosecutor Stevens has no other choice than to nollie the murder charge against Petro.

Say the papers:

Judge Hayden who is familiar with the manner in which

foreign witnesses fail to recollect facts when testifying against their own countrymen, commended the prosecutor on the stand he took in the matter saying it was the best thing to do.

Had a record been kept of the testimony offered before the grand jury, there is little doubt but that some witnesses could be punished for perjury, an action the prosecutor would like to bring in the present case. *The Evening Telegram, October 21, 1909.*

The total cost associated with the case: $122.41.

Petro returns to work once he's released. On November 2, he leaves for the saloon at 11:00am as usual, but doesn't return. Mrs. Petro says that it's not all that unusual since he often left town on business without telling her ahead of time, but that this time she's worried considering the trouble he's been in over the past few months and the rumors that his life has been threatened.

The saloon owner returns home, unharmed, two weeks later. On November 19, one day later, Deputy Sheriffs Salisbury and Van Dusen try to levy a judgment upon Petro for attorney fees involved with his murder trial. Petro becomes so enraged and threatening that Van Dusen is forced to pull his revolver.

The lawmen withdraw, procure a warrant, and arrest Petro on the charge of resisting a police officer. He is out that same day on $200 bail.

Attorney Harvey E. Gougler, member of the law firm Gougler and Adams that defended Petro, files suit against him to recover $500 in legal fees incurred while defending him in court. An attachment is also filed charging Petro with trying to dispose of property to defraud his creditors.

Petro agrees to make good on the legal fees and his other monetary problems. The officers drop their charge of resisting.

Petro's Saloon is in business, at least until the end of the year, when the establishment is mentioned in a story where yet other man has received a severe beating, but this time at the hands of a customer and not the owner.

1909, October 12, Tuesday:

Several years back Mr. and Mrs. William Elliott moved their family from Elyria's West River Road to a farm in Pittsfield Township. They figured it was a better place to raise their kids. Of late they aren't so sure. Their daughter, Clara (20, "brunette, rather full faced and good looking") has taken up with 22-year-old Roy Hines, a hand on the nearby Pitts farm.

The boy has family in the area: Sisters Mable Carruthers and Iva Hines up in Oberlin and his grandfather, Edison Hastings, over in LaGrange, but Roy is something of a drifter. He never keeps a steady job, preferring to move from place to place, doing what Clara's parents consider simple-minded work.

Clara and her sweetheart are engaged despite her parents being dead set against the relationship. Mom and Dad are pushed over the edge upon discovering that Hines has taken advantage of their Clara. They threaten to send her off to the "industrial school" if she doesn't break her engagement (likely the Girls' Industrial Home, a farm in Delaware County, Ohio).

When confronted with his vile behavior, Hines is man enough to confess his guilt. He then proclaims his love for the young woman and runs from the house shouting "I'll marry Clara or kill myself!" He then he's off to his father's farm, Chauncey Hines, in Ashtabula, Ohio.

Clara returns to her work as a housekeeper for widower Thomas Crabtree and his children on Cortland Street over in Wellington. Relative calm returns. Clara's parents, while disappointed with their daughter's serious lack of judgement, consider the matter closed.

Then Hines returns from Ashtabula and without permission visits his Clara at the Crabtree's. The two are alone in the house.

Neighbors hear gunshots: two—two more—and two more after that. A dazed and bloodied Roy Hines emerges from the Cortland Street home and stumbles into Charles T. Jamison. Roy declares that he has shot himself and asks to be taken to a doctor. Neighbors rush into the house where they find a wounded Clara Elliott and the weapon, a fully-loaded, 4-shot, Iver-Johnson .32 caliber pocket revolver. Coroner Miller will come to figure it would've been reloaded at least twice in the process of firing bullets into both Clara and Roy's heads.

Both shooting victims are placed on the Green Line car that speeds them to Elyria. Clara has been wounded twice in the head. One bullet entered her right cheek and lodged itself in the bone under her right eye. The other, to her right temple, passed through her brain end exited the other side. She cannot be roused and dies soon after arriving in Elyria.

Roy is in extreme pain but semi-conscious and still able to speak, though it's mostly nonsense. He has been shot three or four times in his head, both to his forehead and in his left ear. Despite multiple gunshot wounds, his brain suffers no significant damage. He is given some chance for survival due to the minimal power of the firearm that was used.

Clara's funeral services are held at Rimbach and Friday's parlor.

Conducted by Rev. T.W. Grose, they are well attended by upwards of sixty people. She is buried in Wellington.

Within a week Roy Hines, a very good and appreciative patient, is able to walk. Rumors abound that the suspect has been caught in several escape attempts. Doctors and hospital staff ridicule that idea, saying he's hardly strong enough to walk let alone run.

Justice J.C. Conway and Constable Cahoon visit Hines in his hospital room to charge him with murder in the first degree. By October 30, he is well enough to be taken to the County Jail as long as he remains under a doctor's care.

Hines tells reporters that he's being treated well in jail besides that he "doesn't get enough to eat." The truth is quite different. Hines is despondent and depressed. He tries to kill himself by drinking a large quantity of disinfectant that makes him sick but isn't fatal. His attempted suicide is kept from the public until after his trial.

Roy Hines is nervous at the November Grand Jury and complaining of pain in his head and jaw:

> Hines was a dejected looking mortal as he awaited the opening of court, the scars from the gunshot wounds showing plainly through the whiskers which covered portions of his face, and connected with the hair on his head which has no evidence of ever having been brushed or combed. Powder burns were in evidence around his ears and a long scar on his forehead showed where a bullet had furrowed along his skin and spent itself in some unknown spot. *The Evening Telegram, November 11, 1909.*

He has no money. The court assigns attorneys Charles Adams and Clayton Chapman to defend. Hines pleads not guilty.

It's noted that Hines has changed his story since his arrest. At first he tells authorities that he shot Clara and then himself at her request, in a murder-suicide pact. At the Grand Jury he says a despondent Clara used the revolver to shoot herself with the expectation that he would soon follow.

William Elliott, father of the victim, strongly refutes any notion of a double suicide. The brother-in-law of the accused, H.G. Carruthers, disagrees with Elliott, saying Clara's family interfered with the engagement and forbade their daughter from marriage. Says Carruthers, "Better judgment on the part of the young people and her parents who denied them the right to marry would have saved both sadness and trouble and all would have been happy today."

No matter the actions of the living, dead, and wounded, Hines is indicted for murder in the first degree. His criminal trial starts December 6 with Judge Washburn presiding. It is expected that the case will be one of the defense trying to obtain a recommendation of mercy from the jury to avoid execution.

In the court room. Hines complains of being cold and accepts the offer of a raincoat as he moves his chair closer to a radiator.

There is some trouble seating a jury because of scruples against the death penalty. This doesn't impede progress since, after six jurors are seated, Hines pleads guilty to murder in the second degree.

Defense attorney Chapman believes the accused's state of mind at the time of the shooting justifies the plea. "It is evident that public sentiment is against the death sentence."

Prosecutor Stevens had his sights set on a first degree charge, but agrees to accept murder in the second. "I consented to this plea largely on account of the defendant's dull face and apparent lack of mentality. The accused scarcely seemed aware of what was going on around him. He is a rural and simple man, clinging to 'sun time' in reckoning the hour of the day."

Judge Washburn sentences Roy Hines to life in the Ohio Penitentiary in Columbus plus court costs of $234.61. Instead of keeping the guilty man at the County Jail for a few days after sentencing, Hines is hustled to the Ohio Penitentiary in Columbus within hours of hearing his fate. The reason? Sheriff Ward is afraid Hines will kill himself while in the County Jail.

The last statement Hines makes to the sheriff is to the effect that he'll be out in a few years as long as he behaves himself. That turns out not to be true. In early June of 1915, Hines is denied parole despite his assurance that "he has received sufficient punishment" for the murder of Clara Elliott.

1909, September 20: *Elyria Evening Telegram:*

Women Should Hide Spavins—Imperfections Reason For More Modest Bathing Suit Crusade:

Alderman George Emener of Queens, New York, who had considerable to do with the recently passed ordinance that women bathers should wear more clothes, said today; "Our beaches are sights. New York women are anything but lovely in bathing suits. There is an average of 50 ladies with the spavin, 23 who are bow-legged, five or six weighing less than

100 pounds, very skinny; seven or eight with elephantiasis, and 18 with knock-knees. I don't see why these women are so anxious to exhibit their imperfections. It is a horrid example for children."

So you know... A "bone spavin" is a growth within the lower hock joint of horse or cattle. I think in this context, it's meant to refer to much-less-than-attractive knees.

1909, December 28: *Elyria Evening Telegram:*

Auto is Used to Haul Sleigh Party—New Wrinkle In Bob Sled Practice Becoming Popular as the Snow Improves:

No it was not a horning which attracted the attention of residents of this city Tuesday evening, just a merry party enjoying a bob sled ride. The bob being hauled about the streets by means of a small auto of the runabout type. The next thing Elyrians will behold will be a sled attached to the anchor rope of an airship, with the aerial craft furnishing the horse power for the atmospheric coast line.

I think a "horning" is the insistent blowing of a car's horn.

1910 – 1919: County Population = 75,037

1910: Haley's Comet's going to end the world, according to Camille Flammarion. It doesn't. Chicago doctor James Herrick identifies sickle cell anemia. *The Firebird.* Edward VII dies. Long live George V. Congress attempts to control prostitution with the Mann White Slave Act. A ten-year revolution in Mexico kicks off with a nine-year border skirmish with the U.S. Sun Yatsen and others merge their interests to become China's Nationalist Party. Japan annexes Korea. Revolution in Portugal deposes their king. 76 lynchings: 67 Blacks, 9 others. $1,000 is worth $24,920 modern.

1910, March 29, Tuesday: *Elyria Evening Telegram:*

> Notorious Man and Woman Removed by a Triple Shooting—Ruby Richards and David Vesper Dead as Result of Night Tragedy: Third Victim Also—Sister of Richards Woman is Found Dead Across Her Body—Vesper Did Shooting and Finished by Sending Bullet Into His Own Head While Upon the Bed.

> A double murder and suicide at Lorain, Monday night, removed Ruby Richards and David Vesper, two characters well known in the county court. The third victim is said to be Miss Bessie Mitchell, aged 35, a sister of Mrs. Richards. Vesper did the shooting as the result, it is believed, of the woman's refusal to give him money. The bodies of the two women lay upon the floor, with that of Miss Mitchell on top, while Vesper, gun in hand, was propped upon the bed.

> Ruby Richards had often been indicted and fined as the result of keeping a house of prostitution in Lorain. Vesper was a gambler and sporting man. In one case he was made defendant by a woman whose husband had lost money through his operations.

> Passersby heard three shots in the house. The front door was locked but the rear door was open. A light was seen in Mrs. Richard's room. Here Mrs. Richards was found, her head in a pool of blood with a bullet wound in the left side of her head above the ear. A part of her left forefinger was shot off, indicating that she had raised her hand in a feeble attempt to protect herself. She was attired in street dress. In the forehead

of the body of Miss Mitchell was a bullet hole just above the left eye. She was clothed in night attire. On the bed was the form of Vesper, propped against the footboard. Blood flowed from a wound in the right side of the head, just above the ear.

The police department was notified and ambulances were called. The bodies were removed to the Wickens Company's, Helfrich's, and Reichlin, Reidy and Scanlan's morgues. Coroner Miller and the police are investigating.

Ruby Richards has operated resorts in Lorain for years. Her home was in Braddock, Pa.

At the first of this year when Mayor King took his office, he ordered all keepers of resorts to quit business. Since that time Mrs. Richards has been living with her sister, Vesper boarding at the same house.

Bessie Mitchell came there about Christmas and had resided with her sister. Vesper has been a hanger on at the Richards place for several years and has been a familiar figure in police circles.

When the police examined the body they found that Mrs. Richards had $5,330 in cash tucked in her stocking. There were two $2,000 [*sic*] bills and others of high denomination.

For several days, neighbors say, Vesper and the women have been quarreling—Vesper had repeatedly demanded money of Mrs. Richards and she had as often refused the request.

Within an hour after the killing, hundreds of people flocked to the morgues to see the victims. Half a dozen special police were necessary to keep the crowds out of the buildings.

Mrs. Richards was formerly a resident of Cleveland. She was forty-two. She had always had a fad for diamonds and is said to have worn more of these gems than any other woman in Lorain. At one time recently she was closeted in her rooms with a Cleveland jeweler and $20,000 worth of diamonds were examined before a choice of several stones was made. She had been notorious in police circles for years.

There is a report among the friends of the trio that recently there has been a coolness between the woman and Vesper and that the former has made several efforts to drive Vesper out of the city and away from her.

Vesper was arrested about a month ago on the charge of keeping a gambling establishment. He was convicted and fined $50. Since that time he has spent practically all his time about the Richard's place.

Investigation by the police last night showed that Mrs. Richards came here from Cleveland about eight years ago and married William Richards, who died a few years ago. The police found numerous letters and souvenir cards from Braddock, Pa. None of them contained any facts which had any bearing up the tragedy.

In the room were two half-pint whiskey bottles partly emptied. The apartment was in perfect order and there was no evidence of a scuffle.

1910, June 2: *Elyria Evening Telegram:*

Was Pittsfield Farmer Murdered? Note Found On Supposed Suicide Not His Writing:

Coroner S. E. Mailer is making further investigations as to the cause of the death of S.E Johnson, who it was believed had shot himself in the temple last Friday. Residents of Pittsfield, where the death occurred, are inclined to the belief that Johnson was murdered and that the note left for the dead man's family, supposed to have been written by himself, was written by another.

The note which was found in a book carried by Johnson, read: "I hope you will be satisfied when you find me." This, Pittsfield residents say, was not in Johnson's handwriting. Figures and notes in the book do not compare with the letters in the note.

Coroner Miller began his inquest this afternoon. The gathering of evidence, he says, will require several days.

Outcome: Cause of death was ruled a suicide.

1910, August 4, Thursday, 9:30pm:

John Francis "Frank" Walkinshaw, of Pennsylvania, marries the beautiful Mary Kell(e)y, of Ohio, on June 16, 1896. The couple lives in Altoona, Pennsylvania, where he works as a telegraph operator, before moving to Lorain, Ohio. Older brother, Vincent, already works in the Lorain City Safety

Department. Younger brother, Frank, already something of a drinker, takes a job as a saloon-keeper. Mary, also known as "Mayme," is admired and well-liked in her community. She is a daughter of Dave Kelley, a successful real estate dealer with political aspirations.

In 1908, eight years after arriving in Lorain, Mary Walkinshaw appears before Probate Judge Hinman to swear an affidavit of insanity against husband Frank who "has been acting queerly for some time past."

Walkinshaw is taken into custody by Deputy Sheriff Ray Van Dusen. Once in his cell, Frank is examined by Judge Hinman and Dr. French who decide the bulk of Walkinshaw's problems are caused by his hitting the bottle a little too hard. The judge and doctor are of the opinion that a little enforced sobriety will greatly improve Frank's sense of reality. Sure enough, a few days on the wagon render him very nervous but talking and acting in a sane manner.

Later that year, July 25, a month past their twelfth anniversary, Mary files for divorce. She alleges that Frank has been a habitual drunkard for the past three years and refuses to hold a steady job, though he is capable. What's more, he's hocked their valuables to pay for his drink. Under the circumstances, Mary asks for custody of their four sons and one daughter.

Frank begs Mary not to go through with the divorce. He promises to give up the liquor and support their family. They agree to reconcile. Mary cancels the proceedings.

Almost exactly two years later, July 22, 1910, Mary re-files for divorce. She claims all efforts to reform Frank have proved futile. His brother Vincent, now Lorain's City Safety Director, has money owed to Frank. Mary asks it be given to her so she can, at least, retain her family's furnishings.

Frank has been out of the house and is living in central Pennsylvania when he's served papers on both the divorce and injunction his soon-to-be ex-wife has obtained to keep him out of and away from their home on Lorain's Livingston Street. He's on the next train to Ohio.

Walkinshaw disembarks at Pittsburgh long enough to buy a revolver. Then it's on to Cleveland. He arrives in Lorain on the Green Line a few minutes after 9:00pm, Thursday, August 4.

Less than a half-hour later all five of the Walkinshaw children are awakened by the sounds of gunfire. They run, screaming, to the neighbors who summon the police.

Mayme is found face-down at the top of the stairs. Shot through the heart, she is breathing but beyond help. Frank, downed by two severe scalp wounds, has fallen across her body.

At first, Frank says he shot his wife, then tried to commit suicide. He claims remorse for failing to "finish the job." As he recovers, he tells a different story: that he was trying to kill himself, that Mary tried to grab the gun and was accidentally shot during the tussle.

Police doubt this to be true since powder burns on Mary's dress are insufficient to support Frank's assertion that the woman was shot at point-blank range. Mary Walkinshaw is buried from Lorain's St. Mary's Church on August 8.

The September Grand Jury indicts Frank Walkinshaw on charges of murder in the first degree. He is not present for the arraignment because of a paperwork foul-up by his lawyer. When Frank does appear, a week later, he pleads not guilty.

Sheriff Ward of the County Jail calls Frank a "model prisoner who is at all times polite and obedient." He also shows no fear or concern about his upcoming trial—with good reason.

On November 11, Frank pleads guilty to murder in the second degree in front of Judge Washburn. A petition is presented with hundreds of signatures of Lorain and Elyria businessmen stating that justice would be served with the second degree charge.

Frank Walkinshaw, along with brother Vincent, sign a statement stipulating that they will never seek parole or commutation of the mandatory life sentence. Vincent also promises to raise his niece and nephews.

Prosecutor F.M. Stevens advises the court that it is almost impossible to convict a man of first degree murder "in this day and generation" without ending up with a recommendation of mercy, which results in a life sentence anyway. Stevens states he will accept the plea to save the county the money always involved in a capital case.

Judge Washburn sentences John Francis Walkinshaw to life in the Ohio Penitentiary in Columbus, plus court costs of $22.34.

On November 14, the day before Frank Walkinshaw is transported to prison, the *Elyria Telegram* prints an editorial saying, in part, that it's a sad case when a man can "deliberately stalk into the home and shoot down the woman he swore at the altar to protect" and get away with it.

The paper goes on to call the judgment "questionable mercy" since "a good many men who have looked into the stuffy cells at the Ohio Penitentiary would take the electric chair in preference to a life sentence."

Mary Walkinshaw's killer never finds out what that's like.

1917, July 18: *Elyria Telegram:*

> Man who Killed His Wife to Enjoy Freedom Once Again: Frank Walkinshaw, of Lorain, who shot and killed his wife at their home in this city about seven years ago has been pardoned from the Ohio Penitentiary in Columbus by Governor Cox.
>
> Walkinshaw was given his freedom on condition that he attend church regularly, keep out of saloons, leave intoxicants alone and report monthly to the prison warden.

Parole, it seems, was recommended by the Board of Pardons for Frank and more than thirty other murderers that term. Frank Walkinshaw served fewer than 7 years for the planned shooting death of his wife and mother of five children, the beautiful Mary Kelly.

Walkinshaw dies in Cleveland, Ohio, on January 18, 1935.

1910, September: Lake Shore Railroad abandons the telegraph for the telephone, despite increased cost, because telephones produce "better results."

1911: Indianapolis 500. Ray Harroun beats the pack. Baseball pitcher Cy Young retires. Wurlitzer builds his first movie theater organ. Irving Berlin's *Alexander's Ragtime Band.* Jelly Roll Morton. Italy invades Libya. Taft sends marine back to Honduras to protect U.S. banana plantations. Germany starts poking the bear by sending warships to Agidir, a French-controlled port in Morocco. Edward Carson stumps for forceful protection of Protestants in North Ireland. Widespread revolution in China. The word "Vitamine" is coined by Casimir Funk for substances that prevent diseases of deficiency, like rickets and scurvy. Roy Rogers is born in Cincinnati, Ohio. 67 lynchings: 60 Blacks, 7 others.

1911, January 8, Sunday: Location: South Lorain, Joe Sabb's Saloon. Victim: Peter Johansye (Johansyi, Janosy). Suspect: Joe Farkas. Act: Shooting. Charge: Murder in the second degree. Plea: Not guilty. Outcome: Not guilty. Cost: $164.29.

1911, March 17, Friday: Location: One mile west of Oberlin along the tracks of the Lake Shore Railroad. Victim: Unknown White male infant. Act: Suffocation. The body is found in a paper-wrapped shoebox by two young boys, Fred Evans and James Herkley(?). They take the package to the Oberlin freight depot and the coroner is summoned. Findings are inconclusive: either the baby was born prematurely and dead at the time of birth or it died of "suffocation due to the negligence of an unidentified mother." Outcome: Unsolved.

1911, June 18, Tuesday, early morning hours: Location: South Amherst, in "the Hungarian settlement." Victim: Ameil Kolander. Suspect: Bronislav Gursk aka Benesel Gerski aka Bronislar Gurski. At first, papers have the crime completely backwards, with Kolander doing the stabbing and Gursk the victim. Even when that error is corrected, news stories are completely at odds with what's reported in court.

Papers say: One Mary Ketchut was engaged to victim Kolander, and the bridal party was travelling to Lorain to tie the knot. On the way, the woman met one "John Utrich" and decided not to marry Kolander who agreed to give up his bride-to-be as long as he was reimbursed for the cost of the wedding and reception party (such a romantic, this Kolander).

Kolander, who gave up his bride, then became exceedingly drunk at the reception he wasn't paying for, went to the home of a man named "Gursk," and began a quarrel during which Gursk grew so enraged that he slashed Kolander, opening a wound several inches long.

Gursk then took off for the woods. He was described as five feet, six inches tall, sandy hair and moustache missing one finger (or part of a finger) on his right hand. Bloodhounds were brought in to track him. Heavy rains turned the woods into a series of small lakes that the dogs could not manage. Nearly a hundred men searched around the quarries but were unable to find the suspect.

A $100 reward was offered for the capture, dead or alive, of Bronislav "Will-'o-the-Wisp" Gursk, who foiled professional trackers and bloodhounds and hid himself in the "wilds of South Amherst."

Gursk surrendered to Justice E.C. Schuler of Amherst at 5:30pm, Wednesday, June 28. He said he had hidden for so long because he feared a lynching and had concealed himself in "the old quarries."

During the September Grand Jury, newspapers report that a jealous Gursk killed Kolander at the wedding as Kolander and Mary Ketchut walked to the altar. This in front of more than twenty witnesses. Gursk is indicted for murder in the second degree.

Plea: Not guilty. *Changed to:* Guilty of manslaughter. Outcome: Ohio State Reformatory at Mansfield, until discharged by law, plus costs of $228.79.

1911, September 16, Saturday: Location: Lorain, on one of the "business streets." Victim: Tom Sugey (35, "a Croatian"). Suspect: Eli Brecki. Act: Sugey attacked Brecki with a knife before Brecki killed him in self-defense. Per police, the crime was the result of a long-standing quarrel. Charge: Murder in the first degree. Plea: Guilty of murder in the second degree. Sentence: Life in the Ohio Penitentiary in Columbus.

1912: Iceberg off the starboard bow! W.C. Handy's *Memphis Blues.* The Republic of China with Sun Yatsen as its president and the abdication of the Child Emperor Puyi. Tibet declares its independence after the fall of China's imperial rule. Revolution against Turkish rule kick-starts the Balkan War. Lenin forms the Bolsheviks with himself as the leader. In Italy, Benito Mussolini, Socialist, becomes the editor of his party's newspaper. The Negro Rebellion in Cuba. Taft sends marines because of the island's political unrest. Nicaragua gets a visit, too. A short one, for now. Vitamin A. Presidential Candidate Theodore Roosevelt is shot. Undeterred, he finishes his 90-minute speech. Woodrow Wilson (New Jersey Democrat) wins the Election with 41.8% of the popular vote. In the Docket: Horse stealing. New Mexico. Arizona. And, that's it for new states until 1959 when Alaska and Hawai'i are added to the pile. 64 lynchings: 62 Blacks, 2 others.

1912, September 3: Voters approve 33 of 41 amendments to create a new Ohio State Constitution. *Among the winners:* Voter-led referendums; giving the Governor line-item veto power in appropriation bills; giving the legislature the power to fix daily hours of labor, minimum wage, and establishing a workers compensation system. *Among the losers:* Giving women the right to vote in State Elections; removing the word "white" from the State Constitution when specifying certain rights; the use of voting machines; state regulation of outdoor advertising; and an end to the death penalty.

1912, January 15, Monday: Location: South Amherst, Kendeigh Corners (near the intersection of Middle Ridge, Quarry, and Rice roads). Victim:

William Uckinick. Suspects: Martin Frenolan (Fernolan, Fernoland) and Frank Barosky (Boroski). Act: Shotgunned.

Uckinick is killed at a wedding celebration in a battle between guests and party crashers. Witnesses say Frenolan opened fire with a shotgun, taking out one of Uckinick's knees. That is the wound he dies of several days later.

After the shooting, one guest takes the shotgun from Frenolan and uses it to crack him over the head. A different guest beats him with a shovel. Frenolan is hospitalized, then develops pneumonia from which he must recover before a trial can take place.

Children playing in the snow find a blood-spattered shovel and "choked and exploded" double-barrel shotgun believed to be the murder weapon.

At trial, the accused, Frenolan, is still in tough shape from his beating and illness. Charge: Murder in the second degree. Plea: Not guilty. Jury deliberates ninety minutes. Outcome: Not guilty.

All charges against the other accused man, Barosky, are nollied by the Prosecutor when Frenolan is found not guilty. Court gives defense attorneys Adams and Resek, of Lorain, $500 and not the $1,000 they asked for because only one of the two accused was tried.

1912, January 14, Wednesday: Location: Lorain. Victim: Steve Horvath (Horvach, Harvath). Suspect: John Fejes. At first, newspapers have victim and suspect reversed.

Victim Horvath has won the hand of a pretty, young lady who spurned suspect Fejes as "too old to wed." The newly-married Horvath is killed not long after the wedding while trying to eject the recently-rejected Fejes from an unnamed drinking establishment.

Charge: Murder in the second degree. Plea: Not guilty. Found: Guilty of manslaughter. Outcome: Ohio Penitentiary, 6 years, plus costs of $111.82.

Says the *Elyria Evening Telegram (Feb, 28, 1912)*:

> It is becoming more and more common for juries to be lenient with foreigners as long as they shoot their fellow countrymen instead of selecting some American for their victims, but consensus of opinion is, that inasmuch as it is such an easy matter for an alien to become a citizen of the U.S. the courts should not be criticized for not being over anxious to shoulder the responsibility of transforming them into law abiding citizens.

1912, March 5, Tuesday: *Elyria Evening Telegram:*

Lorainites who happened to be out of doors Sunday evening (March 3) were witnesses of a remarkable spectacle. In the southeastern heavens there appeared a large meteor bar, probably the largest and most vivid ever seen here. It rose rapidly towards the zenith and was visible for five or eight minutes. There were no spots apparent, but the light formed a long bright bar, resembling a "white hot" steel rail.

Many saw the spectacle and marveled at it. It was visible for such a long time that the news spread rapidly and from homes in all parts of the city there were interested watchers.

I think the phrase "meteor bar" is what we might call a "fireball." A check of other papers turned up no reports of unusual sky activity on March 3, 1912. I also checked several historical records of meteor(ite) sightings and found bupkis.

1912, May 18, Saturday: Location: South Lorain, the basement of Fertalji's Saloon, East 28th Street. Victim: Tony Bodanger (Banyak, Banjuk) (28). Suspect: Peter Harambasic (Aranbasic) (21). The act takes place at a dance where partiers had been "indulging in liquid refreshments until the male members of the party were in a condition to [either] dance or fight."

Suspect Harambasic is captured almost immediately a few blocks from the scene after knifing Bodanger. The victim is hospitalized for three deep cuts and dies Monday (May 20) after considerable suffering from punctured lungs and loss of blood. Witnesses say there was absolutely no provocation for the act.

There is an indictment for murder in the second degree by the July Grand Jury. Defense is Attorney A.E. Lawrence. Plea: Not guilty. Found: Guilty as charged after 15 minutes deliberation in what is still one of the speediest murder trials in the history of Lorain County. Outcome: Life in the Ohio Penitentiary in Columbus, plus costs of $306.23.

Elyria Evening Telegram (August 2, 1912):

The crime was of a cold blooded nature and if the fact that Harambasic will spend the rest of his natural life behind prison walls serves as an example to other foreigners, society will have secured some compensation, but at an awful cost to the unfortunate foreigner.

1912, October 12, Saturday: Location: South Lorain. Victim: Simon (the "Giant of South Lorain") Stamibola (Stamibula). Suspects: Andrew (Andy) Bobic (Bodic) and Vasil (Stencil) Bobic (Bodic).

Stamibola, as his nickname implies, is a large and strong man. He has been in Lorain only a few weeks when, boasting that he can win the favor of the bride, he tries to invade a boarding house where a wedding celebration is underway.

Lorain Police Office Feldcamp has been keeping watch over the party. When there is no trouble by midnight, he decides to leave. As he reaches the sidewalk he hears a commotion on the porch. Looking back, he sees Stamibola, lying on his back, feet hanging down the steps, and "literally carved to pieces" by the men angered by his attempts to crash the party.

The victim is hauled inside. His dying statement names his attackers as party guests Andrew and Vasil Bobic. Vasil is found in an agitated state, hiding in the basement. A blood-smeared Andrew is located in an upstairs bedroom, fully dressed except for his shoes. At the January, 1913, Grand Jury, both are indicted for murder in the second degree.

At the criminal trial younger brother Andrew takes ownership of the crime, pleads guilty to manslaughter, and describes how the victim choked him until he drew his blade to begin cutting.

There are prosecution witnesses who say the brothers shared in the killing but Vasil, with Andrew in his corner, maintains his innocence. The court decides that only the two brothers know who is guilty, take Andrew at his word, and accept his plea of guilt. Suspect: Andrew Bobic. Charge: Murder in the second degree. Plea: Not guilty. *Changed to:* Guilty of manslaughter. Outcome: Ohio Penitentiary in Columbus, 5 years, no solitary, plus costs of $330.88.

The second degree murder charge against Vasil Bobic is nollied by the prosecutor once brother Andrew is convicted of the crime.

1913: Amendments to the *U.S. Constitution: Sixteenth:* Removes restrictions preventing Congress from directly taxing income. *Seventeenth:* Popular vote elections for U.S. Senators. State governors can only make temporary appointments of senators until a special election can be held. The "Great Lakes Hurricane." Erector Set. Arthur Wynne publishes the first crossword puzzle. Work is completed on the Ohio Reformatory for Women in Marysville. No more female prisoners for Columbus. Jim Backus (Mr. Magoo and Thurston Howell, among others) is born in Cleveland, Ohio. The U.S. begins a 21-year occupation of Nicaragua. In the Docket: Begin seeing "Concealed Carry." 52 lynchings: 51 Blacks, 1 other.

1913, May 19, Monday: Location: Oberlin, Mechanic Street (may be Locust or "Frankfort," depending on the house number). Victim: Infant. Suspect: Mrs. Clayton (Francis or Mary) McConico (29). Mrs. McConico and her husband, Clayton, have been separated for two years. She and at least three children were living alone in near destitution. Child in question is born sometime the evening of May 19. Dr. Hutchins, "township physician," is called to the home the morning of the May 20 and finds the infant's body in a pail of water. The post-mortem leaves some doubt as to whether the baby was actually born alive. The suspect was home alone at the time.

Mrs. McConico is arrested May 20 by Marshal Paden but, because of her physical condition, is allowed to remain at home until she is arraigned before Oberlin Mayor Yocom. Mrs. McConico is then placed in the Elyria Jail in default of a $1,000 bail. She is indicted by the October Grand Jury on the general charge of "Murder" to which she pleads not guilty. Outcome: Found not guilty.

Clayton McConico (41) plead guilty to a charge of "nonsupport of a minor child" on April 4, this same year. He received a suspended sentence on payment of $,1000 bond.

1913, August ?: Location: Lorain. Victim: Mark Lanar, saloon porter. Suspect: James White (Colored). A saloon shooting. White is about to kill a (Colored) woman. Lanar steps between them and takes a bullet to his head for his troubles. Shooter White, "the son of civil war slaves, had no education and [is] considered a dangerous man by those who knew him," is captured a few hours after the crime. The October Grand Jury indicts for murder in the first degree. All preparations for trial are made when the accused pleads guilty to second degree murder. Say the papers:

> Although White was indicted on a first degree murder charge, it has been the custom for many years to permit them to plead guilty to second degree murder, as juries seldom return a verdict on the first count without recommending mercy at the hands of the court. *(Elyria Evening Telegram, October 25, 1912)*

Charge: Murder in the first degree. Plea: Not guilty. *Changed to:* Guilty of murder in the second degree. Outcome: Life in the Ohio Penitentiary, plus costs of $85.48.

1913, September 28, Sunday, about 10:00pm: Location: Lorain, corner of Lexington Avenue and 13th Street. Victim: William Chrospowski (50). Act: Trauma. Chrospowski is found by William Hunter, brewery wagon driver. Police and ambulance are called. Chrospowski never regains consciousness. He dies at St. Joseph's Hospital of a skull fracture at the base of the brain. Outcome: Unsolved.

1913, October 14: *Elyria Evening Telegram:*

May Remove Phones From School Rooms at an Early Date—School Board Deplores the Trivial Messages Which are Received:

The discarding of the school telephones is being seriously considered by the city school board. They are so generally used for the transmission of trifling messages or the directing of children to do unimportant errands that they seriously interrupt the teachers in their work. School officials find the 'phones a practical necessity, but on the other hand they are used by people generally as a mere convenience.

The principals of the buildings, who are regular teachers, are interrupted in their work by every call, and the chances are that some other teacher must also stop her work to take a message—for herself or for some pupil. The senders perhaps all think their messages important, but as a matter of fact they range all the way from appointments to meet after school to small errands to be made at the store.

At a recent meeting of the Board it was decided to restrict the use of the phones, to school officials and for school purposes. It will be granted that in extreme cases, as sickness or death, the schools may be called and the message given the principal to be delivered to the proper person. If the publication of this ruling does not very materially diminish the trouble complained of the phones will be discontinued.

It's not the technology. It's the people.

1914: George Ruth is nicknamed "Babe" when he joins the Baltimore Orioles. Robert Galambos is born in the City of Lorain. His research will prove that bats find their way, and their prey, thru the use of sound. He coins the phrase "echolocation." His later research lead to the development of tests that allow for cochlear implants for those who are profoundly deaf. Tinkertoys. A gallon of gasoline costs 18 cents—don't forget to adjust for inflation! The Bluff Indian War against the Ute and Paiute in Utah. The heir to the Austro-Hungarian throne and his wife are assassinated in Sarajevo. Europe tips into *The War to End All Wars*. Wilson send marines to Haiti to restore order after a series of political assassinations. The Panama Canal opens for business. St. Pete to Tampa, in Florida, is the route of the first scheduled airline flight. Ford Motor introduces the assembly line for its Model T, cuts its standard workday from 9 to 8 hours, *and* bumps wages from $2.90 to $5.00 a day. Charlie's *Tramp*. Bernie's *Pygmalion*. Electric traffic lights are installed in Cleveland, Ohio. 55 lynchings: 51 Blacks, 4 others.

1914, August 28, Friday: Location: South Lorain. Victim: Joseph Serdi (Sardi). Suspect: Mike Szakacs (Szakas). Victim Serdi is a musician at a wedding party. A bottle thrown during a fight strikes him in the right eye, fracturing his skull and causing death. The criminal trial before Judge Redington crawls due to the fact that each witness needs an interpreter. "As expected," each tells a different story of the beer bottle battle.

On the witness stand, one of the musicians claims his bass fiddle was ruined "during the fistic bombardment." Szakacs, the accused, claims self-defense since it was the musicians who attacked when he criticized their playing. Charge: Murder in the second degree. Plea: Not guilty. Found: Guilty of manslaughter. Outcome: Ohio Penitentiary, until discharged by law, plus costs of $181.73.

Judge Horace Greeley Redington:
H.G. Redington was born in Amherst, Lorain County, Ohio, on July 10, 1858. A farm boy, he was educated in public schools in both Amherst and Oberlin, then attended Oberlin College, but left to read law in 1880.

He was admitted to the Ohio Bar in 1884 and hung his shingle in Amherst. After serving 8 years as Mayor of Amherst, he was appointed as a Common Pleas Judge from September to November of 1914.

The November election of 1914 resulted in a tie between him and fellow contender W.R. Thompson. Redington kept the judgeship (**because possession's nine-tenths of the law, I suppose**). The general election two years later resulted in another term, ending in 1929 when he refused re-nomination due to poor health. H.G. died May 13, 1937, at the age of 78 after a long illness. He was laid to rest in the family mausoleum in the Crown Hill Cemetery in Amherst, Ohio.

1915: The northern portion of Avon Township separates to form Avon Lake. Black boxer Jack Johnson loses to Jess "The Great White Hope" Willard. "Typhoid Mary" Mallon is arrested in new York. *Pack Up Your Troubles* by George Asaf and Felix Powell. Yet another version of the Ku Klux Klan is founded in Atlanta, Georgia. Raggedy Andy and his better-known sister. You know they're siblings 'cause they're cut from the same cloth! William (Billy) Strayhorn is born in Dayton, Ohio. If you've never listened to his music, you should. In Chicago, 844 people die when the S.S. Eastland rolls over while taking on passengers. Wilson tell the Germans to quit poking the bear. Everyday automobiles grow fast enough to "turn turtle." Iron and steel workers strike for an eight hour day and higher wages, y'know, like Ford provides its crews. In the Docket: Still seeing "horse stealing," but on November 13, Harry O'Connor is apparently the first in the county charged with "Operating [a] Motor Vehicle without Owner's Consent." He pleads guilty. His sentence of ten days in the County Jail will be suspended if he pays court costs of $10.13. 69 lynchings: 56 Blacks, 13 others. $1,000 is worth $24,422 modern.

1915, February 13, Saturday: Location: Lorain, Black River. Victim: Martin Lasko (Latsko). Suspects: Tom Derzaj (37), Steve Yonowich, George Valkovan, Tom Sugaj, and Steve Bofea. A drunk Lasko leaves his home, is seen staggering towards the Black River, and vanishes. He may have drowned or, perhaps, met with foul play since he was known to have been carrying a considerable sum of money.

Lasko is found floating in the Black River near the pump house at National Tube on April 23, more than two months after he disappeared. His skull is fractured over the right ear and his pockets are empty.

All five suspects are arrested. Only Derzaj is held for trial. Charge: Murder in the second degree. Plea: Not guilty. Outcome: Grand Jury does not indict. Tom Derzaj is set free. Crime is unresolved.

Suspect Derzaj was suffering from tuberculosis before his confinement. Being in jail aggravates the illness. National Tube (where he worked as a "pipe straightener") sends him to St. Anthony's Hospital in Columbus for treatment. He dies in late June, 1915, leaving a wife and two children in Austria.

1915, February 18: *Elyria Evening Telegram:*

Eugenist [*sic*] Tells How to Get a Child of Any Desired Type.

According to Mrs. Viola Mizell Kimmel of Bellville, Ontario, lecturer on eugenics, all the mother need do is "get a picture of a child who has the admired characteristics and look at it longingly at regular intervals for several months before the baby is born. Any desired color scheme involving the eyes and hair or formation of features frequently can be controlled in this way."

1915, December 26, Sunday: Location: Lorain. Victim: (Harriet) Centuria Lewis (14 or 15 or maybe 16). Suspect: Ernest Crutchfield (33 or 39, Negro). Shooting. Suspect Crutchfield claims he was cleaning a revolver when it accidentally discharged and struck Lewis in the abdomen. He didn't know the gun was loaded. Witnesses say Crutchfield pointed the revolver at Lewis, asking if she "dared" him to shoot, and then pulled the trigger.

Victim Lewis dies at St. Joseph's Hospital on December 28. Suspect Crutchfield is taken to the County Jail on December 30.

Criminal trial is halted on February 10 when the accused suffers a grand mal seizure. The defense then tries to prove the accused is an epileptic and, at times, mentally irresponsible. The Prosecutor's physicians testify that the accused is "too old to be subject to epilepsy."

Charge: Murder in the second degree. Plea: Not guilty. Outcome: Guilty of manslaughter. Sentence: Ohio Penitentiary from 1 to 20 years, plus costs of $157.69. Appeal for new trial is overruled.

September 26, 1916: Crutchfield dies in the penitentiary. According to prison officials, while in his cell, he experienced a seizure, took a header from his cot, and fractured his skull. The dead man's friends say his death proves he was not always able to control what he was doing.

1916: Thirty-four female inmates are transferred from the Ohio Penitentiary in Columbus to the brand-new Woman's Reformatory near Marysville, Union County, Ohio. The National Park Service. The R.O.T.C. American Elms start dying in earnest. Measles kills 12,000 in the U.S. The majority of victims are under five years old. Polio kills more than 6,000 and cripples thousands more. Many summer amusements are closed out of fear of both diseases. President Wilson sends marines to occupy the Dominican Republic as that that county slides towards civil war. They'll stick around for eight years. October brings extra-deadly storms on Lake Erie. Woodrow Wilson (New Jersey Democrat) wins the Election with 49.2% of the popular vote. 54 lynchings: 50 Blacks, 4 others.

1916, March 30: *The Union County Journal, Marysville, Ohio:*
Woman Was Murdered.

Elyria, O., March 28—The mutilated body of a women was found in the woods on the Albert Mills farm, four miles east of this city, by a boy employed by the Mills. The body lay face down in a deep ditch in the heart of the woods. Coroner C.G. Garver says he believes the woman was killed two weeks ago. There is no mark of identification on the body.

1916, March 28: *The Times-Democrat, Lima, Ohio*
Slain Woman Camp Employee, Opinion: Lorain County Officers Seek Pipe Line Layers as Witnesses.

ELYRIA, March 28.—County authorities are trying to find members of a labor camp, located until several weeks ago near Ridgeville, in an effort to solve the mystery of the death of a woman, about 30, whose body was found partly covered with earth in a ditch near that village Saturday evening.

Officers are working on a clew [*sic*] that the woman was a cook at the camp and that probably she was hired through a Cleveland employment agency. The camp was composed of employees of a gas company, laying a pipeline from Berea to the National Tube Co.'s mills in Lorain. The camp was abandoned upon the completion of the line.

The woman's head had been crushed and her body bore five knife wounds. A calico dress that she wore had been torn to shreds, leading the officers to believe she had struggled with her assailant.

The murder is believed to have been committed some distance from the scene of the finding of the body and the body then carried to the ditch for concealment.

Coroner Garvey declared the woman had been dead at least a month.

1916, March 29, Wednesday, about 3:50am:

An engineer confused by severe fog and what seems to be a misbehaving caution light near Amherst stops the eastbound Buffalo Limited. Minutes later, there is a collision from behind by another eastbound train. Not long after, the westbound Twentieth Century Limited, the fastest train on the planet, crashes into the wreckage.

Considering the size and circumstances of the accident, the human toll seems relatively light: 27 killed and 47 injured. Of the dead, five are unable to be identified at least in part because of ghouls who robbed the pockets of both the freshly killed and injured. The five unknown are buried in a common grave in the Amherst Crownhill Cemetery. One is later exhumed and identified by his family.

Human beings take the brunt of the early blame, particularly Herman Hess, engineer of the second train. It's eventually decided the overriding cause was a combination of the foggy weather and a malfunctioning track switch.

It's difficult to find local newspapers published in the days immediately after the wreck. That's why you see murder references to sources outside of Lorain County.

1916, March 29: *The Sandusky Star-Journal:*

Lorain county officials expect to have substantial clues on which to trace the murderer of the woman whose body was found in a wood at Ridgeville Sunday, by Wednesday night. The woman is supposed to have been a native of Lorain and married to a Columbus man.

The clothing on the dead woman's body is eventually used to positively identify her as Mrs. Anna Mouff, of Ridgeville, Ohio. She and her husband had gone from that small town several weeks prior. As might be expected, authorities have great interest in finding and questioning Mr. Mouff.

1916, April 3, Friday, evening hours:

It's always tough in Amherst, Ohio, when the quarries are on strike. It leaves too many hard-working men with too much time. Idle hands are the Devil's workshop.

Martin Bischoff (Bishop) owns a set of those idle hands. He usually keeps busy as a hoister in one of the largest sandstone pits in the world, Amherst Quarry Number 6. With nothing to occupy his attention besides the hubbub and confusion surrounding the big train wreck, Bischoff has managed to work his way up to just this side of outrage.

He can be a difficult man at the best of times. He's in constant pain with severe rheumatism. His English is poor and his near-deafness turns all conversations into shouts. His poor behavior earlier in the day finds him booted out of Mischkas, down on Park, by the retired baseball pitcher Cy Young who plays as a ringer on Amherst's town team.

Several hours of stewing over his perceived maltreatment at Mischkas and the spur-of-the-moment purchase of a revolver, brings an angry, well-armed, and revenge-seeking Bischoff to the Young house on Church Street.

There he accosts Young's brother-in-law, Harold Brown. When he suddenly realizes his mistake, Bischoff leaves as abruptly as he arrived. Harold Brown reports the incident to the police.

Amherst's Marshal, William Miller, begins a search for Bischoff. All Miller wants to do is to disarm the man and return him to his home. Miller has with him Rupert Becker, an Amherst Township constable who works as a night watchman for businesses in the village. He's a good, solid man, who's serious about his work and does it well. But since two-to-one odds aren't quite good enough when dealing with Bischoff, the Marshal also deputizes Amherst native Henry Fields, the former editor of the *Elyria Evening Telegram* back when it was *The Elyria Reporter.*

The men split up. It's Marshal Miller who finds Bischoff in front of the Amherst Telephone Exchange at 280 Church Street. As Miller prepares for the confrontation, the door to the building opens and out walks telephone operator Mrs. Herman Subjenske. Bischoff takes his revolver, puts it in under her nose, and attempts to force the woman back into the building. Miller talks with Bischoff, trying to defuse the situation.

In the midst of the conversation and without warning, Constable Becker appears from around a corner of the building. Bischoff panics, turns, and fires at the now-retreating Becker. The constable is hit twice in the back, one shot each to his right lung and right kidney.

Bischoff takes off. Miller pursues. The commotion draws Deputy Henry Fields who joins the chase. Running full speed, Bischoff turns and fires. The deputy is struck in the right shoulder and goes down. Another of Bischoff's shots ricochets from the sidewalk. One of Bischoff's shots hits Miller in the right foot.

Left behind, Constable Becker, with two bullets in him, staggers into town for help. He makes it to the office of Dr. A.F. McQueen, 200 Park, where he collapses. Henry Fields arrives to gather Amherst doctor Washington Foster, just down the avenue, to assist.

O.H. Baker's ambulance is used to haul the two injured men to St. Joseph's Hospital in Lorain where the gravely wounded Becker is patched up as much as possible. Henry Fields' injuries are minor, relatively speaking.

Bischoff holes up behind St. Peter's at 582 Church, where authorities keep him trapped while reinforcements are called. They appear an hour later in the form of Deputy Sheriffs Jerry Gray, Charles Cahoon, and Henry Haywood plus Elyria Police Officers Clare Sayles and Max Balt. They arrive via "Haywood's machine," driven by Leland Leser who, it is noted in the papers, makes the nine mile trip in a remarkable twelve minutes *(45 mph)*.

Martin Bischoff threatens to kill anybody who comes near but grows distracted by the sheer number of lawmen. He is finally overpowered and captured by Constable Grover Ormsby and Dr. W.H. Turner of Elyria, who sneak up on him from behind.

Planting season makes it difficult to find enough jurors for the April Grand Jury. Once in session, it indicts Bischoff for shooting with intent to kill and wound. At the same time the hospital is reporting that Becker simply cannot recover from his injuries. The doctors say that the bullet that struck the right lung has caused "paralysis of the vital organs."

Constable Rupert Becker (55) dies on April 7, 1916, four days after the shooting. He is buried on April 11, with funeral services held in Amherst's St. Peter's Church. Businesses in town close for the afternoon. Hundreds attend the services held in both German (Rev. J.G. Zeigler) and English (Rev. J.H. Smith).

Martin Bischoff, now charged with murder in the first degree, is allowed to plead guilty to murder in the second. Judge Thompson sentences him in accordance with the law. That means life in the Ohio Penitentiary in Columbus plus court costs of $63.25.

The justification for accepting the plea is that Bischoff does not have a "criminal heart" but, instead, took a human life in a fit of anger. In reality, it's uncertain if the man even understands what's happening.

In 1917, former temporary deputy Henry Fields, recovered from his shoulder wounds, applies for "Workingman's Compensation." Fields' application is refused. Representative W.L. Hughes introduces a bill in the State Legislature to gain recompense. It is voted down.

It's interesting to imagine what might've happened if the armed Martin Bischoff managed to confront his intended victim, Cy Young. Though out of his prime,

the baseball player was a big man, self-assured, strong, and known to be a little stubborn...

Judge William B. Thompson:

W.B Thompson was born in Columbia Township, Lorain County, on September 6, 1863. A graduate of Baldwin-Wallace College, he studied law in the offices of Cleveland's Judge Barber and Lorain County Judge A.R. Webber and was admitted to the Ohio Bar in 1888.

He served as the Mayor of the City of Lorain from 1890 to 1894. By 1896, Thompson was assisting Lorain County Prosecutor Thomas and then, in 1901, Prosecutor Stroup.

Thompson serves as Lorain County Common Pleas Judge from 1915 to 1935 with his first term an appointment to fill a second judgeship created by the Ohio State Legislature due to the increased population of Lorain County.

Thompson left the bench at the end of his term in January, 1935, while suffering mightily from lumbago (severe low back pain). He returned to a few years of private practice and then retired. W.B. Thompson died October 26, 1945, and is buried in Ridge Hill Memorial Park, Elyria, Ohio.

Judge William Thompson is not to be confused with Judge Malcom Thom(p)son of Lorain City Municipal Court who sat, starting in the 1940s.

1916, April 14: *Elyria Evening Telegram*:

Supposed Dead Woman Visits Old Neighbor. Mrs. Anna Mouff and Husband Put in Appearance at Ridgeville. Mysterious case is more of a riddle now. Probable that identity of dead woman will never be positively established.

Who the woman is who was found dead at Ridgeville, several days ago, is more a mystery than ever, as Mrs. Anna Mouff, who was supposed to have been the dead woman, put in an appearance in Ridgeville, Thursday.

The remains had been positively identified as Mrs. Mouff, even to the shirtwaist, which was identified as one given her by her mother.

That the dead woman worked about a camp of men engaged in laying a gas main, is again the limit of police information. Apparently no one knew the woman except by sight.

Sheriff Whitney dispatched Deputy Sheriff Gray, to Ridgeville, to make sure that Mrs. Anna Mouff was alive and the deputy reported that she was and that her husband was with her.

Now that this has been established beyond a doubt, the prospects of identifying the slain woman are not very bright. Where she came from and how she happened to be in the out of the way place her body was found, will probably never be known.

The murdered woman found on the Albert Mills farm in Ridgeville Township back in late March is never identified. The case remains unsolved.

1916, September 27, Wednesday:

Mrs. Minnie Hoffman hasn't been seen for several days. A neighbor finally raises a window in her Lorain house, crawls in, and finds the 46-year-old woman dead on the floor. Her throat's cut, the head almost severed from the body by a gash six inches long and three inches deep. There is, also, a stab wound to the chest. Her condition indicates that she suffered a beating before being cut. The woman lived alone, but there are two whiskey glasses on the table in the room where her body is found. One glass is empty; the other, full. Analysis of the liquor shows no drug or poison.

Police find a bloody footprint on a carpet and a bloody fingerprint on an inside door. The weapon? A gore-covered butcher knife left inside the house. There's no readily apparent motive for the killing, except that it was not robbery—the contents of Mrs. Hoffman's house are undisturbed.

A suspect is arrested on October 3 as he picks up his mail at the Lorain Post Office. Authorities will not disclose what evidence led them to their man and withhold his name, identifying him only as a "foreigner." Jealousy is now thought to be the cause. A second man, named Miller, is held as a witness. Both are in the County Jail.

Within the week, police obtain a confession. The suspect, 25-year-old Nick Shoshetti (Shiochetti), says that he had visited Minnie Hoffman and during that visit the woman stole thirty dollars from him. He grew angry, they quarreled, and he killed her by cutting her throat.

In front of Judge Redington at the November Grand Jury, when indicted for murder in the first degree, Shoshetti pleads not guilty despite his previous, full confession. "The silence that prevailed in the room was noticeable." Lorain Police Chief A.A. King and Plain Clothes Officers David Beatty and Frank Lenahan assure Prosecutor Guy Findley that they have a written confession from Shoshetti. The defense knows there are no witnesses to the killing and is more than ready to fight it out in court.

Shoshetti's story, now, is that the woman, of unsavory character, lured him into the house and then tried to rob him using his own revolver. Her death was the result of his defending himself against her crime.

The papers are disgusted. "Robbery followed by attack, seems to be the story told by most Italians who kill women and girls in this section of the country," says the *Elyria Evening Telegram*.

Shoshetti had told police that he figured he would be convicted of manslaughter and receive 10 to 20 years in the penitentiary. On February 10, 1917, as he predicted, Shoshetti is allowed to plead guilty to manslaughter. Outcome: Judge Thompson does not comment on the crime, but orders the man to the Ohio Penitentiary in Columbus for one to twenty years.

Per the *Elyria Evening Telegram (February 10, 1917):*

> Opinion differs as to whether or not he had ought to have paid the penalty supposed to be accorded those who take human life, but at any rate, it was agreed about the court house, that Lorain County could well spare the gun toter and throat slasher.

Keep an eye out for Policeman Frank Lenahan.

1916, November 18, Saturday: Location: Lorain, boarding house at 2100-block East 28th Street. Victim: Samuel Jansik (50, steel worker). Suspect: Michael Komadina (35, Croatian).

About 10:30pm, two steel workers heading home find Samuel Jansik crumpled with a bad head wound at the foot of his boarding house's exterior fire-escape. He lives for several hours and is able to make a statement to St. Joseph's hospital staff. An autopsy by Drs. David Thomas and F.C. Ward indicates a skull fracture plus numerous small bruises.

Jansik had been drinking the night of his death. Police think the victim was struck over the head with a hatchet and then tossed, head first, down the fire escape. The motive, authorities say, is "the love of a woman." Michael Komadina, who runs the boarding house, is arrested on the basis of Jansik's death-bed statement, even though the now-dead man said he was struck by a female.

Komadina emphatically denies any guilt. He is held without bail and pleads not guilty to murder at December's Grand Jury, which decides the evidence is too scanty to indict. Outcome: Unresolved.

1916, December 4, Monday, shortly before 3:00am: Location: Lorain, 2100-block East 29th Street. Victim: Mrs. Julia Minda. Suspect: Vasily Nagy (41). Nagy is accused of "criminally assaulting" Julia Minda, then saturating her clothing with kerosene and setting her afire to cover his crime. She is completely engulfed in flames but lives for several hours at St. Joseph's Hospital. Newspapers are full of grisly details. Reports are that the victim said "he did it," referring to the suspect, before she dies. Minda's husband was at work when the crime took place.

The warrant for Nagy's arrest is sworn by victim's sister, Mary Valascuk. Trouble is that Prosecutor A.C. Cahoon and police are convinced there is no foul play. Coroner Charles Garver agrees, finding the cause of death accidental and due to an unintentional explosion of kerosene or gasoline. Outcome: Nagy is released.

1917: The Lorain Lighthouse starts operation. Sort of. It won't be completed until 1919. The Original Dixieland Band. Puerto Ricans are granted U.S citizenship. Britain's Foreign Secretary declares his country's (conditional) support for a Jewish homeland in Palestine. Germany allows Lenin to travel home to Russia. They hope his presence will upset the Russian war effort. It sure does: Russia falls into revolution and, by the end of the year, the KGB is in place and suppressing all political opposition to the Bolsheviks. The U.S. severs diplomatic ties with Germany when they invite Mexico to attack to the north and then proceed to sink several U.S. merchant ships. Wilson tells Germany to put up their dukes. Radio Flyer, the wagon, that is. Dean Martin is born in Steubenville, Jefferson County, Ohio. Arthur Schlesinger, Jr. is born in Columbus, Ohio. In the Docket: Non-Support of Family and Children. 38 lynchings: 36 Blacks, 2 others.

April 2, 1917: R.T.J Martin, the owner of the American Shovel and Stamping Company of South Lorain, and his chauffeur, Frank Marshall, are apparently, the first in county to be charged with "Driving Automobile While Intoxicated."

Driver Frank Marshall pleads not guilty, stating he'd only had two glasses of beer and, therefore, could not be considered intoxicated.

R.T.J. Martin starts off by complaining about the filthy condition of the jail and states that building's renovation should be the first order of the day's court. Then, pleading not guilty, he claims that he took the wheel only after determining that Marshall, his chauffeur, was too drunk to drive, and, besides, they were heading home when they were stopped by police.

Martin bails both himself ($500) and his chauffeur ($250). At the close of the trial, the case is taken from the jury with charges nollied by the Prosecutor.

April 16, 1917: R.T.J.M. is back on the same charge. He pleads not guilty (again). Bond is set at $500. The charged is (again) nollied by the Prosecutor, this time because the charge said he was driving on Broad Street when it was actually West Avenue.

May 23, 1917, same guy, same charge, same outcome: Nollied.

All of this must have been hard on his R.T.J.'s brother, A.J.S. Martin, who was, you see, a local, prominent, and vociferous proponent of living the "clean life."

1917, April 2, Monday: Location: Lorain, Carolina Avenue. Victim: Benjamin Musk (Mosk) (stepson). Suspect: Antone Lester (Loster) (45, stepfather). Suspect Antone Lester was released from jail the previous Thursday (March 29) after being held on a charge of assaulting his wife. He becomes involved in an argument with his wife, Mary, and stepson, Benjamin Musk. Lester is "crazed with anger" and shoots both his wife and stepson. Mary, wounded in the arm, runs to a neighbor who calls the police.

Policeman Frank Lenahan responds. He forces a window and starts through it. Lester fires and the bullet creases the cop's abdomen. Undeterred, Lenahan continues after his man. Lester also takes shots at Lorain Police Captain Hugh Reilly and Patrolmen Amos Smith, Charles Wright, and George Carson before making an unsuccessful attempt at suicide by shooting himself in the side. Lester is straightjacketed.

All those suffering from gunshots, including the suspect, are transported to St. Joseph's Hospital where Benjamin Musk dies. A few hours later, with the failed-suicide-bullet still in him, Lester slips his straightjacket, escapes the hospital, and flees back to his home where he barricades himself with a shotgun.

Officers Reilly and Carson make their second visit of the day, breaking down the front door of the house. As they enter, Lester aims his shotgun and pulls the trigger. It misfires. Lester is overpowered and hauled to the County Jail. From there he's transported, under heavy guard, to Elyria Memorial where the bullet from his self-inflicted wound is finally removed from his side. His health improves rapidly.

April's Grand Jury indicts for murder in the first degree. One day into his criminal trial the prosecutor and Judge H.G. Redington allow the accused to change his plea to guilty of manslaughter. Outcome: Ohio Penitentiary, 1 to 20 years, plus costs of $86.67.

Papers note that the court is having trouble gathering jurors. They're not showing up for duty.

1917, April 13, Friday: Location: Ridgeville. Victim: Russell Emmons (18). Victim is from Ridgeville, but born in Elyria. Parents are Arthur I. and Alice Lackorish Emmons. Two siblings, Marjorie and Willard.

Russell is a popular, young man, a senior at Elyria High. He has spent the evening at a youth church meeting. He has escorted a friend home, east of Ridgeville Center, and is riding his bike to his own home when he is struck by an automobile.

Young Emmons is discovered by Elyria taxi driver, Harry "Circus" Miller. The boy is alongside the road, coat buttoned up and wrapped in a blanket—meaning somebody had tended to him before he was found. He is unconscious upon arrival at Elyria Memorial with little hope of recovery. He dies three days later. Cause of death is a skull fracture. Buried in Ridgeville Cemetery from Ridgeville Congregational Church.

Locals observed two cars racing along the road about that time, 11:00pm. Tire tracks are plain to see on the highway. Police think the vehicle may have been a Packard from Cleveland and are working the case.

The May Grand Jury investigates the death. Now it's a Buick Roadster with its owner subpoenaed. The evidence is too weak to indict. The suspect is never named. Outcome: Unresolved.

June 6: Victim received high school diploma posthumously.

1917, April 14: *Elyria Evening Telegram:*

> Record Breaking Number of Marriage Licenses Demanded—Young Men Are In Love Or In Fear Of Having To Enlist.
>
> Dan Cupid is breaking all records for April. So far this month 40 licenses to wed have been issued by the probate court, as compared with 43 issued for the entire month a year ago.

Sixteen licenses were issued for the first half of April last year with almost three times that number being issued for the same period this year.

Truly, "In the spring a young man's fancy softly turns to thoughts of love," and it might be added, to escape enlisting.

1917, April 19: *Elyria Evening Telegram*:

Order Aliens to Turn Over All Weapons—Chief Stankard Issues Notice to the Unnaturalized Citizens of This City to Turn In Guns, Revolvers, Bombs, or Instruments Written in Code.

This in response to President Wilson's Proclamation of April 6, 1917, making it illegal for "alien enemies" to have such items. Several hundred non-citizens in Lorain County begin the process of applying for citizenship.

1917, May 16: *Elyria Evening Telegram*:

Mexicans are Invading Lorain in Droves, Says The Chief of Police—Twenty of Villa's Countrymen Discovered in an Old Building:

Lorain is becoming distinctly cosmopolitan, according to Police Chief A.A. King, who watches closely the influx of new people drawn to this city by the wave of industrial expansion and progress.

The police department thus far has been able to cope with the constant tide of certain kinds of new-comers whose chief dereliction appears to be the result of a bibulous fondness [drunkenness].

What the police are unable to account for is the appearance here of so many Mexicans. They have come to Lorain in droves since the first of the year. Sanitary Officer James Price the other day was called to inspect a building and found more than a score of Mexicans housed in an old frame building in the suburbs where the windows had been out and the place unoccupied for years. The Mexicans are employed in local construction work. many of them at the Lorain electrical building and plant.

There are today probably a score of languages spoken in Lorain, including Chinese and Japanese.

1917, June 7: *Elyria Evening Telegram:*

Might Recover Breath; Cash? Well Scarcely—John Ammenhauser is Alien Enemy Of The Country, Says Court.

Because he is of German birth and not a naturalized American, John Ammenhauser of Amherst is not only classed as an alien enemy, but he has no standing in the courts in the country in which he resides.

He filed suit to recover the sum of $500 but he will be lucky to recover his breath when he realizes the position he occupies as long as the U.S. is at war with Germany.

1917, September 1, Saturday, early afternoon:

There's something wrong with Ed Hazen according to his wife, Ella, and she should know. They were married in Pittsburgh, Pennsylvania, on the first of July, 1912. Soon she was carrying a child who turned out to be their son, Edward Jr. But it was right after she became pregnant that things got a little weird.

In January of 1914, Ed up and joined the U.S. Navy to get the $150 signing bonus. Thing is, he used the assumed name of "Thomas Reno." Then he deserted. Well you couldn't do something like that and not expect consequences. Ed was captured and placed in the Navy Prison at Portsmouth, New Hampshire, for almost two years. "Thomas Reno" then received a dishonorable discharge.

Ed had a married sister in Cleveland, Ohio, and so the Hazens moved there to make a fresh start. Ella had just become pregnant with her second child, little Mary Jane, when Ed turned so terribly mean that she was forced to take the children and move to Lorain.

Ed has been bothering the three of them ever since. First, he promises to change. Then he makes threats of violence. It's reached a point where Ella can't stand being in the same room with him. On August 23, 1917, she sues for divorce. He's cruel and does not provide for his family. She has to sell her jewelry to feed her children and herself. As part of the case, Ella seeks to keep him from disposing of their furniture, and for support to dun the salary he earns as a clerk with the Cleveland office of the New York Central Railroad. That's $100 a month.

It takes a while for divorces to work through the courts. Her case is finally scheduled for mid-September. As far as Ella's concerned, it can't be over soon enough.

It's a week after she files, a pleasant Saturday. Ed stops by to visit the kids which is fine with Ella, as long as he stays on the porch. She won't let him in the house where the neighbors can't see what he does. Ella stays inside, keeping her contact with him to a minimum.

Ed's always been pretty good with the kids, smiling and content in their company. He paces the porch floor, carrying 5-month-old Mary and talking with Ed, Jr., who's almost 5 now. He places the baby in her carriage and calls his son to him, father and children sharing a moment, together.

The father suddenly pulls a revolver from his pocket. He places its muzzle near his baby daughter's heart and pulls the trigger. Quickly throwing his arm around his son, he sends a bullet through the boy's body. Turning his weapon on himself, Edward C. Hazen fires again.

All three are near death by the time Ella makes it outside. Father, son, and daughter are taken to St. Joseph's Hospital in Lorain. Of the three, only the shooter survives. Ed managed to kill his kids, but he missed his own heart.

From his hospital bed, Hazen says he does not want a lawyer. "I want the maximum penalty." On September 13 he is released from the hospital to the Lorain County Jail. Doctors expect a complete recovery.

He is charged with two counts of murder in the first degree. Despite his earlier request for the maximum penalty, Hazen pleads not guilty when bound over to the Grand Jury. There is no bail.

Hazen remains weak and pallid and insists on seeing his wife. "She would come to see me, if you would ask her to. After the shooting and after I had shot myself, she came to me, took my head into her arms, and said she forgave me."

Ella does not visit. Instead, she sues her husband's place of work for allowing him to carry a concealed weapon. She seeks $1,000. She does not win the case.

The Grand Jury indicts Ed Hazen for murder in the first degree. Hazen's defense attorney, C.F. Adams, files a "suggestion of insanity" with the courts. Ed is examined on November 3 by Drs. G.E. French and W.B. Hubbard. Both pronounce the man insane and judge him unable to give testimony on his own behalf.

Says the *Elyria Evening Telegram (November 7, 1917):*

The fact that Edward Hazen, who murdered his two

children in the Port City, has been pronounced insane, takes some of the odium off that city. Lorain of course, can't be held responsible for the acts of an insane man.

Prosecutor Findley believes none of it. He is certain that Edward Hazen has been "shamming insanity" since the killing. Still, on the testimony of five different physicians, the Probate Court sends Hazen off to the Lima State Hospital for the Criminal Insane, where he will likely stay for the rest of his life. If he does ever recover, he will be returned for trial.

1918, June, nearly a year after the shootings, doctors at Lima deem Hazen to be in a "normal mental state." He is returned to the Lorain County Jail on June 14 to be tried on June 21. But, first, it's a trip to Washington D.C. in the company of Sheriff William Whitney to witness the deposition of Jack Burton who was Hazen's keeper during the his first stay in the County Jail.

The law requires those charged with murder in the first degree be present on every occasion when any proceedings are had which may affect the case. Prosecutor Findley and defense attorney Charles Adams are along for the journey. The prisoner is not handcuffed at any time during the trip and his behavior is good.

Hazen's criminal trial starts on June 24. It takes only 35 examinations to fill the jury box. This is considered remarkably quick in the face of pre-formed opinions and scruples against the death penalty.

Everyone is expecting an insanity defense. A number of "alienists" (psychologists) are lined up to testify, though the State maintains that Hazen faked his insanity and was always aware of the enormity of his crime.

The accused is alert and takes interest in the proceedings. His sister, Mrs. L.B. Bryant, of Cleveland, is sitting with him. It is expected that the trial will occupy several days and attract a large number of spectators.

Eyewitnesses describe the facts of the killings. It comes to light that, while lying wounded on the porch, Ed asked his estranged wife for a kiss and forgiveness. Ella, supposing him to be fatally wounded, said nothing, but she did kiss him.

Defense agrees the killings took place as described, but they say he was in the grip of insanity at the time of the killing and so cannot be held responsible for his actions. The first of the alienists has testified when Hazen's defense convinces the State to accept a plea of guilty of murder in the second degree.

The judge sends Hazen to the Ohio Penitentiary for life. He is later transferred to the London Prison farm in Madison County, just west of Columbus, Ohio.

1928, September 27: After ten years of incarceration, the 42-year-old Hazen escapes the farm by stealing a car owned by one of the prison officials. He gets as far as Delaware, Ohio, a distance of 50 miles before he is captured. It's back to the farm pending action by Warden Thomas to return him "inside the walls" for the escape.

1930, June 5: Edward C. Hazen (number 46835) has been recommended for clemency by the Warden and Chaplain of the Ohio Penitentiary. He is deemed eligible in September of 1931. That works out to be about seven years of his life for each of his murdered children.

FILICIDE: The killing of one's child or children.

1917, October 16, Tuesday: Location: Lorain, "near Stop 48 on the Green Line" (the southern outskirts of the city, on Broadway near Baerenwald Park, later known as the Lincoln Park nightclub). Victim: Mary Kocher (Kocker) (13).

Mary, the daughter of Mr. and Mrs. George Kocher, leaves for school but never arrives. Her father makes a search then, unable to find her, calls in the sheriff and Lorain police. The girl is found 2:00am the next morning about 20 feet off the path she took to and from school. She has been raped and strangled to death. An unusual crime for Lorain County.

A $500 reward is posted by County Commissioners. Sheriff Whitney puts up an additional $100. Several suspects are questioned but nobody is arrested or charged. Police figure it may have been a crime of opportunity and that the attacker hopped a car at the nearby stop and left the area.

October 19: An unnamed man, seen in the vicinity the day of the crime, is picked up by police. They search his belongings for a pair of boots to match the tracks found at the scene. He is released.

October 24: It's reported that Deputy Sheriff Hugh McCrae has arrested a Lorain railroad detective, Otto C. Dieschley, at the home of his parents in Garrett, Indiana and charged him with the attack. Dieschley had taken a few days off, he says, to visit with his family before reporting to the Draft Board. He fights extradition. A trip to Columbus is needed to obtain the proper papers. Once in custody, Dieschley is kept separate from all other inmates at the Lorain County Jail. Sheriff Whitney refuses to discuss the case other than to admit the evidence, so far, is all circumstantial.

It's thought whoever killed Mary Kocher also assaulted another young girl in Lorain, Mary Szabo, on September 22. It's hoped she and several other Lorain residents can help identify him.

October 30: Witnesses are unable to pick the suspect out of a line-up as the person spotted near the scene of the crime. Some, including young Miss Szabo, are adamant that Dieschley is not the man. Police are disappointed.

Since the suspect had entered a plea of not guilty at his arraignment, he is released from custody to report for service at the Lorain Draft Board and leaves with the next contingent due for Camp Sherman, Chillicothe, Ohio.

Outcome: Unsolved.

1917, October 30: Ohio legislators give Ohio women the right to vote but those against it force the matter to a general vote. In November, Ohio male voters deny women the right to vote in general elections. And a state-wide prohibition on booze is narrowly defeated.

1917, November 27, Tuesday: Location: Elyria, Depot and East streets, near the Henry Haywood Saloon. Victim: James Baldwin (40). Suspect: George Decker (41). George Decker is a machinist at the Willys-Overland Company. James Baldwin is employed by Garford Manufacturing.

Baldwin is married but not living with his wife. He takes a room in the Decker home, 102 Cleveland Street, Elyria, and becomes infatuated with Mrs. Decker. There is some insinuation that, perhaps, she does not discourage him as strenuously as might be considered proper.

Trouble starts Friday, November 23, when the George arrives home to a locked door with his wife and James behind it. Decker blackens both of Baldwin's eyes and calls the cops. It's Baldwin, *who has been beaten*, who's fined $15 and ordered by Mayor Tucker's Court to stay the heck away from the Decker house. Baldwin is back the next night. Decker tosses him out on his ear.

On November 27, the men happen to meet on the east side of the Public Square and argue. Instead of yielding to good sense, they continue to the Bank Café, where they argue some more, then to the Post Office, then to Martin's Café, and finally to the Haywood Saloon on West Broad.

The two, still arguing, leave the Haywood and walk towards Depot. With witnesses Jude Jones and Dr. G.E. French standing several steps away on Broad Street, Decker produces a recently-purchased revolver and fires five times. Baldwin is struck once in the right hip and twice in his left side.

Police Patrolman Patrick Crehan, stationed at the Andwur corner (Court and Broad), is on his way at the sound of the first shot. He finds Decker standing near the dying Baldwin.

"Here I am, Pat," Decker says as he hands him the revolver. "He forced me to it." George Decker is arrested and held without bail.

James Baldwin is dead before the patrol wagon arrives. His body is taken to Wadsworth's Funeral Parlor. He is survived by his estranged wife, one sister in Grafton, and two in Cleveland.

The January, 1918, Grand Jury takes up the case. It's generally thought that, once facts are known, Decker will be allowed to plead to manslaughter in order to avoid the expense of a trial.

Decker justifies his actions with "the unwritten law." He is said to be penniless. His friends have appealed to the *Bartender Union* to supply part of defense funds which will be bolstered by his relatives. Mrs. Decker, in the meantime, is with her father in New York.

Grand Jury indicts on murder in the first degree. George Decker pleads not guilty.

Early February; jurors are drawn for the criminal trial, but the case is held up when defense attorney C.F. Adams petitions the court to take the deposition of witness Wilbert Tobin who's being processed by the army draft in Ft. Meyer, Virginia. The trip is not needed when Tobin is rejected by the army for not measuring up during his physical exam.

The trial is never held. The accused cops a plea to manslaughter. "George Decker saved the county two or three thousand dollars in court costs, so that there was something mutual in the consideration shown each by the other." Outcome: Decker is sentenced to the Ohio Penitentiary in Columbus for an indeterminate term of one to twenty years. It is supposed that any early release will likely be opposed by the local court officials. That supposition proves inaccurate. Within a year his friends are working to have him freed. Their first attempt at one year fails. They do better the second time around.

On March 31, 1920, and on the recommendations of the Prosecutor, the Judge, the Mayor, and many other prominent Elyrians, model prisoner George Decker is set free. He served less than three years for killing a married man who kissed the wrong wife.

1918: 51.4% of Ohio voters (all male, mind you) approve "Prohibition of the Sale and Manufacture for Sale of Intoxicating Liquors as a Beverage." Every saloon in the state will close on May 26th of 1919. After years of protests and several deaths, British women are given the right to vote—if they're over 30, that is. The 1918 Act also gives the vote to all male citizens over the age of 21 without regard to property or class. In Russia, the Bolsheviks change their name to the Russian Communist Party. Tsar Nicholas II, his wife, and kids are executed. As *The War To End All Wars* winds to a close a world-wide influenza pandemic begins. 30,000,000 (again, *30 million*) die within the year. Dorothy Maguire is born in LaGrange, Lorain County. She will go on to become an All-Star Catcher and Outfielder during her 1943-1949 career in the All-American Girls Profession Baseball League and be part inspiration for the catcher Dottie Hinson in the 1992 movie *A League of Their Own*. Jack Paar is born in Canton, Stark County, Ohio. In the Docket: Selling Cigarettes to Minors. Publishing Obscene Writing. 63 lynchings: 60 Blacks, 3 others.

1918, June 1: Battle of Belleau Wood with more than 1,200 U.S. deaths. Shortly after, all German citizens over the age of 14, who are within the U.S. are required to register with local police as German aliens.

1918, June 27, Thursday, about 9:00pm: Location: Lorain. Victim: Andrew Miller. Suspect: Andrew Genshure (Genshur, Gunshur, Gunchen, Genshuer). Both Andrews are employed at National Tube Company. They live next door to each other in a duplex. The victim and his wife have a seven-year-old son. The suspect and wife have five kids, the youngest, a baby, and the oldest about ten years old.

Both families own chickens over which the wives argue frequently. The birds belonging to one travel to the other's back yard and ruin vegetables there. On the day of the crime, a routine chicken argument between the women escalates to include "personal adjectives and expletives." The men, now returned from work, take up the argument. "They talked plain United States, in the employment of epithets, that gave expression to the contempt they held for each other."

Things reach the point of Genshure fracturing Miller's skull with a club, eluding police and vanishing. Officials circulate photographs of the suspect throughout the region. The July Grand Jury indicts the suspect without his presence for murder in the second degree.

September 16, 1918, Sheriff William Whitney and Prosecutor Guy B. Findley head to a small town in Arkansas to retrieve the accused from authorities. He was identified via his wanted picture printed in a local paper.

Once arraigned on second degree murder charges, to which he pleads not guilty, the accused is released on $4,000 bond.

His criminal trial is before Judge Redington on October 22. The widow Miller, dressed in black, her son, and the defendant's wife and kids make a sad sight in court.

All agree Genshure killed the victim. The trial hangs on who struck first.

Prosecutor Guy Findley and the victim's witnesses insist Genshure was the aggressor, and armed with a club crossed into the victim's property, knocked him to the ground, and beat him until he was dead.

Defense attorney G.A. Rosek and his witnesses maintain Miller was the aggressor and that the motive of the killing was self-defense.

The trial moves slowly. There is some doubt as to the veracity of the translator employed. Witnesses, speaking in Hungarian, give answers requiring dozens of words that are reduced to a half dozen in English.

Jury is out a short time then returns a verdict of guilty of manslaughter. Outcome: Ohio Penitentiary for 1 to 20 years, plus costs of $160.50. Appeal for new trial filed and then withdrawn.

1918, October 2: *Elyria Evening Telegram:*
> At this term of court nothing but criminal cases will be tried. War gets preference over courts and lawyers are busy with [draft board] questionnaires.

1918, September 26: Meuse-Argonne: more than 100,000 killed.

1918, November 11: Cease fire and the beginning of the end of the Great War: Total killed/wounded/missing: *39million+.*

1919: Amendment to the *U.S. Constitution: Eighteenth:* National prohibition of the making, transporting, and selling of alcoholic beverages. Pogo Stick. Jess "The Great White Hope" Willard has his jaw broken in defeat by Jack Dempsey. Babe Ruth is sold to the New York Yankees. The Boston Red Sox get $125,000 for the deal. The end of *The War to End All Wars.* The Irish Republican Army. Mussolini opposes the rise of Socialism in Italy. The Russian Gulags open for business. Adolf Hitler joins the obscure, anti-Semitic, German Workers' party. Afghanistan is recognized as an independent country. Nancy Astor is the first woman to take a seat in Britain's House of Commons. Woodrow Wilson suffers an incapacitating stroke. The country is run by his wife, Edith Bolling Galt Wilson, and Wilson's own Cabinet through the last half of his term. In late April, *The Elyria Chronicle* and *Elyria Telegram* merge to form—what else—*The Chronicle Telegram*. In the Docket: Overloading Trucks, Selling Liquor to Minors, Non-Support, and Concealed Carry. On August 15, Thomas Gendio is, apparently, the first in county charged with "Motorcycle Theft." 83 lynchings: 76 Blacks, 7 others.

1919, January 15, Wednesday: Location: Lorain. Victim: Mrs. Mable Cluley (wife). Suspect: William Cluley (36 husband).

Both are well known and have family in Lorain. They have no children and have suffered marital strife for some time. She leaves him during the Christmas Holidays but returns home.

After another brief, but intense argument, he grabs her, bends her backwards, pulls "an exceedingly sharp" knife from his pocket, and cuts her throat "from ear to ear." Freeing herself from his grasp she runs to a neighbor's and calls for help. "Just before she fell [over dead] her wedding ring dropped from her finger."

Cluley stands on his own porch, watching. After his wife dies, he goes into his home, takes his .38 caliber revolver, and dies by suicide with a gunshot to his head.

1919, January 16: Nebraska becomes the thirty-sixth state to ratify the prohibition amendment. Missouri also votes for ratification later that same day. The nation will go dry July 1, 1920. With ratification, brewers immediately increase the price of a barrel of beer from $10 to $20 a barrel. Ohioans opposing National Prohibition raise a state-wide referendum to reverse the State Legislator's approval of the amendment. It passes, state-wide, by 479 votes and Ohio's approval of the amendment is, uh, amended. The people have spoken. Except, in 1920 the U.S. Supreme Court rejects the referendum, reinstating Ohio's ratification of Prohibition.

1919, March 8, Saturday, 6:30pm: Location: Lorain, 2100-block East 28th Street. Victim: Louis Rovos (Rovis) (44, uncle). Suspect: Dave Vido (25, nephew). Clevelander Vido pleads with Rovos to give up a woman in Lorain and go back to supporting his wife and three children in the old country.

Papers flip-flop over the facts of the matter. At first, the two are cousins, then uncle and nephew. Later, they are brothers-in-law. Also the story changes from one of the suspect being infatuated with the victim's woman to the suspect being disgusted with her. Two things are certain—the deep knife wounds Louis Rovos suffers: one in the neck, the other in the side which pierces the heart. He lives for fourteen hours at St. Joseph's Hospital in Lorain before expiring.

Papers report Dave Vido pleads guilty to murder in the first degree in front of Lorain Municipal Court Judge William P. Duffy in Criminal Court. The docket says he is charged with murder in the second degree, pleads not guilty, then changes his plea to guilty of manslaughter. Outcome: Mansfield Reformatory for 1 - 15 years, plus costs of $92.96. Applies for parole April 30, 1919 and is rejected. He is later released.

AVUNCULICIDE: Killing an uncle.

1919, May 16, Friday:

A railroad worker is making his early-morning rounds walking the Nickle Plate tracks in Lorain when he comes across a badly mangled body. It happens fairly often, what with all the half-drunk tramps staggering along the right-of-way. This beat-up dead body is a little unusual. It has its head on one rail and its feet on the other. Trains are never that neat. There's only one conclusion. This corpse hasn't been struck—it was placed on the tracks in hopes of masking a crime committed elsewhere.

Authorities identify the body as 42-year-old Rocco Tratea (Tropea, Tropia). His throat is slashed, and he's been hacked with what must've been a large knife, meat cleaver, or small axe. Even the coroner and undertakers are shocked, saying that, except for train victims, they've seen few dead bodies in as bad of shape as this one.

A search of the victim's home yields a hidden set of blood-stained bedclothes. Police think the victim was murdered in his sleep with a cut of his throat, then mutilated and hauled to the track to create the impression he was struck and killed by a train. The killing happened quietly enough that none of his six children, sleeping in the adjoining room, were disturbed.

Arrested are the victim's wife, Elizabeth Tratea, and his cousin, James Tratea. There are rumors that the two are involved. Both suspects are held without bond. Both are charged with murder in the first degree. Both plead not guilty. Charles Adams is their attorney.

Five of the six children are placed in the very crowded Lorain County Children's Home in Oberlin. The youngest, an infant, is sent to godparents in Cleveland.

The accused are tried separately. Elizabeth's trial begins December 8. Her first trial ends in a hung jury; the second yeilds a conviction of guilty of murder in the second degree. Judge Thompson asks the individual jurors to confirm the verdict and each answers "yes" in turn.

A motion for a new trial is overruled. Elizabeth Tratea is sentenced to the Reformatory for Women at Marysville for a term determined by the law plus court costs of $315.91.

James Tratea's trial begins August 4. The jury is impaneled in less than an hour. Lorain Police Chief King testifies, exhibiting the victim's blood-stained mattress and clothing. James swears he was nowhere near the murder scene the night of the killing and that he had gone to South Lorain to visit a woman. Problem is defense lawyers are unable to produce the woman, saying she has moved away and that they can't find her.

On direct examination, a witness testified she heard the accused say of the victim, "There goes Rocco. He has horns on his head and I am going to cut them off."

The jury takes only one hour of deliberation to find James Tratea guilty of murder in the second degree. Judge Thompson's sentence: The Ohio Penitentiary in Columbus, with a term determined by the law, plus court costs of $153.14.

Elizabeth Tratea's lawyers make occasional appeals for her release but all fail. She is granted an unconditional pardon by Ohio Governor Frank J. Lausche on August 11, 1954. I found no record of any similar action for cousin-in-law James.

1919, May 19, Monday: Location: Lorain, near Vine and East 35th Street. Victim: Vandel Gynrovisici (42). Suspects: Mike Kezcver (Knezevich) and Peter Kovasish aka Imbra Kandusaka aka Steve Kovacich aka Steve Kocacicik. Gynrovisici is known to carry large sums of money. His dead body is found in the street when it is run over by an early morning milk wagon. He has been robbed with pockets turned inside-out. The victim has dozens of wounds, some of which pierced his entire body.

The suspects own a coffee house on East 28th Street in Lorain, where the victim was last seen and where he flashed a roll of bills amounting close to $1,000.

A long butcher knife covered with blood to the hilt is found in bushes about a hundred feet from the body. Suspect Kezcver admits the murder weapon is the same knife they use in their business to "sharpen pencils."

Charles Adams is defense attorney. No bond. Charge: For both, Murder. Plea: For both, Not Guilty. Outcome: For both, the prosecutor nollies the charges for unrecorded reasons. Case is unresolved.

1919, May 20: *Elyria Chronicle*:

Lorain Swept by Tidal Wave.

A strange phenomenon took place at Lorain late yesterday afternoon when a tidal wave swept into the harbor and flooded things. It was about two feet high and first showed up in the shape of a comber, or wave that, went over the docks and flooded the lifesaving station. Just what caused the occurrence is unknown but it is laid to some disturbance resembling an earth quake.

1919, May 26: *Elyria Telegram*:

Saloons Here Close Saturday Eve.

Approximately 6,000 in State End Career.

A Few Will Remain Open in Cleveland and in Other Cities Until Tonight; No Undue Disturbances Occurred in Elyria.

In Elyria and throughout the greater part of the state old John Barleycorn is dead. At the stroke of 12 o'clock Saturday night approximately 6,000 saloons throughout the commonwealth closed doors. The state is not entirely dry today owing to the fact that a number of saloonists in Cleveland, Toledo, Columbus, Cincinnati and other large cities paid the extra tax to remain open until tonight. Tuesday, however, Ohio will be as dry as the Sahara desert.

The closing here was accompanied by no undue disturbances contrary to expectations, only twelve persons having been arrested for intoxication. All of those discharged in police court Sunday morning without fine by Acting Judge Neiding.

All cafes opened early Saturday and until the closing time bartenders were kept busy satisfying the wants of the thirsty. Many of whom laid in as large a supply as their pocketbooks would permit in anticipation of the long dry regime. The big rush occurred in the evening when every saloon in the city was filled to its capacity. Augmented by the regular Saturday night crowd the streets were literally packed, and strange to say not a single accident occurred notwithstanding the fact that there were many women and children.

Never before were so many men seen carrying jugs on the streets. Round packages were to be seen in the arms of others while there was a multitude seen walking bent under the weight of heavily loaded suit cases. No rush on a department store by bargain hunters ever assumed larger proportions than the eleventh hour liquor bargain hunters. Display windows of the different saloons were the mecca for hundreds, each having its throng of men looking at prices and the brands displayed. By 8 o'clock several of the cafes were entirely sold out with the result saloonists regretted their inability to lay in larger stocks. And back of all this was the specter of the camel, which stands for drought, and which materially aided to swell the sales.

According to information given out this morning by the former saloonists very few of the buildings occupied by them will remain empty. They will be metamorphosed into restaurants, pool rooms, cigar stands and soft drink establishments. Many bartenders will continue with old employers in their new trades.

AND THIS...

Charity Began at Home.

"I can't complain" said a prominent business man, Saturday. "I helped do it."

"I voted dry the first two times to save the other fellow," he added. "The last time I voted dry to save myself."

AND THIS...

Catching Up With Oberlin.

J.W. Metcalf of Oberlin, son of one of the founders of the Anti-Saloon League, and himself an active supporter of it, was in town, Saturday.

"Come over to help close up?" somebody asked him.

"Yes, I came over to see the rest of the world catch up with Oberlin," he said. "Oberlin has been seventy-five years ahead of the times."

1919, August 31, Sunday: Location: Elyria, Gully below Glendale Court. Victim: Arthur Schultz. Victim Schultz was a recently returned soldier from overseas. The crime is thought to be the result of two men fighting over a woman. Schultz is found at the entrance to Cascade Park with a .38 caliber bullet and corresponding wound in his chest. He dies on the way to Memorial Hospital.

A light gray cap is found at the scene. A bareheaded man was seen walking up Glendale Court with a woman running the other direction. Both are unidentified but police think they know who the woman is and that she was seen with Schultz in front of Elyria's American Theater. Witnesses are unable to identify anybody involved in the murder but say the shooter bent over the victim and cursed him before walking away. Outcome: Unsolved.

1919, September 13, Saturday: Location: Elyria, 200-block of West River Road. Victim: Steve Sumegi (Sumanzi, Sumacz, Sumerge) (new husband). Suspect: John Hammersak (old husband). Act: Shooting.

1919, June 9: Sumegi, a boarder in Mr. Hammersak's home, runs off with Mrs. Hammersak. They take the two Hammersak children and $275 of the family's savings. Mr. Hammersak accuses the duo of kidnapping and theft.

July 4: Sumegi and Mrs. Hammersak are arrested in Alliance, Ohio. The children are with them. Each adult receives $200 fine and is placed in the County Jail.

July 5: Mr. Hammersak files for and gains divorce on the ground of desertion. He asks his ex-wife be barred from any interest in their property.

September 13: Sumegi and the ex-Mrs. Hammersak are released from jail. They marry two hours later. Shortly thereafter, Mr. Hammersak makes a visit to the newlyweds, shoots and kills his ex-wife's new husband and then shoots and kills himself. Neighbors say he originally planned to kill his ex-wife and two children as well, but was thwarted in that plot.

The new Mrs. Sumegi is expecting a third child by her new husband.

Say the papers: "An investigation disclosed that housing conditions at Western Heights are largely responsible for the tragedy and immoral turpitude." It seems a total of four adults and two children slept in the same room. In three beds.

1920 – 1929: County Population = 90,612

1920: Amendment to the *U.S. Constitution: Nineteenth:* The federal government cannot deny women the right to vote. Sheffield Township loses its northern third when citizens there vote to form the Village of Sheffield Lake. The American Professional Football Association forms in Canton, Ohio. Twelve teams each pay $100 to join. Jim Thorpe is the first president. Cleveland Stone Co. & Ohio Quarries Co. merge to form the Cleveland Quarries Co. The German Workers' Party changes its name to the Nazi Party. LEGO® = Awesome. More violence in Ireland. Mexico's ten-year revolution ends with a successful coup. The League of Nations grants Britain responsibility for Iraq, Transjordan, and Palestine while France takes control of Syria and Lebanon. Things won't work out so good. The U.S. starts three years' worth of mucking about in the Russian Civil War. The Associated Press. Charles Ponzi builds a scheme. Elyria police begin ticketing for speeding. Warren Harding (Ohio Republican) wins the Election with 60.3% of the popular vote. 61 lynchings: 53 Blacks, 8 others. $1,000 is worth $12,780 modern.

1920, May 23, Sunday: Location: Lorain. Victim: Stanislaw (Stanley) Jacoboski. Suspect: Mike Martini. This killing is the culmination of a fight over a game of cards played in the home of the suspect.

According to Prosecutor Findley; there was a ten-dollar bill on the table that both men claimed to own. Martini told Jacoboski that he would be killed if he touched it. An undeterred Jacoboski reached for bill. True to his word, Martini produced a revolver and shot the other man dead.

According to defense attorney Adams; Martini was a victim of a drunken row in which three men assaulted him and he shot in self-defense.

The September Grand Jury indicts for murder in the second degree. In the criminal trial, Lorain Police Chief Theodore Walker identifies the bloody clothing worn by Jacoboski at the time of the shooting. Walker says he talked with the victim before he died and that he said he was shot in a fight over a game of cards. The Chief also testifies that the suspect, Martini, had previously spent time in prison, that he changed his name after release, and that he was a lake sailor who ran a "fast and loose rooming house in Lorain" where the shooting occurred.

Jury deliberates about three hours before returning a guilty verdict. Outcome: Ohio Penitentiary for life, plus court costs of $835. Motion for new trial overruled. Court of Appeals confirms sentence.

1920, June 30, Wednesday: Location: Lorain, near the Wabash Railroad. Victim: Peter Paul. Suspect: Christ (Kris) Lazos. Act: Shooting. Charge: Murder in the first degree. September Grand Jury indicts for same. Plea: Not guilty. Outcome: Guilty of Murder in the second degree. Sentence: Ohio Penitentiary for life and court costs of $205.83. Motion for new trial overruled.

1920, July 27, Tuesday, at night:

David Barnes is a detective for the New York Central. He's a big man, over 6-foot tall and well able to handle the often-drunk tramps and so-called tough guys that ghost the NYC tracks that run through Elyria.

It's a typical July night. Barnes has just finished up rousting several men messing around the cars a short distance past the East Bridge undercut. Neighbors to the tracks hear two quick gunshots, a pause, then a third. Racing toward the sounds, they see two men, one tall and one short, running from the scene. They also find the 48-year-old Barnes who's been hit twice: once in the left groin, and a fatal shot directly to the right temple. Powder burns on the victim's head and spent ammunition indicate an execution-style killing with a .38 caliber revolver.

Police figure Barnes was somehow ambushed while arresting a group of men for vagrancy. The first shot went wide. The second struck him in the groin and brought him down. The third shot, at such close range, proved deliberate murder.

One of the men in custody, who remains unnamed, is released. Three are held. Henry Michalak (29) and Joe Kusky (18), are from Berea, Ohio. Richard Ballenir (23), aka Adrian Michigan is late of Detroit.

Authorities think the three know more about the murder than what they're telling, but nobody can prove that as fact. All are held without bond until police check their alibis. Then each is released after paying a $10 fine.

In the meantime, Barnes is buried in Berlin Heights, Ohio. His fellow railroad detectives acts as pallbearers.

Investigators grow convinced that the well-known Cleveland criminal George "Jiggs" Losteiner is somehow involved in the killing. He's been on the run from the law for more than a year for a combination of robbery and murder and is known to travel along the Lake Erie shoreline on a regular basis. That conviction grows when night watchman Ned Worthington picks Losteiner out of a photo line-up as a tall man who asked for shelter the night of Barnes' murder. There is no hesitation on Worthington's part, "I would know him among a thousand." Police still have no idea who the shorter man seen fleeing the crime might be.

On October 21, 1920, George Losteiner, along with others in his gang are arrested after a gun-battle following a robbery of $50,000 from the Cleveland Trust Bank in Bedford, Ohio.

At the November *Cuyahoga County* Grand Jury, George Losteiner pleads guilty to bank robbery, but not murder. Elyria authorities say they are certain Losteiner knows something of the Barnes' murder, but that they do not have enough evidence to indict in a Lorain County Grand Jury.

Cleveland's criminal courts send Losteiner to the Ohio Penitentiary in Columbus for life. It is safe to say that number 49043 is not a model prisoner. In November of 1926, he leads an unsuccessful prison break. By 1927, he's in permanent solitary confinement for repeated escape attempts. His own mother has to ask for permission to visit. Outcome: Losteiner is dead in prison by 1944, but the murder of David Barnes is, technically, unsolved.

"Jiggs," and "Giggs" were once common nicknames for "George."

1920, November 29, Monday: Location: South Lorain, 1951 East 28th Street. Victim: Lem Sanders (Souder) (50 or 60, Colored). Suspects: Wilbur (Warren, Joe) Alexander and John Walker (both Colored).

Victim Sanders, a citizen of Lorain for about three years, is a teamster and known to carry large sums of money. He is found dead by co-workers in the barns of his employer, the Ohio Engineering Company, where he usually sleeps. His head is "brutally beaten with an ax or spade" with four deep gashes on his head. Police find blood-stained clothing, a blood-stained axe, and bloody claw hammer nearby.

Coroner Garver holds an inquest on November 30. The joinery between the bloody hammer's head and handle holds hairs that are found to match that of the victim.

Alexander and Walker are charged with murder in the first degree. Both plead not guilty in front of Judge W.B. Thompson.

The two are held in the Lorain County Jail for more than three months, then, this: 1921, June 9: *The Chronicle-Telegram*: "Prosecution Witness Goes Insane, Results in No Murder Trial: Two Men Held in Connection With Lorain Slaying Go Free After Being in Jail 112 Days."

Outcome: The indictments against the accused are nollied by Prosecutor Webber due to lack of evidence. Upon release, Alexander is quoted as saying, "Man, man! It seems good to see the sun shine once more."

1921: Ohio's *Bing Act* requires children to attend school until the age of 18. The Band-Aid® is invented by Earle Dickson. Lenin proves extraordinarily brutal when it comes to quelling unrest. A youngish FDR is paralyzed by polio. Hitler becomes leader of the Nazi Party. Mao Zedong is a delegation leader to the First Congress of the Chinese Communist Party. In Tulsa, Oklahoma, close to 300 people of varying colors, but mostly not White, are killed in race riots. More than 10,000, mostly Black, are left homeless in the resulting fires. Enrico Caruso dies. John Glenn is born in Cambridge, Guernsey County, Ohio. Ohio Legislators pass, and Ohio voters overwhelmingly approve, the "Crabbe Act." This provides extra money to law-enforcement and elected officials who arrest and convict those breaking the liquor laws. 64 lynchings: 59 Blacks, 5 others.

1921, January 22, Saturday, 9:45pm:

Police are called to the 1600-block of East 32nd Street in Lorain. There, they find longtime city resident Mary Kosco, 38 years old and mother of eight (5 to 22 years old), dead, shot through the heart. Her four youngest, Steve 11, Helen 10, Georgia 7, and Mary 5 are found huddled in a corner of one of the rooms with their arms around each other.

Steve tells police:

> I was on my way to Shiff's Jewelry store on Vine Avenue to get a watch that a neighbor had left to be repaired, when I saw my father coming down the street.
>
> Daddy had been away from home since last September and I was glad to see him. I ran to him. Daddy pushed me aside and said "Get out of my way, I am not your Pa anymore!"
>
> I then knew he was mad, and I ran home to tell mother to run because Pa was coming home to hurt her. But Papa was too quick for me and with a knife he cut the telephone and electric light wires.
>
> I tried to phone the police for help but the phone would not work. The light in the house went out and mother ran out the front door.
>
> Dad told her to get into the house so there would be no witnesses, but mama was afraid to go back.
>
> Then I saw Pa reach in his hip pocket for his gun and start towards Mother. I tried to trip him, but he kicked me out of the way. He then fired a shot at Ma who ran to a neighbor's

house. He then shot at her three times. As Mother reached the neighbor's house, Pa ran up behind her and struck her several times over the head with the butt end of the pistol.

Then Mama fell and I ran up to her. I took her head in my lap but she could not talk to me. I yelled for someone to bring some water for her to drink. Someone did, but Mama was choking and could not drink it.

In a few seconds I knew Mama was dead, so I ran back to the house to get my big brother's shotgun so I could shoot Pa for hurting my Mama. In the house I saw Pa lighting some papers and trying to set the house on fire.

After he lighted several papers he ran through the back of the house toward 33rd Street.

I found brother's gun but when I got it loaded, I could not see Dad.

And that's all I know. My mama's gone now and I don't know what to do. *The Chronicle Telegram, January 21, 1921.*

The body is taken to undertaker George B. Wickens. Autopsy shows a single bullet passed from the front through the lower part of victim's heart. The bullet is found beneath the skin of the victim's back.

Police know that Mary Kosco had obtained an uncontested divorce from her husband two months prior on the grounds of physical and mental cruelty. The neighbors say she's been spending time with Mike Barzeko (Barzenko) who lives over on Denver at 32nd.

The cops arrive at Barzeko's place at 6:35 the next night intending to interview him. There, they find an armed man matching the description of Michael Kosco but who identifies himself as "Mike Maximen."

When questioned, Maximen cannot account for his presence at Barzeko's home. He denies having anything to do with the killing of Mary Kosco. But, once arrested, he admits he's Kosco and gives a rambling account of the murder, saying he had fired two shots from his revolver from the alley, but only to frighten, not strike or kill her.

Besides a "Spanish revolver" with one spent shell, he's carrying a little money and an obituary, written in Polish that he hoped would be published after his planned killing of Barzeko and suicide (neither of which took place).

It says:

When I was sued for a divorce in the Elyria courts, by

my wife, I was not given a chance to say a word in defense of myself. The court gave the children to my wife and I was put out of my home.

I went to friends in Perth Amboy (New Jersey).

I have no home, wife, children anymore and have no place to lay my head, so I am going to kill the man who is responsible for my trouble, kill my wife and put a bullet through my own heart. *The Chronicle Telegram, January 21, 1921.*

Kosco says had been in New Jersey. When he returned he found his ex-wife and Barzeko in a compromising position. It was then that he determined he would kill them both.

He says he always provided for his large family, and all was well between him and his wife until she met Barzeko. She had invited him to dinner and prepared special meals for him. That Barzeko ate like a dog, sometimes consuming eight or ten eggs in one meal.

Kosco tells police he shot twice when he confronted his wife, but never intended to kill her. Then he replaced one of the spent shells with new ones and went hunting for his rival. He was waiting to kill him when the police arrived and took him into custody. The shooter seems not as upset about killing his wife as he is about *not* being able to kill Barzeko who he was planning on murdering as the cause of his divorce.

Kosco suggests he may still kill himself. His suspenders are removed before he is placed in his cell, and he's carefully watched.

The Kosco's other children are Mrs. Veronica Yarmon (Yarmen), 20, Mike 18, Andrew 16, and Anna Kosco (the eldest), 22, who works at the Union Station lunch counter in Cleveland, Ohio.

Anna tells authorities that both of her parents were from Austria-Hungary and arrived in the U.S. in 1896. They were married in Perth Amboy, New Jersey, in 1897. The family, with newborn Anna, arrived in Lorain 21 years ago.

The marriage had always been contentious, but in the last few years her father had been cruel to her mother and sometimes the kids, and that was the cause of the divorce. The divorce was not contested once it was revealed her mother had corroborating evidence of his cruelty. Her father didn't even show up for the hearing. The house had been awarded to her mother, but the deed was not yet transferred.

Anna said their father drank heavily and sometimes seemed demented, especially after the divorce. She and her older siblings were convinced the man was set on killing them all by arson since a number of rolls of partially-burned papers had been found stuffed under the floor of the home last week.

Her father had moved back to New Jersey and wanted to return to Europe. He kept mailing his ex-wife for money so he could make his trip, but she had no extra cash to send. The letters grew more and more threatening to the point that her mother showed them to Elyria Attorney G.B. Findley. "The last letter came about two weeks ago, and in it Dad said it would be the last letter, and that if she did not send the $500 that some 'niggers' would get her."

Upon appearing before Lorain Municipal Judge Harding, Kosco states: "If she were a good woman I would not have shot her. I did not try to escape. Instead I kept the revolver with which I shot my wife, to show to the court. I do not care what the police do with me now."

He then tells the papers this story:

> I have been a hard-working man and have lived in Lorain for over 21 years, during which time I bought and paid for a home.
>
> During the last few years my wife has been intimate with other men and I have been broken hearted.
>
> The man directly responsible for the breaking up of my home is Mike Barzenko, who kidnapped three of my children last October (Kosco had pressed charges). That man would not leave my wife alone, although I pleaded with him to do so, and leave me with my children.
>
> Finally he persuaded my wife to get a divorce, and I was thrown out into the street.
>
> I left Lorain for Perth Amboy, N. J., hoping to be able to forget and begin all over again. I had hard luck in that town and I could not forget. So I came back to Lorain determined to end all my trouble, and kill Barzenko, my wife and myself.
>
> I bought the revolver in Pittsburgh and paid $14 for it.
>
> I suppose my little children hate me now, but it is only the turn of fate that has been bringing me bad luck ever since that man entered my life. *The Chronicle Telegram, January 21, 1921.*

In response, the older children deny their father's accusations, saying it was he who was cruel and that she was faithful to him until the divorce was clear.

Mary Kosco is buried from Holy Trinity Church in Lorain at 9:30am,

January 25 in Calvary Cemetery. Steve, who held his mother as she died, has to be forcibly removed from the grave after the ceremony. He's taken in by his married sister, Mrs. Lattimer Yarmon of 3638 East 38 Street, Cleveland, Ohio.

At the January Grand Jury (2 days after the crime) Anna Kosco tells the court that a second man, also named Mike, who lives on East 23rd, between Elyria Avenue and Broadway, encouraged her father to kill her mother and threatened to do so himself if the act were not carried out.

Says Anna, "My father could not have committed the crime if someone else had not urged him on."

"Little Steve" is also on hand for the proceedings, drawing pictures for which he shows considerable talent, and generally charming the policemen in charge of him.

January 27: The *Chronicle-Telegram* reports on the younger children's visit to their father in jail:

> For the first time since the murder of their little mother on the porch of their home on East 32 Street, Saturday night, Little Steve, 11 years old, in whose arms his mother died, talked with his father in the county jail at Elyria yesterday.
>
> With big tears streaming down the little fellow's face, he looked up into his father's eyes and said: "Daddy, I am sorry."
>
> That is all the little boy could say, for his voice was choked with emotion as he put his little arms around the neck of his "Daddy."
>
> Mike Kosch [*sic*], the wife murderer, cried as though his heart would break. Little Steve was his favorite son, and the father and son had always been close to each other's heart until the bullet from the father's revolver had crashed through the heart of Steve's mother.
>
> Steve and his little 5-year-old sister were taken into the cell to see his father by his sisters Anna and Veronica. A reunion the sadness of which will never be forgotten by county jail attaches [*sic*] was enacted in the small cell.
>
> Anna told her father that she was sorry for him and said she wished he could come back and live in the little house.
>
> The father told how sorry he was for them and said: "Little children, if I ever get free from this, I will work hard to bring

you all up right. I am not sorry that I killed your mother, for she was a bad woman."

As the little kiddies passed out of the big Elyria jail there was not a dry eye among the jail inmates.

January 27. A true bill for murder in the first degree is returned against the accused who pleads not guilty. That night Anna calls the police to guard/ check their house for prowlers that have been seen on the porch and walking up and down the street, peering into the windows. This has upset everyone inside the house to the point that the oldest brother has armed himself. Authorities investigate, but come up blank.

As the criminal trial starts in early March, Anna, dressed in mourning black, greets her father in the court room. Attorney Adolph Resek, who also defended during the Grand Jury, has volunteered to represent the accused, who is destitute.

March 5: Kosco pleads down to murder two. Resek presents his client's side of things, saying Kosco did, in fact, work hard to provide for his family. It's true that he might've been cruel on occasion, but things weren't all that bad until the other man came into the picture. Kosco could not overcome his antagonism towards Barzeko and so acted upon it. It was a something he would carry to his grave.

At the same time, the papers hint, but never outright state, that the ex-wife was perhaps not the paragon of virtue as represented by the children and that she may have left her husband for the interloper.

Judge Thompson, in sentencing, says he thinks it strange that a man would maltreat his wife and then kill her because someone paid attention to her. If a wife does wrong, a husband should not bring violence to her, and if he does, society demands that he should suffer the penalty of doing wrong. Kosco is sent to Ohio Penitentiary in Columbus for life, plus court costs of $12.51.

Kosco is cool during his sentencing and after turns to police and tells them he was ready to return to his cell. The kids are able to make one last visit with their father in Elyria before he is taken to Columbus.

1927, March 22. Kosco is pardoned by Ohio Governor A. Victor Donahey after serving six years and nine days. Commutation was recommended by the eight children, the Ohio Board of Clemency, Judge W.B. Thompson, former Prosecutor Lawrence Webber, "and a number of others." Kosco is instructed by the parole board to "abstain from using intoxicating liquor and to attend church regularly."

I found the name "Kosco" in the Ohio Death Records. The Elyria papers have it as "Kosch."

1921, January 27: *The Chronicle-Telegram:*

Uncle Sam's Weasel Skin Well Filled:

WASHINGTON. Jan. 27—Acting treasurer Allen announced today that a total of $13,883,819,826.36, two-thirds in cash and securities was found in the treasury as a result of the count necessitated by the resignation of John Burke as treasurer.

This total is about $10,000,000,000 greater than usual and is accounted for by approximately that amount of notes deposited by foreign governments for war loans.

1921, February 9, Wednesday, 6:30pm: Location: Lorain, 1900-block East 30th Street (Frank Sarezin's boarding house). Victim: Mrs. Julia Pausen (32, ex-wife). Suspect: Demeter Popp (34, ex-husband).

Stick with me now. This one's a little complicated… Mr. and Mrs. Popp are married and boarders in Sarezin's house for two months. Mrs. Popp drives her husband from the house and files for an annulment when she discovers he has another wife and family in Hungary. An hour after the Popp's marriage is annulled, the now-ex-Mrs. Popp turns around and marries Neaslie Pausen who, it is reported, she has been seeing secretly throughout her now-annulled marriage to the bigamist Popp.

The now-spurned Mr. Popp is upset over the turn of events, but tells a friend, Steve Feche, 1924 East 30 Street, that he and his ex-wife are on reasonable terms and that she has invited him to visit any time as long as he "behaves himself."

February 9: Brand new husband Pausen comes home from National Tube Company with a head injury. The new Mrs. Pausen insists on taking him to St. Joseph's Hospital where is admitted.

Mrs. Pausen returns home about 5:00pm to find ex-husband Popp waiting for her. She invites him up to her room. Sometime later, other boarders in the house can hear screaming and the victim crying. One boarder suggests to landlord Sarezin that he should go up and help her to which he replies, "No, let them fight their own battles." As those words leave his lips, there are five gunshots.

Sarezin runs upstairs to the room and then calls police.

Dr. Frank Young conducts an investigation: The condition of the room indicates a struggle. Mrs. Pausen's torn clothing is taken as evidence that she has been "mistreated."

Mrs. Pausen suffered three gunshots: right breast, left shoulder blade, and a fatal shot through the head from the right to left temples. Her ex-husband, Mr. Popp, then turned his .38 caliber revolver on himself, firing into his chest and through his heart to cause instant death.

Outcome: The bodies are taken to Reichlin, Reidy, and Scanlan Funeral Home. Hospitalized Neaslie Pausen, the victim's new husband, takes the news with little change in emotion, but spends the night awake "gazing into the semi-darkness of the ward."

1921, February 22, Tuesday, 4:45am: Location: Lorain, on the sidewalk in the 1200-block of 8th Street. Victim: James Capogreco (27). Capogreco is walking to his work in the steel mills from his place in the 700-block of Brownell when he is attacked and shot multiple times. The victim begins running through back yards, hurdling fences and porches, covering half a block before falling dead in someone's back yard.

The killer fired seven times. Capogreco is shot four times: three in his back and once in his head (or hand, depending on the newspaper). Police claim the victim had fired back, but missed.

The now-dead man was recently out on $2,500 bond on an arrest for the alleged criminal assault of a 15-year-old, Livingston Avenue, Lorain school girl. He was arrested and charged on January 27 when police found him under the girl's bed. He said he'd hid there because he thought it was the girl's father coming up the stairs. The young man had been rooming at the girl's home and said he would do the right thing and marry her.

Knowing that, officials believe Capogreco's death is revenge by the girl's family, especially since, when he was arrested for assault, the girl's father, armed with both knife and revolver, admitted to hunting for the victim to kill him. But the father was released when he promised to let the law take care of the young man. Police immediately arrest Tony Richichi and his son Dominick (father and brother of the 15-year-old girl) on suspicion of murder. They are later released.

Then the theories are put forth that the killer may be another sweetheart of the pregnant girl or perhaps a fellow criminal who is seeking revenge for other reasons. Guards are posted at every street car and railroad station to "watch for suspicious characters." Authorities search for a short, stout man with a dark complexion. He is smooth shaven, with black hair and has two facial scars, one running across his left cheek and another over either his left or right eye.

Capogreco is buried in Lorain's Calvary Cemetery on February 24, from St. Peter's Church. His sweetheart, meanwhile, is in a Cleveland home expecting the birth of their child. Outcome: The smooth-shaven, scarred man is never found. Unsolved.

1921, March 27, Sunday: Location: Elyria. Victim: Unknown infant girl.

Fourteen-year-old George Berkline, son of Police Officer Berkline, 800 East Avenue is playing along the East Branch of the Black River in Elyria near 7th Street, off East Avenue, and watching the water rise from the spring melt. The boy sees what he thinks is a pretty doll floating in the river. He pulls the object ashore using a long stick and picks it up. When he realizes it is a baby, he drops it back into the water and rushes home. He says to his father, "I don't think I'm seeing things, and if I'm not, there is a dead baby in the river."

The tiny body has floated off but is retrieved by Frank Smith of the Henry H. Smith Company and placed on the bank along the 700-block of East Avenue, high enough so the rapidly rising water won't reach it.

Coroner M.E. Perry rules the death as "homicide by drowning." The baby girl was alive when thrown into the river. The back of the newborn's head is crushed in, and the body is covered with bruises. She is naked except for a weighted cloth tied about her neck. The coroner suspects the infant was tossed into the river from either the LaPorte or Coonville (Fuller Road) Bridge.

The child is "plump, good looking, and fully developed," blond, and appears to be of "white, civilized parents." Condition of the body is such that no doctor had been at the birth. The tiny body is taken to Beal and Hearne Undertakers and is provided a coffin for a burial "befitting a human being" in the "baby plot" of Potter's Field at Ridgelawn Cemetery. Many flowers are sent by the public, but no mourners attend the little girl's service. Outcome: Unsolved.

Just so we're clear, here... The "Coonville Bridge" is name after C.E. Coon, an early property owner on the east side of the river in Carlisle Township.

1921, April ??: Location: Lorain. Victim: John Eutcher. Suspect: John Ellis (Eles, Elees). Eutcher runs a boarding house where Ellis either stays, or works, or both. There is a mutually drunken argument of some sort over money. Ellis fatally stabs Eutcher. April Grand Jury indicts for murder in the second degree. Plea: Not guilty. *Changed to:* Guilty of manslaughter. Outcome: Ohio Penitentiary 1-20 years, plus court costs of $12.35.

1921, April 18: Ohio state senate passes a bill raising the pay of grand and petit jurors from $2.00 per day to $3.00. Average factory pay for men is $3.00 to $8.00 each day.

1921, November 12, Saturday afternoon: Location: Elyria, Warren Avenue. Victim: Andy Roman. Suspect: Valentine Snezik. Roman is killed with a shotgun for "wrecking the home" of the suspect. Snezik states he was not sorry that he killed the victim whom he found with his wife.

Roman is buried in a pauper's grave by friends who all disagree with what he did to the Snezik family. Snezik grows despondent and threatens to kill himself over his problems. He is watched carefully in the lockup.

Prosecutor Webber and stenographer Walter Watts take the following statement:

> I was born in Croatia, Poland in 1892. I have known Andrew Roman for over two years. I have a wife and four children. Roman came to my house one day recently and I saw him talking to my wife I over-heard him say, "That kid is not his, it is my kid." My wife answered, "you're drunk." Tuesday I come home from work at dinner time and I asked my wife if it was true what Andrew said. I had treated it as a joke at first but she did not answer. When I came home at night I again asked her if it was true, as I had heard him say and as he had told other people. She would not answer and I then saw my relatives and ask them about it. They would not tell me and said I should get my information elsewhere as they did not want to get mixed up in it.
>
> Wednesday I said to my wife, "listen, tell me true if you did it or not." She did not say anything for a while and then said "yes." I could not speak for a while and got very nervous I could not work for it was a great grief to me. This happened about fourteen months ago when we lived on Shear Street

and I had lost my job at the Columbia Steel Company. I went to Pennsylvania and got a job for six weeks I told her she had spoiled my life and had put a great shame on me and the children. She cried and said she would not do it again. Lately he has been coming to my house nearly every day. I did not suspect him lately. I asked my wife if she wanted a divorce and she said she did not. I said I had to stay here on account of my children. Then I told him to keep away.

Wednesday I talked to my friends as to what to do and they told me I would have to help myself. I left it to my wife to go, but she wouldn't. Wednesday evening he came and I was lying on the bed. My wife was in the kitchen and he came in to see me. I said, "don't come here anymore, you're no good. I don't believe my wife." Then he left.

Friday I went to the police station and told the Chief of my trouble and asked him to do something, and he said he would. On my way home I went in a store and bought a single barreled shotgun for $11 and some shells for $1. I bought it because I didn't want Roman at my home. If he come I think I shoot him, and I did. I come home from work at 2:30 Saturday and found Roman in the kitchen with my wife. I took off my coat, went and got my gun and loaded it. I went into the kitchen and told my wife and children to get out. Then I said to Roman, "What are you doing here? You tell everyone my wife is bad." He said. "No. I didn't say that." He got nervous when he saw the gun, and I kept it pointed at him from my hip. Then I shot him.

I am not sorry, because his blood wiped my shame from my family. *The Chronicle Telegram, November 14, 1921.*

Officials and friends sympathize with Snezik, but the law must be carried out no matter the motive for killing. Outcome: 1921, December 15, per docket: "Transcript from Mayor's Court filed. A warrant to discharge from custody is issued."

HONOR KILLING: Killing someone who has brought shame to your family.

1922: Insulin for Diabetes. Vitamin D. Egypt is an independent kingdom as long as the British run the Suez Canal. Gandhi is arrested and sentenced to six years in prison. Lenin's second stroke ends his political career. Joseph Stalin is the General Secretary of the Communist Party. In the Irish Free State you can be executed for possessing a pistol. Harding nearly drowns, politically, in a Teapot. The Bombardment of Samsun (Turkey). Mussolini prepares to take Rome. King Victor Emmanuel II invites him to form a government. Mussolini's happy to be Prime Minister. The last Ottoman Emperor goes into exile as his sultanate is dissolved by the government. The American Professional Football Association changes its name to the National Football League. Dorothy Dandridge is born in Cleveland, Ohio. Doris Kappelhoff is born in Cincinnati, Ohio. You likely know her as Doris Day. A juicy local divorce can still make the front-page. In the Docket: Burglary, Larceny, and Receiving Stolen Property. 57 lynchings: 51 Blacks, 6 others.

1922, July 31, Sunday, about 4:00am: Location: Grafton, beside the Big Four tracks between the water tank and the railroad bridge. Victim: Andy Kuccovich. Suspect: Paul Citck. The "Big Four" is the Cleveland, Cincinnati, Chicago, and St. Louis line. Victim Kuccovich is found, dead, beside the track by a railroad employee and taken to Sudro Funeral Home on orders of Coroner Perry.

Kuccovich is 35 to 40 years old and well dressed. A pair of glasses are found in his pocket along with a ticket to New York City bought in Cincinnati, Ohio. Pocket contents suggest he may be from Monroe, Michigan, or Toledo, Ohio. Injuries include a smashed skull and a hole in his side. Death was instantaneous. The Coroner cannot determining if there was foul play involved or if, perhaps, the victim fell or jumped from the train. Some suggest he may have been "a sleepwalker."

Kuccovich is positively identified on August 1 by son, Pete, of Monroe, Michigan. The son says that Kuccovich's been working as a coal miner in Lynch, Kentucky, since his wife died two years ago, had saved $1,000 for a return to Poland, and was on his way there. Only $35 was found on the body.

Authorities discover that Kuccovich had bought two tickets and two baggage claims at the railroad office in Cincinnati. That means the victim had a traveling companion. Lorain County Sheriff N.D. Backus wires New York City police to be on the lookout for somebody claiming the bags.

Paul Citck is arrested in New York City's Grand Central Station when he presents baggage checks to claim both his and the victim's luggage. The suspect is carrying $2,400 dollars when apprehended. He is immediately extradited to Ohio by the state of New York. Prosecutor Webber presents his case to the September Grand Jury. There is not enough evidence to warrant an indictment.

Outcome: Paul Citck is set free. The case is unresolved.

1922, September 27, Wednesday, about 2:00pm: Location: Lorain. Victim: Peter Gust (26, of Elyria). Suspect: Larry Frank aka Larry F. Santa aka Frank Santo(s) (25, of Lorain). Santos is a shoemaker from Steubenville, Ohio. He and his wife are staying at the Commonwealth Hotel on Livingston, Lorain, while looking for a shop location. Victim Peter Gust lives at the Miller Hotel, Clark Street, Elyria.

Gust thinks that Santos and his wife stole over $140 from his coat when he visited them at the Commonwealth. He decides to confront Santos but does not go alone. He takes Max Slutzker (Elyria barber) as muscle, and G.V. Chinque (Elyria storekeeper on East Broad) as an interpreter.

After an argument at the Commonwealth, all of the men travel towards Tony Patiallo's Barber Shop in Lorain to settle their differences. The Elyrians, including victim Gust, drive: Gust and Max Slutzker in the front of the car, Chinque is in the back. Santos, the alleged thief, elects to walk.

The automobile containing Gust, et. al., stalls at the Nickle Plate railroad crossing. Santos approaches the vehicle from the rear, produces a revolver, and fires five times. G.V. Chinque is not injured. Max Slutzker is struck in the arm. Peter Gust is shot both in the arm and in the back with that bullet passing through his liver.

A nearby policeman, William Babcock, hears the shots and comes a'running. Santos fires once at him—the bullet hits the officer's shoe but does no harm. Santos escapes but is traced to a nearby restaurant and arrested when found hiding beneath a wagon box.

All those injured are taken to St. Joseph's Hospital. Peter Gust is well able to make a statement, but refuses. When told he is going to die, Gust replies, "Well, go on away, then and let me die."

Mrs. Rose Santos (21) and Sam Fiora (36) are held as possible witnesses. Slutzker and Chinque are placed under bond for the same reason.

September 29: Rumors circulate that Santos' many friends might try to obtain his freedom from the lockup in the city of Lorain. He is moved to the more secure County Jail. The October Grand Jury indicts for murder in the first degree. Santos pleads not guilty.

Several venires are required to pull enough jurors for the trial. Once in front of Judge Redington for his criminal trial Santos changes his plea to guilty of murder in the second degree. Outcome: Life in the Ohio Penitentiary in Columbus, plus court costs of $77.18. As he is sentenced, the guilty man turns and smiles to his friends in the courtroom.

January of 1924, wife Rosie Santos files for divorce citing her husband's life sentence as reason.

1922, November 16, Thursday: Location: Lorain, on the Lake Road. Victim: Sophia (Mary) Stesner (ex-wife). Suspect: Carl Stesner (ex-husband).

Sophia Stesner files for divorce in July of 1922 on the grounds of gross neglect of duties and adultery. She claims Carl never properly supported her or their child and committed adultery with the wife of Ignatius Teska. In response, Carl successfully kills Sophia but fails at suicide. Stesner is indicted for murder in the first degree by the Lorain County Grand Jury.

1923, February 2: Sophia Stesner's 19-year-old sister Stella Chopinski, an important part of the case, dies in an automobile crash as she travels to Sandusky in search of witnesses against the accused.

March 12: Stesner's criminal trial starts in Court Room 1. Judge W.B. Thompson is sick with a bad cold, but is on the bench. Prosecutor: Lawrence Webber assisted by Dan B. Symons. Defending are attorneys Don Myers and Roy Vandemark. Stesner is clearly showing the "prison pall" but is neatly dressed and not outwardly nervous. Mrs. Mary Petelczyk, sister of the murdered woman, represents her family.

The court room is filled to capacity with people standing along the walls.

It's a long, slow slog to pick a jury. Several venires are required to pull enough people. Many have read newspaper accounts and have already formed strong opinions. The State is asking for the death sentence, which almost always slows jury selection.

March 15: In opening arguments, the prosecutors describe Carl Stesner as a brutal and unfaithful husband with no regard for the welfare of his family. He beat Sophia in front of their 11-year-old daughter, blackening the woman's eyes and dragging her around the house by her hair. He had threatened to kill not only the woman, but their child and her family, too.

According to the prosecution, on the day of the murder Stesner broke down the door of her brother-in-law, where she was staying, knocked a man, Anton Chopinski, to the floor, chased, captured, and kidnapped his ex-wife, beat her, forced her into his automobile, and shot her three times before driving off. Stesner was followed to Kolbe Road where he shot himself in a suicide attempt. There is some debate over his state of mind at the time of the crime, but doctors agree he was then, and is now, sane.

According to police, when captured, Stesner said "I did it. I shot myself and my wife. My wife ran away three times with an east side coal dealer." Defense attorney Don Myers twists "the unwritten law" into a justification for the killing. He accused the dead woman of an illicit affair with Lawrence Nokum, the east side coal dealer Stesner referred to in his confession. Defense says they have proof of the affair and that Sophia and Nokum were about to run away using $1,300 of Stesner's own money. The idea is to cast enough of a shadow on the victim to keep the accused out of the electric chair.

In closing, the prosecution pushes hard for the death penalty, carefully defining the notion of premeditation.

The defense urges the jury not to make a decision that cannot be recalled. They say that Stesner told the whole truth in the trial and was at their mercy.

March 23, Friday, 4:20pm: The trial goes to jury. Deliberations continued until 11:00pm when rooms are assigned to them in an unnamed Elyria hotel. The jury reconvenes at 8:30 the next morning and continues deliberation for several more hours. The long debate is, the jurors later say, over the notion of premeditation. They were deadlocked with four of the twelve for execution, but a compromise was finally reached with a first degree murder verdict with a recommendation of mercy.

Carl Stesner does not flinch when the verdict is read, but grows angry back in his cell. "I don't want any God Damned mercy," he shouts. "I would like to go back and tell them I don't want mercy. I would rather go to the electric chair than have a life sentence." He also complains about his defense lawyers, saying they and the prosecutor are "riding the same horse." Stesner is further outraged when his remarks make it into newsprint.

March 26: Judge W.B. Thompson, now in the end-stages of his cold, sentences the man to life in the Ohio Penitentiary in Columbus, plus court costs of $572.36.

After judgement, Stesner apologizes to his lawyers, saying they had worked hard for him. Then, turning to a reporter he snarls "put that in your paper!" The *Chronicle-Telegram* does just that while noting that it took Lorain County two weeks and $4,000 to convict a confessed killer.

March 28. Lawrence Nokum (Nocum), the man Sophia Stesner allegedly carried on with, is arrested with two other men while operating a still in Brownhelm Township. The rig was given to the three arrested men by Fred Regal, one of the witnesses in the Stesner murder case.

1934, October 19: Carl Stesner's name appears on a list sent to the U.S. State department for deportation back to his home country, wherever that happens to be—the name is most common in today's Czech Republic.

Suffrage, and More

Ohio was the fifth state to ratify the *Nineteenth Amendment* to the United States Constitution granting women the right to vote. It took effect in 1920, but it was a while before women finally found their way onto juries in Lorain County. Doubters thought women too tenderhearted to endure the stress and horror of criminal cases. This, despite the obvious fact that they were the most faithful of courtroom spectators during the most gruesome of the county's murder trials.

It soon became evident to local attorneys that women were unafraid to forgive *or* convict. Sought by both prosecution and defense, it didn't take long for the "gentler sex" to become active participants in the legal system of Lorain County.

Carl Stesner, in the story above, was the first person indicted for murder by a Lorain County Grand Jury that contained women jurors: Mrs. Alson L. (Lillie) Hill of Lorain and Mrs. J. Wesley (Myrtle) Smith of Elyria.

Lillie Hill was born in Ohio, was about 50 years old at the time of the trial, and lived on Lorain's East Erie Avenue.

Myrtle Smith, in her early 50s, was also born in Ohio. She was living on East 2nd Street, Elyria, when she was called to jury duty.

At the close of the session, Judge W.B. Thompson "took occasion to thank the jury for their faithfulness, and said that the work of the two ladies on the jury were but a foretaste of what was to come as other women would be called upon to serve from time to time." Prosecutor Webber "spoke to the court and said that in view of the fact that this was the first time women had been used on the jury he wished to thank them especially for their intelligent work, and their faithfulness to duty."

It happens that two women jurors also helped pass judgement in Carl Stenser's criminal trial: Florence Brackett and Florence Hannaford.

Ms. Brackett was a member of Avon's pioneering Root family and in her mid-40s at the time. A member of the Eastern Star, she would go on to live more than 75 years in the same small, modest home at the near end of Water Street, Elyria, before dying there at the age of 98 on April 26, 1975, after a short illness. Her long life, combined with a sharp memory, made her an asset to local historians and the occasional newspaper reporter.

In contrast, Florence Hannaford, also in her mid-40s when she sat on the Stesner murder trial, was well-known and as mover and a shaker in Lorain County's business and social circles. In her youth, her father, Elyria hardware mogul and banker William Heldmeyer, was the president and then director of the Elyria Saving and Bank Company—a job that passed to Ms. Hannaford upon his death in July of 1912—eight years before women were able to vote in the U.S.

Among Mrs. Hannaford's many accomplishments: organizer and past president of the Elyria YWCA, a Girl Scout Commissioner from 1936 to 1938, and Chair of the Girl Scout Council finance committee. She and her husband also helped establish the Elyria American Legion Post.

Florence Hannaford died April 25, 1949, at the age of 72 as a result of head injuries suffered in a fall down the basement steps of her home in the 300-block of 5th Street, Elyria. At that time she was President of the Elyria Hardware Company (founded by her deceased husband), secretary-treasurer of the Heldmeyer Hardware Company (founded by her father), and a director of the Elyria Savings and Trust.

1923: Bessie Smith's *Downhearted Blues* sells 2,000,000 copies in one year. If you've never heard it, you should. The IRA agrees to end the Irish Civil War but the violence continues. The USSR arrives, complete with a newly-inked constitution—interesting reading. Turkey finally comes to terms of peace with the Allies and becomes a republic. When Hitler agitates for a new national government, things don't go so good. He flees gunfire but is captured and tossed in the clink where he (and ghostwriter Rudolf Hess) author *Mein Kampf.* In Ohio, the "Bender Bill" makes it murder in the second degree if you kill somebody with poisonous liquor. National Tube recruits 1,300 workers from Mexico. The Posey Indian War with, again, the Ute and Paiute in Utah. In the Docket: Abandonment of Families and Children, plus booze-related crimes; Manufacturing of Distilled Liquors; Selling intoxicating Liquors; Transporting and Possessing Liquor. Warren Harding dies. Calvin Coolidge is President. 33 lynchings: 29 Blacks, 4 others.

1923, June 13, Wednesday, 7:30pm: Location: Lorain, 1500-block Broadway. Victim: Otis Rallie (29, Colored). Suspect: James Pleasant. Act: Gunshot. Victim Rallie and suspect Pleasant are fellow boarders. Pleasant was shaving, says witness Anna Berry, when Rallie came to his room. The two men exchanged increasingly angry words over one of many of Rallie's get-rich-quick schemes (or an alarm clock, depending on the paper). Rallie called Pleasant "crazy and ignorant."

In response, Pleasant shot Rallie three times in the head and then fled the scene. Police were called by another boarder, Robert Tate.

Patrolman John Early apprehends Pleasant a few minutes after the shooting, on Reid Avenue, near 18th Street. Upon arrest Pleasant states that he "shot the man because he wanted to and did not like him anyway."

James Pleasant has a previous criminal record: fourteen months in the Ohio Penitentiary in Columbus on assault with intent to kill in Akron, Ohio. He was also held by Toledo, Ohio, authorities on suspicion of shooting a police officer but released for lack of evidence.

Pleasant is indicted by the September Grand Jury with trial set for November 19. Charge: Murder in the first degree. Plea: Not guilty. Criminal trial begins. Two days in, after securing a jury and opening statements, the plea is changed to guilty of murder in the second degree. Outcome: Life in the Ohio Penitentiary plus costs of $102.95.

1923, August 12, Sunday, 6:00pm: Location: South Amherst. Victim: Joe Biro (52, a Hungarian). Suspect: Joseph Chepol (Chopel, Chopol, Chepal) (46). Act: Shooting. Victim Biro and Chepol are Amherst quarry workers with wives in Hungary. Both men are drinking when an argument develops. Brio calls Chepol "a vile name and then did the same thing regarding his mother" (always a bad idea). More words follow. Chepol threatens to shoot Biro. Biro tells him to go ahead (an even worse idea). Biro is, as a result, shot the head with a .32 caliber revolver.

Upon arrest, Chepol tells Sheriff Underhill, "I fired point blank at him, hitting him squarely in the forehead, and he fell over dead. I don't care. He called me names." Joseph Chepol is indicted for murder in the second degree but is allowed to plead guilty to manslaughter. Outcome: Ohio Penitentiary, minimum of 1 year, maximum of 20, plus costs of $26.51 modern.

Four days after the shooting, Adolph Houluvich, boarding house keeper where the killing occurred, is fined $500 for possessing fifty gallons of illegal wine. The man is jailed and put to work there until he pays the fine.

1923, October 5, Friday afternoon: Location: Lorain. Victim: Richard Atwood (29, Colored). Suspect: Mack Manning (28, Colored). Both men formerly lived in Gary, Indiana and were friends until Atwood ran away with

Manning's clothes, money, and wife. Manning swore he would kill Atwood and began searching for them.

Manning catches up with his wandering wife in Sandusky, cuts her five times on the shoulder and body, robs her of $65, and flees the authorities. Manning then trails the couple to Lorain. Before he can act, he is arrested on possession of liquor. While in the county jail he tells the sheriff his story and threatens, again, to kill Atwood.

The sheriff tells him to "let it go," and then the sheriff lets Manning go. When Manning finally sees Atwood on the street, he pulls his revolver and shoots him four times in the body. Once Atwood falls, Manning puts a final bullet in his victim's head.

Manning is bound over to the Grand Jury already in session and indicted for murder in the second degree. In something of a surprise, he is allowed to plead to manslaughter. Outcome: Judge Thompson sends Manning to the Mansfield Reformatory for 1 to 20 years, until discharged according to the law, plus costs of $27.50. The sheriff who let Manning go free, despite repeated threats against Atwood, doesn't seem to get into any trouble at all.

1923 October 23, Tuesday:

Neighbors have called the authorities on 42-year-old Alice Hall. Everyone knows she's fallen on hard times, being a widow and all for the last four years. But she gets close to $7.50 a month from charity. Her son's making $25 a month working other farms, and there's also the cash her daughter earns, doing the same. Yes, she needs all the help she can get working her plot of land. Still, that does not excuse her from sending her children to school. After all, it's November, well past harvest.

Constable Jack Howlett makes the trip up Pitts Road, a mile or so north of Wellington, to the old school house that Alice Hall and her kids call home. The officer stops to get a little more information from a neighbor before dropping in for his visit. It's then he learns of a seventh child, a girl named Doris, born on October 20, who's not been seen since.

Really, as if she didn't have enough mouths to feed and out of wedlock, to boot. The woman was once a nurse at the old Elyria Hospital—you'd think she'd know better. No... folks aren't sure who the father is, but the rumors sure are flying.

When confronted, Alice Hall admits that Baby Doris was born, but died. The woman's behavior suggests there's more to the story. Sheriff Underhill and Coroner Perry are called. The thin, exhausted woman doesn't know where the baby is buried. She says neighbor Lewis Cowles can tell them.

They travel to his farm a little less than a mile away, over on the Oberlin Road. Cowles (55) points to a ditch near the back of his barn. Ordered to dig it up, the man does so, and inside a toolbox-like chest is found a tiny body dressed in baby clothes. The coroner finds the 6-pound girl to be perfectly developed. There are some abrasions around the forehead and back of the head as if there had been pressure there.

Cowels refuses to give an explanation for the child's death or how the baby ended up buried on his property. He is arrested and jailed on November 15. When questioned by Prosecutor Webber and assistant Dan Symons, the November 16 *Chronicle-Telegram* reports:

> He said after the child was born he and the woman talked it over, and that he said, "I'm going to take the brat out and knock its brains out against a tree." She said. "You'll do nothing of the kind."

According to Cowles, Alice Hall suggested getting some chloroform. So he went to Wellington, procured the drug, and brought it back. He retrieved a small tool chest from his farm. They put the child in alive, saturated cotton batting with chloroform, placed it in the box with the baby, and closed the lid. He took the chest home with him, leaving it in the barn overnight. The next morning, without opening the box, he buried it. A week later he dug the box up, made the grave deeper, and reburied it.

With this, Alice Hall's four youngest children are placed in the care of neighbors (they are later moved to the Oberlin orphanage) and Alice is arrested. She tells the authorities almost the same story that Cowles has.

Both plead not guilty to first degree murder when arraigned in front of Elyria Municipal Judge S.J. George. Both are bound over to the Grand Jury.

> The authorities state that for diabolical wickedness it is the most cold blooded affair they have had anything to do with for some time. *The Chronicle-Telegram, November 16, 1923.*

The "gingham-clad" Alice is quoted:

> I loved the little thing, but it never seemed like a real baby to me! It never nursed. If it even had cried once I could not have let it be killed! It only whined like a little sick kitten. It doesn't seem possible that this thing has happened to me. I can't realize that my baby has been born and murdered. I wasn't

in my right mind at the time. *The Chronicle-Telegram, November 21, 1923.*

As to her conceiving the child—she says Cowles came to deliver a charity load of wood in the depths of last winter. Her kids were in bed, she was cold and crying. That's how it started. "I know it was a dreadful thing to do, but I was at the end of my tether. At the end of life, almost, it seemed."

Dr. C.B. Weidman of Wellington tells authorities that Alice fainted when told she was carrying the child. The baby was born around midnight on October 20. It's the doctor's opinion that Alice's weakened condition, destitution, possible melancholia, and pain from fibroid tumors weakened her resistance to Cowles' insistence the newborn be killed.

Defense attorney Lee Stroup asks for bail for the woman. She is not a risk because she would never leave her children or her property where she has raised her own crops. Three neighbor women, Mrs. Mildred Miller, Mrs. Wilson Miller, and Mrs. Elizabeth Conkel, tell the judge that Alice certainly would not leave the area or her children.

Alice Hall is released on $10,000 bail the day before Christmas. The bond is signed by her brother, E.R. McConnell, a prosperous farmer of Wellington Township. Judge Thompson admits it's unusual to bail somebody charged with first degree murder, but says that a petition signed by twenty-five of her neighbors, public sentiment, and the needs of Hall's children led him to believe it was the right thing to do.

Lewis Cowles remains in jail.

The January, 1924, Grand Jury indicts both for the first degree murder of their illegitimate child by chloroform and suffocation. Both plead not guilty. The defendants will be tried separately.

Alice Hall is re-arrested and re-released on $15,000 bond, once again on the signature of E.R. McConnell.

As before, Lewis Cowels remains in jail.

It takes several tries to draw enough people for the jury pool. Cowels' criminal trial starts February 22 before Judge Thompson with Webber and D.B. Symons prosecuting, and Guy Findley defending.

Mrs. Cowles is there and has been visiting him in jail, too. Many people are attending as spectators. The case draws a huge crowd to Court Room 1. Most of the spectators are women. Many bring meals so as to not lose their seats over the lunch hour.

Careful questioning of potential jurors spins out the selection to a day and a half. A thirteenth juror is selected as an alternate in case one of the original twelve becomes ill.

The prosecution maintains that Cowels was intimate with the woman in January 1923, but broke off their relationship soon after, that it was Alice Hall who suggested the chloroform, and Cowles accepted the idea. He bought the drug in Wellington. Then on October 26, they killed the child as they described when arrested.

Defense Guy Findley counters with Lewis Cowles' good reputation and that, even though he bought the chloroform, the baby was dead of malnutrition before it was ever put in the box. The baby was born, says Findley, into conditions of squalor and destitution and had died because of those conditions. Cowles had buried a dead body and nothing more.

Wellington drug store owner, E.R. Lehman, identifies Cowels as a buyer of chloroform, "to kill a dog," as it was explained at the time.

Local doctors testify to Cowles actions and the condition of the baby at time of death. But it's Dr. John G. Spencer, of Cleveland, "an eminent expert on poison analysis," who puts a big dent in the defense claim that little Doris was dead before she was placed in the box by testifying that an analysis of the baby's vital organs showed traces of chloroform. She was still breathing when the lid was closed.

Alice Hall is placed on the stand to testify, but her attorney, Robert Rice strenuously objects to her being there, saying that she is also facing a charge of murder. She cannot be expected to incriminate herself. Judge Thompson agrees and excuses her from the witness chair.

The defense brings a large enough number of witnesses to testify to Lewis Cowels' reputation as a good and honest citizen that the State agrees to admit the fact.

Cowles takes the stand on February 28 and denies any knowledge about the death of the child. He says he lives on the farm where he was born. At the age of 35 he married a widow who had two children of her own and, despite doing nothing to prevent it, never became a father himself. The man tells the court how he had met Alice Hall about twenty years back and what he knew of her falling on hard times.

In February of 1923, she had sent her two oldest children to his farm to say they were out of fuel. He took a load of firewood to her and then visited about twice a week. They were intimate between February 10th and 15th. Not before, and not after.

He says he was stunned when she told him she was carrying his child.

He didn't know how it could be his when he'd been married two decades to an obviously fertile woman without producing any children of his own. He says Alice Hall told him, "I *think* it's yours."

The box the baby was buried in is entered as evidence.

Cowels testifies that the child was not strong, that Alice did not want it, and that she was the one who suggested they chloroform it. Yes, he bought the drug, saying it was "to kill a dog," but when he went to the house, Alice told him the baby was already dead. Yet, she insisted they use the chloroform.

When asked about his confession upon arrest, Cowels maintains he would've never opened his mouth if he had been allowed an attorney. He did ask for one several times but those requests were denied by the police and prosecutor. Cowels says that attorney Symons, working for the State told him he'd "give him any legal advice he needed."

The papers describe Cowles as a "poor witness." Cranky and irritable, he contradicts his own story several times.

Meanwhile, women spectators faint from the lack of air. People in the corridors try to buy seats from those inside. "Bailiff Chas. Hyman is nearly worn out trying to keep order, attend to the ventilation, call and swear witnesses, and wait on the attorneys and Judge Thompson."

The Prosecution wraps up the case with a recapitulation of the facts.

Surprisingly, the Defense makes no closing argument.

The jury is charged at 2:15pm, February 29. It returns 45 minutes later to find Lewis Cowels guilty of both charges (death by chloroform and death by suffocation) with a recommendation of mercy—at least there'll be no electric chair.

Cowles visibly pales when the verdict is read. Defense attorney Myers does not make a motion for a new trial. The guilty man is sentenced to life in the Ohio Penitentiary in Columbus.

Alice Hall's criminal trial is scheduled to start on March 31. Through the papers, Bailiff Chas. Hyman advises spectators to bring their "camp chairs." He says he'll try to serve tea at noon for those who bring their dinners.

The entire panel of fifty prospective jurors is exhausted by objections. Rather than wait to draw more in the usual way, the judge and both sets of lawyers agree to question court spectators and seat the last five in that way.

Lee Stroup is defending. A.R. Webber is prosecuting. Judge Thompson is on the bench. The trial starts with a jury visit to where the murder was committed, the schoolhouse-home of Alice Hall. Automobiles can only be taken to within a mile and a half of the home's location out in the wilds of

Wellington Township before the mud stops them. The balance is crossed via hay wagon.

There's a lot of overlap with the previous trial with same witnesses giving the same testimony.

Lewis Cowels does not testify at Hall's trial, but she is an excellent and sympathetic witness for herself. Tears run down her face as she tells of her life of destitution and self-neglect, working herself nearly to death for the sake of her children. Alice says Cowels was kind to her when she was so cold and poor. She was intimate with him, but after several times, she told him to stay away. He kept hanging around her property, but she would not admit him to her home. When she discovered she was carrying his child, Cowels tried to convince her to pin it on "some bachelor," saying he hoped "Shorty" (a pet name for his wife) would not find out.

Alice blames Cowles for everything. It was Cowles who was angry at the birth of the child. Cowels who offered to kill it, first by bashing out its brains, and then by chloroform. He was half-drunk when he showed up with the box and the drug.

Why, then, had she confessed to the killing of her own child when she was arrested? Because she was alone and afraid and had no attorney.

Dr. Weidman of Wellington testifies to Alice's broken medical and mental condition. The State objects, saying the doctor is no expert in mental health. Judge Thompson allows the testimony to stand.

The defense brings in experts to describe how Alice Hall was suffering from "puerperal insanity" (postpartum psychosis) when the baby was killed.

The prosecution counters with experts of their own who testify she was sane, but all the same, the State can clearly see that Alice Hall has won the hearts of everyone in the room.

Just before deliberation, juror Thomas Artress, of Lorain, is taken ill with "an acute attack of indigestion." No alternate had been selected, as was in Cowles' trail. The fate of Alice Hall is decided by eleven men.

Like Cowles, the jury is out for less than an hour. When they return, Alice Hall appears to be in prayer. Unlike Cowels, Alice Hall is acquitted of all charges. The one hundred women present in the court room cheer, loudly applaud, and must be gaveled to silence. When Hall is set free, she thanks each juror in turn.

Cowles is in jail a little more than two years. On May 5, 1926, he is granted clemency by Ohio Governor A. Victor Donahey. With that, Lewis Cowels returns to his farm.

I found it more than a little curious that Alice Hall seemed to be starving to death while having a brother well-off enough to provide large amounts of money for bail. If true, I wonder why he didn't help before things grew so desperate.

Cowles' trial is the first for which I saw an "alternate juror" mentioned.

Finally, the newspapers refer to the Cowles-Hall baby as "Doris" and list the date of death as October 26. Ohio's records have her as "Hall, Unnamed," who died October 23, 1923.

1923, November 9, Friday: Location: Elyria, National Tube Plant. Victim: Jesus Guzman. Suspect: Bandeloo Cruz aka Baudelia Cruze aka Bendall Kruze aka Bendelia Cruz aka Radelia Cruz (Mexican [Guatemalan, actually]). Not much in the papers except for the trial. Brought before the January, 1924 Grand Jury. Indicted for second degree murder. Criminal trial starts February 18.

Defense is one of accidental shooting. Leading witness for the prosecution is Simeon Walkrain who says he saw the two men fighting and later, when he heard a man had been shot, went to the location of the fight and found a revolver and shells. It is a slow trial since some of the witnesses are Mexican and an interpreter must be used.

Plea: Not guilty. Found guilty as charged after the jury deliberates a little over a half-hour. A motion for a new trial was made by defense. It's overruled on February 23.

Defense attorney is W.S. Hurley who says the guilty man is a fatalist. "Whatever happens was meant to be, and that's all there is to it."

Outcome: Sentenced by Judge W.B. Thompson: Life in the Ohio Penitentiary, plus costs of $146.35.

This is one of the first of many Lorain County murder trials in which the defense questions the methods the county uses to select potential jurors.

1923, November 20, Tuesday, late night: Location: Lorain, along the Nickle Plate tracks between Oberlin and Leavitt roads. Victim: J.W. Laicy (Lacey, Laicey), Nickle Plate railroad detective. Suspect: Charles L. Wright (Colored). Plainclothes Railroad Detective Laicy confronts Wright "and several colored companions in the rail yards" to roust them from a box car. The situation escalates. Both Laicy and Wright pull revolvers and fire. Both are hit: Laicy, in the guts; Wright in the jaw, neck and hand.

Laicy staggers a half-mile before finding help. He is transported to St. Joseph's Hospital in Lorain. Wright, who claims to be from Richmond, Virginia, ends up there, too, once he is found in the railyard, weak from the loss of blood. When searched, Wright carries no weapon, but two .32 caliber cartridges are found in his pockets.

Laicy's story is that Wright fired first. Wright's is exactly the opposite.

Wright survives. He is held in the hospital until he is charged with murder in the first degree upon Laicy's death at 10:00pm on November 26. It's the detective's 25th birthday.

Laicy was a veteran of the World War, returning from two years of duty, shell-shocked and gassed. After 18 months of treatment at John Hopkins Hospital in Baltimore, Maryland, he had moved to Lorain with his wife, Martha, and son, Jack, not quite six months prior, living in the 1500-block of Maine Avenue. The detective is buried with full military honors in the Elmwood Cemetery.

Charles Wright is brought before the January, 1924 Grand Jury and indicted for first degree murder. He pleads not guilty.

1924, March 3: At his criminal trial Wright denies having shot at Laicy, testifying that more than one man in the boxcar had opened fire on the unfortunate detective. The signed confession produced as evidence? No way could've he made it—he was unconscious at the time, unable to speak.

Then, Wright backtracks to his original story. He shot Laicy only when fired upon. Laicy was in plain clothes but never identified himself as a man of the law. Wright says he feared for his life. After all, a White man who pulls a gun on a Black man has just one thought in mind.

At 10:00am, March 11, after several hours of deliberation, the jury finds Charles Wright guilty of murder in the first degree with a recommendation of mercy. Outcome: Life in the Ohio Penitentiary plus court costs of $243.72.

1923, December 23, Sunday:

It starts out like most other days for 18-year-old Walter Thomas: up early for his shift at the steel mill, out about 3:00pm, back to his place in south Lorain for a bath and a nap before heading out for a night of fun.

First, it's to 11th Street for some booze. Then, over to "Soldier Boy's" for some cards and dice. Then back to 11th for more power drink and maybe dancing with the pretty girls. That's when things start to go wrong. He argues with three jerks who haul him out onto the porch and rough him up pretty good. It takes three because Walter is no weak, little man.

Now, maybe it's the liquor urging Walter on, but three against one is wrong, plain and simple. He heads back to his place and retrieves his gun. With the pistol stuck in his belt, the young man hops a bus at 28th for the ride back to 11th. He'll show those three so-and-sos what happens when you pick a fight with a proud son of Alabama.

As Walter is boarding the bus at 28th, the owner of the Nickel Plate Restaurant, where the tracks cross 11th, has grown tired of an inebriated customer who refuses to shut his loud mouth. Lorain Police Office Ed Sage manages to get the lout out of the diner before calling for an assist to haul the drunk to the station.

Patrolman Fred Webber (no close relative of Judge A.R. Webber) and Patrol Wagon Driver August J. Mackerty are dispatched. It's nothing more than an out and back. The two men joke and kid as they ride along.

Meanwhile, a guy sitting on the bus next to the angry Alabaman, Walter Thomas, notices his pistol and asks him why he's carrying it. Walter pulls the weapon and yells to the people on the bus "three guys jumped me and I'm going to kill them all!"

It's no surprise that Walter Thomas' fellow passengers assume the seemingly crazy man with the weapon is threatening them. As the bus reaches the 11th Street tracks, Thomas leaps to his feet, points the revolver at bystander Edward McAndrews and shouts "damn you, you're the law and I'm going to blow out your brains."

McAndrews grabs the young man's wrist and deflects the gun towards the floor just as it goes off. He then shoves Thomas out of the door of the bus that speeds off. Thomas stands on the west side of 11th, on the south side of the tracks, half drunk, all the way angry, shouting at the top of his lungs, and waving his handgun in the air.

At this exact moment policemen A.J. Mackerty and Fred Webber arrive to assist Ed Sage with his disruptive diner. The two cops spot Walter Thomas flourishing a revolver. Webber jumps from the wagon, dashes across 11th, and starts grappling with the larger man.

Thomas fires several shots. Says Mackerty later, "When I heard the shots, I could feel a bullet speed by me. I drew my gun and fired at Thomas and by the time I had reached them, both men were wrestling on the pavement each appearing wounded." Mackerty blackjacks Thomas' head and puts him out of action.

Officer Sage leaves his prisoner at the Nickel Plate Restaurant and rushes across the street to assist. He orders the driver of a stopped bus to haul the badly wounded Fred Webber to St. Joseph's Hospital. Webber says his last words as he's carried aboard the vehicle; "He's got me, take me to the hospital."

Fred Webber is dead on arrival, the first Lorain Policeman killed in the line of duty. The 37-year-old, 10-year veteran of the Lorain Police leaves behind a wife, Rosia, 34, and daughters Mary, 12, and Elisabeth, 8.

In response to Webber's death, politicians, both in office and newly-elected, pledge a cleansing of not only the 11th Street district "but all others of similar repute." Lorain chief of Police Theodore Walker issues shoot to kill orders to his force with no consideration shown to crazed, armed suspects. "Shoot first," says the chief.

Authorities hear rumors of mobs planning to lynch the supposed shooter, Walter Thomas. The 18-year-old is quickly moved to the County Jail for his own safety.

Webber is buried the day after Christmas in the Calvary Cemetery. The entire Lorain police force is in the crowd of nearly a thousand that overflows the 10:00am services at St. Joseph's Church.

Said Father Charles Reichlin in his sermon, "Office Webber died a hero to his duty—he was faithful unto death. He died protecting your security and mine, at the hand of one of the many in this country today who lack respect for all laws, whether of God or man."

The community at large responds by setting up a $2,500 trust fund for the Webber children.

Coroner Perry Miles post-mortem shows that Fred Webber was struck by three shots: one grazed his neck, a second entered his back, and the third entered his left side and pierced his heart. But there's a problem… The revolver used by Walter Thomas contained lead bullets that should have left fragments within the dead man. Since none can be found, Coroner Miles has no choice but to very reluctantly conclude that Patrolman Fred Webber was killed by the steel-jacketed ammunition from Patrol Wagon Driver A.J. Mackerty's service pistol.

Both Walter Thomas (manslaughter) and policeman Mackerty (murder) are brought before the January, 1924 Grand Jury that considers their fate in light of evidence from the Coroner's Report.

No indictment is brought against Mackerty since the shots he fired were in the line of duty. On the other hand, because of a lack of evidence, Walter Thomas cannot be charged with anything more severe than carrying a concealed weapon and shooting to kill both Webber and Mackerty.

Thomas gladly pleads guilty to both. Outcome: A one-year term in jail. **Ed Sage, the cop with the drunk at the 11th Street eatery, remains a Lorain**

City Policeman for 32 years, retiring in 1948. He passes away on March 15, 1958, at the age of 73.

August J. Mackerty eventually rises to the rank of Lorain Police Lieutenant before having charges filed against him, in 1943, that he obtained his job under false pretenses. Seems he represented himself as a U.S. citizen, a citizenship the current District Attorney claimed Mackerty never obtained after arriving in 1901 from Germany. Mackerty dies in early December, 1972.

1924: *Rhapsody in Blue.* The National Party in South Africa protects White privilege. The U.S. state of Virginia—after sixty years of forgetting who just might be whose grand-pappy or grand-mammy—passes the Act to Preserve Racial Integrity. A shame there were no DNA tests available to determine exactly who might be carrying that "one-drop!" Mussolini's thugs kill Italy's Socialist leader. In the Docket: Possessing Liquor nets you a $500 fine. Transporting Liquor costs twice that. Repeat offenders spend time in the county jail. Calvin Coolidge (Massachusetts Republican) wins the Election with 54.0% of the popular vote. 16 lynchings: 16 Blacks, 0 others.

1924, January 13, Sunday: Location: Lorain. Victim: George Karvoch (Harvoch, Horvath). Suspect: Kathleen Zvosecz. Act: Gunshot. Karvoch is shot through the heart by Zvosecz who claims it was in self-defense to stop an assault. She is brought before the January Grand Jury. Outcome: No indictment.

1924, January 20, Sunday, shortly before 6:40pm: Location: Lorain, 18th Street, near Washington Avenue. Victim: Alfonso Stillitano (32, of Youngstown, Ohio).

Lorain Police Detectives David Beatty and William Johnson along with Office John Brusk are called to investigate a still-warm body lying in the tree lawn of 18th Street about 125 feet west of Washington. The man is dead from five gunshot wounds—one to his jaw and four to his body. Any footprints or other evidence on the snowy ground have been obliterated by the crowds that gathered around the body before the cops arrived. The corpse is hauled to Royce's morgue and identified by items in his pockets.

Stillitano is known to the local Italian community. Robbery does not seem to be a motive. Authorities suspect the action of one tall and one short "Black Handers." Several suspicious characters are taken in for questioning.

All are released except two who are handed over to officials from U.S. Immigration. Outcome: Unsolved.

1924, January 23: *The Chronicle-Telegram:*

Women Named Sheriff for Crawford Co.—Is First of Her sex to Be Thus Honored in Ohio—Succeeds Husband Who Was Killed Saturday:

Mrs. Ira F. Freese, widow of the late sheriff of Crawford County (Ohio), was today appointed sheriff for the unexpired term of her husband. She is the first woman sheriff in Ohio.

Her husband was killed last Saturday when his auto was struck by a passenger train.

1924, February 14, Thursday: Location: Lorain, 1800-block of East 28 Street. Victim: Wallace Moore aka William L. Anthony. Suspect: Keouas (Thomas, Robert) E. Crenshaw (Grenshaw, Cranshaw) (28 Colored). Crenshaw hails from Amherst and has been living in the 2900-block of Pearl Avenue. The killing is the end result of an argument over the winnings during a game of "craps."

Wallace Moore is shot three times: right jaw, left cheek, left breast. Crenshaw escapes to Cleveland, Ohio, where he is apprehended and returned. He is bonded for $100 and released on own recognizance. Charge: Murder in the second degree. Plea: Not guilty. He is allowed to change it to guilty of manslaughter. Outcome: Ohio Penitentiary, 10 years, plus court costs of $227.

1924, February 20: *The Chronicle-Telegram:*

Lands Many **Convicts.**

The Salvation Army is carrying on a revival meeting at their hall. A.L. Carey, of Cleveland, is in charge of the work. Last night there were twenty **converts.**

Emphasis is mine. Typos sometimes make me smile.

1924, February 20: *The Chronicle-Telegram:*

Joe Sex Dies at Niles, Ohio.

Mrs. Annie Sex, 220 Seventh Street, received word yesterday of the death of her son Joe Sex at Niles, Ohio. No particulars as to the cause of his demise were given, and she left at once for Newark, Ohio, where the body was to be taken. Mr. Sex formerly lived in this city, and at that time was assistant superintendent of the Longwear Rubber Co.

Yes, it's juvenile. That doesn't make it any less funny.

1924, April ??: Location: Lorain, "in the middle of a little residential street." Victim: George Temasch. Suspect: Paul Fuga. Act: Knifing. This case is a mystery from the start. Temasch's body is found in early morning. Fuga is arrested when stains, believed to be blood, are found in his cellar. He denies all knowledge from the start. Paul Fuga is still in jail in late June. His lawyers seek his release because he is being denied a "fair and speedy trial." Probate Court Judge Wilcox refuses. The June Grand Jury does not indict Fuga and he is set free. Outcome: Unsolved.

Probate Judge Harvey Clyde Wilcox:
H.C. Wilcox was born, September 27, 1872, in LaGrange, Lorain County, Ohio. He was educated in the LaGrange Public School and was a graduate of Baldwin University, Berea, Ohio, and the Cleveland Law School (which later merged with Marshal Law School and is now affiliated with Cleveland State University).

A Republican, he was elected to Lorain County Clerk of Courts in 1902, then to serve as Probate Court Judge 1913-1937. In Lorain County, at that time, that also carried responsibility as Juvenile Court Judge. Retirement brought him to practice law with is son, Hubbard. H.C. Wilcox died, March 7, 1971, and was buried in the Brookdale Cemetery, Elyria, Ohio.

Judge H.C. Wilcox should not be confused with Judge Frank M. Wilcox who served as the Elyria Municipal Judge from 1955 (at the inception of that court) until 1972, when he retired.

1924, May 3, Saturday: Location: Lorain, field on Eagle Avenue, near B&O tracks. Victim: Unknown man "pounded on the head with an axe or club." Outcome: Unsolved.

1924, May 22, Thursday: Location: Lorain. Victim: Unknown infant boy, ten days old. Act: Strangulation. Baby was thought to be from Elyria, but was found floating in the Black River in Lorain. Well-developed. Believed to be born alive. Handkerchief tied around the infant's neck tight enough to choke. Buried from the Thompson Funeral Home in Lorain. Outcome: Unsolved.

1924, June 15, 5:00pm, Sunday: Location: Lorain, 2834 Palm Avenue. Victim: Nicholas Spanich (36, boarding house owner). Suspect: John Spanich (38, brother). Act: Knifing. Drunken fight between bothers. Witnesses see the start of the action but abandon the siblings to their battle. Police are unsure what happened. They find Nicholas, the victim, on the floor, bled to death, with one arm nearly cut off and a stab wound in the side. Brother John, the suspect, is also wounded and is placed in St. Joseph's Hospital, under guard. He is bonded at $20,000. Outcome: The June Grand Jury does not indict.

FRATRICIDE – Killing a brother.

1924, June 28, Saturday, late afternoon:

A tornado forms over Sandusky Bay, Ohio, and strikes that city, destroying twenty-five businesses, nearly one hundred homes, and killing eight. The storm heads east over Lake Erie, causing huge, damaging waves at Vermilion, and then roars ashore at Lakeview Park.

The wind cuts a three-mile-wide swath through the city of Lorain, demolishing a large section of downtown. Automobiles are shoved through buildings. Some vehicles are blown out and into Lake Erie. Hundreds of homes are destroyed.

The tornado skips into the air after visiting Lorain, then bounces into both Sheffield and Avon on its way east. With all the damage it's something of a miracle that the official death toll will eventually be set at seventy-two.

The estimated damage to the city of Lorain is $12 million. Martial law is declared. Street are patrolled by the State Militia. Curiosity-seekers are either turned away or pressed into service as rescuers, but not everyone comes out of the post-storm drama alive…

1924, June 30, Monday: Location: Lorain. Victim: Sam Turboreck. Suspect: John S. Tenerty. Suspect Tenerty is a self-appointed guard at a storm-damaged Lorain hotel and shoots Turboreck for stealing wood. He is indicted by the June Grand Jury. Charge: Murder in the first degree. Plea: Not guilty. *Changed to:* Guilty of manslaughter. Outcome: Sentenced to the Ohio Penitentiary for 5 years, plus court costs of $40.45. Parole hearing November of 1929.

1924, ? ?: Location: Lorain. Victim: Adam Ratenchuk (Rayenchuck). Suspect: Fred Bender (19) and two others. Three men rob Ratenchuk's store. He resists, pulling a banana knife which is taken and used against him. Bender confesses his part in the crime while under arrest in Cleveland, Ohio, on a forging charge. Police investigate. Outcome: Nothing in docket. No further information in the papers.

A banana knife, akin to a linoleum knife, has an up-and-back, sharpened hook at the tip.

1925: The world is supposed to end, according to Margaret Rowen. It doesn't. In Chicago, trumpeter Louis Armstrong forms the "Hot Five." Mussolini's political opponents are arrested as he abolishes freedom of the press. He's happy to be the dictator. The first volume of *Mein Kampf* is published. The *Geneva Protocol* bans the warfare use of poisonous gas and biological weapons. Reza Khan mounts a coup in Iran and declares himself The Shah. Paul Newman is born in Cleveland, Ohio. Jonathan Winters is born in Dayton, Ohio. In the Docket: "LIQUOR" is the catch-all phrase for cases involving booze. In North College Hill, Hamilton County, Ohio, Ed Tumey is arrested for possessing liquor by his mayor, A.R. Pugh who also turns out to be the Prosecutor and Judge in the case. The Crabbe Act allows the Police-Mayor-Prosecutor-Judge to collect an extra $12 from the $100 fine levied against Ed Tumey. Mr. Tumey doesn't like the idea, not one, doggone bit. 17 lynchings: 17 Blacks, 0 others. $1,000 is worth $14,258 modern.

1925, January 11, Sunday, about 3:30am: Location: Lorain, 1800-block East 28th Street. Victim: Jose Perez (30, Mexican). Suspect: Benido (Benito) Padillo. Benido Padillo and his wife are arguing. Padillo grows violent. Wife flees to an upstairs room in the boarding house and asks the man there, Jose Perez, to intervene. Padillo crashes through the door. Jose Perez stands up to the angry husband and is shot for his bravery.

The wounded Perez then, depending on the newspaper, either jumps or falls through the room's window onto the roof of the building next door, and then again either jumps or falls through the skylight in the roof of that building, hurtling down and into a restaurant below.

Shooter Padillo returns to his room, dresses in his best clothing, and flees the scene taking $70 dollars with him. Police are called. Padillo's room is found to contain the smoked remains of marijuana.

Police find Jose Perez on the floor of the restaurant and think he's only stunned and bloody from his fall through the skylight. He is taken to Lorain Police Headquarters where the bullet wound is discovered. Perez is transported to St. Joseph's Hospital where he dies six hours later.

Coroner Perry returns a finding of homicide after an autopsy by Drs. Peebles and Adrian. Perez was struck in the right side by a single bullet from a "Mexican .38." The projectile passed through a vertebra punctured a lung and lodged in the left arm.

Suspect Padillo is trailed to Cleveland where, it is claimed, he's been seen twice in the B.&O. rail yards. He is indicted, in abstentia, by the January Grand Jury for murder in the first degree.

Padillo is found and arrested *in late 1927*. He pleads not guilty to murder, then agrees to guilty of manslaughter. Outcome: Sentenced by Judge W.B. Thompson to the Ohio Penitentiary for a minimum of 1 year, plus court costs of $49.79.

This was not Padillo's first run-in with the law. He had been arrested a few weeks before shooting Perez on a charge of trying to cut a man's throat, but was released due to lack of evidence.

The above killing was the first I saw mentioning marijuana as part of the action. The newspaper article that followings appeared the very next day.

1925: January 12: *The Chronicle-Telegram:*

Coroner Plans to Ask Law on Drug—Dr. Perry Will Enlist Prosecutor and Legislators in Move to Obtain Regulatory, Ohio Statute Covering Marijuana, a Deadly Mexican Opiate.

Legislation to place the deadly Mexican opiate, Marijuana, under an Ohio statute, will be asked of State Senator William R. Comings and Representative Elmer F. Cotton by Coroner Myles E. Perry the coroner, said today.

Marijuana abounds in Mexican rooming houses and "joints" in South Lorain and has figured prominently in recent deaths from violent causes in other criminal affairs in this alleged vice district, police say.

Coroner Perry said he would communicate with Prosecuting Attorney Dow Baird to enlist his aid in getting a statute into the Ohio general code to regulate or prohibit the importation, sale or use of this drug.

"The drug is deadly in some cases and drives many who use it into lunacy. Smokers have been known to become as raving maniacs from its effects. It is more powerful than opium and more dangerous than many other drugs now regulated by law," the coroner says.

But due to its scarcity and to the fact that little has been known about it until recent years, no law has ever been passed to control Marijuana.

Lorain police have confiscated large lots of the drug. As much as five pounds has been accumulated at once. But there is no law to curb its use.

The drug resembles a small leafed weed with a tiny berry. It is dried and smoked in pipes and cigarettes.

At the time of the investigation into the death of Juan Fransto from acute alcoholism in his room on East 25 street, December 26, police learned that Fransto and his companions were in the habit of brewing a tea from the marijuana and mixing it with their liquor.

In the room where a man was shot Sunday morning, police found many cigarette stubs lying about the floor containing the remains of what had been smoked of the drug [*see case listed just above*].

"The drug is a menace and ought to be controlled," Dr. Perry said. "Under the Ohio law, it is necessary for a specific statute to be enacted covering marijuana before its use can be prohibited."

A little *Reefer Madness*, anyone?

1925, February 8, Sunday, about 2:00am: Location: Lorain, 300-block 14th Street. Victims: Dominic Griffa and Mike Verano.

Police are called at the sound of shooting. Griffa is found dead, shot in the back, slouched on the floor near the kitchen door. Verano's lying on a bed, bleeding from two chest wounds. All bullets are from a .32 caliber weapon. Verano is taken to St. Joseph's in Lorain and lives for several hours but refuses to make any statement to the police for fear of retribution against his family and friends.

Potential witnesses either give conflicting stories or "answer questions with shrugs." A nine-year-old boy, Josephino Courareo, says the victims were shot by two men. Police think the suspects may be the boy's uncles, but have no proof. Outcome: Unresolved/Unsolved.

1925, March 30, Monday, about 1:40am: Location: Oberlin, Frankfort Street, James Wright residence. Victim: Clarence Stevens (24, Colored, of Oberlin). Suspect: Homer "Bighead" Clement (Colored).

A total of six men have been playing poker all day long with Homer Clement losing steadily. Clarence Stevens calls Clement, who is drunk, a name. Clement draws a revolver and fires. The bullet enters Steven's forehead slightly over the left eye. It does not exit.

Clement scoops the money from the table, about $35, and flees. When asked by the sheriff why none of them stopped the killer, one of the other card players replies, "We did not want that man. That gun was as big as a cannon!"

Both Clarence Stevens and Homer Clement are well-known to authorities. Stevens was shot, and then served time a few years back, when he attempted to rob an undercover policeman in Cleveland. Last year (1924) Clement fought with and cut up Butler Durham. His most recent arrest was for carrying a concealed weapon.

Clarence Stevens is buried from Rust Methodist Church by Rev. C.T. Parker in Oberlin's Westwood Cemetery on April 1.

Homer Clement vanishes from the area. If found, he will be charged with murder in the first degree. Outcome: Suspect never found. The case is nollied by the prosecutor in April, 1926, after four continuances.

Names Not Used:

The scene of the killing described above, "Oberlin, Frankfort Street, James Wright residence," no longer exists. It's not that the house is gone—the entire street is missing!

People tend to think that place names are fairly permanent, but that's not true. House numbers, street names, even entire towns are created, change, and vanish without leaving much of a trace. Most people living in Lorain County have no idea what happened to Rawsonville or where Nickle Plate or Charelston used to be. *Not* forgetting is part of what makes history important.

Be sure to note the year of a story before assuming you know exactly where the murder occurred. Just because a story says "1325 Broadway, Lorain," doesn't mean that it was where *you* see as that address. Many cities and towns have renumbered their lots at least once. Not only that, but for most small villages, house numbers are relatively new. Really… Why would your house need a number when everyone simply knew where you lived?

Some places, like the City of Lorain, reset the names of their streets. The

8th you know might be different from the 8th of the past. Your Vine might very well be the past's Mill. If you're trying to figure out if a street name might have changed, consider its tie to history. Would there be a reason to name a street "Edison" before old Tom became famous?

As far as Oberlin's "Frankfort Street" goes… Traces of it can still be seen. Go south on Spring Street from East College. Just before you reach the bike trail (where the railroad ran), look to your right. A careful eye will discern where Frankfort used to be that, before it was Frankfort, was part of Mechanic Street, which is now called "Locust." I think. The other stuff about Rawsonville, Nickle Plate, and Charleston? That's your problem!

1925, June 10, Wednesday: Location: ? Victim: Ricardo Luard (a Mexican). Suspect: Pilar Outiga (Outega, Ontiga) (a Mexican). Ricardo Luard is shot in the neck by Pilar Outiga during an argument and dies of infection three weeks later. Outiga's criminal trial for murder in the second degree ends October 27, during which, evidence was presented that it was the victim, Luard, who attacked and shot first. Outcome: Outiga is found guilty of manslaughter and sentenced by Judge Thompson to 10 years in the Ohio Penitentiary, plus court costs of $86.50.

Pilar Outiga serves about four-and-a-half years of his sentence when he dies, along with more than 300 other prisoners, in the Penitentiary's fire of April, 1930. Others convicts from Lorain County that perish in the fire are John Niciceki of Grafton (on a one-year sentence for his third offense for the possession of liquor) and Frank Miller aka Raymond Miller of Elyria (on a three-year sentence for check and bank fraud). Both Niciceki and Miller had been at the prison for six months.

1925, July 10, Friday: Location: Lorain. Victim: William (Wilbur) Nance. Suspect: Luther Young. Nance is killed (in a manner unspecified) during an argument over a card game. Suspect Luther Young flees and is indicted, in abstentia, by the July Grand Jury for murder in the second degree.

1928, May 14: Luther Young is arrested by Officers Knapp and Meister in Buffalo, New York and returned to the Lorain County Jail to stand trial.

June 14, Grand Jury re-indicts on the charge of murder in the second degree. Young is allowed to plead guilty of manslaughter. Outcome: Sentenced to the Ohio Penitentiary for 1 year, plus court costs of $48.94.

The original 1925 indictment was continued until March 29, 1937, when it was nollied by the Prosecutor because of the suspect's 1928 conviction of manslaughter.

1925, September 6, Sunday: Location: Lorain. Victim: Mildred Vouchovich (Oukovich) (wife). Suspect: Mike (Milos) Vouchovich (Oukovich) (husband). Wife shot in spine. Husband, suspected of the crime, escapes and is never arrested. Outcome: Case is nollied by Prosecutor on May 14, 1935.

1925, September 24 or 25, Thursday or Friday: Location: Elyria, 500-block Delaware Avenue. Victim: Jim McCoy (67, a recluse). Suspect: Joseph Hackendorn (67). McCoy is a bachelor and known as a candy maker, but has worked other trades from railroading to sailing. He also makes his own wine and is very drunk at the time of his death. Neighbor Joe Baki is the last to see victim alive.

Victim McCoy, who has been flashing a lot of cash in downtown Elyria, is found with his head crushed by an eight-pound sledge-hammer. Police theorize he may have been murdered during a robbery of $100, but because there's a gold watch still in his pocket, the motive could be jealousy over his relationship with Joseph Hackendorn's ex-wife.

Hackendorn, who lives in the 200-block of Case Avenue, Elyria is arrested by Chief of Police E.J. Stankard when he tells conflicting stories during questioning. He is then released when witnesses confirm his alibi.

Hackendorn was himself the subject of a potential robbery around the time the murder occurred and had frightened off the thieves with four shots from a gun. He puts forth the theory that the murderers may be his own ex-wife and in-laws. Those charges are denied.

McCoy is buried on September 28.

Says Chief Stankard:

> We are hampered in investigating this mystery because the crime happened in a remote part of the city and there were few if any people around who could have known anything about it. There wasn't a thing disturbed in McCoy's house and even the ground about the dwelling was bare that there are no footprints of any kind. *The Chronicle-Telegram, Sep. 28, 1925.*

Outcome: Unsolved.

1925, September 26: Because of crowding at the Massillon Hospital, Lorain County insane will be sent to the Toledo Asylum instead.

1925, September 30: *The Chronicle-Telegram:*
>   North Part of County is Peeved.
>   A persistent rumor is in circulation that an effort is being made to have the north part of this county split and another county formed with Lorain, Black River, French Creek, Avon and Brownhelm in it. Dissatisfaction with the county officials who it is alleged are not paying enough attention the north part of the county is said to be the reason of the agitation.

1926: Miniature golf. Vitamins B1 and B2. Jelly Roll Morton and the Red Hot Peppers record *Black Bottom Stomp*. A 23-year-old Bing Crosby records *I've Got The Girl*. Hitler Youth. Hirohito, now 25, takes his place on the Imperial Throne of Japan. In Mount Vernon, Ohio, Paul Lynde is at the very start of his journey towards the Center Square. In the Docket: Rape with Consent. This was most commonly used for what we know as "Statutory Rape." Plus, various charges with trials never taking place because suspects escape the law. 30 lynchings: 23 Blacks, 7 others.

1926, January 1, Friday: Location: Lorain, 1600-block East 32nd Street. Victim: George Fairvody (Fefezaria, Fehervary), a Hungarian (29, former boarder). Suspects: Mary Major and Bert (Bertie) Major (wife and husband). December, 1925, Bert orders Fairvody from the house because of his alleged attentions to Mary. A few nights before Christmas, Bert Major and his brother, John, give Fairvody a beating on the street in South Lorain. In response, Fairvody tells Bert Major that he's a dead man who will be "shot on sight."

December 27, Bert answers a knock at the kitchen door and is nearly struck by two shots from a revolver. The shooter races to the front of the house and fires twice more in through the windows, causing damage but not harming anyone. Nobody sees the person's face, but everyone assumes it's Fairvody.

January 1, about 9:00pm, Mary Major hears a knock at the kitchen door. She sneaks a peek through the window and sees that it's Fairvody. She hurries to her bedroom to retrieve a revolver that she then hides beneath her apron. When she opens the door Fairvody bulls his way into the house and demands to see her husband, saying "I am going to kill him." Mary says, truthfully, that her husband is not home but refuses to tell Fairvody where Bert is. The outraged intruder turns on her and threatens to end her life if the doesn't cooperate.

Mary Major pulls her revolver. She will tell police: "I fired three times at him and then ran out of the house and as I ran I think I shot once more."

Bert has returned to his home by the time police arrive at the scene. They are sitting in the kitchen, close by the body of the victim. Mary's revolver is handed over when asked for. It contains one bullet and four spent cartridges. By way of comparison, Fairvody's head contains two bullets. Examination of the body turns up a knife, but no firearm.

Mary Majors is arrested and charged with second degree murder. Three days later police return to arrest Bert Majors when boarders at the house, Mike Kaferejo and his son, tell authorities that Mary made up her entire story. It was Bert who did the shooting, not his wife.

The case is taken to the Grand Jury, mid-January of 1926. The charge against Mary returns without a true bill. Bertie is indicted for manslaughter, the papers report first, and then second degree murder with $2,500 bond. Bert Majors pleads not guilty. Outcome: There is no criminal trial. Charges are dropped.

1926, January 4: *The Chronicle-Telegram:*
>Woman is Grand Jury Foreman.
>
>When the special grand jury convened this morning they elected Mrs. Leon Underhill as foreman. This is the first time in the history of the county that a woman has acted as foreman of a jury. Mrs. Underhill has been serving on the petit jury during the present term of course, and has been in all of the important cases tried this term.

1926, February 25, Thursday about 4:00pm: Location: Elyria, near Lodi Street, New York Central Railway Camp (near Kerstetter Way). Victim: Felix Carvello (Carwell) (30, Mexican). Suspect: James Harris (28, Colored).

Both are section workers for the New York Central Railroad. In Carvello's room are Fannie May, Mrs. Lee Davis (38, cook), and Pauline Allen (25). Everyone is drunk.

The women say Felix Carvello was nodding off to sleep when James Harris entered the room, seized a shovel, and struck the victim three times:

one blow to the left side of the skull and two more in the back, to the base of the brain.

Harris runs from the scene and jumps a freight. He decides he is too lightly dressed for the cold weather, returns for warmer clothing, and is apprehended without a struggle two hours later when surrounded by officers on West River, near Lodi Street (West River and Lake).

Police think the motive may be jealousy over the attentions of Mrs. Lee Davis, who is the section cook and whose husband is in the County Jail, working out a fine for bootlegging.

The law says Carvello's body has to be kept for 36 hours. No relatives claim the body and it is buried at the county's expense.

The women are held in jail as witnesses, each being paid $48 with an additional $7.00 at the end of the trial.

James Harris is indicted by the April Grand Jury for murder in the second degree. Harris says he saw Carvello reach to draw a knife. Not so, say the female witnesses. Besides, says Coroner Perry, while it's true the victim had a knife, it was hardly larger than a pen knife and it was not drawn.

Charge: Murder in the second degree. Plea: Not guilty. *Changed to:* Guilty of manslaughter. Outcome: Sentenced to the Ohio Penitentiary, 12 year minimum, plus court costs of $54.41.

1926, April 10, Saturday, just past midnight: Location: Lorain, 1770 East 28th Street. Victim: Jose Garza (?, Colored). Suspect: Paul Martinez, aka Paul Lopez (22, Mexican).

Garza is a dishwasher in a restaurant at 1770 East 28 Street and will not allow Martinez into the restaurant's kitchen. With the words "I will kill you," Martinez draws a knife and attacks Garza, stabbing him more than a dozen times. Two of the wounds pierce the victim's heart. He lives a short while but is unable to make a statement.

The manager of the place, Louis Pulido, tries to keep the suspect from escaping, but the suspect pulls a .32 caliber revolver, points it at Pulido, and says "I will kill you, too." However, he does not fire and escapes the scene.

Martinez is arrested the afternoon of the killing when he returns to the scene of the crime. He denies all knowledge of the killing despite numerous eyewitnesses accounts. Charge: First degree murder. Plea: Not guilty. Outcome: Nothing in either the criminal docket or newspapers about a trial.

1926, July ?: Location: Elyria, The "Jungle" near the New York Central tracks (likely the Lodi Street area). Victim: Unknown Man, assumed to be the victim of a "tramp fight." Coroner Myles Perry unable to identify the victim since there are no distinguishing marks that can be used. Outcome: Unsolved.

1926, July 3, Saturday: Location: "In the woods" of Highland Park in west Lorain. Victim: Unknown infant boy (about one week old). Body is clothed in an underskirt and wrapped in several layers of Lorain newspapers published on July 3. The infant is found July 18 by Frank Smith, of the 300-block of West 31st Street, who was taking a walk through the woods.

Coroner M.E. Perry is called with an autopsy performed by Dr. M.E. Kishman of Lorain. The cause of death is not specified, but is described as "a most brutal affair." Police search for a young girl who has been seen several nights in a row in the park in hopes that she will be able to shed some light on the mystery. Outcome: Unsolved.

1926, July 19: *The Chronicle-Telegram:*

> Prisoner is Given a Five Year Term—Judge Sentences Lorain Man Who Plead Guilty to Manslaughter Charge:
>
> The traditions of early American history and customs of the colonists who molded the fate of this nation were recalled and portrayed in common pleas court this morning in the pleas of defense attorney for Anthony Garcia, Lorain, who appeared to plead guilty to a charge of manslaughter for the killing of Joseph Guteries. Just before noon Judge Webber sentenced Garcia to the state penitentiary for five years.
>
> A parallel was drawn between the battle of Garcia and Guteries in a woods south of Lorain in the early morning three months ago and with those of the colony days when the pioneers of this nation indulged in hand-to-hand combat on "the field of honor."
>
> The instance of the last notable conflict was cited when Aaron Burr challenged Alexander Hamilton to a "duel of honor." Burr was indicted on a murder charge in two states for the act but fled the country before coming to take hold of the reins of the nation as a statesman.
>
> The customs of Mexico in which both Garcia and Guteries

were raised are today similar to those which were in vogue when the thirteen states were settled, defense attorney said.

The quarrel for which the men fought over at Lorain is said to have developed over the disappearance of some cigarettes. Garcia was indicted by the last grand jury on a charge of second degree murder.

1926, July 22: *The Chronicle-Telegram:*

Find Body of Man in River.

The body of an unidentified man was found floating on the waters of Black River this morning near the [Lorain] Shipyards. The body was badly decomposed and there was evidence that the body had been in the water for several days. Police have been unable in their search to find any clues as to who the man is or where he is from. The body was unclothed when it was found near the bank of the river.

No other articles appear.

1926, September 10, Friday: Location: Lorain, corner of Globe Street and 29th. Victim: Stanley Rockich (Rakich). Suspect: Lazo T. Ralich. Victim Rockich lives in the 1600-block of E 30th Street. Suspect in the 1700-block of E 29th. A fight starts as an argument over a small amount of rent money and escalates from there. Rockich pulls a knife; Ralich wrestles the blade from the victim and strikes him with it. The act is claimed as self-defense.

Arraigned on first degree murder charges. September Grand Jury indicts for second degree murder with the victim's widow at the prosecutor's table.

In trial, the defense claims that during the struggle, Stanley Rockich actually stabbed himself with his own knife, and so the accused is not responsible. Charge: Murder in the second degree. Plea: Not guilty.

Outcome: Guilty of manslaughter. Sentence by Judge A.R. Webber: Ohio Penitentiary, 5 years, plus cost. Cost: $140.81.

1926, October 9, Saturday, 5:00am: Location: Lorain, 500-block West 20th Street. Victim: Joseph Barbatano (33). Barbatano is a foreman at the National Tube Company. He is rushing home to see his newly-first-born child, a girl, and is 100 yards from home when four revolver shots are fired from ambush.

Two shots strike him in the head. He dies instantly. A woman's footprints are found behind the brush from which the shots were fired.

Oddly enough, Barbatano's brother-in-law, John Jazziano, is currently in the hospital recovering from a shotgun blast to the back that was also fired from ambush. Jazziano denies having any knowledge of the fatal shooting.

There are no witnesses to this killing, but a woman neighbor claims to have heard a female voice say "oh, mother" at the time of the shooting. Despite the footprints and the witness, police are sure the killer was a man. They have identified him, but not published his name, saying the suspect has fled the area. Outcome: Unresolved/Unsolved.

1926, October 25, Monday:

Chester, part of the "notorious Durham family of Oberlin," is no angel. Some folks would say it's in his blood. After all, his grandfather, Samuel Durham, spent time in the Big House for the murder of Constable Stone (*see 1881, May 12*).

Chester's been in and out of trouble with the law since he was a kid. His most serious infraction, so far, took place in 1916, when at the age of 33 he interfered with operation of the "Green Line," threatening Conductor Henry Wirscham with two loaded revolvers.

In exchange for pleading guilty to a minor charge of "Pointing Firearms" Judge Thompson sentenced Durham to the Cleveland Workhouse to work off a $300 fine at 60 cents a day. Durham was out in a year and a half.

Shortly after, he was arrested and fined $5 for sleeping off a drunk in the Elyria terminal of the New York City Railroad. No big deal.

In October of 1918, a marriage license was taken by Chester Durham, 34, and Mattie Walker, 27, both of Oberlin. Fewer than five years later, Mattie filed for divorce. The cause was "extreme cruelty;" he frequently beat and choked her. She asked for and was granted a divorce, alimony, and an injunction to prevent him from interfering with her life.

In May of 1924, Chester Durham and Otis Smith (also of Oberlin) were arrested for bootlegging. Justice S.J. George fined them $100 each when they pled guilty.

Likewise, Chester's sometimes friend, the tall and thin William Whiteside, is a tough character. An emigre from the West Indies, he's had several scrapes with the law. For instance, he was arrested in December, 1922, on a gambling charge based in large part on testimony from Rev. J.H. Thompson. At that time, Whiteside threatened to get even, which he did by roughing up the man of God. For that, Whiteside was fined $200 and spent six months in the Cleveland Workhouse.

On Monday, October 25, 1926, William Whiteside, Norman Moore, Frank Blakely, Carl Payne, Chester Durham and his uncle, Butler Durham, are playing cards at Butler's place on the corner of Spring and Railroad streets in Oberlin. It's been an enjoyable, loud, and increasingly drunken several hours.

There are the usual outbursts as the men win or lose a hand. The stakes aren't large, nobody has that kind of money. But, sometimes, it's not the amount of cash that really matters.

Chester Durham clearly beats Whiteside in a particular hand. Whiteside, disputing the circumstances, refuses to pay the 75 cents he wagered. Durham pushes for the money. Whiteside refuses. Durham employs sharper language.

Whiteside retrieves a shotgun from his belongings and threatens an unimpressed Durham who insists Whiteside pay his debt. In reply, Whiteside fires, first one barrel, then the other. Durham takes the first load in the gut but manages to avoid the second blast.

William Whiteside then runs from the building. Uncle Butler Durham, who, in 1902, was nearly shot to death during a drunken craps game by the mostly one-armed and deaf Oberlinian "Dummy" Fox, takes up in hot pursuit. Butler manages to fire both barrels from his own shotgun before losing Whiteside among the houses.

Whiteside runs only a few blocks before stopping at the house of George Sims where George's young son picks pellets from the wounded shooter's arm and leg. Upon discovering the bleeding man in her house, Mrs. Sims angrily orders him to leave, which he does without argument. The Sims later tell police they have no idea where Whiteside went.

Oberlin's Dr. Miller and City Manager Herrick are called to the scene of the crime. It is evident that Chester Durham will not survive. The 43-year-old dies half a day after being shot. He is buried in Westwood Cemetery from the Rust M.E. Church.

Outcome: I found no evidence of a trial. My assumption is that the 57-year-old William Whiteside was never found.

Butler Durham, himself something of an infamous character in Lorain County for his many arrests and minor convictions, is taken into custody less than two years later after running about his neighborhood claiming a man with a pistol was after him. By the time police arrive Butler had shot through his own door, the doors of neighboring homes, and then holed himself up in a shed on the back of his property to hold several men at bay. Durham fired upon officers as they arrived. Luckily for everyone involved, the shells were wet and failed to explode.

Probate Judge H.C. Wilcox would eventually declare Durham insane. Butler Durham died in the early autumn of 1935. He was 69 years old.

But we're not done with the Durham family, yet. Let's step a few years beyond the official range of this book...

1962, November 2, Friday: Location: Oberlin, 200-block of Lincoln Street. Victim: Windom Durham (77). Act: Suffocation.

A neighbor requested a check on Windom Durham due to "suspicious conditions." Police discover that Durham had been robbed and found him, severely beaten, bound, and gagged to the point of being unable to breathe. Several people were interviewed but none arrested. Outcome: Unsolved.

Chester Durham, whose shooting was described above? This man, Windom, sometimes seen as Windham, was his younger brother.

See: 1881, May 20.

1927: U.S. golfer Walter Hagen wins his fifth PGA Championship. Stalin gives his major rivals the boot. Communists take power in China's Jiangxi Province. Right-winger Chiang Kai-shek then launches a campaign against Communism. The IRA assassinates the President of the Irish Free State as he's on his way to Catholic Mass. The U.S. Congress passes laws making it illegal to mail-order concealable firearms. Coolidge says he ain't gonna run in 1928. For the first time, the U.S. Census lists "cancer" as one of the top three killers of those in the U.S. The others are influenza and pneumonia. Remember Ed Tumey, of North College Hill, Hamilton County, Ohio, who was arrested, convicted, and fined in 1925 for possessing alcohol? His lawyers push the case to the U.S. Supreme Court. It agrees that Ohio's Crabbe Act, with its extra dough for law enforcement and judges in actions involving liquor, violates due process since convictions are more likely when a monetary reward is involved. 16 lynchings: 16 Blacks, 0 others.

1927, late February: Location: One mile east of Ridgeville. Victim: Unknown infant boy. On the afternoon of March 6, the tiny body is found at the bottom of a basket. It is wrapped in two Cleveland newspapers dated February 24 and 25, 1927, and covered with several pounds of coal. The discovery is made near the high tension line in Ridgeville by William and George Winfield and Robert Thatcher, all of Ridgeville Heights. The basket has been in place a few days. The body is frozen and in a good state of preservation. Coroner

Myles Perry investigates the case and thinks the baby, about one week old, was not brought a far distance. The tiny victim is buried on March 8 in the Ridgelawn Cemetery. Outcome: Unsolved.

1927, May 14, Saturday: Location: South Amherst. Victim: Mary Sokoloff (30, common law wife). Suspect: Alex Sokoloff (35, common law husband, Russian). Mary Sokoloff, recently of Cleveland, has come to Amherst to stay with her common-law husband, Alex, at the boarding house run by Joe Zezula. On the night before her death, the Sokoloffs, along with Zezula, Tom Shem, Nick Zumkoff, and Mike Smolik drink heavily.

Alex, always violently jealous, suspects affection between his wife and Tom Shem. He accosts the two of them, then begins to beat his wife about her head and shoulders. She falls to the floor. He kicks and stomps her.

When Tom Shem and Nick Zumkoff try to stop Alex, he seizes a nearby hatchet and uses it to strike Zumkoff on the head. Alex is trying for another blow when Joe Zezula jumps him and wrestles the hatchet away. Zezula then runs to obtain more potent firepower.

Alex, now in a fury, grabs a knife, attacks, and cuts Tom Shem. He turns back to his wife who is still on the floor and begins cutting her flesh and slashing at her wrists.

It's the hatchet-wounded Zumkoff, this time, who disarms Alex, tossing the blade out the window. About this time, Zezula appears with a shotgun and somehow manages to restore order without actually shooting anybody.

Zumkoff and Shem wander out into the street. They are found and taken to the hospital by two of their sober neighbors, Mary Simaskevitch and Steve Dano. But, because of their extreme drunkenness, none of those involved in the battle think to care for the beaten and cut Mary Sokoloff.

At 10:00 the next morning the sheriff, tipped off by hospital staff, arrives to investigate the fight. He finds Mary Sokoloff unconscious on the floor and rushes her to the hospital. X-rays reveal that her neck, back, and pelvis are all broken and that she is suffering from a number of internal injuries, all from the beating she had received from her husband.

She soon dies and Alex Sokoloff is arrested on charges of murder in the second degree. The accused pleads not guilty when arraigned before Justice S.J. George. Bail is set at $2,500 but it cannot met.

The defense argues that everyone involved was so "stupefied by liquor" that nobody could testify as to what actually happened or who was responsible for the death.

Assistant Prosecutor Howard Butler agrees to allow Alex Sokoloff to plead to manslaughter. Judge A.R. Webber sentences the guilty man to the Ohio Penitentiary for 5 years hard labor, with no solitary confinement, plus court costs of $44.14. Outcome: 1929, March 2: Prisoner Alex Sokoloff dies of pulmonary tuberculosis while in care of the Ohio Penitentiary Hospital.

1927, June 30, Thursday: Location: Lorain, 11th Street. Victim: A.J. Johnson. Suspect: Jim Bond (Colored). Johnson is shot by Bond as the conclusion of an argument over a girl. Bond is already known to police and had been arrested in August of 1925 for transporting liquor. The September Grand Jury indicts Bond for murder in the first degree of Johnson *and* shooting to kill Milton Easley. Bond pleads not guilty to both charges.

It takes multiple venires to draw a jury. At the start of the criminal trial the plea is changed to guilty of murder in the second degree. Outcome: Bond is sentence by Judge W.B. Thompson to life in the Ohio Penitentiary, plus court costs of $416.91 and transported to Columbus by Sheriff E.G. Mathews the morning of November 16, 1927.

1927, October 7, Friday: *The Chronicle-Telegram:*

Lorain Police Baffled by Mystery—Coroner Believes Unidentified Woman Had Been Killed by Blow on Head:

Police were still mystified today over the discovery of a woman's body on the beach here yesterday, and scanned reports of missing persons in lake cities in an effort to identify her.

Coroner Myles Perry performed an autopsy on the body and expressed the belief that she had been hit on the head with a blunt instrument. The body gave every evidence of being that of a woman extremely careful about her appearance.

The murder theory was advanced by Coroner Perry because of the fact that there was no water in her lungs, and clots of blood in her eyes indicated that she had bled there before being thrown in the water.

She was described by the coroner as being in her late thirties or early forties, about five feet five inches in height, weighing about 120-130 lbs, and having light brown hair. She apparently had been in the water a week or ten days.

When found, she was clothed in a grey suede coat, lined in green, and around her neck was a string of green beads. She was wearing a black crepe dress trimmed in satin, and black four strap shoes of an expensive make that had been half soled.

Her underclothes and hosiery also gave evidence of her having been a well-to-do woman, as they were of light shades of silk, and of the very finest quality.

1927, October 12: *The Chronicle-Telegram:*

Postpone Burial, Continue Probe In Murder Case:

Coroner Myles E. Perry informed the Chronicle-Telegram just before press time today that the burial of the body of the woman who was found murdered on the beach in Lorain last week would be postponed for one or two months, due to the large number of inquiries on hand.

Two Youngstown people called to say they were coming to see if they could identify the body, the coroner said, and numerous other inquiries and reports have been coming in.

Coroner Perry was to go to Oak Harbor this afternoon to investigate a report from that locality that a woman in a car with two men, one of whom hit her on the head with a wrench, was seen in Oak Harbor, Sept. 17.

1927, October 12: *The Chronicle-Telegram:*

LORAIN, Oct. 12. Cleveland police are investigating the report today that the woman whose body was washed up here last week might be Miss Muriel Hutchinson, Cleveland.

The report in the hands of the police indicates that the description of the presumably murdered woman's facial characteristics and dental work tallies with that of Miss Hutchinson.

1927, October 12: *The Chronicle-Telegram:*

YOUNGSTOWN, O. Oct. 12. Believing he can solve the mystery surrounding the finding of a body of a woman on the beach near Lorain a week ago, Tony Demario left for Lorain this afternoon.

Demario said he believed the body was that of his former wife Norma.

Before being divorced the Demario lived at Wydesteel

254

street, given in an anonymous communication to Lorain police yesterday. The letter said at that address police would get information as to the identity of the woman.

Demario conversed with Police Chief Walker at Lorain, before leaving Youngstown, and said the information he obtained convinced him that body was that of his former wife.

1927, October 28: *The Chronicle-Telegram:*
Shoes May Solve Lorain Mystery:
The identity of the woman who was found washed ashore at Lorain a number of weeks ago may never be brought to light but if it is not discovered it will not be because the authorities have not tried.

Robert Vestal was planning to go to Portsmouth (Ohio) today with the women's shoes which were made in a Portsmouth shoe factory. County officials hope these shoes which are of unusual size can be recognized at the factory and that the identity of the woman can be traced through them.

The woman has not yet been buried and numerous letters are still being received by coroner Myles Perry, chief of police Theodore Walker of Lorain, and sheriff E. G. Mathews for her description.

1927, November 8: *The Chronicle-Telegram:*
Believe Lorain Mystery Near Solution:
Coroner Myles Perry believes that the identity of the woman who was washed in from the lake a number of weeks ago will be found in a day or two. The coroner places his hope on discovering the identity of this woman and through her identity perhaps how she came to her death by the unusual pair of shoes she wore.

Robert Vestal has been co-operating with Perry in tracing the shoes and today the coroner received a telegram from Vestal, who is at a shoe manufacturing plant at Portsmouth, Ohio.

The telegram received from Vestal at Portsmouth declares that one of the woman's shoes was taken to pieces here at the Selby plant and numbers were discovered inside which showed that the shoes were purchased from the Arch Preserver Shoe

Shop, New York City. "We have wired them" the telegram declares, "and expect to have reply Tuesday. Will see you Wednesday and hope to have your lady's name."

1927, December 12: *The Chronicle-Telegram:*

Lorain Mystery May Be Solved By Coroner:

Coroner Myles Perry who has been working for months on the identity of the woman found washed up from the Lake last October in an effort to find how she came to her death has reason to believe that his efforts will soon be rewarded. Coroner Perry has been attempting to discover the woman's identity through the shoes she wore and through a bit of unusual dentistry.

Pictures of the woman's teeth were broadcast over the country in the December issue of the Journal of the American Dental Association and today Perry received a letter from Dr. H.C. Houston of 69 Sixth Street, New York City, who declared that if one particular gold crown was missing he thought he could furnish Perry with the woman's name.

Dr. Perry believes that the solution of the mystery may be at hand for the thirteen pairs of shoes traced, of the type and kind worn by the woman, were sold in New York City. The coroner has received ten replies and has three more parties to hear from.

The coroner declared this morning that the casket containing the body of the woman at Lorain will have to be opened to check up on the peculiarity noted by the New York dentist. Perry intends to go to Lorain tomorrow to do this.

1927, December 13: *The Chronicle-Telegram:*

Identify Woman Found on Lorain Beach: New Yorker is Victim of Lake: Miss Elizabeth Sparrow, 44, Had Visited Cleveland: Perry Believes Death From Murder:

That the woman whose body was washed up on a Lorain beach was Miss Elizabeth Sparrow, 44, of New York City has been established. This fact has been determined through a picture of the woman's teeth in a nationally known dental journal and the subsequent correspondence between Lorain

County Coroner Myles Perry and Dr. H.C. Houston, dental surgeon of 69 Sixth Avenue, New York City, who had been the woman's dentist.

Coroner Perry received a night letter from Dr. Houston this morning giving the woman's name after the coroner had examined the body Sunday to make sure of a dental peculiarity noted by the New York dentist. Dr. Houston also furnished the Lorain county coroner with the name of a cousin of Miss Sparrow's, who lives in Cleveland. As soon as Dr. Perry received the desired information he got in touch with the Cleveland cousin, a woman whose name is being withheld by the coroner for the present. Some interesting facts were learned from this relative.

Miss Sparrow, the relative declared, came to Cleveland to visit on July 11 and left the Fifth City in August of this year. The relative had not heard from her since the time she had left. Miss Sparrow is believed to have a cousin in the west and Dr. Perry declares that should the brother not be located within a few days he will ask Cleveland police to broadcast the case.

The Lorain county coroner feels sure that the woman came to her death through murder. He can explain the blow on the head and the fact that she had no water in her lungs through no other way. He intends, if possible, to discover Miss Sparrow's associates in an effort to sift the case to the bottom.

Dr. Perry stated this morning he intended to talk the case over with the Cleveland relative within a day or two and that he would invite a representation of the Lorain, police department to go with him.

In solving the woman's identity the coroner had nothing but her shoes and teeth upon which to work. For more than two months correspondence, telegrams and phones were used in an effort to find her home and name. In, trying to find her identity by her shoes Coroner Perry was assisted by Robert Vestal.

Letters received from ten persons who had been sold the same kind and size shoe as Miss Sparrow included some amusing answers. One woman stated that she could give the coroner little help and that she was sure there was no 'bloody villain' in the case for two reasons. "First: any woman wearing my size shoes would be justified in committing suicide. Second, if she fell overboard accidentally the weight of her shoes would drown her."

1927, December 17: *The Chronicle-Telegram:*

Suicide Theory in Lorain Case:

An anonymous letter received yesterday by Sheriff E.G. Mathews has opened up a new line of investigation of the death of Elizabeth Sparrow, 40, New York City, whose body was washed up at Lorain Oct. 5, and tends to substantiate the theory that Miss Sparrow a victim of suicide rather than murder.

Mathews said the letter, mailed at Columbus, stated that Miss Sparrow had determined to commit suicide. When she left Cleveland she wrote to the Hotel Judson, New York, where she was employed as an accountant, the letter said, saying: "I am going to commit suicide. I am going to jump into Lake Erie. Forward my belongings to Mrs. R. A. Stanton, Columbus."

The letter further stated that Miss Sparrow's body was identified by a member of the family three days after it was discovered at Lorain, but nothing was said on account of the fear of disgrace and publicity.

Sheriff Mathews has written to all of the dead woman's relatives of whom he has any knowledge. They are:

Mrs. Frances Blake, and Mrs. W.W. Starke, both of Cleveland, sisters; Thomas Sparrow, chief executive of the Boy Scouts at Harrisburg, Pa., a brother: William Sparrow, Kansas City. Mo., a brother: and Earl Moore. Cleveland, brother-in-law of Thomas Sparrow.

In addition the sheriff has written to Mrs. R.A. Stanton. of the Fort Hayes Hotel, Columbus. Letters from some of these persons are expected momentarily, and, it is thought, may clear up the mystery surrounding the death of Elizabeth Sparrow.

With his present clues in hand, Mathews is of the opinion that an unhappy love affair earlier in life, hinted at in the letter received, coupled with estrangement from the family, possibly on account of supposed disgrace, point strongly to the suicide theory.

1927, December 19: *The Chronicle-Telegram:*

Miss Sparrow was Suicide Brother Says—Woman Found at Lorain Made Previous Attempt to Take Own Life—Family Disbelieves Murder Theory:

The mystery surrounding the death of Elizabeth Sparrow, 40, New York City, whose body was washed up on the beach at Lorain last October, was solved today when her brother, Thomas Sparrow, arrived from his home in the East in response to a request of Sheriff E.G. Mathews, and said he was sure his sister was a victim of suicide.

"I have not seen my sister for fourteen years," Sparrow told a Chronicle-Telegram reporter in an exclusive interview granted today, "but I kept in touch with her through my sister in Cleveland and knew of her mental attitude."

"I am certain she was a victim of suicide," he continued. "The news came to me last Thursday, out of a clear sky. I was shocked, but not surprised because I knew of a previous attempt she made to commit suicide four years ago at New York."

Regarding the anonymous letter Sheriff Mathews received Friday, telling of a letter Miss Sparrow had written to New York before her death, and stating the body was identified three days after its discovery but not admitted, Sparrow said he knew nothing.

Sparrow and Sheriff Mathews were to go to Lorain this afternoon to determine to their identify of the body to his own personal satisfaction. But the identification of Coroner Perry was not questioned by Sparrow.

Sparrow was to take the body of his sister in charge and be certain that she received a proper burial in Elmwood Cemetery, Lorain.

1927, December 24:

An unnamed Oberlin citizen finds a man's body in a ditch along Oberlin Road "near Stop 91." The discoverer notifies Arthur Brown, 700-block of West Avenue, who calls Coroner Myles Perry and Sheriff Mathews. The dead body is frozen stiff, leading investigators to figure the crime took place the day before with the victim killed and tossed from an automobile. Newspapers report that death was caused by a stab wound to the heart.

On the body is a worker's badge, number X-5367 from the Ford Motor Company's River Rouge Plant in Dearborn Michigan. This is used to identify the victim as John Romano, aka John Trungali, aka John Tringali, aka John Detroit. He's 32 or 33 years old and is identified in the papers, somewhat needlessly, as "Italian."

On December 25, the news is that the victim, recently from Cleveland, was shot three times: once in the head and twice in the chest and that he was murdered where he had been found. Sheriff Mathews believes the dead man had been "taken for a ride" for knowing too much about a gang of rum-runners operating between Cleveland and Detroit.

On December 27, it's reported the victim is from Detroit and that he'd been shot four times with a .32 caliber revolver with fatal damage to his vital organs. It was a mix of bullets, steel jacketed and otherwise. This suggests more than one shooter. Robbery was not the motive since $50 and both wrist and pocket watches were found on the victim.

The victim is positively identified as John Romano by Robert Mayoren, the brother of one of his paramours. Mayoren hails from 2710 Hammond Avenue, Detroit Michigan. That's the southwest side of town, towards Dearborn, down by the tracks.

The dead man is buried in St. Mary's Cemetery, Elyria, by his brother-in-law Frank Srizulla of Monroe, Michigan.

Authorities start searching for Mrs. Anna Michelli, formerly of 4010 Trumbull Avenue, Cleveland, Ohio, who disappeared at the time of the murder. Mrs. Michelli and the victim ran a "booze house" at the Trumbull Avenue address, selling drinks for a quarter-dollar each. The victim was supplying their enterprise by running liquor from Detroit.

December 28. The victim is now "bullet-riddled." Mrs. Michelli has been found and questioned. She ratted out a man named "Joe." She didn't know the guy's last name, but he was, she is sure, the one who committed the crime. "I never trusted him," says Michelli. "He always carried a gun." The woman admits to living with the victim but had done so for less than two weeks, ending the affair when she discovered he'd been sending money back to a wife in Italy. Authorities think Mrs. Michelli knows more than she's letting on. She is placed in the Lorain County Jail as a material witness and held in lieu of $5,000 bond.

December 29. A warrant is sworn for the arrest of one Julio Marco aka Joe Lamarco (also Italian). Deputies have searched rooms at one of his residences, 5025 House Street, Cleveland, Ohio, finding $500 worth of morphine and a quantity of liquor. Much more damaging are a set of blood-stained clothing and bullets matching those found in the victim.

Outcome: Marco aka Lamarco is never found. Mrs. Michelli is free to go. The case is unresolved.

The Cleveland addresses mentioned, Trumbull and House, were on the south side of the city are near the present-day intersections of Interstates 77 and 490.

1927, December 27: *The Chronicle-Telegram:*

Girl Loses in Battle With Death.

OCONTO, Neb.—Alma Overgard, 16, died here today after a corps of volunteer workers had kept her alive for thirty-six days by artificial respiration. Physicians had expected her death almost momentarily for several days.

Infantile paralysis caused Miss Overgard's lungs to cease working. Her parents, two uncles, and several neighbors worked in relays until the moment of her death, keeping her alive by raising her arms above her head and lowering them to her sides. Her arms were raw from the long ordeal.

John French, last of the volunteers, was slowly lowering her arms when physicians pronounced the girl dead at 9 a.m. Physicians said it was the longest case on record of prolongation of life by artificial respiration.

The girl was conscious to the end, and appeared to be trying to thank the persons who had labored trying to save her life. Up until Christmas she had been able to carry on a conversation.

The "iron lung," intended for such victims of polio will be developed in 1929.

1928: We all have something to be better than. Atwater Kent Cabinet Radios are on sale at Van Horn Music, W. 129 Main Street, Elyria for $138.50. An aerial is extra! The term "Boogie-Woogie" is first used on a recording by Pine Top Smith. *American in Paris* by Gershwin. Chiang Kai Shek takes Beijing and eventually establishes a National Government. British women can now vote when they're 21. Stalin now exercises complete control in the USSR. Egyptian schoolteacher Hassan al-Banna establishes the "Muslim Brotherhood" with the goals of Qu'rannic Society guided by Sharia Law. Italy is a one party state. Alexander Graham Bell won't be calling anybody, anymore. In Ohio, you must be able to read street signs if you wish to license yourself to drive. James Lovell, Jr. is born in Cleveland, Ohio. In the Docket: Possessing Liquor and Transporting Liquor. Conviction includes fines between $200-$500 with time in the county jail reserved for repeat offenders. Herbert Hoover (California Republican) wins the Election with 58.2% of the popular vote. There's an attempted assassination of the President-Elect few weeks later during a visit to Argentina. 11 lynchings: 10 Blacks, 1 other.

1928, May 23, Wednesday:

Forty-year-old Florence Grant has lived in the 200-block of North Main, Oberlin, for just over a half-dozen years. To help make ends meet, she runs a laundry business from the basement of her home. Friend "Birdie/Bertie" (Mrs. John) Bertha Robinson helps and yes, it's hard work, but the two enjoy their time together and that lightens the load.

About 3:00pm, May 23, 1928, neighbors see Mrs. Grant's husband, Otis, 60, pull into the driveway, probably from his work as caretaker of the Thomas Henderson home on the east side of town. It's something of a surprise for him to be there.

Mrs. Grant has filed for divorce from her husband on the grounds of non-support, on-going abuse, and threatening conduct. In fact, a court hearing is scheduled on the matter later in the day. It's not the first time she has started proceedings, but this time she's serious. Serious enough that she asked for, and received from Judge W.B. Thompson, an injunction preventing her soon-to-be and sometimes violent ex-husband from entering her home or interfering with her or their thirteen-year-old daughter, Frances.

Those watching are alarmed when they see Mr. Grant exit his small car, carrying a double-barreled shotgun and enter the back door of his home. There are two reports in rapid succession. Grant calmly exits the building, leans the weapon against the outside the structure, and waves a cheery goodbye as he backs his car out of the drive and heads into town.

Neighbors rush into the home to find Mrs. Grant and Mrs. Robinson on the basement floor with 20-gauge wounds to their heads. The women are taken to Oberlin's Allen Hospital where they soon pass away. A shattered wooden laundry basket and splinters in Mrs. Robinson's injury indicate her attempt to lessen the point-blank blast.

Meanwhile, the gray-haired Otis Grant stops at an Oberlin gas station to "fill 'er up" before continuing south. Police think his destination to be either Kentucky or West Virginia where he can lose himself in the mountains. Regional authorities are told to keep a lookout for the suspect. His vehicle is later found in Columbus, the city where a brother lives. A belt containing nineteen 20-gauge shells is found in the abandoned car.

A description and arrest warrant are sent throughout the country. Deputy Sheriffs Claud Bivins and Harvey Crehore travel to West Virginia in an effort to apprehend the suspect but report failure. County Commissioners post a $500 reward. Oberlin City Council adds $200 to that amount.

The women are buried in Oberlin's Westwood Cemetery from the Mt. Zion Baptist Church. Florence Grant, in Potter's Field, leaves behind her 13-year-old daughter. For Birdie Robinson, whose grave is marked, it's a husband and seven children.

1929, August 21: The still-missing Otis Grant is sued by Oberlin undertaker (and furniture dealer) G.T. Sedgeman to recover $326.85 for services rendered. He asks that the Grant property on North Main be sold and the proceeds be applied to payment of the owed amount.

1930, June 24: A man thought to be Otis Grant is arrested in Clayton, New Mexico. Sheriff Clarence E. Adams sends Deputy Fred Underhill to identify the man. It's not the suspect.

Outcome: The case is nollied by the Prosecutor on April 14, 1935.

Thirteen-year-old Frances Jeanette Grant goes on to a very different life than that of her mother. She marries and becomes Frances Harris. Passing away in her mid-80s in December of 2000, she is buried in the Forest Lawn Memorial Park of • Covina California. Her grave is marked simply: "Beloved Wife."

1928, June 9, Saturday, noon: Location: Lorain, "Little Russia" (the neighborhood of 30th Street and Pearl). Victim: Walter Klukowich. Suspect: Mike Hutera. Together, victim Klukowich and suspect Hutera buy a pint of bootlegged liquor. There is an argument over how the cost is to be split with Hutera refusing to pay what Klukowich thinks is a fair share. A fight ensues. Klukowich is stabbed. His body is found by police when called by neighbors who heard the victim's cries for help.

Hutera is bound over by Lorain Municipal Court Judge J.F. Strenick on June 11. He pleads not guilty. Three witnesses are also held on $300 bond. A true bill is returned by June Grand Jury for murder in the first degree. Before trial, plea is changed to guilty of manslaughter. Outcome: 1929, April 18: Mike Hutera, number 58934, prisoner at the London Prison Farm is recommended for parole.

1928, September 11, Tuesday, 10:00am: Location: Lorain, 300-block Colorado Avenue. Victim: Elizabeth Horvath (Horwath) (38, wife). Suspect: Emery (Emory) Horvath (Horwath) (41, husband). Act: Shooting.

Emery Horvath becomes a naturalized citizen on May 5, 1921. He has five kids—one boy and four girls—by his first wife who dies in the Lorain Tornado (*see 1924, June 28*). There is much trouble in the present marriage. The two have separated five times, divorced in November of 1927, then remarried three months later.

It's one quarrel after another, many over the way he spends his own money. The final argument, over $40 goes on for two days. She spits in his face which makes him "see red." He walks upstairs, returns with a fully-loaded .38 caliber revolver, and empties it at her as she irons clothes. She drops where she stands.

He places the weapon on the kitchen table, covers it with a cloth, then surrenders himself at the police station, shouting "I just killed my wife, go out and get her!" Officer George Jenney and Patrol Driver Elmer Brackett respond. Mrs. Horvath is found in a pool of blood by the ironing board with the electric iron burning a hole through the garment it is sitting upon.

Mr. Horvath gives a complete confession. He is bound over to the September Grand Jury on the charge of murder in the first degree. The Grand Jury returns an indictment of manslaughter and sets bond at $3,000. Before the criminal trial takes place, Horvath pleads to guilty to that charge.

At his sentencing, defense attorney Adams presents the circumstances of the guilty man's life in a "brilliant plea." Soon after the death of his first wife Horvath was approached by the woman he would marry and later kill. She turned out to be a madam in charge of a brothel. On two different occasions this woman approached the victim's daughters "with indecent proposals." On the second occasion, the killer divorced her.

The victim then promised to go straight and they reconciled, but she did not change her evil ways. She went so far as to talk Horvath into buying an old hotel in Lorain that she turned into a brothel. When the killer protested, she threatened to "cut his neck." Each night the man locked himself in the back room of the building fearing for his safety.

The argument on the day of the shooting was not over money as reported, but was Horvath confronting his immoral and unrepentant wife with what she was doing. She attacked him with her iron. He retreated to his room to get his revolver. When he returned, she went for a knife. While it was true he fired five times in self-defense, only the last bullet struck and killed her.

"Your Honor," Adams exclaims at the end of his speech, "there is a limit to human resistance. If it had been I, in Horvath's place, I wouldn't have waited so long to shoot that woman!"

"I can think of nothing more exasperating," replies Judge Webber in passing sentence, "than an attempt to deprive a child of its virtue. It is a difficult thing for me to take this father away from his children." But the judge does just that with a sentence of three years in prison.

1928, November 12, Monday: Location: Elyria, 59 West Avenue, Anderson Restaurant/Pool Hall. Victim: Sanders Biggins (27, Negro). Suspect: "Charley" aka "Sonny" (35, "a negro known to Elyria's colored population") Act: Shooting.

Charley has been in Elyria about two months and keeps a trunk at the Anderson restaurant but does not live there. He works nights, sleeps little, and hangs out in the pool hall in his free time.

Victim Biggins works nights at Fox Furnace. He arrives at the restaurant around 4:00pm and orders food from suspect Charley who has been left in charge by owner Mrs. Martha Anderson. Biggins does not like the food served him and begins a heated argument with Charley. When Biggin's back is turned, Charley pulls out a .38 revolver, shoots his customer twice in the back, and heads for the door. He then turns around and, for good measure, shoots Biggins again, this time in the abdomen.

Charley flees the scene down the railroad tracks and disappears into the elderberry patch along the river known as "the jungles." Authorities are called. Elyria Police Chief E.J. Stankard responds. He arrives to find the place empty, save for Biggins, breathing his last and toppling from his chair.

Charley is described as five feet eight inches tall, medium brown skin, bad front teeth, and slightly pitted face. He is bow-legged and pigeon-toed and was last seen wearing a black overcoat and a hat.

On November 16, Elyria officers Zarnko and Southam make trip to a small, unnamed Pennsylvania town to visit authorities who think they are holding the suspect. It turns out to be a wild-goose chase. The man does fit the description, but it is not Charley. Outcome: Unresolved. The suspect is never found.

1928, November 30, Friday, 5:30am: Location: Elyria, 20-block Chestnut Street. Victims: Mrs. Lizzy (Mattie) Vorhees (Colored) and Emmett Philips (Colored). Suspect: Hugh Thornton (Colored). The crime takes place at the Vorhees home the morning after Thanksgiving at the end of an all-night "crap shooting party attended by both colored and white folks." Everyone present is "more-or-less drunk."

Hugh Thornton and three other men, Al McCalium (White), Pete Cameron (White), and Andy Novak (White) have lost heavily. Thornton accuses Emmett Philips, who is the "star boarder" at the place, of stealing his gold watch and chain as he lay dozing on a couch. Philips denies it.

Thornton leaves, warning that he will return to settle the score. A few minutes later, he reenters the home with a .32 caliber revolver in hand, and begins to "shoot promiscuously." In the ensuing chaos, Lizzie Vorhees, an innocent bystander, is struck in the left temple and falls to the floor, dead. Emmett Philips, supposed watch and chain thief, is hit in the right shoulder and the center of his neck.

Lizzie's eight-year-old son, Henry Allen Vorhees, Jr. (whose father is in the County Jail on charges of possession of liquor) witnesses the shooting, picks up an axe, and goes "after the man what killed my mother." Hugh Thornton flees the building and runs into the street. The wounded Emmett Philips follows and begins shouting for help. This attracts the attention of neighbor "Rabbit" Holloway who calls police.

Thornton is found, quickly walking east on East Broad Street. He tosses his revolver when he sees the cops, but police recover the weapon. Thornton denies the shooting, though he says it was done with his weapon. The suspect is held without bond. The man is described as "more-or-less a transient," having arrived in Elyria a short time back. He has been living on South Prospect.

Emmett Philips dies of his wounds on December 3. A few days later, at the December Grand Jury, Thornton is asked what happened:

> Well, your honor, the houseman short-changed me, and I went and got my gun. When I came in the houseman grappled with me. He knocked me down twice, and when we were wrestling, the gun went off twice. I grabbed the gun, and ran out of the house, and I heard two more shots after I got outside.
> *The Chronicle-Telegram, December 1, 1928.*

Thornton is indicted for first degree murder. He pleads not guilty. The day his criminal trial is to begin, he changes it to guilty of manslaughter. He is sentenced by Judge W.B. Thompson on February 6, 1929, and sent to the Ohio Penitentiary for a minimum of 5 years, plus court costs of $73.70.

Oftentimes, the owner of a boarding house hired a married couple to help. The wife cooked and did laundry. The husband, called a "houseman," took care of heavier duties which, in the case above, included grappling with gunmen.

1929: Yo-yos start, uh, yo-yo-ing. Baseballer Ty Cobb retires with a career record of 2,245 runs. Fats Waller's jazz band is one of the first in the U.S. to be racially integrated. The Vatican becomes a free state. Yugoslavia comes to be. The "iron lung" is developed for polio victims (*see 1927, December 27*). Paul Lauterbur is born in Sidney, Shelby County, Ohio. Think of him the next time you get an MRI. In the Docket: Non-Support of Minor Children. 10 lynchings: 7 Blacks, 3 others.

1929, January 8, Tuesday: Location: Lorain. Victim: Mrs. Katie Wojtowicz (38). Suspect: Theodore (Todor, Tordor) Pruski.

Mrs. Wojtowicz is shot in the abdomen as she enters her house from the back yard. Pruski (a boarder in the home) admits the shooting, saying it was over an argument they had about her insisting he move from his room. The victim's husband, Andrew, is at work at the time. No matter Pruski's confession, the shooting is presumed by neighbors (and the papers) to be the end result of a "love feud."

Mrs. Wojtowicz is hospitalized after the shooting. Police await the outcome of the act before pressing charges. She dies at 2:00am January 9, and Pruski is charged with murder in the second degree with bond fixed at $10,000. Pruski's initial plea is not guilty. *Changed to:* Guilty of manslaughter. Outcome: Ohio Penitentiary for 5 years, plus court costs of $44.50.

Andrew Wojtowicz cannot care for his children. His 6-year-old and 4-year-old set of twins are placed in the Oberlin Children's Home.

1933, December 18: Andrew Wojtowicz, the father, dies in the Oberlin Hospital after being struck by an automobile while walking home after a visit with his children in Oberlin. The vehicle is operated by R.B. Dwire of Longfellow Avenue, Elyria. Coroner S.C. Ward determines cause of death to be concussions of the brain. Sheriff Clarence W. Dick says no charges will be brought against Dwire.

1929, March 15, Friday: Location: Lorain. Victim: San Diego Vega (35, Mexican). Vega lives in the 1700-block of East 28 Street, Lorain, and works in the Tube Mill. On March 16, he is treated by Dr. C.D. Grimm for a cut over the left ear. A few days later, the patient's right arm becomes paralyzed. Dr. Grimm orders him to St. Joseph's in Lorain. Vega dies a few days later. Coroner Perry orders an autopsy that finds death to be caused by a stab wound through the skull over the left ear and into the brain. Outcome: Unsolved.

1929, April 10, Wednesday: Location: ? Victim: ? Suspect: Andrade (Audrade?) Callentano. Charge: Murder in the second degree. Plea: None. Suspect is never arrested. Outcome: Case continued until May 11, 1935, then nollied by the Prosecutor.

1929, June 7, Friday: Location: ? Victim: ? Suspect: Apolinaro Hinozoso aka Polo Zahiona aka Pola Hinijosa aka Apolnar Hingaza aka Apaulino Honezeza. Charge: Murder in the second degree. Outcome: Warrant is issued. Hinozoso is never arrested. Case continued until January, 1935, then nollied by the Prosecutor.

1929, June 20, Thursday: Location: Amherst, 100-block Dane Street. Victim: Mrs. Sophia Bolosky (Berski) (29). Suspect: Mrs. Frances Bakaletz.

Sophia Bolosky is found by her five children, ages 17, 15, 8, 5, and 4, now orphaned since the victim's husband died about six month ago. Cause of Bolosky's death is determined to be alcoholism. Coroner Perry finds a quart can half full of liquor at the scene and suspects it was "bad."

Frances Bakaletz is accused of supplying the liquor. Sheriff Clarence Adams raids the Bakaletz home in the 2500-block of East 32nd Street, Lorain, and finds five quarts of liquor buried about eight feet from the back doorstep. Police believe the accused has been supplying booze to the Amherst area for some time. Mr. Bakaletz is arrested on liquor charges and bonded for $1,000. He admits to driving the car with which his wife delivered liquor to the victim, but claims he did not know his wife was bootlegging. Mr. Bakaletz is fined $500 by Judge A.R. Webber.

The missus is arraigned on a charge of second degree murder and bound by a $5,000 bond. By the time of the October Grand Jury, the charge has been reduced to manslaughter. She is finally indicted for "furnishing intoxicating liquor."

Mrs. Bakaletz pleads not guilty and is released under $1,000 bond to await trial. *Changed to:* Guilty as charged. Outcome: She is fined $100 by Judge A.R. Webber.

1930, May 27: *The Chronicle-Telegram:*

> Lorain Woman Killed by Train—Avon lake, Ohio
>
> Frances Bakaletz, 52 of East 32 Street, Lorain, was instantly killed early this morning when she ran into the path of a west bound freight train on the Nickle Plate railroad here.
>
> Coroner Myles E. Perry and Sheriff Clarence E. Adams who investigated the death, reported that Mrs. Bakaletz had gotten out of an automobile in which she was riding with her husband, and refused to get back in.
>
> She had been drinking, her husband said, and wandered aimlessly in the vicinity of the rail road tracks.
>
> "Look out, there is a train coming," Bakaletz told the officers he warned her.
>
> But, he said, instead of running from the tracks, the woman ran directly into the path of the train.
>
> The woman was fined $100 and costs several weeks ago by Judge A.R. Webber when she pleaded guilty to a charge of possession of liquor.
>
> She had been indicted last year on a charge of manslaughter in connection with the alleged poison booze death of an Amherst woman, but this charge was reduced by county authorities because of insufficient evidence, and the lesser charge placed against her.

1929, June 24, Monday: Location: Lorain, at the Clinton Baseball Grounds (south of the present day "Oakwood Park"). Victim: Frehim (Frank) Berrim (Berrm, Bessim) (37). Suspect: Barian Riza. Frank Berrim, who lives in the 2800-block of Pearl Avenue, Lorain, is shot in what police think is "a result of a love feud." He is taken to St. Joseph's Hospital where he dies two days later. Papers report a witness being held, then a suspect who is charged, then released, but never identified.

1930, early June: Barian Riza is arrested in Lackawanna, New York, and brought in front of the Grand Jury on a charge of first degree murder. He is indicted for murder in the second degree and pleads not guilty. Before the criminal trial starts, Riza changes his plea to guilty of manslaughter. Outcome: By Judge W.B. Thompson, three years in the Ohio Penitentiary.

1929, June 25, Tuesday, 2:00am: Location: Elyria, No. 6 Fox Furnace Apartments. Victim: Pearl Woods (21). Suspect: Lee Miller aka Lee Harvey (40, Negro). For reasons not specified, an armed Lee Miller visits the soon-to-be divorced Pearl Woods at her Fox Furnace apartment. An argument escalates to a fight. He uses a 16-gauge shotgun borrowed from "Big" John Smith to wound her three times: in the right arm just below the elbow, in the right leg, and in the back. She is transported to the Elyria Hospital where doctors hold little hope of recovery.

Police intend to arrest Miller, who's on parole from the Mansfield Reformatory, for shooting to kill. They know he has been in Elyria, on West Avenue, for about one week. The suspect is described as about 40 years old, 5 feet, 6 inches tall, dark skinned, weighing about 200 pounds. He has a Roman nose with a darker spot to the right side of it that resembles a scar from a burn.

June 28: Pearl Woods dies of gangrene as a result of her wounds. The charge against Miller is upgraded to murder in the first degree. Outcome: Lee Miller is never found and the case is unresolved.

1930, October 9: *The Chronicle-Telegram:*
Divorce Case is "Abated by Death."
"Abated by death" was scrawled across the docket for a divorce case scheduled to be heard in common pleas court today. The hearing had been pending for more than a year.
Yesterday one of the attorneys discovered that his client, Mrs. Pearl Woods, who had sued for a divorce from Charles Woods, had been murdered early last summer. Judge A.R. Webber removed the hearing from the docket.
Mrs. Woods was shot three times with a shotgun in the hands of an assailant alleged to be Lee Williams, [*sic*] on June 25th. She died June 27th at Elyria Memorial. Williams made his get-away and police investigated the colored sections of many cities but were unable to find him.

1929, June 25: *The Chronicle-Telegram:*

New Speedboats Will Chase Rummers.

The tightening up of possible "Liquor Leaks" in the Lorain county frontier against Canadian booze was announced by Lieut. Martin W. Rassmussen, chief of the ninth district extending from Buffalo to Toledo.

Two new speedboats capable of making 40 miles an hour, are to be stationed at Vermilion and Huron, thereby making a fleet of three speedboats, including the one at Lorain, and a revenue cutter now stationed at Vermilion. The new additions are to make their appearance July 1, Rassmussen said.

In discussing the situation Rassmussen said the Lorain County area is not as bad as some sections along the lakes but that there are two recognized bad spots between Lorain and Vermilion.

The new boats will each be 34 feet long.

1929, December 16, Monday, 6:45am: Location: Zboray's General Store, Lorain, 2823 Vine Avenue, the "heart of Lorain's east end business district." Victim: John F. Zboray (65). Suspect: Andrew Kader (Kadar) (37). Albert Routh, machinist at the National Tube Company, is passing nearby when he hears breaking glass and sees a man dash down the nearby alley. Routh calls the Tube Company office. They call police.

Within the store, Lorain Police Captain Hugh Reilly finds the body of John Zboray guarded by a dog who will not let him near the body until the victim's son arrives. Zboray is dead behind the glass counter, which is broken. Several red bandanas are scattered about the victim. He was shot twice through the head with the bullets lodged in shoeboxes behind him. The victim had often told friends that, if he were ever held up, he would shoot it out with the robbers. It looks like he tried to make good on that statement: his right hand holds a partially-pulled revolver with its hammer caught on the lining of his pocket.

Police theorize the suspect entered the store, asked to see the bandanas, and produced a weapon when the victim was bent into the glass case. The victim saw he was being robbed, tried to pull his own revolver, and was shot. Zboray's mongrel dog, his constant companion, then attacked the robber and drove him from the store. No actual robbery took place.

Zboray is a widower with five grown children, a son and four daughters, one of which is married to Stephen Kinsey, a Toledo undertaker and former Lorain City Councilman.

Police arrest two young men found in the vicinity. One produces an alibi and is released. The other, under the influence of liquor, cannot account for his whereabouts and is held until authorities are satisfied he had nothing to do with the crime.

The March, 1930, Grand Jury secretly, and surprisingly, indicts one Andrew Kader based on circumstantial evidence. Kader is arrested in Detroit, Michigan, by Lorain Policemen Britt Buda and J.A. Meister and charged with first degree murder. Defense attorney Charles Adams of Lorain is hired. The accused is cool and shows little apparent emotion at his preliminary hearing. Kader is held in the County Jail without bond.

April 12: Kader's criminal trial is postponed "as a matter of convenience and possible further investigation" according to Prosecutor Don W. Myers. It is understood the evidence against the accused is weak.

April 17: The prosecutor nollies the charges against Kader who is released. Outcome: Unsolved/Unresolved.

1930 – 1939: County Population = 109,206

1930: A penitentiary fire in Columbus leaves 319 dead. Gandhi and his followers exert the power of passive resistance in a nearly 250-mile march across India. The U.S. withdraws into isolationism, pulling its troops from the German Rhineland, five years ahead of schedule. Not the best of ideas. The founding of the Nation of Islam within the United States. Neil Armstrong is born in Wapakoneta, Auglaize County, Ohio. George Steinbrenner is born in Rocky River, Cuyahoga County, Ohio. In the Docket: Stealing motor vehicles. Violation of liquor laws. 21 lynchings: 20 Blacks, 1 other. $1,000 is worth $14,425 modern.

1930, February 6, Thursday, 6:00pm: Location: Lorain, 200-block West 29th Street. Victim: Mintora Nichols (35, wife) Suspect: James Nichols (52, husband). Mintora and James Nichols, both raised "in the mountains of Virginia," are married on May 27, 1913 in Pocahontas, Virginia. It is the second marriage for both. They have no children between them, but she has a grown daughter from her first marriage. Mintora sues James for divorce in late December, 1926, on the grounds of extreme cruelty. It seems that James threatened to kill her and chased her with a knife, forcing her to take refuge with their neighbors.

They reconcile, with him promising to treat her better. He does, at first, then slides back into his old habits. The straw that re-breaks the camel's back is a quarrel over a game of bridge that grows violent. The couple separates and Mintora files for divorce a second time.

James has threatened to kill his wife on several occasions since. She has asked for an injunction to keep him away, but the courts have yet to take action on the request.

The night of February 6, Mintora is sitting, talking on the telephone. James approaches the outside of the building and peers through the window at his wife, seated a few feet away. He carefully aims a newly-purchased .38 caliber revolver and fires multiple times though the glass.

Mintora is struck three times in the neck. A boarder rushes downstairs, finds the victim, and calls police who arrive to find that James has turned his gun on himself. His first shot was a misfire. His second, more successful. That bullet plowed a long gash his skull and left itself in his brain.

James is taken to St. Joseph's Hospital in Lorain under police guard. "The case is one absolutely of first degree murder," says Coroner Perry. Outcome:

James Nichols dies of his self-inflicted gunshot wounds on February 14, 1930, Valentine's Day.

1930, March 11, Tuesday:

The Dzouclis and Dineff families have known each other a long time, certainly well before any of them emigrated from Macedonia. They weren't of the same class, mind you, but they were close enough for Antonio Dzouclis' better-off daughter, Sophia, to befriended Vasil, Mial Dineff's poor, orphaned nephew.

That was prior to their move to the United States, but it was one of the reasons they all ended up in Lorain, Ohio—to be with people they knew and trusted.

Antonio Dzouclis, now "Tony," found work in the steel mills and started saving the money needed to bring his wife and daughter over the sea. It took almost ten years. Mial Dineff opened a market on East 29th Street, selling the familiar foods of his homeland, and started saving money to do the same.

It was shortly after Tony's wife and daughter, Sophia, arrived that Mial's nephew, Vasil, came to Lorain. The Dineff's didn't have room for the boy, so the Dzouclis family opened their home—with Mial giving a little money to cover expenses. That was only fair.

It was expected that 22-year-old Vasil and 18-year-old Sophia would rekindle their Macedonian friendship. And it was expected they would spend time together. But it wasn't expected they would run off to West Virginia to marry without permission from either of their families.

Tony Dzouclis reports his dear Sophia's disappearance to police. It is kidnapping, pure and simple. When authorities inform him of the marriage, he is heartbroken and angry. Vasil isn't good enough for his daughter. It's not the way things are done. Not back home and not here. Besides, Sophia had been promised and engaged to a well-established Canadian man. The engagement had even been announced!

A few days after the news of the marriage, the groom's uncle, Mial Dineff, shows up at the Dzouclis home in an attempt to make peace. The elopement was just as much a surprise to him, Mial says. Nobody knew, not even the youngster's best friends. But, what is done is done.

Mial offers money to help Tony deal with the loss of his daughter. It's nowhere near enough, but the $550 is as good as Mial can manage. Like the marriage, for Tony, it's either accept what is offered or get nothing.

Mial tells Tony that he's throwing a wedding party, like back home, to celebrate the marriage of Vasil and Sophia and ease the tension between the families. It'll be like old times, stories, drinking, songs, dancing, tears, and laughter. Tony doesn't want to attend, but his friends talk him into it. Go. See your daughter. She is the most important thing.

The party is well underway when Tony shows up. People hush as he makes his way through the crowd to the newlyweds. He and the young couple greet each other in their native language. Vasil and his new wife stand from their chairs. Sophia, who thought her father would never show, is delighted.

The two men extend their arms, as if to shake hands. Vasil's smile turns to horror. Tony holds a revolver that he empties into the young man's body. The older man turns and runs back through the now-screaming crowd. Vasil falls dead to the floor. Sophia collapses in a faint.

Dzouclis is soon arrested at the home of a neighborhood friend. He freely admits he is the shooter but refuses to give any details or reason for the crime.

March 19, while awaiting the Grand Jury, Antonio Dzouclis is sued in civil court by Mial Dineff for breach of contract. Mial is seeking the return of the $550 he gave Tony the day before the crime to assure his approval of the marriage.

The April Grand Jury indicts on first degree murder. Dzouclis pleads not guilty. The paper describes him as "youthful in appearance, clean shaven and intelligent looking," taking a calm and keen interest in his trial.

Judge W.B. Thompson presides over Dzouclis' criminal trial in mid-May. His defense attorney is Charles Adams. There's been some levity in the courtroom with the struggle to pronounce the defendant's name. Some attempt are bad enough to make the accused smile in response. The court decides the proper pronunciation is "JEW-klis."

There is a large crowd of spectators for the trial, typical for a death penalty case. There is trouble seating the jury, also typical. Sixteen potential jurors are excused for scruples against condemning a defendant to electrocution. The twelve selected are a mix of men and women.

In his opening statement, defense attorney Adams maintains that the accused is not guilty of first degree murder because he acted "according to the God-given impulse to right a wrong to the person he loved most in the world." Adams claims the girl, herself, was in love with the Canadian she was engaged to, and that her elopement was forced upon her by the Dineff family. And the "peace offering" of money offered by Mial Dineff? Tony accepted it in hopes of discovering the location of his precious daughter.

State witness Cecelia Fraico, 16, of the 2000-block of East 29, Lorain, says Vasil and Sophia were often seen together in Mial's market, and nobody ever heard any talk between them about getting married. Fraico also details the plans made at the Dineff home as part of the bridal feast to honor the couple. At the party, Fraico goes on, Dzouclis greeted Vasil in Macedonian and moved to shake his hand. When Vasil stood and extended his arm he was shot several times in the body.

Steve Spiroff, 19, tells much the same story.

Mrs. Mial Dineff, the victim's aunt, testifies through an interpreter. She breaks down and cries several times during her testimony. She claims the two families were never friendly but that there was never any feud between them. At first she says that she didn't know anything about the elopement, then changes her testimony to say she had.

Mial's testimony is much the same, saying he did not know of the marriage until it happened and the couple had returned home. During the youngsters' absence, Dzouclis had come to him, asking if he knew where they were. Mial states that the $550 he gave the Dzouclis was to help pay for the expenses of bringing Sophia from overseas. The girl's father at first wanted $700, but was talked down to the lesser amount.

May 16: Tony's daughter, Sophia Dineff, takes the stand. During her testimony, she repeats, over and over, that she no longer holds any love for her father because he killed her husband just five days into her marriage. As his daughter speaks, Dzouclis puts his head on his trial table with his arms folded beneath his face.

Suddenly, he threw his arms high in the air, straightened stiffly back in his chair, and cried at the top of his voice "Oh Father, Father, Father, believe me Jesus Christ in Heaven, believe me, believe me, believe me. No one believes me. Help me Father, help me oh, God Father, help me! None of these people believe. Oh, Father, Father, Father!"

His cries continued as Judge W.B. Thompson ordered court adjourned at once and the jury to be led out.

Five men, some of them deputy sheriffs, attempted to quiet the man as he waved his arms in the air, moaning and groaning and uttering heart-rending cries. He remained with his head back over his chair and his feet stretched before him as they poured water in his face and gave him more water to drink. *The Chronicle-Telegram, May 16, 1930.*

The pandemonium is no surprise to Sheriff Adams who says he had fears of some sort of outbreak since "the man hasn't slept more than ten minutes since the trial began."

The even more jam-packed trial resumes the next day with the defendant well-rested after 18 hours' sleep in a padded cell, thanks to opiates prescribed by the jail's doctor.

Some spectators suggest that he faked hysteria, but authorities cite his lack of sleep for the outbreak. The proceedings are, once again, put on hold because of Dzouclis' apparent condition. Per Judge Thompson: "The postponement was made to allow the defendant to recover from the illness with which he was attacked Friday."

It is later revealed that when Dzouclis was returned to his regular cell, he began to scream and wave his arms around. He was subdued by another prisoner and placed back in the padded cell, but not before scaring the other inmates so badly that those in the hall returned to their own cells and locked themselves in.

Defense Charles Adams, Prosecutor Myers, Judge Thompson, and jail physician, Dr. G.E. French confer behind closed doors. It is then announced Dzouclis will be examined by Dr. Arthur Hyde, a specialist from the Massillon (Ohio) State Hospital for the Insane.

May 20: Dr. Hyde concludes there is no reason the trial could not continue. The defendant, on suicide watch, has not been allowed a razor for the past few days, and so he appears a little rough, but there are no further outbursts.

Sophia resumes her testimony. She tells how she had only once met the Canadian man to which her father said she was engaged. When asked if she ever intended to marry the man, she said she had never even considered it.

Witness Mike Nakoff says Tony Dzouclis was afraid the Canadian and his friends might come down and shoot him because of what Sophia had done, and that if he could get at least $800 from Mial Dineff he might be able to "make peace."

Police witnesses say that when arrested, Dzouclis surrendered with hands up saying, "Give me the electric chair." In addition, when he identified the Vasil's body as the man he shot, Dzouclis said, "Maybe I should have killed the girl, too."

May 21: Judge Thompson suddenly suspends the trial for five days to allow a sanity hearing for the defendant. The rational for this decision was an appellate court finding, upheld by the Supreme Court, that it is improper to continue with a trial after the attorneys for the defendant have made representation that their client is insane and have supported their contention with the filing of a doctor's certificate.

It turns out that defense attorney Adams has filed such a certificate sworn by Drs. T.A. Peebles and George M. Blank, both of Lorain. Their diagnosis is "Dementia Praecox, Paranoid Form" (sort of like schizophrenia). Defense attorney Adams, who enjoys something of a well-deserved reputation for his flair in court, says to those doubting his veracity:

> I resent the recent suggestion made by officials that I had Dzouclis "stage" the courtroom scene Friday for its effects on the jury. I never have, nor ever intend to resort to underhanded tactics of that kind to win a case. I feel a very real responsibility in this affair, and I am not going to allow them to try an insane man, if I can help it. Any intelligent person can see that Tony Dzouclis is not mentally right. *The Chronicle-Telegram, My 21, 1930.*

May 22: Papers report Dzouclis is eating well and appears to have a good appetite.

May 23: The defendant is to be sent to Lima State Hospital for the Insane for a one-month evaluation with the agreement that he returns for trial if he's found to be sane.

June 21: The report by Dr. Vorban states Dzouclis is sane.

June 23: Trial delayed again because of disagreeing doctors.

Judge Thompson calls for a "special sanity trial" to decide, once and for all, if Dzouclis is sane enough to stand a criminal trial. If insane, then the murder trial is off and the accused goes to Lima Hospital until he dies or regains his sanity. If he does come back to his senses, he will return to stand retrial for murder.

The prosecution doesn't like the idea since they were led to believe the report from Lima would be accepted. Defense, on the other hand, says the Lima report is incomplete and doesn't meet the standards of the court.

June 24: The criminal trial is back on track when defense attorney Adams abandons the idea of a sanity hearing, saying Dzouclis is "remarkably improved" and "his treatment at the Lima State Hospital apparently has restored him to a condition of mental competency, if not complete sanity."

June 26: Sheriff McAdams assigns men to guard against untoward actions Dzouclis may take in court. Defense attorney Adams strenuously objects to the men "surrounding" his client. Adams says they are prejudicial and proof the court considers Dzouclis to be insane and unable to stand trial. Were he sane, they would not be needed and that other, sane prisoners were not treated in like manner.

Dzouclis takes the stand and is either a disaster or star witness for himself. He mumbles answers and must be asked to repeat himself. He answers back-to-back identical questions with different replies. He says his daughter was engaged to a Canadian named "Joe" whose last name he could not recall and that breaking an engagement was like breaking a marriage and would "spoil the family."

Sheriff McAdams, for his part, testifies that he thinks Dzouclis is "trying to act crazy."

June 27: Prosecutor Myers asks for the death penalty. Attorney Adams continues to claim the shooting was manslaughter, if anything at all. Dzouclis sits, stock-still, as if he isn't even hearing what is going on around him.

The case goes to jury at 1:36pm. They are out a relatively short time before returning with a verdict of guilty of murder in the first degree with a recommendation of mercy. Judge Thompson has no choice but to sentence the guilty man to life in the Ohio Penitentiary in Columbus.

Antonio Dzouclis stands silently for his sentencing. When asked if he had anything to say, he remains quiet and motionless until led out of the room without having made a sound.

1932, July 8: Two years after the murder of her first husband, Sophia Dzouclis Dineff Traicoff's second husband, Christ, is wounded in a knife fight with German Karaloff, of Lorain (*his first name is "German"*). The battle is over the attention Karaloff is paying to Sophia. Karaloff is found guilty of assault and battery after being tried for cutting with intent to wound.

1930, May 15: *The Chronicle-Telegram:*

> Permanent Ban On Sightseers At Pen Planned.
>
> COLUMBUS, O, May 15. — Tourists and sightseers will be barred from the Ohio Penitentiary permanently it was understood today as plans for Warden P.E. Thomas to resume complete charge went forward.
>
> Last year about 75,000 persons were conducted on tours through the prison about half of these being school children and like organizations admitted free, while the other half paid

about $9,500 in admissions. Money obtained in this manner has been placed in the state treasury.

Visiting by relatives of prisoners also will be forbidden for at least a month, it was said. Regular visits will not be resumed until all of the men are back in cells or regular dormitories.

1930, late March to early April: Location: Elyria, West Branch of the Black River. Victim: Unknown infant. Act: Unknown. Body found on April 27 by John Radschy, 124 Irondale Street and Paul Haines, 120 Irondale Street as they played on the rocks near the water off West River Road "south of the Fair Grounds." The small body was caught on a willow bush. Using the state of decomposition, Coroner Perry reckons the child had been in the water two weeks to a month. The infant is taken to the Bittner Funeral Home. The baby remains unidentified and is buried in the Ridgeville Cemetery on April 30. Outcome: Unsolved.

1930, April 6, Sunday: Location: Lorain. Victim: Paul Monaco (40). Suspect: Dominic(k) Mannarino (Maunarius, Moreno) (27).

1929, July 9: "Husband Asks Divorce: Paul Monaco, East 28 Street, Lorain, filed suit in common pleas court today asking a divorce from Michelina Monaco, East 20 Street. Lorain, on the grounds of extreme cruelty and gross neglect of duty. The couple were married in 1920 in Italy, and have two children." *The Chronicle-Telegram.*

1930, March 28: "Micheline Monaco was granted a divorce from Paul Monaco, and was awarded $40 a month alimony and custody of the minor children of the couple. Gross neglect of duty was named as grounds for the divorce. A property settlement was also agreed upon." *The Chronicle-Telegram.*

1930, April 6: Paul Monaco returns to what once was his Lorain home, produces a pistol and threatens to shoot his ex-wife and their two children. Boarder Dominick Mannarino tries to take the gun. Several shots are fired during the fight and Mannarino is struck and killed. Another bullet hits boarder Samuel Cutrie who is taken to the Lorain Hospital and survives.

Monaco flees the scene but is captured by police about two hours later. Arrested on a charge of first degree murder with the ex-Mrs. Monaco held as a material witness. The charge is reduced to second degree murder in the indictment of April's Grand Jury (the paper maintains that it's first degree).

Plea: Not guilty. *Changed to:* Guilty of manslaughter. Outcome: Sentenced to the Ohio Penitentiary in Columbus "according to the law," plus court costs of $44.59.

1930, April 12, Saturday: Location: Lorain, 1500-block East 30th Street. Victim: Mike Serra (Senna, Sena, Sierra) (Mexican). Suspect: William Jackson (Colored). Jackson admits shooting Serra, but says it was in self-defense since he was attacked with a butcher knife. The trial is to be held on April 29. The jury is already drawn when Assistant Prosecutor John Harding asks for a postponement because the State's chief witness, Kelly Rosemand, the woman who runs the boarding house, has turned up missing. She said she was going to Cleveland for the funeral of her mother, but a police check shows no such funeral was scheduled.

May 8: During the trial, witnesses Maria Hill and Anna Payne (both Colored) back up the accused's self-defense story. Charge: Murder in the second degree. Plea: Not guilty. Outcome: Found guilty of Assault and Battery. Sentenced by Judge W.B. Thompson to the Toledo Workhouse, 2 months, $150 fine, plus court costs of $233.81.

During sentencing Judge Thompson tells the indigent man: "You got off easy. This fine is just what it cost the county for an attorney to defend you. A man your age should have been able to employ his own attorney."

Vanishing Races

The late 1920s were tough. No jobs. No booze. Riots in the streets. Vigilante lynchings, though dramatically decreased through the decades, began to draw the press they deserved. Increased coverage illuminated how these acts of terror were woven into the fabric of the United States.

In early May of 1930, the little town of Sherman in northeast Texas, descended into chaos when a crowd attacked and burned the Grayson County Courthouse to reach 41-year-old George Hughes, a Black man *accused* of assaulting Mrs. Drew Farlow, who was White. The corpse of Hughes who had "roasted alive" in a second floor room was recovered by the crowd. It was then "dragged in and through the Negro residential district," partially burned, and strung up in a cottonwood tree. It took 300 National Guardsmen to restore order.

The May 13, 1930, *Elyria Chronicle-Telegram* ran a fairly mild editorial condemning the Texans, and then... And then, something remarkable happened. Over the next two weeks the newspaper cleansed itself of all manner of adjectives referring to the race or ethnicity of the people in its articles.

The murder case described above (*1930, April 12*) is the very last for which the Elyria paper lists either the color or ethnicity of those involved. From here on, unless it's important to the story, there is only name, age, and address.

1930, May 19, Monday: Location: In Lake Erie off Avon Lake and Sheffield Lake. Victims: John Snowbrick (22) and Miles Mandick (20). Snowbrick (of Cleveland, Ohio) is found in the water "at about Stop 67, near Avon Lake Village." Mandick (of Detroit, Michigan) is floating "off Stop 87, in Sheffield Lake." The bodies were found by a fisherman who reported it to Avon Lake Marshal Carl Tomasek. The fisherman who discovered the bodies also reports seeing a boat come in near shore. There are later reports of a large automobile in Avon Lake with men inside, asking if a motor boat had been spotted in the area.

The postmortem, held at the Pease Funeral Home, Dover Village, by Coroner Perry, finds no water in their lungs. He says neither of the bodies had been in the water long. Both men died of fractured skulls. Before any information is released to the public, five men appear at the funeral home to identify Snowbrick's body. These men are named as Joe Perish, M. Vichmine, Nick Kordich, Joseph M. Craispik and Andrew Popp, all of Cleveland, Ohio. They said a small boy on the lakeshore had told them where the bodies had been taken.

Police seem certain the floating men were killed in Cleveland as the result of a "bootleg feud," brought off-shore of Avon Lake in a motor boat, and dumped to make it look like a drowning. The two young men were friends says Mrs. Snowbrick who tells how her husband had left early afternoon, Saturday the 17th, saying he was going fishing. She also says she received a tearful call from an unidentified woman the next day telling her that her husband was dead. Outcome: Unsolved.

1930, May 14: *The Chronicle-Telegram:*

    U.S. Forced to Borrow Cash.

    The richest nation in the world is without ready cash and the treasury has been forced to borrow $100,000,000 in short term notes to meet its immediate needs.

    Even with this borrowed money the treasury has no

assurance of ending the fiscal year with a surplus, for $56,000,000 of it must be paid out on May 10 to clear previous obligations.

Moreover, a large deficit is in view when the government closes its bank-book at the end of the present fiscal year, June 15.

1930, May 22: *The Chronicle-Telegram:*

First Jury Composed Entirely of Women Decides Law Suit Here.

For the first time in the history of Lorain County courts a jury composed entirely of women sat in a law suit in the common pleas court of Judge A. R. Webber this morning.

Court officials were deprived of their life-long ambition of determining how long it would take twelve women to agree or agree to disagree, however, because the verdict they returned had been agreed to, and was simply a formality.

The case was that of Christina Zajicek, a minor against Joseph M. Thomas, the former seeking $100 damages for being struck by the latter's automobile on Broadway, Lorain, March 24, 1930. The jury of a dozen women gave the verdict, under court orders to the plaintiff.

The women who made history in this manner this morning were Gladys L. Irish, Josephine L. Austin, Ida Wingard, Elizabeth Abbe, Ada Landon, Grace B. Cook, Lottie Heath, Hazel Van Horen, Jane Setton, Clara E. Lee, Sylvia Curtis, and Edna Caldwel.

The case which they decided was filed in court this morning.

Court records show Zajicek won the suit. Joseph Thomas also had to pay $5.10 in costs.

1930, June 23, Monday, 1:20am: Location: Lorain, 1800-block East 29th Street. Victim: Cresencio Espinoza (33) Suspect: Gregorii (Gregorio) Espinoza. Outside his home, Cresencio Espinoza is shot twice (to his right shoulder, deflecting to the lungs, and into his abdomen) and dies nine hours later at St. Joseph's Hospital. Police think the shooter is the victim's brother and are searching for him. There is no known motive for the crime.

Mrs. Lorenzo Lijua, in the same block of East 29th hears the shots and pursues the shooter a short distance until he turns and fires at her. There are two witnesses to the shooting: Frank Fisher, 1800-block East 29th and Jesus Rosale, 2100-block East 29th.

1931, May 15: The suspect is thought to have been arrested and held in Coeneo, Mexico. He was located when the National Tube Company contacted police after the suspect had written them, asking for money. Extradition papers are requested from the State Department by Ohio Governor White but the suspect is never delivered. Charge: Murder in the second degree. Warrant issued. Was never arrested. Case continued until April term 1935 when it was nollied by the Prosecutor. Outcome: Unresolved.

1931: After years of declining ridership, local, short rail lines begin closing. It's official, the National Anthem of the U.S. is *The Star-Spangled Banner.* Stalin is killing Russians by the millions and nobody seems to care. Japan invades Manchuria and nobody seems to care. The Irish Government declares the IRA to be illegal. Nobel and Pulitzer prize-winning writer Toni Morrison is born in the City of Lorain, Lorain County, Ohio. Don King is born in Cleveland, Ohio. In the Docket: Breaking and Entering Railroad Cars and Receiving Stolen Property. 13 lynchings: 12 Blacks, 1 other.

1931, January 28, Wednesday night: Location: Lorain, near 1818 Broadway, back room of Wallace's Magic Store. Victim: Norman Watte (Watt, Watts) (63). Victim Watte is a well-educated man of a wealthy Chicago family, a graduate of the University of Chicago, and a onetime member of the Chicago Board of Trade. He is popular among the business and professional men of the city who appreciate his learned and keen wit.

Papers state that an "unfortunate marriage" has led to Watte's moral and economic downfall. He is down and out and has been evicted from the Lorain Salvation Army shelter for refusing to follow the rules. Since then, he has been sleeping in the rear of a magic shop run by ex-stage magician Arthur Wallace (30, married father of four) and Maurice W. (Jack) Rice (30, married father of one) who is a demonstrator of magical paraphernalia.

Arthur Wallace tells police the following: He and Jack Rice were in the magic store talking together. Watte was present, and reading. Two young lake sailors entered the building, produced guns, and while holding him and Rice at bay, slugged Watte several times in the head and then dragged him behind the curtain in the back of the shop. The sailors cut off his clothing and slashed it to pieces looking for a large sum of money they said the old man was supposed to be carrying, but found only $3.75. At that point, Wallace says, he began to shout and the two men fled.

Norman Watte dies of head trauma as he is transported to St. Joe's. Because of the crime's location, papers call this the "Magic Shop Murder."

Two Great Lakes sailors, Spencer Stevens, 23, and Edward P. Nolan, 28, are arrested. They admit to beating and robbing the victim. They also tell police that Wallace and Rice, the two magicians, are in on the deal and both received a cut of the gains. Wallace and Rice vehemently deny involvement.

January 30: All four men are charged with first degree murder. Nolan and Spencer own up to the beating and robbery. Wallace and Rice eventually admit to authorities that they set up Watte, but insist it was supposed to be a simple robbery. They never intended the old man be killed. The sailor boys, they say, took things way too far.

All are bound over to the February Grand Jury. All are indicted for murder in the first degree. All plead not guilty. Prosecutor Don. W. Myers says he will ask for the death penalty for each and every one.

The law requires four separate trials. Sailor Ed Nolan goes first. He and Ed Stevens are represented by attorney Milton Friedman, of Lorain. Criminal trials begin on March 23. Jurors are seated within two days. The judge is W.B. Thompson.

Nolan's father arrives from Boston, Massachusetts to support his son. He says his son has worked only two seasons on the lake boats. The boy's mother is dead ("thank God, or this would have killed her"). The old man has political connections back home and carries letters of recommendation for his son from his District Attorney, Mayor, Senators, and various businessmen.

The courtroom is crowded as testimony begins. One witness is called. The trial then comes to a screeching halt when the defense for both Nolan and Stevens announces that the sailors will plead guilty to murder in the first degree and throw themselves upon the mercy of Judge Thompson.

The jury is dismissed. The judge questions each witness to learn the nature of the crime. Prosecutor Myers continues to push for the death penalty. The law specifically states that one who kills another in the perpetration of a robbery is guilty of murder in the first degree, even if the death is unintentional. A surprised Judge Thompson defers sentencing for five days. Says he, "When the matter is given to a jury there are 12 persons who may share the responsibility. But I am not going to shirk my duty. I never have and shall not now." *The Chronicle-Telegram, March 25, 1931.*

A packed room hears Thompson sentence both Nolan and Stevens to life at hard labor in the Ohio Penitentiary in Columbus. Solitary confinement is not part of the punishment. Stevens takes it calmly. Nolan cries as sentence is pronounced, then gathers himself to thank his jailers and the court for their fair treatment and mercy. The sailors are taken to Columbus.

Rumors are that Wallace and Rice will plead to lesser charges. All attorneys are mum. April's Grand Jury sees Wallace and Rice again up for consideration, still with lawyer C.F. Adams, Lorain, defending. Now that Nolan and Stevens have plead guilty to first degree murder, it's thought the charges against the other two men might be reconsidered.

The charge against Wallace is dropped to second degree murder and he pleads guilty. Judge Thompson sentences him to life in the Ohio Penitentiary in Columbus. Rice pleads guilty to manslaughter and draws seven years. Rice and Wallace head to their new home on April 14.

Defense attorneys ask the county for a total of $3,700 in fees. They are paid $700.

Jack Rice is paroled in 1936. Arthur Wallace is released in 1941. By 1956, all but Stevens has been released when Ohio Governor Frank Lausche, Democrat, commutes Stevens' sentence to second degree murder. This makes him eligible for parole.

1931, January 29: *The Chronicle-Telegram:*

Announce Police Radio Plans Are Now Complete.

All preparations for the setting up and operation of a police radio broadcasting station have been completed and there remains nothing now but the purchase of the equipment, Sheriff Clarence Adams announced today following communication received yesterday from the radio commission.

Adams said he was going to take the matter before the county commissioners today. Commissioners recently have approved the plan of erecting a broadcasting station at the county jail and the equipment of county squad cars with receiving sets so deputies may more efficiently cope with lawlessness.

The cost of the station has not been definitely determined, Adams said, but this is to be gone into immediately. It is believed the station can be set up for approximately $1,000, he reported.

Radio equipment on police cars in Lorain and Elyria will be installed when the station is in operation, it is believed.

1931, February 8, Sunday, about 9:00pm: Location: Stop 7 between Elyria and Lorain near the Vincent School (by the intersection of North Ridge and West River Roads). Victim: Steve Zawacski (Zawaczki, Zowalski, Zabotski) (55). Suspect: Nick Muhich (Mubich) (42).

Nick Muhich's wife died in the fall of 1930 from pneumonia which, it was alleged, she contracted because her husband drove her from their home and forced her to sleep in the barn on a bed of straw. A Grand Jury investigation into the death of his wife produced no indictment against him.

Before her death, Mrs. Muhich gave neighbor, Mrs. Stanley Zcak $15 to spend on the Muhich family's six children. Nick, down on his luck, visits Mr. Stanley Zcak to convince him to give back the $15 his now-dead wife gifted to their children.

The discussion grows violent. Nick Muhich draws a jack-knife, cutting Stanley Zcak on the hands. The victim, Steve Zawacski, a friend of Zcak, stands up for his pal. Shortly thereafter, Zawacski is bleeding profusely from a stab wound to the left thigh and soon dies from the loss of blood.

Sheriff Adams and Coroner Thomas Peebles arrive about a half-hour after the fight. The coroner declares death was due to a severed artery in the leg. The sheriff is directed to the Muhich home. Nick admits to doing the cutting and is arrested.

His six children are taken to the Oberlin Home. The victim, Steve Zawacski, is the father of seven. He is buried from St. Stanislaw's Church, Lorain, and interred in Calvary Cemetery on February 11.

The February Grand Jury indicts Nick Muhich on charges of second degree murder. He pleads not guilty on the grounds of self-defense. The criminal trial begins on May 11 with Judge W.B. Thompson, Assistant Prosecutor John Harding, and Basil Dziama for defense. Muhich claims he was attacked by three men and was slashing with his knife in self-defense. He did not mean to kill anyone. All of them had been drinking. The cut was small but happened to be in a fatal location.

The jury finds Muhich guilty of manslaughter. Outcome: Sentenced by Judge Thompson to the Ohio Penitentiary in Columbus for 1 year plus court costs of $86.09. A motion for new trial is overruled.

1931, May 24, Sunday, about 6:45am: Location: Elyria, 500-block North Street. Victim: George Glenn (33, former brother-in-law) Suspect: Sherman Wall (Wahl) (23 former brother-in-law). Police are called to the North Street home of Mrs. Alza Glenn, the divorced wife of George Glenn, who reports her drunk ex-husband is arguing with her mother, Mrs. Flossie Gaters Wall. Alza Glenn says she is afraid that her ex may turn violent and kill her, her baby, and her mother.

Police arrive to find George Glenn with a battered and bleeding head on the blood-slick floor of the front porch. The injured man is taken to Elyria Memorial where he remains unconscious until he dies some hours later. A post-mortem examination reveals hammer strikes to his head, two knife wounds thru the skull, and a three-quarter-inch long end of a broken jack-knife blade lodged in his cranium. The force of the knife strikes are such that authorities conclude they were most likely made by a man. Glenn's body is taken to the Moore Funeral Home in Oberlin.

It turns out that George and Alza Glenn have been married and divorced twice. Police think jealousy over her activities with a new sweetheart drew the ex-husband to his former wife's home where he awaited her return. She knew he was there and purposely stayed away. When she finally did return, the quarrel began.

When questioned, Alza's mother, Flossie Wall admits striking the victim over the head several times with a hammer but claims she knows nothing about the knife. Sherman Wall, Alza's brother, is held pending an investigation. He says he was summoned by his sister and did what was needed to prevent the victim "from doing any damage." Under questioning the suspect admits he wielded the knife that killed George Glenn but insists that he did it to protect his mother and sister from the victim's drunken rage.

Wall says that after the killing he cleaned the knife and gave it to a small boy who was sitting in a car parked on Chestnut Street. Police ask the public for the return of the knife as evidence. It never shows up. Sherman Wall is brought before the May Grand Jury on charges of murder in the second degree. He is not indicted and is released from the County Jail.

1931, July 16: Alza Wall Glenn, 23, Elyria marries James Taborn, 24, craneman, Oberlin.

1933, January 20: Sherman Wall, not indicted for the knifing above, is fined $5 for disorderly conduct against C.H. Phillips, gas station attendant on Oberlin Road, who says Wall threatened him with a blade.

1931, May 30, Saturday, 9:30pm: Location: Sheffield Lake Village. Victim: Mrs. Nellie Schindler (41, landlady). Suspect: Henry Barnes (Barris) (41, boarder and, perhaps, sweetheart). The papers report that Henry Barnes has been "showing affection" toward Mrs. Schindler.

Saturday night, Mrs. Schindler and Mr. Barnes go for a spin in his auto. During the ride, she criticizes his driving. He ejects her from the car. She arrives home about 9:30pm, understandably angry about her forced hike. A drunk Henry Barnes is there to greet her. Another quarrel follows. He orders her back into the automobile. Mrs. Schindler refuses and then threatens to leave him. Mr. Barnes retrieves a shotgun and tells her he will shoot her if she tries.

Mrs. Schindler dares him to. Barnes pulls the trigger and the entire load of shot enters Mrs. Schindler's body slightly below her heart. She drops to the ground. He drops the gun and flees. When captured, Barnes claims he was attacked by the victim and shot in self-defense. Circumstances will show that he *was* attacked, but not by his victim.

The June Grand Jury indicts Henry Barnes for murder in the second degree. As an indigent, Barnes is assigned attorneys George Chamberlin and Richard Horan. At Barnes' criminal trial, the victim's 18-year-old daughter, Wava (one of ten kids) testifies:

> My father left us several years ago, and when Mr. Barnes stayed at our house he provided most of the money to meet expenses. The night my mother was shot they had been drinking considerably. When mother refused to ride in his car they quarreled.
>
> Mother threatened to leave.
>
> He said, "I'll shoot you if you leave this house."
>
> She said, "I dare you to shoot me."
>
> I hit Mr. Barnes over the head with an iron pipe to save mother but that made him raving mad. He pulled the trigger. I screamed and mother said, "oh, my God." *The Chronicle-Telegram, July 7, 1931.*

Defense states that Barnes committed the act under the influence of so much alcohol that he was not aware of his actions. He was so drunk, in fact, that he thought the blow by Mrs. Schindler's daughter was coming from Mrs. Schindler herself. Defense lawyers appeal to the jury for a verdict of manslaughter because there is nothing in the trial to show he purposely and maliciously shot his victim.

The jury of eight women and four men aren't buying it. After three hours of deliberation, they find Henry Barnes guilty of murder in the second degree. Judge W.B. Thompson sentences Barnes to life in the Ohio Penitentiary, plus court costs of $120.39.

Because Mrs. Schindler dared her killer to take action the press ended up calling this the "Dare Murder Case." As previously mentioned and in case you haven't figured it out, it's a very bad idea to dare an armed person to shoot!

1931: June 24: *The Chronicle-Telegram:*

Street Car Rails to be Removed.

Removal of rails of the Cleveland Southwestern Railway company from Wellington to Oberlin is to get underway Monday, it was reported here today. It is understood the work will take about four weeks.

It is also understood that following completion of this section, the rails from Oberlin to Elyria will be removed and that the rails in Elyria, where they are not laid in the pavement, will come next in the salvaging of the tracks.

The company will not take up the rails where they are laid in the pavement because of the expense of replacing the paving, it was stated by Gardner Abbot, attorney for the receiver for the company, in conversation with City Solicitor Harry Redington.

1931, August 12, Wednesday: Location: Lorain, 1700-block East 30th Street. Victim: Mrs. Anna (Anita) Andros (Andres) (45, landlady). Suspect: Mike Caloyanis (32, boarder). Boarder Mike Caloyanis shoots landlady Anna Andros in a dispute over money that he refused to pay and she is suing him for. Andros dies almost instantly. Caloyanis is quickly arrested and freely admits his crime. The September Grand Jury indicts Caloyanis for murder in the second degree. He pleads not guilty.

Caloyanis grows upset when attorney Dziama refuses to work for him pro bono. He dismisses Dziama and sends for County Prosecutor Myers. The prosecutor is more than a little surprised when Caloyanis says he is more than happy to plead guilty to keep his hard-earned money out of the hands of any doggone lawyer.

In the meantime, Judge Thompson assigns Dziama the defense of the case. Dziama meets again with Caloyanis and asks if he is certain he doesn't want to change his plea back to not guilty and stand trial. Caloyanis refuses, telling him, "I am going to plead guilty. If you want your money you will have to work for it!"

Admitting his guilt sends Mike Caloyanis to the Ohio Penitentiary for life. It also costs him $70.44 of his own money to cover the proceedings.

1931, November 19, Thursday, about 3:00am:

Michael Benzak (Bensak) is a farm hand for Harry Hart, out on Durkee Road in Eaton Township. Mike's a good fellow and a hard worker, but he's not the sharpest tool in the shed. It's not that he's lacking in book smarts—so are a lot of the other fellows he works with—it's more that, well… Benzak can be hoodwinked by almost anybody, talked into doing things that nobody with even a grain of common sense would do. The guys don't call him "Crazy Mike" for nothing.

Lately, though, Mike hasn't been teased so much. He's bought himself a sweet ride, a brand new 1931 Willys 6 Coupe, and got himself a girl, Alice Wedic, from over in Grafton. She's Ford Dernier's daughter, recently divorced from that guy from Illinois who turned out to be too mean.

Mike and Alice have been an item almost six month and he's absolutely nuts for her, kind of jealous, too, but that's understandable, considering she's the first serious romance he's ever had. He spends every moment he can with her and plenty of money, too. Fancy shows in Cleveland, dinners, gifts, the whole shebang. Let's not forget Alice's pretty, little 2-year-old daughter, Justine. Mike's goofy for her, too.

The other guys on the farm share glances and grins when Mike tells them he's planning to marry Alice and take her and little Justine out to California where things are hopping. His friends suggest to Mike that maybe he's moving too fast, maybe she's not as serious about things as he is, but guys in love don't always have the sense to listen. Everything's perfect between them, Mike says. Besides, it's Wednesday, that means taking in another show over in the big city.

Cleveland brothers H.H. and C.A. Reynolds are tromping along Durkee, north of Royalton Road in the cold, November, pre-dawn light. The two avid hunters were up hours ago to start the long trip out to the country. The early bird gets the worm, y'know. Or the deer. Or rabbit, pheasant, turkey, or anything else that dares show its furred or feathered face.

Durkee Road is so straight and flat that they see the lights of the automobile well before they reach it. It's a late model Willys Coupe. Odd… The engine's still running.

The hunters find one person on the ground beside the vehicle. Another is half in, half out the passenger side. Neither is moving. One of the brothers rushes to the closest house that's lit. It's farmer Paul Basset, who calls the police.

Deputy Sheriffs Fred Underhill and William Caley are the first to respond. They find 21-year-old Alice Wedic sitting in the passenger seat, facing the door, but crumpled over with her legs hanging out of the car, feet touching the earth. With a bullet through her temple, she's dead, for sure.

Mike Benzak's on the ground, bleeding from what look like bad bite marks on his hands and a severe scalp wound. A .22 caliber revolver is on the ground nearby. The man's alive and mumbling, but extremely confused. Barely coherent, the 22-year-old admits to the shooting and then falls silent.

When X-rayed at the hospital, what the deputies thought was a superficial gunshot wound to Benzak's head turns out to be a bullet lodged at the base of the man's brain. Doctors hold out little hope for his survival.

It's Deputy Underhill's opinion that the shooting occurred about 300 feet from where the car stopped as evidenced from the blood on ground at that distance. Underhill thinks that Benzak shot the girl, drove north to a small creek that passes under Durkee near Giles Road, perhaps to dump the body, but was overcome by remorse and shot himself instead.

Investigation reveals that Ray Ward, a farmer who lives about 1,000 feet from the scene, "was feeding his chickens" at 3:00am when he saw a car with its lights on. He never gave it a second thought—that stretch of Durkee Road is frequently used for parking by couples seeking privacy.

During the police investigation the Dernier family confirms what Mike's fellow farm hands had suspected: Alice had no serious interest in the relationship and, they add, Mike was extremely jealous.

The post-mortem on Alice Wedic finds not one, but two .22 caliber bullets in her brain. One fired into each temple with either enough to cause instantaneous death. Coroner Thomas Peebles figures Benzak first shot the woman in the left temple, drove the car to a place down the road, exited the car, went to the passenger side, and shot her again before shooting himself.

Alice's body is taken to the Taylor Funeral Home. Services are held at the Grafton Immaculate Conception Church on November 21. She is buried in Grafton's St. Mary's Cemetery.

Mike Benzak shows some improvement, but is still unable to speak. He is given a slight chance of recovery by his doctors at Elyria Memorial. The bullet is left inside his skull since any operation to remove is riskier than leaving it in place.

Five days after the shooting, two civil suits are brought against Benzak by Alice's father, Ford Dernier: one for funeral expenses, the other on behalf of the victim's daughter. Both are for $500. Dernier wins both. Benzak's estate has no funds, so Dernier gains the court's permission to sell the young man's bloodied Willys Coupe in a public auction held at the County Court House. The vehicle goes for $210.

The shooting is taken up by the November Grand Jury where Mike Benzak is indicted for first degree murder. He is absent, still recovering in Elyria Memorial from his self-inflicted gunshot wound. Setting a date for his criminal trial depends upon his progress. It isn't until January 23, 1932, that Benzak, now convalescing at the County Jail, is arraigned before Judge A.R. Webber. He pleads not guilty. With appointed co-counsel Richard Horan and Lawrence Webber, Benzak's trial date is set for February 15, then pushed off until February 23.

By February 25 the jury is seated and testimony begins. Spectators jam the court room so completely that Elyria Fire Chief W.N. Bates is called in to clear it. Judge Webber is on the bench. Prosecutor Don W. Myers is pushing for the death penalty. The accused man "appears to be fairly ill." He is uninterested and listless in court.

The defense is one of temporary insanity. Benzak's attorneys contend he "has the mind of an 8-year-old." They describe him as bashful and maintain that he had never "kept company" with a girl before his relationship with Alice Wedic. Defense does its best to paint the victim in a bad light, saying the young woman used their client to get what she could. Benzak had money, a car, and "was just a taxi driver" for the vastly more experienced Alice.

It is true that the accused is known throughout the neighborhood as "Crazy Mike." There is no denial of the shooting, but his actions are attributed to liquor, weak-mindedness, and an argument between the two. Defense contends that the most Benzak could be convicted of is manslaughter, but even then, he should be acquitted.

The trial comes to an abrupt end the next day when defense attorney Lawrence Webber announces that his client is willing to enter a plea of guilty to murder in the second degree. In justifying the move, defense says Benzak had little schooling, was raised in an orphanage, and lacked mental skills. But he was always peaceful and law-abiding. The young man has lost the sight in his right eye and is otherwise suffering from the effect of the bullet to the brain. Benzak is likely to never be himself again.

The plea is accepted by the prosecutor only because the parents of the victim do not want to see their daughter's killer electrocuted due to the guilty man's weak mind. That he'll never fully recover from his self-inflicted wound helps them make that decision.

Judge Webber immediately sentences Michael Benzak to life in the Ohio Penitentiary in Columbus plus costs of $171.09. It's the only term possible for the crime. After judgement, Alice Wedic's weeping parents shake Benzak's hand, express their sympathy, and wish him luck.

He is to be taken to prison on February 29, but requests an extra day so that his sister, a nun in Cleveland, might visit him before he goes. That is granted by his county jailers.

March 4: The full defense bill of $925 will be paid by the county.

As she grows older, Justine Ann(e) Wedic appears as part of plays at the Grafton P.T.A. She graduates from Grafton High School and works for local doctor E.C. Kasper. The young woman eventually fulfills Mike Benzak's dreams of heading west by moving to Hermosa Beach, California, where, in 1950, she marries Fred C. Kircher, a former First Lieutenant of the Army Air Force.

Mike Benzak died at the Lima State Hospital in mid-August of 1968.

1932: Where's the Lindberg Baby? Vitamin B3. Ibn Saud takes control of most of the Arabian Peninsula, and Saudi Arabia comes to be. President Hoover sends troops with tear gas and bayonets to disperse WW I veterans protesting in Washington D.C. in hopes of obtaining their pay bonuses. Newspapers describe local people "motoring long distances," like to Pittsburgh. In the Docket: Arson, Auto Theft, and Manslaughter (as opposed to murder). Let's not forget about Kiting Checks, Non-Support of Minor Children, and Embezzlement. Franklin Roosevelt (New York Democrat) wins the Election with 57.4% of the popular vote. 8 lynchings: 6 Blacks, 2 others.

1932, April 19: *The Chronicle-Telegram:*

>Fatal Shooting Results from Scuffle. 21 Year Old Youth to Be Held For Grand Jury As Result of Shooting of His Father.

>A 21-year-old youth who shot his father in an effort to protect his grandfather is to be held for the grand jury on a homicide charge.

>The incident occurred about 2P.M. yesterday at the home

of William Livingston, Sr., 49, of Walker road, Avon Lake Village.

Livingston senior and Dennis Hoban, 76, father of Mrs. Livingston, were engaged in a heated argument. Fearing harm might come to his grandfather, William junior threatened his father with his 22 caliber rifle.

The father attempted to take the rifle from his son and in the ensuing scuffle the rifle was discharged, the bullet passing through the father's liver.

A doctor was called and he ordered Livingston taken to Saint Joseph's hospital in Lorain. The doctor also notified Marshall Carl Tomanek, who called Sheriff Clarence Adams.

Deputy Sheriff William Hoist was detailed and brought young Livingston to county jail.

The boy was released last night after Sheriff Adams interviewed the wounded father and was requested to release the boy. The father said it was an accident. Sheriff Adams compiled by releasing the boy last night.

The sheriff was notified that the father died at 5A.M. today in the hospital. The matter is now to be brought before the grand jury, the sheriff reported.

Outcome: Suspect was charged with murder but not indicted.

1932, April 22: *The Chronicle-Telegram:*

Woman Granted Parole By Court:

"Do you object to a parole for the defendant?" Asked Judge W.B. Thompson of Utopia Baker, Lorain, who was shot by the defendant more than a month ago.

"I don't object, only I hope that I would get the same break if I were the defendant," she said.

"That is a very unusual spirit. It makes it easy for the court," the judge said.

Hattie Williams, the defendant, who pleaded guilty to shooting with intent to wound, was then placed on probation for one year. Deputy Sheriff William Hoist was named probation officer.

1932, June 3, Friday:

Hattie Williams reports her husband, Oscar, is missing. Two days later he's found in the basement of a nearby abandoned house, dead from severe head wounds. At the July Grand Jury Hattie Williams and her son, Murray Hutchinson, are indicted for murder in the second degree in the death of Oscar Williams.

While in jail awaiting his criminal trial and through his assigned defense lawyers, Basil Dziama and Charles Adams, Murray Hutchinson pleads guilty to manslaughter and takes full responsibility for the crime, saying it was self-defense. His drunken stepfather became violent and threatened him with a heavy iron bar.

Hutchinson says he defended himself with an axe, killing the man. Hutchinson then used a small, two-wheeled cart to move the body to the cellar of an abandoned home in South Lorain.

Judge W.B. Thompson sentences Murray Hutchinson to an indeterminate term at the Mansfield Reformatory plus court costs of $58.84.

Hutchinson is released on parole in September, 1937 on the condition that he goes to Alabama.

Because of her son's confession, murder charges against Hattie Williams are nollied, but she does not get off scot-free. Her arrest violated the terms of her parole from her earlier shoot-to-wound charge involving Utopia Baker. Williams is sent to Marysville Reformatory for Women. She's denied parole in August of 1935 and her case in continued until July 1937.

1932, July 25: *The Chronicle-Telegram:*

Smaller Juries To Be Used Here:

The practice of trying cases before a jury of six instead of 12 persons is to be invoked at the opening of the September term of court as a means of saving court costs. Judge W.B. Thompson said today.

The court said he wished the policy of using the smaller jury would be adopted in every case where such a jury could be used. To prepare for adoption of the plan, the court asked a bar committee appointed for consideration of the "half jury" to meet this week and report its considerations as soon as possible.

Attorneys on the committee are L.B. Fauver, George Glitsch and M.F. Stevens.

The idea didn't take.

Trial by Jury

We typically think of a jury as always made up of twelve people, but it doesn't have to be that way.

State *civil* cases require only eight jurors and only six must agree. If there are twelve jurors in a civil case, Ohio allows a "supermajority verdict." That is, ten or more jurors agreeing to an outcome.

State cases for *criminal misdemeanors* also require only eight jurors, but all must agree. In more *serious criminal cases* (like murder) there must be twelve jurors who present a unanimous decision.

Federal grand juries are usually sixteen to twenty-three people. Federal *civil* "petit" juries can be comprised of six to twelve people who can present a non-unanimous decision, if that is agreed to by the parties involved. A federal *criminal* petit jury is always twelve who always have to present a unanimous decision for a verdict to be rendered.

1932, August 17, Wednesday, about 5:00pm:

Frank Lenahan has been a Lorain cop for 25 years—nearly half his life. He was a good man before drink got its hooks in him. That, combined with a bad temper, is causing all kinds of trouble in his life. He's lost most of his friends on the force, and it's ruined his relationship with his wife, Theresa.

In the middle of another of her husband's benders and in something like a panic, Theresa Lenahan calls out a window to her next-door neighbor and sister, Miss Ella DuRoss, telling her to summon the police.

There is gunfire before DuRoss reaches her telephone. The authorities arrive at the Lenehan home in the 1000-block of Long Avenue, Lorain, to find the body of Lenahan's wife (51) at the foot of the cellar steps. She's been shot through the head. Frank (54) is in the kitchen, a revolver with one spent round nearby. He admits the killing and resigns from the Lorain Police.

He's initially charged with first degree murder, but Lorain legal officials lower it to second degree and release him on $10,000 bond. His bond is revoked and he is rearrested when the September Grand Jury indicts him on charges of murder in the first degree. He pleads not guilty by reason of insanity. Lenahan's lawyer, Charles Adams, claims that his client's excessive drinking over the past years have changed his entire "mental structure," making him crazy.

Prosecutor Don Myers is hearing none of it. "This is a first degree murder charge," he says, "and comes as close to deserving the extreme penalty as any case in which I have come in contact."

Defense attorney Adams has his hands full with the case and not only because of the facts. Lenahan's nephew, Cleveland attorney George Hurley, is also part of the defense, but the two lawyers clash at every turn. Those problems are solved when Lenahan is declared to be indigent and Adams is placed as his sole attorney in the matter.

The criminal trial is first scheduled for October 24, then pushed out to November 10. Adams eventually gains help from his son, Sheldon, and lawyer Lawrence Job.

Prosecutor Don Myers and Assistant John M. Harding only accept jurors who agree they are capable of sending a man to the electric chair. Judge A.R. Webber excuses anybody who cannot, which turns out to be just less than half of the group. Lenahan looks well-rested and refreshed after a month away from the bottle. Dressed in a dark blue suit, he shows little interest in the questioning of potential jurors.

Testimony is scheduled to begin on November 15. It never takes place. On November 14, after jury selection is complete, the defense surprises everyone by making an impassioned presentation to allow a plea of guilty to murder in the second degree.

According to the papers, Adams says:

> For the past four of five years Frank Lenahan hasn't been any more himself that I have been Abraham Lincoln. He has been befuddled with drink.
>
> I am telling you these facts, Judge Webber, in hopes that there may come a time when you are actuated to do something for Frank Lenahan. He didn't intend to kill his wife. She first stabbed him with a fork. He got the gun to scare her. It was her flight that threw her into the path of the bullet which he fired, an act he doesn't remember. Frank was foolishly befuddled with drink. Get the effects of booze out of him and he's just as good a citizen as you have in this county.

To which an angry Prosecutor Myers replies:

> I can't insult my thoughts of justice to say he didn't intend to kill her. Drunk? He had the calmness to call the police and tell what he had done.
>
> "What have you done, Frank?" They asked him. "I shot her and she's deader than Hell," was his answer. *The Chronicle-Telegram, November 15, 1932.*

But Prosecutor Myers ends up taking the plea "with the greatest reluctance. I am actuated by the wishes of Mrs. Lenahan's relatives."

Judge Webber agrees with attorney Adams. "It wouldn't have happened if you were a sober man," he tells Lenahan, who stands calm and silent as the arguments swirl about him.

The ex-cop is sentenced to life in the Ohio Penitentiary in Columbus plus court costs of $72.60. I found no mention of parole.

1932, December 9, Thursday:

Donald Price, 12, is playing along the Lake Erie cliffs at Avon Lake Village when he discovers a body washed ashore. It is identified as Miss Eva Volpe (21) of the 300-block of Kentucky Avenue, Lorain. That's about five-and-a-half miles from where she is found.

The attractive, young woman with short, dark hair and big, dark eyes has bruises on her head, face, and around her temples. Coroner T.A. Peebles finds water in her lungs. A drowning, he rules, with the body in the water for fewer than 24 hours.

Eva's family says she left home two nights before, and the last contact they had was when she visited her sister who lives near their family home. They also tell police that while in high school, Eva had worked in a residence near where her body was found and so was familiar with the area.

The family says the young woman "expressed a recklessness about her welfare and said she didn't care whether she lived or not." Despite this, they are certain Eva is the victim of murder and not suicide and ask for a full investigation. Despite the bruising on her head and face, Lorain County authorities think she took her own life, but are troubled by an apparent lack of motive. Eva Volpe was good-looking, with reasonable finances and in reasonable health. Police speculate that if it was a suicide it was prompted by "personal matters not of a social nature." This is newspaper code for a failed love affair, depression, or insanity, especially since the victim was not reported as being with child.

The dead girl's mother provides a stack of "fervent love letters" written to the girl over a period of several weeks by a man who is hinted to be a wealthy Clevelander, but whose name is kept from the press.

Eva had worked as a governess to three young children in the Derbyshire Road, Cleveland Heights home of the Otto Millers, but had left because of "poor health." The Otto Millers, it turns out, are embroiled in a divorce. Working that angle, authorities closely question Mr. Miller but are unable to shed light on the girl's death. The papers report no connection between Miller and the aforementioned love letters.

Within two weeks all clues have been tracked down. The investigation grinds to a halt. Prosecutor Don W. Myers decides to let the Grand Jury decide if foul play is involved. His replacement, Prosecutor-Elect, John Harding pledges to take the case on if it continues past January 1, 1933.

The matter is brought before the January, 1933, Grand Jury. More than twenty witnesses are called from family members to police authorities. The Otto Millers are there, as well.

Newspapers report that Harry F. Payers, a Cleveland lawyer for the Millers, presents evidence that may help explain the love letters. That information is not divulged to the public.

The Grand Jury's decision is gagged from the press by Prosecutor Harding who says that if an indictment was handed down, he would not want the indicted person to escape. Sheriff Clarence W. Dick isn't so shy and reveals there was no indictment, either because of a lack of evidence, or a lack of crime, or both.

On February 13, 1933, Prosecutor John Harding announces there will be no further investigation into the death of Miss Eva Volpe. The crime, if any, is unsolved. The girl's mother, Mrs. Denise Volpe, remains absolutely certain her daughter, now in Amherst's Ridge Hill Memorial Park, was a victim of murder. Mother and daughter are reunited in early July, 1935.

1933: Amendments to the *U.S. Constitution: Twentieth:* Sets the date on which elected federal officials take office. It's January 3 for Congress. The President and Vice President now take office on January 20. *Twenty-first:* Repeal of the *Eighteenth* thus ending the National Prohibition on alcohol. The City of Lorain removes the fountain from its Civil War monument, placing the statue of the soldier on a low pedestal of its own. In 1967, the statue will be removed from the Public Square and, a year later, sent to its (hopefully) permanent home at the 103rd Ohio Volunteer Infantry Museum, East Lake Road, Sheffield Lake, Ohio. The Ohio Reformatory in Mansfield, Ohio, draws criticism for chronic overcrowding. It will take a Federal Court Order to clear the facility of prisoners in 1990. At the time of this publication, the Reformatory was open for public tours—make the trip! Blues singer Huddie "Leadbelly" Ledbetter is first recorded in the Louisiana State Penitentiary. Hitler is Chancellor of Germany. One of his first acts of government is the forced sterilization of those suffering from mental disease deemed to be inherited. That's followed by a Concentration Camp near Dachau, and that's just the start. The Tennessee Valley Authority begins electrifying and disrupting life for hundreds of thousands of back-wood folks. Spic and Span is invented by housewives Elizabeth MacDonald and Naomi Stenglein in Saginaw, Michigan. In Cleveland, Ohio, Jerry Siegel and Joe Shuster create a fellow more powerful than a locomotive. An assassination attempt on President-elect Franklin Roosevelt. Crime figure Danny "The Irishman" Greene is born in Lyndhurst, Cuyahoga County, Ohio. Comedian Tim Conway arrives in Willoughby, Cuyahoga County, Ohio. In the Docket: No murders, but Rape. Assault and Battery. Larceny. Non-support of a Minor Child. 28 lynchings: 24 Blacks, 4 others.

1934: Gangster John Dillinger is arrested. Bonnie and Clyde are shot and killed. The National Firearms Act regulates the sale and possession of fully automatic weapons. Alcatraz Prison opens for business. The first All-American Soap Box Derby. The board game *Sorry.* Elijah Muhammad now controls the Nation of Islam and will continue to do so for the next forty years. Adolf shows his optimistic side by promising Germans that their new government will last a thousand years. Stalin continues his purges. The Scottish National Party is formed with the goal of Scotland's independence. The U.S. withdraws its troop from Haiti. Actress Mae West is one of the highest-paid people in the U.S. pulling down more than $339,000 a year. Edsel Ford, president of one of the largest companies in the world, earns a paltry $90,000. Charles Manson (yes, *that* Charles Manson) is born as "Noname Maddox" in Cincinnati, Ohio. Gloria Steinem is born in Toledo, Ohio. Virginia Hamilton (children's author) is born in Dayton, Ohio. In the Docket: Manslaughter. Selling Intoxication Liquor. Abandoning a Pregnant Woman. Assault and Battery. 15 lynchings 15 Blacks, 0 others.

1934, August 14, Tuesday: Location: Lorain, Tompko Residence, Delaware Avenue. Victim: Charles Majjessie (49, younger brother). Suspect: Joseph Majjessie (54, older brother).

You could say that Charles, who has served time for manslaughter, and brother Joseph have a complicated relationship. *Serious* trouble has been brewing for the past six years. It started when Charlie borrowed money from Joe. Charlie then gave the dough to Joe's wife who used it to finance a divorce. Joe's ex-wife then promptly married Charlie.

Charlie is cut as the two brothers leave an "old-fashioned wake for a mutual friend" and is the culmination of an argument over the wife of the victim (ex-wife of the suspect). Joe is arrested for "cutting to kill" and released on $10,000 bond.

Charlie and his slashed stomach are rushed to St. Joseph Hospital where he dies three days later. His last words, in front of witnesses, are "I, only, was to blame. Show that brother Joseph, who suffered because of me, was not to blame." When his brother dies, Joe is rearrested on a charge of second degree murder. The September Grand Jury indicts Joseph Majjessie for murder in the first degree. Defense is Lawrence Job, of Lorain along with attorneys C.F. Adams and son Burt Adams.

October 16: Majjessie's criminal trial begins. The jury is selected after examining only 36 potentials. Attorney Walter Watts, serving as the court stenographer, states it took less time to select a jury than in any other murder case in his 40 years of experience. Part of the speed is due to a new selection process by which the jury commissioners weed out people who've been called in the past and brings in registered voters from all parts of the county in proportion to the voters in each respective district. The regular jurors are four women and eight men. The alternate is a woman.

Mrs. Steven Majjessie Sche, sister to both victim and accused sits with her brother Joe. Their mother, Elizabeth, and her third son, John, also attend the trial. Charles' widow (Joseph's ex-wife) weeps silently throughout the proceedings.

Defense claims the act was done in self-defense, that Charles Majjessie was a dangerous man. After all, he had spent time in jail on a manslaughter charge. Joe surrendered to police without a struggle as his brother was rushed to the hospital. Plus, there were Charles' last words, absolving brother Joe of all blame.

Prosecutor Frank E. Stevens and Assistant Prosecutor Malcolm Thomson scoff at that explanation. Joseph made a cold and deliberate attack on his brother. They have witnesses who say the accused ran up to the victim and attacked without provocation.

The jury makes a visit to the scene of the crime on the first day of testimony. Mid-afternoon, the next day, it's announced that Joseph Majjessie will plead guilty to manslaughter, but that he is in no way guilty of murder in either the first or second degree.

Judge Webber puts off sentencing until the next Monday (October 22). Possible time behind bars could be anywhere from 1 to 20 years. Instead, Joseph Majjessie is paroled for 5 years to Lorain attorney E.M. Wickens.

Judge Webber says: "The evidence presented in defense of the defendant was overwhelmingly in favor of his being paroled."

This action is taken over the objection of Prosecutor Frank E. Stevens. "We can't have people think that they can kill with impunity. We have been criticized in this county for our leniency and I think the interests of society and justice would be infinitely better served if he were committed."

Joseph Majjessie's parole is, eventually, extended. It ends in April, 1942, not quite eight years after the killing.

I found no death certificate for a "Charles Majjessie."
See: 1903, October 26 and 1907, November 10.

1934, September 2, Sunday, 10:00am: 1400-block Oberlin Road.

Let's agree that 40-year-old Miss Florence Lee is no angel.

Born Florence Griffin, she had a knack for entertaining. As soon as she was old enough, well, to be honest, a few years *before* she was old enough, she acted, danced, and sang (while scantily dressed) in the many "chicken shows" featured in clubs throughout Lorain County.

At 19 she married, then quickly divorced Howard Shaffer. She took the last name of and lived with Harry Lee for about 10 years before leaving him and moving in with Michael Carreo.

In the summer of 1927, July, she was arrested with Al Morton during a booze raid at his place at 1442 Broadway, Lorain. You'd thing Al would've been smart enough to find a better place to hide his Canadian liquor. That's when Miss Lee decided she'd be better off with a place of her own.

Within the next few years, she and her business partner with privileges, Michael Carreo, are running the 400 Bridge Club. It's one of Lorain County's best known hot spots located just outside the city of Lorain: 3700 Oberlin Road. The place makes money, but things aren't ducky between Miss Lee and Mike. He's taken a turn for the mean. Has started shouting and pushing her around. He's awful when he's drunk, laying into her with the beatings. Her friends have watched it happen, but none of them dare step in. They're all scared of Mike's violent temper.

It's particularly galling to Miss Lee since Mike was nothing but a song-plugger and bootlegger wannabe when she took him in. Now he acts like he's in charge of everything and everyone, like he's her common-law husband, or something.

Their next-to-the-last altercation takes place on a Sunday at sunrise, after a typically busy Saturday night at the club. Mike has tipped a few too many.

He wants to drive home, but is too drunk. Miss Lee tries to hide his car keys and is slapped across the face and roughed up for her troubles. Their club's manager, Joe "Chicken Doc" Yankowsky, offers to make sure Mike makes it safely to his own place out on Oberlin Road.

It doesn't take long for Miss Lee to close up the place. She bums a ride to her own home with Joe Lawrence, who is always telling her to ditch Mike. Then she hops in her own car and drives out to see Mike.

Not long after she surrenders herself at Lorain City Police Headquarters saying, "I just killed a man. Here I am." True to her word, Mike Carreo is dead in the hospital several hours later. How he got that way depends on who you talk to.

Police claim that shortly after Mike and Chicken Doc arrived at their destination, Miss Lee drove up, exited her vehicle, pulled out a .38 long-barrel revolver, and began shooting. The first shot went wild, the second blew a hole in the Mike's left temple, and the third struck Mike in the shoulder. Jealousy was the cause with Mike paying too much attention to "a blond" who frequented the 400 Bridge Club.

Miss Lee claims that she decided to confront Mike about slapping her when she tried to keep his car keys. On her way to Oberlin Road, she found Mike's revolver in her car and thought she could use it to scare Mike. But he went nuts when he saw it, ran towards her, and tried to attack her. She pulled the trigger to keep him away, to keep herself safe.

One thing's for sure. Miss Lee is in near-hysterics for the first 24 hours she spends in her cell, after which she began to regain her composure.

September 17: *The Chronicle-Telegram:*

Miss Lee Dresses Up For Picture:

Vanity stepped in Saturday to rescue Florence Lee, Lorain night club proprietor, from the horrors of a jail photograph.

Miss Lee, who is being held in county jail for the murder of her lover and business partner while in an alleged jealous rage, was requested by Deputy Sheriff Claude Adams, jail photographer to prepare to be "mugged" for the jail's criminal file.

Mindful of her appearance, like all women, Miss Lee begged for an opportunity to dress up a bit before having her picture taken.

"I understand," said Adams, who politely acceded to the request.

The grand jury is to consider Miss Lee's case this week.

The September Grand Jury indicts Florence Lee for murder in the first degree. She pleads not guilty. Her defense is Charles F. Adams and son, of Lorain.

It's a packed court room for the murder trial that begins on October 23 with Judge A.R. Webber on the bench. Selection of jurors is made difficult because of the possibility of sending a woman to the electric chair. The 12 end up evenly split between women and men.

Miss Lee arrives "dressed in an attractive brown dress and wearing a gray coat." Her father, E.B. Griffith (as opposed to Griffin), along with her sisters, Mabel Headwick, Mrs. Marie Parker, and Mrs. John Perry attend. Two other sisters: Mrs. Myrtle Bailey and Mrs. Gertrude Staman are not present that first day.

Defense Adams and son maintain that that Mike Carreo was slowly leveraging away from Florence Lee the business she alone had built, that Miss Lee was brutally beaten several times by Carreo, and that, the morning of the killing she was unmercifully beaten in full view of several witnesses who were afraid to take action. When she confronted the victim with the weapon, he charged her and made several attempts to kick her. Because of her previous beating "she was a bleeding, bruised, helpless and incoherent woman." There can be no other conclusion, her attorneys explain—Miss Lee shot in self-defense.

Prosecutor Frank E. Stevens, assisted by Malcolm Thompson, says the killing was planned, that in front of others, Miss Lee had threatened the victim's life when he was not present, and that she had said to employee James Staman, "I know where he is and I'll get him. And I don't care if I burn."

Several witnesses testify that, shortly before the shooting, Miss Lee had been beaten almost to insensibility by Mike Carreo.

Joe Lawrence tells of driving the accused to her home on the morning of the shooting and how he told her to forget about Mike and his brutality. During that conversation Miss Lee declared several times that she intended to kill the victim. He also testified that, minutes before Mike was shot, Miss Lee had arrived at the club in her own car, retrieved her revolver, and ordered everyone out before heading off.

Chicken Doc Yankowsky, witness to the killing, denies seeing Mike lunge at or try to kick Miss Lee as she described. Then again he had enjoyed a few drinks before it happened and it all went by so quickly.

Miss Lee takes the stand in her own defense and makes a good witness. It's true that she had taken the weapon with her for protection against Mike when she confronted him, but it wasn't hers. She had found it in her car where it had been put by the victim at some earlier time.

She says she was surprised to find Mike at Chicken Doc's house and would have never fired except that she was attacked. "I loved Mike and it is not true that I ever wanted to kill him, or harm anybody."

The trial lasts eight days. In closing arguments, the prosecution calls her cool and calm during the crime and that she did exactly what she told others she was going to do, going as far as telling Chicken Doc to get out of the way before shooting the victim. Holding the murder weapon in front of the jury, Prosecutor Stevens says, "Look at this, ladies and gentlemen, this is no ordinary revolver, this is a cannon."

Defense attorney Adams, senior, throws himself on the court room floor, directly in front of the jury, and asks them to picture the bruised and broken condition of the accused shortly before the shooting. "Let him who is without sin cast the first stone," he quotes, saying there is no justification for any degree of murder, nor even manslaughter, since nobody can prove she shot in anything but self-defense.

The six men and six women deliberate five hours and return a verdict of guilty of manslaughter. The jurors later say they never considered first degree or acquittal, but that there was some argument between second degree and manslaughter. The verdict carries a sentence of one to twenty years. According to Prosecutor Stevens, with the "new criminal laws," the judge cannot sentence, but only order the prisoner to a facility.

Miss Florence Lee weeps in front of a capacity crowd. Judge Webber sends her to hard labor in Marysville Prison, saying, in part:

> In all my experience I don't believe I ever saw a picture such as has been revealed in your case.
>
> The evidence shows that for some years your life has been misspent. You were born with ability but it has been misdirected. It is a sad picture.
>
> The victim became intoxicated from the very liquor from which you received a profit. Your place had a very bad reputation, with drinking, dancing girls, and gambling.
>
> He was engaged in the same business, that of debauching human beings.
>
> The court has no discretion as to your sentence. All the court can do is sentence you to from one to 20 years. If you

want to, you will be released sooner. If not, you will be an old lady before you are released.

You have been your own enemy. Everybody wants you to rise up. If you will do that, everybody will be for you. *The Chronicle-Telegram, October 28, 1935.*

Her case comes up for parole at the one-year mark, in 1935, as is the routine, but is refused, partly because of protests by Prosecutor Howard R. Butler.

Miss Florence Lee is released September 1, 1938, a day shy of the fourth anniversary of the shooting. Prosecutor Butler says he was never notified by the board. "If I had received such a notice I most certainly would have opposed a parole."

1934, September 11, Tuesday, about 10:00pm: Location: Lorain, 28th Street, Fantos Pool Room. Victim: Vincent Moreno (Morrus) (38, steelworker). Suspect: Frank Fantos (Sautos, Santos) (28, pool room owner). The shooting marks the end of an argument in which Fantos accused Moreno of the theft of minor household items. Moreno is shot twice in the back and dies shortly after at St. Joseph Hospital in Lorain. He is survived by several children.

Fantos surrenders peaceably to Patrolman William Johnson who runs to the scene upon hearing the shots fired. The suspect is indicted by the September Grand Jury of murder in the second degree. He pleads not guilty. Following opening argument, that is changed to guilty of manslaughter. Outcome: Paroled, 1 year to B.H. Buda, to report every 30 days, and court cost of $86.87.

1935: The world is supposed to end, according to evangelist Wilbur Voliva. It doesn't. George Gallup starts polling. Oberlin dismantles its tumble-down Civil War monument at the corner of Professor and West College. Marble tablets listing those lost are salvaged. William "Count" Basie starts his orchestra. Hitler says "Ich habe sowas von die Nase voll" in regards to the Treaty of Versailles. Mao Zedong gains control over the Chinese Communists during their Long March to northwest China. Kim Il Sung leads guerrillas against the Japanese occupation of Korea. Early trials of polio vaccines are disasters, causing both the disease and related deaths. American Home Products acquires the rights to produce a "sunburn oil" that is eventually transformed into *Preparation H.* A product used, ironically enough, where the sun don't shine. 20 lynchings: 18 Blacks, 2 others. $1,000 is worth $18,137 modern.

1935, August 14, Tuesday, about 4:30pm:

Steve Meluch sighs as his son Joseph (28), a former boxer, borrows money before heading out to Elyria to look for work. Shortly thereafter they call their brand new daughter-in-law, Dorothy, down for dinner. No response. Not unusual. They have learned in the twelve days that she has been with them that she often naps away the warm summer afternoons.

Sometime later they send their younger son, Paul (13), to get her. He plods upstairs, then returns, pounding down the steps crying, "There is blood on the floor, come quick!"

When Lorain police arrive at the home in the 100-block of West 23rd Street, they are uncertain if they're were dealing with a murder or, somehow, a suicide until it comes to light that Margaret Meluch (22) altered the scene of the crime by hiding a bloody pair of trousers and skirt that had been wrapped around the victim's head. Margaret tells the police it was an attempt to protect her brother, Joe, saying, "You'll probably find him dead, because if he did it, he'll commit suicide."

Police cannot produce a murder weapon at the scene, but believe the young woman was struck with the butt of suspect Joe Meluch's pistol that seems to have gone missing.

An attempt is made by Prosecutor Howard Butler to have Meluch indicted for first degree murder by the August Grand Jury. The jury refuses that charge. Butler accepts this, admitting that to indict would be a waste of money, considering the suspect is still on the lam.

On September 5, suspect Joe Meluch surrenders himself to police in St. Louis, Missouri. He claims to be a graduate of a correspondence course in "how to be a detective" and that it was his advanced knowledge of finger-print techniques that forced him to become a fugitive.

Meluch's story:

> Since I got my correspondence school diploma I had been working as an investigator for a railroad. On July 1, I married Dorothy Flowers of Dearborn, Michigan, and took her to my parent's home in Lorain.
>
> On August 14, I went out for a couple of hours, leaving my wife in our upstairs room. My sister and invalid mother were downstairs. When I returned, I found Dorothy lying face down on our bed. There was blood on the floor. I lifted her head and spoke to her. She was dead.
>
> I glanced around and saw no weapon. I guess it was my

schooling that scared me. My fingerprints were all over her. They'll suspect me. I hurried downstairs, got a clean shirt from my sister and changed my bloody one and left without saying anything about Dorothy to my mother or sister.

I went to Fort Wayne, Indiana, to Michigan, Wisconsin, finally to St Louis. Twice I read in newspapers that I was sought. I gave myself up because I can't stand being a fugitive any longer. I'll gladly take the lie detector or any other test to prove my innocence. *The Chronicle-Telegram, Sep. 5, 1935.*

September 6, back in Lorain County, Meluch admits to police that he killed the victim. He says his intensely jealous wife had threatened him with his own pistol for his association with other women. He had taken the weapon from her and beat her over the head with it.

September's Grand Jury indicts on murder in the second degree. Joe Meluch pleads not guilty. Bond is set at $20,000 but no effort is made to raise it.

The criminal trial starts October 8 with Judge D.A. Cook. Charles F. and Lon B. Adams of Lorain defending, claim self-defense and temporary insanity. Prosecutor Howard R. Butler and assistant William Wickens portray the accused "as a ruthless slayer who tired of his wife after six weeks of married life and took this means of freeing himself of his marital bonds."

Meluch's sister, Margaret, corroborates her brother's claims of Dorothy's extreme jealousy. Saying, in part, "She even hated to have him go into a grocery store where there were pretty clerks." But friend Walter Melosic, 25, testifies that Joe had talked to him about getting rid of his wife two days before the killing. When asked if he was going to leave her, Joe said that "he had another way," but he didn't say how.

When Meluch takes the stand in own defense, he says he had worked as an undercover man for a dozen railroads and other businesses in New York state until it became "too hot for him"—he quit after being shot at and beaten by gangs.

He and Dorothy, he says, had met through a matrimonial correspondence club. They wrote each other for about six months before he went to Dearborn to marry, where he had initially presented himself to her parents as "Government Agent K-23."

His wife was jealous from the start: "The second night after our marriage she slapped my face in a Dearborn beer parlor and led me out of the place because she thought I looked at other women too much."

In retribution, he had played a "kidnapping joke" on her, sending her a letter stating he'd been taken, bound, and gagged to force him to give up "a secret formula worth $10,000." But his wife called the Dearborn Police and he had to confess the hoax.

Meluch grows angry at his intense cross-examination at the hands of Howard Butler. The accused says his wife threatened him with his own gun, saying "you are mine. I would rather see you dead than anybody else's. I am going to kill you and myself." They fought, he took the weapon from her. As he struck his wife, the dead woman's husband says, "I saw red and black spots before my eyes."

The trial goes to the jury October 11. Five hours into deliberations, they ask trial judge D.A. Cook to re-explain the difference between second degree murder and manslaughter.

Seven hours later, the nine women and three men find Joseph Meluch guilty of manslaughter. The guilty man's face lights up with a big smile in contrast to the "stone-like countenance" he had held during the trial. Attorney Lon B. Adams said his client had always been willing to admit manslaughter, but that the prosecution wouldn't take the plea.

The victim's mother, Mrs. W.H. Kline of Dearborn, is present and disappointed at the verdict.

The defense indicates they will not ask for a new trial. Judge Cook gives him one to twenty in the Ohio Penitentiary in Columbus, plus costs of $316.61. When asked if he had any words for the court, Meluch replies "tell the public for me to beware of correspondence loves."

1936, September: Meluch comes up for parole, as is the routine. It is denied. The next hearing for him will be October, 1945. Outcome unknown.

Judge Daniel A. Cook:

Republican D.A. Cook began the practice of law on February 20, 1905, after graduation from the University of Michigan.

He was elected to the bench in 1934 and became the presiding judge in September of 1955. Judge Cook served until 1956 when he retired at the age of 73, nine months before his term was up, to "lessen obligations and take things easier."

After much speculation, J.J. Smythe, of Amherst, was appointed by Ohio

Governor Frank Lausche to replace Cook until the next election, which put LeRoy Kelly in office.

For some time after retirement, attorney Cook returned to limited legal practice in partnership with his son, also named Daniel.

After years of declining health, D.A. Cook died January 30, 1968, at the age of 84. He was buried at the Ridge Hill Memorial Park.

1935, August 27, Tuesday, 2:00am:

Gus Gailus calls Lorain Police to the 1000-block of Broadway Avenue to save his neighbor, Mrs. Stella Bucey (39) from being killed during a fight with her more-than-friend, Mr. Jack Burnett (35). Detective John Meister is not quite quick enough. He is ascending the stairs to the home when he hears shots fired. The officer approaches the scene with weapon drawn.

He, along with everyone else, is surprised to find that it's Jack Burnett who's been shot. Mrs. Bucey claims self-defense, that Burnett was beating her when she grabbed the gun from her bedroom dresser and fired three times. One shot went wide, then she shot the 200-pound Mr. Burnett, her "sailor lover," twice in the back.

Burnett dies several days later at Lorain's St. Joseph's Hospital. On his deathbed, Burnett tells police that he was to blame and signs a statement to that effect. Despite the statement, Mrs. Bucey is soon arrested and charged with second degree murder.

Sheriff Clarence W. Dick calls Dr. F.M. Sponseller, the jail physician, to examine Mrs. Bucey after a week in the county lockup. "It was evident this morning that she was suffering from a serious mental disorder." Sponseller calls in Dr. Stanley Birkbeck. They confer with Probate Judge Wilcox who decides to commit her to the Toledo Hospital for the Insane.

The case is still scheduled for the September Grand Jury. If she is indicted, and then judged to be sane, she will return for trial. Jurors decide to pass on the case, leaving it for later.

Bucey is declared sane in October and is returned for trial. "The prosecutor (Howard R. Butler) stated today that the rapid recovery speaks well for the Toledo institution, where she has been confined for one month." She is released from custody when she agrees to furnish a $10,000 bond, then placed back in jail when the money fails to appear.

The November Grand Jury returns an indictment for murder in the second. Attorney Elias G. Thomas is assigned to defend by Judge D.A. Cook. Unusually, the case is tried in front of Judge Cook without a jury.

It's told that Mrs. Bucey shot four bullets from a "gold-plated, pearl-handled, Spanish automatic pistol during a quarrel." Her attorney has some trouble proving self-defense since her sailor victim was struck twice in the back, near the left shoulder. But, according to Mrs. Bucey, Burnett grabbed a flat iron and came at her whereupon she fired the first two shots that went wide. Burnett then swung the iron at her and missed, turning his back. She then shot twice more and struck with both bullets.

Mrs. Leona Murray, a prosecution witness who lives across the hall, disagrees. She says Mr. Burnett was tugging on the door, trying to escape the apartment when he was shot.

The two-day trial ends with Judge Cook saying prosecution failed to disprove self-defense. Outcome: Mrs. Bucey is set free.

1935, September 29, Sunday, 2:00am: Location: Lorain, in victim's home, near trolley stop 7 and Vincent School (the intersection of North Ridge and West River Roads). Victim: Mrs. Elizabeth Phillips (76, mother-in-law). Suspect: Frank Barath (56, son-in-law).

On March 28, 1921, the year his wife dies, Barath loses his home in Amherst in a foreclosure forced by Florence Walters on a debt of $3,747. Widower Barath and six kids move in with his mother-in-law, widow Elizabeth Phillips who "acts as mother to them all."

Mrs. Phillips is shot in the nose and through the head with a .22 caliber rifle. She is taken to Elyria Hospital where she dies about 5 hours later.

Two of Phillips' grandchildren, Frank (Buddy), 19, and Margaret, 22, live in the Phillip's home, but were not there at the time. Besides them, out of the house are grandchildren Mrs. Carl Bruce and Mrs. Lloyd Reynolds of Elyria and Mrs. William Eaton and Mrs. Stephan Lepatkovics of Lorain.

After the shooting, Frank Barath runs to neighbor Mike Kokr screaming "I have shot my mother-in-law." Kokr and Barath return to the scene to find the bleeding victim on her bed. The suspect picks up the rifle and fires it into a wall of the room. Kokr eases the weapon from Barath's hands.

Neighbors tell police that they believe Barath was drunk and quarreled with Phillips over his inebriated state. He then took a weapon and shot her dead. But Barath says he was not drunk, yet cannot supply a motive.

Neighbor Mrs. John Shivak allows that Elizabeth Phillips had told her that her son-in-law had threatened her life and that she was afraid of him.

Services for the dead woman are held on October 2, 2:00pm at Lorain's

Hungarian Reform Church. She is buried in Elmwood Cemetery from the Wickens Funeral Home.

Barath enters the November Grand Jury charged with murder in the second degree. He exits indicted for murder in the first. Defended by Albert Greulich, of Lorain, Barath decides to waive a jury trial for a 3-judge panel— newspapers says it's a first for the county. The judges will be Guy B. Findley, D.A. Cook (both of Lorain County) and Clarence Ahl of Bucyrus.

The trial moves rapidly. Defense claims Barath "had been drinking heavily on that day and that because of an excess of liquor his mind was fogged and that what occurred was not planned or premeditated—an essential factor in conviction for first degree murder." Defense hopes to have the charge dropped to manslaughter with its 1-20 year sentencing and hope of early parole.

The State maintains that he may have been drunk, but that the shooting was the culmination of a long-standing argument between the two. The prosecution produces witnesses that testified that Barath had called his mother-in-law vile names the day of the shooting. One of the witnesses, Mr. Stanley Demich, says that Mrs. Phillips said Barath made life so miserable that "she wished she could die."

Barath takes the stand in his own behalf calling his victim "Mama." He says he'd come home drunk an hour before the shooting, that she had reproached him for his condition, that he had asked her to leave him alone and that he went to the basement and drank another half pint of liquor and some wine.

"I don't remember anything after that until I found myself some time later in the County Jail," he says, in somewhat broken English.

Miss DeEitte Carpenter, the neighbor who called the ambulance testifies the accused appeared intoxicated and beat his hands against his temples saying over and over "I shot Mama." Other character witnesses stated Barath was an excellent worker and good man when sober.

The judges' panel finds him guilty of murder in the second. Judge Ahl wants to convict on first degree but is convinced by his co-judges to make the decision unanimous. Judge Findley, presiding, sentences the guilty man to life in the Ohio Penitentiary, plus costs of $176.68. Barath says he is satisfied with the outcome, having said all along he "never meant to do it."

MATRICIDE – Killing your mother.

Judge Guy B. Findley:

Born October 10, 1885, local boy Guy B. Findley (Republican) graduated from the University of Michigan school of law in 1908 and immediately joined the Ohio Bar. He served as the Elyria City Solicitor and then two terms as the Lorain County Prosecutor (1917-1920).

Judge Findley was first elected to the bench in 1934. Once established he had little trouble winning another two terms. Poor health forced his retirement on October 15, 1950, not quite 16 years into his judicial career. He recovered from his illness enough to live comfortably until a few weeks before his death on the morning of June 16, 1958, at the age of 72.

Ever hear of Findley State Park, south of Wellington, Ohio? Or, maybe Finwood on North Abbe Road in Elyria? They are the results of gifts to the public by the Findley family.

1935, November 22: *The Chronicle-Telegram:*

Yes, It's News—The Sun Did Shine.

Yes. It's news! Several readers of the Chronicle-Telegram today called attention to the fact that several times the sun broke through the clouds and flooded the city with its welcome rays. "That's news" they said, "for we have seen mighty little of the sun in the past two weeks."

True it is, it's news.

1936: Benny Goodman is crowned the "King of Swing." *Ol' Man River* in *Showboat,* the film, that is. It played on Broadway back in 1927. George V dies. Long live Edward VIII, as long as he's not King, that is. Eddie gives up the throne for the love of his lady, Wallace Simpson. George VI takes up the task. Hitler moves troops into the Rhineland. German youth must join either the Hitler Youth or German Maidens. The Spanish Civil War. Franklin Roosevelt (New York Democrat) wins the Election with 60.8% of the popular vote. 8 lynchings: 8 Blacks, 0 others.

1936, April 16: *The Chronicle-Telegram:*

Follow Murder Theory In Lorain Case.

A murder theory was being investigated by Lorain police today in connection with the death of Angus Joss, 55, stone cutter, whose body was found about 11 a.m. yesterday in the Black River at the foot of Sixteenth Street off Broadway.

With nothing but the appearance of Joss' body on which to base their suspicions, police stated today that there are strong indications that Joss was murdered and not a suicide or the victim of accident.

Police are awaiting a full report of the findings of Coroner S.C. Ward before taking definite action in the case. They reported that Joss had a blackened eye and other bruises on his body.

He was released from Lorain jail two days ago after being charged with intoxication, they reported. He formerly was a resident of Clyde, O.

No other articles appear.

1936, August 14, Friday: Location: Elyria, 100-block Mound Street. Victims: Mrs. William (Pauline) Cecil (24, mother) and Geraldine Cecil (4, daughter).

1936, July 4, William Cecil (32) strikes and slightly injures 11-year-old Ellis Vance Ewing on North Ridge Road and skips the scene. He is arrested, charged, fined $50 and ordered to serve 30 days in the County Jail by Justice of the Peace Joseph Q. Petro. Cecil is taken from his cell early in the morning of July 22 to the Elyria Memorial Hospital for an emergency appendectomy and then returned to the jail.

August 14: The Cecil home burns down around the victims in the early morning hours.

The first person to discover the blaze was Norman Carothers of 115 Quincy Street, who saw Mrs. Cecil in a sitting position at the foot of the stairs through the open door to the outside, but was unable to rescue her because of the flames which surrounded her. He summoned the fire department. It is believed, however, that Mrs. Cecil may have been dead at that time.

The little girl, 4-year-old Geraldine, upstairs, screamed several times before she was overcome and suffocated by the smoke. *The Chronicle-Telegram, August 17, 1936.*

It is first thought that Mrs. Cecil "afflicted with epilepsy" had been overcome with a seizure while walking down stairs with a lit kerosene lamp and, upon falling, set her home on fire. But the open front door leads authorities to think the fire may have set. Elyria Fire Chief W.N. Bates and Detective Lloyd Sweet admit that circumstances point to an accelerant.

The State Fire Marshal's Office investigates. It finds fragments of a letter in which Mrs. Cecil appealed to two Amherst men for help. It suggests that she may have had an unwanted suitor who was trying to force his attentions upon her while her husband was in jail.

The incarcerated William Cecil is questioned. He provides no extra information.

The Fire Marshal's investigation continues for several weeks. Its contents are never released to the press. It is reported that a witness, unnamed by authorities, has been missing since the fire and cannot be found.

1937, January: Police work ends with no definite findings.

1938, January: The case remains open, but at a standstill.

Outcome: Unsolved/Unresolved.

1936, early December: Location: Kolbe Woods, near Amherst, a few miles southeast of Lorain. Victim: Jesse Camera (19).

Jesse Camera is a small, but tough young man. At the age of 13 he boxed 105 pounds for the City of Lorain in the Elks North Central Ohio Amateur Boxing Tourney. He is good enough to have won the year's Golden Gloves Bantamweight Novice Belt.

Camera goes missing on December 5. His body is found December 18 dead from gunshot. There is no doubt that the killing took place at that scene. Authorities first think the murder is gangland related and that the young man had been "taken for a ride." They later abandon that theory when investigation shows the victim had no connections to organized crime. Camera was, in point of fact, held in high regarded by both friends and associates.

Sheriff Clarence W. Dick is due to be replaced by newly elected sheriff William F. Grall (of Lorain). To keep the case fresh, all evidence is turned over to the City of Lorain police who are given complete charge of the crime. It's a move approved by County Prosecutor Howard R. Butler.

1937, June 5: Deputy Sheriff Samuel Paonessa brings in Professor Keeler of Northwestern University and his lie detector machine to interview unnamed witnesses and suspects. Prosecutor Butler had okayed the plan, but Keeler and his machine are in and out so quietly that Butler is never notified and is not present at the questioning. This causes more than a little friction between law and order. No leads are generated. The investigation stalls. Outcome: Unsolved.

1938, December 14: The unsolved Camera case comes up in a bribery trial against the now-former sheriff, William F. Grall who says he allowed Maxine Barbour, aka Penny Morgan, to continue to maintain a house of prostitution because he thought she might collect information that might help solve the Camera murder. His other reason was that such a place "was a biological necessity and helped to serve to protect young women and girls from attacks."

At the end of his trial, Grall is found guilty of accepting three or four $50 bribes and sentenced to the Ohio Penitentiary in Columbus for one to ten years.

The Cardio-Pneumo Psychogram

People lie for various reasons; kindness, deceit, to stay out of trouble. In the grand scheme, most little fibs don't matter much, unless you're trying to figure out who killed whom.

In the very late 1800s, German-born Hugo Munsterberg was a professor of psychology at Harvard in Cambridge, Massachusetts. He and student William M. Marston developed a machine to quickly monitor a subject's blood pressure on a periodic basis. Figuring the stress of lying would change blood pressure, the two ran tests on hundreds of Harvard students. The work convinced Munsterberg and Marston that their machine could detect liars—at least sometimes.

Prickly and unlikeable John A. Larson, a student at the University of California at Berkeley, worked closely with local police to improve existing lie detection technology. In 1921, Larson unveiled his "cardio-pneumo psychogram." As bulky as its name, the contraption continuously monitored and recorded blood pressure, pulse, and respiration. Berkeley police were the first to regularly use lie detectors. But Larson's psychogram was far from perfect. It might catch panicky liars, but well-practiced ones could often fool the machine.

Then along came one of Larson's own assistants, Leonarde Keeler. By 1924, he had made his own lie detector small enough to be portable and added the ability to record "galvanic skin response" (how well the skin conducts a known electrical current). His "emotograph," renamed the "Keeler Polygraph," eventually became what we think of as a lie detector.

Unlike the caustic Larson, "Nard" Keeler was a born showman. He took his machine, which he patented, on public demonstrations around the United States challenging people to try to fool him by lying about inconsequential things, like their age, or what playing card from a deck they were being shown.

Keeler even appeared in documentaries and movies as himself applying his polygraph to help authorities (like *Call Northside 777* with Jimmy Stewart and Lee J. Cobb).

Keeler was invited by police forces around the county to assist in the questioning of suspects. Lorain County called him in at least twice: for the Camera case, just above, and the Hornbeck murder (1937, October 18).

Leonarde Keeler died in 1949 from a stroke at the age of 45, but his lie detector persisted. At one time, Keeler Polygraph results were considered more reliable than eyewitnesses. But the idea of such perfection was difficult for lawyers to swallow. Legal challenges took hold once circumstances produced people able to avoid detection.

Modern courts allow questioning with a polygraph, but some U.S. states disallow the use of any results in court. Other jurisdictions allow findings if their use is agreed upon by both defense and prosecution. In Ohio, polygraph results may be presented as any evidence is, with relative weight determined by the jury.

All very interesting, but we're not quite done. Remember William Marston who, while at Harvard, helped Hugo Munsterberg develop one of the first modern lie detectors? Years later, he and his partners, wife Elizabeth Holloway Marston and their paramour, Olive Byrne, created a comic-book character they called "Suprema."

Suprema grew to fame as "Wonder Woman." And while her invisible plane is pretty cool, her most powerful weapon, by far, is the Magic Lasso she uses to force the bad guys to always tell the truth.

1937: Chicago has the first blood bank thanks to Dr. Karl Dussik. Joe "The Brown Bomber" Lewis becomes boxing's world Heavyweight Champion by defeating James Braddock. Abel Meeropol sees strange fruit hanging from poplar trees. Trombonist Glenn Miller forms his first band. The Neutrality Act prevents the U.S. from *giving* aid to countries involved in war. Neville Chamberlin is British Prime Minister. Stalin's still at it. The Irish Free State is now "Eire." The Ohio River crests at 57.1 feet, almost 30 feet above flood stage. Damage stretches from Pittsburgh to Cairo, Illinois. One million are left homeless with 385 dead and property losses reaching $500 million. 8 lynchings: 8 Blacks, 0 others.

1937, October 18, Monday:

"Pretty." That's the word most often used to describe Miss Ramona Louise Hornbeck. A soft, oval face. Small, cute nose. Big, dark eyes. Symmetrical features framed by stylishly short hair. The 19-year-old, who most folks call by her middle name, is fairly new to the small town of Grafton, Ohio. Her father, Earl, moved to the area as a section crew foreman on the Big Four Railroad bringing his family with him. Louise and her trombone-playing younger brother, Forrest, are well-engaged in the life of their small community.

Miss Hornbeck graduated last year from Ansonia High School, Darke County, western Ohio. Afterwards she completed a correspondence course in secretarial skills and then put her education to good use working the past half-year for Dentists Donald Barber and W.E. Maple on Grafton's Main Street near the northwest corner of Mechanic.

Monday is a late night for her. She leaves the office a few minutes past 9:00pm bundled up against the cool, damp autumn night. Joe Anderson, a Grafton native and long-time barber in town, follows her part way down Mechanic to the corner of Center where she turns for home.

Louise's family smiles when, as usual, the Eberhart's dog gets to barking. It means their daughter has passed by. Smiles turn to concern when the girl doesn't arrive. Louise is never home late from work. Never.

Her father and brother began searching, knocking first on neighborhood doors. Word spreads and, in the space of a few minutes, a large crowd looks for the missing woman.

Evidence of a struggle is found on the Eberhart's sidewalk and lawn. Despite everyone's best efforts, it's not until the next morning that Louise's body is found in a small, untended orchard almost adjacent to her Center Street home.

It's her father and brother, along with Clifford Mole and Willard Rader, who discover her, hidden and face down under an apple tree. She is still wearing her small diamond ring and watch. Two buttons, a hat, and many bloodstains are found on fallen leaves in a circle about her body. The only visible mark is a bruise under her left eye, but her clothing is torn and rearranged in a most disturbing way.

The impact of the violence on the small community is nearly overwhelming. Everyone knows everybody else. Their school graduates a mere handful of students a year. The houses don't even have street numbers—a name on an envelope gets a letter to its destination. Who in their peaceful, little village is capable of such a thing?

Authorities arrive to find the crime scene a mess. A multitude of people have trampled the area with evidence disturbed and scattered. County Coroner Dr. S.C. Ward reports positive evidence of sexual assault with death due to concussion of the brain and intra-cranial hemorrhage due to a blow to the back of Miss Hornbeck's head. Murder during commission of a rape is an unusually violent crime for Lorain County.

Miss Hornbeck is prepared by the Sudro Curtis Funeral Home in Elyria. Services are held on a cloudy October 21 from her home on Center Street with Reverend George Beebe of the Grafton M.E. Church officiating. More than 300 people attend with four deputies detailed to keep order. Burial is two days later at the Hale Cemetery at Mt. Victory, Hardin County, Ohio, from the home of her grandparents Mr. and Mrs. W.G. Butler.

The first place police check for suspects the night of the murder is closer than two miles north along the railroad tracks from that side of town: The Grafton Prison Farm. Officials there declare that all were present and accounted for during the evening roll call. With the failure of that simple solution, authorities are under enormous pressure to solve the crime.

They get their first big break before the victim is even buried. On October 20, one John W. Campbell is arrested in Marshall, Michigan, 210 miles to the west. The 19-year-old is charged with the attempted molestation of a 15-year-old girl in a public park. Police there, having read about the Hornbeck murder, confront Campbell with the crime and report the young man "shivered and shook" when questioned.

After two hours of grilling, Campbell breaks down and confesses. Michigan authorities contend the young man included full details of the crime as corroborated by facts at the scene and summarize it as follows:

> The youth said that he was hitch-hiking from Merchantsville, New Jersey, where he had been working, to Gary, Indiana, where he hoped to find employment, and that he arrived in Grafton Monday night and was in a restaurant there when he saw the girl pass by.
>
> He left the restaurant immediately and followed her until she came to the darkest section of Center Street, near her home, when he seized her around the neck and strangled her. He then dragged her into the bushes where he assaulted

her, after which he struck her with a club which chanced to be handy.

He then went to a nearby filling station where he washed the blood from his hands and hitchhiked to Marshall in two rides. *The Chronicle-Telegram, October 20, 1937.*

Michigan police say Campbell claims that he had previously been arrested on sex charges in Chicago and Quincy, Illinois, and was, at one time, an inmate in an insane asylum.

Campbell's story *seems* to fit the crime, but local police are doubtful from the start. Some details, like the suspect's insistence that he entered Grafton via "Route 60" and ate in a railroad diner are impossible since neither exist.

Says Chief Deputy William G. Smith, "The youth's answers to questions were in many instances not rational, and there are discrepancies in his story." Nonetheless, Lorain County Sheriff William Grall, Deputies Smith and Emil Kubishke, and Hornbeck family friend Anthony Pollock travel to Michigan and collect the young man.

Campbell is placed in the Lorain County Jail in the late evening of October 21. Once there, he denies his confession and any involvement in the killing of Louise Hornbeck, saying he admitted the crime only to stop the ceaseless barrage of questions from his interrogators.

Lorain County Prosecutor Howard R. Butler refuses to file charges until an investigation is complete. All it takes is a day's hard work to convince police that Campbell had nothing to do with the killing. They subject him (and two unnamed Grafton men who are also suspects) to a Berkley Lie Detector test by Professor Bernard R. Higley, a psychologist from the Ohio State University. As far as the machine is concerned, all are innocent.

Ultimately the November Grand Jury dismisses Campbell as a suspect. He is returned to Michigan where he ends up with nine to ten years on local charges of molestation.

On October 23, while police are still checking out John Campbell, Alexander Maneff, a husky, 23-year-old hitchhiker from West Homestead, Pennsylvania, is arrested near Wooster, Ohio, for auto theft. While in custody, he spontaneously admits to involvement in the Louise Hornbeck case.

Examination reveals several apparent bloodstains on his clothing and partially-healed scratches along the sides of his face which could have been inflicted by the victim. Wooster authorities alert Lorain County officials who make the 70-mile round trip to collect Maneff.

Campbell, the old confessor, and Maneff, the new, never meet.

After a couple hours of the third degree by Prosecutor Butler in the Lorain County Jail, the young man admits to being in Grafton the night of the murder. He says he followed the victim to the place she was found, but denies any assault or attack. Instead he stepped from the shadows to ask for directions and she fainted. Rather than leave her on the sidewalk, he dragged her back into the shadows and went to a nearby gas station for a "paper cup of water" to revive her. She failed to respond, so he abandoned her. "I didn't want to get blamed for anything." As he left, the suspect says, he saw another man in a gray Oxford suit and a red tie, walking toward where the body was found.

Then Maneff changes his story, saying he was "overwhelmed" by the beauty of the young woman, wanted to ask her out, but knew she'd refuse. So he attacked her and took what he wanted.

After confessing, the suspect makes a written statement: "I pity the man that has committed the crime for which I am held, and I only hope sooner or later that you people of the law will find the right man, as when I was questioned I did not realize what it would mean."

The next day, after eight straight hours of constant questioning, Maneff is taken to the scene of the crime. The visit is short, partially because residents keep congregating around the prisoner.

The suspect supplies "information helpful to the case" but police refuse to press charges because they are convinced that the confession is incomplete and they are beginning to doubt the available evidence: It's true that some of the spots on the suspect's clothing are blood, but the largest, strategically located on the young man's shirt, is nothing but grease.

Spurred by discrepancies in the confession and results of the first post-mortem, the decision is made to exhume and re-examine the victim's body nine days after burial. William Sudro, the Elyria undertaker, oversees the process. The additional post-mortem provides no new information. Officials are pressured to either move ahead with one of the confessors as the perpetrator or dismiss them and get busy solving the crime.

Maneff is subjected to a lie detector test administered by the machine's inventor, Dr. Leonarde Keeler. The suspect passes. Sort of. The machine shows no indication of guilt. Then again, there's no evidence of any emotion at all. To Dr. Keeler, this points to a severely disturbed mental state.

The November Grand Jury is set to convene. Prosecutor Howard Butler will not comment to the press beyond saying, "We are still working on the case. A special investigator has been working the case from the start."

The jury considers the issue in secret session. More than sixty are subpoenaed for the hearing. There are delays. It is rescheduled for the week of December 7.

The jurors deliberate for days after testimony concludes. The prosecution grudgingly admits that suspicion points to a half-dozen people and that hard evidence against any of them is lacking. All the same, on December 14, the Grand Jury indicts Alexander Maneff on charges of murder in the first degree in the commission of rape.

Nobody seems particularly enthusiastic about prosecuting Maneff. He has confessed, but his story has contradictions. There is a lack of corroborating evidence. Plus, it has become increasingly clear there is something odd about Maneff.

The criminal trial begins December 16. The accused, now said to be 21 by the papers, and without legal representation, enters a guilty plea and waives a jury trial to stand in front of a 3-judge panel. This means either life in prison or the electric chair. The young man is completely unmoved by his fate and shows no more emotion than "had he been ordering pie and coffee in a restaurant."

The paper says:

> As has been expressed by some close to the case and by criminologists, the nature of the arrest, the frankness of the youth's story, his better than average memory of where he has been and what he has been doing, his information about current events, his family, and his plausible method of attack, all taken together, make a situation as fantastic as anything that has ever confronted those engaged in criminal prosecution here. *The Chronicle-Telegram, December 16, 1937.*

The next day, attorney Elias G. Thomas of Lorain is retained through unknown connections to represent Maneff. The first thing Thomas does is tell the court that his client is changing his plea to not guilty. The lawyer also states that he can prove that Maneff was in Portsmouth, Ohio, 200 miles away, until early afternoon the day of the crime, making it almost impossible for the young man to be in Grafton in time to commit murder.

Trial is set by Judge Guy B. Findley for December 29 with he, Lorain

County Judge D.A. Cook, and Judge Charles R. Sargent of Jefferson, Ohio, presiding.

Defense attorney Thomas suggests he will present an insanity defense. Prosecutor Butler says he will oppose any such effort. In response, Judge Findley calls in Dr. Arthur G. Hyde, Superintendent of the Massillon State Hospital, to offer his expert opinion.

December 29, first day of trial: Alexander Maneff arrives with a fresh shave and his thick, black hair recently cut. His father, present in the room, begins crying upon seeing his son bound by manacles. The young man shows no emotion. "Every available inch" of the courtroom is occupied. In the crowd are the parents and brother of the victim, her neighbors, and many of the people who took part in the search in Grafton. Also present are several members of the Grand Jury that indicted Maneff for the crime.

The prosecution claims, that upon arrest, the accused recounted his actions, detailing the facts and confessing fully.

The defense challenges the State to come up with a single shred of evidence, beyond the confession, to prove the accused committed the crime.

It's presented that insanity runs in the family. The young man is known to be a habitual liar. The defendant's father testifies that his son suffered, at the age of two, from "water on the brain" but had improved after an operation that removed more than a quart of fluid from his skull. The father says his son talks "like a big man" to strangers, saying one thing at one time and then something completely different at another.

Mr. L.H. Gerth, of Columbus, a special investigator working for the Prosecutor's Office says he, upon questioning Maneff on various occasions, obtained confessions about fifteen times and denials about half that many. Gerth testifies that he had hoped the Grand Jury would have seen fit to set the defendant free.

Dr. Hyde, Superintendent of the Massillon State Hospital, is called to the stand. His opinion: Maneff is "mentally irresponsible" with a "psychopathic personality allied to dementia praecox" (premature dementia). The youth is a "pathological liar" whose statements cannot be taken as fact. Hyde is certain the young man was never even in Grafton.

When asked point blank by Judge Findley if Maneff was sane, Hyde responds, "No, he is not sane now."

December 30: On the basis of testimony, the judges' panel finds Maneff "not now sane" and sends him off to the Lima Hospital. Prosecutor Butler again states that the accused is guilty and predicts the trial will take place within the next six months.

Maneff absorbs all of this and, with his now-characteristic lack of emotion, is hauled off to Lima to regain his senses so he can stand trial for the rape and murder of Ramona Louise Hornbeck.

This outcome pleases nobody.

1938, February 3, Thursday, 7:45pm:

Miss Bernadette Bater, 22, of Mechanic Street, Grafton, walks home from the evening services of the Church of the Immaculate Conception on Erie Street. She takes Huron towards the tracks—not the smartest move perhaps. The street is fairly empty of buildings, but it's a shortcut to Center Street and then home.

She's avoiding the half-iced puddles left by the last few days of rain and freezing temperatures as she walks not more than two blocks and across the railroad tracks from the scene of the Hornbeck murder (*see case just above*). Along a vacant and particularly dark stretch of Huron, from behind the young woman is seized around her neck. Fighting for her life, she twists to face her attacker. She frees herself and screams.

Harry Matthews, sitting in the tower for the Big Four Railroad about a block away, hears the ruckus and calls police. The town almost instantly swarms with nearly 300 armed men and women. Graftonite Leonard James gives chase to the suspect who, unfortunately, escapes into the dark.

Upon hearing a description of the man, Deputy Smith checks with the Grafton Prison Farm and learns that one man, a 22-year-old trusty, who has been at the Farm for 15 months, has missed the 7:30pm roll call. He is later found by prison guards Ray Taylor and J.M. Rule in the basement of Prison Superintendent Corwin Swan's house where he works as a servant. The prisoner is removing his muddy clothing and collapses when discovered.

The man is held in the Superintendent's basement for two hours before he is taken in for questioning at the Lorain County Sheriff's office. It's discovered that, because of his trusty status, the man has far more privileges than most of the other prisoners at the Grafton Farm. He maintains he did nothing more than walk down the tracks to "get some beer" at Mike Barton's in Grafton.

The suspect denies any involvement in the attack on Miss Bater, who is unable to identify him. After three hours of intense questioning, the suspect finally admits that he intended to rob the girl, that he grabbed her around the throat, but that she surprised him with her strength, managed to turn, fight him off, and scream, whereupon, he ran.

The young man claims to have stolen a .32 caliber revolver from the Superintendent's house to use in his attack on Miss Bater. The weapon is found by a Mrs. Lewis, who happens to be a neighbor of the Louise Hornbeck family. Lewis gives the weapon to Earl Hornbeck who turns it over to the sheriff.

Officers find the suspect's muddy boots stashed under the porch of the Superintendent's house. About 200 feet away from where the attack on Miss Bater took place, matching footprints and a prison cap are found by Mrs. Alfred Hall under a clothesline strung across her back yard.

From the start, the unnamed trusty is a suspect in the recent murder of Louise Hornbeck. Prison Superintendent Swan is asked to take a closer look at his roll-call records to see if there is any possibility that the man who attacked Miss Bater might have been missing from custody the night Hornbeck was killed.

Swan admits that the suspect was not present at roll call the night of the murder. In fact, he was missing until 10:55pm. But, at the time of the Hornbeck murder, when questioned by prison officials, the young man told Swan that he had fallen asleep in the basement of the Superintendent's house. This was accepted as the truth and local authorities were told all were present and accounted for despite the sheriff's specifically asking about the possibility of any missing prisoners.

Prison officials and police lean on the suspect. He eventually confesses to the attack on Louise Hornbeck. He claims to have stolen up behind her and struck her on the back of the head with a beer bottle before dragging her into the shadows of the old apple orchard.

Trouble is, he is the third person to confess to the crime.

Bernadette Bater applies for the $500 reward posted in the Hornbeck murder case, but no money can be disbursed until a conviction is obtained.

The suspect is hauled to the Lima State Hospital to be examined by Dr. Arthur Hyde. It's a precaution to determine the young man's state of mind before proceeding with the investigation. He is found to be sane.

On February 9, a week after the attack on Bernadette Bater, Grafton Superintendent Corwin Swan, announces that "no longer will prisoners be allowed out of the dormitory after dark. We're keeping a closer watch to see that none make beer expeditions to Grafton."

That same day the suspect is named: Edward Hensley. It's reported that he has a checkered past and is described as having an "incorrigible boyhood followed by an adolescence of criminality." At 16 years of age, Hensley was arrested for an attack on a Youngstown girl and sent to the Lancaster Reformatory. Two years later he was sent to the Mansfield Reformatory for robbing a woman and then transferred to Grafton because of good behavior. Newspapers also reveal for the first time that the suspect, Edward Hensley, is Black: not in words, but by publishing a photo of the accused.

Two days later the Grand Jury considers the case with more than 40 witnesses testifying. Never mind the attack on Miss Bater or the fact that Alexander Maneff has already been charged with the crime, Hensley is indicted for the murder of Louise Hornbeck, in the first degree during the commission of rape. When arraigned, Hensley enters a plea of "not guilty."

Criminal trial is set for March 8. It is reported that the National Association for the Advancement of Colored People (NAACP) is watching the case closely to be sure Hensley gets an "unprejudiced trial."

Defense attorneys Dominic Francis Rendinell (veteran of twenty-three first degree murder trials) and M.W. Howard, both of Youngstown, Ohio confer with Judge Guy B. Findley and come away satisfied that Hensley will receive fair proceedings in Lorain County.

With the plea of "not guilty and not guilty by reason of insanity," the defense considers appearing before a three judge panel but ultimately decides on a trial by jury. Near the end of February, defense asks for a continuance. It is denied by Judge Findley.

A few days before trial begins, Prosecutor Butler and Assistant Prosecutor William Wickens admit their biggest problem will be convincing jurors that Hensley's confession is the real deal after having two other people admit to the crime.

Defense, on the other hand, feels certain that once the facts are brought to light, the jury will have no trouble in dismissing their client's previous statement of guilt.

The March 8 trial starts with jury selection that takes relatively little time. Eleven jurors are seated by noon. Some potentials are excused because they admit reluctance to convict to death on the basis of circumstantial evidence.

The courtroom is crowded. Parents of both the victim and the accused (Mr. and Mrs. Sidney Hensley of Youngstown, Ohio) are present. Deputies are placed at every door to assure instructions are properly followed.

Rendinell quickly shows that his tactic throughout the trial will be to establish that the facts of the case, obtained as they were by poor police work, could point to any number of people, not only his client.

March 9: Cuyahoga County Pathologist, Dr. Reuben Strauss is called for the defense. He is the doctor who examined the victim's body upon exhumation from the Mt. Victory, Ohio, Cemetery, nine days after the murder. He testifies that the initial autopsy was botched. There were clear signs of rape, and had the fluids found been collected at the onset they might have been "typed," which could have aided in the identification of the killer. He is certain the cause of death was a brain concussion suffered when the victim was struck on the back of the head. This, at least, agrees with the original autopsy. The jurors are given a full copy of Dr. Strauss' report to consider in their deliberation.

The defense maneuvers to have Hensley's confession dismissed. With jurors absent, the accused tells Judge Findley that he was threatened with "one of the stiffest third degrees ever given a prisoner in Lorain County," and "he knew prisoners who had to go around on crutches and canes after they had been given the third degree." The accused confessed only because he knew it would not stand in court.

Once the jury returns, Dr. Maple, the victim's employer, is presented as someone the police had suspected early on. He testifies that he cooperated with authorities "until they tried to pin it on me. Then I told them to go places." It comes to light that the dentist had been questioned on three consecutive days and was put through a lie detector test, which he passed, but with an extremely elevated heart rate.

The defense pushes hard on the fact that others had confessed, but had been dismissed or found mentally incompetent, and that if Maneff hadn't been declared insane, Edward Hensley wouldn't even be on trial.

The venue is jammed. There is always a large crowd already assembled at 5:00am, well before the room opens. Custodian A.E. Sperry tells reporters that the crowd is so anxious to get inside that they've damaged the hinges and glass of the courthouse storm doors and that no repairs will be made until the end of the trial.

Many spectators bring lunches so they won't have to give up their seats over recess. They are transfixed by the trial. All the same, those who willingly attend are horrified by the testimony. It's reported that the crowd is "shocked" by the defense contention that the girl's rapist/killer "could be a white man."

The State brings Grafton Prison Farm staff to the stand. Guard Jack Carpenter tells the court that the accused returned late to the dormitory the night of the killing, saying he had been reading in the basement of Warden Swan's house, where he worked, and had fallen asleep. Carpenter also says he reported those facts to the Warden the following day.

Farm Superintendent Corwin Swan testifies that he knew Hensley had been out late the night of the murder and told him he might be suspected of it. Swan says he had "censured" the accused because of his absence.

Defense attorney Rendinell states that nobody at the prison really knew where the accused was the night of the murder. With Deputy Sheriff William G. Smith on the stand, attorney Rendinell insinuates a 3-hour grilling took place at the County Jail with an angry mob heard outside. He also implies that Hensley had been threatened with being turned over to the crowd.

Deputy Smith hotly denies such a thing happened. The suspect was questioned for no more than a half-hour and, yes, there were about fifty people outside, but they were not threatening "in any way." The confession, Smith says, was voluntary.

Most damning to the defense is the testimony of Hensley's previous victims: Nurse Marie Lutza, 20, of Philadelphia, Pennsylvania. In 1933, Hensley attacked her as she walked through a field just after 8:00am. He threatened her with a knife, threw her to the ground, kissed, then bit her. He tore off her clothing. She escaped when he started to remove his own.

Mrs. Soule, Youngstown, Ohio: Hensley jumped into her car while she was driving out of a parking lot, held a knife against her side and demanded jewelry. He hit her with the butt of a gun and tried to kiss her. When she lost control of the car and crashed into another automobile, he escaped.

Miss Bernadette Bater, Grafton, Ohio, testifies to her experience. She was dragged into a field, screamed, and then tried to hold onto him when she realized help was arriving. Though, on cross, she admits she was unable to identify Hensley in a lineup.

The defense responds with witnesses of their own like Mike Barton of Grafton who isn't able to recall selling beer to the accused the night of the crime, even though police initially said he could.

The defense hammers at the murder confession. Over the shouted objections of Prosecutor Butler, Rendinell compares it to those wrung from innocent citizens that the Russians accuse of treason, stating that even "strong-willed men" will confess to anything during a third degree.

On March 15, Hensley takes the stand. He flatly denies the confession and testifies he told the story out of fear of both the implied violence from authorities and their threats to turn him over to "the mob" gathered outside.

He's well aware of what happens to Black men accused of assaulting White women. The only reason he confessed to the crime was to avoid a lynching by angry Whites.

If what the accused says about the White mob wasn't true, asks Rendinell, why did police move Hensley and "eight other colored prisoners" from the Elyria lockup to the Lorain County Jail? Wasn't it to prevent a rumored attack from Grafton citizens?

The defense calls Dr. Austin, who declared Alexander Maneff insane, in hopes of showing that the previous confessor was competent when he confessed to the Hornbeck killing.

On March 17, Maneff himself testifies without regard to his sanity. Judge Findley instructs the jurors to "give the testimony as much weight as they deem proper." Maneff says he is completely unable to recall what he had said, or did, in the days leading up to his time at Lima. He is returned to the hospital for care.

March 18: In closing statements, the State points out the previous record of attacks by the accused on women. These crimes show an escalation of violence that could lead to murder. They ask the jurors not to be confused by all the accusations made by the defense. Hensley was the one man that fit the crime.

Rendinell ends with a plea to jurors to consider that his client was framed by authorities desperate to solve the sex-murder case. Defense maintains that the police know who committed the crime but chose to pin it on his client instead of the real killer. He accuses Deputy William Smith of planting evidence at the scene of the Bater attack and accuses Bernadette Bater of cooking up the crime against her to help her collect the $500 in reward. The lawyer says that, even if exonerated of the murder charge, Hensley would still suffer punishment since he bravely decided to testify against his prison guards.

The crowd remains after closing arguments. After seven hours of deliberation, the jury returns at 10:40pm to find Hensley guilty of murder in the first degree with a recommendation of mercy.

They later report they unanimously found the defendant guilty on the first vote and only differed on the question of the death penalty. Initially, the jury sat seven to five in favor of the chair. After debate, and two more votes, the eight women and four men decided to recommend life in prison.

Judge Findley imposes the sentence immediately.

Defense attorney Rendinell: The "colored youth had been an innocent victim of the most astonishing frame-up in the history of Lorain County."

Prosecutor Buckley responds by saying that the defense lawyer had besmirched the reputation of anyone he could to divert attention from Hensley. He also asks for the murder charges against Alexander Maneff be dismissed.

Some among the public never believe the verdict.

But we're not done yet.

March 22: Hensley is taken to the Ohio Penitentiary in Columbus. Rendinell files for new trial alleging the verdict was the result of "passion and prejudice" and against the weight of the evidence.

March 28: Charges against Alexander Maneff are nollied. Maneff is returned to Lorain County and released from police custody. He eventually returns to his hometown, West Homestead, Pennsylvania.

March 31: Elyria's Second Methodist Church collects money for the purpose of funding an appeal for Hensley. The NAACP is gathering funds for the same cause: to take the case to the Ohio Supreme Court.

April 2: Court Reporter Gale Morgan says if the case is carried to appeal it will take at least a month to type up the trial. The record contains "about a quarter-million words."

April 9: In addition to Miss Bater, Mrs. Alfred Hall, of Grafton, finder of Hensley's footprints and hat, has applied for the $500 reward.

May 14: Defense motion for new trial is overruled by Judge Guy B. Findley. This does not prevent the case being taken to the State Court of Appeals. Officials are still awaiting the court reporter's typed record.

May 17: Prison Farm Superintendent Corwin Swan announces that, in light of the "Hensley incident," all prisoners must now work until 8:30pm and then report for roll call. Previously, they could leave work at any time after their tasks were complete, but this made it difficult for guards to tell who was where and when. These new rules also require prisoners to wear their farm overalls at all times which identifies them because there is a red stripe down each leg. Previously, they could wear their own clothes if they so desired. Six prisoners at the Grafton Farm are sent to the Mansfield Reformatory for their protests against these new restrictions.

September 20: The completed trial transcript reaches 1,124 pages and 280,000 words.

1939, March 1: After a total of three years as Superintendent of the Grafton Prison Farm, Corwin Swan is assigned to guard duty at the Mansfield

Reformatory. While it's not announced as such, it certainly appears to be a demotion. Swan eventually returns to Durkee Road, Eaton Township, resuming leadership roles in the Grange and holding a variety of jobs and positions, both private and public.

April 1: The Court of Appeals in Akron, Ohio, is set to hear the Hensley case on April 6. Rendinell plans on arguing that the police and prosecutor "played footsies" in the case to protect each other from scandal.

April 7: The Ninth District Court of Appeals takes the case under advisement. Judges Clarence G. Washburn, Perry Stevens, and Arthur Doyle are on the panel. The trial record is now listed as 3,000 pages long. No new evidence is allowed.

April 21: Hensley's conviction is affirmed by the court of appeals. Now that Hensley's conviction is sustained, there's the matter of the reward. The contenders: Mrs. Bernadette Jakelsky, Elyria, formerly Miss Bater, of Grafton; Mrs. Alfred Hall; Mr. Leonard James; and Mr. Harry J. Matthews all of Grafton. Lorain County Commissioners state that no reward can be paid until after the expiration of the 30-day appeal period allowed by the Ohio Supreme Court.

April 25: Hensley's mother states she intends to take the case to the Ohio Supreme Court. Attorney Rendinell files the action.

August 4: Reward is paid as follows: Mrs. Alfred Hall $50 and Mrs. Bernadette Bater Jakelsky $450. Mrs. Jakelsky indicates that she'll spend the money on medical bills and a vacation. "Furthermore I had planned on giving up my employment in September and become a 100 percent housewife so, of course, the reward, or what's left of it will come in handy then" (*The Chronicle-Telegram, August 4, 1939*). Mrs. Jakelsky and husband Bill eventually move to Carmel, Indiana, where she works as an accountant with St. Vincent Hospital.

1941, October 1: Hensley loses his appeal in the Ohio State Supreme Court. The conviction and life sentence stand.

1948, March 12: It's reported that the State Board of Pardons is looking into the Hensley case after Attorney Rendinell appealed to Ohio Governor Thomas Herbert to examine the circumstances.

1958, February 21: Hensley is up for parole. "The hearing before the commission would be in the nature of recommendation for executive clemency." None is given. Hensley remains in prison.

1973, August 1: *FROM:* The State of Ohio, Office of the Governor. *TO:* Ms. Natalie B. Neeson, Clerk of Court of Common Pleas, Lorain County: *RE:* Edward Hensley, No. 73-764, CCI:

Dear Ms. Neeson: I send you herewith a copy of the warrant of commutation issued by Governor John J. Gilligan to the above named inmate. The warrant commutes the sentence of the inmate from murder first degree to murder second degree, and his assault with intent to rob to time served. Will you please make the appropriate entry on your records to reflect the above change in the status of Mr. Hensley. Sincerely, Robert M. Weinberger, Legal Affairs Coordinator.

1973, August 1: The sentence of Edward Hensley, No. 73-764, CCI, commuted from Murder in the First to Murder in the Second by Ohio Governor John Gilligan with the sentence shortened from life to time served as directed by the Ohio State Parole Board. The vote to commute, with Mr. Nolan Snyder as the chair, was unanimous (7 to 0). After 35 years in prison, Hensley is nearly 60 years.

The jurors in the county's criminal trial, in case you're interested: Foreman Roy Dutton, Lorain. Mrs. Marie Fletcher, Lorain. Mrs. Mabel George, Elyria. Mrs. Vera Goodell, Lorain. Louis Hadaway, Ridgeville. Mrs. Harvey Holcomb, Elyria (alternate). Charles A Houff, Lorain. Mrs. Lottie Kleefield, Lorain. Ethel Lasco, Lorain. Mrs. Ruth Moir, Lorain. Mary Nangford, Elyria. Ralph Reed, Brighton. Mrs. Ruth Rosenberg, Lorain.

I found 125 articles in Elyria papers on the Hornbeck murder. A "typical" murder nets less than ten.

The Third Degree:

I'm willing to bet that you've never heard of New York City Police Inspector Thomas F. Byrnes. This, despite the fact that he was in the 1890s one of the most famous people in the United States. Almost stereotypically, Byrnes (born in 1842), a destitute Irish immigrant, worked and finagled his way from a poor and uneducated start to serve as the top detective of New York City, then one of the biggest, most violent, and crime-ridden cities of the western world.

The mild-looking, heavily mustached and mostly bald Byrnes is usually given credit for establishing the first "modern" police force: the study of criminal actions, use of "mug shots," sharing information between jurisdictions. But, while alive, he was best known for obtaining the confessions of criminals by employing a combination of techniques that came to be known as "the third degree." He punned of giving suspects "Third Degree Byrnes."

There is no doubt that his success was due to a mix of tried-and-true brutality, both psychological and physical. Despite knowing this, newspapers of the era took pains to describe the man's efforts as sly and insightful wars of will between good and evil.

Byrnes served as the head of detectives from 1880 to 1895 when he was forced out of his position by no less a personality than future U.S. President Teddy Roosevelt. T.R. was then head of the New York City Police Commission, and Byrne's resignation was considered part of reducing corruption in the department. While Byrnes was never taken to task for being on the take, his considerable personal fortune of $350,000 built on an annual salary of $5,000 raised plenty of suspicion. This seeming discrepancy was explained away as the result of excellent investments made possible by good connections on Wall Street.

Post-police, Byrnes hung a shingle as a private detective catering to well-to-do-clients. He died in early May, 1910.

Byrnes is sometimes given credit for inventing the term "the third degree," but I'm guessing that's not true.

Before and during his reign in New York, newspapers across the U.S. were full of stories detailing meetings held by the Masons, Knights of Columbus, Odd Fellows, and other, lesser known fraternal organizations. Most such articles listed those moving into the uppermost ranks. Specifics were never given, but the impression was strongly made that a candidate for promotion had to manage heavy questioning by those "giving them The Third Degree" (granting them rank). Hooking such vernacular to criminal investigations seems almost inevitable.

Edward Hensley, the man convicted in the murder of Louise Hornbeck, had good reason to fear getting the third degree from his prison guards. At many institutions beatings severe enough to cripple or kill were routinely doled out to those who ultimately confessed to crimes, whether they committed them or not. Even those held as mere suspects in local lock-ups were often denied legal help, subjected to threats, rough treatment, and days or weeks of solitary confinement, followed by relentless questioning to force admissions of guilt.

We'd like to think those days are long gone. Sadly, that's not true. Even now, the initial steps of arraignment and bail often finds poor and/or unknowledgeable suspects navigating court proceedings without benefit of legal representation. Even more heartbreaking, many would like to see the right to counsel waived for certain types of criminals and crimes.

Repeat after me: "I'm not saying nothin' until I talk to a lawyer."

1937, December 20: U.S. Supreme Court rules, 7 to 2, that evidence gathered through illicit wire-tapping of telephone calls cannot be used as evidence. The case was brought by four New Yorkers convicted of charges of smuggling alcohol on the basis of such surveillance.

1937, December 28: *The Chronicle-Telegram:*
> Six Inch Spoon Removed From Stomach.
>
> Chicago—Bernice Gutevitz, 17, said she was feeling fine today after undergoing an operation for removal of a six inch spoon from her stomach. She swallowed it at a Christmas party while eating ice cream.

Doggone kids. Can't trust 'em with nothin'!

1938: U.S. Tennis player Donald Budge is the first to make a "Grand Slam." The first ballet to Prokofiev's "Romeo and Juliet." Mexico, it turns out, has lots of oil. Their government nationalizes the industry. The House Un-American Committee. The Federal Firearms Act of 1938: gun sellers must obtain a Federal Firearms License (annual cost = $1) and keep records of the names and addresses of their customers *and* firearms may not be sold to those convicted of violent felonies. It all seems so simple, don't it? Hitler and Mussolini seem to be getting along just fine. Germany invades Austria and their minorities begin to suffer. Prime Minister Chamberlain waves a piece a paper in the air and waves his political career goodbye. The View-Master. The "March of Dimes" to fund polio research begins with entertainer Eddie Cantor suggesting to listeners to send dimes to FDR. Within a few weeks the White House has received nearly 3,000,000 of the coins. Ted Turner is born in Cincinnati, Ohio. 6 lynchings: 6 Blacks, 0 others.

1938, February 4: *The Chronicle-Telegram:*
> Borah Declares Anti-Lynching Bill Invades Rights Of States.
>
> Senator William E. Borah, Republican, Idaho, told the Senate today that an "unbroken line" of unanimous Supreme

Court decisions showed that the anti-lynching bill was an unconstitutional invasion of state's rights. "There has never been," he said, "a dissenting opinion against the theory that the federal government cannot impose on the sovereignty of a state."

1938, February 17, Thursday, about 11:00am:

Ruth (14), William (13), Aloha (12), and Bessie (8) Wallace head from school to home for lunch. The place they live, in the 1500-block of New Mexico Avenue in Lorain, is new to them. The youngest kids don't know what Ruth and Bill do—that they recently moved to get away from a big man, named Frank, who keeps bothering their mom.

It's been hard since their dad was sent away for helping kill Norman Watte (*see 1931, January 28*). Their mom has been cleaning houses to earn money. They also get help from their uncles and aunts, and Lorain County. The Department of Aid for Dependent Children says mother Mary Wallace "is an excellent manager and makes a good home for her children."

The kids find no lunch when they arrive that day. What's more, the house is dead quite. It's Ruth who finds their devoted mother, bloodied and unresponsive in her room. They try to call police, but can't. The telephone lines have been cut. They race to the neighbors.

Police arrive. Mary Wallace's room shows evidence of a "terrific struggle:" furniture overturned, windows broken, rug torn up. Her head is bashed in, apparently with the hammer that's found beneath her bed. She has also been choked and her throat cut, but the cause of death is a deep stab to the side of her chest. She is clad in her underwear, but the condition of the body "failed to indicate the motive." At least there's that comfort.

The children are taken in by her sister, Mrs. Bessie Boskey, 37, of Lorain. Mary Wallace also leaves behind two more sisters, Mrs. Ester Ferguson and Mrs. Ethel Becehelere, a brother, Bernie Pratt, and a father, J.L. Pratt. Mary's jailed husband, Arthur Wallace, is temporarily released from prison to attend her funeral held on February 19 from the Boskey house.

Police immediately focus their efforts on finding Mary's persistent admirer, Frank Naiberg. A huge man, well over six feet tall and 200-plus pounds, he had told the victim's brother-in-law, John Boskey, he was going to visit the woman the day of the murder. Witnesses saw him enter the house that morning. Police are certain the motive is jealousy.

A set of the suspect's fingerprints is lifted from a peroxide bottle in the victim's room. The FBI is asked to help.

Despite the efforts of local, regional, state and federal authorities, the suspect cannot be found. Frank Naiberg is not present when he is charged and indicted on first degree murder charges by the Lorain County Grand Jury. Outcome: Unresolved.

1938, March 14:

Wellington Enterprise reports that an annex to the Lorain County Courthouse has been proposed. The 56'x148' building would be connected to the present courthouse by a covered walkway. The first floor would hold the library, probate court, hearing room, judge's and Prosecuting Attorney's offices. Second floor: large courtrooms, hearing rooms, judge's offices, jury and witness rooms, offices for stenographers and bailiffs. Third floor: Grand Jury rooms. The old building would be given over to other county offices. It's never built.

1939: Marian Anderson's concert at the Lincoln Memorial in D.C. helps launch the U.S. Civil Rights movement. Saxophonist Charlie Parker is tagged "Yardbird," or, more simply, "Bird." Germany invades Czechoslovakia. Britain and France say "do that to Poland and you'll have a fight on your hands." Germany does so anyways. Germany builds a treaty with Stalin, secretly dividing Poland and the Baltic states between them. Spain and Portugal say they're staying out of any war that might arrive. Sweden, Norway, Denmark, and Finland agree. Russia invades Finland. The US Coast Guard begins operating the Lorain Lighthouse. They'll run it until 1965. In the Docket: Auto Theft and Non-Support of Family. 3 lynchings: 2 Blacks, 1 other.

1939, March 8, Wednesday: Location: Lorain, 2407 Broadway. Victim: Jesse Dave (63, wife). Suspect: Mike Dave (husband). Police arrive on scene to find the wife dead on the kitchen floor from a wound inflicted by a butcher knife and the husband mortally wounded with knife wound to his abdomen. He was member of the "now-smashed Dave-Koury liquor ring."

In August, 1939, Prudential Insurance refuses to pay on the policy to his estate because his death was ruled a suicide.

1939, April 7, Friday, early morning:

Police are called to the 600-block of East 29th, Lorain, by neighbors reporting a shooting. Inside, they find 50-year-old Anna Brnadech (Brenadies, Brnadeck) dead on the davenport. Her husband, 52-year-old Joseph Brnadech (Brenadies, Brnadeck), a Lorain steel worker, is on the bathroom floor, critically wounded. Both have suffered shots to the head by a brand new .32-caliber revolver found at the scene.

The wife's body is prepared by Reidy and Scanlan Funeral Home with funeral services on April 9 at 10:00am at St. Michael's Church, Lorain. She is survived by her children: Joseph and Nicholas Brnadech, Mrs. Paul Ondeka, Mrs. Fred Sukalac, and Mrs. Andrew Butti, Jr.

Those close to the couple say they have been quarrelling. Investigation turns up a note indicating the man had planned to kill his wife and then himself. The husband may have a chance of survival, though it is believed he will be mentally affected by the fragments of a bullet that are still in his brain. The note he left refers to his wife as a "second Anna Marie Hahn" and alleges that she tried to poison him. Joseph is her third husband. Anna's first husband died by accident. According to Joseph's note, the second hung himself because "he could not live with her."

Joseph Brnadech remains under police guard at St. Joseph's hospital both to keep him from doing himself further harm and to protect him from threats made against his life.

The case is first considered by the April Grand Jury and tabled.

On June 26 Joseph is recovered enough to be taken from the hospital to the County Jail. His brain is still full of bullet fragments. It's thought he may be so mentally damaged that he will not be able to stand trial.

He is charged with first degree murder, though still not processed by the Grand Jury. The problem is that ballistics experts maintain the characteristics of his wound indicate that he did not shoot himself. The case is considered by the June Grand Jury. The lack of powder burns on the husband's skull is convincing evidence that he did not shoot himself, and if he didn't shoot himself last, then how could he have shot his wife first?

Prosecutor Howard R. Butler says there is no explanation of how the crime, if any, occurred. The jury does not indict. Outcome: Unsolved.

Anna Marie Hahn, referred to above, was a "poison slayer" indicted in two deaths but convicted for murdering Jacob Warner, 78. In 1938, Ms. Hahn became the first woman to be executed in Ohio's electric chair.

1939, April 21: *The Chronicle-Telegram:*

Proposes Wires To Hold Courthouse Dome In Place.

Somewhat alarmed over reports of the condition of the dome over the courthouse, Commissioner John E. Davidson suggested today that guy wires be attached to it to prevent it from being swept away by a high wind.

Most of the dome structure is made of sheet metal, fashioned to look like stone. Much of this has rusted and deteriorated and some cases is so loose that it rattles with the wind.

Davidson said today that he is afraid a high wind may rip enough of the metal away to permit the dome to be lifted off As a temporary safeguard, he proposed guy wires.

1940 – 1949: County Population = 112,390

1940: Penicillin is safely used as an antibiotic. Mohammed Ali Jinnah proposes the establishment of independent Muslim states within India. Lehi (aka "the Stern Gang"), a Jewish terrorist organization, is formed in Palestine. Hitler invades the Netherlands and Belgium. Winston Churchill is Britain's Prime Minister. Germany signs an armistice with France, cutting the country east to west. FDR knows he's lying when he makes the campaign promise that no American boys will fight in any European war. Bobby Knight is born in Massillon, Stark County, Ohio. Jack Nicklaus is born in Columbus, Ohio. Franklin Roosevelt (New York Democrat) wins the Election with 54.7% of the popular vote. 5 lynchings: 4 Blacks, 1 other. $1,000 is worth $17,746 modern.

1940, May 27, Monday, late afternoon: Location: South Lorain. Victim: Natalie Minoff (21, wife). Suspect: John (James) Minoff (28, husband). Mr. and Mrs. Minoff have been married 18 months. He is surprised by a deputy sheriff serving him divorce papers. A few hours later he seeks out his soon-to-be-ex-wife, finds her in the kitchen of their home, smashes her head with a flat-iron, and slashes her throat with a razor. Then, with their 5-month-old son asleep in the adjoining room, Mr. Minoff locks up his combination home and barbershop (he's a barber, y'see), walks about a block, flags down a police car containing Lieutenant A.J. Mackerty and Patrolman Charles Springowski, and declares "I just killed my wife."

They drive to the home. There, Mr. Minoff shows them the body lying next to the stove. The officers discover that Mrs. Minoff is still alive and rush her to St. Joseph's Hospital where she dies about a half-hour later.

Minoff describes his actions thus: "I loved her so much I killed her. Now I have to die."

The June Grand Jury hears the testimony of 30 witnesses, including members of both sides of the family, and returns an indictment of murder in the first degree. Mr. Minoff claims he cannot pay for a lawyer and is assigned Basil Dziama as counsel. Plea: Not guilty. *Changed to:* Guilty of murder in the second degree. Outcome: Mandatory life sentence in the Ohio Penitentiary, with possibility of parole, plus court costs of $64.60.

1941: Elyria says "bye-bye" to the Lorain County Fair and Wellington says "boy, howdy," for good, it seems. The brave Amy Johnson is downed under mysterious circumstances. The Lend-Lease Plan—we're not *giving* aid, which is again federal laws, we're *lending* it, y'see? Ho Chi Minh leads the Vietminh guerillas in their fight against Japanese in Vietnam. Hitler breaks his promise to Stalin and invades Russia, murdering minorities as he goes. "The final solution of the Jewish question" is formulated by Reinhard Heydrich who was, I suppose, just following orders. Nazi use of gas against "undesirables" begins thereafter. Britain and the USSR invade Iran and kick Reza Shah from his throne to prevent any alliance with the Germans. Reza's son, Mohammad Reza Pahlavi takes his seat. Emperor Hirohito appoints Tojo Hideki as Japan's Prime Minister. The U.S. is Pearl Harbored into its role in World War II. It's thought that rubella (German Measles) causes birth defects. In the Docket: Selling Tickets in Schemes of Chance. 4 lynchings: 4 Blacks, 0 others.

1941, October 5: Location: 200-block of East 31st Street, Lorain. Victim: Newborn Benson. Suspect: Elsie Benson (20). Neighborhood children playing in the dying embers of a trash fire, find the charred remains of a newborn infant. The kids fetch an adult. He calls the police. Preliminary examination fails to disclose a cause of death. Authorities decide the baby was stillborn.

The mother, Mrs. Elsie Benson, is arrested and convicted of adultery. She is sent to the Toledo Workhouse for a six-month sentence, plus however long it takes her to work off the $200 in court costs.

Lorain Police Prosecutor Austin W. O'Toole is not satisfied with the outcome and reopens the case. He calls in Lorain pathologist Dr. John B. Donaldson who presents information to the November Grand Jury that the baby was alive when placed into the flames. The child died from one or a combination of the following: exposure, suffocation, or burns. Mrs. Benson, is indicted for second degree murder.

In court, without representation, she pleads guilty to the crime, admitting the baby, only 15 minutes old, was alive when she wrapped it in a towel and tossed it on the burning rubbish heap. She has, she says, a husband and another child living in Lancaster, Pennsylvania. Outcome: Sentenced to life in the Marysville Reformatory, plus court costs of $41.55.

Elsie Benson is paroled on March 5, 1951.

NEONATICIDE: Killing an infant within a 24 hours of birth.

1941, October 18, Saturday: Location: Lorain, 200-block Washington Avenue. Victim: Leo Blair (32, ex-husband). Suspect: "Broadway" Julia Blair (41, ex-wife). Act: Gunshot.

1935, June 24: Julia Blair files for divorce from Leo Blair on the grounds of cruelty. On July 18, she withdraws her petition for divorce.

1937, September 27: Julia Blair re-files for divorce from Leo Blair on the grounds of cruelty and is granted one by Judge Guy B. Findley.

1938: Julia Blair (then 35) and ten other women are arrested for prostitution in Lorain and plead guilty in front of Justice C.C. Lord.

1941, October 18: The shooting of Leo Blair takes place behind his house in Lorain during a quarrel following an automobile ride. He dies instantly. Julia Blair is locked up in the county jail and put on a suicide watch. She is under physician's care and given medicine regularly by the deputies.

The November Grand Jury considers the case and indicts on murder in the first degree. The four-day criminal trial opens on December 15 with Judge D.A. Cook presiding. Two full days are used struggling to select the eight men and four women of the jury. By the end of the process, both the defense and the state have used up every challenge available to them.

Prosecutors are William G. Wickens and assistant Stevens who say this of the victim:

> We hold no grief for Leo Blair. He probably was the lustful, unnatural, violent man he was described as being, but that does not give this defendant the right to shoot him in cold blood.
> *The Chronicle-Telegram, December 19, 1941.*

The State says the shooting was caused by jealously. Julia was losing the man she loved to another woman. Mrs. Blair weeps uncontrollably during prosecution's statements and is assisted from the court room by deputies.

Defense attorneys are the father and son team of Charles F. and L.B. Adams. The "highlight of the trial" for spectators is the accused testifying in her own defense and telling of an unhappy childhood and being "unlucky in love." She was born in Pennsylvania as one of 21 children. The family moved frequently. At the age of six, while living in Cleveland, Ohio, she saw her father commit suicide. Her mother then moved to Lorain and remarried. Her stepfather was cruel enough for the Lorain County Social Services to house the children at the Oberlin Home for three years until they were allowed to return home. During her time in Oberlin, Julia was sent to "the girl's reform school in Delaware" for eleven months.

Julia, sobbing frequently through her testimony, tells of being married at 17 years old. She deserted that husband and her three-year-old daughter for another man with whom she lived in a number of cities for about four years. Under cross she admits that she once shot this man when he threatened to kill her. The bullet struck him in the shoulder. She was arrested then acquitted of the charge.

Her second marriage was in 1931. She remained with him for three years. It was through her second husband that she met lake sailor Leo Blair, the victim in this case. She then left her second husband and lived with Blair before obtaining her second divorce and marrying Blair in 1934. She continued living with the victim after her (now third) divorce from him in 1937. She describes life with Blair as "repeated beatings and attacks which kept her in constant fear of him." She says Blair constantly used "marihuana" and that under the influence of the drug he was much worse. "He would beat me severely, and laugh about it and the more I cried the more he would laugh." During this time he prostituted her out to other men so she would earn him money. When asked why she stayed with her cruel ex-husband she responds "because I loved him." She finally shot him in the back yard of his mother's home out of fear of another beating.

Her mother-in-law, Mrs. Leona Blair, says while she had previously witnessed her son striking and kicking the accused, there was considerable shouting but no violence at the time of the shooting.

Defense claims that suspect was *about* to beat the victim once again and that she shot in self-defense despite still loving the man. "If she had planned to kill him would she have taken him to his own back yard and shot him in front of his mother?"

The jury deliberates four hours before finding the accused guilty of first degree murder with a recommendation of mercy. Judge D.A. Cook passes sentence immediately. Outcome: Mandatory life sentence in the Marysville Reformatory for Women, plus costs of $285.63.

But we're not done, yet:

December 22, 1941, the Adams team asks for a new trial for Julia Blair. They state the jury selection process used by Lorain County was illegal and unconstitutional since it did not result in a "representative cross-section of the county without respect to race, religion, or color."

They also charge that:

> …the officials of Lorain County and more especially the
> jury commissioners have, in the instant case and for some

> time past, failed and refused to make said list [of prospective jurors] a constitutional and representative list in that they have excluded therefrom many nationalities and racial groups. *The Chronicle-Telegram, December 22, 1941.*

Of the 70 people selected for the jury pool only 2 were from what might be considered "foreign nationality groups." This despite the fact that election records show that approximately 45 percent of electors are from the under-represented groups.

The Prosecution says there is no evidence to show non-inclusion and that the jury commission did not violate the law which has broad provisions for the selection of "judicious and discrete persons" who are competent to hear cases.

A new trial is denied on December 29, 1941. The defense says there will be no appeal because of lack of funds.

In 1962, Ohio Governor Michael V. DiSalle reduces Julia Blair's conviction of first degree murder to second degree and time served. She is free at the age of 62.

MARITICIDE – Killing one's husband.

The White Bread Barrier

Defense attorney and former Lorain County Prosecutor Charles Adams had good reason to assert that the juries his clients had to face were not a "representative cross-section of the county." Women had been a part of juries since 1922, but a quick look at the juror lists of the late 1930s yields surnames like Cooper, Pearson, Thompson, Miller, Hollen, and McKee. The property deed books for the same period? Marinek, Maravich, Marriott, Maslyk, Magezzeno, and Matzufka—and that's just the "MAs!"

The disconnect of juries to the population was perfectly obvious yet it persisted for a long, long time. Even after jury pools were created from the voting rolls, court clerks routinely cleansed the list of unwanted names. At first it was done to assure that everyone understood and spoke English. With time the reason wasn't quite so clear. Dependable jurors were called back over and over again. Some reasoned that such anchors made trials more efficient since old pros didn't thrash around trying to figure out how things worked.

Throughout the 1940s, Charles Adams continued to challenge the jury selection process—at least in the cases he lost—and that helped create change. How long did it take for juries to match the population of the county? It depends on what you're talking about.

More than one obviously "foreign sounding" name in a grand jury finally appears in January of 1949: Karbowniczek, Matuszak, and Rosso. A decade later there's Butti, Delmonico, Dombroski, Lilak, Sposato, Vidovich, and Visnich. That's a good thing.

People of colors other than White are far harder to find. The first African-American (that I am certain of) served as a member of a Lorain County Grand Jury in September, 1955.

Mr. Willie F. Myricks was born May 2, 1907, in the state of Georgia and came to live on East 22nd Street in the City of Lorain by way of the state of Arkansas, with his wife, Mabel, and brother Joe. Willie enlisted in the U.S. Army on November 6, 1943, and served his term with honor. He died on July 29, 1975.

How about African American women as jurors? I found no evidence for such within the time frame of this book. That doesn't mean it absolutely didn't happen—it may have and I just couldn't find it. Perhaps one of you can tell me!

1941, December 7: Pearl Harbor: Total killed: 2,467

1942: Bing Crosby sings *White Christmas*. Gandhi calls on the population of India to "do or die" to expel the British. He and most of the other leaders of his movement are tossed in jail until the end of World War II. Reinhard Heydrich (the aforementioned architect of the Nazi's "Final Solution") is killed by Czech guerillas who were just following orders. Roger Staubach is born in Cincinnati, Ohio. 6 lynchings: 6 Blacks, 0 others.

1942, April 6, Monday, early afternoon:
Bulgarian Andrew Doinoff (Dorinoff) has buried his mother, Katherine. Following his family's tradition, liquor is on hand for the post-service wake, and Andrew has been drinking heavily ever since making it home to East 29th in Lorain.

Andrew's brother, Nick, their mutual friend, former Lorain City Councilman Ed Sherman, and others are sitting and chatting in the living room when a woman screams in the kitchen.

Brother Nick and friend Ed rush to see Andrew stab his wife, Anna, several times in her stomach with a butcher knife. Ed Sherman grabs Andrew by his shoulders and hurls him into a corner. Then, while Ed calls the cops, Nick keeps his badly bleeding sister-in-law safe from his drunken brother. Nick is, however, unable to keep Andrew from self-inflicting a number of knife wounds to his chest.

Two hours after Mother Doinoff's funeral, her 26-year-old daughter-in-law is dead on her kitchen floor and her 36-year-old son is in critical condition at St. Joseph's Hospital. His doctors say he barely missed his own heart. Andrew Doinoff is transferred from St. Joseph's to the Lorain County Jail eleven days later.

The April Grand Jury hears his daughters Katherine (15) and Anna (14) testify as to their father's cruelty towards both of them and about their good-hearted stepmother. Other witnesses corroborate the stories of violent retributions for petty violations of Doinoff's rules and imagined jealousies.

Doinoff is indicted on first degree murder charges on April 22. The steel worker's criminal trial is set for May 19. While awaiting trial, Doinoff is sued by Dr. Louis Hait of Lorain for $200 for professional services surrounding his treatment of Doinoff's self-inflicted knife wounds.

The court intends to draw a special jury because of the possibility of a death sentence. This does not go well. Doinoff's trial is rescheduled for May 25 when defense lawyers C.F. and L.B. Adams challenge the way Lorain County draws potential jurors. The attorneys maintain the method does not result in a representative sample of citizens as required by law.

Says the *Chronicle Telegram (May 18, 1942):*

> The jury commissions select from the poll lists of the election board the names of persons to be called as prospective jurors but do not, in accordance with instructions by the common pleas court, use the "key" method of selecting the names of prospective jurors, under which system they would make their selection by lot rather than by choice.

The court refuses to draw a different set of jurors. Defense rejects the pool and instead opts for a 3-judge panel. This causes another delay.

Judge D.A. Cook recuses himself, saying he has acted as the family's private lawyer. That leaves Judge Guy B. Findley. Judges C.H. Huston of Mansfield and A.V. Baumann of Fremont are named by Ohio's Chief Justice Carl Weygandt.

Doinoff's criminal trial starts on June 15. The State describes Doinoff as a "jealous European who brought his barbaric instincts with him to this country." Eyewitnesses, including Ed Sherman and Andrew Doinoff's cousin, Mrs. Mary Minkoff, give detailed testimony on the stabbing death of the victim. Mrs. Minkoff says the accused had been drinking the day of his mother's funeral but could not say if he had been drunk. She also describes how the accused was extremely jealous of his wife and daughters. How he refused them the freedom to go anywhere without him.

Neighbor Mrs. Grace Balog of East 29th Street also relates how Andrew Doinoff was so jealous of his wife that he had used a butcher knife to fight duels with men who showed Anna too much attention. Mrs. Balog also testified that a few days before the murder, Anna had tried to poison herself and that Andrew had said he didn't want her to recover.

Daughter Katherine testifies to her father's jealous and violent nature, saying he had choked and threatened to kill all of the women in the house more than once. Defense says this story is told to spite Andrew for disciplining the girl for not returning home before her 9:00pm curfew.

Brother Nicholas is supposed to take the stand, but is unable to due to involvement in a near-fatal automobile accident in Twinsburg, Ohio.

The prosecution is handed a setback when some of their witnesses change their testimony from that given in front of the Grand Jury. Further investigation and questioning brings out that these (unnamed) witnesses have received threatening and intimidating phone calls warning them to not testify against the accused.

Throughout his trial the accused shows no emotion. In fact, according to his jailers, when not in court, Doinoff plays cards with his cellmates without apparent worry over his fate.

Defense points out that it was a custom of the Bulgarians, of which Doinoff is one, to turn a funeral into a sort of celebration which much drinking. They maintain that their client was under the influence of alcohol when he attacked his wife.

Doinoff takes stand in own defense at 10:30am, June 17. Seemingly unmoved by the seriousness of the charges, he testifies without emotion.

The accused says there was much drinking and that everyone was under the influence. That he went into the kitchen where his wife was preparing sandwiches for the guests. His confused story is that they argued about some minor point, she slapped him, then took the knife she'd been using to cut meat and tried to stab herself with it. He had tried to take the knife away and that she stabbed him. They continued to struggle and, during that fight, his wife was fatally stabbed and he stabbed himself.

When asked why he had stabbed her repeatedly once she was on the floor he replies, "I don't remember stabbing her."

The judges deliberate three hours before finding the defendant guilty of first degree murder, with mercy. Andrew Doinoff continues to show no emotion as Judge Huston sentences him to life in the Ohio Penitentiary. Outcome: Doinoff dies in prison, March 17, 1944, of what prison officials say is a heart attack.

1942, April 25: *The Chronicle-Telegram:*

County To Spend $16,150 For Defense.

The county will expand this year's approximately $16,150 in civilian defense activities, according to a computation made in the county commissioners' office yesterday.

It is understood that such an amount will be certified to the county budget commission when it meets next week to consider allocation $44,661 which the state has forwarded to the county for civilian defense expenditure as this county's part of $2,000,000 of state funds distributed for this purpose throughout the state.

The county's listed expenditures for this year, as they appear to date, were itemized as follows: $10,395 in salaries for seven extra deputy sheriffs as special guards for the 21st Street Bridge in Lorain: $70 for deputy bonds: $1,583 for flood lights for the Erie Avenue Bridge: $1,089 for fencing at the Erie Avenue Bridge: $430 for three watchmen's shelters at the 21st Street Bridge: $600 for floodlights at the 21st Street Bridge and $100 for telephones at the bridge.

In addition to these expenditures, the county expended $917 for extra guns and ammunition for the sheriff's department, making the $16,150 total.

1942, June 1: *The Chronicle-Telegram:*

Sterilization Act Unconstitutional.

The Supreme Court today held unconstitutional the Oklahoma Habitual Criminal Sterilization Act which provides for the sterilization of any person convicted in Oklahoma for the third time of a crime involving moral turpitude.

1942, July 12, Sunday: Location: Elyria, Wayne Street, off South Middle. Victim: Charles Glass (42, husband). Suspect: Minnie May (Mae) Fox Glass (42, wife). Husband Charles is shot and killed when he returns home late one night. The June Grand Jury indicts for murder in the first degree. Defense waives a jury for a 3-judge panel. Plea: Not guilty. *Changed to:* guilty of homicide. Outcome: Sentenced to the Ohio Reformatory for Women at Marysville until released by law, plus costs of $68.93.

Minnie Glass is paroled March 2, 1955.

1942, August 18, Tuesday, 7:00pm:

Thirty-nine-year-old Nathan Spuriel is a good-looking fellow, but he's a bad actor. He's spent time in a Michigan prison for burglary and has been arrested in Cleveland on separate charges of narcotics, grand larceny, assault and battery, carrying concealed weapons, and shooting to kill. However, for the time being, he's out on appeal after serving just two days on a conviction for illicit sexual relations with adolescent girls.

That makes Spuriel laugh. Two days—that's what a good lawyer can do for you. He's due back in Cleveland courts this week on charges of running a prostitution ring, but Spuriel's certain that between his attorneys and a little trick he played earlier, he'll get out of that one, too.

In the meantime, he's running women's underwear. Sure, his friends make fun of him for bootlegging bras instead of booze, drugs, or guns, but there's plenty of black market money to be made, what with war-time shortages of silk, nylon, and elastic. Guys looking to impress their ladies are always willing to pay 'way more than what's reasonable for stockings and fancy frills. Plus, there's other business to attend to out here in the sticks, once he's done with his rounds in Elyria.

Spuriel's pleasantly tipsy, having had a few drinks with customers who thought buying him a round would encourage him to lower his prices. He swings his '41 Cadillac Coupe onto East Bridge. Taking the turn a little wide, there's a bang as he bumps front-left fenders with Mrs. Bill Struck, wife of the furniture store owner, who lives a short distance away, in the 200-block of Columbus Street.

It's a minor accident. Nothing, really. Spuriel tries to convince the woman to take cash for her troubles. Something this small, there's no use getting the cops involved... Aw... C'mon, lady....

Mrs. Struck sticks to her guns and insists on a police report. Cash payments and those sorts of under-the-table shenanigans might play in the big city of Cleveland or maybe over in Lorain, but not here in the County Seat. Everything here is always done up properly.

When Elyria cop Howard Taft receives the radio call about a minor accident on East Bridge, he's driving his fellow rookie, Donald Andress, home in a patrol car. They're only a few blocks away and arrive in no time. S.O.P. The two officers talk to a few witnesses, then interview both Mrs. Struck and Nathan Spuriel, who plays it cool but is unusually anxious to see the whole thing over and done with.

Andress and Taft dismiss Spuriel's nervousness as due to the obvious fact that he's been drinking. The cops decide to take the man down to the station where he can sober up a bit before going on his way. The trouble is that Spuriel's had a few too many to drive his own car.

Andress is, technically, off duty. So, he follows in the patrol vehicle while Taft drives the Caddy with Spuriel along for the ride. The two cars travel only a short distance when Taft pulls over, gets out, and tries to bend the damaged left front fender so it'll stop rubbing the tire. Spuriel reaches over from the passenger seat, shuts off the car, takes the keys, and exits the vehicle. To Andress, who's sitting with the windows down in the patrol car, it looks as if Spuriel's trying to help. Then he hears Taft order the half-drunken man back into the Cadillac. An argument ensues, rapidly escalating into shouts and a scuffle.

Witness Arthur F. DuReitz, who lives in the 300-block of East Bridge Street, describes what happens next:

> After Spuriel got back into the car, the officer noticed a gun laying on the floor of the car and the officer picked up the gun. The Clevelander then got out of the car and started to grapple with Taft, who pulled out his gun and fended Spuriel off. The officer fired three times point blank and the man also started shooting.
>
> The officer fell to the pavement, rolling over and over. All the while the other man was shooting at him. The officer shot three times while lying on the pavement and the Cleveland man fell forward against the door of the car and did not move. I then ran over and with the help of another man, we put the officer in the police car and took him to the hospital. *The Chronicle-Telegram, August 19, 1942.*

During the altercation, the unarmed Donald Andress jumps from the patrol car to help his downed friend, but is forced to cover when fired upon by Spuriel.

Officer Taft took the first shots and fell to the ground. From there, he fired three times in rapid succession, striking Spuriel in the chest. Two of the shots went through the standing man and put bullet holes in the side of the coupe.

It is 7:00pm, Tuesday, August 18, 1942: Nathan Spuriel (39) is dead at the scene. The 29-year-old Howard Taft, shot three times, makes it to Elyria Memorial. He dies fewer than two hours later.

Spuriel's body is transported to the Nichols Funeral Home to await the coroner. Authorities are surprised to find the dead man carrying a little over $1,800. But that's nothing compared to the astonishment Police Captain Southam and Patrolman Kenneth Martin experience when they open the trunk of Spuriel's '41 Cadillac and find a woman's naked and badly bruised body.

The motives for Spuriel's actions are suddenly clear: urging Mrs. Struck to take his cash, not wanting police involved, nervousness at the accident, shooting Taft over what was a minor fender-bender. All of it was to avoid discovery of the woman's corpse.

The woman's body is taken to the Sudro Funeral Home and examined by Coroner Ward. Blunt force trauma was the cause of her death. Cleveland Police identify her as Doris McConnell, scheduled to appear as a witness in Spuriel's upcoming prostitution trial. Police track her last movements to a blood-stained apartment on Cleveland's East Side where witnesses describe five minutes of loud crashing accompanied by a woman's screams.

Editorials appears in local and regional papers decrying the leniency granted to criminals and the complicity of their attorneys "who take full advantage of every loophole in the law." Promises are made to investigate the Cleveland court that allowed such an obviously dangerous man to be released pending appeal. Promises, promises.

Policeman Howard Taft is buried in Brookdale Cemetery from Sudro-Curtis with Rev. William Leath of the First Congregational Church officiating. Taft leaves behind his wife of eight years, the former Georgia Watson of Field Corners, and a son, Gary (Garry) Howard, who is not quite nine months old. Also surviving are his mother, Mrs. Ethel Waltzer of Avon Lake, and a brother, Boswell Taft, who is in the U.S. Army.

1943, October 21: Taft's widow is awarded $20,000 from Spuriel's estate for the death of her husband, but it's estimated she'll receive less than $2,300. **Patrolman Donald Andress remained with the Elyria Police for a total of 19** years working his way up the ranks to Sergeant (1956) and Lieutenant (1960), the position he held at his death due to heart trouble, on January 13, 1962, at the age of 48. He was survived by his wife, Dora, two sons, two daughters, two brothers, two grandchildren, and his father.

Howard Taft's wife, Georgia, eventually remarried to become Mrs. Clay Nixon (he was an Elyria barber). Mr. Nixon died in 1972. Mrs. Georgia Watson Taft Nixon died at the age of 79 in Margate Florida on March 16, 1993, leaving three sons, five grandchildren, and three great-grandchildren.

1943: The Lorain County Courthouse loses, in a controlled manner, its sheet-steel dome along with its figure of justice. Oberlin reuses its salvaged Civil War who-died tables when it builds its Memorial Wall at the southwest corner of South Main and Vine. Chutes and Ladders. Race riots by Whites protesting the presence of Mexican Americans... *In Los Angeles.* Mao Zedong is the official leader of the Chinese Communist Party. The Chinese Exclusion Act of 1882 is no more. But only 105 Chinese immigrants are allowed into the U.S., annually, but they are allowed to naturalize. Mussolini is jailed. Hitler has him rescued. James Levine is born in Cincinnati, Ohio. 3 lynchings: 3 Blacks, 0 others.

1943, March ?: Location: Lorain. Victim: Walter Stipe. Suspect: William Varady (17). Stipe suffers a skull fractured when struck on the head during a robbery. He dies weeks later. Varady, who had joined the Navy, is released from duty to face this charge and others, stemming from a different robbery of the William Scher Company of Lorain, Ohio.

Charge: Murder in the first degree. Plea: Not guilty. Outcome: Murder case is nollied by the Prosecutor on January 4, 1944. Varady is then charged with robbery of the William Scher Company. He pleads guilty to that and is sentenced to the Ohio Penitentiary in Columbus.

During this trial defense lawyers file a "challenge to array," that is, they claim the jury is not representative of the electorate from which it is pulled. That challenge is dismissed, but results in a Grand Jury investigation into the way Lorain County jurors are called and selected.

1943, April 26, Monday, about 7:00pm: Location: Elyria, West River and 3rd, outside Kovacs' Café. Victim: William Kovacs. Suspect: Gaston Kableton Francis. Francis, in Elyria only one month, is causing trouble at Kovacs'. Victim William's father, John Kovacs, refuses to serve Francis and orders him from the establishment. The man won't leave. William Kovacs helps Francis find his way to the door.

A fight ensues. William Kovacs is slashed and stabbed. He is taken to Elyria Memorial Hospital where it looks like he will recover. However, at 1:15am, May 2, he dies due to "a blood clot." He leaves behind a wife, Mary, and kids Margaret, 8; Rose Mary, 6; and William, Jr., 4.

Charge: Murder in the first degree. Plea: Not guilty. *Changed to:* Guilty of murder in the second degree. Outcome: Life in the Ohio Penitentiary at Columbus, plus court costs of $125.45.

1943, July 11, Sunday: Location: South Amherst. Victim: Mary Goncheroff (50, wife). Suspect: Nick Goncheroff (54, husband). Act: Gunshot.

Nick Goncheroff arrived in the U.S. from Russia in 1913 to work in the Pennsylvania coal mines. He moved to South Amherst in 1924 for a job in the sandstone quarries. The missus is from Poland, a widow with six kids. The Goncheroffs marry in 1935. He is her fourth husband.

The husband kills the wife with one round from a 12-gauge shotgun after a "weeks-long argument" that started with news reports of the Russians killing 10,000 Poles during the occupation of their country.

The suspect then wounds two neighbors with a second shot. He suffers a self-inflicted wound with a third shot in a possible suicide attempt, then dashes the weapon against the stone steps of the house and runs up the street until stopped by neighbor John B. Egeland who reported the shooter was "a mass of blood."

Nick tells Egeland to call the sheriff and that he "wanted the electric chair." The suspect is taken to Elyria Memorial Hospital for treatment and is placed under guard.

Mrs. Goncheroff's funeral is from her home 9:00am Wednesday, July 14, 1943. She is buried in South Amherst's Evergreen Cemetery, leaving behind four daughters and two sons by previous marriage. One son, Walter Truzak, due to be shipped out with army, is temporarily released from duty because he is a witness.

Mrs. Goncheroff's children tell authorities their mother had been threatened by their stepfather many times, and he had also threatened to take his own life. The Grand Jury indicts on murder in the first degree.

Defense attorney Basil Dziama waives a jury trial, requesting a 3-judge panel: Guy B. Findley and D.A. Cook of Lorain County, plus Walter J. Mougey of Wayne County.

The State is represented by William G. Wickens and Assistant Prosecutor Richard Stevens who are seeking the death penalty. They claim the accused had been drinking the day of the murder, arriving home in a drunken state and in an "angry mood." The victim and accused had argued about the food she served him. He threatened his wife with a butcher knife that was taken away from him by his 20-year-old stepdaughter, Anna Truzak. Goncheroff began smashing plates, then went to his bedroom, retrieved his double-barreled shotgun to blast his wife where she stood in her kitchen.

He pointed the weapon at his stepson, 18-year-old Walter Truzak, who "bolted out of the house." The accused again discharged the weapon; first up the house's stairway and then out through the living room window which injured Mrs. Reien Blazar, 58, and her daughter Betty, 23, standing in the street several houses away. Goncheroff then tried to take his own life, but the shot only grazed his face.

Defense claims Goncheroff was rejected by his wife who continually called him vile names. The accused testifies that his wife had the shotgun first and that the shooting was accidental, taking place during a fight between he and his now-dead wife over the weapon (she was shot in the middle of her back). What's more, the son who claimed to be an eyewitness wasn't even in the house at the time of the shooting.

The papers state the defendant shows no emotion throughout the trial.

Outcome: After 70 minute of deliberation, the judges find the defendant guilty of murder in the first degree with a recommendation of mercy. The mandatory sentence is life in the Ohio Penitentiary, plus costs of $18.60. The sentence seems to make no impact on the guilty man.

Defense attorney Dziama receives $150 for his work.

1943, October 16: *The Chronicle-Telegram:*

Unidentified Body Is Washed Ashore.

Efforts were being made by deputy sheriffs this afternoon to determine the identity of a man whose body washed ashore at Avon Lake today.

Marshal William Arnold of Avon Lake, who notified the sheriff's department, said that the body was badly decomposed. It was thought that it might be the body of one of the sailors who were lost in the sinking of an Allied Oil Co. tug and oil tank barge in that vicinity some months ago.

Coroner S.C. Ward ordered the body taken to Schwartz's undertaking establishment in Lorain.

No other mention of this was found in either the papers or court records.

1944: Copeland's *Appalachian Spring* gets some fancy footwork courtesy of Graham. Remember *The Nutcracker* that was created 'way back in 1892? Well, it finally reaches the U.S. via the San Francisco Ballet. The World Bank. A left-wing revolution in Guatemala. Would-be assassins nearly kill Hitler. Charles de Gaulle strolls through Paris as France is liberated. Greece is freed from occupation. Hungary is freed, sort of, by the Russians who also reach Auschwitz. The brutality they find amazes even their rulers. Franklin Roosevelt (New York Democrat) wins a fourth Election with 53.4% of the popular vote. In the Docket: No murders, but plenty of near misses with a variety of shootings and stabbings. 2 lynchings: 2 Blacks, 0 others.

1944, January 16: Battle of Anzio: 12,000 killed.

1944, February 16: *Common Pleas Journal: Book 114, September 1943 to April 1944, page 201-202: presented as written...*

Rules and regulation of the Lorain County Jail:

Any and all persons entering the Lorain County Jail, including Federal Prisoners are subject to the following rules and regulation, which are to be observed.

Deputy under direction of the Sheriff has full charge of the management of this jail, and he is responsible for the safe-keeping, care, protection, instruction and discipline of all persons confined or employed therein.

The Deputies must see that all rules and regulation[s] are obeyed, and that the sentence of the court is served in an impartial, proper and dignified manner, and that all prisoners shall receive humane treatment under sanitary and healthful conditions.

SECTION 1: Prisoners when admitted shall be searched, required to bathe, their clothes deloused and given medical examination if required. They shall be provided with clean towel, soap, clean blankets. Regular bathing thereafter shall be enforced.

SECTION 2: Prisoners must keep their quarters clean, and if they fail to do so then shall be liable to punishment as provide in paragraph 16. All toilets, sinks, wash basins, floors, halls, stairways, walls, doors, ceiling, cell bars and partitions must be keep clean at all times. No trash or litter shall be allowed to accumulate in any part of the jail.

SECTION 3: Prisoners are required to do all Jail Maintenance work under the supervision of the Deputy on duty, and when not actually at work must be locked in their living quarters.

SECTION 4: All dangerous or harmful articles of any kind shall be excluded from the Jail Cell Blocks. The Deputy in charge shall make a periodic search of the Jail.

SECTION 5: Prisoners are not allowed to keep any money in their possession. All such property is to be kept in Jail Office and disbursement made from there by Deputy on written order from Prisoner.

SECTION 6: Card playing or other games for amusement are permitted, but gambling of any sort is strictly forbidden.

SECTION 7: The Kangaroo Court or similar organization as an agency of management, punishing prisoners or collecting fines is expressly forbidden.

SECTION 8: Importation of food is not allowed. Preparation and cooking of food is allowed only in the Jail Kitchen and to be done only by paid employees or under their supervision.

SECTION 9: Prisoners with syphilis presenting active lesions, or active gonorrheal urethritis, tuberculosis or any other infection disease shall be given intensive treatment by authorized Jail Physicians. Specific authorization for additional or extraordinary medical expense must be secured from the Jail Physician.

SECTION 10: All Prisoners are required to be out of their beds promptly at 7:00 A.M., clean their cells blocks, arrange their bed neatly, and be ready to eat breakfast at 7:30 A.M. promptly. At 9:00 P.M. all Prisoners must be in their beds, cells locked, lights turned off by a Deputy and everyone remain quiet.

SECTION 11: Destruction of property, defacing of walls, or cell bars, throwing cigars, cigarettes, newspaper or any substance in toilets, spitting on floors or throwing trash of any nature on floors is strictly forbidden.

SECTION 12: Each Prisoner shall be held strictly accountable for violation of Rule 11 and also be accountable for the safety and condition of supplies furnished, such as blankets, etc. Upon discharge, the deputies shall have them removed from cell compartments, properly cleansed, laundered and stored until assigned to another Prisoner.

SECTION 13: It is the Deputy's responsibility to designate the Prisoners to work within confines of the Jail in helping maintain and take care of the Jail as proscribed in the Rules. Failure on the part of the Prisoner to perform such duty assigned to him will be reported to the Sheriff who will direct proper punishment.

SECTION 14: Visitors will be permitted only on Wednesday of each week from 1:00 P.M. to 4:00 P.M. All mail is to be censored by Sheriff or Deputy.

SECTION 15: The Deputy on duty must make an inspection of the cell block at least once during his time on duty and any infraction of these Rules, must report them to the Sheriff forthwith.

SECTION 16: All Prisoners are to be subject to strict and impartial discipline. No Special privilege or favoritism is to be granted any Prisoner of class of Prisoners. Brutal or inhuman treatment will not be tolerated. Prisoners violating rules and regulations may be punished as follows; (A) By restriction of privileges. (B) By a restricted diet. (C) By solitary confinement.

SECTION 17: The Deputy has the authority to promulgate any minor rules and regulations that are proper and that may be deemed necessary for the betterment of all concerned and which has not been covered by the foregoing regulations. Any extraordinary situation should be immediately referred to the Sheriff for specific authorization or instruction. All the officials and employees of the Jail should and are expected to carry out their work in an exemplary manner. Their duty is not only to keep the Prisoners in safe custody but, by their own good conduct, to exercise over them an educative influence.

Approved February 14, 1944, D.A. Cook, Guy B. Findley, Judges.

1944, June 6: Normandy begins: 650,000+ total killed.
1944, September 19: Hürtgen Forest: 61,000+ total killed.
1944, December 16: Battle of the Bulge: 33,000+ total killed.

1945: Labor troubles as the war slows and people want more money. The use of the world's first flu vaccine is restricted to the armed services after it was developed in fears of the "Spanish Flu" that killed millions during and after World War I. The Arab League is formed in Cairo, Egypt. Romania is liberated, sort of. U.S. troops discover Buchenwald. The British reach Belsen. Words and images do not represent the horrors. There are those who believe it never happened. FDR dies. Harry Truman is President. Mussolini and sweetheart (Clara Petacci) are shot and strung up by their feet. Hitler marries sweetheart (Eva Braun). Shortly thereafter, the newlyweds commit suicide (she by cyanide, he by pistol-shot). After all he's done, Churchill loses England's first post-European-war election. Truman orders the atomic bombing of Japan. The League of Nations is no more, but the United Nations is. The Japanese surrender. Ho Chi Minh's Vietminh guerrillas take Hanoi, the capital of Vietnam. They don't want to give it up and declare the Democratic Republic of Vietnam, independent of France. The end of World War II. The original Quisling is executed in Norway. In the Docket: Vandalism. 1 lynching. 1 Black, 0 others. $1,000 is worth $13,856 modern.

1945, January 3, Wednesday:

It's cold at 8:00am when a taxi pulls up in front of the Lorain home of Mr. and Mrs. Andrew Raynak. Ralph Brown, the handsome, chin-dimpled passenger, has been bending the driver's ear, telling how he and his beautiful girl are traveling to Columbus to be married. Brown tells the driver to keep the meter running, then exits the cab and bounds up the walk.

A few minutes pass. The door to the house opens. Ralph Brown returns to the vehicle. He takes his seat in the back and asks that he be taken to either the hospital or the police. The driver gets a look at his fare's bloody hands and speeds for the police station. Once there, Ralph Brown, 32, announces he has killed a woman, then immediately asks, "Is Helen hurt?"

Officer Robert Herbert, doubting Brown's sanity, puts the man in a padded cell. When jailers later check their prisoner they finds that Brown has undressed himself.

Police quickly discover that the "Helen" Ralph refers to is more than hurt. Helen Katonak (Kntonak, Katonsk), 28, is dead from multiple stab wounds. Her sister, Ana Raynak, is hospitalized with the same.

The January Grand Jury finds that Brown used a pocketknife to "viciously attack" and kill his sweetheart after she refused to marry him. Her sister, Mrs. Andrew Raynak, was slashed while trying to protect the victim. Brown is indicted for murder in the first degree.

The court assigns attorneys Joseph Provenza and Milton Friedman to the indigent defendant. The initial plea is not guilty. On February 28, this is changed to not guilty by reason of insanity.

The court orders the accused to be examined by Dr. Arthur Hyde, Superintendent of the Massillon State Hospital for the Insane. Dr. Hyde determines Brown to be sane enough to take part in his criminal trial. Dr. E.H. Crawfis from the Cleveland State Hospital also examines the defendant and pronounces the same.

The defense waives a jury trial in favor of a 3-judge panel. Lorain County Judge D.A. Cook withdraws from the case because he, at one time, was a lawyer for the father of the accused. The judges named are Clarence V. Ahl of Bucyrus, A.V. Baumann of Fremont, and Guy B. Findley of Lorain County.

The trial starts March 20 and moves quickly. The accused is shackled to Deputy Charles Mack with Deputies Adams, Kosco, and Reisz attending. Defense objects to the chains and wants them removed because they prejudice their client. The court refuses once deputies tell how Brown has declared multiple times that he will attempt escape at the first opportunity.

Despite the notoriety, far fewer than a hundred people attend the trial. Brown's mother sits at his table, and he takes an active part in the proceedings, conferring with his lawyers as members of the victim's family testify against him.

Knife-scarred Mrs. Anna Raynak, sister of victim and with whom the victim lived, testifies how being with Ralph Brown forced Helen Katonak down a dark path. How the murdered woman went from an upstanding citizen—a soprano soloist at the Emmanuel Evangelical Church in Lorain—to being forced to procure an abortion as a result of her relationship with the accused.

Mrs. Raynak says her sister met Ralph Brown in November of 1943 at the Lorain Shipyards where they both worked. Helen was an electric welder, and he was infatuated with her from the start, calling on her almost every night and sending her two-dozen red roses every weekend. For Christmas he gave her a chenille robe, a toilet set, boxes of candy, and three dozen roses. Oddly enough, these gifts retained their price tags—something that bothered Helen a great deal.

She was also gifted with a string of pearls and matching earrings which Brown said were from his mother in Nashville, Tennessee. This started a string of stories about his wealthy family which, bolstered by photographs, were at first believed, but later discovered to be a pack of lies told to impress Helen and her relatives.

Anna Raynak tells how Helen tried to write to her boyfriend's parents at their Tennessee address but received no replies until one letter was returned marked "Not Found." This led her to the eventual discovery of Brown's real family in Lancaster, Fairfield County, in south-central Ohio. Anna says when she and Helen confronted Brown with the lies about his past, he did not seem to be upset unless the talk involved Helen leaving him. Then he would "cry and wring his hands."

Despite his lies, Brown was allowed to spend the past Christmas Day with the Raynaks. His visit ended when he began to threaten suicide by slashing his wrists and Helen ordered him out of the house.

Anna testifies that Brown next appeared the morning of January 3rd. A borrowed suitcase in hand, he announced that he was there to collect Helen and that they were leaving for Columbus to get married. This astonished Helen who was not yet out of bed. She got up and went downstairs to talk. The two women, Anna and Helen, argued with Brown who hotly accused both Anna and their pastor, Reverend W.H. Herkner, of trying to destroy the relationship.

"Maybe you don't realize my soul has been saved," Brown said. "You don't know what that means. Your religion is just a formality."

Helen asked Anna to go up to her room and get her purse. Once there, Anna heard a noise and rushed to see the accused holding the victim close to him. Neither of them moved nor offered an explanation. Then, Anna said, shortly after returning to her task, she heard Helen scream. She ran to see Ralph Brown striking her sister across the face but did not realize at the time that Brown was slashing with a knife.

Undertaker George W. Cooley and Coroner S.C. Ward both testify to the condition of the victim's body. They found knife wounds on Helen's face, breasts, arms, back, and hands, including several slashes to the neck which severed her jugular veins and windpipe.

Cooley said he had removed broken knife blades from the victim's right elbow and left shoulder. The blades were introduced as evidence. Cooley told of the police bringing the accused to the mortuary at midnight, about eight hours after the murder, and asking him if he didn't want to kneel, pray, and say he was sorry, or if he wanted to kiss the corpse. Cooley said Brown said and did doing nothing in response.

On cross, Coroner Ward said he was called to the shipyard on December 22nd to treat Ralph Brown who had collapsed. Brown was treated for two days at St. Joseph's Hospital to recover from what Dr. Ward calls "a neurosis." Brown's defense contends that, because of this mental illness, the accused did not know what he was doing at the time of the killing.

March 21. Prosecutor Wickens surprises the court by producing witness Mrs. Jean Simpson, 24, "an attractive brunette," of Detroit. Wickens claims Mrs. Simpson met Brown at the Detroit hotel where she lived and that he had sent her money to fund her occasional trips to Lorain.

The presence of Mrs. Simpson is strongly objected to by the defense, and the judges delay her testimony to give them a chance to prepare.

In the meantime, Lorain police officer Robert Herbert testifies to his own doubts about Brown's sanity.

Lorain Detective Vernon Smith, who questioned Brown after his arrest, tells how Brown had said that he loved Helen, that he had lied about his wealth because he knew she wouldn't have had anything to do with him if she knew the truth, and that he "had killed her because he loved her so much."

Brown had told Detective Smith that he had insisted she go to Columbus, Ohio, to marry him that day. Helen refused. He took out his knife and held it to his own throat to kill himself. Helen told him not to do such a thing and grabbed his hand. The next thing he remembered was sitting in the taxi in front of the Raynak home.

Gordon Wellman, convicted automobile thief and forger, now out of jail, was Brown's roommate from January to June in 1944. Under oath, Wellman says Brown always spoke of the victim with the greatest respect, but also told of the rough treatment women received when they double-crossed him. It was from Wellman that Brown borrowed the suitcase for the unilaterally-planned wedding trip to Columbus.

The victim's brother, John Katonak, 31, of Sandusky, Ohio, testifies that Helen sought refuge in his home in December because she was in fear of

Brown. Another brother, George Katonak, of Amherst, Ohio, says Brown had visited his home and created a scene, trying to pull the victim from the building until he, George, "grabbed him by the throat."

In the witness chair, Reverend Herkner says the victim was a member of the church choir and an interested and valuable member of the congregation. The Reverend states he thought that Helen and Ralph were going to be married until Helen told them of her troubles with Ralph's lies and his hospitalization for neurosis.

Helen told her pastor that she was afraid of Brown. She said he always put on being sweet in the reverend's presence. Helen said that she discovered Brown was previously married and had been arrested for both adultery and beating his now ex-wife.

The pastor told how Brown threatened Helen with plastering her name all over Broadway whenever she tried not to "submit to him." Because she was pregnant, Reverend Herkner says he advised the couple that they marry. Brown was in favor of tying the knot, but Helen refused, saying she was afraid he'd kill her in the end. Brown had already threatened her with a gun on the night of November 28th to force her to stay at his apartment and again on December 11th when she was at her brother George's home in Amherst.

According to the reverend, "Ralph admitted all that she accused him of, but said, that he had gone to some church with a friend, that his soul was saved and that he was reformed, was a new man, and that he wanted to start all over again. I believe he meant it." Reverend Herkner said he advised Brown to leave Helen alone for a while and try to win her back by being a gentleman.

After the State rests its case, defense attorney Milton Friedman moves that the court dismiss the first degree murder charge on the grounds that premeditation was not proved. He urges the court to consider a charge of murder in the second degree, which carries a sentence of life in prison.

That motion is overruled by the judges with the reservation that it will be considered later. The court also prevents the prosecution from questioning witnesses who might provide facts about the accused's previous relationships with women, but would allow them as rebuttal witnesses after the defendant had testified.

Kirby Arter, of Lancaster, Ohio, Brown's stepfather takes the stand. As a boy, Brown had failed eighth grade, spending two years there, and attended high school for only six months before dropping out to work and earn money to buy clothes. "He liked good clothes and the girls," the stepfather says.

Besides a quick temper, the boy seemed normal. Though, Arter does know the boy's biological father and does not think him in his right mind.

March 23, Good Friday: Ralph Brown takes the stand and tells a story of infatuation and a courtship built upon lies and the revelation of the truth.

He grew up poor in Lancaster, Ohio, and was married and divorced. Brown says he started using the stories of being from a wealthy family shortly after arriving in Lorain in 1943 because he learned, "that people here didn't like hill-billies" and was afraid that he would lose Helen if she discovered who he really was. He continually urged Helen to marry, but she always put him off. A month before the killing he grew greatly upset by a cooling of their relationship. The stress and worry put him in the hospital.

He could not sleep the night of January 2nd. He read the bible and prayed for guidance. Then, instead of going to work, he went to see her. "Something told me that if I went to Helen's house and asked her to come with me and get married, that she would."

He packed a suitcase he borrowed from roomie George Wellman and headed over to his sweetheart's. Once again, Brown says darkly, she refused. Helen's sister, Anna, confronted him, saying, "You aren't a man. You have threatened several times to commit suicide. I don't believe you have nerve enough." Brown testifies that he pulled his knife and that the victim and her sister had tried to stop him. He remembers nothing else.

Under cross examination he admits to being intimate with two other women and of beating one of them.

This opens the door for the attractive Mrs. Simpson of Detroit. She states that she met Brown in a hotel of that city in March of 1943. Of course, she was not married at the time. He had invited her to Lorain and on three occasions sent her traveling money. Mrs. Simpson says Brown told her the same lies about the rich family in Tennessee and, when confronted with the truth, he beat her unmercifully, to the extent that he was arrested for assault and battery.

On the stand, Dr. E.H. Crawfis, Superintendent of the Cleveland State Hospital is of the opinion that Brown's actions are "more impulsive than reasoned" and that the accused suffers from physical and emotional disturbances that could influence his judgment. The doctor maintains that the accused is presently sane and was sane the day of the murder, but Crawfis believes that Brown is telling the truth when he says he cannot remember the killing.

After two hours of closing arguments, at 11:00am, the judges take the case under advisement. The next day, March 24, The court finds Ralph Brown guilty of murder in the first degree, without mercy.

That verdict provides only one outcome… Execution.

Defense lawyers Provenza and Friedman immediately file a motion for a new trial on the grounds that the verdict was not sustained by the evidence. Sentencing is postponed until a decision on that motion is decided.

The defense says they will appeal if a new trial is denied.

March 28: Deputy James Elemes is sent to Brown's cell in the County Jail to remove the leg shackles he has worn almost constantly since his arrest. When he arrives, Brown smilingly tells him, "You don't need to bother. They are already off!"

Sure enough, the half-inch steel leg irons are on the floor, cut through with a hacksaw, a trace of which cannot be found. Brown refuses to tell them how he had got the saw or where it was saying, "The Good Lord gave it to me and took it away."

His only visitors have been his parents and his pastor. Brown is left in his skivvies as every inch of his cell is fruitlessly searched. All the trusties on the block are locked up on suspicion. The sheriff would like to be done with him, but Brown cannot be moved to Columbus until the court has sentenced him.

The hacksaw mystery is solved two days later when Lorain County prisoner Andrew Simko, 27, is transported to the Ohio Penitentiary in Columbus to begin a 10 to 25 year sentence for the pre-Christmas armed robbery of McCarvel's jewelry store and Spike's Food Store. Simko cheerfully confesses to providing Brown with the hacksaw blade. As proof Simko produces it from an inconspicuous hole at the back of one of his shoes.

Simko says he always carried it in case he was caught and jailed, but he never had a chance to use it to escape from the Lorain County lockup. As a career criminal, he knows he'll be carefully searched and given prison garb upon his arrival in Columbus and so wanted to rid himself of the blade before reaching The Big House.

Ralph Brown's motion for a new trial is denied on April 7. He's back in leg shackles for sentencing. It's death by electrocution. The condemned man, with two-week's beard, takes the news calmly. "I have nothing to say. I will leave it up to the Good Lord. I have nothing to fear."

As soon as possible he is taken by automobile to Columbus.

Brown's execution is scheduled for August 3. He is the first death sentence for both Judges Findley and Baumann. He is the sixth for Judge Ahl.

Defense appeals the decision. Appeal Court judges Clarence Washburn, Perry Stevens, and Arthur Doyle sustain the conviction and sentence.

Defense takes the case to the Ohio Supreme Court which reviews and refuses to consider the case. A stay of execution is granted by Ohio Governor Frank Lausche to give the Ohio Board of Clemency an opportunity to hear final appeals on January 23. The appeal is dismissed with "no debatable question involved."

1946, February 9, 7:07pm, more than a year after his crime, Ralph Brown (32) is executed in Ohio's electric chair for the murder of Helen Katonak. Gordon Wellman, who was his roommate around the time of the murder, is a witness to the electrocution.

Brown's attorneys eventually divide $900 for their work. Court costs are $337.45.

1945, October 23: As the case of Ralph Brown wends its way through the appeals process, his roommate and prosecution witness, the handsome, dimpled, and wavy-haired Gordon Wellman, shows up in the office of Prosecutor Wickens.

It seems that Ralph Brown, in preparation for leaving with the woman he ultimately murdered, had borrowed Gordon's suitcase. Wellman tells Wickens he's planning a wedding trip of his own and asks for his suitcase back, please.

A somewhat amazed Wickens denies the request and tells Gordon Wellman that the suitcase will be held as evidence until Brown exhausts all appeals. When asked how long that might be, Wickens replies weeks, or months. Maybe years. Wellman indicates that he does not have that much time and leaves the office angry and upset.

Wellman's visit is something Prosecutor Wickens will remember for the rest of his life.

Helen's sister Anne (Anna) Katonak Raynak Reinke is the last of her generation to pass, dying at the end of June, 1996, at the age of 88.

1945, March 27, Tuesday:

Lorain County Prosecutor, William G. Wickens, receives a telephone call straight out of a crime novel. It's the FBI. On the other end of the line is an agent who thinks Lorain County might be interested in a man they've taken into custody in Los Angeles, California: truck drive Harry A. Harlan.

Mr. Harlan had been routinely fingerprinted so that he could earn a little extra money making deliveries to a war materiel plant in California. During the background check, the prints were found to match those submitted to the FBI by Lorain County, back in February of 1938.

It seems the Feds have snagged Frank Naiberg, the alleged murderer of Mary Wallace (*see 1938, February 17*). What's more, upon apprehension, Naiberg spontaneously confessed to killing the woman seven years prior.

Immediate steps are taken to bring Naiberg, now 45, home for a trial. He is very large, an inch shy of six-and-a-half feet and weighing 292 pounds. The dark haired, dark eyed man is always shackled and handcuffed to a heavy belt around his waist so that he can neither run nor raise his arms.

Naiberg is retrieved by automobile by Lorain Police Chief Theodore Walker and Inspector John Meister at a travel cost of $393.37, including $50 to replace a windshield pitted by a sandstorm encountered on their cross-country travels.

The suspect makes a full confession upon his return and is arraigned on charges of murder in the first degree in Lorain County at 9:00am, April 23.

His confused wife of two years, Mrs. Harry A. Harlan soon arrives from Los Angeles to be with him. She claims to know nothing of her husband's past, and it's not until she's here that she realizes the severity of the charges against him.

Virgil Burgett and Basil Dziama, Lorain Attorneys assigned as counsel, have the accused enter a "general plea" which must be changed before trial. It's reported Naiberg will try to enter a plea of guilty to murder in the second degree. Prosecutor Wickens says he will oppose that plea or any other effort to "try and soften the charge" of murder in the first.

On May 14, the accused makes the plea of guilty of murder in the second degree. Dziama says there are mitigating circumstances: the accused suffers from heart disease. He has collapsed twice in the county jail in the past week. If allowed to plead guilty he could avoid a trial that might kill him. Defense also points out that the accused has kept a good record, even giving up booze. Besides, there was no way the State could prove the premeditation required for a first degree charge.

Untrue, the State counters, they have plenty of evidence to prove premeditation. Not only that, but since the murder of Mary Wallace, Naiberg had been arrested and served 29 months for robbery in South Dakota. It was only because nobody had ever asked that the prints taken for that crime weren't checked against the files at the FBI. Besides, says Prosecutor Wickens, the victim's husband, Arthur Wallace, wants a first degree charge and Wallace has experience with pleading guilty to second degree murder since he was paroled from a sentence for the same after only ten years in prison for his part in the 1931 "Magic Shop Murder" of Norman Watte.

Judge Guy B. Findley tells both defense and prosecution to save their arguments for the trial. The 1938 Grand Jury indicted Naiberg for murder in the first degree, and murder in the first is what it will stay.

Jury selection begins on May 28. It takes one day to seat the jury: Carl Dietz, Avon lake; Carl Gutman, Oberlin; Sophia Tite, Bertha Boothroyd, Agnes Mitchell, and Councilman James C. Scott, all of Elyria; Luella Steiner, Anna Joynson, Agnes McVey, Anna Parkman, Lilly Mobille, and Ruth Nathan, all of Lorain.

The victim's children are summoned for the trial: Mrs. Ruth Bryant, 21; Aloha, 19; Bessie, 15; and William, 20, a petty officer with the U.S. Navy, home on leave after extended service in the Pacific Theater. Their father, Arthur Wallace, attends every court session.

The State says that Naiberg had made statements that he intended to marry the victim, and wouldn't take no for an answer; that if he did not get her, no other man would because he would cut her throat; that there were other suitors and the killing was done out of jealousy; that the accused had been in Detroit before the crime, but returned for the single purpose of killing the woman.

Not so, says defense attorney Dziama. The crime was committed in the heat of passion and not as a premeditated act. The accused and the victim had talked about her divorcing her then-jailed husband so she would be free to marry. They had fought over the matter, yes, that was true, but that he had returned from Detroit for a reconciliation. When he arrived, the victim threw a flower pot at him, the violence escalated, he lost his temper, and the woman was killed.

The victim's daughter, Mrs. Ruth Wallace Bryant testifies: It was her brother, William, who first met Naiberg. As a child he used to play along the lakefront and encountered the unemployed Naiberg, who was staying at "Todd's Boat House."

Naiberg began calling on them in their Lorain, Lakeside Avenue home. He kept calling when they moved to 8th Street even though her mother told him to stay away. He followed them to New Mexico Avenue despite Mary Wallace's demands that he leave them alone. The situation was bad enough that, two weeks prior to her murder, her mother had purchased a revolver as protection against Naiberg who was lurking about the neighborhood.

When asked about what she saw the day of the murder when she discovered her mother's body, Ruth breaks down on the witness stand, unable to continue. When asked what kind of person her mother was, the quiet reply is "she was as nice as any mother could be."

Police Inspector John Meister tells the jury of Naiberg's confession of the crime on April 23 in the Lorain Police station. Meister reports that the accused said, "he was glad to get it off his mind."

Naiberg told them that he'd met the victim in 1937, was enamored by her, and extremely jealous when other men paid her attention, a statement corroborated by other witnesses. When she finally rejected him he "went to Detroit and, in a period of two days, drank a half gallon of liquor." He then determined to "choke her to death and then commit suicide."

Naiberg had said he hitch-hiked to Lorain and visited the New Mexico Avenue home of the victim. She grew angry with him and threw a flower pot at him. He flew into a rage, choked her, and then cut her throat with a butcher knife that he had found in the kitchen and had used, earlier, to cut the telephone lines. The accused man told police that he then fled the house, going to the Nickel Plate Railroad Bridge to jump and drown himself in the river, but was chased from the bridge by a man there. He then went to Toledo, then Cincinnati, and on to California. The confession held no mention of jail-time in South Dakota.

Frank Naiberg takes the stand in his own defense. He had been married before meeting the victim. After his first wife died in 1928, he hoboed around the country, working odd jobs and riding freights, sleeping where he could. He met the victim in 1937, lived in her place for a while, and fell in love with her.

The two had fought on the day of her death. She threw a flower pot at him. He flew into a rage. He choked her and cut her throat. During their fight, he said, "I went stone blind. Then I proceeded to put my darling out of the way by choking her to death. I was completely out of my mind." He testifies he had no recollection of cutting her throat. He didn't even know he had killed her until he read it in the Toledo paper the next day. He said he also later tried to kill himself by taking three (mercury) "bi-chloride tablets" but they were counteracted by the whiskey he'd consumed prior to the attempt (not likely).

Mrs. Harry Harlan testifies, saying the person she was married to was in no way like the man on trial. Her husband was a good, sober man who never touched liquor. She maintains that she knew nothing of the crime until he was arrested. All of this, she sobs, is a complete surprise.

Prosecution calls the crime the "foulest, most vicious thing that has ever happened in our county" and urge the jurors to find the man guilty as charged. Defense admits the killing, but maintains it was never planned. The crime does not meet the premeditative standard of first degree murder.

June 2: The case is placed into the jurors' hands. It doesn't take long for the nine women and three men to return a verdict: Murder in the first without mercy. If Naiberg's weak heart doesn't kill him, the State will.

Judge Findley sentences the guilty man to death, with the execution to be held at the Ohio Penitentiary in Columbus on September 17.

His lawyers ask for a new trial. It is denied.

August 9: The District Court of Appeals grants a stay of execution until the Appeals Court determines the validity of the verdict and sentence. The Appeals Court meets on September 20 with judges Clarence Washburn, Perry Stevens, and Arthur Doyle. Naiberg's sentence is upheld.

December 11: Naiberg's case is reviewed and rejected by the Ohio Supreme Court. Governor Frank Lausche grants a stay of execution until the Ohio Board of Clemency can hear final appeals. All appeals fail. The Governor takes no further action.

1946, February 9, 7:26pm: Frank Naiberg (48) is executed by the State of Ohio for the murder of Mary Wallace Brown. His electrocution takes place less than twenty minutes after that of Ralph Brown from the case just above. It is the state's first double execution in six years, both men on sentences from Lorain County.

Naiberg's attorneys divide $900 for their efforts.

Arches and Loops and Whorls and Composites:

Your fingerprints are the result of genetics and happenstance. Formed before you're born, the basic, general shape of the lines and ridges on your fingers (and toes) are controlled by your chromosomes. But, your unique, detailed patterns are thought to be furnished by various factors such as your motion inside the womb and even the density and composition of the amniotic fluid in which you floated.

Nobody (including identical twins) has matching fingerprints, making them ideal as a means of identification. The trouble is this: how do you categorize millions (or billions) of somethings that are all different from one another? And, once categorized, how do you retrieve the one set of recorded prints that match the ones you've just collected?

In 1896, English police officer Edward Henry, building on the work of British anthropologist Francis Galton, devised a system of fingerprint classification based on values assigned to each finger, then altered by the basic shape of the print on that finger.

Arches: Ridges that run from one side of the finger to the other with little or no disturbance, although they may display a tent-like pattern.

Loops: Ridges that run from one side of the finger to the other but bend upwards like an upside-down "U" and may tilt to the left or right.

Whorls: Circles or spirals in the middle of the print that are disconnected from the ridges that run from side to side.

Composites: Combinations of the three, previous, basic patterns.

The Henry System is best used on sets of prints, all from one hand. The actual calculation is complicated and looks as if it were concocted by somebody who spent too much time out in the noonday sun. Even then, it doesn't produce a unique value for each set of prints. Instead, it gives a general classification that can be used to exclude a huge number of potential matches and allows an investigation to focus on the details of a more manageable collection of fingerprints.

The FBI began using a Henry-based system when it started, in the 1920s, to compile what would become a 200 million-plus collection of fingerprint cards from various agencies around the U.S. When a new set of prints arrived, they were categorized and filed. When a set of prints was to be matched, it would be categorized and, any one of hundreds of analysts (mostly women) would begin the work of comparing the fine details of individual fingers in hopes of finding that needle in a haystack made much more reasonable by the Henry Classification.

In the case described above, "a set" of Frank Naiberg's prints were lifted from a peroxide bottle found in the bedroom of his victim, Mary Wallace. Assuming the set was five good prints they could have been used by the FBI to match against the set Naiberg gave as the truck driver "Harry Harlan." Or, it could be that Naiberg had highly unusual fingerprints, such as perfectly vertical or horizontal ridges.

Whatever the case, Frank Naiberg's apprehension, trial, conviction, and execution for the seven-year-old murder of Mary Wallace is proof that, sometimes, things happen just like they do in the movies.

1945, February 16: Iwo Jima: 26,000+ total killed.

1945, April 1: Okinawa: 200,000+ total killed.

1945, May 8: Formal acceptance of Germany's surrender.

1945, August 6: Hiroshima: 100,000+ total killed.

1945, August 9: Nagasaki: 60,000+ total killed.

1945, August 15: Japan announces its intent to surrender.

1945, September 2: World War 2 ends with the formal acceptance of the Japanese surrender. The toll from military actions… Service: 24million+. Civilians: 4.5million+. Add the millions more killed in various genocides and the human race doesn't make a very good showing for itself. Does it?

1945, September 7, Saturday: Location: Lorain, C.I.O. Hall. Victim: Joseph L. Lasky. Lasky, 38, is a fireman on the B&O railroad. He dies September 10 at St. Joe's of a broken back sustained in a fight during an "end of the war party" at the C.I.O Hall. (*C.I.O. is either the "Congress of Industrial Workers," or "County Industrial Workers," depending on the article.*) Victim Lasky is found 5:00am in a courtyard beneath the hall's third floor by George Yepko who lives adjacent to the hall.

The March, 1946, Grand Jury investigates the matter. "We wish to further report that the grand jury has investigated the death of Joseph Lasky and at this time find there is insufficient evidence to determine the circumstances surrounding his death." Outcome: Unsolved.

1945, October 12, Friday: Location: Lorain, East 29th Street. Victim: Michael (Mike) Falls (Fallis) (57 of Lorain). Suspects: Haywood Donald (18 of Lorain) and Frank Haynes (20 of Lorain). While being robbed on east 29th Street, Lorain, victim steelworker Falls is struck over the head with an iron bar. He later dies of a fractured skull. Both Donald and Haynes are charged with first degree murder after making statements to the police. The November Grand Jury indicts both for murder in the first degree.

Frank Haynes declares poverty and is assigned recently discharged armed forces veteran Harold Ewing, of Elyria, as an attorney. Donald and Haynes both plead not guilty. Both change to guilty of manslaughter. The two had planned to rob the victim, but did not carry out the act once he was felled. It was Frank Haynes who struck the victim with the iron bar. Outcome: Both receive terms of 1-20 years in Mansfield, plus costs. Costs, when combined, are $55.95.

Haywood Donald is paroled on April 30, 1952.

October 24, 1945:

It's getting near the end of another long day for William "Bud" Heilmann, owner of a diner and sweet shop at East Erie and California in Lorain. A little before 10:00pm, the curly-headed and vivacious Helen Duffield makes an appearance—she always brightens things up. Bud's known Helen for about three years and considers her a friend. She's a regular customer: breakfast, lunch, and dinner. She always has a good appetite, but he knows she has to be careful with her diet because she has The Sugar.

She orders one of her favorites, a big "Dagwood Sandwich," plus a lunch to take home for her next day's work as a stenographer for the Lorain Products Company.

Bud and Helen talk a while. She's happily chatty, rambling a little about the return of her husband, Paul, who's served these past few years in the Pacific as a Navy radar operator. She tells Bud how she's recently moved out of Ruby Miller's place and back to her and Paul's pre-war home, a bungalow in the 2700 block of North Jefferson. Then, with a smile and a wave, Helen leaves the store at about 10:15.

Moments later there's a scream. Heilmann runs from his building. Across the street is a fairly late-model Buick coupe with someone, a woman, falling from the open driver's side door. Another scream. There's the flash and report of a single gunshot. Then another, maybe?

The traffic is too heavy for Bud to reach the car. Helpless, he watches as the hapless woman is pulled inside the vehicle and a hunched-over man appears from the passenger's side, quickly walks around the car, gets in the driver's side, and speeds east on Erie.

Two brothers in Heilmann's store, Jimmy and Paul Romoser (*initially "Redinoser" in the Elyria papers*) also hear the ruckus. Jimmy calls the cops. Paul jumps in his own car and takes off in pursuit.

They race east on Erie and take right on Kansas. Paul's keeping up, driving 80 miles per hour, and more. But once they make the left onto Colorado, that's all she wrote. The faster, more powerful Buick pulls away into the dark, continuing east towards Avon.

Harry Siegfield, 17, a bystander, is the only one capable of giving police a description of the killer. It's not much to go on. Medium height. Medium build. Good-looking. Dark, wavy hair. Dimples. Tan overcoat. Harry also tells police that a woman exited Heilmann's shop, crossed the street, and got into her car. The man then climbed into the vehicle from the passenger side. She tried to flee, but was pulled back in and shot at least once.

About forty-five minutes after the car-jacking, on the west side of Abbe Road, a little south of Detroit, Ellis Hoag (like Heilmann, also known as "Bud") comes across a Buick sitting a ways into the entrance of his family's commercial greenhouse. He exits his own car to investigate and is somewhat surprised to find the vehicle empty, but with its engine running. He walks around the automobile, stops, then returns to his office to call the police. Hoag tells them he's found a car, but there's more. There's also what looks like a body, half-submerged in the icy, water-filled ditch alongside the road.

Police arrive at the scene. The body is Helen Duffield (24), dead from four .25 caliber gunshots to her head and body. Detectives surmise the killer must've fled in a heck of a hurry since inside the Buick are a tan coat, a scarf, hat, a cameo ring, and a cigar lighter monogrammed with the initials "G.E.W." There are bloody fingerprints on the car's steering wheel. It is removed to be sent to the FBI in Washington, D.C., for examination and testing. There are also footprints, apparently from a man, who hurried northwest through Bud Hoag's asparagus patch.

At about 2:00am the next morning, October 25, Warren Crisp (21) is working third shift at the National Tube Company along the lake in east Lorain. A somewhat bloody and extremely muddy man appears out of the darkness to threaten him with a .25 caliber semi-automatic pistol. Crisp is astonished when he recognizes the nearly-crazed man as someone his sister dated, co-worker Gordon Wellman.

Crisp is forced to dress an injury on Wellman's hand. Then the gunman breaks into the locker used by Willie Katronica to steal a shirt, trousers, and coat. The gunman tells several men that he's already killed a girl, showing them the partially emptied clip in his firearm as proof, and states that he'd have no trouble killing anybody else who doesn't cooperate. Wellman takes a shower and changes into Katronica's clean clothes before forcing Crisp to burn the filthy, cast-off clothing. Wellman instructs another worker to buy him two sandwiches and a glass of milk at the Tube's cafeteria.

After his meal, Gordon Wellman takes the time to bury his pistol somewhere on Tube grounds before fleeing shortly after 5:00am. Warren Crisp then calls the cops.

Authorities are surprised by the news that their alleged killer is 23-year-old Gordon Wellman. Police know he served 10 months in the Chillicothe, Ohio, Federal Prison for forgery and transporting a stolen vehicle across state lines. But he's better known as the roommate of Ralph Brown, the recently condemned murderer of Helen Katonak (*see 1945, January 3*).

Wellman had been a prosecution witness at Brown's trial. What's more, it was only yesterday that Gordon Wellman appeared in Prosecutor Wickens' office looking for a suitcase that Ralph Brown had borrowed before killing his victim. At that time Wellman told Wickens that he needed the suitcase back because he was going away with a girl to get married. Could the now-dead Helen Duffield be that girl?

Police race to Wellman's Lorain boarding house in the 500-block of East Erie, where they find evidence of a hasty departure. Among the items retrieved is a letter from the condemned killer Ralph Brown that says, in part, that Wellman should "seek out God and correct your ways or you will end up here with me. Please don't put it off, but go to church someplace at once and ask the Lord to forgive you and repent. He is willing to forgive our sins."

Wellman's gun is recovered from its burial place at National Tube and matched to slugs taken from the body of the dead woman. Police are tipped off that Wellman boarded a Cleveland-bound bus several hours after the murder, about a block away from where the car-jacking had taken place. Two days later he's spotted in Portsmouth, Ohio, near his previous home in New Boston, Scioto County, along the Ohio River.

That same day Sergeant A.J. Lashley, of the Columbus Police, arrests Wellman as he walks down a street of that city with two women who turn out to be his sisters. "Good-looking, with dark, wavy hair and dimples" turns out to be an adequate description, as long as you've seen a photo.

There is still no clear motive for either the car-jacking or killing. Lorain Police Detective Vern Smith says he's working the theory that the killer was a suitor angered by the victim's preparations for her husband's return from duty in the Pacific. Smith has established that the victim and killer were well acquainted and "frequented the same places," but he has no actual proof that there was any affair taking place.

Detective Smith's theory is dismissed when, after his arrest, Wellman confesses to the crime. He says he wanted to elope, not with Duffield, but an 18-year-old Lorain woman that he refuses to name. He had stood across the street from Bud Heilmann's store for several nights in a row watching for a suitable victim. His choice of Helen Duffield was happenstance. They had no previous acquaintance. His only interest was her automobile.

In the car he threatened the woman with the gun, she fought back, and the weapon discharged accidentally. He commandeered the vehicle, and while eluding pursuit, happened to drive to the entrance of Hoag's Nursery on Abbe Road where he parked to think. Once there, he pulled the wounded, but still-living Helen Duffield from the automobile and tossed her into the water-filled ditch. He returned to the car to smoke a cigarette to calm his nerves and try to figure out what he should do next.

Wellman says the injured woman's moaning and gasps "disturbed him." So he returned to where she was floating, straddled the ditch, and killed her by firing a few more shots into her body. He panicked with the approach of Bud Hoag's car and fled on foot to the National Tube Company, where he entered the plant over a railroad bridge. There he forced a worker to dress a hand injury he had suffered while fleeing. Then he broke into a locker, obtained clean clothes and ordered the young man, under threat of death, to dispose of his cast-off, muddy, and bloodstained clothing.

He obtained food, took a shower, buried the gun, and returned to his boarding house where he remained until taking a bus to Cleveland. He continued by bus to Portsmouth to visit his mother. Then went on to Columbus where he was arrested Saturday night as he walked along the street with his two sisters.

Police say Wellman's confession is fully confirmed by the evidence they have on hand. He is charged with first degree murder and placed in a cell of his own at the Lorain County Jail where deputies check on his well-being every hour. The confessed killer behaves himself. The sheriff deems him "a good prisoner."

Wellman pleads not guilty to the charges. He also pleads indigence, he has no money for his defense. The court assigns him Lorain attorneys Walter Harland and Edward Conley, both fresh from military service.

The State is represented by Prosecutor Wickens and his assistant, Robert Vandemark. Wellman's criminal trial starts in front of Judge D.A. Cook on January 8, 1946. Proceedings are a sensation from the start with the courtroom packed. As usual, many spectators bring lunches so they don't need to abandon their seats at the noon recess.

A new system of calling people for jury duty is based on voter registration. It provides a more representative cross-section of citizens. But most of those called are unfamiliar with legal proceedings. This adds to the confusion and slows progress in seating jurors. It's clear that the prosecution is seeking the death penalty. So many prospective jurors are excused because of their opposition to electrocution that the court has to call an additional thirty people to seat the jury of four men and eight women.

In opening statements, the prosecution points to the killer's confession. They go through the crime, matching Wellman's statement to evidence. How, after the initial car-jacking and kidnapping on East Erie Avenue, Lorain, Wellman drove to Abbe Road where he shoved Helen Duffield into a ditch and deliberately killed her by firing bullets into her body. How, after being chased from the scene by an approaching car, Wellman fled and broke into the National Tube Company where he forced a young man to assist him. How he returned to his room in Lorain and then left town, and his flight and eventual arrest. To the State, there is no case more clear-cut. There is no question that Gordon Wellman is guilty of murder in the first degree. There is no question of premeditation. There is no question that Gordon Wellman deserves death.

In their opening, defense lawyers state that Wellman's original confession about eloping with an 18-year-old girl was false. It was the victim, Helen Duffield, that he was going to run away with. Wellman and the married Mrs. Duffield had been intimate. She was shot during a lover's quarrel. What took place was not premeditated, but the result of an argument and "hot blood." The original story about an 18-year-old was to protect Helen Duffield's reputation, but now that his own life was on the line, Gordon Wellman had decided to tell the whole and absolute truth. This line of defense throws the trial into a whole, new light, and sends the prosecution scrambling.

Throughout the remainder of the nine-day trial the focus of the State remains on the facts of the crime. But the defense works to plant seeds of doubt in the killer's previous statements about the lack of relationship he had with his victim.

Prosecution walks the jurors through the crime, verifying, step-by-step, the veracity of Wellman's initial confession and how it matches the facts at hand. Why would he tell the truth about every, single detail except his alleged relationship with his victim?

Besides witnesses to the crime and forensic experts, husband Paul Duffield (31) testifies for the prosecution. Gordon Wellman sits, looking at the floor with his hand to his face during the husband's testimony.

Described as "quiet mannered and calm under questioning," Paul Duffield testifies to being aboard ship in Okinawa when he received a radio message that his wife had died. How he didn't know until November 17, when he arrived in Lorain to find that she'd been murdered. Duffield says he and his wife, the former Helen Ireland, were married September 2, 1940. They purchased a four-room home on Jefferson Boulevard which Helen rented once he left for military service in June, 1943.

Helen had written to him daily, or every other day, during his time away, mentioning that she planned to move back into their home on Jefferson on October 19. She seemed happily anxious for him to return.

On cross, defense attorney Conley asks Paul Duffield if his wife had written that she was going out with other men. Did he know from any other source that she was stepping out? Did he know if his wife had gone to see any lawyers about getting a divorce? All of these questions are answered with a flat "no."

The prosecution continues to pound away on proving Wellman's original confession. On the stand, Mrs. Josephine Siegfried, a witness to the crime, says she saw a man shoot a woman and walk around the car, while putting the gun in his pocket. Her son, Harry, ran toward the car but the man look menacingly enough at him to make him take refuge behind a tree.

Mrs. Siegfried did not recognize Wellman at the time of the shooting because of darkness and distance but that she had noticed him standing in the doorway of the grocery at East Erie and Colorado Avenue on the two nights preceding the crime, as if he was watching for someone. She said she knew him because he had tried to rent a room at her house, but that she had sent him to Mrs. Murphy's home, nearby, where he'd taken up residence.

Mrs. Glen Murphy, of Lorain, related how Wellman had told her that he was leaving on October 25 to be married and that he was planning a honeymoon in Georgia. Mrs. Murphy collapses on the witness stand as she tells of how Wellman kept a gun in his room. Wellman had requested she call the police because he feared a man who was angry about his relations with the man's daughter. Murphy testifies that Wellman had a number of girlfriends and frequently received phone calls from young women.

Corwin Callatino, also a roomer at Mrs. Murphy's, said on the night of the killing, he had seen Wellman in a barbershop on East Erie. Wellman told him he was going to visit his girl and expected to see her around midnight. It was a short time later that Wellman shot Mrs. Duffield.

Julius Toth, of the Employees Transit Company in Lorain, testifies that he had sold Wellman 20 rounds of ammunition for a .25 caliber automatic pistol only a few days before the crime.

On January 14, FBI fingerprint expert M.C. Wilson is called to show that prints found on the steering wheel of Duffield's 1941 Buick belonged to Wellman. Judge D.A. Cook leaves his bench to stand by the jury box to watch the expert's testimony of how they obtained the bloody prints and the 12 points of similarity found between those prints and ones taken from the accused.

That same day ballistics expert, Cleveland Police Inspector David Cowels, shoots live rounds from the murder weapon into a steel cylinder lined with cotton to catch the slugs. "The crowded room of spectators, the majority of which were women, got a thrill. Several of the women screamed when the gun went off."

Inspector Cowels says the pistol lacks a safety and therefore is prone to firing if carried in a cocked position. Not only that, but to be fired, the weapon has to be manually cocked and that requires both hands. The State contends Cowels testimony proves that Wellman had to use both hands to use the pistol. There is no way it could have "gone off accidentally."

Wellman's former roommate Jack Volpe (23), who works at the Lorain Shipyard, testifies he and the accused had roomed together and were good friends until they had a "falling out" over Wellman threatening to kill him for a supposed debt. Volpe says Wellman told him that he loved "Lucille Gurstak" and that Lucille was the girl Wellman intended to marry and go away with the day of the killing. Volpe said that Wellman once said to him, when hearing something about Lucille being friendly with a merchant marine, that he would kill anyone he caught going with his girl. Volpe also told about how he and Wellman met Lucille Gurstak and one "Clara Kunaday" in Columbus, and then going to Portsmouth, Wellman's former home.

Cross examination reveals Volpe as discharged from the Navy after being court martialed. Volpe denies his discharge was dishonorable.

Another of Wellman's friends, Santo Russo, said that on October 21 Wellman showed him the murder weapon and said he was going to get a car, marry Lucille Gurstak, and go to Florida on October 25.

Lucille Gurstak, now 19 and a grocery store employee, is called to testify. She met Gordon Wellman in June, 1944, and went with him until August of 1945 when they broke up. She says he had proposed to her several times but that she repeatedly refused because she did not love him. When she told him she was going to marry someone else, he threatened that if he couldn't have her, nobody could. Another time, when he thought she was cheating, he slapped her a half-dozen times. He took her door key away from her saying, that without it, she couldn't stay out late with any other guy because she'd have to get home early while her landlady was still up.

Gurstak admits to the story of staying in a motel with Wellman, Volpe and Kunaday. She says Wellman had said to her the last time she refused to marry him that he would force her to her go with him. She said she knew he carried a gun and was scared of him.

When asked why she went around with such a violent man, Gurstak says Wellman is "good company until he gets jealous, and then he gets mean."

The last time she saw him was the Friday before the killing. She was driving her employer's grocery truck, saw him on the street, and gave him a ride home. At that time he told her he would meet her following her bowling session on Wednesday night, October 24, and that he'd have an automobile. He failed to show that night. The next morning, about 9:30, she received a phone call from him. He said he was in Cleveland. He apologized for not keeping their date and told her he would write to explain. Then he told her he had heard there had been a murder in Lorain and asked if she knew the victim and that was all that was said about it.

Gurstak testifies that she and Wellman were in a lunch room once when they saw Mrs. Duffield. Wellman had commented on how Duffield had told him she "wanted to get a man to drive her car" but the two made no recognition of each other that day.

On the stand, Clara Kunaday (19) tells how Wellman told her he wanted to marry Lucille and take her away. Kunaday said she knew Wellman carried a gun because she had seen him with it.

The State rests its case on January 16. Almost all of their entire last day is spent showing the jury crime scene photographs and reading parts of Gordon Wellman's confession. In resting his case, Prosecutor Wilkens flatly denies that Gordon Wellman and Helen Duffield were anything more than casual acquaintances. Wilkens states there is absolutely no evidence to corroborate Wellman's statement that the two were intimate.

The defense takes over. Since the State was allowed to read just selected parts of Wellman's statement, defense is allowed to do the same. Their case is only starting when the trial is halted for several minutes when a young man, about 20, standing near the rear of the courtroom, faints.

So many spectators are attending the trial that courthouse custodian, Albert Sperry, reports collecting "a bushel of cigarette butts a day."

> The proceedings… Packed 'em in better than "Oklahoma" and, even more, holds them spellbound and standing in the aisles from morning until night.
>
> Judge Cook likes his cigars as much as the spectators love cigarettes, but smoking is not allowed in the courtroom. But, the second recess is declared, spectators light up and smoke starts belching from the windows that are open like an old country smoke house.

Elyria has a smoking ordinance but it has apparently been forgotten in these busy times. As far as the fire hazard, well, there are some in the courthouse who are in favor of a new building. *The Chronicle-Telegram, January 17, 1946.*

The courtroom is jammed to the point of not even having standing room when a visibly nervous Gordon Wellman takes the stand January 17.

Wellman tells of his father, who was religious and strict, and then about his incarceration at 19 for auto-theft and forgery. He describes his discharge from the Army for theft and then being assigned to work in the Tube Mill by the U.S. Employment Service in Portsmouth, Ohio. He then talks of his relationship with Lucille Gurstak. How they had a "falling out," though they did occasionally go out together after that. He gave up any thought of marrying her because he knew she didn't love him.

He said he had dated Mildred Crisp (relative of Warren Crisp), who had testified about sending the accused several "amorous letters." When asked if he ever intended to marry Mildred, Wellman replies "that is absurd."

Gordon Wellman says he met Helen Duffield over time at Heilmann's. That she had told him she was working hard and was tired and wanted to "find a man to drive her car" for a trip to Cleveland. With Paul Duffield listening, Wellman tells of the relationship that grew between him and Helen. How they'd begun dating. The places they'd gone: A dinner party at the William Howard's. A place called "The Musical Bar" in Cleveland. How they'd spent V-J day together. Wellman's testimony about the day of shooting is delayed several times because he begins to cry, breaking down and weeping when asked to provide the details.

Mr. and Mrs. William Howard testify that Gordon Wellman had, in fact, brought a woman to their house in May of 1945 and introduced her as "Miss Duffield." And Miss Tony Cameron, vocalist at The Musical Bar in Cleveland testifies for the defense that she had seen Wellman in the bar with Duffield and that Duffield had lost a rhinestone bracelet.

Nonsense. All nonsense, says the prosecution. The State brings in the owners of "The Musical Bar" who say that witness Cameron wasn't even employed at the time in question. They produce Miss Margaret Pastulka, of Lorain, who testifies that it was her, not Helen Duffield, who had been in Cleveland with Wellman that night. It was Pastulka who lost the rhinestone bracelet. Pastulka also refutes Wellman's testimony that he had spent V-J day with Duffield, saying it was she, Pastulka, who was with Wellman "from 7:00pm until 3:00am the next morning."

But the defense contends killer and victim were lovers. The shooting was accidental. The fatal wounds George Wellman inflicted on Helen Duffield as she floated in the ditch on Abbe Road were made in mercy. "To put her out of her misery."

Judge Cook provides prosecution and defense a total of one hour, each, to make their final arguments. Neither side takes the whole time allotted.

Assistant Prosecutor Robert Vandemark makes sure the jury understands that "premeditation" does not mean days of planning, but can mean only a fraction of time. The law implies a killer "need only consider the results of the act before committing the crime." Wellman, Vandemark says, "knew when he left his rooming house that night and he put his gun in his pocket that there was going to be a killing."

Defense lawyer Conley points out that Wellman admits the killing, but that "it was purely the result of a lover's quarrel. She called him a foul name and slapped his face, and in the heat of that encounter she was shot." That, yes, Wellman dated a number of women but "that did not prove that Wellman was not familiar with Mrs. Duffield."

Conley speaks of Wellman as a boy. How he was kicked out of his home when he was 16. Then kicked out of the Army because of trouble there. He describes Wellman as being "stoned and pilloried" since his youth. Conley closes his argument with the Biblical admonition made by Jesus: "Let he who is without sin cast the first stone," adding, "don't throw any more stones at this boy."

Lawyer Walter Harlan concludes defense arguments by charging there was an illicit love affair between Gordon Wellman and Helen Duffield. Harlan then does a fine job of blaming the victim by stating that, Duffield would still be alive if only she had remained true to her marriage vows. "This case does not warrant the death penalty," says Harlan. "This boy is entitled to his life."

Prosecutor Wickens concludes the arguments by pointing to Paul Duffield. Wickens says it is Duffield and other men in the armed services who fight to preserve a system whereby law and order is maintained. That the jurors in this case have the responsibility of seeing that law and order prevail. "By all the tests and the evidence, this was a deliberate and premeditated murder."

"There are two Gordon Wellmans," Wickens sneers. "The cringing, cowardly type you saw on the witness stand yesterday, and the other, the swaggering bully, who has no regard for life and who has the heart of the killer. Helen Duffield saw that other side." It makes no difference to the law if he knew Helen Duffield or not. "He killed her and he did it deliberately and with premeditation, and that is all the jury has to know." Gordon Wellman's first story is the truth, but during his three weeks in jail he thought it over and changed it and said that he'd been intimate with an innocent woman he hardly knew if at all. "He changed that story because he thought that if he cheapened and defamed Helen Duffield that he might save his own cheap soul. This is not a case for mercy. He granted none. He is unworthy of any recommendation of mercy."

The jury is charged at 1:00pm on January 19. They have their own struggles, asking to have the Court Recorder read back part of the testimony of Warren Crisp who was the first person to talk to Wellman after the murder. They also ask for reinstruction on the legal meaning of "premeditation."

The verdict comes in eight hours later, at 9:00 that night. When Gordon Wellman stands for judgement "his lips tremble and his hands shake, although his right wrist is still shackled to Deputy Sheriff Charles K. Mack."

Judge Cook asks jury foreman Theodore Johnson for the verdict. Johnson replies, "guilty of murder in the first degree with a recommendation of mercy." Some of the jurors are clearly angry at the outcome, but when questioned by Prosecution Assistant Vandemark, all say they agree.

Judge Cook does not criticize the decision but says to Wellman, "The jury has been generous to you in this verdict." Cook then asks the guilty man if he has anything to say. Wellman stands mute until his attorney, Edward Conley, whispers to him to say something to thank the court and the jury. Wellman mumbles "I thank the court and the jury."

Judge Cook then sentences Gordon Wellman to life in the Ohio Penitentiary in Columbus to begin immediately. Following sentencing, Cook takes the unusual step of officially commenting on the case by announcing from the bench that the evidence presented in this case completely cleared Mrs. Paul Duffield of any mark against her character.

Paul Duffield is not there to hear Judge Cook's statement. The widower had attended the entire trial and had previously stated he felt his wife was vindicated by the testimony, but he misses the verdict and sentencing.

Wellman's sister Thoma and brother, Lester, a soldier, are present at the trial's end. Both siblings say they are grateful for the verdict. Thoma embraces Gordon in the hall and the two weep. Lester returns to the family in New Boston, Ohio; Thoma, to Columbus, Ohio, where she lives.

After being discharged, Jury Foreman Theodore Johnson describes the jurors as deeply divided and the verdict as a compromise. Johnson says that at one point there were two for manslaughter, two for second degree murder, two for life, and six for the death sentence.

Another juror reports that an even dozen ballots were taken and that almost all of the discussion centered around whether Wellman would be put to death. In the end eight were for death and four for life. They decided to agree on a life sentence rather than have the case become a mistrial.

Perhaps it's an indication of how lucky the defense considers itself that there is no motion for a retrial and no appeal of sentence. Wellman's lawyers ask for $2,670.66 for their work. The court gives them $900. Costs for court are $738.48.

1946, February 9, 7:07pm: Ohio Penitentiary lifer Gordon Wellman, knowing how close he came to meeting the same fate, watches as his former roommate, Ralph Brown, is executed in Ohio's electric chair for the murder of Helen Katonak. Twenty minutes later, murderer Frank Naiberg, also from Lorain County, is sent to meet his Maker in a similar fashion. Wellman knows if the majority of jurors had managed to sway the minority in the case of Helen Duffield, he might have followed up twenty minutes after that.

1969, December: Gordon Wellman's sentence comes up for review. It is revealed that, during his time in the penitentiary, the prisoner has sent repeated threats against the lives of those involved in the investigation and prosecution of his case, including then Sheriff Vernon M. Smith. Through the papers, Smith says:

> This isn't just talk in his case. With 34 years in the field of law enforcement, I have never had cause to fear any threats expressed by persons sent [to prison] on evidence I compiled, the one exception being Wellman.

> I remain convinced that upon his release, Wellman's one objective will be to carry out his repeatedly expressed intentions to murder this writer. *The Chronicle-Telegram, December 4, 1969.*

Gordon Wellman is eventually released from prison after serving more than a half-century. He does not make good on his threats. He dies in Portsmouth, Ohio, on June 5, 2000 at the age of 78.

This is the first Lorain County murder trial that fingerprints are used as evidence, beating Frank Naiberg's trial (described just above) by four months.

FEMICIDE: The killing of women. Could also be termed: GYNECIDE, GYNAECIDE, or GYNOCIDE.

1945, November 26: *The Chronicle-Telegram:*
    Beautiful Home and Grounds Offered to City:
    Judge and Mrs. Guy B. Findley have offered to give to the city for park purposes their home and attached garage and service building. The buildings are situated in a 41-acre wooded tract along a beautiful ravine and adjoins on the east side of Abbe road with a 19-acre tract on the west side of the road which they gave to the city in 1936 for park purposes. Their gift is subject to their life use of the $65,000 property, during which time they will pay the taxes and upkeep.

1945, December 3: *The Chronicle-Telegram:*
    New Drug Promises Relief For Hay Fever And Allergies:
    Relief for hayfever sufferers and victims of asthma, hives and other allergies is promised in a new drug, Benadryl, announced today by the University of Illinois School of Medicine.
    The drug was said by its discoverer, Dr. Earl R. Loew, associate professor of pharmacology at the University, to bring relief in 30 to 60 minutes.
    Dr. Loew said the new compound prevents ill effects from histamine, a chemical released by the body cells during an allergic attack and considered the cause of allergy symptoms. Loew said that one out of every 10 persons suffers from one of the major allergies.
    Dr. Loew emphasized that experiments with the new drug assured marked symptomatic relief but promised no cure. He estimated that three doses daily, would be necessary for continued relief.
    The anti-histaminic properties of the drug first were demonstrated by Dr. Loew in 1943 and first produced by Dr. George Rieveschi Jr., of the Parke-Davis Laboratories in Detroit.
    The drug, known chemically B-dimethly-amincethyl Benzhydryl ether hydrocholoride, has not yet been released for general use.

1945, December 11: *The Chronicle-Telegram:*

Fate Of 27 Navy Airmen Unsolved:

The Navy listed as an unsolved, mystery today the fate of 27 Navy airmen who disappeared aboard six planes off the Florida coast.

Naval officials called off its greatest peacetime search party yesterday when planes and surface craft reported they had found no trace of the missing planes.

Five of the planes carrying 14 men were missing on a routine training flight since last Wednesday. The sixth plane, a Mariner patrol bomber, disappeared with 13 men aboard during the early hours of the search for the other planes.

1945, December 29: Dr. Perry, Lorain County Coroner from 1920 to 1930 has decided to retire from practice and retire to St. Petersburg, Florida. He's a dentist.

1946: Tonka Trucks. Syria becomes independent when France withdraws her troops. Britain establishes medical care for the sick, old, and unemployed. Hirohito says he ain't divine with General Douglas MacArthur helping him to realize that fact. France and the Vietminh start fighting the Indochina War. Churchill coins the phrase "Iron Curtain." Steven Spielberg is born in Cincinnati, Ohio. 6 lynchings: 6 Blacks, 0 others.

1947: "It Is Certain" with the Magic 8-Ball. The National Tube Company recruits 500 workers from Puerto Rico. Jackie Robinson becomes Major League Baseball's first Black player, sort of (*see 1856*). The C.I.A. is formed, at least that's the rumor. Truman says we'll help any country fighting Communism. Britain divides what was India along sectarian lines with Muslim Pakistan led by Mohammed Ali Jinnah and Hindi and Sikh India with Jawaharlal Nehru as Prime Minister. The United Nations proposes partitioning Palestine into separate Arab and Jewish states. Terry Anderson is born in the City of Lorain. He'll grow to be a journalist but gains unwanted fame when taken hostage by Iranians in 1985 and is held until 1991. 1 lynching. 1 Black. 0 others.

1947, January 2, Thursday:

It's late morning. Russia Township brothers, John (13) and Nick (14) Yacysyn are making a visit to 79-year-old James "Josh" Peters. They like the old man with his stories and such, but are kind of afraid of him, too. Their mom always makes sure they never visit without somebody else along. Not that Josh would ever do anything bad... it's, well, it's that he's a little odd is all, living alone like he does in his boxcar home near the railroad crossing on Butternut Ridge.

Josh earns his living doing odd jobs for area farmers. One thing he's good at is butchering animals. In fact, that's why the Yacysyn boys are on their way over, to pay him for slaughtering a goat. The kids figure the money will go into that big pile of cash that everyone says the old man carries.

The recluse doesn't respond to their repeated knocks, but the door's unlocked. The boys figure, maybe, they'll leave the money inside where it'll be safe. They push their way into the boxcar to find Josh dead and frozen stiff beside an unlit woodstove. He's been gone long enough that rats have worked their way along the right side of his face.

The boys run the whole way home to tell their folks.

Police take the body to the Sedgeman Funeral Home in Oberlin. Undertaker G.H. Cowling begins preparation of the remains and is shocked to discover that the wound in the dead man's face is full of wadding and pellets. The old man wasn't chewed by rodents after his death from exposure, he was shot-gunned at close range.

Authorities begin their investigation. They quickly decide the victim did not commit suicide since there is no similar weapon at the scene. Despite the rumors of the old man carrying large amounts of money, not much is found in the boxcar. A search turns up two empty pocketbooks along with a third that contains $26.

The date of death is fixed as December 23 or 24 by the frozen condition of the body and the fact Peters had not been seen since December 23. His last known visitor was 30-year-old labor foreman George Payne of the 200-block of Spring Street, Oberlin.

Prosecutor William Wickens has Payne arrested after receiving the ballistics report on the pellets found in the victim's face. It seems Payne owns a matching-gauge shotgun. Investigators check for, but fail to find any sudden influx of money into their suspect's life.

The father of four vehemently denies any wrongdoing. Defense lawyers Adams and Adams insist their client be allowed to take a lie detector test, which he passes. On January 31, 1947, Assistant Prosecutor Robert Vandemark drops the charges against Payne and he is released. The investigation, it is promised, will continue. Outcome: The case is unsolved.

1947, February 8, Saturday, 3:15am: Location: Elyria, 20-block Chestnut Street. Victim: Beulah Simmons (29). Suspect: Robert Bowens (24, of Elyria). Simmons and Bowens have previously lived in common law marriage. In 1944, she presses charges against him for disorderly conduct for which he is fined $10 and costs. They continue to live together but have frequent, violent arguments. In one, Miss Simmons takes a stab at the suspect's head with an ice pick and misses "by only an inch."

Suspect Bowens tips off police about a card game where heavy gambling is taking place. Police make a raid in which victim Simmons is present. She and Bowens then quarrel. Bowens fatally stabs Simmons and is held in the county jail without bail.

February Grand Jury: Bowens is indicted on murder in the first degree. Plea: Not guilty. *Changed to:* Guilty of murder in the second degree. At sentencing, defense lawyer Basil Dziama says the guilty man is a "victim of circumstances that could not help but lead to violence." Outcome: Life in the Ohio Penitentiary at Columbus, plus court costs of $65.30.

1947, November 28, Friday, 5:25pm: Location: Lorain, 1760 Elyria Avenue, "in front of the Rocky River Café." Victim: Willie Butler (45). Suspect: Thomas A. White, Jr. (28) of Akron. The victim and suspect quarrel over a card game. Victim Butler throws a snow shovel at White, narrowly missing him. Both men leave the scene.

Suspect White, on parole from Summit County, Ohio, but living in Lorain, goes to his home and retrieves his revolver. Upon returning, he finds Butler in front of the Rocky River Café and opens fire striking Butler several times. The December, 1947, Grand Jury indicts White on a charge of murder in the first degree. Trial scheduled for January 22, 1948. The accused pleads not guilty. *Changed to:* Guilty of manslaughter. Outcome: Sentence by Judge D.A. Cook: Ohio Penitentiary—indeterminate term of 1-20 years, plus court costs of $88.48.

1948: The Cleveland Indians win the World Series! Fans hoping for a repeat are in for a loooooong wait. Conditions in the Ohio Penitentiary improve, but the food is horrible and stays that way for a long, long time. Alfred Butts'

Scrabble. Cootie! Gandhi is assassinated by a Hindu extremist during a prayer meeting. The Communists take over in Czechoslovakia. Israel proclaims its independence and displaces 700,000 Palestinians. The U.N. moderator in Palestine, Folke Benadotte, proposes a peace plan involving partitioning. He is assassinated by the Zionist group, Lehi, which opposes the plan. The Muslim Brotherhood strikes out against Egyptian and British troops. Britain's National Health service provides free medical and dental care to its entire population. The Soviets pull out of "their" half of North Korea and Kim Il Sung becomes Prime Minister. The Soviets blockade Berlin. The west begins flying in needed supplies. The DTP (diphtheria, tetanus, and pertussis) vaccine. In the Docket: Concealed Carry. Harry Truman (Missouri Democrat) wins the Election with 49.6% of the popular vote. California is the second U.S. state to legalize marriage between Blacks and Whites. Ohio was the first—*in 1887!* 2 lynchings: 1 Black, 1 other.

1948, April 7, Wednesday:

Thirteen-year-old David Leonard crawls out of bed at 4:00am and heads to the bathroom. He notices a light on in the kitchen. There he finds his mother, Frances Leonard (39), on the floor with a gunshot wound. The bullet fired into her forehead exited her left temple. The projectile is found embedded in a cupboard door. A semi-automatic pistol is on the floor beside her. The clip is in it, but the weapon is dead empty.

Police are called to the home in the 1000-block of Leavitt Road, Lorain. The fully clothed victim is rushed to St. Joseph Hospital where she dies at 5:45am without regaining consciousness.

Besides young David, police find in the house David's friend, Paul Driscoll (12), who is staying overnight, the victim's daughter, Phyllis (8), and Uncle Clarence Daniels (who is deaf). All claim they were asleep when David discovered his wounded mother.

There is a single plate of spaghetti and one cup of coffee on the kitchen table. A packed lunch sits nearby. Her car, a 1940, gun-metal gray Plymouth, is gone.

Investigation reveals that Frances Leonard, widowed for one year, was employed by the National Tube as a housing agent. After work on the night of her death, she visited the Saxon Club in Lorain at Apple Avenue and East 29th. Leaving there, she proceeded to the Liedertafel Club on Apple near 23rd for a couple beers and arrived home sometime later. The working theory of the Lorain Police is that she was murdered by a jilted lover.

Alex Lengyel (19) arrives at Lorain Police Headquarters about 5:00pm the day of Frances Leonard's death. He says that he was with the victim moments before the shooting, but that he has committed no crime.

His story: Mrs. Leonard had picked him up at 10:42pm, the end of his workday as a crane-man at the National Tube. They went to her home. Then to her bedroom. The teenager gives vague and contradictory details of their time there together.

Lengyel takes pains to make one point perfectly clear, and that is the pistol belonged to the victim. They had taken it from her bedroom. He had shot it out-of-doors, then removed the clip, and returned both the weapon and the clip to her. He then started for home, walking about "a mile towards the Nickle Plate" before discovering he had forgotten his own lunchbox. Returning to the Leonard house, he found Frances on the floor apparently dead from a gunshot wound to the head.

The young man says he panicked. He took his things and fled the scene in her car, driving around for the rest of the day, trying to figure out what to do. He finally abandoned the automobile on East 34th Street, near Vine, and turned himself in to police.

Lengyel says that both of them believed the weapon to be unloaded. They didn't know there was a bullet still in the chamber. He figures Frances Leonard, in placing the empty clip back into the pistol, somehow managed to accidentally shoot herself in the forehead. It's a story he sticks to, even after hours of questioning. Police hold the young man while arranging for a lie detector test, which he passes.

Outcome: Though the story is vague, it is the opinion of examining doctors and police authorities that it is, in fact, the truth. Alex Lengyel is released without charge.

Young Alex eventually marries and has a son, but dies at the age of 49 "following an illness of several weeks."

1948, June 1, Tuesday:

It's about 9:30 of a pleasant June evening. Jim Bohach (39) and his 9-year-old, Eugene, return to their home in the 3800-block of Clifton Avenue, near South Lorain, after a walk to a neighborhood store for the essentials: milk, beer, and ice. The house is quite. That's kind of unusual for a Tuesday night since there are plenty of radio shows that Jim's wife, Margaret, enjoys. The two call for her. There is no answer.

Jim tells his son to stay put and then climbs the stairs to their bedroom.

There on the floor, the husband finds his wife wounded in the head. Beside her is his nine-shot .22 caliber revolver. Jim hurries downstairs. Father and son run to the home of a neighbor, Mrs. Jane Fox, and tell her that it looks like Margaret has shot herself.

Police find no evidence of an intruder or a struggle. There is one discharged cartridge in an otherwise full set of chambers. It looks as if 34-year-old Margaret Bohach chose to end her own life. But Deputy Sheriff Howard Van Buren has two big reasons to turn up his nose at the suicide angle: first, there are no powder burns on the victim's head; second, the victim was right-handed and that makes the single, supposedly self-inflicted wound behind the left ear about as unlikely as it could possibly be.

There's also the Bohach's marital history. Jim and Margaret were married in Napoleon, Henry County, Ohio, on September 6, 1943. By April of 1948 she had filed for divorce, charging that she'd been beaten several times, had her life threatened, and that her husband refused to earn a living, choosing instead to force the family to live on what she made at The National Tube Company.

Her allegedly-brutal husband had recently found a job as a janitor in a Lorain clothing store at $30 a week and they had reconciled, apparently. But Mrs. Fox, the next-door neighbor, tells police that Margaret said she was, once again, planning on leaving her husband. The day of her intended departure was June 1st. The day she was found shot dead.

With means, motive, and opportunity in his pocket, Deputy Van Buren arrests Jim Bohach on suspicion of murder. When confronted with what police know, it takes fewer than 20 minutes of questioning for Bohach to confess. Turns out, he is the first murder suspect in Lorain County to have his deposition taken by both a human being and a wire recorder.

Bohach's story: He starts with the fact that he hasn't had the best of luck with his marriages. A friend introduced him to his first wife, Irene, who died shortly after giving birth to Eugene. He met wife number two in 1943 through a lonely-hearts correspondence club. Francis Cushman of Pennsylvania had traveled to Ohio to marry him when authorities discovered that she was already hitched to a Pennsylvania coal miner and arrested her for attempted bigamy. The woman was released on probation to return to her home state and care for her family. Bohach returned once again to lonely hearts correspondence. That's where he met Margaret from New York state. He pointedly asked her if she was then or had ever been married. She assured him that she had always been single. The two were married, as police already knew, in September of 1943.

Immediately after her suing for divorce this past April and throughout their reconciliation, Bohach says he went back to the lonely hearts club and started writing to a woman in Imlay City, near the base of Michigan's "thumb." He says he is sure Margaret knew nothing of the correspondence between him and the Michigan woman, just as he had no idea that Margaret was planning to leave him, as Mrs. Fox, the neighbor, told police.

Bohach says he and his wife had fought the night of the killing. The shooting had taken place when, in the heat of an argument, she called him a "Bluebeard."

It wasn't the first time she had compared him to the legendary villain who disposed of multiple partners. Says Bohach, "I always got very mad over that when she called me this name." He grabbed his .22 revolver from the dresser planning to kill himself. Margaret rushed him and he accidentally fired at her instead.

"I had the gun and pulled back the trigger. She had her back partly turned from me. The gun discharged and I shot her. I was about two or three feet away." The projectile struck his wife behind her left ear and she dropped, dead, to the floor. Bohach attempted to arrange his wife's body on the floor and dropped the gun by her right side. "I must have been in a daze, because I don't remember too well."

He gathered his 9-year-old and suggested they go to the boy's grandmother, Mrs. Mary Bohach, who was staying at the David Krause residence on Arkansas Avenue in Lorain. It was after that visit that he and Eugene had stopped by the store and then returned to their own home to "find" Margaret's body.

It's the first time a Lorain County Grand Jury is able to hear a killer's confession in his own voice as the wire recording is played back by Assistant Prosecutor Richard Horan.

Sheriff Carl R. Finnegan says he prefers the charge to be murder in the first degree. Defense attorney Charles Adams disagrees, saying a study of the crime shows no premeditation, warranting a second degree plea. He adds that it's his opinion that James Bohach is not mentally well, but could not be called insane under the legal definition of the term.

The Grand Jury indicts Bohach for murder in the second. Bohach pleads guilty. Judge D.A. Cook accepts the plea, in part, because Prosecutor William G. Wickens and Assistant Horan "would not take it were it not proper."

Bohach is calm as he is sentenced to life in the Ohio Penitentiary plus court costs of $53.79.

His son, Eugene grows up to be Lorain steel worker. He marries and has a family of his own.

1948, June 1, Tuesday: Location: Lorain, Central Lorain Café. Victim: Salmon Dixon, of the 1400-block Broadway, Lorain. Suspect: Neal Rhodes (36), of the 200-block 14th Street, Lorain. Suspect Rhodes stabs victim Dixon in the midst of a card game during a quarrel over who was going to pay for the drinks. Rhodes claims he stabbed in self-defense after Dixon pulled a knife. Charge: Murder in the first degree. Plea: Not guilty. *Changed to:* Guilty of murder in the second degree. Outcome: Mandatory sentence by Judge D.A. Cook: Life in the Ohio Penitentiary, plus court costs of $42.65.

1948, June 11: Acting on tips that conditions in the Lorain County Jail are less than ideal, the Grand Jury makes an unannounced inspection of the facility. They are "assaulted by foul odors" and find "dirt, filth, and vermin" in both the women's and men's quarters. The lockup is filthy. "The mattresses were black, toilets unclean, walls very dirty, and the hall covered with tin cans, bread, rubbish, etc." Said one juror, "It is no fit place for human beings no matter what their offense might be."

1948, June 29: *The Chronicle-Telegram:*

> More Cells To Be Added To Death Row:
>
> A shortage of cells in death row at Ohio penitentiary has forced an expansion of the 14-cell area where prisoners awaiting death in the electric chair are held, Warden Ralph W. Alvis disclosed today.
>
> "We're filled up now, and inclinations are we will be needing more cells in the immediate future" Alvis said. "In view of this, seven more cells are being readied to take care of the record-breaking number of condemned killers now on, or passing through, that gloomy corridor of death."
>
> Two tiers of cells, seven in a row, house the condemned prisoners in the penitentiary's "L" block and annex. The new quarters will be added on top of the present two tiers, Alvis said.

1948, November 14, Sunday, about 11:45 pm: Location: Elyria, Mrs. Ruth Sharp's Rooming house, RD2 Linwood Street. Victim: Daniel Chunn (28). Suspect: John H. Roach (30). Victim Chunn is single, a native of Decatur, Alabama, who arrived in the area about two years back. He works for the Holmes Construction Company of Lorain. He and suspect Roach, an Elyria foundry worker, live in Mrs. Sharp's Rooming house. The two men are drinking together when they argue. Roach strikes Chunn over the left ear with a thrown bottle.

During the ruckus Mrs. Sharp, the boarding house keeper, runs into her own room and locks the door out of fear. She emerges a short while later to find Chunn on the floor, moaning and bleeding from the head with Roach standing over him. Roach remains motionless for a few moments before fleeing the scene. Mrs. Sharp then hurries to the home of neighbor Gussie Smallwood. Charles Blair and Emil Brazil, both of West River, take Chunn to Elyria Memorial Hospital where he dies at 12:53am, November 15, from a stab wound to the left temple.

Deputies say the wound indicates the stabbing may have been done with an icepick. A search finds the weapon—a knife with a thin, 5-inch blade. Police in Elyria and Lorain search for Roach but cannot find him. Justice James Horn puts out a warrant for the suspect. A statewide bulletin is released. Deputy Sheriff Albert McWilliams seeks an indictment against the suspect so that the FBI may be brought into the search. The case is continued until March 11, 1955, when it is nollied by the Prosecutor due to the death of an unnamed material witness and the fact that Roach is never apprehended. Outcome: Unresolved.

1949: Get a Clue, Candy Land. After defeat by the Communist Chinese, Chiang Kai-shek leaves mainland China to set up his government on the island of Taiwan. Meanwhile, in Beijing (or "Peking" as the west used to call it), Mao Zedong announces the People's Republic of China. NATO is born. Nelson Mandela becomes a force to be reckoned with. Eire is renamed the Republic of Ireland and severs ties with the British Government. Britain declares Northern Ireland will remain British. The Ohio General Assembly authorizes the formation of the Ohio Turnpike Commission. The roadway will be named after the first chairman of the commission, James W. Shocknessy. In the Docket: Concealed Carry. 3 lynchings: 3 Blacks, 0 others.

1949, January 4, Tuesday: *The Chronicle-Telegram:*

Man Believed To Have Shot His Wife Dies:

LORAIN—Homicide and suicide was expected to be the final entry of police in the slaying of Mrs. Katie Cimesa, 44, Wednesday, a result of the death in St. Joseph's Hospital at 9:45 p.m. yesterday and of her husband, Samuel, 57.

The daughters of Mrs. Cimesa, Mary, 24, and Velma, 17, found their mother dead on the living room floor when they returned home Wednesday afternoon, and their stepfather mortally wounded on the couch. Several bullets found about the new and neatly kept home indicated a wild shooting affray. Police said the shooting occurred Wednesday morning.

Cimesa told police before he lapsed into a coma that two masked men entered the home and shot them. Police found his own revolver in a drawer with some of its shells discharged and blood on the gun. It was a 38.

Evidence led police to conclude however, that Cimesa shot his wife and then shot himself. An examination of bullets taken from her body and also from his body will be made, Lieut. Det. Vernon Smith said, as a routine check on whether his gun or some other gun was used.

Police had placed a first degree murder charge against Cimesa following the shooting.

Funeral services for Mrs. Cimesa were set for Monday.

Other newspaper articles have the name as "Cimasce."
I wonder who put the revolver back in its drawer after both of these people were shot—the mortally wounded Mr. Cimesa?

1949, September 17, Saturday, Early Morning: A man's body is found in a Lorain alley off Livingston Avenue, near Broadway and 17th. Head beaten, throat slashed, wallet empty, shoes removed. The victim is identified as Alan F. Feeley (45). A manager for a Cleveland finance company, Feeley had moved from that city to work in a local branch office just two weeks prior to his violent death. Quite a welcome.

Police work the area looking for witnesses: apartments, late-night businesses, houses, questioning people of both good and questionable repute, anybody who might've seen or heard anything unusual the night of the crime.

Police question seventeen possible suspects in the first few days of the investigation. None of them pan out. As far as a killer goes, authorities are left empty-handed. The Lorain County Commissioners put up a reward of $1,000 for those providing information leading to the arrest and conviction of the killer. It's no help.

In April of 1950, seven months after the crime, Lorain Vice Squad Inspector Maurice Mumford and Patrolman Michael Dernyan are approached by an irate Thelma Evans. The 28-year-old tells Mumford and Dernyan that Clevelander James "Kilrock" Winston is the man they should be looking for in connection with the death of Alan Feeley. She also makes it clear that, while the reward money would be nice, the reason she's ratting out Winston is because of his rude treatment of her. (Woman scorned and all that.)

Acting on that tip, Winston (47) is arrested on April 13, 1950, in his Cleveland rooming house at 3839 Central Avenue. He's hauled into the April Lorain County Grand Jury. Material witnesses Thelma Adams, Paul "Pretty Papa" Berry of Lorain, and William Banks of Baton Rouge, Louisiana, are held in the Lorain County Jail to prevent flight. Police know William Banks owned the knife Winston used to cut Feeley's throat.

James Winston is indicted for murder in the first degree. His criminal trial is scheduled for May 15, 1950. He pleads innocent of any charges when arraigned before Judge D.A. Cook. He also claim indigence. The court assigns defense attorneys Robert Corts of Elyria and Basil Dziama of Lorain.

At the start of his criminal trial, after jury selection begins, Winston and his lawyers decide to go with a three-judge panel. The plea is changed to guilty of the general charge of homicide with the judges to decide the degree.

Three days later, May 18, Judges D.A. Cook and Guy B. Findley of Lorain County, and H.E. Culbertson of Ashland gather to hear testimony.

Defense attorney Dziama starts off with a bang when he reveals that William Banks, presently held as a witness against Winston, was actively involved in the crime. This is the first anybody besides defense has known this.

Winston's story: He and Banks had been drinking in the Black Diamond Cafe near the scene of the crime. They came across Alan Feeley, drunk in the alley, and decided to rob him for gambling money.

William Banks took hold of Feely. Winston went through the victim's pockets. Feeley broke free and struck Banks, who took a knife from his pocket, handed it to Winston and told him to cut their victim. Winston said he was drunk and didn't know what he was doing. He complied when Banks told him to cut Feeley, but he never meant to kill the man.

Prosecutor Paul J. Mikus with assistants Harold Ewing and James Christie scoff at this. "Winston said he did not intend to kill Feeley," Mikus says. "[Yet,] He cut his throat."

Witnesses Paul Berry and Thelma Evans tell the court that Winston had told them about the crime immediately after committing it. Berry says he did not believe the story until Winston drove him to the scene and showed him the lifeless body there in the alley.

The State does not argue for the death penalty because of Winston's "frank admission of slashing the throat of the victim when he resisted robbery." (The truth doesn't always set you free. Sometimes all it does it keep your butt the heck out of the electric chair!)

The judges find James Winston guilty of murder in the first degree with mercy, and sentence him to life in the Ohio Penitentiary, plus costs of $90.34. Winston shows little emotion at the pronouncement.

Thelma Evans and Marshall Berry are released at the close of the Winston's trial but former witness William Banks (26) is held on a charge of murder. He is indicted by the May Grand Jury for his part in the killing of Alan Feeley. Banks tries to plead guilty of murder in the second, but that is refused.

Banks' criminal trial begins June 13, 1950, represented by Charles F. and Lon B. Adams. Like Winston, Banks enters a general plea of guilty of homicide and will let a 3-judge panel decide the degree of the crime.

James Winston is brought back from the Ohio Penitentiary to serve as a State witness. The prosecution also brings in 29-year-old Martha Selvage (by plane!) from Baton Rouge, Louisiana, and hold her in the county jail. Also called is Mrs. Teresa Hogan (aunt of Banks) of the 2300-block of East Avenue, Lorain.

William Banks has the same judges as Winston: D.A. Cook and Guy B. Findley of Lorain County and H.E. Culbertson of Ashland.

Banks' story: He came to Lorain in 1947 because he heard that's where he could find good jobs at good wages. He met James Winston the night of September 16, 1949, while gambling at the Black Diamond pool room in Lorain, on Broadway, near 15th. While there Winston borrowed his knife—that is Winston already had the knife when they encountered the victim. Banks says they left the pool hall and that it was Winston who saw and approached Alan Feeley in the alley off 17th. Banks went into the alley to see what Winston was doing and was handed an empty wallet that Winston had taken from the victim.

Winston struck Feeley to the ground and removed his shoes to see if money was hidden in them. While the victim was on the ground, Winston took the knife he had borrowed earlier and used it to slash Feeley's throat. At that point, Banks testifies, he turned and ran from the scene. James Winston called Banks up short, saying he was just as much in it as Winston was.

Banks, then afraid of both arrest and Winston, fled to Louisiana where he was apprehended in Baton Rouge, his former home.

Mrs. William Banks testifies she and her husband, the accused, had three children with another due in five months and that Banks had always been good to her and maintained steady employment following his discharge from the service.

Not so fast, says Prosecutor Mikus. His witness, Martha Selvage says that's not what Banks had told her, at all, as far as the murder went.

Selvage testifies that William Banks was living with her in Lorain after Mrs. Banks returned to Baton Rouge. At the time of the killing, Banks said he and James Winston had killed a man. That made Banks an accomplice and not a person who happened to stumble into a crime. James Winston backed that up, saying yes, he was the knife-wielder, but that it was Banks who held Feeley. It was Banks who had the idea to cut the victim.

The judges find William Banks guilty of murder in the first degree with a recommendation of mercy. He is sentenced to life in the Ohio Penitentiary on May 9, 1950.

The considerable reward is claimed by Thelma Evans and Marshall Berry—both of whom were held in jail for 45 days as material witnesses for the trial of James Winston.

1958, July 7: James Winston, 57 (say the papers), dies in the penitentiary "of natural causes."

1968, March 31: William Banks, 46, dies in the penitentiary after contracting pneumonia following a dining-hall stabbing by Robert Wynn, 33, a second degree murderer from Hamilton County, Ohio. Banks' cellmate, Jesse Scott, 19 was also stabbed, but survived. "The motive was reported to be jealousy over the friendship between the two victims."

1950 – 1956: County Population = 148,162

1950: British researchers Austin Hill and Richard Doll link lung cancer to smoking. It takes a half a century for tobacco companies to admit the fact. Senator Joe McCarthy hunts for Commies in the U.S. Government. Remember how Tibet declared its independence with the fall of China's Emperor? Seems like China wasn't keen on the idea, so they invade. The Korean War, aka the "Fatherland Liberation War." Various uncoordinated hate groups begin using the name "Ku Klux Klan." During an assassination attempt on President Truman, White House Policeman Leslie Coffelt is killed. The surviving attacker is sentenced to death. Truman commutes the sentence to life in prison. In 1979, then-President Jimmy Carter will commute that to time served. In the Docket: Charges of "Statutory Rape" begin to appear. 2 lynchings: 1 Black, 1 other. $1,000 is worth $10,496 modern.

1950, April 19, Wednesday, 6:00pm:

Bertha Brown Knight, 45, and James Knight, 42, have been married going on two years now. He has a considerable temper, but she still loves him despite being "chased down the street many times." It's been rough, but never bad enough to call the cops.

It's safe to say Bertha's 25-year-old nephew, O.B. Jordan (Jordon) has never been a favorite of husband James. He didn't like the kid before marrying into the family, and O.B.'s giving his Aunt Bertha a revolver for a wedding present didn't really help the young man's standing with his new uncle.

Tensions have been running high in the month since O.B. left his home in Huntington, Tennessee, and moved in with his Aunt Bertha and Uncle James in the 200-block of West 14th Street, Lorain. That the youngster has never found a job and likes having his pals over adds to James' aggravation.

About 6:00, the Knights are readying their home for a visit of their church's Wednesday night prayer group. It so happens that O.B. and a few friends are playing cards. James tells the youngsters to wrap up their game and either get ready for the church group or scoot.

O.B. wants to finish their hand. James insists they stop now—right now. O.B. gives him lip. An argument ensues and heats up quickly. James Knight goes silent, abruptly turns, and heads upstairs. The kid gets it in his head that the old man will return with the wedding present revolver he gave his Aunt Bertha. So he goes to the kitchen, takes a large butcher knife, quickly sharpens it on a stone, and hides it beneath his sweater. He then waits in the living room for his uncle to reappear.

When James Knight comes downstairs and walks towards him, O.B. stabs him once in the abdomen. The wounded James runs from the house with O.B. in pursuit. Once outside, O.B. stabs his uncle seven more times before returning to the house, hiding the knife in a warm-air register, and leaving for a local cafe where he orders a beer.

Well before his nephew finishes his suds, James Knight dies on his own front lawn of a severed aorta. He holds his own open knife in an outstretched hand.

By the time Lorain police Michael Bulzomi and John Kochan arrive, O.B. Jordan has returned to the house and sits on the sofa awaiting arrest. Police find he is carrying a long-bladed pocket knife.

O.B. pleads innocent when charged with first degree murder in the Lorain Municipal Court. The May Grand Jury indicts him on that same charge. He maintains his innocence, claiming self-defense.

At his late June trial, Prosecutor Paul Mikus claims that Jordan (now spelled "Jordon" in the newspapers) became incensed when James Knight told him and a woman friend that they needed to stop playing cards because the church group was coming to call. When Knight went upstairs to prepare for guests, O.B. armed himself with the butcher knife, returned to the front room, and resumed his card game, all the while making statements he would kill the old man if he bothered him again.

The nephew stabbed the uncle without provocation, pursued him outside, and finished him off in a violent fury. The pocket knife found in the victim's hand, Prosecutor Mikus continued, was there "as if he had gotten the knife out to defend himself but was unable to use it."

Mikus, assisted by Harold Ewing, push for the electric chair "because of the premeditated and willful nature of the murder."

Defense attorney Henry P. Webber argues that James Knight attacked O.B. Jordan with a knife and had threatened to kill him. The younger man was defending himself, that's all.

During testimony, O.B. says Knight approached him in the kitchen to tell him there was to be no more card playing and at the time had a knife in his hand. When his uncle went upstairs, Jordan thought he was going to retrieve a gun, so he picked up the butcher knife, sharpened it, and put the knife in his belt, concealing it with his sweater.

When James returned, he walked rapidly towards O.B. who slashed at him with the butcher knife. Knight immediately ran for the door. Jordan said he thought the older man was going to his car to get his gun, so he followed him and cut him several more times. He didn't mean to kill his uncle. It was an accident that one of the wounds was fatal.

Defense paints the victim, James Knight, as a dangerous man who had the reputation of being overbearing and violent and who was known to usually carry both firearm and blade. William Scott, a boarder in the house testifies to those facts, as does Bertha Knight, the victim's wife.

According to attorney Webber, Jordan armed himself with the butcher knife because he was fearful of Knight, not because he wanted to kill him.

Judge D.A. Cook tells the jury of seven men and five women that they may find on anything from acquittal to execution. The case is turned over to them 9:35pm, June 30.

It takes fewer than 5 hours to find O.B. Jordan guilty of first degree murder with no recommendation of mercy. All juror express agreement when polled by the court.

Judge Cook's immediate sentence is death by electric chair at the Ohio Penitentiary on October 19, 1950, plus court costs of $349.68. A motion for new trial is made. Judge D.A. Cook denies it.

The date of O.B. Jordan's execution is pushed to April 20, 1951. Court of Appeals considers the case. The conviction and sentence is upheld. The Ohio supreme Court refuses to review the case. Defense attorney Henry Webber appeals to Ohio Governor Frank Lausche for clemency.

Jordan's execution is rescheduled to June 8, 1951 while the Governor ponders. The sentence is commuted to second degree murder and a life in prison with the Governor stating: "There is incontrovertible evidence that the victim, through provoking words and actions and the possession of an open knife found in his hand by police, contributed in some measure to his own end."

Sometime in the late 1950s, O.B. Jordan is transferred from the Ohio Penitentiary to the Lima State Hospital. On March 2, 1961, he is moved to the Apple Creek State Hospital in Wayne County, Ohio.

1950, May 16: *The Chronicle-Telegram:*
> Grant Permission For Memorial In Courthouse Yard.
> County commissioners today granted permission to the
> Amvets here to erect a memorial on the north west corner

of the court house property for men and women who served during World War II.

The memorial is to be erected as a joint project for the Elyria and Lorain Amvets groups and dedicated to all Lorain county veterans of the last war. It is to be dedicated on Memorial Day.

1950, July 22, Saturday: Location: Lorain, intersection of Vine and 28th Street. Victim: Joseph Turner (43, steelworker, of Lorain). Suspect: James Thorpe (40). Shooting due to a lover's triangle. Thorpe kills Turner with three shots from a revolver when the two men happen to meet in the street.

Miss Alice Marcella Reed (30) of Lorain, "for whose attentions the two men were rivals," plus Red and John Frazier are held as material witnesses at $5,000 each. Lee Penn, Albert Jackson, Michael Prince, and Jessie Martin are held as the same at $11,500 each.

The August Grand Jury indicts for murder in the first degree. Thorpe tells the court he has no money to hire counsel. Bruce Alexander of Elyria is assigned to case, but withdraws due to his association with the Prosecutor's Office as attorney with the Humane Society. Judge Guy B. Findley then assigns David Goldthorpe of Amherst, and Steven Nagy of Elyria.

Fifty-seven names are drawn for the jury pool. Then the jurors are told not to show up due to a change of plea to "guilty of homicide" as the defense decides to go with 3-judge panel: Lorain County's Guy B. Findley and D.A. Cook, plus Charles D. Hayden, Knox County as assigned by Ohio Chief Justice Carl Weygandt.

The starting plea is "Guilty of Homicide." *Changed to:* Guilty of manslaughter. Defense claims Thorpe was a hunted man in a dangerous rivalry for Miss Reed and had purchased the revolver only for his protection; that the man on trial had suffered a terrific beating at the hands of Turner and witness John Frazier the day before the shooting and that Turner had threatened the life of the accused.

The principal witness is Miss Reed who says she had tired of her relationship with Thorpe and had fallen in love with Turner. Probate court records show Thorpe and Miss Reed had made an application to get married January of 1950 but that no license was ever issued.

Outcome: Judges find Thorpe guilty of murder in the first degree with mercy and sentence him to life in the Ohio Penitentiary, plus court costs of $454.24.

1972, March 6: Ohio Governor John J. Gilligan commutes Thorpe's sentence to murder in the second degree. This makes him eligible for parole.

1950: August: Battle of Pusan Perimeter: 4,599 U.S. soldiers killed.

1950, December 25, Monday: Location: Elyria, 300-block South Maple Street, home of Oscar Davis. Victim: Charles Fields (53). Suspect: George Mell Williams (37). Williams is described as a "quiet man" who holds his feelings in check until they boil over. Both he and victim Fields are foundry workers.

Defense attorneys Frank Wilcox and John C. Edwards are appointed because the accused has no funds. The case goes to the Grand Jury on January 15, 1951. The State is represented by Prosecutor Paul Mikus and assistants Ewing and Christie. Williams is indicted on first degree murder charges. The defense waives a jury trial in favor of a three-judge panel: D.A. Cook and John Pincura, Lorain County, and W.E. Kellogg of Medina County. Williams pleads guilty to a general charge of homicide; the court will decide the degree of the crime.

Testimony is that Williams and his wife were separated for about eight years, then had lived together until three months ago when she left him to travel to St. Louis and live with their 18-year-old daughter there. Prior to her leaving, Charles Fields, the victim, was making up to Williams' wife and teasing Williams about his domestic troubles. Williams simply lost his temper and shot Fields at the neighborhood Christmas party.

Mrs. Williams corroborates her estranged ex-husband's testimony, which aids in his defense. The judges find the accused guilty of murder in the first degree with mercy after one hour of deliberation. Outcome: Life: Ohio Penitentiary and court costs of $95.46. Williams takes his sentence "with the same stoic calm that characterized his two-day trial."

Judge John D. Pincura:

John Pincura, born in Lorain, Ohio, was the football quarterback at Lorain High School. He continued playing the sport throughout college.

The 1932 graduate of The Ohio State University Law School was elected as Lorain City Solicitor for eight consecutive terms starting in 1936. In November, 1950, Ohio Governor Frank J. Laushe (Democrat) appointed the then 46-year-old Pincura to fill the gap created by the illness-caused retirement of Lorain County Common Pleas Judge Guy B. Findley.

According to the *Chronicle-Telegram* (November 18, 1950, p2) Pincura was only the second Democrat to hold a judgeship in the history of Lorain County. He went on to be elected to four successive six-year terms and was the first Lorain County Common Pleas Judge to consistently wear black, judicial robes while on the bench.

Outgoing, respected, and well liked, Pincura served until forced to retire in 1977 because State Law prohibited him from running after reaching the age of 70. But his retirement was busy since he sat in assignment as late as 1986, substituting for vacationing judges or in cases where a justice recused himself.

After a long illness John Pincura died April 17, 1987, at 82 years. He was buried at Ridge Hill Memorial Park, Lorain.

1951: Amendment to the *U.S. Constitution: Twenty-second:* Limits an elected president to two four-year terms, but a person may serve up to a maximum of ten years if they take over an exiting president's term for two years and then go on to win two elections. Alan Freed aggravates White parents when by playing Black rhythm and blues music on Cleveland, Ohio, radio. Guatemala aggravates the U.S. by seizing the land of the United Fruit Company. Iran aggravates Britain by seizing oil assets. Palestinians aggravate Jordan when they assassinate their king, Abdullah, on Jerusalem's Temple Mount. Libya is independent of Italy. Churchill returns as Prime Minister of England. Colorforms! Musician Chrissie Hynde is born in Akron, Ohio. 1 lynching. 1 Black, 0 others.

1951, February 18, Sunday:

Three Lorain boys, Mitchell Corey (15), Edward Molnar (14), and Edward Beresh (14) are checking muskrat traps in the vicinity of the Clinton Avenue rifle range south of Lorain. The boys round a bend to find at the base of a tree a man's hat carefully placed atop a neatly-folded coat. A clothes line tied to that same tree has its other end attached to the ankle of a man's body floating in the water of the adjacent creek.

The youngsters run home to call the cops. Authorities arrive. A drowning? No. An exam reveals the unfortunate fellow has shot himself through the mouth with a .38 caliber pistol. The contents of his pockets identify him as 55-year-old Manuel Maltos and provide his home address.

It's never easy to deliver such news. Police detectives somberly approach and knock on the front door in the 1700-block of East 30th Street, Lorain. No answer. The cops circle the house and try the back door. Locked. They peer through the windows, then break and enter upon seeing what looks like blood on the kitchen floor. Following the stains to the basement, they discover the poorly concealed bodies of the dead man's wife, Mercedes Maltos (52), and stepdaughter, Angela Ramirez (18), both axed to death.

Coroner Paul Tillman says they died between 5:00 and 8:00pm Thursday, February 15. That's three days before Manuel Maltos' creek-side suicide. Investigation suggests the murders were planned. Before and after the crime, Maltos talked to others about going to Mexico and had the home's telephone removed a few hours prior to the killings. Police disclose that the man had suspected his wife of being unfaithful, going so far as asking friends to help monitor her activity when he wasn't around. No evidence of infidelity is found.

The coroner decides Maltos was, apparently, deranged. The man killed the two women and later shot himself out of guilt or fear, or both. The county prosecutor closes the case as a double murder-then-suicide.

Such events make it difficult to settle estates. The wife and husband had jointly owned their home. Since she died first, her half went to him. Had he lived to be tried he would have lost her half *if* there had been a conviction. Since he took his own life there could be no trial. The property is in limbo.

With attorney Joseph Svete working as the Maltos' estate representative and Prosecutor Paul Mikus for the estates of the victims, property rights had to be decided by other means. One thing seemed certain, none of the killer's family should benefit from the death of the victims. More than four years later: $2,792 was paid to the family of stepdaughter Angela Ramirez. The rest, $2,558, went to Mrs. Maltos' sister and two brothers.

FAMILICIDE – Killing a spouse and all children.

1951, August 21, Tuesday:

Leonard and Larry Hill are walking through a ravine off of Quarry Road about a mile north of North Ridge Road. They find two suitcases, clothing, a passport, three hand-painted landscapes, and a sickle covered with what appears to be blood. They report what they've found to Amherst Patrolman Groff, who turns the matter over to the sheriff.

Deputies Chalmer Davidson and Manuel Gomez determine the property belongs to a Reverend John DeBlair Staley of Cleveland (the one in Tennessee, that is).

Police there are called. It seems Rev. Staley had been robbed by a hitchhiker who put him out of the car and then drove off in the preacher's 1948 Plymouth. Authorities surmise the thief tossed the items because they meant nothing to him and were incriminating to boot.

The car and thief are never found.

1951, August 27, Monday: Location: South Lorain, East 30th and Vine. Victim: Benito C. Peystel (25). Suspect: Jose Delores Padilla Arroyo (31). Both victim and suspect arrived in Lorain from Puerto Rico "a short time ago." They share a basement room in the 1500-block of East 29th in Lorain, sleeping side-by-side on cots. Peystel is in a barroom brawl with a man other than the suspect. Padilla enters the fray. Peystel is, somehow, knifed in the left chest. His heart is pierced. He dies ten minutes after reaching St. Joseph's Hospital in Lorain. A few hours after the death, Padilla walks into the Lorain Police Station and admits the stabbing. Charge: Murder in the second degree. Plea: Not guilty. *Changed to:* Guilty of manslaughter in the first degree. Outcome: Sentence by Judge D.A. Cook to a 1-20 year term at the Ohio Penitentiary, plus court costs of $49.40. Padilla out on parole December, 1954.

1951 August 28: *The Chronicle-Telegram:*
> Stricter Marriage And Divorce Laws In Effect:
> Ohioans who want a "quick" divorce or an easy marriage had better travel to another state for their martial adventures.
> Starting today, more stringent divorce and marriage laws will become effective in Ohio, and court observers say many prospective divorcees and marriage applicants will go elsewhere for their problems.
> Already a rush has developed in one Ohio city in an attempt to beat the new laws. Sidney Douglas, deputy clerk in the domestic relations division of common pleas court at Toledo, reported that 13 divorces were filed yesterday by attorneys as well as two answers and cross petitions.
> The strictest of the new provisions enacted by the recent general assembly deals with divorce cases where children under 14 years of age are concerned.
> Under the new law, the court is required to investigate

the character, family relation, the past conduct and financial conditions of contestants with minor children.

Court officials say the investigations will require additional office clerks, especially during the peak divorce and marriage months of June and July.

Another aspect of the new divorce law states that a divorced person intending to marry again must furnish the probate court with a complete record of past marriages and divorces.

In case either party has been previously married, the law now states, "The (marriage) application shall include the names of the parties to any such marriage, any minor children, and if divorced the jurisdiction, date and case number of the decree."

No marriage license will be delivered unless that information is obtained. Another amendment to the law requires a 90-day residence in the county of the application, instead of the former 30-day waiting period.

Blood test requirements will also be a little more strict.

1951, November 23, Friday:

On November 10, 1951, Raymond Mattingly (38) starts a new job out on Marks Road in Columbia Station as a hand for bachelor-farmer Walter Konarski (65). Konarski tells Mattingly he has replaced a 20-year-old Clevelander named Larry Smith who worked fewer than two weeks before getting the boot for being untrustworthy.

The night of November 23, Mattingly and Konarski finish up their evening chores in the dairy barn and return to the dark farmhouse. Scraping and removing their boots, the two tired men enter through the back door. They flip on the light to find Smith, the fellow who Konarski recently fired, brandishing the old farmer's small, single-barreled 410 shotgun.

Smith orders Mattingly and Konarski to raise their hands. Mattingly is forced to remove his belt and use it to bind the farmer's hands. Without another word, Smith shoots Mattingly in the back. The injured farmhand falls to the floor immobilized by the pain but still aware.

Smith hurries to reload the weapon. Konarski, arms bound behind him, rushes the shooter who strikes the old man in the head with the butt of the gun. Konarski staggers back. Smith shoves the business end of the shotgun against the center of the farmer's chest and pulls the trigger. Instant death.

Smith steps over the dead Konarski and the possum-playing Mattingly to head to the garage to steal the farmer's truck. The vehicle refuses to start. The shooter returns to the house and rifles through the pockets of both of his victims. He finds $2.00 and leaves both men for dead.

Once he's sure Smith has gone, Mattingly pulls himself to his feet and staggers to the nearby home of Charles Harle who calls authorities. From his bed at the Berea Hospital, Mattingly tells police that Konarski had hired Larry Smith through the Cleveland offices of the Ohio State Employment Service. Police are at those offices the next day at noon when Smith breezes in seeking another job.

Once arrested, Smith is hauled to the Berea Hospital by Deputy Sheriffs Joseph Crunda and Joseph Guzik and Assistant Prosecutors Ewing and Christie to obtain an identification from Mattingly. It's apparent from the get-go that Irvin (Laurence, Larry) Smith isn't very sharp. He willingly submits to questioning, saying that he had returned to Konarski's farm "to borrow a shotgun," but as he walked along, conceived a plan of robbing the farmer of the wad of dough he always carried. He'd seen the old man pay cash for a $200 feed bill when he was working for him, after all.

The farm house was empty when he arrived, just as he hoped it would be. He picked up Konarski's shotgun, loaded it, and waited to rob his ex-boss. That other guy that was there, Mattingly, threw him a curve ball, and things went downhill from there.

Smith tells the cops he had been in a "state feeble-minded institution in Columbus for six years and had run away twice." Police check that story and find it true. Smith is a former inmate of the state mental institution in Columbus. Assistant Prosecutor Ewing admits the young man is "dull, mentally, as his questioning disclosed."

Walter Konarski is buried from the Berg Funeral Home in Berea with services held at 10:00a.m., November 27, 1951, at St. Adelbert's Catholic Church in Berea. He is survived by two brothers and four sisters.

Larry Smith is bound over to the Grand Jury on charges of first degree murder and held without bond in the Lorain County Jail. A plea of innocent is entered for him since he is not represented by counsel. Judge John D. Pincura appoints Henry G. King of Lorain and J.P. Henderson of Elyria to defend Smith. His lawyers convince him to change his plea to guilty of first degree murder. Defense asks for three-judge panel to hear evidence in mitigation of sentence with the case to be heard March 26, 1952. The judges hearing the facts are Lorain County Common Pleas Court Judges D.A. Cook and John D. Pincura, and Judge H.E. Culbertson of Ashland County.

Probate records do show Smith to be feeble-minded and that he ran away from Columbus so often that authorities there grew weary of chasing him. Defense testimony emphasizes Smith's sub-normal intelligence in hopes of winning a life imprisonment behind bars. The three-judge panel finds Larry Smith guilty as charged with a recommendation for mercy because the defendant's mentality is "slightly above that of a child." There will be no electric chair for Smith. He is sentenced to life in the Ohio Penitentiary, plus court costs of $1,045.

Deputy Sheriff Eugene Finnegan, in charge of the jail, says that following sentencing, Smith, with tears in his eyes, threatens to commit suicide rather than spend the rest of his life behind bars. He is taken to the penitentiary on March 28, 1952. Appeals begin almost immediately and continue for the next several years.

New lawyers for Smith claim the court-appointed attorneys did not provide satisfactory representation. There is another appeal based on new evidence. The grandson of one of the convicting judges, D.A. Cook, Lorain County attorney Daniel A. Cook, appeals the verdict because Smith's original attorneys did not plead insanity as a defense. All appeals are denied.

In 1972, Ohio Governor John Gilligan commutes the sentence of the now 41-year-old Irvin L. Smith from murder in the first to murder in the second, thus making him eligible for parole. The action is based on a unanimous recommendation of clemency from the six-man state parole board.

1952: It takes a prisoner riot to improve the quality of food at the Ohio Penitentiary in Columbus. More than 57,000 polio cases are reported in the U.S. A cautious Jonas Salk begins testing his polio vaccine. It's a year before it's declared effective. DNA's structure is obvious to Watson and Crick. King George VI is dead. Long live Elizabeth II. Cars as big as a Matchbox. Heads the size of Potatoes. The throat spray "Chloraseptic" is inspired by drinks at a cocktail party. **(Must've been serving Jeppson's Malört—if you've not tried it, you should—at least once in your life!)** In the Docket: Sodomy. Dwight Eisenhower (Kansas Republican) wins the Election with 55.2% of the popular vote. *0 lynchings*—for once.

1952, July 3: A fire in the Lorain County Courthouse, in the Treasurer's Office. It is discovered at 5:27pm when "janitress" Mrs. Rose Francis, working on the floor above the office hears shooting, smells smoke, and sends janitor Harold Howe to investigate. At the same time, Chief Deputy Treasurer Carl Schmitkens, in the basement Tax-Map Room, hears what he thinks are firecrackers going off and goes to take a look. Turns out the shots are cartridges in a pistol in the cashier's cage exploding from the heat. According to County Treasurer Walter J. Wright, the fire was caused by defective or overloaded electrical wiring. No records are lost.

1952, July 5, Saturday:

It is just after 3:00am, Saturday. Lillie Mae West, not quite 40 years old, and Cleveland musician Jimmie Hemphill, 23, clean the bar area of the Maplewood Inn on Fuller Road, Elyria. They work around Bob Davidson, 48, who lives down the road a piece. Old Bob's too drunk to be of help.

Mrs. West and her husband Edward (42) bought the business from Tony Frabotta about six weeks back, though the liquor license remains in Frabotta's name. There was an initial struggle with cash flow until they hired pianist Hemphill. Jimmie's clever and lively playing has brought plenty of new customers. There is a downside to Jimmie, that being Edward West's jealousy of the relationship between his wife and the young, talented, and good-looking man. Mr. West thinks Jimmie is moving in on *both* his business and his wife. Mrs. West reassures her husband it's a simple friendship, but she isn't sure he's listening.

Mr. West says he has some errands to run and leaves the building. Bob Davidson slouches against the bar as Mrs. West counts the register and Jimmie Hemphill stacks chairs.

Mr. West enters unseen through the building's back door and uses a nickel-plated, nine-shot .22 revolver to shoot the piano player at close range. The kid hasn't a chance. The bullet enters Jimmie's left chest, pierces the arteries to his heart, and embeds itself in his right chest wall. Mrs. West approaches her somewhat inebriated husband. She grabs the gun's barrel with her left hand, controlling its aim. The weapon discharges and the bullet draws blood as it grazes the skin between her thumb and index finger. Holding tight to the revolver, she backs the man out the front door whereupon he fires one more shot into the air, jumps into his car, and speeds off.

Lillie May West calmly calls the police and then returns to her husband's victim. Jimmie Hemphill tells her he is dying, and he proves himself correct within the next few minutes. Deputy Sheriffs Manuel Gomez and John

Wircenske arrive to find Davidson intoxicated, Hemphill sprawled on his back, and Mrs. West waiting patiently.

Edward West surrenders to authorities at the Lorain County Jail about two hours later. He is accompanied by his brother-in-law, the Reverend Joseph Carter of the 100-block of Wood Street. Reverend Carter says the suspect had sought out his sister, Mrs. Carter, immediately following the shooting and had asked the Reverend to take him to jail.

The Maplewood Inn remains open, as always, catering to a rough-and-tumble set of customers. Two days after the killing, Perry Watkins of West 14th, Lorain, reports a "minor stabbing incident" after a shoving match in the parking lot.

On July 8, Edward West is charged with murder in the first degree in the death of Jimmie Hemphill. He is bound over to the Grand Jury. A friend, Sonny Williams, is held as a material witness with his bond set at $1,500.

Trouble continues at the Maplewood. On July 17, Mrs. West reports a burglary of six cases of beer, some wine, and potato chips. Entry was not forced so she assumes the crime was committed by someone possessing a key. She changes the locks. On August 8, Clifton Gilmore, 19, Garden Avenue, Lorain, reports to police he was struck by a thrown bottle while crossing the Maplewood Inn parking lot at 1:00am. The resulting injury takes several stiches to close. October 6, police investigate another burglary. Mrs. West says she locked up as usual at 12:45am. Upon arriving at 8:30am the next morning, she discovered the rear door had been forced. The coin drawer of the juke box had been pried opened and emptied; the cigarette machine had been tampered with, but not opened; and $9.40 was taken from the cash register. Also pilfered: three cases of beer, six bottles of wine, a box and a half of cigars, and six pounds of pickled pigs feet.

Edward West is indicted on first degree murder charges later that same month. On October 27, when arraigned, he pleads guilty to manslaughter in the first degree and is sentenced to the Ohio Penitentiary for a term of 1 to 20 years. West maintains he shot the victim in self-defense, even though the victim was unarmed.

In a year's time, Mrs. Lillie Mae West is granted a divorce from Edward West, of the Ohio Penitentiary.

November 21: The Ohio State Liquor Board suspends Tony Frabotta's beer and wine permits for the Maplewood Inn on charges of improper disturbances and the homicide. Furthermore, they refuse to transfer the liquor license from Frabotta to Mrs. West because they are in suspension. In

1954, Mrs. West renames her business "The Rose Room" and continues there until the mid-1960s. The place continues to cater to a rambunctious crowd and is the scene of a number of minor assaults and robberies.

1992, February 19: *The Chronicle-Telegram:*

> Lillie Mae West, 78, of Elyria, died Tuesday at Elyria Memorial Hospital and Medical Center, following a brief illness. Born in Ridge Spring, S.C., she lived in Elyria for 50 years. A graduate of Dunbar High School in Washington, D.C., she attended Howard University in Washington, D.C. For many years she owned and operated the Rose Room in Elyria. A licensed beautician, she operated several other businesses in Elyria…. Burial will be in Brookdale Cemetery, Elyria.

Of all the people in this book I think I would've most liked to have met Mrs. West. Imagine the stories she might've told!

1952, July 17, Thursday, around 6:08pm: Location: Lorain 28th Street and Vine Avenue. Victim: William H. "Pee Wee" Jackson (24). Suspect: Lester "Baby Face" Brown (32). While sitting in his car listening to a baseball game on the radio, William Jackson is shot once through the abdomen with a .38 caliber pistol. Witnesses say the shooter fled the scene on foot.

Jackson is taken to St. Joseph Hospital in Lorain where he dies about a half-hour later. He had worked at National Tube and is survived by his widow, Zeter May. He is buried from the Finley Funeral Home in Lorain.

Jackson had earned extra money by running numbers (carrying cash and results for illegal, private lotteries) for former Cleveland Councilman Thomas J. Davis. Lorain police can find no connection between the victim's death and the numbers racket.

Moments before expiring, Jackson utters the words "Baby Face." Police are certain this refers to Lester "Baby Face" Brown who has made himself scarce. In the end, Lorain authorities are unable to located their man.

October, 1953: El Paso, Texas. The FBI arrests Lester Brown for the possession of a dozen marijuana cigarettes. Brown is brought back to Lorain County at a cost of $662.43 to be arraigned on first degree murder charges. Brown admits to the shooting, but claims it was accidental. He evaded authorities, he says, because he "was scared stiff."

Upon hearing the details of his side of the story, charges against Brown are reduced to manslaughter. He is indicted on that charge by the October, 1953, Grand Jury. Judge D.A. Cook assigns attorney Phillip Johnson as defense who earns $50 for his efforts. Outcome: Brown pleads guilty to manslaughter and is sentenced to an indeterminate term of one to twenty in the penitentiary.

1953: The Korean Conflict sort of ends. Civilian dead: 1.6million. Military dead: 1.26million. Military wounded: 2.04million. Sounds like a war to me. Stalin dies of a stroke. If there's a hell, he's there. The FBI opens a file on Malcolm X as he expands his involvement with Nation of Islam. The Iranian Prime Minister is removed from office in a coup sponsored by U.S. and British secret services. The first commercial electric wheelchair. Salk and his associates develop a potentially safe, injected polio vaccine. *0 lynchings.*

1953, July 11, Saturday: Location: Lorain, "Bar X Tavern," Vine Avenue. Victim: Manuel Pimetal (Pimentol). Suspect: Felix Santiago Rodriguez (26). Act: Shooting. Santiago is bonded for $4,000. Andy Rodgers acts as interpreter. Case is considered by the July Grand Jury that indicts on murder in the second degree. Plea: Not guilty. *Changed to:* Guilty of manslaughter in the first degree. Outcome: Sentenced by Judge John D Pincura to the Ohio Penitentiary. Indeterminate sentence of one to 20 years, plus court costs of $34.85.

1953, July 12, Sunday, early morning: Location: Lorain, Vine and 29th. Victim: Juan Marquez (23), is found lying on the sidewalk. Suspect: Pedro Cardenas Leiva aka Pedro Cardenas Leiba aka Pedro Cardenas Leibas (papers use Pedro Leivas) (25). Both victim and suspect are Lorain steel workers. Marquez, the victim, has lived in Lorain about a year. A native of Mexico, he has a wife and small child there and was planning to travel to visit them that Christmas. He dies of a single, small pocket knife stab wound to the chest which severed his aorta.

Leiva, the suspect, of the 100-block of Lakeside Avenue, Lorain, is picked up the afternoon of that same day by Lorain Police using information provided by witnesses who had seen them leave a bar together.

Leiva is charged with murder in the first degree in commission of a robbery. The July Grand Jury considers the case. The accused pleads innocent by reason of insanity. He is committed to Lima State Hospital for mental examination and returns in October, 1953, with a report that states "although his mentality is subnormal, he is not insane, and that in the opinion of Lima physicians he is mentally qualified to stand trial."

Defense waives jury trial for a three-judge panel: Lorain County's two Common Pleas Judges: John D. Pincura and D.A. Cook, and Judge James L. McCrystal of Sandusky.

The State, represented by Prosecutor Paul Mikus and assistants Harold Ewing and James Christie opens the trial by reading an agreed-to statement that the two men had been drinking together at the "Cozy Corner Tavern" at Vine and 30th until that place closed at 3:30a.m., Sunday. The two men left together, walking to Vine and 29th, where the fatal stabbing occurred.

With the killing stipulated, the court must decide whether the defendant intended robbery since "a death resulting from the perpetration of a robbery is punishable by death in Ohio."

The State maintains the suspect killed the victim to rob him. Victim Marquez had been paid that week and had displayed a $50 bill at the tavern. Leiva took the victim's coat, thinking the money was in it, but the money was in his trouser pockets. The coat was found some distance away, where the Leiva tossed it after discovering it contained only $5.

"Veteran criminal lawyer" Charles F. Adams and Meyer Gordon (of Lorain) describe the stabbing as "the result of too much liquor and an argument between the men." They say Marquez had insisted Leiva accompany him home, Leiva had refused and they argued. The argument escalated to violence and the stabbing occurred. There was a single, small wound which was only accidentally fatal.

The case moves rapidly. There are only five witnesses, three by state and two by defense, including the defendant.

Police had obtained a statement from Leiva that he had taken the victim's coat. At trial, he testifies that confession was obtained by threats of violence on the part of police. He was not physically mistreated, but abused psychologically. Leiva says the victim gave him the coat after they left the bar and that the victim invited him to his home. When he had refused, an argument had ensued. The victim struck at him and called his mother a "vile name." Leiva says he was infuriated. He made a single thrust at him with his pocket knife, striking only in self-defense and with no intent to kill.

The accused is found guilty of murder in the first, with mercy. The "mercy" saves Leiva from the death penalty. Somewhat unusually, Judge J.L. McCrystal of Sandusky declines to sign the verdict. His questioning during the trial suggested he may have favored a lighter sentence.

Outcome: Life sentence in the Ohio Penitentiary, plus court costs of $99.33. Leiva is taken to the Penitentiary on November 27, 1953 by Deputies Claude Adams and John Judge.

1952, August 5: *The Chronicle-Telegram:*
> 615 Divorce Suits Filed Here In Past 12 Months:
>
> A total of 615 divorce suits were filed in common pleas court here for the 12-month period ending June 30, according to a report prepared by County Clerk of Courts H. E. Agate and released today.
>
> During the period the courts decided 576 divorce actions. There were 269 divorce suits pending at the close of the period as compared with 230 pending at the end of the preceding fiscal year.
>
> The report shows that three-fourths of all divorce actions are brought by the wife and approximately one-third of all suits brought by the wife are dismissed by her before trial. Approximately 20 per cent of the suits brought by husbands are dismissed before trial.
>
> Principal grounds charged are gross neglect with extreme cruelty trailing a poor second. Out of a total of 845 cases pending and filed. 647 charged gross neglect and 161 charged extreme cruelty. Other grounds were as follows; 26 for willful absence, three for fraud, five for drunkenness, two for adultery and one for imprisonment.

1954: The world is supposed to end, according to UFO cult leader Dorothy Martin. It doesn't. Ohio is among the top states for polio cases along with Texas, Florida, and Michigan. These four states account for 6,440 cases, 43% of the nation's total. Almost two million children participate in the field trials of Salk's Polio Vaccine. What's a kidney between identical twins? Why, if you're the Herrick boys, it's the first successful organ transplant between human beings by Dr. Joseph Murray. Bill Haley & His Comets *Rock Around the Clock.* Elvis Presley, erstwhile truck driver, cuts his first recording for Sun Records in Memphis, Tennessee. Joe says it's so—he'll marry Marilyn Monroe. Senator McCarthy continues stomping on rights guaranteed by the *U.S. Constitution.* Guatemala's government is overthrown with help from the CIA. France says "l'enfer avec elle" and gives up claims to

Cambodia, Vietnam, and Laos. Postwar occupation of Germany ends. Gamal Abdel-Nasser stages a coup to become president of Egypt and then narrowly dodges an assassination attempt by the Muslim Brotherhood. In the Docket: Extraditions of criminals to other states. *0 lynchings.*

1954, March 11, Thursday: Location: Elyria, 200-block Griswold Road, shortly before noon. Victim: Mary Durisek (28 daughter). Suspect: Andrew Durisek (54 father).

Andrew is born in Czechoslovakia and comes to the United States in 1922. He is a World War II veteran and for the past five years has been a crane operator at the National Tube Company. He buys his property on Griswold from Michael Gluhank in March of 1951 and transfers part of it to wife, Maria Durisek, in August of 1953. Then he transfers another section to Ohio Edison, in February of 1954.

His daughter, Mary, is born in Daisytown, Pennsylvania (east of Pittsburgh) in 1925. As a small child she is taken to Europe by her mother. The two return in 1952. The young lady is a member of the Slovak Evangelical Women's Lodge No. 29 and was employed as a seamstress at the Weitz Company in Lorain until laid off in the Fall of 1953.

Neighbors claim there has been trouble at the house since the daughter divorced and moved back in with her parents. Things have been bad enough that the family was in court two weeks prior when the mother, Mrs. Durisek, had the father arrested on a charge of assault and battery for which there was a $25 fine.

The day of the killing there is an extended period of intense argument, the climax of which is the father shooting his daughter twice—in her chest and head.

The Sheriff is called at 11:35am after neighbors report gunshots. He arrives to find the suspect barricading himself in the house. Deputies Joseph Guzik, Claude Adams, John Judge, Chalmer Davidson, Roy Niece, and Edwin Mitchell rush to the scene to discover the suspect has fled the house, gone into his garage, locked the doors, and hung himself. He is cut down and rushed to the Elyria Memorial Hospital, but cannot be revived.

Besides his wounded daughter, the father leaves behind a wife, three sons, and a brother, John, of Lorain. His funeral service is held March 13 at 1:00pm from the Mathews Funeral Home in Lorain with Rev. J.V. Turcsanyi officiating. He is buried in Elmwood Cemetery, Lorain.

The daughter is dead on arrival at Elyria Memorial from the bullet wound to her head. She is survived by her mother, Mrs. Mary Durisek and three brothers: Andrew, Stephen, and John, all in Czechoslovakia. Her funeral services are held March 15 at 1:00pm from the Emil Dovala Funeral Home in Lorain and at 1:30pm from Christ Evangelical Lutheran Church, where she is a member. Rev. J.V. Turcsanyi officiates. She, too is buried at Elmwood.

1954, August 29, Sunday, early morning: Location: Lorain, Highland Park. Victim: Emmett Tollett (23). Suspect: James (Jim) Harmon (25). Victim Tollett and multiple friends are in the Highland Grill(e), 341 West 23rd Street, Lorain, when suspect Jim Harmon and one friend arrive to order ten beers. They take the beer and leave—without paying.

Victim Tollet knows something of what can happen when you do such a thing. Earlier in the year, he and friends were arrested and fined for ordering $2.22 worth of food at the Coffee Cup restaurant on West Bridge, Elyria, and leaving before it arrived. Tollett catches Harmon outside the grill, hauls him back inside, and forces him to pay.

Harmon strikes Tollett who then agrees to continue the fight at Highland Park and decide the matter "without interference from the police." Seven carloads of people who know the men, mostly Elyrians, leave the grill for the park.

At Highland Park, William Tollett (19), brother of the victim, takes a monkey wrench from Harmon. To assure it is a fair fight, Emmett Tollett gives up his knife.

Harmon knocks Tollett to the ground with a blow to the head, then jumps on him and strikes the downed man at least four more times about the head. With the fight over, Harmon and friends leave the scene. The victim's friend are hauling him to St. Joseph's Hospital when they are stopped by Lorain Police to whom they report what has happened.

Tollett is pronounced dead at St. Joseph's with a brain hemorrhage listed as the cause of death.

Lorain Police notify authorities in Elyria who pick up and question both William Heyd Jr., 21 of the 200-block of Marselles Avenue and James Hambly, of the 300-block, 49th Street. Hambly admits watching the fight and identifies the winner as a man named "Jim" whose last name starts with an "H." Hambly tells police that he had followed the suspect and one Joe Cook (31) to their Broad Street home in Elyria where the suspect had washed blood from his face.

About 9:30, later that morning (Sunday), police are tipped off that one

Joe Cook's car has been spotted south of Elyria, on Route 57, near the LaPorte Inn. Sure enough, the car is parked at the Methodist Church. Cook and Harmon are nabbed trying to crawl away through tall weeds nearby. Harmon admits to having fought the now-dead Tollett.

Harmon lives in the 400-block of Oberlin Road. He had been released 12 days prior to the fight after serving time on a charge of assault and battery. He was also on probation from Federal charges of "moonshining" near Oberlin.

In all, eight men and two women are held as material witnesses as part of the investigation. All eventually have bonds set at $500 each. All but two are able to pay.

Charge: Per Municipal Judge LeRoy Kelly it's murder in the second degree. The accused pleads innocent. Harmon is unable to pay $10,000 bond and so is placed in jail. The September Grand Jury reduces the charge to manslaughter in the first degree.

December 6: Trial starts before Judge John D. Pincura.

Witnesses Shirley Thompson (20) and Barbara Davis (18), both of Elyria, describe Harmon as kicking the victim during the two-minute fight.

Harmon says yes, he fought, but maintains he "meant no particular harm" towards the victim. Outcome: Acquitted of all charges by a jury of six men and six women.

Victim Emmett Tollett was born in Crab Orchard, Tennessee (between Nashville and Knoxville), September 19, 1931, had lived in Elyria for two years, and was a machine operator at Ridge Tool. He lived in the 100-block of Water Street, Lorain. He was survived by his parents and several brothers and sisters and was buried in Crossville Tennessee, near his birthplace.

Note: The two "girl witnesses" who were unable to make their bond were paid $297 each. That's $3 for each of the 99 days they were held.

1954, December 1:

Six years after the formation of the Commission, the first 22-mile stretch of the Ohio Turnpike opens from the state's eastern border to near present-day exit 218 (I-76 and I-80). Following a snow plow, of course, patrol cruisers, officials, and several hundred drivers form a caravan that includes the first private citizens to drive the highway. The section from exit 218, west to Indiana, opens on October 1, of the next year. Construction costs $326 million and it is, up to that time, the biggest project in state history with 10,000 employees, more than 2,300 bulldozers, graders, loaders, and other machines utilized over a 38-month period.

1954, December 26, Sunday, very early morning: Location: Lorain, 28th Street and Oakwood Avenue at the "Wonder Bar." Victim: Joseph J. Ribich (Kibich) (52). Suspect: William Howard Willis (45). Victim Ribich is a bachelor, living with parents in the 3100-block of Norfolk Avenue, Lorain. Suspect Willis lives in the 1900-block of East 32nd Street.

Wonder Bar waitress Leona Kay Gray tells police that William Willis and another man, Mike Vignovich of the 2300-block of East 29th Street, became involved in a drunken brawl. The victim, Joseph Ribich, was sitting with Vignovich but had nothing to do with the original fight.

Willis, takes his wife and two kids home, then returns to the bar. At that time, Vignovich stands up to him, demands, and receives an apology from Willis. Vignovich then leaves the bar.

Later, bartender LeRoy Smith (30) investigates a ruckus in the men's room and discovers the previously apologetic Willis kicking the stuffing out of Joe Ribich. The bartender breaks up that fight.

Willis leaves by the back door. When Ribich exits the bar, he and Willis take up their fight, only this time in front of the building. Bartender Smith breaks this up, too. Ribich collapses, dead, as he's lead back into the building. The cause? A stab wound to the heart courtesy of the knife-wielding William Willis who flees the scene.

Police arrive. At first nobody can provide an address for Willis. Then a woman in the crowd says she was sent a Christmas card by him. She retrieves it and the return address leads police to the suspect. The officers enter his home with weapons drawn. They find Willis, who has continued to drink, sitting, wearing a topcoat, all ready to go. Upon arrest Willis says "I did it." He is permitted to kiss his children goodbye. When asked the location of the weapon, he says he dropped it somewhere.

The dead Joe Ribich has lived in Lorain for 45 years and worked as a charger in the Pipe Mills of National Tube. He was a member of St. Vitus Church and the Eagles Lodge. Besides his parents, he leaves three brothers and two sisters. He is buried in Calvary Cemetery from St. Vitus Church, Reverend Simon Nekic officiating.

Charge: Willis faces murder in the second degree in front of Municipal Judge LeRoy Kelly. Plea: Not guilty. Willis posts bond of $5,000 and is released on December 28. *Changed to:* Guilty of manslaughter in the first degree. Outcome: Sentenced by Judge D.A. Cook to five years' parole, plus court costs of $22.59. Records show probation ending January 7, 1960.

1955: Gumby! Yahtzee! Miles Davis forms his quintet. The Ohio Penitentiary in Columbus reaches its maximum population of more than 5,000 prisoners, many times more than it is designed to hold. An armed uprising helps convince France to give up claims to Morocco. Churchill retires at 81. The Warsaw Pact counter-balances NATO. South Vietnam declares itself a country separate from the north with the U.S. kind of egging things on. Rosa Parks won't sit in the back of the bus, nor should she, says Martin Luther King. Large-scale polio vaccinations halt after hundreds of children are paralyzed and nearly a dozen die. Faulty manufacturing is blamed, but after correction, some parents refuse to have their children inoculated. Even so, within the next two years new cases of polio in the U.S. fall nearly 90%. That's what science can do for you! Ralph Treuel is born in Elyria—he will become a major league baseball coach. Because of its growing population, Lorain County gets a third judge for its Common Pleas Court. 3 lynchings: 3 Blacks, 0 others. $1,000 is worth $9,238 modern.

1953, December 19:

1955, January 9, Virgil Cunningham is once again doing a favor for his sister, Dorothy. She has called and asked him to get some clothing from her house trailer to send to her down in Cumberland, Maryland, where she and her new husband, Bob Shipe, are visiting his family.

The thing is, the trailer isn't theirs anymore.

See… Dorothy and Bob had reached Bedford, Pennsylvania, when their junker car gave up the ghost. It cost them all their dough to get the old jalopy running again. They did make it to Cumberland—by the skin of their teeth—but ended up dead broke in the process. Because of that and other financial woes, they were unable to make the payments on their mobile home. That led to Thornburg's Trailer repossessing it from W.E. Miller's camp over on Routes 2 and 6. The single bright spot in this whole mess is that Thornburg's has been kind enough to give Virgil access to the trailer to retrieve the clothing his sister wants.

The stink hits Virg at the front door. It takes him a moment to recognize what it is. Man, that's all he needs, a dead raccoon or possum. Just his luck that something else has gone wrong. When it rains, it pours. He hopes the stench hasn't got in Dorothy's clothes. No woman would be happy about that! The odor grows stronger as he moves to the back of the trailer. He has to cover his mouth and nose with a hand when he opens a closet door. There he finds a suitcase that's the source of the foul smell.

419

Virgil legs it to Thornburg's office and calls the police. Deputy Steve Mohowski arrives a short time later. He enters the trailer and opens the suitcase to find the decomposing body of an infant.

Lorain County Deputies Donald Smith and Joseph Stitzher travel to Maryland. When confronted by the facts, the 22-year-old Dorothy tells the deputies that she was already pregnant when she traveled from West Virginia to Lorain, Ohio, back in 1953. She found a job at Neisner's "five and dime" and hid the fact that she was carrying a child.

Dorothy goes on to say that she visited a Lorain doctor twice during her pregnancy. On her last visit she was told that her baby may be dead and that she should return before the birth. She did not. She delivered her own stillborn baby on December 19, 1953, in a rented room in the 400-block of Washington Avenue, Lorain. About a week after the birth she went to a "woman doctor" in Lorain who treated her for the physical injuries she'd suffered during her ordeal. She wasn't married, had no place to turn, and didn't know what to do. She wrapped the dead child in a sheet, put it in a suitcase, placed it the clothes closet, and never told a soul. She never disposed of the small body because she couldn't figure out how.

Her husband, Bob Shipe, is floored by the news. Dorothy confirms that he knew nothing of her baby.

Deputy Coroner Charles Chesner disagrees with one important aspect of Dorothy's story. His examination shows the baby to be fully developed. It is his opinion that the child was alive at birth and then suffocated to death shortly after its arrival. How, he's not sure.

Once in the Lorain City Jail, Dorothy Shipe agrees with the Deputy Coroner. She admits to Police Detective Maurice Mumford that her child was alive at birth. She is charged with murder in the second degree and pleads not guilty. Lorain Municipal Judge LeRoy Kelly sets bond at $10,000. It is not met. The February, 1955, Grand Jury indicts for manslaughter in the first degree. Dorothy pleads guilty to that charge. Outcome: Five years of probation.
Compare to: 1941, October 5.

1955, July 2, Saturday: Location: Lorain. The Palm Garden, 1606 East 28th. Victim: Ennis Price (41), 1600-block East 28th, Lorain. Suspect: Willie Burrell Vinton (Venton) (40), 1700-block Livingston Avenue, Lorain. Victim Price is stabbed in the stomach and right side and dies several hours later at St. Joseph's Hospital.

Vinton is arrested, charged with murder in the second degree, and held without bond. He is indicted by the September Grand Jury. Plea: Not guilty. *Changed to:* Guilty. Outcome: The Ohio Penitentiary for life, plus cost of $46.50. Vinton is released by 1968.

1955, August 6, Saturday: Location: Route 10, just west of Route 76, in Ridgeville. Victim: Mrs. Elizabeth Hester Duncan (21, girlfriend). Suspect: John Paul Berger (21, boyfriend).

John Berger is a veteran of the U.S. Army having enlisted for three years starting in August, 1951. In 1953, he was promoted to corporal while serving at the Army's 151st General Hospital in Fukuoka, Japan, a 1,000-bed facility caring for U.N. personnel evacuated from Korea.

Elizabeth Duncan tells Berger she is leaving him for another man. Berger responds by stabbing her a total of 17 times in her abdomen and throat. Charge: Murder in the first degree. Plea: Not guilty.

John Berger has no money for defense and is assigned attorneys J.W. Dilgren and James Parobek. The criminal trial is set to start October 4.

On September 30, Berger is sent to the Lima State Hospital for the Criminally Insane for one month's observation. Berger resents the action even though Lorain County Deputies say he attempted to commit suicide while in their custody. Despite the suicide attempt, defense attorneys Parobek and Dilgren tell the court they believe their client is sane.

One month later Berger is returned for trial with Superintendent of Lima, R.E. Bushong, declaring him sane, though the man suffers from "some instability and insecurity" and "emotional panic."

Trial by jury is waived for a 3-judge panel with his plea changed to not guilty by reason of insanity. Testimony reveals that the victim, former telephone operator, Elizabeth Duncan was, in fact, a married woman from West Virginia. At the time of her killing she was separated from her husband who had custody of their 20-month-old child.

Everyone, including Berger, is shocked by the turn of events. He claims that he did not know, that she never told him.

During the trial, he is allowed to plead guilty to manslaughter in the second degree. Outcome: Judge John Pincura sentences suspect to Ohio Penitentiary, "according to law," plus court costs of $80.45, not including the $900 divided between the defense lawyers.

August, 1963, John Berger is operated on in the Ohio Penitentiary for "low grade throat cancer." Officials are optimistic about the operation and his survival. He is out of prison by the 1980s but dies of cancer in 1988 leaving behind a family of his own.

AMICICIDE: Killing a friend.

1956: Another fire in Lorain County courthouse. North Eaton looks to sell the stock of its telephone company. Vermilion begins looking at sites for a new school. Arthur Miller and Marilyn Monroe? Poor Joe, say it ain't so. *Heartbreak Hotel* is at the top of the charts. Nikita Khrushchev says Stalin was a no-good-nik. Egypt gives England and France the boot when it nationalizes the Suez Canal. Hungary gets uppity. Russian and Warsaw pact troops put it back in its place. Fidel Castro begins to organize Cuban fighters against Batista. Arsenio Hall is born in Cleveland, Ohio. In the Docket: "Traffic Manslaughter" appears. Dwight Eisenhower (Kansas Republican) wins the Election with 57.4% of the popular vote. *0 lynchings*, but, over the next 10 years there will be at least 7 more. 4 Blacks, 3 others.

1956, May 21, Monday, shortly before 5:00pm: Location: Lorain, Clinton near East 39th. Victim: John V. Barnes (28 husband). Suspect: Annie Lee Barnes (18 wife). Both lived in the 100-block of Surf Road, near Lorain. Husband and wife, John and Annie Barnes, publically argue over the attention John has been giving another woman. Husband slaps wife.

Once home, husband slaps his mother-in-law, Anna Pearl Charlton. Then husband fights with wife's stepfather, Fletcher Charlton. Also present is a friend of the husband, Booker Caldwell (19, of the 900-block of DeWitt Street), who hustles the husband into a car and drives him away.

The wife retrieves a .32 caliber pistol from under her bed. The wife, her mother, and her stepfather jump into his car to search for Booker Caldwell and the husband. They find the two men sitting in their car at the stop sign on Clinton, near East 39th.

The wife jumps from her stepfather's car, runs up to the other vehicle, and fires five times. Four shots are wild with two passing completely through the car. The fifth strikes the husband in the side of the chest. The bullet punctures both lungs.

Booker Caldwell drives away. The wounded husband, the guy with punctured lungs, tells Caldwell he isn't driving well. *The two trade places.* The husband then drives himself to St. Joseph's Hospital in Lorain. There, in the Emergency Room, before dying from internal bleeding, he tells nurses Mary Ellen Eschen and Eleanor Citak that his wife has shot him.

While waiting at the hospital, Booker Caldwell, the guy who couldn't drive, gives his statement to Deputies Eugene Miller and Robert Vinovich.

The deputies arrest Annie Barnes at a rooming house in the 1500-block of Lorain's East 28th Street. She tells the officers that the gun is hidden in a box under some clothes. The weapon is not loaded, but a quick search in the vicinity of the shooting produces the empty cartridges.

Annie tells deputies Edward Gawlik and Lloyd Secki of the county jail that she had married the victim in 1950 (**at the age of 12?!**) in Cleveland to give "a name" to the child she was expecting by him. She had lost that child and they had no others. Annie says John had been beating her. She purchased the gun on May 12 for $17 and told her husband, point-blank, that she'd kill him if he ever beat her again.

It is true that the dead man was no angel. County records show Annie had called the Sheriff on November 11, 1955, to report John beating her and threatening her with an axe. Besides the previous wife-beating complaint, he'd also been arrested for driving while intoxicated and leaving the scene of an accident (September 16, 1955) and the unlawful discharge of firearms (March 13, 1956).

On May 24, Annie Barnes waives preliminary hearing in Lorain's Municipal Court with Judge LeRoy Kelly. She is charged with murder in the first degree. On June 14, an exam is requested by her defense attorney to determine if Annie is pregnant. Physician L.Z. Hoffer, of Lorain, states that she is not.

The June Grand Jury indicts her for murder in the first degree. Fletcher Charlton and Booker Caldwell are held as witnesses. Annie Barnes pleads not guilty. *Changed to:* Guilty of murder in the second degree. She is sentenced by Judge John D. Pincura to life in the Marysville Reformatory for Women, plus court costs of $51.25 with some hope of parole in 10 years.

1956, June 13, Wednesday about 6:00pm: Location: Lorain, in front of 2064 East 28th Street. Victim: William Cornelius Tayborne (40) Suspect: Amanzie Lee Williams, Jr. (23). Act: Gunshot.

Papers say William Tayborne came from Bluefield, Tazwell County, Virginia. (**On the border with West Virginia and pretty much in the middle of** nowhere.) He has lived in the City of Lorain for three years, most recently in the 900-block of DeWitt.

Mr. Amanzie Williams lives in the 1300-block of East 29th Street. He says he purchased an automatic pistol because his wife has been bothered by Tayborne "for quite a while."

Williams finds Tayborne on East 28th and begins talking/arguing with him. Tayborne goes for his pocket. Williams fires at the ground near the victim to scare him, but can't remember how many times.

Victim Tayborne is standing beside his car at time of shooting, then runs out into the street where he falls, two feet from the center line. Police find three spent and one live shell at the scene. The victim is struck in the head and leg. A live bullet is found in his pocket as he is prepped for surgery at St. Joseph's Hospital, but he carries no firearm.

Upon seeing Tayborne down, Williams flees the scene. He is on East 29th when he spots an approaching police cruiser. Williams walks over and tosses the pistol onto the front seat of the car. He is also found to be carrying a large butcher knife and several more live shells.

On June 19, St. Joseph's upgrades Tayborne's condition from critical to poor. On June 20 it's back to critical.

Initial charge: Shooting with Intent to Kill. Initial plea: Innocent. Suspect is held on $10,000 bond as set by Lorain Municipal Judge LeRoy Kelly.

Tayborne dies June 22 leaving behind wife, Lena, daughter, Mrs. Daisy Lynette Tayborne, and sister, Mrs. Della Prieto. He is buried in the Brookdale Cemetery from the Sudro-Curtis Funeral Home, Elyria, with the Reverend R.J. Gordon officiating.

Now charged with murder in the first degree, Williams pleads not guilty. For the December Grand Jury, the prosecutor changes the charge to first degree manslaughter. Williams pleads not guilty. *Changed to:* Guilty. Outcome: Probation for five years.

And... Finally...

1972, August 7: *The Chronicle-Telegram:*

Historical Society Seeks State's Electric Chair:

The Ohio Historical Society is interested in obtaining the state's electric chair for display in an exhibit "on torture and punishment."

Although state officials have not yet decided whether to

discard the chair that has been used to kill 315 persons since 1897 at the Ohio Penitentiary, historical society director Daniel R. Porter said his organization would accept the device.

He said the chair would not be permanently displayed because "it's too grisly," but would be part of a temporary exhibit on torture along with whipping posts.

At the time of this publication, The Ohio State Reformatory in Mansfield, Ohio, held the state's long-retired electric chair.

And There You Have It

One hundred and thirty-two years of murder and mayhem. It's up to you to decide what lessons (if any) you choose to take away from this book. As for me, the following were reinforced:

- The well-to-do find other ways to get even.

- You already know the person you're most likely to murder.

- Too much booze is a bad thing but drunkenness is no excuse.

- Women who kill men, even dangerously violent men, don't always get off the hook. Men who besmirch a female victim's reputation sometimes do.

- A "life sentence" isn't, often.

- Justice is determined by skin color and ethnicity. Sometimes.

- There are men who make me ashamed that I am one.

- Papers sure do like to describe crimes as "the most bloodthirsty ever."

- People who think the present is violent don't know the past.

- It used to be 'way easier to run and hide.

- Most murders can be solved. A jury accepting the solution? That's another thing, entirely.

- Most (all?) of us have done things that others have been murdered for.

- Violent people remain violent until an outside force acts upon them.

- "People kill people" but a quickly and easily procured gun sure does help.

- Juries don't always understand the idea of premeditation.

- It's a bad idea to blame the victim because, someday, it may be you!

By The Numbers: Even if You Don't Like Math

The Big Picture

Right off, you need to know that there are holes in the information presented below. So, if you're one of those people who likes to cross-check the math (you know who you are), the numbers won't match!

Population, Killings, and Killings per Thousand People by Decade

Years	Population	Killings Found	Killings/Thou
1824-1829	3,695	-	-
1830-1839	5,696	-	-
1840-1849	18,467	1	.05
1850-1859	26,086	-	-
1860-1869	29,744	2	.06
1870-1879	30,308	5	.16
1880-1889	35,526	4	.12
1890-1899	40,294	17	.42
1900-1909	*54,856*	*46*	*.84*
1910-1919	76,037	35	.46
1920-1929	*90,612*	*65*	*.72*
1930-1939	109,206	33	.30
1940-1949	112,390	23	.20
1950-1956	148,162	20	.13
1951-1956	-	16	-
Total		**267**	

Generally speaking, the number of killings increased with the number of people living in an area, but this relationship was not perfect, as seen in the chart above. After 1929, the number of murders dropped despite a growing population. This followed a nation-wide trend that started with the end of Prohibition.

The two decades in which I found the most murders were 1900-1909 and 1920-1929. These represent vastly different times. The early 1900s were marked by extremes. Worldwide "panics" in the economy, a dramatic shift from agriculture to manufacturing, internal migration into cities and external European immigration into the U.S. produced huge numbers of people out of their element: easy prey for those looking to take advantage. There was little in the way of welfare available to the poor. The reasons for crime often revolved around overcrowding and the control of resources.

On the other hand, the 1920s were part of the between-wars boom. The economy was good. Immigration was down, comparatively speaking, but the male population was exceeding mobile. The crimes were ones of opportunity, misunderstanding, and those involving liquor.

The years leading up to 1930 were among the most violent for not only Lorain County, but much of the U.S. Local killings weren't really tied directly to the organized crime that controlled the booze industry, though there was some of that. It's more that people seemed to drink until they were stupid—and guess what? Stupid people do stupid things.

One look at the *Month of Year* chart tells you that there wasn't a whole lot of variability based on the season.

There was no real variation in these numbers over time. That is, people in the early history of the county killed others all year round, just like those who arrived later.

Though, for some year, those out in the sticks of Lorain County sometimes saw an slight up-tick in murders in March and April. Sort of cabin-fever taken to the extreme.

Month of Year	Killings Found
January	19
February	21
March	19
April	22
May	20
June	21
July	23
August	18
September	21
October	21
November	24
December	17
Unknown	6
Total	**252**

Week of Month	Killings Found
First	36
Second	68
Third	53
Fourth	50
Remainder	19
Unknown	25
Total	**251**

The second week of the average month was definitely the most dangerous, murder-wise.

Different industries paid on different schedules: daily, weekly, semi-monthly, monthly. But bills, especially rent was almost always due the first of the month. Less money = less mayhem = less murder.

I was expecting a big difference between the days of the week, with many more murders on Friday, Saturday, and Sunday. This was clearly not the case and I'm not sure why.

I *suspect* this was the result of many different businesses with varying pay schedules and so the money, with its accompanying trouble, ended up spread

Day of Week	Killings Found
Sunday	34
Monday	35
Tuesday	25
Wednesday	29
Thursday	31
Friday	37
Saturday	35
Unknown	25
Total	**251**

throughout the week. Still, Tuesday was the least lethal. That sort of matches my expectations.

For the murders for which it was given, the time of day was about what you expect: You were safest during the day and more likely to be killed late at night and very early in the morning. However, a surprising number of killings happened in the afternoon/early evening.

Time of Day	Killings Found
Midnight:01 – 4:00am	27
4:01am – 8:00am	10
8:01am – Noon	5
Noon:01pm – 4:00pm	23
4:01pm – 8:00pm	24
8:01pm – Midnight	36
Unknown	126
Total	**251**

Location, Location, Location

Location	Killings Found
Lorain City	144
Elyria City	34
Oberlin	15
All Others	64
Total	**257**

At the end of this section there's a listing of all murders in all locations. Here's a summary.

Suffice it to say that the majority of murders took place in the county's two largest cities: Lorain and Elyria. Part of this was due to the number of people, and some of it was due to the wider range of semi-legal and illegal activities to be found in cities (booze, gambling, prostitution, etc.), but a surprising amount had to do with crowding and human nature.

A large number of murders could be tied directly to jealousy and anger (more on that below). Crowded and over-intimate living conditions led to both. The inability to escape a stressful situation didn't help—at all.

These numbers were not the result of large groups of immigrants in the cities, leastwise not in the way people usually think. We'll get to that in a bit.

Age of Perpetrators and Victims

The most striking thing about this chart? The number of killed children. This is thought to be a modern plague, but it's nothing new. Our youngest citizens have always been at risk.

The most dangerous people were 21-30 year-olds. The most

Age Range – Years	Perps	Vics
0-10	-	25
11-20	13	10
21-30	41	48
31-40	27	40
41-50	17	29
51-60	12	14
61-70	5	10
71-80	1	2
Total	**116**	**178**

dangerous ages for victims was 21-40. Look carefully and you'll see that perpetrators, as a whole, tended to be younger than those they killed. Impulsive youth. Again, nothing new.

Running counter to this is older husbands killing younger wives.

ETHNICITY AND RACE ARE SLIPPERY

The next two charts and subsequent comments concerning ethnicity and race are based on newspaper descriptions of those involved in the murders described above. Remember that the bulk of this information is pre-1930.

"Foreign" was a term used by the newspapers to describe somebody who was not a citizen—especially if they lacked spoken English. It was more about language skills than color, ethnicity, or place of origin.

"White" is also from the newspapers. It was used for people who were considered White, or *looked* White. Typically, such a person was a U.S. citizen, but it could be any English-speaking, light-skinned person.

"Non-White" is a term I use to categorize people for whom the newspapers used something other than "Foreign" or "White." *Do not assume all of these people are African-American!*

For the period described, more Whites killed and were killed than the other groups. This is to be expected, since there were more Whites in Lorain

Ethnicity	# Perps	# Vics
Foreign	54	54
Non-White	33	28
White	70	64

County than any other group. Because of the imprecise buckets of data, I am unable to say if any of the groups are over- or under-represented in this chart.

Ethnicity and Race of Perpetrators and Victims

Ethn of Perp	Ethn of Vic	Killings Found
Foreign	Foreign	43
"	Non-White	2
"	White	7
Non-White	Foreign	2
"	Non-White	24
"	White	5
White	Foreign	4
"	Non-White	-
"	White	64

I am certain that the idea of faceless hordes of "them killing us" was used by the very first bigot to stir up trouble for those who were different. Sadly, it's still used to great effect by those wishing to generate fear, votes, or both.

But look at the statistics! In Lorain County, like elsewhere, those committing murder did so against others like themselves. Think about it… You're most likely to kill somebody you know. Aren't most of the people you know mostly like you?

What we tend to remember in the news (one ethnicity/race killing another) is an inaccurate reflection of what's actually happening. That's as true now as it was a hundred or more years ago.

The exceptions to this rule are officers of the law. Their job takes them into any and all populations, no matter the danger to whom.

The Gentler Sex

Despite there being very nearly equal number of males and females, murderers were overwhelmingly male.

Perp's Sex	#M Vics	#F Vics	Total
Male	162	55	217
Female	13	3	16
Total	175	58	233

In Lorain County, for the time covered, over 90% of murderers were men. It's a shame that's not more surprising. The only good thing about that was, most of the time, they were killing other dangerous males. But men also killed a fair number of females: wives, girlfriends, lovers and ex-es of all of those. Raise your sons to know there's strength in kindness and teach your daughters that it's much safer to *avoid* bad men than it is to try to restrain them with a court order. *A jealous man can be a very dangerous creature!*

Who Killed Who

Relationship	#M Perps	#F Perps	#M Vics	#F Vics
Acquaintance	79	3	75	7
Spouse	27	5	5	27
Friend	32	-	28	4
None	22	-	19	3
Business	14	2	15	1
Lover	11	2	2	11
Child	5	5	4	2
The Law	6	-	6	-
Relative	3	2	5	-
Step-Relative	5	-	4	1
In-Law	3	-	2	1
Parent	2	1	2	1
Sibling	3	-	2	1
Co-Worker	2	-	2	-
Total	214	20	117	59

Note the numbers that are in ***bold italics***. You know the person most likely to murder you. Or, you know the person you're most likely to kill. With friends, spouses, and lovers like these, who needs enemies?

Modus Operandi

Act	#M Perps	#F Perps	#M Vics	#F Vics
Shooting	105	7	117	33
Beating	50	2	59	10
Knifing	47	2	38	12
Strangulation	4	1	2	5
Suffocation	1	2	2	2
Poison	2	3	4	1
Burning	1	1	-	3
Inaction	1	1	2	-
Drowning	-	1	-	-
Exposure	-	-	1	-
Malnutrition	-	-	1	-
Hanging	-	-	1	-
Total	**211**	**20**	**227**	**66**

The preferred ways to murder are obvious; shoot, beat, and cut. Gunplay accounted for nearly half of all Lorain County murders. Many of those weapons were purchased less than a day ahead of the crime. Cooling off period, anyone?

It Goes to Motive

Motive	#M Perps	#F Perps	#M Vics	#F Vics
Anger	80	5	69	16
Jealousy	47	3	27	23
Robbery	35	-	32	3
Money	9	-	8	1
Gambling	9	-	9	-
Revenge	4	2	6	-
Fear	3	3	4	2
Total	**187**	**13**	**155**	**45**

An interesting chart, this. Look at the motives for #F Perps (number of female perpetrators). They were driven by emotions between people. Males had those, but added theft, greed, and gambling to the list. No wonder all of these things are part of the "Seven Deadly Sins!"

Something you can't see here was the impact of booze. The percentage of the top two motives fueled with liquor? Anger = 46%. Jealousy = 37%.

434

COURT REPORTING

Excuses, Excuses

For males, denial was the most common defense against a charge of

Defense	#M Perps	#F Perps
Innocent	44	5
Self-Defense	37	8
Accidental	34	-
Drunkenness	13	-
Insanity	11	2
Honor	11	-
Total	150	15

murder. Females tended to go with self-defense, especially when killing males. Smart, considering how often they were killed by males.

Pleading to a Lesser Charge

"Plea Deals" are often thought to be a modern phenomenon, but they have been a part of Lorain County courts from the very start. For the 186 cases where such information was reported, 32% involved a plea to a lesser charge. For the defendant

Charge	Total	Plead Down
1st Degree	98	19
2nd Degree	74	24
Murder	14	-
Total	186	43

it avoided a trial and the possibility of increased jail time or execution. For the prosecution plea deals guaranteed results while saving time and money. The "Murder" listed here is for the non-jury trials where a judge or judges decided the degree of murder. There was no pleading out to lesser charges once that process began.

Note that the cases brought directly before judges resulted in convictions almost exactly in line with jury trials. 30% of judge-only defendants (v. 32% with jury) were found guilty of something less than the original charge.

Make the Punishment Fit the Crime

Charge	Found 1st	Found 2nd	Found Mansltr	Not Guilty	Nollied	Other
1st DM (96)	24	32	23	1	9	7
2nd DM (74)	-	12	37	4	10	11
Murder (14)	1	1	2	4	3	3
Total (184)	25	45	62	9	22	21

Of the 96 first degree murder trials, only 25% resulted in a conviction for the same. Second degree murder did even worse. Of 74 such trials, a mere 17% resulted in that conviction. It's interesting to note that 29% of those accused of murder said they didn't do it. The courts found only 5% not guilty.

I was able to track 41 of the killers sent to prison. *59% did not serve their full sentence.* This is especially true of those sent away for "life" but later paroled or pardoned. It seems that getting away with murder is nothing new.

A total of 13 murder cases (about 7%) brought before the Grand Jury resulted in no indictments.

A TALE OF TWO COUNTIES

This is my second book on capital crime. The first, *Murders, Mysteries and History of Crawford County, Pennsylvania 1800-1956*, listed all the killings I could find in my home county of my home state.

How does Lorain County, in north-central Ohio, compare with northwestern Pennsylvania?

The two counties are similar in certain ways. Both contained two major cities early in their histories (Elyria and Lorain / Meadville and Titusville) with one as the county seat and the other vying for attention. Most killings took place in those cities. Both counties hold an excellent 4-year, private, liberal arts college (Oberlin and Allegheny). Many of each county's best known lawyers and judges attended those respective schools. The career path of attorney to assistant prosecutor to prosecutor to judge also existed in both places. Judges were re-elected until they chose to move on or died.

Lorain County is blessed with an excellent record-keeping system. Microfilmed court dockets begin at the start of the county's history. Many county newspapers can be found online and those that can't are in the collections of a number of wonderful public libraries.

At best, Crawford County's criminal court records are nearly impossible to reach. The people are extremely helpful, but the lack of court dockets is not. Murders have to be found by secondary means. The newspapers at the county seat are not online and this makes searching them difficult and slow.

Despite the 24-year head start of the Pennsylvania book, I found far more murders in Lorain County. Some of this is because of the better and more accessible records, but most of the increase is due to the fact that there were (and are) far more people here in Ohio. Generally, more people equals more murders.

The types of people were very different. To a large extent, widespread immigration to my home county ceased after the first World War. A much wider variety of people arrived in Lorain County, and for a considerably longer time. Some of the Lorain County groups maintained traditions of vendettas against those who did them wrong. But, as shown above, it's never been one ethnic/racial group killing another. It's victims killed by someone similar. That was true in both Ohio and Pennsylvania.

Pennsylvania is one of the original thirteen colonies. The early settlers of Crawford County carried the opinions and actions of that stock. No real man would shoot or knife another. Only a coward (or a woman) would do such things. This attitude, prevalent almost until Prohibition, kept the number of early murders low since it's far more work to beat someone to death than to shoot or cut them dead. Likewise, drunkenness was not considered an excuse for *any* action, let alone murder. Allowing booze to control you was a sign of weakness that should, in and of itself, be punished. Plea bargaining, while allowed by law, was nearly non-existent in cases of murder. Such deals were never offered and rarely requested.

In contrast, Lorain County had shootings, knifings, leniency for drunkenness, and pleading to lesser charges from the very beginning.

In both counties the majority of murders were men killing men, and for much the same reasons. Both counties found women killed by abusive men at an alarming rate. Both had their share of abandoned and drowned babies. In each location there were rare female defendants in cases of murder. Lorain County tended to send these women to prison. Crawford County almost always excused their actions—even when they confessed!

Sentencing was similar, though Crawford County sent a higher percentage of murderers to execution. But a life sentence usually was not, and some of the worst killers received paroles for reasons that were never made completely clear.

Though there were differences, it's important to point out the one constant across both geography and time—the part drunkenness played in the crime of murder. One-third to one-half of the killings I found in either counties happened, at least in part, because the victim, perpetrator, or both were boozed up.

If you take any single lesson from the preceding pages, it should be: *Don't hang out with angry drunk men!*

SOURCES AND SUNDRIES

Finding a Murder

Haul yourself to the Lorain County Justice Center in Elyria and try to find a spot to park. On second thought, since you're going to be there a while, it may be best if you park down by the river so you don't have to leave every couple hours to move your car!

Stroll into the records department and politely ask one of the ever-kind staff members how to find a criminal case for the year in which you have an interest. If the crime happened of late, then it's probably in the "computerized" records and you're in luck because those are exceedingly easy to search. If it's an older case, the Criminal Dockets are preserved on rolls of microfilm indexed by year. Mount the film on a reader (hoping, of course, that one of the ancient machines is in working order), spin the film to the beginning of that year's docket, and find the index that lists some variation of the last name of the person charged with the crime. The name will be cross-referenced to a case or page number. Advance the film to that location, and there you are. You cannot find a crime if all you have is the name of the victim.

Docket entries are usually fairly complete but present "just the facts." There is no mention of the victim but you'll find charges, the name(s) of the accused, usually the defending lawyer, dates of proceedings, outcomes of the same, and a listing of costs. Be aware that many things are abbreviated in Court Recorder-Speak. Older dockets are handwritten and often poorly so. To make matters worse, they are negative images. This saved production costs, but makes them difficult to read. If you don't need bifocals when you start, you may before you're finished.

If you're doing a survey, like this book, you start at the beginning of the first docket. There is no "index of crimes," so you mount the reel, set the machine to slow forward, sit back, and right-brain cruise the charges as they go by. Luckily, "MURDER" tends to stand out. Unluckily, the work may make you motion-sick, but that wears off after the first mile, or so, of film.

Once you have court data, it's off to the newspapers. Always remember that papers are capricious sources of information *because they print the news and news changes with time.* You cannot trust a single article in a single paper since it can take three or more news pieces for the facts to begin to settle.

This is especially true of older papers. Both Elyria and Lorain had multiple publications with strong political filters: Democrat, Republican,

Constitutionalist, and Independent. All present the same story from differing points of view. Smaller cities also ran multiple papers, except theirs didn't typically announce their editorial slant on their mastheads. Never allow your preconceived notions to color what a town's publications might be like! A community you consider liberal might've had staunch conservatives as editors, and vice-versa.

(While we're on the topic, newspapers appear to have a startling need to add and remove the word "The" to their masthead: *Elyria Republican* versus *The Elyria Republican*. I tried to keep track and then threw up my hands at the seeming capriciousness of it and abandoned all hope. I'm sorry if I mistakenly added, or neglected to add the leading *The* in my cites. It was all simply too much for me to bear.)

It takes a fair number of articles to fill in the blanks left by the spare nature of the court records. For example, what you read in this book was gleaned from well over 3,000 separate news pages (that's the reason there is no bibliography). Heaven only knows how many pages I looked at to find the ones I used—I don't think I want to know!

But, looking through all those newspapers has an upside. You see, the Criminal Dockets list only killings for which there were court proceedings. In this book a very large percentage of murders have no docket record because they were committed by people who skipped, or killed themselves, or who were unknown because the crimes were never solved or prosecuted. Such murders had to be stumbled upon while researching known cases.

The task was made easier by modern technology. Area newspapers, especially Elyria's, are available in on-line form and searchable by key word. It's far from a perfect system, but it does make finding murder articles a little more practical. Though, honestly, all it typically does is reduce the number of articles from soul-crushingly large to "kripes, look at all that stuff." It helps to have a touch of O.C.D.

Articles on one killing sometimes refer to another with something like "similar to the _____ murder mystery of April, 1940." News summations printed at the end of the year also provide an excellent synopsis of major crimes with murder being one of them.

Was I able to find every murder? No. Definitely not. In point of fact I found and added two more while the book was with my editor. But I am willing to bet I snagged most of them.

Sources of History

Information on general history was collected, as needed, from sources old and new. Some of it was found in the entertaining, wonderfully biased, and sometimes inaccurate books *History of Lorain County, Ohio,* William Brother, 1879, and *A Standard History of Lorain County Ohio,* G. Frederick Wright, Supervising Editor, 1916.

I also recommend; *They Stopped in Oberlin,* 2002, William E. Bigglestone, for an interesting history on some of the early settlers of Lorain County. *Historical Lights and Shadows of the Ohio Penitentiary,* 1899 edition, Dan J. Morgan, for a harrowing description of 19th century prison life. Lastly, in order to save yourself from dying in a state of ignorance, you should read Lewis Clarke's 1845 book, *Narrative of the Sufferings of Lewis Clarke, During a Captivity of More than Twenty-Five Years, Among the Algerines of Kentucky, One of the So Called Christian States of North America.* It can be found online.

Biographical information on judges was found in newspaper pieces leading up to elections (one of the least trustworthy sources) and obituaries (the most scrutinized articles printed). It was difficult to find *any* past article that threw a bad light on a local judge or attorney. Remember, these men, no matter how human, wielded *tremendous* social and political power. They were rarely criticized. Nobody, including newspapers, wanted to anger a sitting or retired judge or the lawyers heavily involved in criminal or civil cases.

Most other historical information was gleaned from the plethora of ".gov" and "oh.us" web sites. Stuff from them isn't necessarily more accurate, but it is more legitimate. That seems to be important.

Fact Checking

I always tried to cross-reference what I found with at least one other source. If opposing Elyria papers agreed, I figured I was pretty close. If in doubt, there were the Lorain papers to consult. The Wellington Enterprise was published twice a week through much of the period covered and turned out to be a fine reference. The Oberlin-area papers, some of the first in the county, were great up until several decades past the Civil War. Then, over time, they grew so fanatically local in focus that anything outside the city, including the dropping of the first atomic bomb, was pointedly and somewhat proudly ignored.

There were times when all I had was a single newspaper article or an entry in the Criminal Docket. That's why a number of listings included question marks—information wasn't there to be found.

To the Census!

There are cases when I made the effort to track an individual through time: a particularly sympathetic spouse, or child left behind. This was done mostly through documents held in the U.S. Census.

The data contained in the Census are dependent on both the subject and the taker and, as a result, are often flawed. Is the wife listed in 1900 as Arabella the same as the Arvella of 1910 and the Avie of 1920, or are they two or three different people? The listing for my own father's family in the 1920 Census contains errors for three out of the five children!

The "slipidy" nature of race is driven home by careful tracking of some citizens. It is of extreme interest to watch over the decades as the children of parents listed as Black and White pinball between Mulatto, Black, back to Mulatto, to White, and then (perhaps) back again. Many of us are obviously One Thing or The Other and self-identify as such, but an amazingly large number of us, perhaps you, are the result of a choice made somewhere along the line.

What Follows

To round out the book, the crimes I've described are listed in sundry ways. They start with a simple Location/Year table, then continue with various combinations of Year, Victim, and Suspect.

Enjoy!

List by Location

Location (#found):	In the Years:
Unknown (12)	1840, 70, 73, 79, 95, 96, 1901, 01, 02, 25, 29, 29.
Amherst (3)	1916, 29, 36.
Avon (1)	1894.
Avon Lake V. (5)	1930, 30, 32, 32, 43.
Black River Twp (1)	1865.
Brighton	None found (*this notation doesn't mean there weren't any*)
Brownhelm Twp (1)	1895.
Camden	None found
Carlisle Twp (1)	1935.
Columbia Sta. & Twp (2)	1894, 1951.
Eaton Twp (3)	1882, 1907, 31.
Elyria (34)	1883, 93, 1902, 04, 07, 07, 09, 17, 19, 19, 20, 21, 21, 23, 25, 26, 26, 28, 28, 28, 29, 30, 31, 31, 36, 42, 42, 43, 47, 47, 48, 50, 52, 54.
Grafton & Twp (5)	1862, 94, 1902, 22, 37.
Henrietta Twp	None found
Huntington Twp	None found
LaGrange Twp (1)	18??.
Lorain (City) (144)	1895, 95, 99, 99, 1901, 02, 03, 03, 03, 03, 04, 04, 04, 05, 05, 06, 06, 06, 07, 07, 07, 07, 07, 07, 08, 08, 08, 08, 08, 08, 09, 09, 10, 10, 10, 11, 11, 12, 12, 12, 13, 13, 14, 15, 15, 16, 16, 16, 17, 17, 17, 18, 19, 19, 19, 19, 20, 20, 21, 21, 21, 21, 22, 22, 23, 23, 23, 23, 24, 24, 24, 24, 24, 24, 24, 24, 25, 25, 25, 25, 26, 26, 26, 26, 26, 26, 26, 27, 27, 28, 28, 28, 29, 29, 29, 29, 30, 30, 30, 30, 30, 31, 31, 32, 32, 32, 34, 34, 34, 35, 35, 36, 38, 39, 39, 40, 41, 41, 42, 43, 45, 45, 45, 47, 48, 48, 48, 49, 49, 50, 50, 51, 51, 51, 52, 53, 53, 53, 54, 54, 55, 56, 56.
(New) Russia Twp (4)	1881, 1927, 34, 46.
Oberlin (15)	1875, 81, 81, 87, 89, 90, 90, 1900, 03, 03, 11, 13, 25, 26, 28.
Penfield Twp (1)	1907.
Pittsfield Twp. (1)	1910.
N. Ridgeville & Twp (7)	1870, 1900, 00, 16, 17, 27, 55.
Rochester	None found
Shawville (1)	1905.
Sheffield(1)	1954.
Sheffield Lake V. (1)	1931.
South Amherst (5)	1911, 12, 23, 27, 43.
Wellington & Twp (7)	1883, 90, 90, 92, 98, 1909, 23.

MASTER LISTS:

1840 – ? – Gilmore	1900 – Morrison – ?
1862 – Burton – Fryar	1900 – Trebisky – Svoboda
1865 – Mitchell – Long	1901 – ? – ?
1870 – Jones – Jones	1901 – Kovacs – Nagi
1870 – Mieden – Schleifeinbaum	1901 – Larson – Worden
1873 – ? – Williams	1901 – Larson – Worden
1875 – Cooper – Scott	1902 – ? – Caine
1879 – Cook – Faulkner	1902 – McCoy – Tate
1881 – Stone-LO – Durham	1902 – Russell – Russell
1881 – Walker – ?	1902 – Washburn – ?
1882 – Fishburn – Fishburn	1903 – ? – ?
1883 – Brenner-LO – Young	1903 – ? – ?
1883 – Brenner-LO – Tirey	1903 – Bennett – Bennett
1883 – Ryan – Bruce	1903 – Black – Butler
1887 – ? – ?	1903 – Reichlin – Walser
1889 – Johnson – Johnson	1903 – Richards – Majesse, C
1890 – Blakenay – Waring	1903 – Richards – Majesse, S
1890 – Hutchinson – Jacobs	1903 – Richards – Vig
1890 – Sage – Hoke	1904 – Nelson – Nelson, C
1892 – Arnold – Arnold	1904 – Nelson – Nelson, E
1893 – Manning – Manning	1904 – Nelson – Nelson, R
1894 – Gletzer – Geska	1904 – Securro – Dimente
1894 – Hoeline – Mertaugh	1904 – White – Williams
1894 – Schaf(f)er – Nichols	1905 – ? – ?
1894 – Schaf(f)er – Waldecker	1905 – James – Torney
1895 – ? – Aleck	1905 – McFadden – ?
1895 – Champsey – Shipley	1906 – Bruc – ?
1895 – Champsey – Snyder	1906 – Elders – Williams
1895 – Drugaen – Palgot	1906 – Rasin – Bunda
1895 – Moon – ?	1907 – ? – ?
1896 – ? – Authoro	1907 – Caperillo – ?
1898 – Packenbush – Fox	1907 – Dominski – Gordon
1899 – Myers – Wheeler	1907 – Dominski – Seslia
1899 – Rider – Sagi	1907 – Dominski – Shea

1907 – Koch – Brown	1913 – McConico – McConico
1907 – McAlpine – McAlpine	1914 – Sardi – Szakacs
1907 – Norfa – ?	1915 – Latsko – Bofea
1907 – Schwarz – Schwarz	1915 – Latsko – Derzaj
1907 – Smith – Goohs	1915 – Latsko – Sugaj
1907 – Washtak – Thomas	1915 – Latsko – Valkovan
1907 – Wilson – Juren	1915 – Latsko – Yonowich
1908 – ? – ?	1915 – Lewis – Crutchfield
1908 – Berta – Cepis	1916 – ? – ?
1908 – Berta – Garvey	1916 – Becker-LO – Bischoff
1908 – Berta – Pap, D	1916 – Hoffman – Shoshetti
1908 – Berta – Pap, E	1916 – Jansik – Komadina
1908 – Berta – Pap, J	1916 – Minda – Nagy
1908 – Dovisak – Dick	1917 – Baldwin – Decker
1908 – Washnack – Doneski	1917 – Emmons – ?
1908 – Washnack – Sknoicki	1917 – Hazen – Hazen
1908 – Yung – Connors	1917 – Hazen – Hazen
1908 – Zernikow – McLane	1917 – Kocher – ?
1909 – Elliott – Hines	1917 – Musk – Lester
1909 – Francis – Moore	1918 – Miller – Genshure
1909 – Szantaj – Petro	1919 – Cluley – Cluley
1909 – Watson – Williams	1919 – Gynrovisici – Kezcver
1910 – Johnson – ?	1919 – Gynrovisici – Kovasish
1910 – Mitchell – Vespers	1919 – Rovos – Vido
1910 – Richards – Vespers	1919 – Schultz – ?
1910 – Walkinshaw – Walkinshaw	1919 – Sumegi – Hammersack
1911 – ? – ?	1919 – Tratea – Tratea, E
1911 – Johansye – Farkas	1919 – Tratea – Tratea, J
1911 – Kolander – Gursk	1920 – Barnes-LO – Losteiner
1911 – Sugery – Brecki	1920 – Jacobski – Martini
1912 – Bodanger – Harambasic	1920 – Paul – Lazos
1912 – Horvath – Fejes	1920 – Sanders – Alexander
1912 – Stamibola – Bobic, A	1920 – Sanders – Walker
1912 – Stamibola – Bobic, V	1921 – ? – ?
1912 – Uckinick – Barosky	1921 – Capogreco – ?
1912 – Uckinick – Frenolan	1921 – Eutcher – Ellis
1913 – Chrospowski – ?	1921 – Kosco – Kosco
1913 – Lanar – White	1921 – Pausen – Popp

1921 – Roman – Snezik
1922 – Gust – Frank
1922 – Kuccovich – Citik
1922 – Stenser – Stenser
1923 – Atwood – Manning
1923 – Biro – Chepol
1923 – Guzman – Cruze
1923 – Hall-Cowels – Cowels
1923 – Hall-Cowels – Hall
1923 – Laicy-LO – Wright
1923 – Rallie – Pleasant
1923 – Webber-LO – Mackerty-LO
1923 – Webber-LO – Thomas
1924 – ? – ?
1924 – ? – ?
1924 – Karvoch – Zvosecz
1924 – Moore – Crenshaw
1924 – Ratenchuk – Bender
1924 – Spanich – Spanich
1924 – Stillitano – ?
1924 – Temasch – Fuga
1924 – Turboreck – Tenerty
1925 – Griffa – ?
1925 – Luard – Outiga
1925 – McCoy – Hackendorn
1925 – Nance – Young
1925 – Perez – Padillo
1925 – Stevens – Clement
1925 – Verano – ?
1925 – Vouchovich – Vouchovich
1926 – ? – ?
1926 – ? – ?
1926 – ? – ?
1926 – Barbarano – ?
1926 – Carvello – Harris
1926 – Durham – Whiteside
1926 – Fefezaria – Major
1926 – Fefezaria – Major

1926 – Garza – Martinez
1926 – Guteries – Garcia
1926 – Rockich – Ralich
1927 – ? – ?
1927 – Johnson – Bond
1927 – Romano – Marco
1927 – Sokoloff – Sokoloff
1927 – Sparrow – ?
1928 – Biggins – "Charley"
1928 – Grant – Grant
1928 – Horvath – Horvath
1928 – Klukowich – Hutera
1928 – Philips – Thornton
1928 – Robinson – Grant
1928 – Vorhees – Thornton
1929 – ? – Hinozoso
1929 – Andrade – Callentano
1929 – Berrim – Riza
1929 – Bolosky – Bakaletz
1929 – Vega – ?
1929 – Wojtowicz – Pruski
1929 – Woods – Miller
1929 – Zboray – Kader
1930 – ? – ?
1930 – Dineff – Dzouclis
1930 – Espinoza – Espinoza
1930 – Mandick – ?
1930 – Monaco – Mannarino
1930 – Nichols – Nichols
1930 – Serra – Jackson
1930 – Snowbrick – ?
1931 – Andros – Caloyanis
1931 – Glenn – Wall
1931 – Schindler – Barnes
1931 – Watte – Nolan
1931 – Watte – Rice
1931 – Watte – Stevens
1931 – Watte – Wallace

1931 – Wedic – Benzak
1931 – Zawacski – Muhich
1932 – Lenahan – Lenahan-LO
1932 – Livingston – Livingston
1932 – Volpe – ?
1932 – Williams – Hutchinson
1932 – Williams – Williams
1934 – Carreo – Lee
1934 – Majjessie – Majjessie
1934 – Moreno – Fantos
1935 – Burnett – Bucey
1935 – Meluch – Meluch
1935 – Phillips – Barath
1936 – Camera – ?
1936 – Cecil – ?
1936 – Cecil – ?
1936 – Joss – ?
1937 – Hornbeck – Campbell
1937 – Hornbeck – Hensley
1937 – Hornbeck – Maneff
1938 – Wallace – Naiberg
1939 – Brnadech – Brnadech
1939 – Dave – Dave
1940 – Minoff – Minoff
1941 – Benson – Benson
1941 – Blair – Blair
1942 – Doinoff – Doinoff
1942 – Glass – Glass
1942 – Taft-LO – Spuriel
1943 – ? – ?
1943 – Goncheroff – Goncheroff
1943 – Kovacs – Francis
1943 – Stipe – Varady
1945 – Duffield – Wellman
1945 – Falls – Donald

1945 – Falls – Haynes
1945 – Katonak – Brown
1945 – Lasky – ?
1946 – Peters – Payne
1947 – Butler – White
1947 – Simmons – Bowens
1948 – Bohach – Bohach
1948 – Chunn – Roach
1948 – Cimesa – Cimesa
1948 – Dixon – Rhodes
1948 – Leonard – Lengyel
1949 – Feeley – Banks
1949 – Feeley – Winston
1950 – Fields – Williams
1950 – Knight – Jordan
1950 – Turner – Thorpe
1951 – Konarski – Smith
1951 – Maltos – Maltos
1951 – Peystel – Padilla
1951 – Ramirez – Maltos
1952 – Hemphill – West
1952 – Jackson – Brown
1953 – ? – Shipe

1953 – Marquez – Leiva
1953 – Pimetal – Rodriguez
1954 – Durisek – Durisek
1954 – Ribich – Willis
1954 – Tollet – Harmon
1955 – Duncan – Berger
1955 – Price – Vinton
1956 – Barnes – Barnes
1956 – Tayborne – Williams

Victim – Suspect – Year

447

? – ? – 1887

? – ? – 1901

? – ? – 1903

? – ? – 1903

? – ? – 1905

? – ? – 1907

? – ? – 1908

? – ? – 1911

? – ? – 1916

? – ? – 1921

? – ? – 1924

? – ? – 1924

? – ? – 1926

? – ? – 1926

? – ? – 1926

? – ? – 1927

? – ? – 1930

? – ? – 1943

? – Aleck – 1895

? – Authoro – 1896

? – Caine – 1902

? – Gilmore – 1840

? – Hinozoso – 1929

? – Shipe – 1953

? – Williams – 1873

Andrade – Callentano – 1929

Andros – Caloyanis – 1931

Arnold – Arnold – 1892

Atwood – Manning – 1923

Baldwin – Decker – 1917

Barbarano – ? – 1926

Barnes – Barnes – 1956

Barnes-LO – Losteiner – 1920

Becker-LO – Bischoff – 1916

Bennett – Bennett – 1903

Benson – Benson – 1941

Berrim – Riza – 1929

Berta – Cepis – 1908

Berta – Garvey – 1908

Berta – Pap, D – 1908

Berta – Pap, E – 1908

Berta – Pap, J – 1908

Biggins – "Charley" – 1928

Biro – Chepol – 1923

Black – Butler – 1903

Blair – Blair – 1941

Blakenay – Waring – 1890

Bodanger – Harambasic – 1912

Bohach – Bohach – 1948

Bolosky – Bakaletz – 1929

Brenner-LO – Young – 1883

Brenner-LO – Tirey – 1883

Brnadech – Brnadech – 1939

Bruc – ? – 1906

Burnett – Bucey – 1935

Burton – Fryar – 1862

Butler – White – 1947

Camera – ? – 1936

Caperillo – ? – 1907

Capogreco – ? – 1921

Carreo – Lee – 1934

Carvello – Harris – 1926

Cecil – ? – 1936

Cecil – ? – 1936

Champsey – Shipley – 1895

Champsey – Snyder – 1895

Chrospowski – ? – 1913

Chunn – Roach – 1948

Cimesa – Cimesa – 1948

Cluley – Cluley – 1919

Cook – Faulkner – 1879

Cooper – Scott – 1875

Dave – Dave – 1939

Dineff – Dzouclis – 1930

Dixon – Rhodes – 1948

Doinoff – Doinoff – 1942

Dominski – Gordon – 1907

Dominski – Seslia – 1907

Dominski – Shea – 1907

Dovisak – Dick – 1908

Drugaen – Palgot – 1895

Duffield – Wellman – 1945

Duncan – Berger – 1955

Durham – Whiteside – 1926

Durisek – Durisek – 1954

Elders – Williams – 1906

Elliott – Hines – 1909

Emmons – ? – 1917

Espinoza – Espinoza – 1930

Eutcher – Ellis – 1921

Falls – Donald – 1945

Falls – Haynes – 1945

Feeley – Banks – 1949

Feeley – Winston – 1949

Fefezaria – Major – 1926

Fefezaria – Major – 1926

Fields – Williams – 1950

Fishburn – Fishburn – 1882

Francis – Moore – 1909

Garza – Martinez – 1926

Glass – Glass – 1942

Glenn – Wall – 1931

Gletzer – Geska – 1894

Goncheroff – Goncheroff – 1943

Grant – Grant – 1928

Griffa – ? – 1925

Gust – Frank – 1922

Guteries – Garcia – 1926

Guzman – Cruze – 1923

Gynrovisici – Kezcver – 1919

Gynrovisici – Kovasish – 1919

Hall-Cowels – Cowels – 1923

Hall-Cowels – Hall – 1923

Hazen – Hazen – 1917

Hazen – Hazen – 1917

Hemphill – West – 1952

Hoeline – Mertaugh – 1894

Hoffman – Shoshetti – 1916

Hornbeck – Campbell – 1937

Hornbeck – Hensley – 1937

Hornbeck – Maneff – 1937

Horvath – Fejes – 1912

Horvath – Horvath – 1928

Hutchinson – Jacobs – 1890

Jackson – Brown – 1952

Jacobski – Martini – 1920

James – Torney – 1905

Jansik – Komadina – 1916

Johansye – Farkas – 1911

Johnson – ? – 1910

Johnson – Bond – 1927

Johnson – Johnson – 1889

Jones – Jones – 1870

Joss – ? – 1936

Karvoch – Zvosecz – 1924

Katonak – Brown – 1945

Klukowich – Hutera – 1928

Knight – Jordan – 1950

Koch – Brown – 1907

Kocher – ? – 1917

Kolander – Gursk – 1911

Konarski – Smith – 1951

Kosco – Kosco – 1921

Kovacs – Francis – 1943

Kovacs – Nagi – 1901

Kuccovich – Citik – 1922

Laicy-LO – Wright – 1923

Lanar – White – 1913

Larson – Worden – 1901

Larson – Worden – 1901

Lasky – ? – 1945

Latsko – Bofea – 1915

Latsko – Derzaj – 1915

Latsko – Sugaj – 1915

Latsko – Valkovan – 1915

Latsko – Yonowich – 1915

Lenahan – Lenahan-LO – 1932

Leonard – Lengyel – 1948

Lewis – Crutchfield – 1915

Livingston – Livingston – 1932

Luard – Outiga – 1925

Majjessie – Majjessie – 1934

Maltos – Maltos – 1951

Mandick – ? – 1930

Manning – Manning – 1893

Marquez – Leiva – 1953

McAlpine – McAlpine – 1907

McConico – McConico – 1913

McCoy – Hackendorn – 1925

McCoy – Tate – 1902

McFadden – ? – 1905

Meluch – Meluch – 1935

Mieden – Schleifeinbaum – 1870

Miller – Genshure – 1918

Minda – Nagy – 1916

Minoff – Minoff – 1940

Mitchell – Long – 1865

Mitchell – Vespers – 1910

Monaco – Mannarino – 1930

Moon – ? – 1895

Moore – Crenshaw – 1924

Moreno – Fantos – 1934

Morrison – ? – 1900

Musk – Lester – 1917

Myers – Wheeler – 1899

Nance – Young – 1925

Nelson – Nelson, C – 1904

Nelson – Nelson, E – 1904

Nelson – Nelson, R – 1904

Nichols – Nichols – 1930

Norfa – ? – 1907

Packenbush – Fox – 1898

Paul – Lazos – 1920

Pausen – Popp – 1921

Perez – Padillo – 1925

Peters – Payne – 1946

Peystel – Padilla – 1951

Philips – Thornton – 1928

Phillips – Barath – 1935

Pimetal – Rodriguez – 1953

Price – Vinton – 1955

Rallie – Pleasant – 1923

Ramirez – Maltos – 1951

Rasin – Bunda – 1906

Ratenchuk – Bender – 1924

Reichlin – Walser – 1903

Ribich – Willis – 1954

Richards – Majesse, C – 1903

Richards – Majesse, S – 1903

Richards – Vespers – 1910

Richards – Vig – 1903

Rider – Sagi – 1899

Robinson – Grant – 1928

Rockich – Ralich – 1926

Roman – Snezik – 1921

Romano – Marco – 1927

Rovos – Vido – 1919

Russell – Russell – 1902

Ryan – Bruce – 1883

Sage – Hoke – 1890

Sanders – Alexander – 1920

Sanders – Walker – 1920

Sardi – Szakacs – 1914

Schaf(f)er – Nichols – 1894

Schaf(f)er – Waldecker – 1894

Schindler – Barnes – 1931

Schultz – ? – 1919

Schwarz – Schwarz – 1907

Securro – Dimente – 1904
Serra – Jackson – 1930
Simmons – Bowens – 1947
Smith – Goohs – 1907
Snowbrick – ? – 1930
Sokoloff – Sokoloff – 1927
Spanich – Spanich – 1924
Sparrow – ? – 1927
Stamibola – Bobic, A – 1912
Stamibola – Bobic, V – 1912
Stenser – Stenser – 1922
Stevens – Clement – 1925
Stillitano – ? – 1924
Stipe – Varady – 1943
Stone-LO – Durham – 1881
Sugery – Brecki – 1911
Sumegi – Hammersack – 1919
Szantaj – Petro – 1909
Taft-LO – Spuriel – 1942
Tayborne – Williams – 1956
Temasch – Fuga – 1924
Tollet – Harmon – 1954
Tratea – Tratea, E – 1919
Tratea – Tratea, J – 1919
Trebisky – Svoboda – 1900
Turboreck – Tenerty – 1924
Turner – Thorpe – 1950
Uckinick – Barosky – 1912
Uckinick – Frenolan – 1912
Vega – ? – 1929

Verano – ? – 1925
Volpe – ? – 1932
Vorhees – Thornton – 1928
Vouchovich – Vouchovich – 1925
Walker – ? – 1881
Walkinshaw – Walkinshaw – 1910
Wallace – Naiberg – 1938
Washburn – ? – 1902
Washnack – Doneski – 1908
Washnack – Sknoicki – 1908
Washtak – Thomas – 1907
Watson – Williams – 1909
Watte – Nolan – 1931
Watte – Rice – 1931
Watte – Stevens – 1931
Watte – Wallace – 1931
Webber-LO – Mackerty-LO – 1923
Webber-LO – Thomas – 1923
Wedic – Benzak – 1931
White – Williams – 1904
Williams – Hutchinson – 1932
Williams – Williams – 1932
Wilson – Juren – 1907
Wojtowicz – Pruski – 1929
Woods – Miller – 1929
Yung – Connors – 1908
Zawacski – Muhich – 1931
Zboray – Kader – 1929
Zernikow – McLane – 1908

Suspect – Victim – Year

? – ? – 1887
? – ? – 1901
? – ? – 1903
? – ? – 1903

? – ? – 1905
? – ? – 1907
? – ? – 1908
? – ? – 1911

? – ? – 1916
? – ? – 1921
? – ? – 1924
? – ? – 1924
? – ? – 1926
? – ? – 1926
? – ? – 1926
? – ? – 1927
? – ? – 1930
? – ? – 1943
? – Barbarano – 1926
? – Bruc – 1906
? – Camera – 1936
? – Caperillo – 1907
? – Capogreco – 1921
? – Cecil – 1936
? – Cecil – 1936
? – Chrospowski – 1913
? – Emmons – 1917
? – Griffa – 1925
? – Johnson – 1910
? – Joss – 1936
? – Kocher – 1917
? – Lasky – 1945
? – Mandick – 1930
? – McFadden – 1905
? – Moon – 1895
? – Morrison – 1900
? – Norfa – 1907
? – Schultz – 1919
? – Snowbrick – 1930
? – Sparrow – 1927
? – Stillitano – 1924
? – Vega – 1929
? – Verano – 1925
? – Volpe – 1932
? – Walker – 1881
? – Washburn – 1902

Aleck – ? – 1895
Alexander – Sanders – 1920
Arnold – Arnold – 1892
Authoro – ? – 1896
Bakaletz – Bolosky – 1929
Banks – Feeley – 1949
Barath – Phillips – 1935
Barnes – Barnes – 1956
Barnes – Schindler – 1931
Barosky – Uckinick – 1912
Bender – Ratenchuk – 1924
Bennett – Bennett – 1903
Benson – Benson – 1941
Benzak – Wedic – 1931
Berger – Duncan – 1955
Bischoff – Becker-LO – 1916
Blair – Blair – 1941
Bobic, A – Stamibola – 1912
Bobic, V – Stamibola – 1912
Bofea – Latsko – 1915
Bohach – Bohach – 1948
Bond – Johnson – 1927
Bowens – Simmons – 1947
Brecki – Sugery – 1911
Brnadech – Brnadech – 1939
Brown – Jackson – 1952
Brown – Katonak – 1945
Brown – Koch – 1907
Bruce – Ryan – 1883
Bucey – Burnett – 1935
Bunda – Rasin – 1906
Butler – Black – 1903
Caine – ? – 1902
Callentano – Andrade – 1929
Caloyanis – Andros – 1931
Campbell – Hornbeck – 1937
Cepis – Berta – 1908
"Charley" – Biggins – 1928

Chepol – Biro – 1923
Cimesa – Cimesa – 1948
Citik – Kuccovich – 1922
Clement – Stevens – 1925
Cluley – Cluley – 1919
Connors – Yung – 1908
Cowels – Hall-Cowels – 1923
Crenshaw – Moore – 1924
Crutchfield – Lewis – 1915
Cruze – Guzman – 1923
Dave – Dave – 1939
Decker – Baldwin – 1917
Derzaj – Latsko – 1915
Dick – Dovisak – 1908
Dimente – Securro – 1904
Doinoff – Doinoff – 1942
Donald – Falls – 1945
Doneski – Washnack – 1908
Durham – Stone-LO – 1881
Durisek – Durisek – 1954
Dzouclis – Dineff – 1930
Ellis – Eutcher – 1921
Espinoza – Espinoza – 1930
Fantos – Moreno – 1934
Farkas – Johansye – 1911
Faulkner – Cook – 1879
Fejes – Horvath – 1912
Fishburn – Fishburn – 1882
Fox – Packenbush – 1898
Francis – Kovacs – 1943
Frank – Gust – 1922
Frenolan – Uckinick – 1912
Fryar – Burton – 1862
Fuga – Temasch – 1924
Garcia – Guteries – 1926
Garvey – Berta – 1908
Genshure – Miller – 1918
Geska – Gletzer – 1894

Gilmore – ? – 1840
Glass – Glass – 1942
Goncheroff – Goncheroff – 1943
Goohs – Smith – 1907
Gordon – Dominski – 1907
Grant – Grant – 1928
Grant – Robinson – 1928
Gursk – Kolander – 1911
Hackendorn – McCoy – 1925
Hall – Hall-Cowels – 1923
Hammersack – Sumegi – 1919
Harambasic – Bodanger – 1912
Harmon – Tollet – 1954
Harris – Carvello – 1926
Haynes – Falls – 1945
Hazen – Hazen – 1917
Hazen – Hazen – 1917
Hensley – Hornbeck – 1937
Hines – Elliott – 1909
Hinozoso – ? – 1929
Hoke – Sage – 1890
Horvath – Horvath – 1928
Hutchinson – Williams – 1932
Hutera – Klukowich – 1928
Jackson – Serra – 1930
Jacobs – Hutchinson – 1890
Johnson – Johnson – 1889
Jones – Jones – 1870
Jordan – Knight – 1950
Juren – Wilson – 1907
Kader – Zboray – 1929
Kezcver – Gynrovisici – 1919
Komadina – Jansik – 1916
Kosco – Kosco – 1921
Kovasish – Gynrovisici – 1919
Lengyel – Leonard – 1948
Lazos – Paul – 1920
Lee – Carreo – 1934

Leiva – Marquez – 1953

Lenahan-LO – Lenahan – 1932

Lester – Musk – 1917

Livingston – Livingston – 1932

Long – Mitchell – 1865

Losteiner – Barnes-LO – 1920

Mackerty-LO – Webber-LO – 1923

Majesse, C – Richards – 1903

Majesse, S – Richards – 1903

Majjessie – Majjessie – 1934

Major – Fefezaria – 1926

Major – Fefezaria – 1926

Maltos – Maltos – 1951

Maltos – Ramirez – 1951

Maneff – Hornbeck – 1937

Mannarino – Monaco – 1930

Manning – Atwood – 1923

Manning – Manning – 1893

Marco – Romano – 1927

Martinez – Garza – 1926

Martini – Jacobski – 1920

McAlpine – McAlpine – 1907

McConico – McConico – 1913

McLane – Zernikow – 1908

Meluch – Meluch – 1935

Mertaugh – Hoeline – 1894

Miller – Woods – 1929

Minoff – Minoff – 1940

Moore – Francis – 1909

Muhich – Zawacski – 1931

Nagi – Kovacs – 1901

Nagy – Minda – 1916

Naiberg – Wallace – 1938

Nelson, C – Nelson – 1904

Nelson, E – Nelson – 1904

Nelson, R – Nelson – 1904

Nichols – Nichols – 1930

Nichols – Schaf(f)er – 1894

Nolan – Watte – 1931

Outiga – Luard – 1925

Padilla – Peystel – 1951

Padillo – Perez – 1925

Palgot – Drugaen – 1895

Pap, D – Berta – 1908

Pap, E – Berta – 1908

Pap, J – Berta – 1908

Payne – Peters – 1946

Petro – Szantaj – 1909

Pleasant – Rallie – 1923

Popp – Pausen – 1921

Pruski – Wojtowicz – 1929

Ralich – Rockich – 1926

Rhodes – Dixon – 1948

Rice – Watte – 1931

Riza – Berrim – 1929

Roach – Chunn – 1948

Rodriguez – Pimetal – 1953

Russell – Russell – 1902

Sagi – Rider – 1899

Schleifeinbaum – Mieden – 1870

Schwarz – Schwarz – 1907

Scott – Cooper – 1875

Seslia – Dominski – 1907

Shea – Dominski – 1907

Shipe – ? – 1953

Shipley – Champsey – 1895

Shoshetti – Hoffman – 1916

Sknoicki – Washnack – 1908

Smith – Konarski – 1951

Snezik – Roman – 1921

Snyder – Champsey – 1895

Sokoloff – Sokoloff – 1927

Spanich – Spanich – 1924

Spuriel – Taft-LO – 1942

Stenser – Stenser – 1922

Stevens – Watte – 1931

Sugaj – Latsko – 1915
Svoboda – Trebisky – 1900
Szakacs – Sardi – 1914
Tate – McCoy – 1902
Tenerty – Turboreck – 1924
Thomas – Washtak – 1907
Thomas – Webber-LO – 1923
Thornton – Philips – 1928
Thornton – Vorhees – 1928
Thorpe – Turner – 1950
Tirey – Brenner-LO – 1883
Torney – James – 1905
Tratea, E – Tratea – 1919
Tratea, J – Tratea – 1919
Valkovan – Latsko – 1915
Varady – Stipe – 1943
Vespers – Mitchell – 1910
Vespers – Richards – 1910
Vido – Rovos – 1919
Vig – Richards – 1903
Vinton – Price – 1955
Vouchovich – Vouchovich – 1925
Waldecker – Schaf(f)er – 1894
Walker – Sanders – 1920
Walkinshaw – Walkinshaw – 1910
Wall – Glenn – 1931
Wallace – Watte – 1931
Walser – Reichlin – 1903
Waring – Blakenay – 1890
Wellman – Duffield – 1945
West – Hemphill – 1952
Wheeler – Myers – 1899
White – Butler – 1947
White – Lanar – 1913
Whiteside – Durham – 1926
Williams – ? – 1873
Williams – Elders – 1906
Williams – Fields – 1950

Williams – Tayborne – 1956
Williams – Watson – 1909
Williams – White – 1904
Williams – Williams – 1932
Willis – Ribich – 1954
Winston – Feeley – 1949
Worden – Larson – 1901
Worden – Larson – 1901
Wright – Laicy-LO – 1923
Yonowich – Latsko – 1915
Young – Brenner-LO – 1883
Young – Nance – 1925
Zvosecz – Karvoch – 1924

PGIL2020USA